Affect Regulation, Mentalization, and the Development of the Self

Affect Regulation, Mentalization, and the Development of the Self

Peter Fonagy
György Gergely
Elliot L. Jurist
Mary Target

OTHER

Other Press
New York

This book was set in ITC Bookman.

10 9 8 7 6 5 4 3 2

Library of Congress Cataloging-in-Publication Data

Affect regulation, mentalization and the development of the self / by Peter Fonagy ... [et al.].
   p. cm.
   Includes bibliographical references and index.
   ISBN 1-892746-34-4
   1. Affective disorders. 2. Affect (Psychology). 3. Self. I. Fonagy, Peter, 1952–
   RC537 .A283 2002
   616.89—dc21   2001058026

Contents

About the Authors

Peter Fonagy, Ph.D., F.B.A., is Freud Memorial Professor of Psychoanalysis and Director of the Sub-Department of Clinical Health Psychology at University College London. He is Director of the Child and Family Center and of the Clinical Outcomes Research and Effectiveness Center, both at the Menninger Foundation, Kansas. He is also Director of Research at the Anna Freud Centre, London. He is a clinical psychologist and a training and supervising analyst in the British Psychoanalytical Society in child and adult analysis. He is Chair of the Research Committee and Vice-President of the International Psychoanalytic Association, and a Fellow of the British Academy. He is on the editorial board of a number of major journals, including *Development and Psychopathology* and the *Bulletin of the Menninger Clinic*. He has published over 200 chapters and articles and has authored or edited several books. His most recent books include *What Works for Whom: A Critical Review of Psychotherapy Research* (with A. Roth; published in 1996 by Guilford Press), *Psychoanalysis on the Move: The Work of Joseph Sandler* (coedited with A. Cooper and R. Wallerstein; published in 1999 by Routledge), *Attachment Theory and Psychoanalysis* (published in 2001 by Other Press), and *Evidence-Based Child Mental Health: A Comprehensive Review of Treatment Interventions* (with M. Target, D. Cottrell, J. Phillips, and Z. Kurtz; to be published by Guilford Press).

György Gergely, Ph.D., is Director of the Developmental Psychology Laboratory of the Psychology Institute of the Hungarian Academy of Sciences and Senior Lecturer at the Cognitive Developmental Doctoral Program of the Eötvös Lóránd University in Budapest. He is a clinical psychologist and is on the visiting faculty of the Max Planck Institute for Psychology in Munich, the Child and Family Center at the Menninger Clinic, the Department of Psychology at University College London, and the Department of Psychology at Berkeley. He is on the Panel of the European Cognitive Neuroscience Initiative at Trieste, Italy. He is the author of *Free Word Order and Discourse Interpretation* (published in 1991 by Academic Press of Budapest) and he serves on the editorial boards of several major journals.

Elliot L. Jurist, Ph.D., Ph.D., is a Professor in the Department of Philosophy, Hofstra University, and a Lecturer in the Department of Psychiatry, College of Physicians and Surgeons, Columbia University. He is the author of *Beyond Hegel and Nietzsche: Philosophy, Culture and Agency* (published in 2000 by MIT Press) and of numerous articles in philosophy and psychoanalysis. He is a Member of the Neuropsychiatry Service, New York Presbyterian Hospital, and a Member of the Ethics Committee of the New York State Psychiatric Institute.

Mary Target, Ph.D., is a Senior Lecturer in Psychoanalysis at University College London and an Associate Member of the British Psychoanalytical Society. She is Deputy Director of Research at the Anna Freud Centre, Member of the Curriculum and Scientific Committees, Chairman of the Research Committee of the British Psychoanalytical Society, and Chairman of the Working Party on Psychoanalytic Education of the European Psychoanalytic Federation. She is Course Organizer of the UCL Master's Course in Psychoanalytic Theory and Academic Course Organizer of the UCL/Anna Freud Centre Doctorate in Child and Adolescent Psychotherapy. She is on the editorial board of several journals, including the *International Journal of Psycho-Analysis,* and she is Joint Series Editor for psychoanalytic books at Whurr Publishers and an Associate Editor for the New Library of Psychoanalysis, Routledge. She has active research collaborations in many countries in the areas of developmental psychopathology and psychotherapy outcome. She is author and editor of several books, including *Attaccamento e Funzione Riflessiva* (with P. Fonagy, published in 2000 by Raffaello Cortina Editore of Milan) and *The Outcomes of Psychoanalytic Treatment* (edited with M. Leuzinger-Bohleber; to be published by Whurr).

Acknowledgments

We would like to acknowledge first of all our gratitude to our patients; some of the ideas in this book have been prompted by our clinical work, and one important yardstick in judging the ideas is whether they can help us better to understand our experiences with patients past, present, and future. We hope that our efforts toward new theoretical understanding have sometimes benefited them in turn.

This book could not and would not have been produced without the outstanding contribution of Dr. Elizabeth Allison, the Publications Editor of the Psychoanalysis Unit at UCL. Her contribution went very significantly over what might be expected from someone in this role. She effectively conceived and organized the project, as well as offering superb advice on the integration of the chapters and the dovetailing of arguments. We are sure that many gaps have remained, but the level of integration we were able to achieve is in large part due to her remarkable intellectual abilities and brilliant editorial skills. What is more, she was able to impose her editorial and intellectual discipline on all of us with charm and sensitivity. Liz, we are all immensely indebted to you.

In writing this book we have been immensely fortunate. Liz's predecessor in the Publications Editor post was Kathy Leach, whose contribution was enormously valuable, not only in the planning phases of the project, but also in preparing for publication many of the pieces on which the present work relies. Our only regret is that despite ingenious, tactful, and sometimes desperate efforts to keep the production of this book to schedule, we were not able to reward her with a complete manuscript.

We are also grateful to our publisher, Dr. Michael Moskowitz, whose vision about a new kind of psychoanalytic press we share and are extremely pleased to be participating in. We are particularly grateful for his patience, as this book, born of work in four countries and on two continents, slowly progressed to final completion. In terms of intellectual debt, more people deserve acknowledgment than we could possibly list. The contributions of two people, however, have been clearly formative: John Watson of the University of California at Berkeley has collaborated for many years with one of us (GG), but all of us have benefited from his writings and wisdom. Even in these days of virtual workplaces, this collaboration would not have been possible without a common workplace that at least three of the four of us share. Dr. Efrain Bleiberg's leadership of the Menninger Clinic during the time that the work reported here was undertaken has made it possible for us to work together in the Child and Family Center of the Menninger Clinic, which Dr. Bleiberg created and supervised in a truly free intellectual spirit. Others at the Child and Family Center, particularly Dr. Jon Allen and Dr. Helen Stein, have offered inspiration and advice. Two additional colleagues have been a source of inspiration and guidance: Dr. Susan Coates has followed our work over the years, as indeed we have followed hers with admiration. She has set a path in developmental clinical psychoanalysis that has been a true inspiration. Dr. Arietta Slade has inspired us not only in her research work, clinical skills, and scholarship, but the integration of all these into one personality with exceptional spirit and charm. We are grateful to her for her friendship as well as her guidance.

Earlier but somewhat different formulations of some of the ideas contained in this book have appeared, or will shortly appear, in the following publications:

Chapter 1 incorporates some material from "Attachment and reflective function: Their role in self-organization" by Peter Fonagy and Mary Target, which appeared in *Development and Psychopathology, 9* (1997), 679–700.

Chapter 4 incorporates some material from "The social bio-feedback model of parental affect-mirroring" by György Gergely and John Watson, which first appeared in the *International Journal of Psycho-Analysis, 77* (1996), 1181–1212.

A shorter version of chapter 5, "The development of understanding of self and agency" by György Gergely, will appear in U. Goshwami (Ed.), *Handbook of Childhood Cognitive Development.* Oxford: Blackwell (in press).

Chapters 6 and 9 incorporate material from Peter Fonagy and Mary Target's "Playing with reality" series of papers, which appeared in the *International Journal of Psycho-Analysis, 77* (1996), 217–233; *77* (1996), 459–479; *81* (2000), 853–874.

Chapters 1 and 8 incorporate some material from "Attachment and borderline personality disorder: A theory and some evidence" by Peter Fonagy, Mary Target, and György Gergely, which first appeared in *Psychiatric Clinics of North America, 23* (2000), 103–122.

The concluding chapter incorporates some material from "An interpersonal view of the infant" by Peter Fonagy and Mary Target, which first appeared in A. Hurry (Ed.), *Psychoanalysis and Developmental Theory* (pp. 3–31). London: Karnac, 1998.

Introduction

Numerous paths come together in this book. Drawing from a wide range of sources, we ambitiously aim to address multiple audiences: research psychologists, clinical psychologists, and psychotherapists, but also developmentalists from across other disciplines. From the most general perspective, we wish to highlight the crucial importance of developmental work to psychotherapy and psychopathology. We offer an account of psychotherapy that seeks to integrate our scientific knowledge of psychological development with our experience as clinicians, working with children and adults. We believe that the interests of our patients are best served by a constant effort on the part both of individual therapists and of the profession collectively to bring about such an integration. The value of this kind of integration is by no means immediately accepted (see Green 2000; Wolff 1996), nor should it be. The psychotherapist offers clinical help, mainly though language, to people looking for help not (just) from medication, but from someone who is willing to have their minds in mind. It cannot be assumed that scientific progress in adjacent disciplines will benefit psychotherapeutic practice. For example, we can well imagine that progress in Hullian or Skinnerian learning-theory research in the 1940s and 1950s would have been of little help to psychodynamic therapists at that time. Learning theory benefited quite a different kind of psychological therapy, less concerned with meaning and the person than with behavior and the environment.

Our work can be located within the well-established tradition of interest within psychoanalysis in developmental theory and research found among giants like Anna Freud, Melanie Klein, Mahler, Brody, Emde, Stern, and many others. A particularly inspiring example of the seamless integration of developmental and clinical thought may be found in a book by Anni Bergman (1999), Margaret Mahler's well-known collaborator. Many of the ideas in Bergman's book will be found here, perhaps cast in somewhat different perspective. All developmental orientations to psychotherapy must share many important features as they are all based on the observation of human development. At the same time, we believe that a number of the ideas discussed in this book—such as the social biofeedback theory of parental mirroring, the teleological and intentional stance, reflective function, the psychic equivalence and pretend modes of psychic reality, the alien self, mentalizing, affectivity, and, of course, affect regulation and mentalization—suggest a genuinely new direction for psychoanalysis and psychotherapy.

From another perspective, however, this book is not limited to psychoanalytic ideas and concerns. We apply a philosophy-of-mind approach in order to capture and specify the process by which infants fathom the minds of others and eventually their own minds. The notion that we fathom ourselves through others has its source in German Idealism and has been articulated further by analytic philosophers of mind (Jurist 2000). The use of philosophy of mind in this way is common in the field of social cognition. What differentiates our approach is the attention we give not just to cognition, but to affects as well. In this regard, we rely on attachment theory, which provides empirical support for the notion that an infant's sense of self emerges from the affective quality of relationship with the primary caregiver. Indeed, our work does not just borrow from attachment theory, but offers a significant reformulation of it. We shall argue that attachment is not an end in itself; rather, it exists in order to produce a representational system that has evolved, we may presume, to aid human survival. Another way to think about the contribution of this book, therefore, is as an effort to resolve some of the historical tensions between psychoanalysis and attachment theory (Fonagy 2001).

Let us say a little more about the main theme of this work and its relation to the trio of terms found in our title. Our main focus throughout is on the development of representations of psychological states in the minds of infants, children, adolescents, and adults. Mentalization—a concept that is familiar in developmental circles—is the process by which we realize that having a mind mediates our experience of the world. Mentalization is intrinsically linked to the development of the self, to its gradually elaborated inner organization, and to its participation in human society, a network of human relationships with other beings who share this unique capacity. We have used the term "reflective function" to refer to our operationalization of the mental capacities that generate mentalization (Fonagy, Target, Steele, and Steele 1998).

Mentalization is intimately related to the development of both the agentive and the representational aspects of the self: both the "I" and the "Me" described by W. James (1890). A great deal of attention has been paid to the development of self-representation, James's "Me" or the "empirical self" (Lewis and Brooks-Gunn 1979), which encompasses the development of the set of characteristics that we believe to be true of ourselves even if this knowledge is inferred from the reactions to us from our social environment (Harter 1999). Thus, this aspect of mentalization is a concept with a rich history in both psychoanalytic theory (Fonagy 1991) and cognitive psychology (Morton and Frith 1995). However, the self as a mental agent—or, as we have referred to it elsewhere, the psychological self (Fonagy, Moran, and Target 1993; Fonagy and Target 1995)—is a relatively neglected subject of study. The relative neglect by psychologists and psychoanalysts of the developmental processes that underpin the agentive self may be seen as a residue of the traditionally powerful Cartesian doctrine of first-person authority that claims direct and infallible introspective access to intentional mind states, rather than seeing this access as a hard-won developmental acquisition. The work of Marcia Cavell (1988, 1994, 2000), among others, serves as a reminder of the limited extent to which psychoanalytic metapsychology has been able to distance itself from Cartesian doctrine. Both psychoanalysis and developmental science have often adhered to the Cartesian tradition in their assumption that the experience of mental agency is innately given. In this book we attempt a radical break with this dominant philosophical tradition, arguing that mental agency may be more usefully seen as a developing or constructed capacity.

Developmental and philosophical studies of the representation of intentional action have revealed that the representation of intentional mind states may have a rather complex internal structure. Conscious access to these structures may be at best partial and could be totally absent. It seems to us important that we map the process by means of which the understanding of the self as a mental agent grows out of interpersonal experience, particularly primary-object relationships. Mentalization involves both a self-reflective and an interpersonal component. In combination, these provide the child with a capacity to distinguish inner from outer reality, intrapersonal mental and emotional processes from interpersonal communications. In this book we present both clinical and empirical evidence in conjunction with developmental observation to demonstrate that the baby's experience of himself as an organism with a mind or psychological self is not a genetic given.[1] It is a structure that evolves from infancy through childhood, and its development critically depends upon interaction with more mature minds, who are both benign and reflective in their turn.

Our understanding of mentalization is not just as a cognitive process, but developmentally commences with the "discovery" of affects through the primary-object relationships. For this reason, we focus on the concept of "affect regulation," which is important in many spheres of developmental theory and theories of psychopathology (e.g., Clarkin and Lenzenweger 1996). Affect regulation, the capacity to modulate affect states, is closely related to mentalization in that it plays a fundamental role in the unfolding of a sense of self and agency. In our account, affect

---

[1] For economy and clarity, we refer to the child as "he" and to either the parent or the therapist as "she." This is not meant to suggest any difference between male and female babies or male and female parents or therapists.

regulation is a prelude to mentalization; yet, we also believe that once mentalization has occurred, the nature of affect regulation is transformed. Here we distinguish between affect regulation as a kind of adjustment of affect states and a more sophisticated variation, where affects are used to regulate the self. The concept of "mentalized affectivity" marks a mature capacity for the regulation of affect and denotes the capacity to discover the subjective meanings of one's own affect states. Mentalized affectivity lies, we suggest, at the core of the psychotherapeutic enterprise. It represents the experiential understanding of one's feelings in a way that extends beyond intellectual understanding. It is in this realm that we encounter resistances and defenses, not just against specific emotional experiences, but against entire modes of psychological functioning; not just distortions of mental representations standing in the way of therapeutic progress, but also inhibitions of mental functioning (Fonagy, Edgcumbe, Moran, Kennedy, and Target 1993). Thus we can misunderstand what we feel, thinking that we feel one thing while truly feeling another emotion. Moreover, it is even possible that we can deprive ourselves of the entire experiential world of emotional richness. For example, the inability to envision psychological and psychosocial causation may be the consequence of the pervasive inhibition and/or developmental malformation of the psychological processes that underpin these capacities.

Our theory of affect regulation and mentalization enables us to enrich the arguments advanced by theorists such as John Bowlby about the evolutionary function of attachment. We argue that an evolutionary function of early object relations is to equip the very young child with an environment within which the understanding of mental states in others and the self can fully develop. We propose that self-reflection as well as the ability to reflect on other minds are constructed capacities that have evolved (or not) out of the earliest relationships. Since mentalization is a core aspect of human social functioning, we can infer that evolution has placed particular value on developing mental structures for interpreting interpersonal actions. Language is, of course, the major channel for symbolic interaction. Yet, in order for language to function adequately, the subjective world requires organization. Internal states must have a meaning in order to be communicated to others and interpreted in others to guide collaboration in work, love, and play.

It should be readily apparent that this book places considerable emphasis on early social experience as a primary moderator of the mental capacities centrally involved in psychological disorders and their psychotherapeutic treatment. In this respect the work is a continuation of a psychosocial tradition that has seen parenting practices and the early social environment as the key to developmental psychopathology (Cicchetti and Cohen 1995; A. Freud 1981; Masten and Braswell 1991; Rutter 1993; Sameroff 1995; Sroufe 1996). We recognize that this perspective, while undoubtedly dominant in psychiatry and social science during most of the past century, has come under increasing critical scrutiny in the light of more recent evidence from behavior-genetic adoption and twin studies (Eaves et al. 1997; Hewitt et al. 1997). It is very probably true that past studies might have overestimated the influence of the social environment on development because they failed to control for genetic influences. We note, however, that current psychiatric literature is showing signs of a return of a naively nativist perspective, where genetic data are viewed as indicating that a psychological level of analysis cannot be productive. Consequently, early environment is given little significance, and such significance as is accorded to it is from a physical rather than a psychological perspective (e.g., Marenco and Weinberger 2000).

While it is clear that psychological principles cannot violate the limitations set by the neurophysiological capabilities of the systems that subserve them, this does not imply the reduction of psychology to biology. In this book we take issue with the "geneticization" of human behavior. We adopt a position in line with that of the evolutionists Dobzhansky (1972) and Gould (1987). We consider that nature (genetics or genes) operates as a "potentialist" rather than as a "determinist." Since biological determinism is frequently clothed in the language of malleability and interactionism, we note that in reality, behind these more palatable portrayals of biology, genes are still considered the primary ruling force. While changeability of evolved dispositions is acknowledged, these inherited traits are then seen as predominant. We suggest that this tendency can occur because of the absence of convincing data on gene–environment interaction. Yet modern genetics has provided ample room for the contention that biology has culture on a "loose" rather than a "tight leash" (Gould 1987).

We attribute the failure of behavior geneticists to find convincing evidence for gene–environment interaction to their predisposition to study the "wrong" environment: the physical rather than the psychological. We suggest that the decline of interest in subjectivity, in the mechanism that interprets the social world, is partly to blame for this gap in our knowledge. We argue that it is the manner in which the environment is *experienced* that acts as a filter in the expression of genotype into phenotype. The intrapsychic representational processes that underpin the agentive self are not just the consequences of both environmental and genetic effects. They may acquire additional importance as *moderators* of the effects of the environment upon the unfolding of genotype into phenotype. We place mentalization at the heart of this process of moderation, since it is the interpretation of the social environment rather than the physical environment that governs genetic expression.

These considerations have led us to reformulate our understanding of the impact of early social relationships on later experience. We move away from the model where an early relationship is principally seen as the generator of a template for later relationships (e.g., Bowlby 1980). Instead, we argue that early experience, no doubt via its impact on development at both psychological and neurophysiological levels, determines the "depth" to which the social environment may be processed. Suboptimal early experiences of care affect later development by undermining the individual's capacity to process or interpret information concerning mental states that is essential for effective functioning in a stressful social world. Insecurity in attachment relationships is a signal of limitation in mentalizing skills. We find that the traditional classification of attachment patterns may be helpfully reinterpreted in this context as indication of a relatively good (secure attachment), or relatively poor (insecure attachment) capacity to manage or cope with intimate interpersonal relationships. An absence of mentalizing capacity under stress is signaled by the disorganization of the attachment system.

So what aspect of the environment can be specified as critical to the healthy development of an agentive or psychological self? Attuned interactions with the parent (Jaffe, Beebe, Feldstein, Crown, and Jasnow 2001; Stern 1985) often involve affect-mirroring—that is, the parent's use of facial and vocal expression to represent to the child the feelings she assumes him to have in such a way as to reassure and calm rather than intensify his emotions. We see parental affect-mirroring as instrumental in fostering the capacity for affect regulation, through the creation of a second-order representation for constitutional affect states. The image of the caregiver mirroring the internal experience of the infant comes to organize the child's emotional experience. Thus the self is not merely open to environmental influence: it is in part *constituted* through its interactions with the social environment. Freud, arguably, saw infancy as a time when the self saw others as extensions of itself (e.g., Freud 1900a). Our emphasis is the reverse—we see the self as originally an extension of experience of the other.

We propose two intimately connected developmental theories. Both concern the relationship between the acquisition of an understanding of the representational nature of minds on the one hand and affect regulation on the other. The social biofeedback theory of parental affect-mirroring explores the way in which the infant's automatic emotion expression and the caregiver's consequent affect-reflective facial and vocal displays come to be linked in the infant's mind through a contingency-detection mechanism identified by John Watson and colleagues (Bahrick and Watson 1985; Gergely and Watson 1996; Watson 1972, 1994). (This mechanism is described quite fully in chapter 4.) The forging of this link has two important effects: (*a*) The infants come to associate the control they have over their parents' mirroring displays with the resulting improvement in their emotional state, leading, eventually, to an experience of the self as a regulating agent. (*b*) The establishment of a second-order representation of affect states creates the basis for affect regulation and impulse control. Affects can be manipulated and discharged internally as well as through action; they can also be experienced as something recognizable and hence shared. Affect expressions by the parent that are not contingent on the infant's affect will undermine the appropriate labeling of internal states, which may, in turn, remain confusing, experienced as unsymbolized, and hard to regulate.

For affect-mirroring to serve as the basis of the development of a representational framework, the caregiver must somehow indicate that her display is not for real: it is not an indication of how the parent herself feels. We describe this characteristic of the parent's mirroring behavior as its "markedness." A display that is congruent with the baby's state but lacks markedness may overwhelm the infant. It is felt to be the parent's own real emotion, making the infant's experience seem contagious, or universal, and thus more dangerous. In the short term, the infant's perception of a corresponding but realistic negative emotion is likely to escalate rather than regulate the infant's state, leading to traumatization rather than containment.

Our second theory concerns the nature of subjectivity before recognition of the representational character of the human mind. We suggest that the infant's and young child's early awareness of mental states is characterized by the equation of the internal with the external. What exists in the mind must exist out there, and what exists out there must invariably also exist in the mind. Psychic equivalence, as a mode of experiencing the internal world, can cause intense distress, since the projection of fantasy to the outside world can be terrifying. The acquisition of a sense of pretend in relation to mental states is therefore essential. The repeated experience of affect-regulative mirroring helps the child to learn that feelings do not inevitably spill out into the world. The child's mental state is decoupled from physical reality. We suggest that children whose parents provide more affect-congruent contingent, and appropriately marked, mirroring displays facilitate this decoupling. In contrast, the displays of parents who, because of their own difficulties with emotion regulation, are readily overwhelmed by the infant's negative affect and produce a realistic unmarked emotion expression disrupt the development of affect regulation. A major opportunity for learning about the difference between representational and actual mental states is lost. We argue that the equation of external and internal continues to dominate the subjective world of individuals with severe personality disorders.

Affect-mirroring can take pathological pathways, because the caregiver is overwhelmed by the negative affect generated in response to the infant's reaction and presents an overly realistic emotionally arousing display. This undermines not only the infant's possibility of creating a secondary representation, but also the sense of a boundary between self and other—an internal experience suddenly becomes external through the experience equivalent to contagion. We believe that this corresponds to the clinical characterizations of projective identification, the habitual defense particularly associated with borderline personality disorder (BPD). Sustained experience of this kind might, we argue, play an important role in establishing projective identification as the dominant form of emotional experience in the development of borderline personality. It should be noted that we use the term "borderline" in this book in the sense of a form of pathological personality organization that could be a likely factor in all serious personality disorder, rather than just the more specific DSM-IV category of personality disorder, Borderline Personality Disorder. The model advanced in this book is intended to explain borderline phenomena in many patients, not just those who meet formal diagnostic criteria. Our aim is to cast light on the nature of the mental functioning of a larger group of patients—perhaps those who fit Otto Kernberg's (1967) classical description of borderline personality organization—whose thinking and emotional experience often becomes massively disorganized and regressed in the clinical setting, evoking intense feelings in the therapist (e.g., Rey 1979). The emotional lability that is a hallmark of these patients is generally regarded to be a clue to the nature of their disturbance. Their therapy rarely takes place without dramatic enactments—their own and sometimes their therapists'—and their intense dependence on the therapist increases the difficulties of the treatment process.

A second type of deviant mirroring structure is one that we feel predisposes to narcissistic personality disorder rather than to borderline states. When affect-mirroring is appropriately marked but is noncontingent, in that the infant's emotion is misperceived by the caregiver, the baby will still feel the mirrored affect display to map onto his primary emotion state. However, as this mirrored state is incongruent with the infant's actual feelings, the secondary representation created will be distorted. The infant will mislabel the primary, constitutional emotional state. The self-representation will not have strong ties to the underlying emotional state. The individual may convey an impression of reality, but as the constitutional state has not been recognized by the caregiver, the self will feel empty because it reflects the activation of secondary representations of affect that lack the corresponding connections within the constitutional self.[2] Only when psychotherapy generates mentalized affectivity will this fault line in the psychological self be bridged.

We have attempted to specify in greater detail the psychological mechanism that underpins the processes by which parental affect-mirroring deviates from its normal course in terms of our concept of the *alien self.* In general we might say that the self as agent arises out of the infant's perception of his presumed intentionality in the mind of the caregiver. Where parental caregiving is extremely insensitive and misattuned, we assume that a fault is created in the construction of the psychological self. We follow Winnicott's (1967) suggestion that the infant, failing to find *himself* in the mother's mind, finds the mother instead. The infant is forced to internalize the representation of the object's state of mind as a core part of himself. But in such cases the internalized other remains *alien* and unconnected to the structures of the constitutional self. In the case of chronically insensitive or misattuned caregiving, a fault is created in the construction of the self, whereby the infant is forced to internalize the representation of the object's state of mind as a core part of himself.

In early development this "alien self" is dealt with by externalization; as mentalization develops, it can be increasingly

---

[2] By "constitutional self" we mean an individual's biologically determined experiences associated with emotional expressivity as well as temperamental manifestations of affect.

woven into the self, creating an illusion of cohesion. Thus, the young child showing disorganized attachment will frequently control and manipulate the parent's behavior. This is part of a projective identificatory process whereby he achieves his need to experience his self as coherent, and the alien part of his self-structure as outside his mind, by perceiving these elements within other selves, normally within a parent. The disorganization of the self disorganizes attachment relationships by creating a constant need for this projective identification—the externalization of the alien self—in any attachment relationship.

The alien self is present in all of us, because transient neglect is part of ordinary caregiving; with the development of mentalization, and given a mid-childhood environment relatively free of trauma, the gaps in the self corresponding to noncontingent parenting are covered over by the self-narratives that the reasonably functioning mind can create. The alien self is mostly pernicious when later experiences of trauma in the family or the peer group force the child to dissociate from pain by using the alien self to identify with the aggressor. In these cases the gaps come to be colonized by the image of the aggressor, and the child comes to experience himself as destructive and, in the extreme, monstrous. Thus we see inadequate early parenting as creating a vulnerability that may become destructive of development and seriously pathogenic if later experience is unfavorable, either in terms of failing to facilitate the later development of mentalization or explicitly calling for the use of the faults in self-development for defensive purposes. These factors interact, and the likelihood of surviving psychological assault improves if mentalizing is freely available to interpret the perpetrator's behavior (Fonagy, Steele, Steele, Higgitt, and Target 1994). However, brutalization in the context of attachment relationships generates intense shame. This, if coupled with a history of neglect and a consequent weakness in mentalization, becomes a likely trigger for violence against the self or others, because of the intensity of the humiliation experienced when the trauma cannot be processed and attenuated via mentalization. Unmentalized shame, which remains unmediated by any sense of distance between feelings and objective realities, is then experienced as the destruction of the self. We have called it "ego-destructive shame." The use of the alien, dissociated part of the self to contain the image of the aggressor and the unthinkable affect generated by their abusive actions is a survival strategy for many individuals, some of whom we try to describe in this book.

The defensive use of the alien part of the self is deeply pathogenic, although initially adaptive. In our view it marks the development of serious personality problems. It involves three important changes: (*a*) a further repudiation of mentalization, at least in attachment contexts, (*b*) disruption of the psychological self by the emergence of a torturing other within the self, and (*c*) vital dependence on the physical presence of the other as a vehicle for externalization. These features, in combination, account for many aspects of disordered functioning in borderline patients. Abused and traumatized individuals, unable to conceive of the mental states that could explain the actions of the abuser, voluntarily and defensively sacrifice their thinking about internal states. While able to think of mental states in self and other in the context of ordinary social relationships, they inevitably become conflicted and entangled once a relationship becomes emotionally intense, organized by mental structures that are involved in attachment relationships. The abandonment of mentalizing leaves them with an internal reality that is dominated by psychic equivalence. These individuals, like all other patients, organize the therapeutic relationship to conform to their unconscious expectations, except that for them these expectations have the full force of reality and there is no sense of alternative perspectives. The inability to think about mental states removes the possibility of "narrative smoothing" of the basic gaps in the self-structure, and the alien self emerges in a manner much clearer for the therapist to see and experience. Splitting becomes a dominant defense and projective identification—the externalization of the alien self—an essential part of survival. The vehicles for the projective identification must be present for the process of externalization to function, and total dependency on these individuals turns into a dominant theme.

Our reformulation of the significance of the early social environment has important clinical implications. Psychotherapy with individuals whose early experiences have led to a compromised mentalizing capacity should be focused on helping them to build this interpersonal interpretive capacity. One way of conceptualizing the entire psychotherapeutic enterprise may be as an activity that is specifically focused on the rehabilitation of this function. The work of many previous theoreticians can be reread in the light of our reformulation. Throughout the book we often point out that the ideas being advanced here were anticipated in the work of great psychoanalytic theoreticians, not least those in the object-relations tradition. For example, we make many connections with Bion's (1959) thinking about containment. The interpersonal interpretive stance of the human brain is an overarching biological construct (Bogdan 2001). Its limits are as yet unexplored. Our concerns in this book are principally with reflective function and mentalization—capacities that are likely to turn out to be specific instances of this more general capacity.

An important aim of psychotherapy, then, if not its central aim, is the extension of mentalization. With some patients, particularly those at the borderline end of the spectrum, the therapist's task may be considered to be similar to that of the parent who intuitively engages with the child's world of psychic equivalence to emphasize its representational character. Integrating the concrete and dissociated (pretend) modes of functioning can only be achieved through focused work on the patient's current experience of the transference. Some enactments on the part of both therapist and patient are an inevitable part of this work, since the patient cannot remain psychologically close to the therapist without externalizing the alien parts of the self. It is at these moments, when the therapist is enacting the split-off part of the patient's experience, that the patient's true self may be most accurately observed. Sadly, almost invariably the therapist will have extreme difficulty in communicating insight and understanding at such times. It is far more likely, in the middle of such turmoil, that the therapist's rage or terror or both will obscure her vision of the patient. Nevertheless, persistence and a determined focus on understanding the moment-to-moment changes in the patient's experience usually pays off, and the psychotherapeutic treatment of even quite severely impaired patients can be surprisingly effective (Bateman and Fonagy 1999) and lasting (Bateman and Fonagy 2001).

Not all borderline patients are as severely disturbed as the above description implies, although most have features contained in it. If the caregiver has presented affect displays to the infant that correspond poorly to the child's constitutional self-state, affect regulation will be based on second-order representations of affects that do not have strong connections with constitutional self-states. Inaccurate mirroring by the caregiver will lead to emotional experiences that cannot be experienced as "true." Consequently, the secondary representational structures will not provide a means for accessing and attributing emotion states to the self. So words will not form the basis for the child's emerging ability to think about his or her real thoughts and wishes. The aim of psychotherapy for these individuals is to regenerate the connection between the consciousness of an affect state and its experience at the constitutional level. We have labeled this "mentalized affectivity"—a term intended to indicate the capacity to connect to the meaning of one's emotions. The clinical emphasis on experiential understanding of one's feelings in a way that ensures "meaningfulness" is crucial because it serves to establish congruent connections between primary and secondary affect-representational structures. The focus on emotion ensures that the secondary representational structures used to think about or to reflect on affect are reconnected and that misconnections where displayed affect was tied to a different nonconscious affect state are corrected.

This book is divided into three parts. The first part (chapters 1–3) is theoretical; the second part (chapters 4–8) is developmental; the third part (chapters 9–11) is clinical. The book concludes with an Epilogue. The tripartite division is primarily a matter of convenience; it is not meant to convey that the components of the content are separate. The reader will find, for example, that in the theoretical part there is considerable discussion of developmental material; that in the developmental part there is important theoretical material on the self as well as the introduction of some clinical material. This is deliberate. Throughout this work, we attempt to integrate theory, development, and the clinical sphere. We are committed to forging a theory that is inspired by clinical observation and rooted in the findings of systematic research. Our aim is to bring both theory and research to bear on clinical practice.

The content of the chapters is as follows: Chapter 1 offers an overview of the major themes to be covered in the book. We survey the links between attachment theory, studies of early social development, and studies of cognitive development that focus on one approach to mentalization—the study of the acquisition of a "theory of mind." We sketch an outline (to be filled in later) of what we know about the developmental course of self-organization and the developmental deviations that can result from an adverse early environment, later trauma, or both. We introduce the notion of mentalization as a potential mediator of psychosocial risk.

In chapter 2, we consider broad intellectual trends in theories of affect, across a range of disciplines. We suggest that the dialectic between those who see affect as inevitably disorganizing and external to cognitive influence and those who attempt to integrate affect as a form of cognitive activity may be addressed through the concept of mentalization and—more narrowly— mentalized affectivity. We introduce a distinction between first- and second-order representation of affect and argue that this distinction is consistent with data from psychology, neurophysiology, and psychoanalytic theories.

In chapter 3, we address the challenge posed by recent arguments about the relative importance of genes and the early environment to a mainly psychosocial model of personality development. It may seem foolhardy to advance a model in which the capacity for mentalization is rooted in an attachment relationship, at a time when social cognitive capacities are increasingly seen as being genetically determined rather than as products of the early environment. We counter this challenge by arguing that the human capacity for interpreting the social environment is a key moderating influence in the expression of genes in phenotypes. Mentalization and the family of capacities to which it belongs (deriving from the "interpersonal interpretive mechanism") can be either facilitated or retarded by attachment experiences and can play a key role in creating an *experienced environment*. As part of this argument, we propose a reorientation of attachment theory, from an emphasis on templates for relationships, fixed in early infancy, to a model that views attachment as the context provided by evolution for the development of interpersonal understanding.

Chapter 4 presents in detail our developmental model of how an interpersonal interpretive mechanism for affect might evolve intersubjectively, in the context of the infant–caregiver relationship. This is a parsimonious model. Traditionally, psychoanalytic developmental models have made extravagant assumptions about infants' capacities. This was one of the major foci of the Controversial Discussions between Anna Freud and Melanie Klein (King and Steiner 1991). In contrast, our more parsimonious model is based on Gergely and Watson's (1996) Social Biofeedback Theory, which is, in turn, rooted in Watson's work on the developmental functions of the human infant's sensitivity to contingent relationships between his proprioception (of intentional movement) and the external world. We argue that the internal representation of affect develops around the mother's mirroring of the infant's expressions of affect. The caregiver's mirroring display is internalized and comes to represent an internal state, but it can do so only in certain conditions, which include sufficient attunement, together with signaling to the infant that the affect the caregiver is expressing is not her own but the child's. This account will help us to understand a range of severe pathologies.

In chapter 5, we review developmental research concerning the development of the self as agent rather than as representation. We consider a five-phase model of gradually increasing sophistication concerning the mental world, both of the self and of others. In this chapter we confront the critical issue of intersubjectivity, a fraught notion within developmental theory. We argue that interpersonal awareness is a relatively late developmental acquisition. Assuming a developmental progression toward full interpersonal awareness offers us a rich range of developmental explanations for psychological disturbances. In general, we maintain throughout this volume that personality disturbances often reflect the reemergence of rudimentary forms of interpersonal awareness—an argument that is incompatible with the assumption of an inherent (primary) intersubjectivity.

In chapter 6, we attempt to apply the findings from early developmental research more directly to construct a psychoanalytic model of the growth of subjectivity. Using clinical as well as empirical evidence, we identify two incompatible and probably alternating ways in which young children treat their inner experiences. The mental world can feel either totally real or totally unreal to a young child, and we suggest that playing with reality, making the real unreal and vice versa, is the principal avenue for the development of mentalization. We introduce the cases of two young children, both treated in psychoanalytic therapy. "Rebecca" was the loved child of young single mother, a child who learned in therapy to play with her painful image of her father. This idea had initially been too real to be played with, and the feelings it generated obstructed her otherwise normal development.

In chapter 7, we introduce "Mat," a far more deprived child. Mat's experience of inadequate mirroring left him with uncontained and uncontainable affect, which he experienced as part of his bodily self, in an effort to create an illusion of self-control. His encopresis and his quasi-autistic features both responded to a playful therapeutic stance.

In chapter 8, we consider the special case of adolescence, a time of high risk for the emergence of serious disturbance. We argue that this is the consequence of an increased load on the mental world of the adolescent, brought on by the sudden leap in cognitive complexity, simultaneously with pressure for separation from the primary attachment figures. We consider two cases, "Tony" and "Glen." Both were challenged by the sharply increased complexity of their interpersonal worlds, but once again they followed quite different paths. We maintain that this reflected critical differences in their early experience, which equipped one with a far more robust mentalizing capacity than the other.

In the two following chapters, we discuss severe personality disorder in adults, which we see as the developmental continuation of poorly established mentalized subjectivity.

In chapter 9, we outline the theory that borderline personality disorder results from the inhibition of mentalizing due to maltreatment in childhood. We expect that this kind of inhibition is more likely to occur if, because of inadequate early parenting, the precursors of mentalization were not firmly established. Interpersonal interpretive processes that developmentally antedate mentalization appear to govern the behavior of individuals with BPD, at least within attachment relationships. In chapter 10, we link the failure of mentalization to a distortion in the structuring of the self; failures of early attunement are expected to cause disorganization within the structure of the self-representation. Combined with trauma, these limitations in the integrity of the self can cause massive disruption in relationships. Two cases are presented. In the first case, "Emma," lack of mentalization was evident in her treatment of her own body—her suicidality and mismanagement of her chronic physical illness. The disorganization of her self-structure, when externalized onto her body, led to a profound distortion of the link to her physical experiences. The second case, "Henrietta," had a history of violence against a lover, as well as self-destructiveness. Her functioning at a prementalistic level profoundly colored her analytic relationship. In this chapter we also consider the implications of a disorganized self-structure, with very limited capacity for mentalization, for our understanding of certain transference and countertransference phenomena.

Finally, in chapter 11, we consider four more therapeutic encounters. Each illustrates in a different way the centrality of mentalized affectivity in the course of psychoanalytic therapy. The aim of this chapter is to illustrate the way misconnections between primary and second-order representation of affect can generate disturbances of self-development, which were earlier argued to be the consequences of inaccurate mirroring. To address such pathologies, the therapy must simultaneously activate primary and secondary representations of affect. The cases illustrate the importance of the integration of affect and cognition in the practice of psychoanalytic psychotherapy. Through developing second-order representations for emotional states we can come to experience our subjectivity in a way that bridges two fundamental needs in human beings. On the one hand, we need to maintain a sense of the internal equilibrium between mental forces—a struggle that was at the heart of Freud's journey of discovery. On the other, we need to be integrated into the social world, in which we must respect the separateness of other minds, while being able also to build flexible bridges across that separateness, to create close emotional and working relationships. Therapy only works when both intrapsychic and interpersonal aims are achieved, and this is where we believe that mentalizing affectivity plays a vital role.

The Epilogue explores some of the implications of our ideas for psychopathology and psychotherapy in general.

THEORETICAL PERSPECTIVES

In Part I, we offer an introduction to some of the main theoretical concepts used in this book. The first chapter can be thought of as an overture. We offer definitions of self-reflective function and mentalization and, in particular, make the argument that the capacity to mentalize is a key determinant of a psychological sense of self. Yet, mentalization is not simply a cognitive concept, and thus we turn in the second chapter to focus in detail on different perspectives on affects and affect regulation. We clarify the meaning of affect regulation and emphasize the distinction between a basic form of affect regulation where the object is needed to modulate an affect or affects and a more complex form, altered by the development of mentalization, where the aim is to be able to regulate the self. Finally, in the third chapter, we stake out a defense of an environmental position concerning early development, which does not contest the evidence for a genetic–biological position but does challenge some of the inferences that are made from it—especially as they are mistranslated into the clinical realm. We also propose here a crucial reformulation of attachment theory: according to our view, a major goal of attachment is to produce a representational system for self-states through mentalization.

1

Attachment and Reflective Function: Their Role in Self-Organization

This chapter introduces the idea of a relationship between attachment processes and the development of the capacity to envision mental states in self and others—the capacity that is referred to in this book as mentalization or reflective function. Throughout this book, we develop the argument that the capacity to mentalize is a key determinant of self-organization and affect regulation, and we maintain that this capacity is acquired in the context of the child's early social relationships. Here we give an overview of the evidence for an association between the quality of attachment relationship and reflective function in the parent and the child. We offer some hypotheses about the development of reflection in the context of the infant–caregiver relationship. We then interpret these data and speculations in the context of current models of theory-of-mind development.

REFLECTIVE FUNCTION OR MENTALIZATION: A HISTORICAL CONTEXT

Concepts and ideas around the notion of affect and self abound and have an extraordinarily rich history in philosophy and psychology. Even without a comprehensive historical perspective, it seems apparent that the concept of the self and allied ideas have, more recently, been experiencing a considerable revival of interest from social scientists and developmentalists (e.g., Bracken 1996; Cicchetti and Toth 1994). Psychological interest in the self is usually traced to W. James's (1890, 1892) distinction of two aspects of the self: the "I" (self as subject) and the "Me" (self as object). The "I" is the active agent responsible for constructing the self-concept of "Me." To paraphrase in the terms of current cognitive neuroscience, the "Me" is the mental representation, while the "I" embodies the self as agent, the mental processes or functions that underpin representations of the self (Mandler 1985). The "I" organizes and interprets experience, ensures the experience of continuity through time, creates a sense of freedom or initiative, and generates the experiences leading to the distinctness of oneself as a person (see chapter 5). Modern developmental psychology has brought us closer to a full understanding of the mental processes that combine to organize the representation of selfhood.

Developmentalists over the past ten years have drawn our attention to the near-universal and remarkable capacity of young children to interpret their own and others' behavior by attributing mental states (see chapters 3 and 4). Reflective function, referred to in developmental psychology as "theory of mind," is the developmental acquisition that permits children to respond not only to another person's behavior, but to the children's *conception* of others' beliefs, feelings, attitudes, desires, hopes, knowledge, imagination, pretense, deceit, intentions, plans, and so on. Reflective function, or mentalization, enables children to "read" other people's minds (Baron-Cohen 1995; Baron-Cohen, Tager-Flusberg, and Cohen 1993; Morton and Frith 1995). By doing this, children make people's behavior *meaningful* and predictable. Their early experiences with other people enable them to build up and organize multiple sets of self–other representations. As they learn to understand other people's behavior better, they become able flexibly to activate the representation(s) from these multiple sets that are best suited to respond to particular interpersonal transactions. The term "reflective function" (RF) refers to the operationalization of the psychological processes underlying the capacity to mentalize—a concept that has been described in both the psychoanalytic (Fonagy 1989; Fonagy, Edgcumbe, Moran, Kennedy, and Target 1993) and cognitive (e.g., Morton and Frith 1995) psychology literatures. Reflective functioning or mentalization is the active expression of this psychological capacity intimately related to the representation of the self (Fonagy and Target 1995, 1996; Target and Fonagy 1996). RF involves both a self-reflective and an interpersonal component that ideally provides the individual with a well-developed capacity to distinguish inner from outer reality, pretend from "real" modes of functioning, and intrapersonal mental and emotional processes from interpersonal communications.

The interdependence of understanding applied to others and to the self was highlighted by the second pioneer of psychological self theory, Cooley (1912): "The thing that moves us to pride and shame is not the mechanical reflection of ourselves, but an imputed sentiment, the imagined effect of this reflection upon another's mind" (p. 153). Developmentally, this may be thought to imply that a mental operation is required in early childhood to derive the self-state from the apperception of the mental state of the other. Exploring the meaning of others' actions is then a precursor of children's ability to label and find meaningful their own psychological experiences. This ability arguably underlies the capacities for affect regulation, impulse control, self-monitoring, and the experience of self-agency—the building blocks of the organization of the self. This book attempts to trace the stages of acquisition of reflective function or mentalization, its roots in attachment, the relationship with the development of self-organization, and the particular role of emotional experience. This is highlighted in the final chapter, on mentalized affectivity.

The notion of reflective function is rooted in Dennett's (1978, 1987, 1988) proposal that three stances are available in the prediction of behavior: the physical stance, the design stance, and the intentional stance. He takes predicting the behavior of a chess-playing computer as his example. At its simplest this can be based on knowledge of the physical properties of the machine (the physical stance). The design stance would be based on knowledge of the design of the computer, including the programming that had gone into its development. The third approach consists of predicting what might be the computer's most rational move. Here we attribute to the computer certain beliefs and desires—in other words, regulation by intentional states. Dennett's thesis is that explanation in terms of such states of meaning provides good grounds for predicting human behavior— the only grounds accessible to all of us—this knowledge is embodied in the theory of mind of folk psychology (Churchland 1986; Fodor 1987; Mele 1992).[1]

"Theory of mind" is an interconnected set of beliefs and desires, attributed to explain a person's behavior. The theory-of-mind concept has great explanatory value. Philosophers of mind (Hopkins 1992; Wollheim 1995) have extended Dennett's approach to examine unconscious processes. They illustrated that one of Freud's substantive contributions was to extend folk psychology to unconscious mental states, a theory of unconscious mind, thus making those aspects of behavior meaningful that—using the ordinary constructs of intentionality—make little sense (e.g., dreams, neurotic symptoms, humor). These behaviors may be understood if we add unconscious beliefs, thoughts, feelings, and desires to our everyday model of the mind.

For research purposes, we have operationalized mentalization as reflective function (Fonagy et al. 1998): we have developed a tool by means of which the ability to give plausible interpretation of one's own and others' behavior in terms of underlying mental states can be measured. This implies awareness that experiences give rise to certain beliefs and emotions, that particular beliefs and desires tend to result in certain kinds of behavior, that there are transactional relationships between beliefs and emotions, and that particular developmental phases or relationships are associated with certain feelings and beliefs. We do not expect an individual to articulate this theoretically, but to demonstrate it in the way they interpret events within attachment relationships when asked to do so. Individuals differ in the

---

[1] Dennett's formulation is perhaps unnecessarily restrictive (Bolton and Hill 1996). It does not address predicting the behavior of systems that do not function rationally.

extent to which they are able to go beyond observable phenomena to give an account of their own or others' actions in terms of beliefs, desires, plans, and so on. This cognitive capacity is an important determinant of individual differences in self-organization as it is intimately involved with many defining features of selfhood such as self-consciousness, autonomy, freedom, and responsibility (Bolton and Hill 1996; Cassam 1994). Intentional stance, in the broad sense considered here (i.e., including apparently irrational unconscious acts), creates the continuity of self-experience that is the underpinning of a coherent self-structure.

It is important not to conflate reflective function with introspection. Bolton and Hill (1996) note that the weakness of introspection is to define mental states in terms of consciousness or self-report rather than, as here, in terms of their capacity to make sense of, and thus regulate, behavior. Introspection or self-reflection is quite different from reflective function as the latter is an automatic procedure, unconsciously invoked in interpreting human action. We see introspection as an overlearned skill, which may be systematically misleading in a way that is much more difficult to detect and correct than mistakes in conscious attributions would be. The shape and coherence lent to self-organization by reflective function is entirely outside awareness, in contrast to introspection, which has a clear impact on experience of oneself. Knowledge of minds in general, rather than self-knowledge, is the defining feature; introspection is the application of the theory of mind to one's own mental states.

The Psychoanalytic Concept of Reflective Function

Various notions have been introduced in the psychoanalytic literature to denote mental processes that overlap with the construct of mentalization, underpinned by RF. Space does not permit an exhaustive review, but some of these should be mentioned, as they may assist the reader in making links between the current constructs and those proposed by other writers. Mentalization has been described in the psychoanalytic literature under various headings (see the excellent review by Lecours and Bouchard 1997). All such notions derive from

Freud's initial concept of "*Bindung*" or linking. In his distinction between primary and secondary processes, Freud (1911b) stressed both that "*Bindung*" was a qualitative change from a physical (immediate) to a psychic associative quality of linking and that the psychic working out or representing of internal state of affairs (conceived of in energic terms) failed in various ways (Freud 1914c). Some might argue that Melanie Klein's notion of the depressive position (Klein 1945) is at least analogous to the notion of the acquisition of RF, which necessarily entails the recognition of hurt and suffering in the other as well as that of one's own role in the process. Wilfred Bion (1962a, 1962b), in describing the "alpha-function," delineated the transformation of internal events experienced as concrete ("beta-elements") into tolerable thinkable experiences. Similarly to the current conception, Bion also saw the mother–child relationship as at the root of the symbolic capacity. Winnicott (1962) also recognized the importance of the caregiver's *psychological* understanding of the infant for the emergence of the true self. Winnicott was also foremost among psychoanalytic theorists of self-development (e.g., Fairbairn 1952; Kohut 1977) in recognizing that the psychological self develops through the perception of oneself in another person's mind as thinking and feeling. Parents who cannot reflect with understanding on their children's inner experiences and respond accordingly deprive their children of a core psychological structure, which they need to build a viable sense of self.

Independently, French psychoanalysts developed a notion of mentalization that was largely formulated from the economic point of view. Pierre Marty discussed mentalization as a protective buffer in the preconscious system that prevents progressive disorganization (Marty 1968). He considers mentalization as connecting drive excitations and mental representations and thereby creating both "fluidity" and "constancy" (Marty 1990, 1991). Mentalization ensures freedom in the use of associations as well as permanence and stability. At the same time Pierre Luquet (1981, 1988) discussed the development of different forms of thinking and the reorganization of inner experience alongside this development. In his chapter on a theory of language (Luquet 1987), he distinguished primary mentalization (which we would consider the absence of RF) from secondary symbolic mentalization. While this form of mentalization was still seen as closely connected to sensory data and primary unconscious fantasies, it was nevertheless also seen as representative of these processes and observable in dreams, art, and play. His third level was verbal thought, which he considered most distant from bodily processes. Similar ideas were proposed by André Green (1975), Hanna Segal (1957), and Joyce McDougall (1978), and, more recently, by Auerbach (1993; Auerbach and Blatt 1996), Busch (1995), and Frosch (1995).

Theories Concerning the Development of Mentalization

Baron-Cohen and Swettenham appropriately ask: "how on earth can young children master such abstract concepts as belief (and false belief) with such ease, and roughly at the same time the world over" (1996, p. 158)? Their answer is that of *modularity theorists,* along the lines of Chomsky's solution to the problem of the acquisition of a knowledge of syntax. They postulate an innate (learning) mechanism with a specific location in the brain (see also Baron-Cohen 1995; Leslie 1994; G. Segal 1996). Other current psychological theories stress the cognitive precursors of theory of mind. Some favor the folk-psychology, *theory–theory,* approach, which assumes that the child evolves a scientific-theory-like network of interdependent propositions about the mind on the basis of experience (e.g., Botterill 1996; Gopnik 1996). Others assume that theory of mind is acquired via *simulation* of the mental state of the other, either through making inferences from what we ourselves would do in the imagined circumstances (e.g., Goldman 1993; P. L. Harris 1992) or an even more radical assumption of imagined transformation into the other which does not involve introspection or inference (Gordon 1992, 1995). These, and other theories, are considered in greater detail in chapter 5.

Both simulation and theory–theory models may at first glance appear to emphasize social-learning aspects of the development of mind-reading, but on closer scrutiny their focus is at the level of mechanism rather than content. They question how and when the child acquires knowledge of other minds in an abstract sense and do not ask what the child feels about the mental states he encounters in others. Yet, in this context at least, the question of knowledge and that of emotional investment are evidently closely related. The child may know what the other feels but care little or not at all about this; alternatively, this information may, for some youngsters, be an issue of survival. The emotional significance of mental states determines the evolution of the capacity or structure available for processing, but this is not usually addressed. Current models of theory-of-mind development tend to portray the child as an isolated processor of information, who constructs a theory of mind using biological mechanisms that have an expectable failure rate where the child's endowment is less than optimal.

From the viewpoint of developmental psychopathology and its psychosocial treatment, this is a barren picture, which ignores the central role of the child's emotional relationship with the parents in fostering the capacity to understand interactions in psychological terms. The development of children's understanding of mental states is embedded within the social world of the family, with its network of complex and often intensely emotionally charged relationships, which are, after all, much of what early reflection needs to comprehend. Therefore it should not surprise us that the nature of family interactions, the quality of parental control (Dunn, Brown, Slomkowski, Telsa, and Youngblade 1991), parental talk about emotions (Denham, Zoller, and Couchoud 1994), and the depth of parental discussion involving affect (Dunn, Brown, and Beardsall 1991) are all strongly associated with the acquisition of the intentional stance in observational studies. The involvement of the family in the child's acquisition of a theory of mind is further highlighted by the robust finding that the presence of older siblings in the family appears to improve the child's performance on a range of false-belief tasks (Jenkins and Astington 1996; Perner, Ruffman, and Leekam 1994; Ruffman, Perner, Naito, Parkin, and Clements 1998).

Modular accounts of theory-of-mind development have difficulty with such data. Neither the theory–theory nor the simulation account adequately covers the social origins of this critical aspect of self-organization. In the theory–theory account, mental concepts are thought to develop within a network of interdependent concepts on the basis of data from the social world, but the social world does not generally "give" concepts to the child; rather, it provides him with data for concept-building. In the simulation model, mental-state concepts are thought to arise from introspection, but this begs the question of how children come to think of their own mental states as feelings, beliefs, wishes, and so on. This chapter and the book as a whole explore the role of parent–child relationships in the transformation of prereflective experience of mental states into reflective understanding of them. Both social models of mind-reading may have their place here; the predominance of one or other route to understanding the mind may be a function of individual differences between children, but, in our view, a satisfactory model must be rooted in the child's relationships with attachment figures.

THE DEVELOPMENTAL ROOTS
OF REFLECTIVE FUNCTION IN INFANCY

The "Teleological" Stance

There is general agreement that self-organization initially entails the integration of body-related experiences, defining the physical boundaries of self and world (e.g., Brownell and Kopp 1991). Once the physical self has been established, social exchanges, the identifications of social boundaries, and, somewhat later, the identification of social causality become central self-functions. The parent's recognition of the child's intentional stance (Dennett 1978), however, is communicated nonverbally, beginning at birth. Between birth and the age of 5 months, face-to-face exchanges of affective signals between infant and caregiver (Beebe, Lachmann, and Jaffe 1997; Tronick 1989) play a key role in the development of the child's representation of affect.

For example, using a microanalytic observational paradigm, the program of work reported by Beatrice Beebe, Frank Lachmann, and Joseph Jaffe over the past two decades has demon-strated, among other things:

1. that the human infant enters into interaction with the care-giver, which involves both self-regulation and sensitivity to the state of the other;

2. that at the level of facial expression there is a rapid, mutually influencing process where the infant's behavior over a twelfth-of-a-second time period is predicted by the mother's and vice versa, presumably on the basis of schemata of the anticipated reaction of the other;

3. that the space and degree of contact between infant and caregiver is systematically altered by both, again apparently on the basis of expectancies;

4. that a higher degree of coordination predicts precocious cog-nitive performance, whereas lower levels of coordination are optimal for secure attachment and easy temperament;

5. that interaction (coordination) with a stranger at 4 months is *more* predictive of the infant's behavior with the mother in the Strange Situation (SSn)[2] at 1 year than is the same measure with the mother herself.

Interactions at this stage may be argued to be presymbolic in that they are not mentalized; the infant is not required to repre-sent the thoughts or feelings of the caregiver. However, they involve reference to future states, such as goals, in explaining the behavior of the other. Thus they can be used to predict behavior, although these structures would be limited in their capacity to modify behavior. The mental models thus created (Johnson-Laird and Byrne 1991, 1993) do not have the informa-

---

[2] The Strange Situation is a 20-minute laboratory test where the child is exposed to two "minuscule separations" of a maximum of 3 minutes each. Mary Ainsworth and her colleagues (Ainsworth et al. 1978) found that the majority of middle-class 1-year-old children respond to the mother with proximity-seeking and relief at reunion (securely attached—B infants), but about 25% respond with subtle signs of indifference (anxious avoidantly attached—A infants), and a further 15% respond with proximity-seeking but little relief at reunion (anxious resistantly attached—C infants).

tion required to change the other's state of mind. This would require an intentional stance (Dennett 1983) where, in addition to prediction, the person's beliefs and desire states are represented. Work by Gergely and Csibra (1996; Gergely, Nadasdy, Csibra, and Bíró 1995) suggests that by the second half of the first year infants' perception of social contingencies is "*teleological*" in that they make reference to future states (goals) as explanatory entities in the interpretation of behavior based on the principle of "rational action." (This work is reviewed in full in chapter 5.) Infants apply the teleological stance to human and nonhuman objects alike. Studies by Gergely and Csibra (1997) demonstrate that infants express surprise when nonhuman but moving objects (e.g., various-sized disks in a computer-generated animated display) appear to act "irrationally"—not choosing the optimal action, given specific goals and reality constraints.

The infant is assumed to extend teleological models beyond the prediction of human behavior. Teleological models, however, evolve into mentalizing ones in the restricted domain of human action. They become fully mentalizing once representations of future goal states come to be thought of as desires and constraints on reality come to be thought of in terms of the agent's belief about physical reality. The infant's behaviors in dyadic interactions are underpinned by their evolving model of rational action on the part of the caregiver. We argue that the development from teleological to mentalizing models will depend on the quality of interpersonal interactions between the infant and the parent. It should be noted that while such models may merely represent rational action, it is the perceived rather than actual rationality of an act that defines the teleological model. Thus, misapprehension of reality constraints (e.g., assumed dangerousness) will provide and create a model where action that is clearly irrational from an external standpoint is nevertheless seen as based on the principle of rational action. The predictive significance of the infant's response to a stranger (Beebe et al., 1997) suggests that representations (working models) of self–other relations, even when not yet mentalized, begin to vary in quality in the first year, and this quality is related to infant–parent interactions, as observed in the laboratory situation. If sufficiently coherent to be generalized to other relationships in characteristic ways, they may index processes that are crucial to the creation of a secure mother–infant bond.

Representational Mapping

Representational mapping is likely to underpin the gradual move in infancy from teleological to mentalizing models of mind. Between the ages of 6 and 18 months, the child becomes increasingly able to match his mental state with that of the caregiver vis-à-vis a third object or person, as, for example, in requesting joint attention (Bretherton 1991a). The communication is evidently deliberate (goal-oriented) since children may be observed at this phase trying to repair failed communicative bids (Golinkoff 1986) and thus showing at least rudimentary recognition of awareness and agency in self and other, including feelings, perceptions, and intentions (Wellman 1993). Neisser (1991) suggested that, based on perceptual processes, two preconceptual aspects of the self emerge: the ecological and the interpersonal. While the former involves self-awareness in reference to visuo-spatial, tactile, auditory, and other perceptual information concerning the child's nonsocial surroundings, the latter is generated via the coperception of actions of the self and related contingent actions of others. Taking Stern's (1985) and Neisser's formulation of the interpersonal self together, we can identify three aspects of the intersubjective development of the self, which Mundy and Hogan (1994) term "instrumental action states," "sensory or perceptual action states," and "affective action states." Rogers and Pennington (1991) offered a model of the cognitive basis for such an intersubjective process in their concept of representational mapping (the process of coordinating representations of self and other), which is thought to underlie the sharing of affect, attention, and higher-order aspects of cognition such as beliefs. The existence of imitation skills from the neonatal stage represents strong evidence for the model (Meltzoff and Gopnik 1993). The acquisition of an appreciation of mental states, however, goes beyond mirroring.

The development of an understanding of affect in self and other may be a good illustration of the role of representational mapping in the development of reflective abilities (Gergely and Watson 1996; Target and Fonagy 1996). Anxiety, for example, is for the infant a confusing mixture of physiological changes, ideas, and behaviors. When the mother reflects, or mirrors, the child's anxiety, this perception organizes the child's experience, and he now "knows" what he is feeling. The mother's representation of the infant's affect is represented by the child and is mapped onto the representation of its self-state. The discrepancy between these is helpful insofar as it provides organization for the self-state, and thus the caregiver's mirroring can become the higher-order representation of the child's experience. Within this model, mirroring would be expected to fail if it is either too close to the infant's experience or too remote from it. If the mirroring is too accurate, the perception itself can become a source of fear, and it loses its symbolic potential. If it is absent, not readily forthcoming, or contaminated with the mother's own preoccupation, the process of self-development is profoundly compromised. We may presume that individuals for whom the symptoms of anxiety signify catastrophes (e.g., heart attack, imminent death, etc.) have metarepresentations of their emotional responses which cannot limit their intensity through symbolization, perhaps because the original mirroring by the primary caregiver exaggerated the infant's emotions.

Although this idea is speculative, it is empirically testable. It might help to answer the thorny question of why individuals with panic disorders are so threatened by physiologically relatively mild disturbances of their equilibrium. The suggestion here is that the metarepresentation, or symbolic representation, of affect in these cases contains too much of the primary experience; hence, instead of labeling the experience in such a way as to enable the individual to attenuate its intensity, it tends to stimulate and exacerbate symptoms of the affect state, which in turn accentuates the secondary expression, in a cycle of escalating panic.[3] In one study (Fonagy, Steele, et al. 1995), we have confirmed that mothers who soothe their distressed 8-month-olds most effectively following an injection rapidly reflect the

---

[3] In terms of linguistic theory, one may say that the signifier is not sufficiently "demotivated"—in other words, it resembles the signified too closely.

child's emotion, but this mirroring is contaminated by displays of affect that are incompatible with the child's current feeling (smiling, questioning, mocking display, and the like). In displaying such "complex affect" (Fónagy and Fónagy 1987), they ensure that the infant recognizes their emotion as analogous, but not identical, to their experience, and thus the process of symbol formation may begin. In this way, the representational mapping between affect of self and emotions of others, the exchange of affect between young child and caregiver, provides a unique source of information to the child about his own internal states. We suggest that the meaning or sense of affect develops out of the integrated representation of the affect in self and other. The combination of the representation of self-experience and the representation of the reaction of the caregiver elaborates the child's teleological model of the mind and ultimately enables him to understand affective displays in others, as well as arriving at the regulation of his own emotions. The representational mapping of emotion displays and self-experience is seen here as a prototypical instance of caregiver sensitivity, which, as we attempt to demonstrate, is likely to be an important component of the development of mentalizing. The sensitivity of the caregiver prompts the child to begin organizing self-experience according to clusters of responses that will eventually come to be verbally labeled as specific emotions (or desires). The high contingent response is the means by which this mapping can take place. The child's affective experiences are given further meaning by becoming associated with clusters of reality constraints within the parent–infant interaction (leading to rudimentary beliefs about the causes and consequences of his emotional state).

REFLECTIVE FUNCTION
AND ATTACHMENT SECURITY IN THE PARENT

Attachment theory, developed by John Bowlby (1969, 1973, 1980), postulates a universal human need to form close affectional bonds. At its core is the reciprocity of early relationships, which is a precondition of normal development probably in all mammals, including humans (Hofer 1995). The attachment behaviors of the human infant (e.g., proximity-seeking, smiling, clinging) are reciprocated by adult attachment behaviors (touching, holding, soothing), and these responses strengthen the attachment behavior of the infant toward that particular adult. The activation of attachment behaviors depends on the infant's evaluation of a range of environmental signals, which results in the feeling of security or insecurity. The experience of security is the goal of the attachment system, which is thus first and foremost a regulator of emotional experience (Sroufe 1996). In this sense it lies at the heart of many forms of mental disorder and the entire psychotherapeutic enterprise.

None of us is born with the capacity to regulate our own emotional reactions. A dyadic regulatory system evolves where the infant's signals of moment-to-moment changes in his state are understood and responded to by the caregiver, thereby achieving their regulation. The infant learns that arousal in the presence of the caregiver will not lead to disorganization beyond his coping capabilities. The caregiver will be there to reestablish equilibrium. In states of uncontrollable arousal, the infant will come to seek physical proximity to the caregiver in the hope of soothing and the recovery of homeostasis. The infant's behavior by the end of the first year is purposeful and apparently based on specific expectations. His past experiences with the caregiver are aggregated into representational systems that Bowlby (1973) termed "internal working models" (IWM). Thus, the attachment system is an open biosocial homeostatic regulatory system.

PATTERNS OF ATTACHMENT IN INFANCY

The second great pioneer of attachment theory, Mary Ainsworth (1985; Ainsworth, Blehar, Waters, and Wall 1978), developed the well-known laboratory-based procedure for observing infants' internal working models in action. Infants, briefly separated from their caregiver in a situation unfamiliar to them, show one of four patterns of behavior: (*a*) Infants classified as *secure* explore readily in the presence of the primary caregiver, are anxious in the presence of the stranger and avoid her, are distressed by their caregiver's brief absence, rapidly seek contact with her afterwards, and are reassured by this contact, returning to their exploration. (*b*) Some infants, who appear to be made less anxious by separation, may not seek proximity with the caregiver following separation and may not prefer her over the stranger; these infants are designated *anxious/avoidant*. (*c*) *Anxious/resistant* infants show limited exploration and play, tend to be highly distressed by the separation, and have great difficulty in settling afterwards, showing struggling, stiffness, continued crying, or fuss in a passive way. The caregiver's presence or attempts at comforting fail to reassure, and the infant's anxiety and anger appear to prevent him from deriving comfort from proximity. Secure infants' behavior is based on the experience of well-coordinated, sensitive interactions where the caregiver is rarely overarousing and is able to restabilize the child's disorganizing emotional responses. Therefore, they remain relatively organized in stressful situations. Negative emotions feel less threatening and can be experienced as meaningful and communicative (Grossmann, Grossmann, and Schwan 1986; Sroufe 1996). Anxious/avoidantly attached children are presumed to have had experiences where their emotional arousal was not restabilized by the caregiver, or where they were overaroused through intrusive parenting; therefore, they *overregulate* their affect and avoid situations that are likely to be distressing. Anxious/resistantly attached children *underregulate*, heightening their expression of distress, possibly in an effort to elicit the expectable response of the caregiver. There is a low threshold for threat, and the child becomes preoccupied with having contact with the caregiver but is frustrated even when it is available (Sroufe 1996). (*d*) A fourth group of infants exhibits seemingly undirected behavior, such as freezing, hand-clapping, head-banging, and the wish to escape the situation even in the presence of the caregiver. These infants are referred to as *disorganized/disoriented* (Main and Solomon 1990). It is generally held that for such infants the caregiver has served as a source of both fear and reassurance, and thus arousal of the attachment behavioral system produces strong conflicting motivations.

Not surprisingly, a history of prolonged or repeated separation (Chisolm 1998), intense marital conflict (Owen and Cox 1997), and severe neglect or physical or sexual abuse (Carlson, Cicchetti, Barnett, and Braunwald 1989) is often associated with this pattern.

THE ATTACHMENT SYSTEM AS A DETERMINANT OF LATER INTERPERSONAL RELATIONSHIPS

Bowlby proposed that internal working models of the self and others provide prototypes for all later relationships. Such models are relatively stable across the lifespan (Collins and Read 1994). Because internal working models function outside awareness, they are change-resistant (Crittenden 1990). The stability of attachment is demonstrated by longitudinal studies of infants assessed with the Strange Situation and followed up in adolescence or young adulthood with the *Adult Attachment Interview* (AAI) (George, Kaplan, and Main 1985). This structured clinical instrument elicits narrative histories of childhood attachment relationships. The AAI scoring system (Main and Goldwyn 1994) classifies individuals into *Secure/Autonomous, Insecure/Dismissing, Insecure/Preoccupied,* or *Unresolved* with respect to loss or trauma—categories based on the structural qualities of narratives of early experiences. While *autonomous* individuals value attachment relationships, coherently integrate memories into a meaningful narrative, and regard these as formative, insecure individuals are poor at integrating memories of experience with the meaning of that experience. Those *dismissing* of attachment show avoidance by denying memories and by idealizing or devaluing early relationships. *Preoccupied* individuals tend to be confused, angry, or fearful in relation to attachment figures, sometimes still complaining of childhood slights, echoing the protests of the resistant infant. *Unresolved* individuals give indications of significant disorganization in their attachment-relationship representation in semantic or syntactic confusions in their narratives concerning childhood trauma or a recent loss.

Major longitudinal studies (C. Hamilton 1994; M. Main 1997; Waters, Merrick, Albersheim, Treboux, and Crowell 1995) have shown a 68–75% correspondence with attachment classifications in infancy and classifications in adulthood. This is an unparalleled level of consistency between behavior observed in infancy and outcomes in adulthood, although, obviously, such behavior may well be maintained by consistent environments as well as by patterns laid down in the first year of life. Moreover, attachment relationships play a key role in the transgenerational transmission of deprivation. Secure adults are three or four times more likely to have children who are securely attached to them (van IJzendoorn 1995). This is true even where parental attachment is assessed before the birth of the child (Steele, Steele, and Fonagy 1996; Ward and Carlson 1995). Parental attachment patterns predict variance in addition to temperament measures or contextual factors, such as life events, social support, and psychopathology (Steele, 1991).

The attachment system (Bowlby 1969, 1973, 1980) is intimately connected with the process of representational mapping and the development of the reflective function of the self. There is general agreement that, as the self exists only in the context of the other, the development of the self is tantamount to the aggregation of experiences of self in relationships (e.g., Crittenden 1994; Sroufe 1990). Psychoanalytic object relations (Kernberg 1982; Winnicott 1965) and attachment (Bowlby 1980) theorists are in agreement that repeated, invariant aspects of self–other relations are abstracted into internal representational mental models (Johnson-Laird 1983) and structured, to use Kernberg's term, into self–other–affect triads or internal working models, according to Bowlby. Although in its original formulation the concept of internal working model lacked specificity (Dunn 1996), more recent empirical work by psychoanalytic clinicians has greatly improved the specificity of this construct (Horowitz 1995; Luborsky and Luborsky 1995).

At the same time, cognitive scientists have elaborated the notion of procedural memories based on the nonconscious implicit use of past experience (Johnson and Multhaup 1992; Kihlstrom and Hoyt 1990; Pillemer and White 1989; Schachter 1992; Squire 1987; Tobias, Kihlstrom, and Schachter 1992).

There is general agreement that the memory system is at least of a dual nature with two relatively independent, neurologically and psychologically homogeneous systems underpinning it. In addition to the autobiographical memory, which is at least in part accessible to awareness, an important additional component to memory is a nonvoluntary system that is implicit, principally perceptual, nondeclarative, and nonreflective (D. L. Schachter 1992; Squire 1987). It is possible that it is, at least in certain respects, more dominated by emotional and impressionistic information than its autobiographical counterpart (Pillemer and White 1989; Tobias et al. 1992; van der Kolk 1994). It stores the "how" of executing sequences of actions, motor skills being prototypical instances. The procedural knowledge that it contains is accessible only through performance. It manifests itself only when the individual engages in the skills and operations into which knowledge is embedded. Given these features, it seems likely that the schematic representations postulated by attachment and object-relations theorists are most usefully construed as procedural memories, the function of which is to adapt social behavior to specific interpersonal contexts.

The classification of patterns of attachment in infancy (Ainsworth et al. 1978) taps into procedural memory (Crittenden 1990; Fonagy 1995a). The strength of the Strange Situation as a method of psychological assessment is that it provides a powerful analogue of past situational contexts within which knowledge concerning the "how" of behavior with a specific caregiver is accrued. In this sense attachment is a skill, one that is acquired in relation to a specific caregiver and encoded into a teleological model of behavior. In the London Parent–Child Study we investigated the question of how well the Adult Attachment Interview, administered before the birth of the first child to 100 predominantly middle-class primiparous parents, could predict the classification of the infant's attachment at the age of 12 months to mother and at 18 months to father (Fonagy, Steele, and Steele 1991). There was only a marginally significant association between the attachment classification with mother and that with father. However, both test results were powerfully predicted by the attachment classification of the respective parent on the AAI (Steele et al. 1996). The small overlap between the two sets of classifications could be equally well accounted for by assuming a temperament factor or by the generalization of the child's behavior with the mother (reflecting her attachment classification) on his behavior with the father. The results suggest that the infant develops independent models (self–other schemata) for its major attachment relations based on its past history of interactions with each of those individuals. These interaction experiences are, in turn, indexed by the caregiver's representation of their attachment history.

There has been considerable research on the manner in which representations of attachment might influence the caregiver's behavior with the child. Van IJzendoorn's (1995) comprehensive review identifies a "transmission gap," to the extent that the variability that AAI narratives and SSn classifications share is not accounted for by observational data concerning the sensitivity of caregiver behavior. Indeed, studies of the AAI–SSn association, which concurrently measured the sensitivity of caregiver–infant interaction, have yielded negative (Ward and Carlson 1995) or inconclusive (van IJzendoorn, Kranenburg, Zwart-Woudstra, Van Busschbach, and Lambermon 1991) results. Previously, we have suggested that the transmission gap may be a consequence of the limitations of measures of sensitivity (Fonagy, Steele, Moran, Steele, and Higgitt 1992; Fonagy, Steele, et al. 1995). Sensitivity is a generic construct covering a wide range of parental behaviors (Belsky, Rosenberger, and Crnic 1995). Not all of these may be equally relevant in engendering secure attachment. If secure attachment is conceived of as the acquisition of procedures of goal-oriented rational action for the regulation of aversive states of arousal within an attachment context (Carlson and Sroufe 1995; Cassidy 1994; Sroufe 1996), we argue that these would be most consistently acquired and coherently represented when the child's acute affective state is accurately, but not overwhelmingly, reflected back to the child.

The child who looks for a way of managing his distress finds in the response of the caregiver a representation of his mental state that he may internalize and use as part of a higher-order strategy of affect regulation. The secure caregiver soothes by combining mirroring with a display that is incompatible with the child's affect (thus perhaps implying coping). This formulation of sensitivity has much in common with the notion of British psychoanalyst Wilfred Bion (1962a), of the role of the mother's capacity to mentally "contain" the affect state that feels intolerable to the baby and respond in terms of physical care in a manner that acknowledges the child's mental state, yet serves to modulate unmanageable feelings. The finding that the clarity and coherence of the mother's representation of the child mediates between the AAI and mother's observed behavior is certainly consistent with this model (Slade, Belsky, Aber, and Phelps 1999). Ratings of the quality of the reflective function of each caregiver were found independently to predict the child's security of attachment in the London Parent–Child Study (Fonagy, Steele, Moran, Steele, and Higgitt 1991).

If secure attachment is the outcome of successful containment, insecure attachment may be seen as the infant's identification with the caregiver's defensive behavior. Proximity to the caregiver is maintained at the cost of reflective function. A dismissing (Ds) caregiver may altogether fail to mirror the child's distress because of the painful experiences this evokes for her or because she lacks the capacity to create a coherent image of the child's mental state. In contrast, the preoccupied (E) caregiver may represent the infant's state with excessive clarity or in a way that is complicated by responses to the parent's ambivalent preoccupation with her own experience, so much so that the symbolic potential of the exchange is lost. In both cases the infant internalizes the caregiver's attitude and "this dysynchrony becomes the content of the experience of the self" (Crittenden 1994, p. 89).

We may speculate as to the impact of such a state of affairs on the development of the child's sense of self. We know that avoidant infants respond to separation with minimal displays of distress while experiencing considerable physiological arousal (Spangler and Grossmann 1993). Crittenden (1988; Crittenden and DiLalla 1988) reports that 1-year-old maltreated children display falsely positive affect that does not match their true feelings. At an extreme, the internalization of the caregiver's defenses can lead not only to a failure to represent and display actual emotional experience adequately, but also to the construction of an experience of self around this false internalization (Winnicott 1965).

While the conscious experience of "putting on an act" may be a fairly general experience, particularly in adolescence (Harter, Marold, Whitesell, and Cobbs 1996), in the current context we are referring to the highly distressing experience of severely personality-disordered children who experience a sense of alienation from their core self (Bleiberg 1984, 1994). A strategy adopted by many such children somewhat later in development is to attempt to externalize this false part of their self-representation and manipulate the behaviors of others around them so that these match the incongruent self-representation. We would argue that this model explains the strangely coercive behavior with the caregiver of preschool children whose attachment at the stage of infancy was classified as disorganized (Cassidy, Marvin, and The MacArthur Working Group on Attachment 1989; Crittenden 1992; Main and Cassidy 1988). These children—and adults—become quite skilled and sensitive in manipulating others to get them to behave consistently with their internal representations. These are not their representations of self–other relationships, which we all try to actualize. In a far more desperate way these children and adults try to provoke behavior consistent with a part of the self-representation experienced as "alien," which they feel forced to externalize in order to achieve a more coherent perception of the residual self (Fonagy and Target 1995).

ATTACHMENT SECURITY IN THE CHILD AND REFLECTIVE FUNCTION

There is general agreement that the "harmoniousness of the mother–child relationship contributes to the emergence of symbolic thought" (Bretherton, Bates, Benigni, Camaioni, and Volterra 1979, p. 224), and the idea has a long and distinguished history (Mahler, Pine, and Bergman 1975; Vygotsky 1978; Werner and Kaplan 1963). Bowlby (1969) recognized the significance of the developmental step entailed in the emergence of "the child's capacity both to conceive of his mother as having her own goals and interests separate from his own and to take them into account" (1969, p. 368). Moss, Parent, and Gosselin (1995) reported that attachment security with mother was a good concurrent predictor of metacognitive capacity in the child in the domains of memory, comprehension, and communication. The Separation Anxiety Test, a projective test of attachment security, has been shown to be a good predictor of belief–desire reasoning capacity in 3½- to 6-year-old children when age, verbal mental age, and social maturity were all controlled for (Fonagy, Redfern, and Charman 1997).

In a prospective study of the relationship of attachment security to mother (12 months) and to father (18 months) and performance on three tests of theory of mind at 5½ years (Fonagy 1997), 92 of 96 children tested in the Strange Situation at 12 and 18 months were seen. Of those classified as secure at 12 months with mother, 82% passed the belief–desire reasoning task, in which the child is challenged to predict what a character would feel, based on his or her knowledge of the character's belief. (If Ellie thinks the can has coke in it, and likes coke, will she want the drink—even though it is really milk?) In contrast, 46% of those who had been classified as insecure failed. Infant–father attachment (at 18 months) also predicted the child's performance, with 77% of infants classified as secure passing the test, compared to 55% of children classified as insecure. There was some indication of an additive relationship, in that 87% of children with two secure relationships passed the belief–desire task, and 63% of those with only one secure relationship and only 50% of those insecure with both did so. A similar but somewhat weaker pattern could be observed with the second-order false-belief task, which requires the child to reason on the basis of what one character knows about another character's wrong belief. Of those secure with both parents, 36% passed, compared with 23% who were secure with one and 9% who were insecure with both.

In a somewhat smaller but nevertheless careful longitudinal study of mother–infant dyads, Meins and colleagues (Meins, Fernyhough, Russel, and Clark-Carter 1998) reported that 83%

of children who were securely attached in infancy passed a false-belief task at the age of 4, in comparison with 33% of insecurely attached peers. At age 5, 85% of securely attached children and 50% of insecurely attached ones passed a task requiring an understanding of information access. Although the study was not able to replicate our results on the false-belief and emotion task (probably because of its small sample), the general trend of the findings confirms that security of attachment is significantly linked to symbolic abilities in general and to precocious mentalizing in particular.

Both trivial and substantive explanations could be offered to account for these findings. They would be trivial if the association of secure attachment and false-belief understanding were due to an as yet unknown and unmeasured third factor, such as temperament. More plausibly, it could be argued that the facilitative effect of secure attachment is due to a more relaxed, task-oriented attitude, to a general facility to engage in a cognitively demanding task, or to an ability to relate to an adult experimenter in a playful, exploratory way. All these explanations reflect child performance rather than competence. This suggestion could be tested using a false-belief task where implicit and explicit knowledge of false belief is separately assessed (Clements and Perner 1994). If attachment security relates to performance, then securely attached children would be expected to do better only on the explicit (verbal/pointing) task. Implicit, procedural false-belief reasoning would be expected to be facilitated by secure attachment only if this was associated with superior reflective capacity. This remains to be studied. In what follows, we shall cautiously assume that the relationship between false-belief reasoning and security of attachment is nontrivial.

There are two alternative explanations for this relationship: (a) One class of models would suggest that security of attachment in infancy predisposes children to benefit from certain social processes that may be directly involved in the development of reflective abilities and social understanding. (b) The second class of models would suggest that security of attachment is an indicator of that quality of infant–caregiver relationship which generates psychological understanding. In this second model the social processes that accelerate the mentalizing quality of self-organization are the very same as those that ensure security of attachment.

Mediational models would require that two conditions be satisfied: (*a*) compelling evidence that a specific set of social processes is involved in this aspect of the development of self-organization, and (*b*) that such social processes are enhanced in securely attached individuals. At least three candidates meet these criteria.

1.   The first is *pretense*. There is evidence that children in their third year who engage more readily in cooperative interaction (Dunn et al. 1991), and specifically in joint pretend play (Astington and Jenkins 1995; Taylor, Gerow, and Carlson 1993; Young-blade and Dunn 1995), show superior mind-reading and emotion understanding performance. A separate body of observations from longitudinal studies of attachment indicates that preschool children who were securely attached to their mother in infancy manifest stronger engagement in fantasy play than do avoidant children, whose level of engagement is low and whose pretend play is impoverished (Rosenberg, cited in Carlson and Sroufe 1995; Main, Kaplan, and Cassidy 1985). Children rated as securely attached to their mothers during infancy have been reported to engage in more frequent and sophisticated solo pretense (Belsky, Garduque, and Hrncir 1984; Bretherton et al. 1979; Matas, Arend, and Sroufe 1978). Slade (1987) found that maternal involvement in 3-year-olds' play served a facilitating function only for securely attached children. Meins and colleagues (Meins et al. 1998) demonstrated that children who were classified as securely attached in infancy were better able to incorporate the pretense suggestions of an experimenter in their play at 31 months.

It is probable that joint pretend play or playfulness fosters the understanding of mental states. Deliberate role-taking is seen as being integral to the "off-line simulation" model of the performance of mind-reading tasks (Currie 1995; Goldman 1989). Within other models, pretend play is an early manifestation of the theory-of-mind mechanisms (Leslie 1987). The question of why

3-year-olds can understand that someone is entertaining a pretend representation but not a false belief (Harris and Kavanaugh 1993; Harris, Kavanaugh, and Meredith 1994), a pretend/real distinction but not an appearance/reality one (Flavell, Flavell, and Green 1987) is an important puzzle. In the case of pretend, the representations, while they are different from reality, are shared by those engaged in the pretend game. As Astington put it: "they are *inter*mental, not *intra*mental" (1996, p. 193). The sharing of representations that are different from reality may help in understanding situations where representations are not only different from reality but are not shared in a social pretend domain. In joint pretend play or playfulness the adult adopts the child's mental stance and re-presents it to the child in relation to a third object, which is symbolically held in mind by both. Pretending requires a mental stance involving the symbolic transformation of reality in the presence of, and with a view to, the mind of the other. The adult, or perhaps the older sibling, holds the frame of external reality while accurately representing the child's mental state. The scaffolding provided by the child's playmate in pretend play (Vygotsky 1967) not only promotes earlier success but is the mechanism whereby the development of reflection comes about. Lillard (1993) argued that symbolic play may offer a "zone of proximal development" for the skills that subserve mind-reading ability. Children with a secure attachment history may be more likely to engage in an activity that presumes a degree of trust, insofar as the child relies on the other's version or perception of reality.

2. The second is *talking*. There is evidence that conversations about feelings and the reasons behind people's actions are linked to the relatively early achievement of reflective function (Brown, Donelan-McCall, and Dunn 1996; Dunn and Brown 1993). Mothers who spontaneously explained their emotions to 3½-year-olds during laboratory simulation were shown to have children with enhanced emotion understanding over the subsequent 15-month period (Denham et al. 1994). Conversational opportunities concerning mental states appear to improve children's mentalizing performance in experimental studies (Appleton and Reddy 1996).

Strage and Main (cited in Carlson and Sroufe 1995) reported that discourse patterns between mothers and children at age 6 could be predicted from early attachment classification. Secure dyads were more fluent and able to discuss a wider range of topics than those classified as avoidant, who showed little topic elaboration. Patterns of mother–child interaction characteristic of secure dyads—shared play, comforting, or joking—also define the contexts within which the mother's explanations of mental states are found to be particularly facilitative of reflective function (Dunn 1996). Secure children find it easier to deal with emotional issues in an open and free way (Bretherton, Ridgeway, and Cassidy 1990; Cassidy 1988). Mother–child verbal interactions associated with the early acquisition of reflective capacity predominantly concern emotionally charged matters (Dunn 1996). Secure attachment may then engender patterns of verbal interaction between child and caregiver, which in turn support thinking about feelings and intentions.

P. K. Smith (1996) forcefully advanced the central role of language in the acquisition of mentalizing capacity. Using primate evidence, he suggested that the availability of symbolic codes (words) for mental states was crucial for the developing individual to acquire mind-reading abilities, and the explicit use of such codes by caregivers was therefore likely to be important. Even more pertinent in this context is Harris's (1996) proposal that the experience of engaging in conversations *per se* alerts children to the fact that people are receivers and providers of information, irrespective of whether that conversation involves reference to mental states (knowing, thinking, desiring, etc.). The structure of information-bearing conversations (e.g., being told about a past event that one has not witnessed, challenging of information in dissent and denial, or filling in information gaps in questions or when information exchange misfires and repair is needed) strongly implies that partners in a conversation differ in what they know and believe about a shared topic. Effective conversation requires that gaps in shared knowledge and belief are acknowledged and addressed. The measurement of attachment in adults (Main and Goldwyn 1994) strongly endorses the suggestion that secure attachment is associated with greater sensitivity to the rules of conversation as defined by Grice (1975).

3. The third potential mediator is *peer group interaction*. We have already noted that the possibility of interaction with siblings is likely to enhance theory-of-mind performance (Jenkins and Astington 1996; Perner et al. 1994; Ruffman et al. 1998). Importantly, the child's use of mental-state terms with siblings or friends is a better predictor of performance on false-belief tasks than is mother–child conversation (Brown et al. 1996). Likewise, Lewis and colleagues (Lewis, Freeman, Kyriakidou, Maridaki-Kassotaki, and Berridge 1996) demonstrated that false-belief understanding was related to the amount of time that children spent with older siblings, older friends, and older kin, but not with younger persons. There is an independent body of evidence that supports a strong link between secure attachment in infancy and ratings of peer competence (Elicker, Englund, and Sroufe 1992). Children with secure attachment histories are consistently observed and rated more socially oriented, capable of reciprocity, popular, and empathic than those with insecure histories (Lieberman 1977; Pancake 1985; Park and Waters 1989; Sroufe 1983).

Both simulation theory and theory–theory explanations of the development of mind-reading offer good explanations of the facilitative effect of more intense peer-group interaction (Ruffman et al. 1998). Peer-group interaction should increase the opportunities that children have for simulation, imagining what they would see, think, feel, and so on if they were in another person's situation. Equally, interaction with peers or older siblings could be seen from a theory–theory perspective as a rich source of ideas about how the mind works. An alternative view may be that enculturation is itself the source of the child's mental-state concepts (Astington 1996). Bruner (1983) proposed that parents' tendency to treat the infant's spontaneous gestures *as if* they were intentional communications leads to infants seeing themselves as having intentions and starting to communicate intentionally. The social world—in the first instance, the parent—fosters the child's sense of his mental self through complex linguistic and interactional processes, behaving toward the infant in a way that leads him eventually to share the assumption that his own behavior and (by simulation or the observation of similar interactions between the caregiver and others) that of others may be best understood in terms of mental states. Through participation in activities of their culture they come to share their culture's way of regarding others' and their own actions. If children's entry into the folk psychology is viewed as a process of "apprenticeship" in which senior peers and caregivers are seen as encouraging the child's adoption of mentalizing concepts (Astington 1996; Lewis et al. 1996), then secure attachment may be considered as a kind of catalyst to this learning process. The greater readiness with which secure children are willing to explore and engage with the social world could then account for their relative competence in mentalizing abilities.

There is nothing mutually exclusive about these three mediational models. Pretense often involves the use of mental-state language. Interaction with peers often involves both language and pretense. In general, these mediational models suggest that propensity for social engagement across a number of contexts enhances the development of social understanding and that such social engagement is more readily accessible in the families of securely attached young children. However, there is a major problem with such a singular model. Evidence from Dunn's work suggests that these different contexts correlate poorly with one another (Dunn 1996). For example, observational data indicate that individual differences found in pretend play, management of conflict, and discourse about mental states are not correlated among social situations (mothers, siblings, close friend), although each correlates with socio-cognitive assessments (Brown et al. 1996; Slomkowski and Dunn 1992; Youngblade and Dunn 1995). The fact that children's behavior correlates poorly across social partners and situations, although each of those situations relates to test performance, could suggest that there are several independent, simultaneously operating pathways between attachment and social situations.

Alternatively, it is possible that the variables that *prima facie* may be considered to be mediating the attachment/mind-reading relationship are not on the causal path at all, that their correlation with the rate of acquisition of mind-reading is spurious, and that the causal sequence of the relationship does not involve these social experiences but is directly related to the child's attachment status. The early experience with the caregivers in the first year of life may create the bedrock of theory-of-mind competence, ensuring the child's move from a teleological to a mentalizing model of behavior. What evidence do we have to support such a contention? First, it is important to note that in the London data, a mother's attachment classification before the birth of the child was a powerful predictor of the child's theory-of-mind competence at 5 years; 75% of children of secure, autonomous mothers passed the cognitive-emotion task, whereas only 16% of children of preoccupied mothers and 25% of those of unresolved mothers did so (Fonagy 1997). Although on the face of it this could be accounted for by the models already discussed, we believe that there is now evidence that the caregiver brings something to the parent–child relationship, evident even before the birth of the child, which may be critical in the child's establishment of both secure attachment and mind-reading.

What might this be? It is well established that, in infancy, mothers of securely attached children are more sensitive to their children's needs (Ainsworth, Bell, and Stayton 1971; Isabella 1993). We have already touched on the fact that the caregiver's capacity to envision the mental states of her own parents is predictive of the infant's security of attachment to each of his caregivers (Fonagy, Steele, Moran, et al. 1991). In the London project, mothers who were more likely to invoke mental states in their accounts of their childhood attachment experiences had children with superior mind-reading abilities (controlling for verbal fluency in the child). Ratings on the RF scale were found to predict the child's performance on cognitive-emotion tasks also for fathers. Even more important, a path analysis revealed that a mother's capacity to reflect on her own childhood in the AAI shared that portion of the variance with the child's theory-of-mind performance that was predicted by the quality of mother–infant attachment. In a more complex path analysis, we found that the mother's mentalizing ability had a direct as well as indirect relationship with the child's theory of mind. Thus, the child's attachment security was not the only predictor. The mother's capacity to envision the child as a mental entity also seemed to be important.

Such data suggest that common mechanisms underpin attachment organization in the caregiver and the infant and the precocious emergence of mentalizing. It should be remembered that no unequivocal causal paths were identified among mediational models. The relative importance of various potential mediational mechanisms for the attachment–theory-of-mind relationship varies according to context, but intergenerational data may be consistent with at least two of the models (pretense, language). Further experimental research that manipulates parental behavior and explores attachment and theory-of-mind task performance (van IJzendoorn, Juffer, and Duyvesteyn 1995) will be necessary to determine whether specific behaviors that engender secure attachment simultaneously enhance mentalizing. In order for such a study to be feasible, we need a model of how attachment may directly relate to theory-of-mind performance. Next, therefore, we offer one model of how such a mechanism may operate.

Our stipulation is based on the assumption that the acquisition of the theory of mind is part of an intersubjective process between the infant and caregiver (see Gopnik 1993, for a highly elegant elaboration of such a model). In our view, the caregiver facilitates the creation of mentalizing models through complex linguistic and quasi-linguistic processes, primarily by behaving toward the child in such a way that the child is eventually led to postulate that his own behavior may be best understood if he assumes that he has ideas and beliefs, feelings and wishes, that determine his actions, and the reactions of others to him can then be generalized to other similar beings. The caregiver approaches the crying infant with a question in her mind: "Do you want your nappy changed?" "Do you need a cuddle?" The sensitive caregiver is unlikely to address the situation without having the person in mind, so is unlikely to say to herself, "Are you wet around your bottom?" or "Have you been standing alone too long?" The sensitive caregiver can bridge the focus on physical reality and internally directed attention sufficiently for the child to identify contingencies between internal and external experience. Ultimately, the child arrives at the conclusion that the caregiver's reaction to him may be understood as rational, given the assumption of an internal state of belief or desire within himself. Unconsciously and pervasively, the caregiver ascribes a mental state to the child with her behavior, treating the child as a mental agent. This is ultimately perceived by the child and used in the elaboration of teleological models and permits the development of a core sense of selfhood organized along mentalistic lines. We assume that this, by and large, is a mundane process, in the sense of happening every day throughout early life, and that it is a process that is preconscious to both infant and caregiver, inaccessible to reflection or modification. Caregivers, however, execute this most natural of human functions in different ways. Some may be particularly alert to the earliest indications of intentionality, while others may need stronger indications before they can perceive the child's mental state and modify their behavior accordingly.

The child's development and perception of mental states in himself and others thus depends on his observation of the mental world of his caregiver. He develops a concept and is thus able to perceive mental states, to the extent that his caregiver's behavior implies such states. He does this when the caregiver is in a shared pretend mode of "playing" with the child (hence the association between pretend and early mentalization), and many more mundane interactions (such as conversations and peer interaction) will also involve such shared mentation. This is what makes mental-state concepts such as thinking inherently intersubjective; shared experience is part of the very logic of mental-state concepts.

We believe that the caregiver's capacity to observe the moment-to-moment changes in the child's mental state is critical in the development of mentalizing capacity. The caregiver's perception of the child as an intentional being lies at the root of sensitive caregiving, which attachment theorists view as the cornerstone of secure attachment (Ainsworth et al. 1978; Bates, Maslin, and Frankel 1985; Belsky and Isabella 1988; Egeland and Farber 1984; Grossmann, Grossmann, Spangler, Suess, and Unzner 1985; Isabella 1993; Isabella and Belsky 1991).

Secure attachment, in its turn, provides the psychosocial basis for acquiring an understanding of mind. The secure infant feels safe in making attributions of mental states to account for the behavior of the caregiver. In contrast the avoidant child shuns to some degree the mental state of the other, while the resistant child focuses on its own state of distress, to the exclusion of close intersubjective exchanges. Disorganized infants may represent a special category: hypervigilant of the caregiver's behavior, they use all cues available for prediction; they may be acutely sensitized to intentional states and thus may be more ready to construct a mentalized account of the caregiver's behavior. We would argue (see below) that in such children mentalization may be evident, but it does not have the central role in self-organization that characterizes securely attached children. We believe that what is most important for the development of mentalizing self-organization is the exploration of the mental state of the sensitive caregiver, which enables the child to find in the caregiver's mind (that is, in the hypothetical representation of her mind that he constructs to explain her behavior toward him) an image of himself as motivated by beliefs, feelings, and intentions. In contrast, what the disorganized child is scanning for so intently is not the representation of his own mental states in the mind of the other, but the mental states of that other that threaten to undermine his own self. They can constitute within the child's self-representation an alien presence that is so unbearable that his attachment behavior becomes organized around reexternalizing these parts of the self onto attachment figures, rather than around the internalization of a capacity for containment of affects and other intentional states. There is considerable evidence to support the view that secure attachment enhances the development of the self, inner security, feeling of self-worth, self-reliance, and personal power of the emerging self as well as the development of autonomy (Bates et al. 1985; Gove 1983; Londerville and Main 1981; Matas et al. 1978). Disorganized infants, even if they acquire the skill of mind-reading, fail to integrate this with their self-organization.

There may be a number of linked reasons for this: (a) The child needs to use disproportionate resources to understand the parent's behavior, at the expense of reflecting on self-states. (*b*) The caregiver of the disorganized infant is less likely to be reliably contingent in responding to the infant's self-state and, further, to show systematic biases in her perception and reflection of the child's state. (*c*) The mental state of the caregiver of the disorganized infant evokes intense anxiety either through frightening behavior suggesting malevolence toward the child or through behavior suggesting fear, including inexplicable fear of the child himself.

These factors may combine to make disorganized infants become keen readers of the caregiver's mind under certain circumstances but, we suggest, poor readers of their own mental states. Thus, in terms of the rival models of theory-of-mind development, such children may acquire a theory–theory of mind but be unable to use simulation of mentalizing with the same confidence as can children whose attachment (albeit insecure) is coherent and organized. The alternative models may be more usefully thought of as alternative routes to mentalization, the first (theory–theory) accessible to all, the second (simulation) more readily available to children whose early attachment relationships made such a strategy more attractive and desirable.

In chapter 6, we attempt to describe the normal development of reflective function in the child aged 2 to 5 years. We suggest that there is a transition from a dual mode of experience to mentalization. Primarily from a clinical perspective, we advance a number of propositions concerning the development of the psychological part of the self. These are:

1. In early childhood, reflective function is characterized by two modes of relating internal experiences to the external situation: (*a*) In a serious frame of mind, the child expects the internal world in himself and others to correspond to external reality, and subjective experience will often be distorted to match information coming from outside—*psychic equivalence mode* (e.g., Gopnik and Astington 1988; Perner, Leekam, and Wimmer 1987). (*b*) While involved in play, the child knows that internal experience may not reflect external reality (e.g., Bartsch and Wellman 1989; Dias and Harris 1990), but then the internal state is thought to

have no relationship to the outside world and to have no implications for it (*pretend mode*).

2. In normal development, the child integrates these two modes to arrive at the stage of *mentalization*—or *reflective mode*—in which mental states can be experienced as representations. Inner and outer reality can then be seen as linked, yet they are accepted as differing in important ways and no longer have to be either equated or dissociated from each other (Baron-Cohen 1995; Gopnik 1993).

3. We have hypothesized that mentalization normally comes about through the child's experience of his mental states being reflected on, prototypically through experience of secure play with a parent or older child, which facilitates integration of the pretend and psychic equivalence modes, through an interpersonal process that is perhaps an elaboration of the complex mirroring of the infant by the caregiver. In playfulness, the caregiver gives the child's ideas and feelings (when he is "only pretending") a link with reality by indicating the existence of an alternative perspective, which exists outside the child's mind. The parent or older child also shows that reality may be distorted by acting upon it in playful ways, and through this playfulness a pretend but real mental experience may be introduced.

4. In traumatized children, intense emotion and associated conflict can be thought of as having led to a partial failure of this integration, so that aspects of the pretend mode of functioning become part of a psychic equivalence manner of experiencing reality. This may be because where maltreatment or trauma has occurred within the family, the atmosphere tends to be incompatible with the caregiver "playing with" the most pressing aspects of the child's thoughts; these are often disturbing and unacceptable to the adult, just as they are to the child. The rigid and controlling behavior of the preschool child with a history of disorganized attachment is thus seen as arising out of a partial failure on the part of the child to move beyond the mode of psychic equivalence in relation to specific ideas or feelings, so

that he experiences them with the intensity that might be expected had they been current external events.

THE IMPLICATIONS OF REFLECTIVE FUNCTION
FOR SELF-DEVELOPMENT

"Mind-reading" may not be an unequivocally positive experience. Judy Dunn's work, however, gives us an indication that at least the understanding of emotion at the age of 3½ predicts a positive perception of social relations, mature moral sensibility, and the understanding of complex emotions (Herrera and Dunn 1997). Stern (1985) pointed out that a sense of ownership of one's actions—whether derived from the experience of forming plans, proprioceptive feedback, or the objective consequences of physical actions on the environment—contributes significantly to the sense of self-agency. In our view, such agency also crucially depends on the quality and reliability of reflective function, as ownership of action is intimately tied to the mental state (belief or desire) that initiated it. It is impossible to conceive of self-agency as fully established by the actual actions of the child, as such a large proportion of these will fail to achieve their intended objective because of the child's immature physical and cognitive capacities. In fact, it could be argued that if the sense of self-agency were uniquely based on feedback from immature action systems, deficiency in this sphere would be universal. The recognition of the child's intentional stance by (older) others must, then, be critical in making the thought "real" for the child. Interpersonal interaction that permits the registration of perceptions, thoughts, and emotions as causes and consequences of action and the contemplation of these mental states without fear must constitute an important part of the foundation of self-agency. The earliest foundation is presumably the baby's sense that he brings about the caregiver's mirroring behavior (Gergely and Watson 1996). This idea is at the core of chapter 4.

Of course, the core of self-agency must lie in the body, where the infant's effort to be in control often succeeds after the earliest times. However, more complex actions, particularly those that involve others in the child's world, frequently require the reflective caregiver to make sense of the young child's wishes and to express these, if the two-way connection between intentions and action is to be established. Hence, those who have experienced severe neglect or coercive, rigid, frightening, and, at an extreme, abusive parenting will frequently experience their sense of self-agency as massively curtailed and confined to the more firmly established bodily domain (see chapters 9 and 10 for a full exploration of this idea).

The model of the development of mentalizing capacity that we propose has considerable clinical implications. For example, in a study of attachment classification in patients with severe personality disorders, Fonagy et al. (1996) found that the AAI narratives of borderline-personality-disordered patients had lower reflective function, coupled with histories of severe trauma, which was apparently unresolved. The findings suggest that, given a sensitive attachment relationship, which provides the intersubjective basis for the development of mentalizing capacity, trauma (even if severe) is more likely to be resolved. Severe distortion of personality follows when abuse or neglect leads to a defensive inhibition of mentalization. Similarly, evidence is accumulating that among juvenile offenders, where histories of maltreatment are common, capacities for mentalization are severely restricted (Blair 1995; Levinson and Fonagy 2000). The evidence on disturbances of mentalization among clinical groups is elaborated more fully in later chapters (see chapters 10 and 11 in particular).

A DEVELOPMENTAL FRAMEWORK
FOR ABNORMAL REFLECTIVE FUNCTION

It would be undoubtedly overly simplistic to make an absolute connection between developmental disorder and nonreflectiveness. There are variations across situations, or, perhaps more accurately, across relationships. The delinquent adolescent is well aware of the mental states of other gang members, and the borderline individual at times seems hypersensitive to the affective states of mental health professionals and family members. These "anomalies" may be clarified by more sophisticated developmental theory.

Our chosen framework is provided by "dynamic skills theory" (Fischer and Farrar 1987; Fischer, Kenny, and Pipp 1990), which depicts development as a person's elaboration of progressively more complex control systems (skills). Reflective function may be readily conceived of as one such control system, critical to the organization of the self. Within dynamic skills theory, reflective function would be seen as not simply a property of the person, but of the person and situation together, because all skills are composed of both the person's activities and the situations or context within which these occur. Particular tasks, specific events, other people, as well as culture are seen as part of the skill. Furthermore, the development of a skill is not seen as progression along any singular path, determined by maturation. Rather, reflective function, as a skill, evolves through varied pathways, molded by many dynamically interacting influences, such as the individual's emotions, social interaction, family relationships and environment, important social groups, the reactions of the wider social world, and so forth (Fischer, Knight, and Van Parys 1993).

Reflective function is a strand within the developmental web, one of the many distinct control systems that are neither strongly connected with each other nor coordinated or integrated (Fischer and Pipp 1984). The "fractionation" or splitting of all abilities as a function of tasks and domains is well demonstrated, and we might expect reflective function to be subject to the same kind of developmental *décalage* [unevenness] that characterizes the rest of cognitive development (Flavell 1982). "Fractionation" refers to the tendency for a person not to coordinate skills or experiences that are naturally separate but may be thought of as belonging together by some external criterion (Fischer and Ayoub 1994). Just as the understanding of conservation of liquid does not generalize to conservation of area, reflective capacity in one domain of interpersonal interaction should not be expected to generalize to others. Reflective function does not begin as a general capacity, but is a particular skill tied to the task and domain where it is learned—a specific category of relationship. Reflective function as a skill may be more or less present in situations as a function of contextual support and emotional states that push an individual up or down a developmental strand. Differences in the meaning of an interaction as well as its physical context can lead to fractionation. For example, the concept of conservation of liquid may not generalize between the experimental task and one that involves helping a thirsty friend, even if both involve pouring a glass of orange juice (Rogoff 1990). We have noted above that the child's observed use and experience of mental-state language can differ markedly across social contexts (Dunn 1996). Fractionation does not disappear entirely with development, either in general or in the specific case of reflectiveness. It is clearly possible for task-based skills such as reflective function to come to be coordinated, but this should not be seen as automatic. Unevenness across situations is likely to remain prevalent even in adults, especially when they are emotional (Fischer and Ayoub 1994).

Normal development proceeds from fractionation toward integration, which involves the construction of specific coordinations among previously separate skills and provides the foundation for more complex, sophisticated control systems (Bidell and Fischer 1994). Abnormalities of reflective function, the continued use of a teleological rather than a mentalizing model for predictive behavior, should not, then, be seen as either a consequence of "arrest and fixation" at an early stage or a "regression" to that stage. Pathologies in the reflective function of the maltreated child may be expected to develop increased complexity with age and time, in a manner similar to other skills. The skill for limited reflectiveness developed by the child to anticipate and forestall maltreatment and its painful physical and psychological impact would be adaptive in their particular world but would be expected to produce sophisticated forms of difficulty rather than straightforward adaptations in other contexts (Noam 1990). The ability to be reflective in general, but to show only minimal reflectiveness in the context of one's own childhood with reference to the mental states of "caregiving" others or in specific relationships that reactivate the same schemata, could be a result of natural fractionation. Unevenness or splitting of reflective ability could also be the consequence of an active (purposeful, conscious, or unconscious) attempt on the part of the individual not to coordinate or generalize reflective function to specific relationship domains. Here the unevenness is "a developmental achievement," in that the person must create a coordination in order actively to maintain the separation of contexts that would naturally move toward integration. The family might, of course, support such splits with sharp dissociations between their public, proper world and their private tyrannical one. The split is context- and affect-dependent, and skills developed within one context will not necessarily be matched by similar abilities in others. Within an attachment-theory framework we might say that the self is organized so that certain internal working models include considerable reflective components—expectations incorporating the mental states of self and other—while other working models of relationships appear impoverished, indicating only minimal mentalizing skills. In the latter contexts the subject will offer only stereotyped, simple, concrete, low-level descriptions. This does not imply developmental delay or regression; rather, it suggests a remarkably complex ability to coordinate two distinct levels of functioning. It is the function of the abusive or emotionally depriving world within which they developed that engendered in them the sophisticated skills required for such an adaptation. Thus to talk of deficit or absence of a capacity in such individuals would undoubtedly be an oversimplification. Measures of global abilities will not yield difference between these individuals and other groups. Efforts at going beyond mere clinical impression in terms of measurement and quantification have to take on board the unevenness of their abilities and the situational and interpersonal specificity of the failure of reflective function.

In our view, nonreflective internal working models come to dominate the behavior of personality-disordered adults and children when an element of conflict is present within an interpersonal relationship. Conflict—or, rather, its adaptive resolution—prototypically calls for the perception both of the self and of the other in relation to the self, requiring individuals to reconcile their own legitimate claims with concern for the other (Killen and Nucci 1995). Thus, for example, the abnormality of the early family environment of individuals with severe problems of conduct has been most evident in the context of normally expectable conflicts (Patterson 1982; Perry, Perry, and Kennedy 1992). In this context the child with a vulnerable capacity for mentalization experiences no affirmation of his intentional stance and fails to acquire the sense of ownership or inner endorsement of his actions that is essential for a sense of self-agency. Consequently, his sense of autonomy becomes vulnerable, and the importance of his original intention is exaggerated. The characteristics of oppositional defiant disorder (e.g., negativity, disobedience, aggression) may in part be seen as attempts at reasserting self-agency in a relationship where the connection between mental state and action within the self has been undermined by insensitive and coercive parenting.

Abnormalities of parenting represent but one route to limitations on reflective function. The child's biological vulnerabilities, such as hyperactivity, inadequate attentiveness, deficiencies in impulse control, are all likely to obstruct his opportunity for evolving a mentalized reflective model of conflictual interpersonal situations. Within a dialectic or transactional model there is a bidirectional causality inherent to such biological vulnerabilities: they both provoke situations of conflict and gravely limit the child's capacity to handle them flexibly (see chapter 9).

The separation of action from intention undermines the emotional reaction individuals may be expected to have in relation to the consequences of their action, since, as Hart and Killen pointed out, the acquisition of moral emotions requires that individuals are "active contributors to their own development, interpreting their world and making judgments that determine their actions in it" (1995, p. 7). Subsequently, the predominant response to situations charged with emotion will be a nonreflective one, readily disowned by the self. Naturally the absence of reflective function in such situations will give the appearance of rigidity to the person's behavior, as if only a singular pattern of response were accessible. Furthermore, the response may frequently be in conflict with social norms because the tendency to take the perspective of others has been abandoned in that context, and consequently the "moral emotions" used to make judgments about the consequences of actions and to regulate behavior (Arsenio and Lover 1995) are absent. The absence of reflective function may further exaggerate an antisocial response by forcing the individual to see the other not as another intentional agent, but, rather, in nonhuman terms, as a body, as representing a social position or agency, or as an anonymous member of a group.

Maltreatment, or more broadly trauma, is seen as interacting with the domain- and situation-specific restrictions on reflective function at two levels: (a) As we have argued, maltreatment presents the young child with a powerful emotional disincentive for taking the perspective of others because of the actual hostility of the intentional stance of the abuser, as well as the constraints upon self-development imposed by an older person's failure to understand and acknowledge the child's budding sense of intentionality. (b) The child is deprived of the resilience provided by the capacity to understand a traumatic interpersonal situation (Fonagy et al. 1994). Thus individuals traumatized by their family environment are vulnerable in terms both of the long-term maladaptive effect of their reaction to the trauma and of their reduced capacity to cope with it. The predominantly nonmentalizing stance adopted in such situations therefore further impairs the individual and, in the extreme, their nonmentalizing approach will come to dominate all intimate interpersonal relationships. It is at this stage that severe developmental psychopathology—ultimately entrenched personality disorder—becomes the likely outcome.

2

Historical and Interdisciplinary
Perspectives on Affects
and Affect Regulation

In this chapter, we follow out the implications of the argument in the first chapter concerning the developmental mechanisms that produce mentalization and reflective function. Here we examine the relationship of early object relations with mentalization through the lens of affects and affect regulation. This chapter provides a historical overview of academic traditions concerning affects and affect regulation from the perspective of mentalization. The chapter is not intended as any kind of exhaustive review—an ambition that is substantially beyond the scope of this work. Our aim here is to point to key controversies in the study of emotion. The review highlights the fact that analogous dichotomies exist across a number of disciplines. Both philosophical and psychological traditions tend to regard affects in one of two ways: (a) ideally as integrated with cognition, and (b) as inherently independent of, opposed to, and out of the control of rational thought. Certain neuroscientists have suggested that both traditions may have strong foundations in the brain structures assumed to mediate emotional experience. Psychoanalysts, including Freud, have also pursued both lines of thought, with notable individual exceptions. We review the contribution of attachment theorists in some detail, since this framework represents the starting point for many of the ideas in the current monograph. In the attachment theory tradition, there is a commitment to explore precisely how affective experience contributes to the acquisition of self-regulation by virtue of coregulation between caregiver and infant. The present chapter places our approach, which is also based in the developmental tradition already outlined briefly in chapter 1, into a historical frame of reference, insofar as we attempt to integrate the two major intellectual traditions concerning affect.

INTRODUCTION

There is an enormous and growing interest in affects across disciplines. Both in attachment theory and in many other domains in psychology, one important component of this interest in affects centers on affect regulation. Yet, as many scholars have observed, the concept of affect regulation has never been well defined (Gross 1998, 1999; Magai 1999; R. Thompson 1990, 1994). For some theorists, affect regulation, or what is sometimes referred to as "emotion regulation," denotes a process wherein the object of regulation is the affect/emotion itself (Eisenberg and Fabes 1992; N. Fox 1994; Garber and Dodge 1991). For attachment theorists and psychoanalysts, however, the object of regulation is more complex: the regulation of affects is linked to the regulation of the self. More precisely, affect regulation plays a crucial part in the explanation of how infants move from a state of coregulation to self-regulation. The stakes are greater in the way psychoanalysts and attachment theorists conceive of affect regulation.

Affects and affect regulation are not necessarily complementary concepts. Affect regulation entails the capacity to control and modulate our affective responses. However, we shall consider some of the arguments of those who do not agree that affects can be brought under regulation. It is important, therefore, to begin this inquiry by taking a look at various sources and debates concerning the nature of affects and affect regulation. This historical background illuminates the way in which certain beliefs about affects continue to inform contemporary perspectives. We begin, in the first part of this chapter, with philosophical perspectives on affects and affect regulation; we move on to psychological perspectives and then turn to neuroscientific perspectives. In the second part, we examine affects and affect regulation in psychoanalysis and then attachment theory.

PHILOSOPHICAL PERSPECTIVES

In the Western philosophical tradition, the commitment to rationality as the ideal standard to guide action meant that affects were minimized in importance. At the same time, most major philosophers have felt the need to try to have some account of affects, and even philosophers who are staunch defenders of rationality, like Descartes, have had profound things to say about affects.[1] We do not attempt to present a detailed inquiry about how affects have been understood in the history of philosophy in this context. For our purposes, it will be sufficient to emphasize a crucial debate concerning the nature of affect within the history of philosophy that remains extremely relevant today for understanding affects and affect regulation. In chapter 5, on the self as agent, we address contemporary ideas from the philosophy of mind in connection with the theme of intersubjectivity.

For Aristotle, affects are fundamental for the pursuit and attainment of a good and happy human life. He regards affects as beliefs; as such, they provide judgments about the world that can be justified or not. This means that, by themselves, affects are neither harmful nor opposed to reason. As Aristotle sees it, affects become harmful only insofar as our characters are too

---

[1] Descartes is often singled out for criticism concerning his belief that reason, and reason alone, guarantees knowledge. However, Descartes' treatise *The Passions of the Soul* is devoted to the treatment of affects, stressing the importance of the role of the body in affects. For an original perspective on just how seriously Descartes and other seventeenth-century philosophers took affects, see S. James 1997.

weak to counteract and moderate them.[2] He does not deny that affects can become excessive; rather, he stresses that through practice we can learn to have them in the appropriate way—that is, at the right time, in the right way, and toward the right people.

Aristotle is the first philosopher who, it is fair to surmise, postulated a theory of affect regulation. For him, regulating affects depends upon crafting them to occur within the intermediary course between the extremes of either excess or deficiency. In other words, we can distinguish between anger as conforming to the mean and its extremes—excess, which we can call irascibility, and the deficiency, which we can call irritation (Barnes 1984; Rhetoric 1378a31).[3] Aristotle wishes to urge us to cultivate our characters in order to be able to discern how to act in a way that places affects under our control. He appreciates the values of affects, and he particularly stresses how integrally connected pleasure is with affective experience (Gosling and Taylor 1982; Jurist 1998; Stocker and Hegeman 1996). Perhaps, most importantly, he fashions an ideal for human agents of integrating reason and feeling.

Countering Aristotle, the Stoic philosophers challenge the notion that affects can be modulated. In their view, affects are beyond our control and necessarily elude cultivation; this explains why we often feel that affects happen to us, rather than that they are chosen by us. The Stoics regard affects as false judgments and hence as corrupting forces that lead us astray. It behooves us, therefore, to distance ourselves from affects and to strive to act on the basis of rationality alone. If we manage to withhold our consent to the overpowering force of affects, we can achieve the "detachment" and "self-sufficiency" by virtue of which we are able to flourish.

---

[2] The Ancient Greek virtue, *sophrosune*, concerns the regulation of pleasure and bodily appetites. *Sophrosune* has to do with finding the right amount of pleasure, not restricting or devaluing it.

[3] Aristotle makes the point that it is difficult to find the right word for the deficiency of anger, thereby acknowledging that anger is the kind of affect that is more likely to be excessive.

The Stoic view has had a dominant influence on the history of philosophy. This is particularly striking in terms of the philosophical propensity to construe irrationality strictly in terms of being a failure of rationality, rather than as having a meaning in its own right. Moreover, Stoic philosophy has had an important influence on early Christian thinking, wherein affects and the body are portrayed in negative terms. The ambivalence in Christianity toward affects is illustrated by DeSousa in that five out of the seven main vices are affects (pride, lust, envy, gluttony, anger, and sloth, but not avarice and greed), and three out of the four cardinal virtues concern resisting emotional temptations (prudence, fortitude, and temperance, but not justice) (1987, p. 17). Reflecting on the history of philosophy has more than antiquarian interest: the influence of the Stoic view has had real consequences for the self-understanding of our culture.

Generally and somewhat bluntly stated, Aristotelians are friendly toward affects, whereas Stoics are wary of them.[4] Although these appear to be mutually exclusive paradigms, caution ought to be exercised not to reach such a conclusion prematurely. Indeed, in turning to Spinoza, we find a philosopher who accommodates different aspects of both paradigms. Spinoza was greatly influenced by the Cartesian revolution and was particularly attracted to the aim of rendering philosophy more scientific, as is evident from the geometrical form of the *Ethics* (Spinoza, 1677). He departed from Descartes' dualism, however, in conceiving of humans as embodied minds. Descartes' work, *The Passions of the Soul,* had the merit of portraying affects both as sensations that are in the body and as mentalistic; in fact, the emphasis on affects and the body initiates an important new direction, which anticipates psychology, away from Aristotle's conception of them as beliefs. Yet a problem arises for Descartes in having to give an account of how the mind interacts with the body. Spinoza neatly bypasses this problem because he insists that bodily experience is directly accessible to the mind (1677, p. 12).

---

[4] For an excellent discussion of the relation between Aristotelians and Stoics, see Nussbaum's *The Therapy of Desire* (1994).

Spinoza was strongly influenced by the Stoics' view of affects. He regards affects as false judgments and, hence, urges us to strive to resist acting upon them and to accept that they elude our control. Nonetheless, in Part III of the *Ethics*, Spinoza argues that we ought not simply to reject or forsake affects; rather, reason should be used to correct affects without dismissing them. Our self-understanding is improved, according to Spinoza, by understanding our affects. From a clinical point of view, what is especially interesting about Spinoza is his suggestion that the affective state must be preserved in the way reason is applied to it. (We return to this idea later in the chapter.) In appreciating that affects enrich our lives, he exhibits sympathy for the Aristotelian hope of integrating feeling and reason. Thus, it is impossible to place Spinoza neatly into either the Aristotelian or the Stoic camp.

The debate between Aristotelians and Stoics haunts the history of thinking about affects. Can affects be cultivated? Do they give meaning to human life, and are they indispensable to the way we imagine human thriving? Or are they primitive forces that are dangerous to our well-being? One kind of philosophical approach to this debate is primarily to concentrate on those affects that one deems as valuable and as contributing to moral conduct. Hume takes such a position: he does not claim that all affects should be regarded as contributing to morality, but he maintains that morality is based upon feelings and could never be legislated by reason alone. More recently, moral psychologists in philosophy like Stocker and Hegeman (1996), Oakley (1992), Rorty and Flanagan (1990), Greenspan (1988), DeSousa (1987), and C. Taylor (1985) have argued that affects contribute to morality and that it is mistaken to conceive of affects as undermining rationality. In sum, there is a growing appreciation by philosophers of the value of rethinking affects. This does not mean, of course, that there is agreement among philosophers. There remains a divide between those thinkers who wish to define affects in terms of beliefs (like Wollheim 1999) and others who want to reformulate the bodily contribution of affects who are captivated by the burgeoning scientific research on affects (e.g., Griffiths 1997).

PSYCHOLOGICAL PERSPECTIVES

In comparison to philosophy, the field of psychology has always exhibited a keen interest in phenomena besides reason, such as motivation. Nevertheless, during the era of behaviorism and even in the early phases of the cognitive revolution, affects have hardly been at the center of research in psychology. Tomkins (1995a, 1995b) stood as a relatively lone voice in American psychology during the 1950s and 1960s in working to develop Darwin's view that affects are revealed through facial expression and are designed to lead us to action. Tomkins stressed that affects ought to be studied in their own right, and that they constitute an independent sphere of knowledge—distinct from perception, cognition, and memory. According to Tomkins, affects are primary biological motivating mechanisms and can, thus, be understood as having primacy in human agency. Tomkins's work highlights the link between affects and facial expressions, and, in his later writings, he included the importance of skin responses (Tomkins 1995b).

Inspired by his teacher Tomkins, Ekman (1992a; Ekman and Davidson 1994) has, from the 1970s to the present, conducted research that demonstrates that emotions are universal and can be recognized cross-culturally through facial expressions.[5] Ekman argues that there are five "basic emotions"—happiness, sadness, anger, fear, and disgust. These basic emotions are defined in terms of the following nine characteristics: distinctive universal signals, presence in other primates, distinctive physiology, distinctive universals in antecedent events, coherence among emotional response, quick onset, brief duration, automatic appraisal, and unbidden occurrence (Ekman 1992a). Ekman concedes that the evidence supporting these nine characteristics varies: evidence exists for distinctive patterns of autonomic nervous system responses for anger, fear, disgust, and

---

[5] A word about terminology: emotions are biological and universal, whereas feelings are subjective and particular (influenced by culture, family, and individual idiosyncrasy). Affects are inclusive of both emotions and feelings.

(tentatively) sadness, and he claims that unique patterns exist for each emotion in the central nervous system.

Like the Stoics, basic-emotions proponents emphasize that affects *happen* to us. It is the rapid onset of emotions, according to Ekman, that explains why we perceive them as happening to us, as opposed to perceiving ourselves to be choosing them. Yet, unlike the Stoics, basic-emotions proponents value affects as contributing to survival and at least in this sense regard them as salutary. The basic-emotions paradigm offers one possible path to conduct research about affects. There are other paradigms in psychology, growing out of the James–Lange theory (W. James 1884; Lange 1885), which have been influential and which we need to consider. Before doing so, however, two criticisms against Ekman's work need to be acknowledged.

The first criticism of basic emotions presses the question of whether affects form genuinely discrete categories or whether what is really "basic" about affects is their dimensions: levels of arousal, pleasure, and activity. For example, Davidson (1992) argues in favor of the dimensions of "approach and withdrawal" as basic, thus posing an explicit challenge to Ekman's understanding of basic emotions strictly in terms of facial expressions. Davidson rightly notes that nothing in Ekman's studies sustains the invariability of prototypical expressions—especially when these emotions occur spontaneously (as opposed to in the laboratory). As Davidson adds, there is no compelling reason simply to assume that an isomorphic relationship exists between emotions and their expressions—there may well be as much variability within emotions as across them.

The second criticism of Ekman's work concerns its cross-cultural validity. J. Russell (1991) observes that while Ekman's work on facial expressions shows that emotions are *similar* across cultures, we should not assume that emotions are *identical* in different cultures. In a similar vein, Averill (1994) has emphasized that basic emotions are, in essence, a form of classification, and he warns that the adoption of such "prototypes" too often results in overlooking secondary and unusual emotions. Shweder, an anthropologist, develops an even more radical critique of the basic-emotions view. Shweder concurs that some emotions lack characteristic facial expressions and suggests that we ought to understand them as "complex narrative structures that give shape and meaning to somatic and affective experiences" (1994, p. 37). Like Russell and Averill, Shweder rejects the basic-emotions view, regarding it as a construct of language that relies on appraisals of value rather than on anything that is found in nature.

In raising questions about how beliefs can influence affects, the cross-cultural criticism draws our attention to the subjective experience of affects and implicitly to our potential to alter and craft them. Ekman makes it clear that he is primarily concerned with the innate and universal aspects of emotions; he avers that this is the path whereby research can make the most progress. Ekman specifically disavows the subjective experience of affects as unamenable to study "because too little is known about how subjectivity maps on to other aspects of an emotional experience" (1992a, p. 175). However, we may wonder to what extent the presentation of affective experience as found states within the mind is a distortion of its nature, which ignores our capacity to process and regulate affects.

Many psychologists have focused attention on how cognition determines affective experience. Emerging as a response to the James–Lange theory, which stipulated that affects are the perceptual recognition of physiological reactions to the outside world, Schachter and Singer (1962) argued that cognition is necessary in order to help us to label states of general physiological arousal. This perspective shares with the basic-emotions view the fundamental basis of affective experience in the body; however, it differs from basic emotions on the issue of whether affects can be linked to distinctive physiological signs. More recently, Lazarus (1984, 1991, 1994) has stressed the cognitive contribution to affects by arguing that there is no such thing as affective experience without cognition. As he sees it, the startle response differs from the affect of fear precisely on the basis that cognition must accompany the latter. The primacy of cognition over affect was a cornerstone of the theoretical framework that organized the work of early cognitive behavioral therapists (see, for example, Beck 1967; Mahoney and Freeman 1985; Meichenbaum 1997). The notion that cognition determines the nature of the affect is, however, rejected by other psychologists like Zajonc (1984), who, in a widely read debate with Lazarus (1984), maintains that it is possible to have affects without any accompanying cognition.

Much of the Zajonc–Lazarus debate hangs on the issue of what is implied by the term "cognition"—whether it is something fairly minimal, like awareness, or something fancier, closer to logical inference (e.g., Mandler 1984). If cognition indicates nothing more than an accompanying awareness of the affect, it is less controversial than if it is supposed to denote logical thinking. The cognitive view of affects naturally shares an affinity with those who wish to emphasize the concept of affect regulation (Oatley and Johnson-Laird 1987; Power and Dalgleish 1997). Indeed, for a number of psychologists working on "emotion regulation," the basic-emotions paradigm is not wrong as much as it is viewed as telling only part of the story about affects. However, not many of these psychologists have taken on the very difficult question of the knower who knows—that is, the nature of the subject who performs the cognitive evaluation that determines the nature of the affect. In seeking answers to some of the questions raised by philosophical and psychological perspectives, it is helpful to turn to neuroscience.

NEUROSCIENTIFIC PERSPECTIVES

Neuroscience is a new and exciting field for the study of affects. One researcher who has become prominent in the emerging subfield of "affective science" is LeDoux (1994a, 1994b, 1994c, 1995, 1996). His work has dwelt on the emotion of fear in rats, which, he believes, is more or less similar across species, and he has drawn attention to the importance of the amygdala as the focal point in the brain that determines emotional significance. According to LeDoux, there are two emotional response systems in the brain: the first, which has its origin in the amygdala, is described as "quick and dirty" because it occurs automatically and is rather crude in nature; the second, which involves the neocortex, refines our capacity to respond by featuring a cognitive component.

LeDoux does not wish to locate emotion exclusively in these two separate parts of the brain. He is attentive to the interaction between the amygdala and the neocortex as well as to the crucial role of other parts, like the hippocampus. In his book *The Emotional Brain* (LeDoux 1996), he emphasizes repeatedly that there is no single place in the brain where emotion resides. There are pathways from and to the neocortex in the amygdala, which can be activated by thalamic sensory processing (without going through the cortex) at the same time as the cortex is activated from the thalamus. The representation of objects occurs simultaneously, but distinctly from emotional response. As LeDoux puts it: "We can, in other words, begin to respond to the emotional significance of a stimulus before we fully represent that stimulus" (1994a, p. 221).

Emotional processing, thus, has an immediate and a mediate form—the former, while distinct, contributes to the latter. These two response systems are labeled "Type I and II" (LeDoux 1994a, 1994b). Type I emotional responses are immediate and are a product of the evolutionary experience of the species; indeed, LeDoux likens them to fixed action patterns in animals. Basically, in Type I, emotions are automatic responses that occur from an initial, cursory evaluation; they are not under our voluntary control. Type II emotional responses, rather than being elicited, are emitted. They are specific to the individual, not the species, reflecting past experience and judgment about the applicability of the past to the current situation. In contrast to Type I responses, Type II responses are subject to our volitional control.

LeDoux presses the distinction between older, more primitive emotional responses that have the function of being an "early warning system"—allowing us to ward off threatening stimuli, despite being somewhat limited in nature—and more recent and complex emotional responses that have differentiated functions; these more differentiated responses enjoy the benefit of perceptual completeness and are subject to our control. According to

LeDoux, emotional responses can occur in the absence of cognitive systems, since the neural circuits for emotion and cognition, while interactive, are distinct.

Thus, LeDoux's view overlaps with the basic-emotions view, although it points the way to a richer account of affective experience by introducing Type II emotional responses, which are variable, flexible, and voluntary. LeDoux wishes to emphasize that much of emotional processing occurs outside our awareness, and that in his judgment "feelings" emerge merely as a byproduct—"frills that have added icing to the emotional cake" (1996, p. 302). Like basic-emotions proponents, LeDoux minimizes the subjective experience of affects, viewing it as a consequence of behavioral adaptation that has been preserved through evolution, rather than having to do with the "primary business" of affects (LeDoux, 1994c).[6] As a behaviorist and sociobiologist, LeDoux is wary of and refrains from exploring self-reflection. Although he affirms that affects occur unconsciously, he dismisses the psychoanalytic unconscious as "a darker, more malevolent place" (1996, pp. 29–30).

The two-systems view of emotional response described by LeDoux is valuable for mitigating the tension between the Aristotelian and Stoic paradigms. At the risk of oversimplification, we can say that the first system of emotional response captures the Stoic position that affects happen to us and elude our control. The second system of emotional response described by LeDoux helps to clarify that the first system is not the only one and that, as Aristotelians have emphasized, we need to pay attention to our capacity to craft affects once they occur.

LeDoux is aware that his evolutionary account of affects is only a starting point. He casually notes, for example, that Type II emotional responses depend on the existence of some kind of self-organization. Without elaborating, LeDoux observes that "the capacity to have feelings is directly tied to the capacity to be consciously aware of one's self and the relation of oneself to the

---

[6] Not all neuroscientists would agree with LeDoux on this point; in fact, Panksepp has criticized LeDoux for minimizing the importance of emotional feelings (Panksepp 1998, p. 341).

rest of the world" (1996, p. 125). This statement tacitly acknowledges the need to broaden the basic-emotions approach in the direction of affect regulation. In invoking the self, LeDoux is on the verge of opening a door that he opts not to enter.

Other neuroscientists, like Panksepp and Damasio, have taken up the challenge of addressing the relation of affects and the self. For reasons of space, we will concentrate on Damasio's work, although this is not meant to minimize the contribution of Panksepp's *Affective Neuroscience* (Panksepp 1998) to the field.[7] Damasio's neurological research concerns patients with prefrontal brain damage who exhibit an apparent inability to feel, although they are able to reactivate past events into working memory. In contrast to the narrow focus of LeDoux's animal research, which admonishes us to look at very specific functions in our approach to the relationship between emotion and cognition, Damasio welcomes large philosophical questions.

As the title of his first book, *Descartes' Error* (Damasio 1994a), suggests, Damasio wants to reject mind–body dualism and especially the assumption made by philosophers who wish to affirm rationality by rejecting affects. Damasio's argument is that, from the neural perspective, emotions are constitutive of rationality itself. As he observes: "Nature appears to have built the apparatus of rationality not just on top of the apparatus for biological regulation, but also *from* and *with* it" (p. 128). Rationality is shaped by and modulated by body signals; thus, the body provides content to the mind, not just life support in being aware of the condition of the visceral and musculoskeletal state (p. 160). Damasio's claim is not merely that the body and emotions contribute to rationality; he wants to go further and suggest that the reduction of emotion, evident in his brain-injured patients, severely impinges upon the capacity to reason.

Damasio's main thesis is that there is interconnection between cognition and emotion within the brain system, such that

---

[7] Panksepp argues that affective states provide essential scaffolding for all other forms of consciousness; he suggests that the self has its source in the self-representation that comes from primitive motor representation within the brainstem (Panksepp 1998, p. 309).

it is artificial to insist on the difference between them. This stress on interconnection might seem to imply that Damasio's position departs from those—like Tomkins, Ekman, Zajonc, and LeDoux—who assert the primacy of affects.[8] However, while Damasio highlights the interaction between emotion and cognition, he would not deny that emotions can exist without cognition. He endorses a multiple-systems approach to emotions.

In order to clarify the originality of Damasio's view, we need to explore it in more detail. He introduces his own distinction between primary and secondary emotions, where the latter come from acquired rather than innate dispositional representations. Secondary emotions utilize primary emotions, but they also give rise to "feelings"—a technical term that characterizes the experience of changes in the body landscape reflected in the mental images thereby invoked (1994a, p. 145). Damasio ponders why it is that feelings arise, as merely accounting for neurochemical changes or the notion that they are neural representations of the body landscape at the moment seems insufficient. He concludes that we need to understand the many levels of neural circuitry in the body, all of which enable rationality and give rise to the self (pp. 147, 161).

Damasio elucidates the neural basis of the self by probing how emotions are integrated in rationality itself—which he terms the "somatic marker hypothesis." The somatic marker hypothesis shows that our decision-making process incorporates gut-level responses that are, in fact, automatic signals from the body that protect and help us to limit and choose among possible options. Somatic markers—part of the neural system located in the prefrontal cortices—are "a special instance of feelings generated from secondary emotions . . . connected, by learning, to predicted future outcomes of certain scenarios" (1994a, p. 174). But they also serve as a prelude to more abstract decision-

---

[8] LeDoux cites Damasio several times in his book, and Damasio, in turn, cites LeDoux's work on the importance of the amygdala for emotional experience. Both concur that emotions have been given short shrift among cognitive scientists. More significantly, Damasio, like LeDoux, believes that there are two systems of emotions, one subcortical and the other neocortical—which he delineates in terms of primary and secondary emotions. Damasio is also influenced by Edelman's (1992) distinction between primary and secondary consciousness.

making, using attention and working memory. They can occur in an "as-if" manner—without outside stimulation and coming to our awareness. They help us to anticipate outcomes and make new goals, negotiating the future by means of the perception of pleasure and pain landscapes.

For Damasio, the self is implied in a neural account of emotion and especially feelings. He readily acknowledges that this is a biological state that repeatedly recreates itself—a mental construction. Nevertheless, he wishes to affirm our sense of experiencing an ongoing and continuous biological state—of which we feel like "an owner and knower for most, though not all, contents" (1994a, p. 238). He seeks to do so without sounding anachronistic—that is, mistakenly conjuring "a little person, the infamous homunculus, inside your brain contemplating what is going on" (p. 227).

The concept of the neural basis of a self requires early sensory cortices, sensory and motor cortical associations regions, and subcortical nuclei. As Damasio sees it, the neural self does not depend on the function of language, although language does enable a more refined form of subjectivity by means of the creation of verbal narratives out of nonverbal ones. As he formulates this: "Language may not be the source of the self, but it certainly is the source of the 'I'" (1994a, p. 243). Damasio does not explore this suggestive distinction between the self and the I and, in fact, has little to say in his book about what it means to be an "I." We are left to wonder how the neural self is related to what we might refer to as the phenomenological self. Damasio also fails to contend with the influence of the factor of culture in this regard; nor does he discuss human development.

In his recent book, *The Feeling of What Happens*, Damasio (1999) elucidates his earlier work, most importantly by differentiating between three distinct senses of self: the "proto-self," the "core self," and the "autobiographical self." The proto-self is based on "the ensemble of brain devices that continuously and nonconsciously maintain the body state within the narrow range and relative stability required for survival" (p. 22). The second self, the core self, enables us to be concerned with the experience of the here and now. Core consciousness, on which the core self is based, emerges when "the brain's representation devices generate an imaged, nonverbal account of how the organism's own state is affected by the organism's processing of an object, and when this process enhances the image of the causative object, thus placing it saliently in a spatial and temporal context" (p. 169). Damasio stresses the link between the core self and emotions; a reliable correlate of a defective core consciousness, he informs us, is the absence of emotions (p. 100).

The autobiographical self is produced by a more complex kind of consciousness, "extended consciousness." Extended consciousness provides us with an identity and sense of personhood; it makes us aware of being at a point in individual historical time, aware of having both a lived past and an anticipated future. The autobiographical self is predicated on an organized record from reconstructed images of the organism's unique history. Working memory is crucial for the autobiographical self in a way in which it is not for the core self. The autobiographical self, while relying on the core self, adds the dimensions of past and future. According to Damasio, the core self is the foundation of consciousness, and the autobiographical self is its glory (1999, p. 195). In passing, Damasio observes that the sense of self that has preoccupied developmental psychologists, occurring at about the age of 18 months, is the autobiographical self. He does not attempt to address in any further detail the issue of how the self develops. Our work attempts to fill in these stages and mechanisms, thereby underscoring the importance of a developmental perspective to understanding the self.

There are a number of key points to articulate about neuroscience before moving on to discuss affects and affect regulation in psychoanalysis and attachment theory. As we have seen, LeDoux's proposal of two emotional-response systems in the brain helps to reconceptualize the long-standing and seemingly unreconcilable contrast between Aristotelians and Stoics on affects: the first system confirms the Stoic belief that emotional responses are beyond our control; the second system supports the Aristotelian idea that emotional responses can be regulated. LeDoux's proposal also offers a potential resolution of the debate, briefly mentioned above, between the psychologists Zajonc and Lazarus: the first system illustrates how affects can occur without cognition, as the former argues, and the second system shows how affects are influenced by cognition, as the latter argues. LeDoux's view highlights the complexity and range of affective experience: it endorses the basic-emotions view, while offering a more fruitful overall account. Yet in invoking the self without building this into his theory, LeDoux provides a compelling reason to produce such an account. Like other psychological perspectives, LeDoux's rests content with the description of cognition acting upon affects.

Damasio has undertaken an ambitious project of highlighting the interrelated areas of affects, the self, and the brain. His view is sensitive to the interaction between cognition and affects, especially the way in which affects can contribute positively to cognition (as Hume and contemporary philosophers have argued). Damasio develops the notion that affects help to create and sustain the self in an original way. He does not attempt to grapple with the issue of how the self develops—which we shall do later in this book. More specifically, in chapter 5, we focus on the theme of intersubjectivity, concurring with Damasio that aspects of the self do not depend on it, but then moving on to pinpoint its crucial role in the development of the self.

In conclusion, the neuroscientific accounts of LeDoux and Damasio deepen the Spinozistic insight that we are embodied minds. At the same time, they take us beyond most of the philosophical perspectives on affects as either physical or mental (or some combination of both). Neuroscience offers an account of affects that is indispensable, however much more there is to clarify. It would be foolhardy to imagine that all of the problems concerning affects have been or could be dissolved by neuroscience. No doubt, we are still at a relatively early stage of understanding the relation between affects and the brain. We have learned enough, however, to make it impossible for any perspective on affects, including psychoanalysis or attachment theory, to ignore neuroscience. Such a stance does not betoken reductionism. As we shall suggest, the subtle and sophisticated attention paid by developmental theory to the subjective experience of affects and affect regulation has much to offer the neuroscientific as well as other perspectives.

With the background of philosophical, psychological, and neuroscientific perspectives in mind, let us now turn to focus on psychoanalytic and attachment perspectives on affects and affect regulation. In turning to these perspectives, we will concentrate on development as well as the subjective experience of affects. After examining psychoanalytic and attachment perspectives, the final section offers an integration of all of the perspectives that have been considered.

PSYCHOANALYTIC PERSPECTIVES

It has become almost commonplace for psychoanalysts to bemoan the lack of an adequate theory of affects. No one could dispute that affects have occupied an awkward place in psychoanalysis, and that they deserve much closer scrutiny. At the very least, it can be observed that a large disparity exists between the marginal role accorded to affects in the theory of psychoanalysis and their enormous importance in the clinical realm. To understand why affects are only now becoming central in psychoanalytic thinking, we must begin with Freud.

As is well known, Freud never treated affects in their own right, and he modified his views several times, usually without trying to reconcile his new views with previous ones. Moreover, Freud never addressed the question of how affects could be closely tied to drives on the one hand, and yet be so omnipresent and crucial to what occurs in the interaction between analyst and patient in the clinical setting on the other. Nevertheless, Freud does offer numerous richly nuanced descriptions of affects—especially in some of his writing on aesthetics—even if they are not the centerpiece of any of his works.

There are two main competing tendencies in the way Freud portrays affects, and these two tendencies have dominated the history of psychoanalysis. According to the first tendency, affects discharge energy and must be comprehended as the psychic manifestation (along with ideas) of drives. Closely connected to this tendency is that, ultimately, affects have their source beyond the realm of consciousness—in the id. In his earliest writings, Freud developed the view that affects discharge energy; he then modified it in the metapsychological papers, in particular the essay "The Unconscious" (Freud 1915e), in order to affirm the relation between drives and affects (and also to move away from the implication that affects have a merely pathological function).[9] Of course, the shift to the view that affects are the manifestations of drives left Freud to struggle against the perplexing notion that affects must be conscious, whereas drives are unconscious.[10] Although Freud's view evolved, the overall direction of the first tendency is to affirm that affects are powerful, elemental biological forces.

According to the second tendency, affects are signals and are subject—at least to some degree—to the control of the ego. This certainly carries the implication that affects are regarded as contributing to adaptive functioning. The second tendency, which has its source in Freud's *Inhibitions, Symptoms and Anxiety* (Freud 1926d [1925]), has been extended further with the introduction of the language of the self and the concept of affect regulation in psychoanalysis. It is fair to say that through the influence of object-relations theory and particularly developmental theory, the second tendency has flourished in recent years.

Nonetheless, there are some psychoanalytic thinkers, like André Green, who wish to question the emergence of the second tendency, arguing that only the first tendency represents a uniquely psychoanalytic view. Green (1999) suggests that placing too much importance on the regulatory control of ego obscures the power of the unconscious to generate affects. He also worries about the diluting effect on psychoanalysis of importing ideas from biology and/or developmental theory (Green 1999). In our view, though, the assumption that a choice must be made between the first and second tendency is questionable. Both are important in psychoanalysis.

Although our interests are mainly consistent with the second tendency, we do not think that this entails any slight to the first one. It is incumbent, though, upon anyone who wishes to develop the first tendency to reformulate Freud's ideas within the frame-

---

[9] There are good accounts of the development of Freud's view of affects in Green (1999), R. Stein (1990), and Rapaport (1953).

[10] Pulver (1971) grapples with this issue and concludes that affects can be unconscious.

work of current scientific knowledge. Consider, for example, Green's defense of the first tendency, which stresses how affects are particularly oriented toward the inside of the body (1999, p. 163). This directly follows Freud's belief that the affect "manifests itself essentially in motor (secretory, circulatory) changes of the subject's own body without reference to the outside world" (Freud, 1915e, p. 179). On the face of it, such a view seems to contradict the psychological and neuroscientific views that we have encountered, which explain affects in terms of responses to the world. It is also relevant in this connection that developmental research has shown that infants are turned outward to the world from the time of birth in a way that departs from the assumptions of classical psychoanalysis. (Research on this topic is discussed in chapters 4 and 5 on infant development).

Does this mean that we must conclude that Freud's intuitions about affects are wrong? Not necessarily. It is possible to qualify what he means by appealing to Damasio's discussion of the "internal milieu" and his "somatic marker hypothesis," wherein the brain constantly monitors what is occurring in the body, as a way to understand the internal experience of affects. Although this might help us characterize the sense in which affects are internal, it would still not be a negation of the idea that they are stimulated externally. Interestingly enough, one of the earliest psychoanalytic thinkers on affects, Brierley (1937), specifically addresses this point, urging psychoanalysts to appreciate that affects can be either internal or external.

As a general point, it is worth stressing that psychoanalysis has much to gain from opening itself up to define and develop itself with reference to views from other, related fields. It is our impression that psychoanalysis has suffered from being isolated from other perspectives on the subject of affects. As is already apparent, many of the issues about affects that have been raised within psychoanalysis echo debates from historical and other perspectives.

For Freud, affects have both physical and mental aspects. They occur within the body, but they have psychic significance. Like Spinoza, Freud defined the mind as embodied, and he articulated the nature of psychic experience in such a way as to avoid the pitfalls of Cartesian dualism. Freud's approach to the study of affects seeks to affirm biology without forsaking subjective experience. Although many questions remain unresolved about what this really means, it constitutes a distinctive and fruitful approach to the subject. For instance, one might raise the question of whether the body is a necessary component of all affective experience—or is affect experience possible without it? Freud clearly appreciated the biological basis of affects and saw them as contributing to survival. However, Freud also ascribed a mental function to affects—for example, that along with ideas, they are the manifestations of drives. He implied that affects play a role in how we interpret and find meaning in the world, although he never ventured to explore this point explicitly.

Let us take a step further in formulating how psychoanalysis follows and yet can be distinguished from other points of view on affects. Insofar as Freud links affects to discharge and the manifestation of drives, we may discern the Stoic orientation: affects are strong and dangerous forces that are not subject to our conscious control. But insofar as Freud sees affects as signals that are subject to the mediation of the ego, an Aristotelian orientation is also present. Freud's special emphasis on the single affect of anxiety marks his view as quite different from Aristotle. Yet he is certainly not as suspicious of affects as the Stoics were. Indeed, a psychoanalytic approach to the mind is often read as challenging the hegemony of reason that defines the Western philosophical tradition.[11]

Some psychoanalysts, like Emde (1983) and Gaensbauer (1982), explicitly register their agreement with the basic-emotions view. The position of psychoanalysis in relation to basic emotions remains open to question, however. One might note that psychoanalysis is naturally allied with the dimensions criticism of basic emotions, given its commitment to pleasure and unpleasure as basic. One might argue, alternatively, that pleasure and unpleasure are transformed into basic emotions—a point of view that is in the spirit of Jacobson (1953). In this connection, too, it is worth noting that there are a number of psychoanalysts who have become interested in neuroscientific

---

[11] Sherman (2000) offers a strong argument on this point, contrasting psychoanalysis with the philosophical tradition.

views of affects (Kaplan-Solms and Solms 2000; Schore 1993, 1999).

Freud construes anxiety in a way that expands the meaning of this affect. In one sense, it is almost as if he conceives of it as akin to a general state of physiological arousal. In another sense, he chooses to dwell upon this one affect because of its clinical prominence. The concern with anxiety is problematic in that it lends credence to the notion that Freud was, from the time of his original understanding of affects as discharges of energy to his later point of view, preoccupied with negative affect. Indeed, Jacobson (1953) was the first analyst squarely to confront the fact that attention to the salutary dimension of affective experience was missing from Freud's theoretical account. Nowhere does Freud grapple with the Aristotelian appreciation for how affect regulation is crucial, not just for survival, but for well-being. This is all the more curious in light of the strong interest that Freud developed in the affective bond between analyst and patient.

Damasio's work is particularly relevant to psychoanalysis for a number of reasons, such as his interest in the neurobiological basis of the self, especially his emphasis on the relation between affects and the self (which coincides with the second tendency in psychoanalysis). Moreover, Damasio's work supports the idea that we need not choose between what we have described as the first and second tendencies in psychoanalytic conceptions of affects. Damasio's concerns range from the neurobiology of moment-to-moment internal, homeostatic regulation to the sophisticated integration of the past, present, and future autobiographical self. Underlying his understanding of regulation is biology. Damasio persuasively draws our attention to the complexity of the notion of regulation by demonstrating how regulatory processes are not necessarily subject to the ego or self.

In the final section of this chapter, we focus in greater depth on the meanings of the term "regulation." For now, let us observe that a psychoanalytic approach to regulation highlights the ongoing struggle that it entails. Once achieved, regulation is not automatically maintained. Characteristically, it is lost and regained even for the most capable people. While it belongs to the nature of a self to modulate affective experience, this is not simply a matter of applying cognition to name and determine the nature of a single affect. Understanding regulation means heeding the subtleties of subjective experience. More specifically, it means grappling with the elusiveness of our affects and the difficulty of understanding their meaning. Clinical experience makes it abundantly evident that we do not always know how we feel. We are often deceived about our affects, believing that we feel one thing, when in fact it turns out that we feel something else. Moreover, we can and often do feel different things at the same time.

Psychoanalysts have ample experience with the subjective experience of affects. This does not mean that a theory of affects must be clinically based, as some have maintained (Westen 1997). It does suggest that the basic-emotions paradigm, however necessary, will not be sufficient. Psychoanalysts are comfortable with how unobvious and complicated affective experience can be. Yet the aim of psychoanalytic treatment in all cases must include the facilitation and maintenance of affect regulation. It is impossible, we think, to imagine psychoanalysis as not addressing itself to one's relation to one's own affects. Regulation goes to the very heart of change that is produced by psychoanalysis.

ATTACHMENT THEORY PERSPECTIVES

It is somewhat ironic that in the literature on attachment affects are so fundamental that questions about what they actually are have been overlooked. Affects are crucial to attachment theory because the attachment relationship between infant and caregiver is itself an affective bond. Affect regulation has enjoyed prominence in attachment theory and research; in fact, the focus on this concept can be used as a partial explanation of why affects themselves have not garnered more specific attention. However, this explanation only goes so far. It does not satisfactorily explain, for example, how little Bowlby concerned himself with affect and motivation in general. Bowlby defined attachment in terms of an "affectional" bond without explicating what he meant by this term. His comments on emotions, while highlighting their importance for attachment, are not particularly insightful. For example, Bowlby asserts that

> Many of the most intense emotions arise during the formation, the maintenance, the disruption and the renewal of attachment relationships. The formation of a bond is described as falling in love, maintaining a bond as loving someone, and losing a partner as grieving over someone. Similarly, threat of loss arouses anxiety and actual loss gives rise to sorrow; while each of these situations is likely to arouse anger. The unchallenged maintenance of a bond is experienced as a source of security and the renewal of a bond as a source of joy. [1980, p. 40]

His interesting idea that fear is an inevitable response to certain innately encoded stimuli—such as novelty, suddenness—that triggers the attachment system, whereas anxiety is the same affective response once the attachment system has been triggered but not responded to adequately by the caregiver, is not strongly supported by research. There is no indication that Bowlby fully appreciated how affect regulation ensues from attachment. Happily, the tendency in recent attachment work is to pay more attention to affects in relation to affect regulation, and so we turn now to examine this development.

In attachment theory, the regulation of affects serves to foster the emergence of self-regulation from coregulation. Or, put into the alternative language that Sroufe uses, this means that the regulatory system of the infant is transformed from being "dyadic" to being "individual." Sroufe's focus is on the role of emotions in development. He observes that Bowlby did not adequately conceptualize affects, and therefore he undertakes this task (Sroufe 1996, p. 177). He maintains that emotions arise during the second half of the first year of life. To some extent, this offers a challenge to the basic-emotions position. Sroufe specifically rejects the view put forth by Izard that infants are born with basic emotions, stressing instead that such emotions come into being through the input of a caregiver. Sroufe's point is that emotions exist from birth only in a precursor form; a shift then occurs during the second half-year of life whereby emotions become more differentiated and less global. Emotions are thereby experienced subjectively and are imbued with meaning in a new sense. As Sroufe claims, during the second half of the first year, "regulation of arousal and emotion no longer depend simply on what the caregiver does, but on how the infant interprets the caregiver's accessibility and behavior" (p. 170).

Sroufe grounds his notion of affect regulation in the capacity to maintain organization in the face of tension. He is careful to emphasize that this is not a matter of cognition influencing affects. Sroufe makes the proposal that the regulation of affects ought to be seen as an "*Anlage*" or prototype of self-regulation. Self-regulation is understood as part of a nexus that includes self-reliance and self-esteem. Sroufe traces the movement of how "confidence in the caregiver becomes confidence in the self with the caregiver and, ultimately, confidence in the self" (1996, p. 186). Although Sroufe would seem to be receptive to postulating intrapsychic structures that are produced by attachment—given that he was responsible for the shift away from Bowlby's notion that the goal of attachment is proximity to the caregiver to the goal of "felt security" (Sroufe and Waters 1977a)—he does not attempt to articulate what underlies the idea of self-confidence.

Another attachment theorist whose work has focused on the role of affects is Magai (1999). (For her earlier work on this topic, published under the name Malatesta, see Malatesta, Culver, Tesman, and Shepard 1989.) Like Sroufe, Magai acknowledges that Bowlby did not pay much attention to affects themselves. Nevertheless, she points out some similarities between Bowlby and Tomkins, who developed their respective views at around the same time. Although Magai is more sympathetic than Sroufe to the basic-emotions position, her special interest lies in how parental affective style influences the capacity for regulation.

A key aspect of Magai's work is drawn from Cassidy, who proposes a connection between styles of attachment and regulation. Yet, to her credit, Magai cautiously resists the supposition that emotional traits/dispositions completely overlap with attachment style.

According to Cassidy, affect regulation can be linked to the quality of attachment (1994, p. 247). The anxious/avoidant style of attachment tends to minimize affects and thus can be understood in terms of the overregulation of affect; the anxious/ambivalent style tends to heighten affects and thus can be understood in terms of the underregulation of affect. The secure style of attachment manifests an open and flexible kind of regulation. More specifically, Cassidy maintains that in anxious/avoidant attachment, the aversion to negative affect means that negative affect is not expressed, but not that it is not felt. In anxious/ambivalent attachment, it is unclear whether the greater responsiveness to negative affect means that it is expressed to a degree beyond how it is actually felt. Cassidy's work offers a promising way to think about affective experience for attachment theory and has been developed further by Slade (1999), who suggests how problems in dysregulation can be tied to various types of pathology.

As attachment theory has evolved, so the concept of affect regulation has become increasingly central. Interest in affects themselves has been slower to evolve and is still in the process of developing. There is clearly an Aristotelian bias in attachment thinking about affects—they are, by nature, understood to be subject to modulation. There is not much evidence that attachment theorists give much credence to the Stoic orientation to affects. Indeed, attachment theorists have not contended with the first system of emotional response as depicted by LeDoux and supported by Damasio. Hofer's (1984, 1990; Polan and Hofer 1999) work with rat pups and mothers comes closest to doing so, as it offers an account of regulation through attachment that emphasizes hidden dimensions that are not subject to conscious control. Hofer warns us, in fact, that regulation should not be conceived of strictly in terms of affects.

There continue to be differences among attachment theorists in the way they think about affects. Some are more explicitly sympathetic to the basic-emotions position than are others. A number of attachment theorists have come to adopt what is referred to as a "functionalist" position. This emphasizes, not just that affects themselves are regarded as subject to regulation, but that they serve as regulators as well (N. Fox 1994).

Others have tried to articulate a systems point of view that features the interdependence of all processes (Fogel 1993; Lewis and Granic 2000). What attachment theorists and researchers share is a commitment to follow out in development how affective experience contributes to the acquisition of self-regulation through coregulation between caregiver and infant.

A problem area in attachment theory that bears on the topic of affects and affect regulation has been its conception of internal structure, or what is termed the "internal working models." Initially, the idea of working models was understood in a way that was close to being a reduplication of external interaction. Mary Main (1991) rendered the idea of working models more complex with her emphasis on metacognition—the higher-order capacity to appraise and reorganize memories. The notion of internal structure is developed even further in subsequent chapters with the ideas of mentalization, and particularly the unfolding of the capacity for mentalization. From the same epistemic tradition, this volume aims to make a contribution to the reconceptualization of attachment theory beyond Bowlby's notion of proximity to the caregiver and Sroufe and Water's (1977a) important qualification of "felt security." In the following chapter (chapter 3) we attempt to show that the realm of representation is not merely derived from, but constitutive of, the evolution of attachment. MacLean's (1990, 1993) theory of the triune brain, which distinguishes three stages of the brain's evolution—the reptilian, paleomammalian, and neomammalian—might be usefully applied to the difference between Bowlby's idea of proximity to the caregiver (which can be associated with the paleomammalian brain) and our focus on mentalization or reflective function (which can be associated with the neomammalian brain).[12] In the next section, we elaborate on the impact of reflective function on affective experience, introducing a new term— "mentalized affectivity"—to characterize this. In conclusion,

---

[12] MacLean observes that the paleomammalian brain is distinguished by the separation cry, the most primitive and basic mammalian vocalization; the neomammalian brain is produced through expanded memory and intelligence. MacLean's theory of the "triune brain," while provocative, has not been universally accepted. See, for example, Pinker's (1997) criticism of it.

attachment theorists have made progress in focusing on affects themselves, though some of the tensions between affects and affect regulation deserve greater exploration.

AN INTEGRATED PERSPECTIVE
ON AFFECTS AND AFFECT REGULATION

In this concluding section, we sharpen our discussion of the relation between psychoanalysis and attachment theory on the subject of affects and affect regulation, leading us to reconsider the meaning of affect regulation and to reflect upon the closely related concepts of self-regulation and mentalization. Finally, we move on to introduce the notion of "mentalized affectivity," the adult capacity to regulate affects, which will be discussed more fully in chapter 11 in connection with clinical material.

Psychoanalysis and attachment theory dovetail in their depiction of the important role played by affect regulation in early development, in facilitating the emergence of the sense of self and the transformation of coregulation to self-regulation. Both perspectives also concur in understanding affect regulation as a balance between positive and negative affect; in particular, they uphold the value of negative affect as opposed to assuming that it ought to be expunged. Yet, some tensions between psychoanalysis and attachment theory have been uncovered as well (for a conceptual review see Fonagy 2001). Classical psychoanalysis views affects as connected with drives, and even in more contemporary versions of psychoanalysis there remains an affinity with the notion that affects are powerful, primitive forces. Insofar as affects are located in bodily experience, it makes sense that there will be limits to our awareness of them. Attachment theory, in contrast, distances itself from this way of thinking about affects. Affects are regarded as adaptive, and, moreover, affect regulation ensures that this is the case.

It is tempting to conclude that while *affects* have primacy for psychoanalysts, affect *regulation* is cherished for attachment theorists. However, it would be a mistake to ignore the fact that affect regulation is important in psychoanalysis as well. As already discussed, affect regulation in psychoanalysis is a concept with distinct connotations of struggle. It is subject, as every mental activity is, to the inherently conflictual nature of the mind: conscious experience is bound to run up against the unconscious. Affect regulation in attachment theory is conceived of more optimistically: secure attachment means that affect regulation can work well—that is, flexibly and reliably. Of course, attachment theory envisions less desirable forms of regulation (or dysregulation) in insecure attachment. Still, there is a difference between psychoanalysis and attachment theory in how affect regulation is understood.

The tension between how affect regulation is understood in psychoanalysis and attachment theory reflects a larger confusion about the meaning of the concept. As a term, affect regulation is used in numerous senses and without much precision. Recent attempts in psychology to clarify the meaning(s) of affect regulation deserve our attention. Gross (1999) offers the definition of affect regulation as "processes by which individuals influence which emotions they have, when they have them, and how they experience and express these emotions" (p. 275). He endorses a "process-oriented approach" in which affect regulation embraces situation selection, situation modification, attention deployment, cognitive change, and response modulation. Underlying Gross's point of view is an evolutionary perspective that construes emotions as "flexible response systems." The sources of affect regulation lie in both psychoanalysis and the stress and coping tradition, both of which, according to him, emphasize the reduction of negative affect. Gross claims, on the contrary, that affect regulation ought to include increasing, decreasing, and maintaining positive and negative affect. He also argues that affect regulation is best restricted to one's own relation to one's affects, rather than how one influences others' affects (how others' influence one's affects is not mentioned). Gross fails to take seriously the developmental ideas we have considered, wherein the infant's own affective experience is determined by the interaction between himself and the primary caregiver.

Anticipating Gross, Ross Thompson (1990, 1994) attempts to grapple with the lack of a clear definition of affect regulation. He claims that we ought to think of affect regulation as "heterogeneous," not as a "unitary phenomenon." Nevertheless, Thompson moves on to formulate a definition that encompasses all of its many aspects. According to Thompson, affect regulation "consists of the extrinsic and intrinsic processes responsible for monitoring, evaluating and modifying emotional reactions, especially their intensive and temporal features, to accomplish one's goals" (1994, pp. 27–28). Affect regulation serves adaptive purposes and, as Thompson makes clear, is closely connected to socialization. Thompson's sympathies for attachment theory mean that he is not willing to detach the issue of one's own relation to one's own affects from the issue of others' relation to one's affects.

At the center of Thompson's investigation is an enumeration of the various objects of affect regulation: (*a*) neurophysiological processes underlying emotional arousal and its management, (*b*) attention processes, (*c*) informational processes—such as the reinterpretation of events (which is linked to defense mechanisms), (*d*) encoding of internal cues, such as of the internal indicators of emotional arousal, (*e*) enhancing access to coping mechanisms, (*f*) helping to predict and control commonly encountered settings, and (*g*) expressing emotions in a satisfactory way—that is, concordant with one's personal goals for the situation. This comprehensive list conveys the broad range of aims that coincide with affect regulation—from the neurobiological basis of regulation to its role in successful adaptation to the social world. Although Thompson acknowledges an internal dimension of affect regulation (*d* above), his explanation focuses on experiences like the reinterpretation of rapid heart rate, breathing rate, and/or perspiration. The example he provides concerns an actor who manages stage fright by reinterpreting emotional arousal to signify the expected anticipation of public performance, rather than impending dysfunction. Thompson's understanding of the internal dimension of affect regulation is insightful, as it underscores that the concept should not be limited to its manifestation in action. Yet, as we will show, Thompson does not go far enough in capturing affect regulation viewed through the lens of mentalization.

Our contribution to the project of clarifying the concept of affect regulation consolidates the earlier perspectives that have been discussed with the views presented above. At the lowest level of regulation, we must think of the organism's equilibrium, to which neuroscientists like Damasio and psychobiologists like Hofer have drawn our attention. On this level, affect regulation is equivalent to homeostasis; it occurs approximately and largely outside conscious awareness. Regulation prompts us to alter our state and to act expeditiously in circumstances where this is necessary—such as extreme situations in which survival is at stake. Choice can become part of this level of affect regulation, although the ensuing action can be spontaneous and without accompanying reflection.

On another level, regulation occurs in connection with our relation to others. Regulation serves to help us to craft affects and to communicate them (at times in lieu of acting on them). Indeed, at this level, we are moving to deal with self-regulation as much as affect regulation. Affect regulation concerns the regulation of affects, but it has implications for the self since it helps to bring the self into existence (see Gergely and Watson 1996, and chapter 4). Self-regulation occurs when the object of regulation is the self; this can be, but is not necessarily, achieved through affects. In one sense, self-regulation can be considered as a higher kind of affect regulation; in another sense, it constitutes a change in form. In order to clarify the change that takes place between affect regulation and self-regulation, it will be necessary to say more about what it means to be a self.

Affect regulation on the second level is about the meaning that affects have for particular individuals. Insofar as regulation involves the capacity to remain within an affective state as one considers it, we have a different model from those found traditionally in philosophy and psychology, wherein cognition acts upon the affect. A precedent for what we have in mind here is found in Spinoza: while he stresses the use of reason over the affect, he emphasizes the value of allowing the affect to be felt for self-understanding. Like others, we appreciate that there must be a cognitive contribution to regulation—whether this is cast in terms of appraisal, attention, or informational processing—but we wish to posit the distinctive possibility of doing so while preserving the affective state. The state might be adjusted upward (increased) or downward (decreased), and it might not be altered at all.

Our point is certainly not to challenge the possibility of affect regulation leading to outward action. Our intention is merely to draw attention to a specific function of affect regulation that is predicated upon mentalization and that has not been described in the literature on regulation. Mentalization is the larger category that includes self-regulation. Like self-regulation, reflective function does not necessarily concern affects. However, insofar as it does concern affects, affective experience will be processed in a more complex way. Just as reflective function brings about a new kind of interest in one's own mind, mentalization with affects brings about a new kind of relation to one's own affects.

Let us try to distinguish and label this ultimate form of affect regulation. The concept of "mentalized affectivity" marks an adult capacity for affect regulation in which one is conscious of one's affects, while remaining within the affective state. Such affectivity denotes the capacity to fathom the meaning(s) of one's own affect states. This is a goal that is no less significant, evolutionarily speaking, than is the goal of acting upon one's emotions. It is worth noting how close the notion of mentalized affectivity is to what happens in psychoanalytic (and other kinds of) psychotherapy. It is widely appreciated by clinicians that it is crucial to understand one's own feelings experientially in a way that is emotionally meaningful (vs. intellectually). There is an especially deep appreciation in psychoanalysis for how difficult it can be to understand one's own affective states and experiences. Not only do we misunderstand what we feel, thinking that we feel one thing while we really feel another emotion; but we often feel more than one emotion, even contradictory emotions, at the same time. Mentalized affectivity enables us to be human—or, ironically put, to become even more human.

3

The Behavior Geneticist's Challenge
to a Psychosocial Model
of the Development of Mentalization

In this chapter, we consider the recent challenges to the psychosocial approach taken in this book. The assumption that the quality of mentalizing is related to the quality of early object relations is a common thread throughout the volume. We argue that many of the known consequences of sensitive as opposed to neglecting and maltreating early environments might be understood as having an impact on the child's capacity to mentalize. However, such assumptions concerning the influence of the child's family environment have recently been challenged by evidence from behavior genetics. Findings from studies of twins and from children adopted early in life are used to claim that past work has exaggerated the influence of parenting on child development. If substantiated, these critiques would remove the logical foundation of most psychodynamic or psychoanalytic approaches, rendering the present proposals, among others, untenable.

It is therefore incumbent upon us to review these critiques and to attempt a vigorous defense of the environmentalist position. In the course of this defense, we will argue that the role of early experience is critical in determining gene expression and that the influence of early environment, as a moderator of the progress from genotypic potential to phenotypic outcome, may therefore be very substantial. We place mentalization at the heart of this process of moderation, arguing that the interpretation of the environment rather than the actual environment governs genetic expression. These considerations lead us to reformulate the influence of attachment on later development. Moving from a model where the early relationship was seen as offering a template for later relationships—a model that appears naive in the light of more recent evidence—we argue that it is the quality or "depth of processing" of the psychosocial environment that can be set by early experience. We posit that the evolutionary function of the early relationship might indeed be to equip the child with the mentalizing skills necessary to function effectively in a stressful social world. Insecurity in attachment relationship may be a signal of some limitation in mentalizing skills. The self-representation is then not so robust to social relationships, and the child or adult needs special strategies to cope with intimate interpersonal relations. We recognize these strategies as the common types of insecurity: the avoidant or dismissing strategy on the one hand, and the resistant or preoccupied strategy on the other. The complete failure of mentalization is no longer characterized by a clear attachment strategy. Disorganization of attachment may be the indication of exceptionally poor mentalization.

INTRODUCTION

Over the past ten years we—developmental professionals as well as the lay public—have unconsciously switched from a primarily psychosocial model of child and adult development to a genetic-biological frame of reference that often a priori excludes consideration of child–parent relationships. In an informal study, we asked twenty parents referred to an outpatient child community mental health clinic consecutively about the likely cause of their child's problems. It surprised no one that they all put brain chemistry at the top of the list. It was more surprising that "bad genes" came second, peers third, and early life experiences a poor fifth, just ahead of food additives. Why is this happening?

The excitement of novelty, of scientific discovery, must have something to do with it. But this is not a sufficient explanation. The reduction of the mind to a genetically prefigured constellation of brain chemicals is appealing. While our consciousness, our free will, our mind is undoubtedly our most treasured possession, it is also the source of all our sadness, conflict, pain, suffering, and misery. The reduction of models of pathology to a principally genetic mode of causation is undoubtedly a relatively comfortable solution for all of us—but like all comforts, it comes at a price.

A fault line runs through modern developmental psychopathology. Environmental enthusiasts, such as the authors of this volume, continue to pursue their agenda of identifying key socializing processes in development with a view to designing ever-improved psychosocial treatment and prevention strategies. They work (in attachment research, for instance), apparently oblivious to the work of behavior and molecular geneticists (the new nativists), who have in the meantime settled the entire issue of developmental causation, at least in principle, and are busy trying to find the genes and proteins to explain pathological brain development. Those who try to bridge the gap—Michael Rutter (Rutter, Silberg, O'Connor, and Simonoff 1999a, 1999b), David Reiss (Reiss, Neiderhiser, Hetherington, and Plomin 2000), Robert Plomin (Plomin, Fulker, Corley, and DeFries 1997)—are relatively few in number. As paid-up members of the gradually thinning group of environmental enthusiasts, we, too, are trying to forge links, while remaining quite aware of what happens to those who try to build bridges across fault lines.

Where has all the mystery gone? Recently, one of us saw three new male cases on the same day. They were very different: a depressed journalist with sexual problems, a young man soon to be married but worried about his history of bipolar illness, and an adolescent with violent behavior problems. During initial assessments it is interesting to try to elicit the patients' theory of their problems and ask something like: "Why do you think this has happened to you?" or "Why do you think people like you get depressed?" On this particular day, surprisingly, all three men came up with identical answers: "I think from my mother I inherited a tendency to look for the negative," said the journalist;

"I think it is well established to be a chemical imbalance caused by my genes," said the groom with the bipolar disorder; and "I've been told I have bad genes that make me hit people," replied the adolescent.

In each case, as they answered, time seemed to collapse. There was no space between the moment their father's sperm penetrated their mother's ovum and the present moment. Of course, in each case it was possible to call upon the natural human desire to create a meaningful life narrative and to explore how their experiences had assisted or hindered their capacity to cope with the difficulties they brought. Psychotherapy is based on biological forces that are rooted more deeply than any intellectual conviction about the origin of a patient's difficulties. But while they expounded their respective naive nativist views, there was no room for dialogue. There was just one simple message: Don't ask what causes my problems, don't probe my memories or thoughts or feelings; there is nothing to know, the answer lies in my genes. There was no room for human mystery! This inability to envision psychological and psychosocial causation is both at the root of the psychological problems these individuals brought into the consulting-room and at the core of the naive nativist perspective.

THE DEMISE OF SOCIALIZATION: PARENTING VERSUS GENETICS

There are three primary agents of socialization of children in Western society: families, peer groups, and day-care centers or schools (Maccoby 2000). The emphasis, both professional and cultural, has been on the family as an agent of socialization. For the best part of the past century, both psychological theories (e.g., Alexander and Parsons 1982; Bowlby 1958; Patterson 1976; Winnicott 1963) and commonsense psychological views (Leach 1997; Spock and Rothenberg 1985) agreed in identifying experience with parents as pivotal in shaping an individual's values, beliefs, character, and, naturally, dysfunctions in adaptation. It is interesting to note that, of the two psychological approaches—learning theory and psychoanalysis—that dominated the last century, it was the latter that retained some emphasis on the constitutional delimiters to socialization (e.g., Freud 1912–13, 1920g; Neu 1992).

The last quarter of the twentieth century saw a dramatic realignment of developmental theories. The emergence of a cognitive mental science (e.g., Barasalou 1991; Johnson-Laird 1983) prompted the translation of some learning and many psychodynamic principles into the language of information processing, with presumed mental operations on past experience creating predictable biases and distortions (what used to be called psychic defenses) in mental representations (e.g., Bandura 1977; Mischel 1973). Cognitive behavioral approaches to development and psychopathology were ultimately saved from tautology and circularity by two factors: (*a*) the theory inspired a whole series of brief and effective psychosocial interventions (cognitive behavioral therapy—e.g., Beck 1976; Meichenbaum 1997); and (*b*) the introduction of a dialectical model into developmental theory (e.g., Chess and Thomas 1979; Kagan 1989).

The views of socialization that emerged from cognitive social learning theory have underscored that the child plays an important role in determining his own socialization experience. Clearly, mothering an infant high in emotionality must elicit quite a different set of maternal behaviors than would the mothering of a sociable, unemotional infant. This realization was critical in radically and helpfully moderating the parent-blaming tendency of early psychopathologists. Although these transactional models of child-to-parent effects were later used to support the argument of those proposing a nativist revival, for the most part cognitive social learning theory maintained the environmentalist tradition of psychoanalytic theories. The simultaneous independent emergence in the late 1960s of the family systems perspective (e.g., Minuchin et al. 1975) and Bronfenbrenner's (1979) influential ecological ideas in the 1970s increased the explanatory power of socialization and further reinforced the focus of developmentalists on the social environment.

Developmental psychopathology, permeated with the dialectic of social learning theory, came to dominate child psychiatric epidemiology, under the leadership of Norman Garmezy, with other giants such as Michael Rutter, Alan Sroufe, Robert Emde, and Dante Cicchetti. The key research question came to be the mysterious unfolding, integration, and interaction of person and environmental characteristics in the generation of psychological disturbance through ontogenetic development. Notwithstanding the explicit commitment to a dialectic transactional model (e.g., Garmezy, Masten, and Tellegen 1984), developmental psychopathology always retained its emphasis on socialization, particularly intrafamilial socialization (e.g., Cicchetti 1987; Rutter 1993; Sameroff 1995). Attachment theory became one of the guiding frameworks of the approach (e.g., Cicchetti and Cohen 1995; Sroufe and Rutter 1984), and John Bowlby was, to some degree posthumously, recognized by many as one of its pioneers (Sroufe 1986). Thus, notwithstanding the dominance of cognitive psychology and social learning theory, developmental psychopathology remained a broad church, and many psychodynamic concerns—in particular a focus on early relationships (e.g., Cicchetti 1987), on affect regulation (e.g., Sroufe 1996), on relationship representations (e.g., Dodge 1990), and on processes of identification (e.g., Crittenden 1994), internalization (e.g., Fonagy et al. 1995), and self-organization (e.g., Fischer and Ayoub 1994)—were retained.

In the last quarter of the twentieth century, developmental psychopathologists were mostly concerned with risk factors—risk factors associated with the family occupying a most important role (e.g., Masten and Garmezy 1985). Developmental psychopathology of the early years of development was particularly concerned with social and cultural facets of risk (e.g., Masten and Braswell 1991), parent–infant relationships, epistemic and motivational mental states that influence parenting (e.g., Belsky 1984), the interaction of economic and social disadvantage with parenting (e.g., McLoyd 1990; Quinton, Rutter, and Liddle 1984), the distorting influences of past experience on emotional and cognitive structures of the child (e.g., Fox, Platz, and Bentley 1995; Parker, Barrett, and Hickie 1992), and parental behaviors as mediators of the gross social inequalities that became an increasing source of concern for social scientists of the Thatcher and Reagan years (e.g., Conger, Ge, Elder, Lorenz, and Simons 1994; McLoyd 1998; Petit, Bates, and Dodge 1997). Permeating all these ideas was the notion that the unfolding of psycho pathology occurred in the context of the child's primary socialization environment: the family. The family, the parents in particular, provided the backdrop against which this unfolding occurred—their characteristics were crucial to the developmental choices the child would make, their actions and collaboration critical to both treatment and prevention.

However, over the last decade of the twentieth century, perhaps in part triggered by the excitement of the human genome project, but also by research designs of increasing statistical sophistication, quantitative behavior genetics was unleashed on early development research. At a certain point it seemed as though research in genetics had all but eliminated the place for classical socialization theories that placed an emphasis on parenting, such as attachment theory, and had refuted all theories that advocated the key role of early family experience (see Scarr 1992). For example, the behavior geneticist Rowe wrote: "parents in most working to professional class families may have little influence on what traits their children may eventually develop as adults" (1994, p. 7). He went on to say that he doubted whether any undesirable trait displayed by a child can be significantly modified by anything a parent does. In fairness, it should be noted that these comments were published before data became available from research that gave equal weight to both genetic and social influences on development.

The Findings from Behavior Genetics

The biological (genetic) movement of the 1990s highlighted a number of issues that seemed to threaten the validity of the kinds of environmentalist claims we are making in this book.

1. The overall connection between early parenting and socialization outcomes turns out to be quite weak, and in longitudinal studies parenting accounts for negligible proportions of the variance. There is very limited evidence that might link early relationship experiences to the development of personality and psychopathology. Furthermore, the implicit assumption that

genetic influences occur only in early life, and therefore that later emerging differences between individuals can be safely assumed to be environmental, turns out to be false. Genetic influences are just as changing and as dynamic as environmental influences. For example, genetic influences on IQ are relatively small in early years but increase considerably as the child moves toward adolescence (Rutter et al. 1997) and conversely the influence of parenting on aptitude test scores declines (Plomin, Fulker, Corley, and DeFries 1997). As we shall see, it is quite possible that at the molecular level some genes are dormant in early phases of development but their activity is promoted in subsequent stages. In fact, genetic influences predisposing to the same trait—such as antisocial behavior—can change over the course of development without altering the size of the genetic component. Thus, the heritability of antisocial behavior is 63% in early adolescence and 68% in late adolescence, but only about a third of this variability overlaps (i.e., is the same part of the genetic makeup at each stage) (Neiderhiser, Reiss, and Hetherington 1996).

2.   Behavior-genetic models of twin and adoption studies partition variability into genetic (h) and environmental (E) components by subtracting the proportion of variability on a specific trait accounted for by genes (h^2) from 100 ($E = 100 - h^2$). In most domains h^2 is 50–60%, with less than half left to E. For attention-deficit hyperactivity disorder (ADHD), heritability is estimated to vary from 55% to 82% (Nigg and Goldsmith 1998; Smalley 1997) As large-scale studies continue to emerge, the proportion of variance that is left after subtracting genetic influence is diminishing.

3.   Behavior-genetics research has revealed that influences that had previously been considered environmental (such as children whose caregivers read to them learning to read earlier than those who are not read to) were actually mostly mediated by the shared genetic predisposition of caregiver and offspring (Kendler et al. 1996). Apparently environmentally mediated family influences are in fact explained by the shared genetic predisposition of caregiver and offspring and therefore are possibly in them-

selves unimportant (J. R. Harris 1998; Rowe 1994). Recently, an analysis of the Colorado Adoption Project showed that many of the milder adverse effects on social adjustment associated with parental divorce are in fact genetic: children who are adopted away from parents who later get divorced develop adjustment problems even if they are adopted into nondivorcing families (O'Connor, Caspi, DeFries, and Plomin 2000). The quality of the environments that are thought to be so important to development, including stress, life events, and trauma (and probably also maternal attunement and sensitivity), can all be inherited. It is likely that personality characteristics that we had often thought of as—and what the child might experience as—the consequence of the parents' behavior toward the child are in fact genetic predispositions. It might be that the particular personality trait in the child and the associated form of parenting (criticism, warmth, or even abuse) are both consequences of the same genes in the parent and the child or that the prodromal version of the child's trait might elicit—say, by evocatory projective identification (Spillius 1992)—a particular way for the parent to be with the child.

4. Correlations between characteristics of early parenting and later child behavior can be reinterpreted given that any association may be attributable to the 50% of genetic overlap between a parent and a biological child. This has been termed *passive genotype–environment correlation.* As genetic factors influence the independent variables (measures of the social environment) and the dependent variables (measures of social adjustment), there is a potential for confounding. In the majority of published socialization studies this possibility is not acknowledged. Reiss, Neiderhiser, Hetherington, and Plomin (2000), in a landmark investigation of genetic and environmental influences on adolescent development, found that of 52 statistically significant associations between family relationship (e.g., parental warmth or sibling relationships) and measures of adjustment (e.g., depression and antisocial behavior), 44 showed genetic influences that accounted for more than half of the covariance. In almost half of the 52, little association between family relations and adolescent functioning remained once genetic influence was taken into con-

sideration. In the Colorado Adoption Project, the parents' report of warmth versus negativity in the family and the child's report of achievement orientation appear associated, but achievement orientation turns out to be genetically determined, suggesting that aspects of the family environment are susceptible to the influence of the child's genetically rooted characteristics—the so-called child-to-parent effects (Deater-Deckard, Fulker, and Plomin 1999).

5.   Insofar as behavior-genetic studies showed family environment to matter, it was the environment specific to each child within the same family (*nonshared environment*) that mattered (Plomin and Daniels 1987). Environment may be partitioned into a shared and a nonshared component. Shared environmental influences may be estimated in adoption studies by comparing the correlation of adopted children and their adopted siblings with children in other households. If shared aspects of the environment, such as parenting, were indeed formative, then adopted siblings living in the same home should be significantly more alike than unrelated children across households. After the genetic and shared environmental components are estimated, what remains is the nonshared environment ($E_{us} = 100 - h^2 - E_s$). The nonshared environment appears to be the bulk of the environmental component; shared environment, an instance of which would be parental sensitivity, accounts for almost no variance (Plomin 1994). Adopted children, it seems, are no more like their adopted siblings than are unrelated children growing up in a different household (Plomin and Bergeman 1991). This is important because the relatively weak observed effects of the shared environment have been used to suggest that environments generally assumed to be toxic by developmental psychopathology (such as high level of parental conflict, parental psychiatric disturbance, or even relative social disadvantage) are either of less importance than previously thought or, more probably, are actually genetically mediated (Plomin, Chipuer, and Neiderhiser 1994). Plomin put this quite elegantly:

> So often we have assumed that the key influences on children's development are shared: their parents' personality and child-

hood experiences, the quality of their parents' marriage relationship, children's educational background, the neighborhood in which they grow up, and their parents' attitude to school or to discipline. Yet to the extent that these influences are shared, they cannot account for the differences we observe in children's outcomes. [1994, p. 23]

6. It has been argued that even nonshared environmental effects may be better understood as being genetic in origin. Genetically influenced aspects of children's behavior may be responsible for provoking specific observed responses in parents and other people. This is sometimes termed *evocative covariance*, when children with different genetic predispositions elicit complementary responses from the caregiver. Thus, the child's nonshared (specific) environment may sometimes have been erroneously attributed to parental behavior rather than to his genes (O'Connor, Deater-Deckard, Fulker, Rutter, and Plomin 1998). Some studies of adopted children suggest that authoritarian parenting, which has been thought to account for oppositional behavior in children, may be elicited by the child's resistive or distractible behavior (Ge, Conger, Cadoret, Neiderhiser, and Yates 1996).

Thus, it seems that over the past ten years we—developmental professionals as well as the lay public—have unconsciously switched from a primarily psychosocial model of child and adult development consistent with psychodynamic ideas to a genetic–biological frame of reference that often a priori excludes consideration of child–parent relationships. We will now argue that the case for reducing the emphasis on parenting, particularly the emphasis on the early attachment relationships, is based on false evaluations of behavior-genetic data, and that perhaps in the past our emphasis on the role of parenting was somewhat naive in trying to see the parents' influence simply in terms of relationship quality, internalization, introjection, identification, and so on. We try to show that (a) early attachment experiences may well be key moderators of the expression of individual genotype, and (b) the primary evolutionary function of attachment may indeed be the contribution it makes to the ontogenetic creation of a mental mechanism that could serve to moderate psychosocial experiences relevant for gene expression.

Scrutinizing the Case for Genetics

As demonstrated earlier, the case for genetic determinants rests on two pillars: (*a*) the weakness of the socialization evidence, and (*b*) the findings of quantitative behavior genetics. We will just touch on the first and focus on the second.

Classical reviews extensively cited by behavior geneticists (e.g., Maccoby and Martin 1983) tended to reveal weak correlations between parenting and socialization outcomes open to alternative, genetic interpretations. However, there have been substantial methodological improvements in studies of socialization, in terms both of the breadth and of the depth of measurement, and correspondingly effect sizes have also increased. For example, Martin Maldonado-Duràn and his colleagues, in a study at the Menninger Child and Family Center (Maldonado-Duràn, Helmig, Moody, and Millhuff, in press; Maldonado-Duràn et al. in press), carried out operationalized clinical ratings of almost 150 infants. Over 70% of the children have so far been followed up two to four years later. Infant behavior problems strongly predicted later behavioral difficulties in a number of areas. Parenting observed in infancy predicted preschool emotional difficulties. In particular, parents who were both neglectful and hostile had children with more behavioral problems. This remained true even when behavioral problems in infancy were controlled for. Observed neglect and hostility toward the child correlated 0.36 with the child's behavioral problems noted at age 4 years, even when infant behavior was already controlled for. This implies that parenting had a predictable effect beyond that which could be explained in terms of the parent responding specifically to the precursors of the child's behavioral problems. Better-controlled studies, such as this one, are accumulating, and current reviews of the socialization literature tend to yield more encouraging conclusions (Maccoby 2000).

A considerable complexity is introduced into the interpretation of social environment to behavioral-outcome correlations by the recognition that the parenting environment varies in significance across development and even within each developmental phase across time. Therapeutic experience shows us the exceptional influence of certain "key moments" of interaction between therapist and patient, when experience brought into clear relief by a confluence of circumstance and intrapsychic factors suddenly enables therapeutic change. (This idea is fully elaborated in the work of Daniel Stern, Ed Tronick, Karlen Lyons-Ruth, and the Boston group on therapeutic process—Fonagy 1998; Lyons-Ruth 1999; Stern 1998; Stern et al. 1998.) They argue that change in therapy might be a function of special moments of attunement between therapist and patient. More generally, the same could apply to special moments of influence of parents on children—naturally with both a positive and a negative valence—moments of parenting influence, however key and formative, that might be the needles in a socialization haystack. It is difficult to imagine how observational research, focusing on aggregate or time-sampled behaviors, can hope to capture significant numbers of such key moments. The correlations between observed parenting and child outcome may never reflect the true influence of parenting.

In any case, however strong the associations between parenting and socialization, the possibility that the more parsimonious explanation is genetic cannot be ruled out. It is the apparent strength of genetic findings, the massive proportion of variability accounted for, no matter how specific the trait, that casts such a dark shadow over developmental psychopathology. But are the genetic findings as unequivocal as they seem? Let us offer a brief, robust rebuttal of quantitative behavior genetics.

The evidence from behavior genetics should be interpreted with caution. The reasons are: (*a*) methodological, (*b*) conceptual, and (*c*) empirical. Methodologically, the contrast of identical and fraternal twins confounds genetic similarity and environmental influence. It has been claimed that identical twins have more similar environments than do fraternal ones (e.g., they have more friends in common, they are treated more similarly by the parents—Reiss et al. 2000). The status of inferring environmental effects by a process of subtraction using the additive model has also been questioned (Elman et al. 1996; Turkheimer 1998).

In particular, E is estimated without any direct measure of environmental factors. If the estimate for heritability, G, is high, E must be low. In reality, G and E combine to generate a phenotype. In simple additive models, however, this interaction would be pooled with genetic effects. The use of parents as a source of data about themselves as well as their child creates an inbuilt genetic bias. Heritability estimates are inflated by the use of parents' reports of child behavior rather than behavioral observation or self-reports. It is not surprising that when parents rate a child's aggression, the correlation with the parent's aggression should increase (Cadoret, Leve, and Devor 1997; Miles and Carey 1997).

At a conceptual level, we may certainly question the notion of nonshared environment, since it merely refers to intersibling differences, not to their environment. In fact, shared environments could as easily serve to make children in the family different from one another as to increase intrafamilial similarity, since shared environments may be experienced very differently by two children. A further conceptual problem concerns heritability estimates based solely on individual differences—estimates that remove shared environmental effects such as secular trends and are strictly restricted to the environment studied. Height, IQ, as well as the prevalence of a number of psychological disorders (such as delinquency and eating disorder) have increased markedly over the last century, undoubtedly as a consequence of environmental changes, yet current behavioral-genetic methods of estimating environmental effects preclude consideration of these.

Empirically, we could point to studies where environmental determinants revealed substantial effects *after* genetic influences had been excluded (Johnson, Cohen, Brown, Smailes, and Bernstein 1999). We could raise questions about the actual—rather than assumed—differential responsiveness of caregivers to siblings. Evidence on just how differently siblings are treated is actually quite mixed. In one of the only behavioral-genetic studies to actually look at the child's environment rather than simply infer it, Reiss, Plomin, Hetherington, and colleagues found direct evidence for the notion of the nonshared environment (Reiss et al. 2000). The difference between the degree of coerciveness of parenting between a pair of twins was more predictive than was the absolute level of negativity (Reiss et al. 1995). However, Judy Dunn's naturalistic observational studies of siblings actually suggest that while cross-sectionally parents may appear to be treating siblings differently, looked at longitudinally children at various ages receive comparable treatment (Dunn and McGuire 1994). The obvious implication here is for a more systemic approach.

Regardless of the ultimate conclusion concerning the differing treatment of siblings, the fact that studies of social development have tended to look at single children implied that they have on the whole underestimated the impact of parenting and other shared environmental influences. As we shall see later on, there may be specific pressures in family systems for different responses of siblings as part of the need for each person within the system to have a unique role. Interestingly, the pressure for difference may be greater when genetic differentiation is least. In a recent study, Pasco Fearon and Peter Fonagy attempted to establish the role of genetic influence on patterns of attachment (Fonagy, Fearon, and Target 1999). The question concerning genetic influence was raised by transgenerational studies of consistency in attachment patterns (mothers whose attachment was secure before the birth of the child tended to have babies securely attached to them one year later—van IJzendoorn 1995). Is this another example of a genetic effect? In a study of identical and nonidentical twins, we found very little evidence for greater concordance of attachment patterns among monozygotic twins. However, we found that the likelihood of concordance in attachment patterns was predicted by mothers' assessment of the temperaments of their twins. Briefly, the more similar the mother rated the two infants' temperaments, the more likely it was that the twins' attachment classifications were to be dissimilar. Conversely, the more the mother differentiated between the temperaments of her twins, the more likely they would be congruent in terms of their attachment classification. In interpreting these results, we tentatively suggest that if the mother fails to differentiate between her children consciously, she is more likely to project unconscious expectations onto one or other twin, forcing them to be different in relation to her. Alternatively, being seen as different at some level may mean that the twins do not feel that they have to find a place for themselves in the family system. If the mother is able to see their individuality, then they can behave consistently with their predispositions.

Furthermore, on occasion experimental manipulations of the environment as part of treatment and prevention interventions have yielded relatively large effects. It is noteworthy that neither of the two major attacks on the importance of family on socialization (J. R. Harris 1998; Rowe 1994) covers parent training. The average effect size of parent training for children with Oppositional Defiant Disorder is around 1 (Serketich and Dumas 1996), which means that the average treated child is better off at the end of treatment than at least 84% of the controls. More relevant in this context is the fact that accumulating evidence supports the usefulness of experimental interventions with parents, such as home visitation (e.g., Olds et al. 1998), with long-term beneficial effects in reducing the risk of criminality and delinquency. Of course, the impact of environmental manipulation is often not as large as one would hope; moreover, long-term follow-ups in treatment studies are relatively rare, and even quite impressive changes initiated by experimental interventions dissipate (Fonagy, Target, Cottrell, Phillips, and Kurtz 2000).

As clinicians, our main objection to behavior-genetic data would not be methodological, conceptual, or empirical but, rather, pragmatic. Genetic effects may well be indirect as well as direct. Even a high genetic loading for a certain environmental hazard does not mean that the consequences associated with that risk factor would necessarily be genetically rather than environmentally mediated. For example, if child abuse were found to have a large genetic component, its toxic effects would still be via the destruction of trust in the world for the abused child rather than via a purely genetic process. The implications of behavior-genetic data for clinical intervention are thus quite limited. But the continuing tension between perspectives based on genetics research and environmental studies should not be played out on the battlefield of the assumptions underlying the genetic model. The findings from behavior genetics appear quite robust, and the burden is on environmentalists to integrate the genetic data with their theories. What follows is a very modest preliminary attempt at the integration of selective genetics findings with environmentalist observations arising from the field under consideration in this volume: the relationship of mentalization and early attachment relationships.

SUBJECTIVITY AT THE INTERFACE OF GENE AND ENVIRONMENT

The Role of Experience in the Expression of the Genotype

It is universally acknowledged that developmental psychopathology involves a gene–environment interaction. In the case of honeybees, the reproductive and social roles of colony members are fixed by events that occur during the first few days of larval development. Worker or queen bee status is apparently not encoded in the genotype but follows from the differential treatment of larvae by worker bees, resulting in differential gene expression—both up-regulation and down-regulation (Evans and Wheeler 2000). Some quantitative human behavior-genetic studies also strongly suggest interactive processes whereby environmental exposure triggers genetic vulnerability. For example, the classic Finnish adoptive-family study of schizophrenia suggests that children with a schizophrenic biological parent were more likely to develop a range of psychiatric problems if, and only if, they were adopted into dysfunctional families (Tienari, Wynne, Moring, Lahti, and Naarala 1994). Bohman (1996) reported that criminality appeared to be associated with a genetic risk only if children whose biological parents were criminals were adopted into dysfunctional homes. So genetic risk may or may not become manifest, depending on the quality of the family environment to which a child is exposed. But if this is such a pervasive process, then why is the quantitative behavior-genetic evidence for gene–environment interaction so sparse? Empirically, this interaction term has proved to be quite hard to find. Plomin's (Plomin, DeFries, McLearn, and Rutter 1997) systematic review of the literature, now admittedly somewhat dated, found evidence only for relatively isolated examples.

We suggest that the answer lies in the fact that behavior genetics sometimes studies the "wrong" environment, because the environment that triggers the expression of a gene is not objective. Gene expression is not triggered by the observable, objective environment. The child's *experience of* the environment is what counts. The manner in which environment is experienced will act as a filter in the expression of genotype into phenotype. And here we touch on the pivotal importance of psychoanalysis and attachment theory, the primary concern of which is with the interaction of multiple layers of representations in generating developmental outcomes. Data from genetics call for exactly such sophistication in understanding the way genes may or may not be expressed in particular individuals.

The pathway between genes and phenotypes is a tortuous one, with genetics and environment constantly interacting (Elman et al. 1996). At the molecular level, evidence suggests that positive and negative environments may alter gene expression—that is, the rate at which genes are transcribed into RNA and subsequent protein synthesis that can, at least in principle, influence the structure and functioning of the human brain. Internal and external stimuli, steps in the development of the brain, hormones, stress, learning, and social interaction all alter the binding of transcription regulators (Kandel 1998). Of particular interest are animal studies that suggest that various forms of learning in animals reflect a process whereby environmental stimuli—such as songs and calls from one bird to another—may activate the transcription of RNA from dormant genes, leading to new proteins being synthesized and changes of synaptic structure and function (Chew, Vicario, and Nottebohm 1996; Nguyen, Abel, and Kandel 1994). The very process of learning may be genetically controlled. Environmental stimuli involved in the conditioning of gill reflexes in Aplysia act to turn off memory suppressor genes (Abel and Kandel 1998). Perhaps more relevant to us from an attachment standpoint are the classic studies of rat pups separated from their mother in the first two weeks of life, who appear to incur a permanent increase in the expression of genes controlling the secretion of CRF (corticotrophin-releasing factor) (Plotsky and Meaney 1993). While the maternally deprived rat pups may acquire a life-long vulnerability to stress through this permanent increase in gene expression, dams who showed increased care of their pups by licking and grooming them during nursing seemed to provide them with a life-long protection from stress. This latter process appeared to be mediated through the enhanced expression of genes regulating glucocorticoid receptors and the consequent suppression of genes regulating CRF synthesis (Liu et al. 1997).

There is substantial individual variability in response to stress and adversity. Much of this variability is poorly understood (Rutter 1999), but it underscores the potential importance of intrapsychic variables. Whether or not specific environmental factors trigger the expression of a gene may depend not only on the nature of those factors, but also on the way the infant or child experiences them, which will be an intrapsychic function that is determined by conscious or unconscious meaning attribution to these experiences. The quality of the experiential filter that attachment provides may, in turn, be a function of either genetic or environmental influences, or their interaction (Kandel 1998). Thus intrapsychic representational processes are not just the consequences of environmental and genetic effects—they may be critical moderators of these effects.

This has substantial clinical significance, since the understanding of an environment by the child is more readily modifiable than are the environment itself or the genes with which the environment interacts (Emde 1988). An attachment-theory intrapsychic perspective may be helpful in considering not just what precipitates personality and its disorders, but also which processes influence the course of the disorder for better or worse. Until the last five years this was theory, but now the collaboration of molecular geneticists and attachment theory is making it a reality. We will offer three examples of this powerful paradigm.

There is excellent evidence from Rhesus monkeys (Suomi 2000) that individuals who carry the "short" allele of the 5-HTT gene are significantly more severely affected by maternal deprivation than are individuals with the "long" allele (Bennett et al., 2002). Actually the full story is somewhat more complicated. The work of Suomi's laboratory over the last decade demonstrated that peer-reared (maternally deprived) infants grow up to be socially anxious in nature, to have a reactive temperament (a tendency to become emotionally aroused, aggressive, impulsive, and fearful), and to drop to the bottom of dominance hierarchies (Higley, King, et al. 1996; Suomi 1997). If their early attachment experiences are poor, then their neuro-endocrine functioning will become highly abnormal; they will have lower CSF (cerebrospinal fluid) concentrations of 5-HIAA (Higley, Suomi, and Linnoila 1996), indicating decreased serotonergic functioning. They will also consume larger amounts of alcohol (Higley, Hasert, Suomi, and Linnoila 1991) and will develop tolerance to it faster, in line with their serotonin turnover rates (Higley et al. in press), which, in turn, is associated with serotonin transporter availability (Heinz et al. 1998). The 5-HTT is the serotonin transporter gene that has been implicated in impaired serotonergic function (Lesch et al. 1996) for the short allele of the gene (Heils et al. 1996).[1] In the Suomi rhesus-monkey colony, 5-HIAA CSF concentration was lower in monkeys with the short allele of 5-HTT—*but only for peer-reared monkeys.* For mother-reared subjects, 5-HIAA concentrations were identical for monkeys with either allele (Bennett et al. 2002). The experience of an inadequate early environment triggered the expression of the 5-HTT gene.

The reversibility of genetic vulnerability was indicated in studies where the foster-mothering of specially bred high-reactive monkey infants was experimentally manipulated. Reactive infants assigned to nurturant foster-mothers appeared to be

---

[1] The literature reveals four studies that found an association between the short allele and harm avoidance and/or high anxiety measures (Greenberg et al. 2000; Katsuragi et al. 1999; Osher, Hamer, and Benjamin 2000; Ricketts et al. 1998). Two further studies showed mixed findings (Gelernter, Kranzler, Coccaro, Siever, and New 1998; Rosenthal et al. 1998). Nine studies, however, found no association (Ball et al. 1997; Deary et al. 1999; Ebstein et al. 1997; Flory et al. 1999; Gustavsson et al. 1999; Hamilton et al. 1999; Herbst, Zonderman, McCrae, and Costa 2000; Jorm et al. 2000; Kumakiri et al. 1999). Thus, as in many instances in this complex new area, the real significance of the short allele of 5-HTT is not known.

behaviorally precocious and unusually secure. When moved into a larger social group, they were particularly adept at recruiting and retaining other group members as allies, and they rose to and maintained high positions in the dominance hierarchy (Suomi 1991). The maternal style of high-reactive females raised by nurturant mothers reflected the style of their nurturant foster-mothers rather than their own temperament. Thus the benefits of nurturant foster-mothering can evidently be transmitted to the next generation, even though the mode of transmission is nongenetic in nature (Suomi and Levine 1998). Calm mothering of these genetically vulnerable individuals not only will reduce the risk associated with this genotype, but there is some evidence that if they receive particularly sensitive caregiving, these individuals will develop special capacities of resilience.

A further example of the same kind of gene–environment interaction comes from our collaborative studies at the Menninger Clinic (Fonagy, Stein, and White 2001). We have focused on the alleles of the second dopamine receptor (DRD2). The A1 or A1A2 allele exists in only a minority of normal subjects (usually no more than 20%). Its prevalence has been shown to be elevated in a number of clinical groups, particularly those with problems of alcoholism (Blum et al. 1990; Gelernter, Goldman, and Risch 1993), gambling (Comings, Muhleman, and Gysin 1996), substance misuse (Uhl, Blum, Noble, and Smith 1993), and eating disorders (Comings 1997). Accounts of these findings mostly invoke the observations of reduced numbers of D2 receptors. We have been able to replicate these results in a traumatized borderline-personality-disordered sample at the Menninger Clinic, many of whom naturally have dependency and other similar problems. As part of a study on the effect of early trauma, we are collecting retrospective information on childhood trauma using Toni Bifulco's Childhood Experience of Care and Abuse Instrument (Bifulco, Brown, and Harris 1987). Concurrently, childhood data were collected on a substantial subgroup of the individuals assessed, as these individuals attended the Menninger therapeutic preschool.

A very preliminary analysis of a relatively small sample (n = 78) suggests that the A1 allele may be a biological marker for the effect of certain types of trauma. Based on largely retrospective information, we found that the impact of trauma on adult personality functioning as measured by Jonathan Hill and colleagues' APFA measure (Hill, Harrington, Fudge, Rutter, and Pickles 1989) was restricted to the subgroup who had the A1 allele. However, the effect appeared to be limited to certain kinds of interpersonal trauma, namely physical and sexual abuse. This is a very preliminary analysis on quite a small sample, so these findings might very well not hold. It is introduced here merely to illustrate a specific type of gene–environment interaction. It is, however, consistent with the mixed evidence that sometimes (but not invariably) links DRD2*A1 with susceptibility to trauma (Comings et al. 1991, 1999). The implication is that early trauma activates the gene, which, through reducing the capacity for interpersonal adaptation, makes the individual vulnerable to later traumata. We have some evidence consistent with this hypothesis. As part of our battery we used Simon Baron-Cohen's "reading the mind in the eyes" test (Baron-Cohen 2000). We found that subjects with traumatic experiences were less sensitive on this test. Furthermore, when we controlled for mentalization using the eyes test score as a covariate, the previously observed gene–environment interaction disappeared. This implies that sensitivity to mental states may indeed have been the mediator of the selective effect of trauma. Those with the A1 allele, either as a consequence of trauma or associated with a genetic predisposition, had less interpersonal sensitivity and showed greater trauma-related impairment in social functioning.

The A1 allele is probably a marker for low dopamine transporter binding, which predicts, among other things, a detached personality in healthy subjects (Laakso et al. 2000), vulnerability to relapse in alcoholics (Guardia et al. 2000), and social phobia (Schneier et al. 2000). It is at least possible to argue that the D2 alleles provide a marker for a certain kind of interpersonal vulnerability. In our sample, the A1 allele was, in the absence of trauma, coupled with significant elevation of personality dysfunction, but dysfunction associated with trauma was evident in the presence of trauma. It is either trauma that leads to the expression of the gene that generates pathology, perhaps via the reduction of D2 receptors, or else the other alleles mark an individual's capacity to metabolize early traumatic experience adequately and avoid the diverse forms of sequelae that might be expected to follow early traumatization. It should be emphasized that these data come from the analysis of pilot data from an ongoing study; the ultimate results might not support these provisional conclusions.

Finally, an important result has recently been published from the Budapest Infant–Parent Study (Lakatos et al. 2000). These workers found an association between the DRD4 receptor III exon polymorphism and disorganized attachment classification in 12-month-old infants. Over the years, considerable evidence has linked behavioral problems in both children and adults with the 7-repeat allele of the DRD4 gene. In particular, ADHD has been implicated (Faraone et al. 1999; LaHoste et al. 1996; Rowe et al. 1998; Smalley et al. 1998; Swanson et al. 1998), although not all studies concur (Castellanos et al. 1998). The review by Swanson and colleagues (Swanson et al. 2000) confirmed the likely role of the 7-repeat allele of this gene in making the postsynaptic receptor subsensitive, thus possibly reducing the efficiency of neural circuits for behavior inhibition. Comings et al. (1999) report findings related to impulsive, compulsive, addictive behaviors that indicate a greater complexity than does a sole focus on the 7- versus non-7 alleles of the DRD4 gene. In view of recent findings, which have linked disorganized attachment in infancy to clinical conditions in middle childhood, it may be particularly important that in this study 71% of the infants classified as disorganized were found to have at least one 7-repeat allele, in contrast with only 29% of the nondisorganized group. Thus infants classified as disorganized were more than four times more likely to be carrying this allele.

This finding is consistent with observations that neurological (Pipp-Siegel, Siegel, and Dean 1999) and neonatal (Spangler, Fremmer-Bombik, and Grossmann 1996) behavioral organization may anticipate a disorganized attachment classification. It might at first sight seem at odds, however, with the classical observation that disorganized infant attachment was linked to unresolved loss or trauma in the mother (Lyons-Ruth and Jacobovitz 1999; Main and Hesse 1990). A recent prospective study led by Pat Hughes confirmed that mothers with a history of perinatal bereavement were far more likely to have disorganized infants than were controls. Whereas almost 45% of the mothers who had lost their last baby during pregnancy had infants classified as disorganized at 1 year, only 20% of the control mothers matched for age, SES (socioeconomic status), and education did so. Adult attachment interviews collected before the birth of the child picked up the risk for disorganization. Lack of resolution of mourning mediates the association of stillbirth experience and disorganization of the "replacement infant" in the Strange Situation.

But only 62% of the mothers with unresolved AAI classification had infants classified as disorganized, although specificity was relatively high (over 80% of disorganized infants had unresolved mothers). It seems that lack of resolution of mourning may be a necessary but not a sufficient condition for disorganization. Since only a third of the children in the Budapest study with the 7-repeat allele showed disorganized attachment, checking for the presence of the 7-repeat allele might, of course, explain the discrepancy. It is possible that the abnormalities in infant–mother interaction, assumed to be associated with lack of resolution of bereavement, may impact more on individuals whose mesolimbic dopamine system is functioning less efficiently, for which the 7-repeat allele of the D4 receptor may be a marker. The mesolimbic dopamine system has been proposed to control behavior motivated by reward (Robbins and Everitt 1999), and less sensitive D4 dopamine receptors (Van Tol et al. 1992) could further distort the signal value of the mother's response. The review by Swanson and colleagues (Swanson et al. 2000) suggests that dopamine underactivity compromises attentional systems, which might exaggerate the impact of subtle anomalies of the mother's behavior in relation to her infant (e.g., momentary dissociation, frightened or frightening behavior, etc.—see Solomon and George 1999). This is clearly speculative, but it is a readily testable hypothesis that is in line with the general interactional model that we propose.

To summarize, we have identified three instances where data from molecular biology might be illuminated by study of the early family environment, particularly parenting and attachment. In one case, lack of adequate parenting was clearly linked to the penetration of one of the alleles of the 5-HTT gene, causing dysfunction in serotonergic activity. In the second case, those whose experience included psychological (and physical) abuse and the A1 allele of the D2 gene showed the greatest personality dysfunction. In the third case, a posttraumatic state in the mother might possibly interact with another dopamine receptor, causing dysfunctional attachment organization and subsequent psychological disturbance. All these findings are rather tenuous at the moment, but all three are consistent with the hypothesis that early experience with the object is formative, even for genetically determined predisposition through the triggering of gene expression. Taken together, they suggest quite a fruitful line of investigation, which, given the relative facility with which samples can be collected and analyzed, might become an important adjunct to most of our work in developmental psychopathology.

The Genesis of an Appraisal Mechanism

So far, we have argued that the importance of family environment may have been underestimated in behavioral genetics research, for methodological and conceptual as well as empirical reasons. We have also tried to construct a *prima facie* case for a representational system that forms an active filter between the genotype and the phenotype. In other words, the mental processing of experience is critical for the expression of genetic material, and therein lie substantial interactions between gene and environment. We will now argue that the genesis of the representational system that forms an active filter between the genotype and the phenotype is intrinsically linked to the quality of early object relationships. Perhaps more than shaping the quality of subsequent relationships (for which evidence is lacking), the early relationship environment serves to equip the individual with a processing system. The creation of this representational system is arguably the most important evolutionary function for attachment to a caregiver. Adopting this perspective helps to redress the prevailing bias against the centrality of the family as the major force in socialization, but it also shifts the emphasis from content of experience to psychological structure or mental mechanism and involves expanding on current ideas of the evolutionary function of attachment.

John Bowlby, a major Darwin scholar (Bowlby 1991), was impressed by the obvious selection advantages of infant protest at separation—that is, protection from predation (Bowlby 1969). Given that phylogenetically and ontogenetically infancy is a period of extreme risk, it is unarguable that natural selection would favor individuals with a capacity for attachment. There has been a revolution in evolutionary theory since Bowlby's time. We now realize that "survival of the fittest" cannot guarantee the natural selection of a behavior. Only the reproduction of genetic material can achieve this (W. D. Hamilton 1964). This is the theory of inclusive fitness. One does not need to survive and reproduce oneself in order for one's genes to be replicated. For example, some organisms will forgo reproduction in order to ensure the reproductive potential of their *genetically* close relatives. The concept of "inclusive fitness" places attachment theory at the center stage of evolutionary sociobiology as a key behavioral mechanism mediating the establishment of genetic proximity, for attachment is the process that ensures that we know whose survival will advantage the reproduction of our genes. Of course, it may have additional evolutionary functions. Freud's (1900a) principle of multiple determination works in evolutionary theory just as much as in dream interpretation and symptom generation. It is possible that attachment marks individuals with whom we should *not* mate because of the biological risks associated with interbreeding and incest. Adult attachment may also be a marker for reciprocal altruism. Altruism and cooperativeness (Axelrod 1984; Trivers 1971)—the "quid-pro-quo" strategy of helping non-kin if, and only if, they have done something for one—might also be underpinned by the mechanism of attachment. Attachment is likely to minimize the adverse effects of "cheaters"—individuals who do not reciprocate equitably in groups over time and to whom we are unlikely to become attached. This would be a good example of a further interesting facet of evolution: how a mechanism that evolved for one purpose (the protection of the vulnerable infant) may be put to good biological use in the context of the adaptive problems of subsequent developmental phases. But all these potential biological functions would apply as readily to animal models of attachment as to the human infant. If the biological function of attachment is to be a pillar in our argument for the importance of parenting, we need to restrict ourselves to uniquely human capacities.

The generally recognized components of attachment behaviors that serve to establish and maintain proximity are: (*a*) signals that draw the caregivers to their children (such as smiling), (*b*) aversive behaviors (such as crying), which perform the same function, and (*c*) skeletal-muscle activity (primarily locomotion), which brings the child to the caregiver. But there is a fourth component that provides a better evolutionary rationale for the entire enterprise of human attachment, going beyond the issue of physical protection: (*d*) according to Bowlby, at about the age of 3 years behaviors signifying a goal-corrected partnership begin to emerge. The central psychological processes for mediating goal-corrected partnerships are the internal working models.

Bowlby's original concept has been thoughtfully elaborated by some of the greatest minds in the attachment field (Bretherton 1991b; Bretherton and Munholland 1999; Crittenden 1990, 1994; M. Main 1991; Main et al. 1985; Sroufe 1990, 1996), and no attempt to duplicate this will be undertaken here. However, it might be helpful to summarize the four representational systems that are implied in these reformulations: (*a*) expectations of interactive attributes of early caregivers created in the first year of life and subsequently elaborated, (*b*) event representations by which general and specific memories of attachment-related experiences are encoded and retrieved, (*c*) autobiographical memories by which specific events are conceptually connected because of their relation to a continuing personal narrative and developing self-understanding, and (*d*) understanding of the psychological characteristics of other people (inferring and attributing causal motivational mind states such as desires and emotions and epistemic mind states such as intentions and beliefs) *and differentiating these from those of the self.* Thus a key developmental attainment of the internal working model is the creation of a processing system for the self (and significant others) in terms of a set of stable and generalized intentional attributes, such as desires, emotions, intentions, and beliefs inferred from recurring invariant patterns in the history of previous interactions. The child comes to be able to use this representational system to predict the other's or the self's behavior in conjunction with local, more transient intentional states inferred from a given situation.

Classically, in attachment theory this phase change from behavior to representation is generally regarded as a modification of the attachment system propelled by cognitive development (Marvin and Britner 1999). Our contention here is the reverse: rather than seeing the biological role of attachment shifting ontogenetically as a consequence of other, biologically driven maturational changes, we propose that a major selective advantage conferred by attachment to humans was the opportunity it afforded for the development of social intelligence and meaning-making. The capacity for "interpretation," which Bogdan defined as "organisms making sense of each other in contexts where this matters biologically" (1997, p. 10), becomes uniquely human when others are engaged "psychologically in sharing experiences, information and affects" (p. 94). The capacity to interpret human behavior—to make sense of each other— requires the intentional stance: "treating the object whose behavior you want to predict as a rational agent with beliefs and desires" (Dennett 1987, p. 15).

The capacity for interpretation in psychological terms—let us call this the "Interpersonal Interpretive Mechanism," or IIM—is not just a generator or mediator of attachment experience; it is also a product of the complex psychological processes engendered by close proximity in infancy to another human being—the primary object or attachment figure. It is not Bowlby's IWM; it is just a part of the IWM (Bowlby, 1980) and perhaps Kernberg's self–object–affect triad (1983). It does not contain representations of experiences and is not a repository of personal encounters with the caregiver. Rather, it is a mechanism for processing *new* experiences, more like Bion's (1962a) alpha function. The IIM is closely related to the notion of a "theory of mind"—the ability to attribute independent mental states to others in order to explain and predict their behavior (Leslie 1987). Earlier in this volume, we introduced the concept of reflective function and mentalization (chapter 1) to broaden the rather narrow scope and operationalization of the theory-of-mind construct. We see the IIM as an overarching hypothetical neural structure, a processing system for social information that underlies reflective function or mentalization but may have many functions beyond these. In the present chapter, we use IIM as the assumed neural mechanism that interacts with the genotype to enhance or reduce the likelihood of genetic expression. In later chapters, we restrict ourselves almost entirely to psychological observations and mark this by using the terms "mentalization" or "reflective function"—the latter when referring to mentalization as it is operationalized in our work. We assume that the quality of functioning of the IIM is reflected in the quality of mentalization. In chapter 4 we outline how the development of the IIM is facilitated by sensitive and attuned early care, and chapter 5 gives a comprehensive account of the ontogenesis of mentalization as it relates to the formation of the self.

The IIM may be a final step in the transcription of genetic influence into a pattern of behavior, in a way analogous to RNA. The interpretive mechanism encodes genetic information in the form of biases, but, we would suspect, of a very specific and situational character. Interpreting social behavior in one context may correlate poorly with understanding of another. For example, from the work of Mary Target with Arietta Slade and her colleagues on the PDI (Parents Development Interview—Slade, Bernbach, Grienenberger, Wohlgemuth-Levy, and Locker, unpublished manuscript), we are finding that parental reflective function is specific to each parent–child relationship. In our twin study, parents' representation of each twin was independently predictive of Strange Situation observation. The IIM, or a mechanism like it, is responsible for the moderation of genetic influence by modifying the child's perception of his social environment. Thus given a genetic predisposition for antisocial behavior, for example, positive behaviors in the family can protect the child from becoming antisocial (Reiss et al. 2000), because such positive behaviors enhance the functioning of the interpersonal interpretive mechanism in that child, which, in turn, helps in generating less malevolent interpersonal attributions. Of course, such warmth may, in turn, be the consequence of inherited characteristics in the child, such as physical attractiveness, easy temperament, and so on. Our proposal for environmental influence does not entail a return to naive environmentalism.

The Ontogenesis of the IIM

How is the IIM created out of the secure base? Clearly there must be biological preparedness, but in our view this is not separable from the infant's experience of the caregiving environment. In answering this question we are drawing on George Gergely and John Watson's model (Gergely and Watson 1996, 1999). A core proposition in this book is the rejection of the notion that the conscious apprehension of our mind states through introspection might be a basic, direct, and probably prewired ability of our mind. We do not believe that knowledge of the self as a mental agent is innately given. Rather, we see it as a developing or constructed capacity that evolves out of the earliest relationships. In chapter 4 the developmental roots of our model of the apprehension of emotional states is described in full, and in chapter 5 some of the problems of the nativist intersubjective position are critically considered. In the current chapter, we anticipate these arguments with a brief outline of the ontogenetic model and focus on the broader implications of the assumption of an interpersonal interpretive processing system that moderates genetic influences on personality.

Our core idea is that the attachment context provides the setting in which the infant can develop a sensitivity to self-states, through what Gergely has termed "psycho-feedback" or social biofeedback—a mechanism that is fully described in chapter 4. The child acquires this capacity for sensitivity by developing a second-order symbolic representational system for motivational and epistemic mind states. What initiates the development of this representational system is the internalization of the mother's mirroring response of the infant's distress (caregiving behavior), which comes to represent an internal state. The mother's empathic emotion provides the infant with feedback on his emotional state. The infant internalizes the mother's empathic expression by developing a secondary representation of his emotional state, with the mother's empathic face as the signifier and his own emotional arousal as the signified. The mother's expression tempers emotion to the extent that it is separate and different from the primary experience, although crucially it is recognized not as the mother's experience, but as an organizer of a self-state. It is this "intersubjectivity" that is the bedrock of the intimate connection between attachment and self-regulation.

As shown in chapter 5, however, intersubjectivity in this context may be a misnomer. At this stage the infant is unaware that he is seeing the other's subjective state. It is likely that the infant does not yet know that others have internal feelings. At this level of human proximity the other's subjective state is automatically referred to the self. In infancy the contingent responding of the attachment figure does far more than provide reassurance about a protective presence. It is the principal means by which we acquire understanding of our own internal states, which is an intermediate step in the acquisition of an understanding of others as psychological entities—the intentional stance. We believe that when relational analysts such as the brilliant late Stephen Mitchell (2000) describe intersubjectivity in the context of therapy, they are invoking this mechanism.

In the first year the infant only has primary awareness of being in a particular internal, emotional state. Such awareness is noncausal or epiphenomenal in that it is not put to any functional use by the system. It is in the process of psychofeedback between infant and mother that these internal experiences are more closely attended to, evolve a functional role (a signal value), and acquire a function in modulating or inhibiting action. Thus it is attachment processes that ensure the move from primary awareness of internal states to functional awareness. In functional awareness a feeling of anger may be used to simulate and so to infer the other's corresponding mental state. This is achieved not through reflection but by action: the child "knows" that acting in a particular way will result in a specified outcome but does not need to—or is not yet able to—make the further inference that the outcome is a consequence of the internal state he generated in the object. Functional awareness of internal states can also be used to serve a signal value to direct action. The next level of awareness is reflective awareness, where the individual can make a causal mind state become the object of attention without it causing action. Whereas functional awareness is intrinsically coupled with action, reflective awareness is separate from it. It has the capacity to move away from physical reality and may be felt to be not for real. A final level is autobiographical, where the child is able to place records of experiences imbued with psychological states into a sequence that represents his history as an individual. These stages of the development of self as agent are detailed in chapter 5.

Many studies provide evidence consistent with this model (see chapters 1 and 5). For example, a study mentioned earlier showed that the rapid soothing of distressed 6-month-olds could be predicted on the basis of ratings of emotional content of the mother's facial expression during the process of soothing: mothers of rapid responders showed somewhat more fear, somewhat less joy, but most typically a range of other affects in addition to fear and sadness. Mothers of rapid responders were far more likely to manifest multiple affect states (complex affects). We interpreted these results as supporting Gergely and Watson's notion of the mother's face being a secondary representation of the infant's experience—the same, and yet not the same. This is functional awareness with the capacity to modulate affect states.

A further set of studies performed by Gergely and his colleagues in Budapest as well as our laboratory in London and with an ongoing replication in Topeka, Kansas, explored 1-year-olds' understanding of conflicting affect (Koós, Gergely, Gervai, and Tóth 2000). In one study, 12-month attachment classification—particularly secure and disorganized—was found to be predicted by infant behavior at 6.5 months in a modified still paradigm (Koós et al. 2000). The paradigm involves the mother being instructed according to the still-face protocol but facing a mirror, where the infant has a choice between looking at the mother's face or looking at a perfectly contingent image (themselves). Infants classified as securely attached engaged six months later in significant amounts of active testing of their mirror self-image only when their mother became temporarily inaccessible (the still-face period). In contrast, babies who went on to manifest disorganized attachment six months later were drawn to the image of their fully contingent self movements throughout the laboratory testing. Interestingly, the Koós et al.

(2000) study also demonstrated that following the still-face period the infants who engaged in more contingency testing while
looking at their self-image showed more positive affect following
the procedure. This led to more successful affect regulation in
disorganized infants than in secure ones. Yet seeking for perfect
contingency in attempts at detecting internal states in the context of human interaction will be of limited effectiveness in the
long run. It characterizes the dissociative style of attention organization that is typical of disorganized attachment.

In chapter 5 we consider the developmental move from a stage
when the infant seems to prefer stimuli that are perfectly contingent with his actions to a stage when infants indicate greater
interest in stimuli that only partially mirror their actions, which
are contingent but clearly not perfectly so. The preference for
perfect contingency that characterizes the infant of less than 5
months clearly orients him toward his own physical self. It
establishes the parameters of his body as proprioceptive and
provides him with visual experiences that are perfectly contingent, and also contingent with rudimentary volitional states
related to action. In chapter 5 we argue that the developmental
step entailed by the preference for high but imperfect contingencies after the age of 5 months turns the human infant toward
social interaction with his attachment figures. Human beings are
incapable of responding with perfect contingency. An orientation
to the social world entails a greater tolerance for imperfect
contingencies, as the caregiver fails to respond to a high proportion of the infant's signals (Tronick 1989, 1998). Notwithstanding
the biological preparedness for imperfect contingency, the interpersonal learning environment within which the IIM can develop
probably requires a minimum level of contingent responding for
the experience of "*nearly, but clearly not the same*" to evolve—the
experience that is undoubtedly key to the creation of interpersonal symbolic capacity. Disorganized attachment perhaps
marks the historical absence of an interpersonal context that
failed to meet the tolerance limits of the infant's capacity
to absorb imperfect contingency. Thus, the experience of mis-
attunement (or noncontingency), which causes all of us to internalize an "other within the self" (the part of the self we will be
calling the "alien self"), goes in some cases beyond what the

infant can tolerate and still feel a sense of coherent, continuous identity. For most us, the experience of unresponsiveness or inappropriate response can be incorporated within our self-structure through mentalization, which lends an illusion of coherence, normally through creating a narrative self. This coherence becomes a functional reality as we weave incompatible experiences together into one identity. Arguably, the nagging sense of incongruity and of "loose ends" within the self-structure supplies some of the motivation for seeking out further attachment relationships throughout life, in a search for greater integration and understanding. For other people, the alien experience within the self remains an inassimilable core that creates an even more powerful need for integration through later attachment relationships but that also gets in the way of forming and maintaining such relationships. The vulnerability of reflective function may then be compounded by later attachment trauma, which, in an effort to restore a feeling of control, may lead to identification with the abuser's state of mind. This sequence is explored further in chapter 10.

Evidence for the Interpersonal Interpretive Mechanism

Is there any evidence for an IIM that evolves out of the attachment relationship, with its efficiency conditioned by attachment security?

1. There is unequivocal evidence from two decades of longitudinal research that secure attachment in infancy is strongly associated with the precocious development of a range of capacities that depend on interpretive or symbolic skills, such as exploration and play, intelligence and language ability, ego resilience and ego control, frustration tolerance, curiosity, self-recognition, social cognitive capacities, and so on. Attachment security foreshadows cognitive competence, exploratory skill, emotion regulation, communication style, and other outcomes. In our view, this is not because of the general impact of attachment security

on the child's self-confidence, initiative, ego functioning, or other broader personality processes but, rather, because attachment processes provide the key evolutionarily prepared paths for an interpersonal interpretive capacity to develop.

Thus it is not the first attachments that are formative, it is not attachment security per se that predicts good outcome on this dazzling array of measures; rather, the features of the interpersonal environment that generate attachment security during the first year of life also prepare the ground for the rapid and competent ontogenetic evolution of interpersonal interpretation. One problem in attempting to trace some of the long-term outcomes of secure attachment in infancy has been the appropriately conservative strategy of controlling for numerous aspects of this interpretive capacity. Controlling for verbal fluency or even IQ removes a part of the variability in which the attachment relationship arguably plays a causal role. But this is an issue for another time.

2. A number of specific findings in the literature link attachment to the development of an IIM. Laible and Thompson (1998) reported that securely attached children have higher competence in understanding negative emotion. A unique study by Jude Cassidy and colleagues (Cassidy, Kirsh, Scolton, and Parke 1996) found that securely attached kindergarteners were less likely to infer hostile intent in stories with ambiguous content. This bias appeared to mediate their superiority in sociometric status. In the London Parent–Child Study Peter Fonagy, Miriam and Howard Steele, and Juliet Holder (1997) reported precocious performance on theory-of-mind tasks among 5-year-olds with a history of secure attachment in infancy. This finding has also been reported by other investigators since then (Fonagy 1997; Meins et al. 1998).

3. In a relatively full exploration of findings linking early attachment and later development, Ross Thompson concludes that "the strength of the relationship between infant security and later socio-personality functioning is modest" (1999, p. 280). The associations are stronger contemporaneously than they are predictively. Within the context of the present theory, it is not the

content of internal working models that is likely to be determined by early experience; rather, the presence of a model or the quality or robustness of the model determines later socio-personality functioning. Thus, attachment classification might or might not be stable from infancy through middle childhood to adolescence. As prediction comes from the IIM, not from attachment security per se, this is of no great concern.

The focus of study should not be attachment security, which achieved significance as a correlate of the IIM but has little stability and possibly little predictive value. Within the context of the present theory, it is not the nature of self–other representations that is thought to be determined by early experience. Rather, the focus of the present enquiry is the extent to which early experience may jeopardize the very existence of a structure to represent object relationships, the processing skills required to deal with interpersonal interaction, the robustness of the model, the extent to which this interpretive mechanism can function under stress and process emotionally charged information, and so forth. The mechanism of predictive significance is the interpersonal interpretive mechanism, which is a genetically defined capacity that is probably localized in the medial prefrontal cortex. Studies of patients with orbital-frontal and medial-frontal lesions have repeatedly suggested specific deficits in tasks that call for thinking about mental states in others (Channon and Crawford 1999, 2000; Stuss, Gallup, and Alexander 2001). Both PET (positron emission tomography) and fMRI (functional magnetic resonance imaging) studies in which subjects were asked to make inferences about the mental states of others found activity associated with mentalizing in the medial prefrontal cortex. In addition, activity was elicited in the temperoparietal junction (Gallagher et al. 2000; Goel, Grafman, Sadato, and Hallett 1995).

There is independent evidence for the developmental vulnerability of this structure from PET-scan studies of Romanian adoptees who were deprived of the interpersonal experiences that we think might generate the IIM (B. Perry 1997). Damage to these frontal areas (Adolphs, Tranel, Damasio, and Damasio 1995; Alexander, Stuss, and Benson 1979; Brazzelli, Colombo, Della Sala, and Spinnler 1994; Channon and Crawford 1999,

2000; Damasio 1994; Rogers et al. 1999) has been consistently associated with social and personality deficits that are consistent with the notion of the loss of interpersonal interpretive capacity: impaired social judgments, impaired pragmatics, deficient self-regulation, and impoverished association of social situations with personal affective markers (e.g., Craik et al. 1999; Stuss 1983, 1991). Independently, we know, of course, that the attachment classification of these adoptees remains disorganized at the age of 3 years and their social behavior is abnormal at age 8. We also have evidence that the mentalizing capacity of individuals maltreated in early childhood continues to have significant limitations.

4. Myron Hofer's work with rodent pups identified regulatory interactions within the mother–infant relationship that have clear analogies to what is proposed here (Hofer 1995; Polan and Hofer 1999). Hofer's work over three decades has revealed that the evolutionary survival value of staying close to and interacting with the mother goes far beyond protection and may be expanded to many pathways available for regulation of the infant's physiological and behavioral system. Hofer's view is analogous to ours in that he proposes that the attachment "relationship provides an opportunity for the mother to shape both the developing physiology and the behavior of her offspring through her patterned interactions with her infant" (Polan and Hofer 1999, p. 177). Attachment is not an end in itself—it is a system adapted by evolution to fulfill key ontogenetic physiological and psychological tasks.

Hofer's reformulation of attachment in terms of regulatory processes, hidden but observable within the parent–infant interaction, provides a very different way of explaining the range of phenomena usually discussed under the heading of attachment. The traditional attachment model is clearly circular. The response to separation is attributed to the disruption of a social bond, the existence of which is inferred from the presence of the separation response. We argue that what is lost in "loss" is not the bond but the opportunity to generate a higher-order regulatory mechanism: the mechanism for appraisal and reorganization of mental contents. We conceptualize attachment as a process that brings complex mental life into being from a complex and adaptable behavioral system. Some, but by no means all, such mental function is unique to humans. The mechanisms that generate these (attachment relationships) show evolutionary continuity across nonhuman species. Just as in rat pups the ontogenetic development of biological regulators crucially depends on the mother–infant unit, so in human development psychological interpretive capacity evolves in the context of the repetitive interactions with the mother.

5. In a series of studies at the Menninger Clinic we explored the factor structure of a number of self-report measures of adult attachment. On both community and clinical samples we found very similar results across three investigations. In the first study (Allen et al. 2000), two measures of adult attachment style—the Relationship Questionnaire (Bartholomew and Horowitz 1991) and the Adult Attachment Scale (Collins and Read 1990)—were administered to 253 individuals (99 female trauma patients and 154 community controls). The factor space provided a reasonable two-dimensional solution with a secure–fearful axis and a dismissive–preoccupied axis.[2] We found the same two factors—a secure–fearful axis and a dismissive–preoccupied axis—in a replication study by Stein and colleagues, which used five adult attachment-questionnaire measures, again on a mixed population. When we plotted the subjects in the sample—both patients and community controls—on the same two principal components, it was clear that while the secure–fearful axis was excellent at distinguishing the community sample from the patient group, the dismissive–preoccupied axis did not distinguish the groups well. What was also clear was a somewhat unexpected relationship between component scores. Although the overall correlation between the two scales was negligible, as you would expect, the discrimination between dismissive and preoccupied was somewhat greater toward the middle point of the secure–fearful dimension.

---

[2] In a principal-component analysis, a two-component solution accounted for all eigen values greater than 1 and for 67.2% of the total variance.

One way of interpreting these data is to assume that security represents an experience of safety in closeness, whereas fearfulness relates to a disorganization of attachment. The fearfulness appears to be specific to attachment relationships, as non-attachment relationships rarely score highly on this dimension. The dismissing attachment style appears to offer protection to the self by isolation, whereas in enmeshed preoccupation self-protection is perhaps afforded by an amplification of the other, by a denial or subjugation of the self.

We would argue that the safety-to-fearfulness dimension corresponds to the quality of functioning of the IIM. At the high end, the individual is well able to represent complex internal states of the other and of the self. With a well-established higher-order capacity for distinguishing psychological states of the other and the self, they need no additional strategies for conducting productive interpersonal relationships. When the psychological mechanism crucially underpinning attachment is somewhat weaker (as a function of attachment history or biology), the capacity for sustaining a clear distinction between self and other also becomes weaker. In such a situation the individual will require specific strategies to accommodate to interpersonal encounters. The two prototypical strategies are the avoidant and resistant strategies.

But why are such strategies necessary? Both serve to protect the self in the context of intense interpersonal relations. We assume that these strategies may be necessary because the self, which is, as we have seen, the product of the other, always remains vulnerable to social influence. To avoid such instability, against a background of a relatively insecure internal working model, the individual can either deliberately withdraw and enhance the self-representation relative to the other representations (dismissing) or protectively overamplify and exaggerate the other representation (preoccupied). In either case, the strategies in representational terms are about deliberately separating the other from the self-representation.

Neither of these strategies is inherently pathological, although both signal a certain degree of weakness. At the extreme end of the safety-to-fearfulness dimension, there can be no strategy because the attachment system is not there to sustain a consistent set of defenses. In these cases the interpretive mechanism that sustains social relations functions so poorly that the capacity to arrive at representations of the motivational or epistemic mind states of the other, independent of those of the self, is profoundly compromised. This is attachment disorganization or, rather, the absence of the mental function that sustains attachment. Thus we conceive of attachment disorganization as lying at the opposite end of the scale to attachment security and as an indicator of the regular failure of the interpersonal interpretive mechanism. As we argue throughout this book, we consider the quality of interpretive capacity to vary substantially across normal and clinical groups. At the low end of this scale are individuals who use a teleological rather than an intentional stance in interpreting their own and others' behavior (see chapters 5 and 8). As we shall see, the reasons for this weakness might be linked to early suboptimal environments that could create a vulnerability through undermining the robustness of the IIM (see particularly chapter 4) or the failure to appropriately integrate developmentally early forms of representations for subjectivity (see chapter 6) due, for example, to a lack of playful interactions with parents or frank maltreatment at much later ages (see chapters 10 and 11).

To summarize, we feel that there are at least five strands of converging evidence to suggest that a key selective advantage of attachment might be the development of an understanding of internal states: (*a*) that secure attachment is associated with favorable outcomes across a wide range of relevant tasks; (*b*) that secure attachment predicts precocious performance in tasks specifically calling for symbolic capacity; (*c*) that the class of early attachment classification has less predictive weight than whether attachment experiences occurred; (*d*) that attachment has been demonstrated to have other ontogenetic biological functions in mammalian species that have analogies or may parallel the evolutionary function for attachment proposed here; (*e*) that the factor structure of adult attachment scales separates out a factor to do with type of attachment (perhaps the internal working model) and the quality of attachment (perhaps the interpersonal interpretive mechanism).

THE NEURO-ANATOMICAL BASIS OF IIM-a AND IIM-c

So far we have discussed the IIM as if we thought of it as a singular and unitary system. In chapter 5 we present evidence that the acquisition of an understanding of desires might antedate the acquisition of a capacity to understand epistemic states (such as beliefs) by as much as 18 months. This discrepancy in the developmental timetable suggests that separate mechanisms for interpersonal understanding concerning emotions and belief states should be considered. In this section we present some neuropsychological evidence that points in the same direction. We believe that the IIM subdivides anatomically into two substructures: the IIM-a (a for affect) and the IIM-c (c for cognition). Emotional resonance (empathy) may exemplify the former, while reasoning about epistemic states might be prototypical of the latter. The term "theory of mind" or "mentalization" as currently used covers both these aspects, although there is a bias in the literature toward equating mentalization with the understanding of belief states.

The concept of empathy has been variously defined. In this context the availability of a mechanism that allows one individual to assume another's perspective and to infer and, to some degree, experience their emotional state of mind is central. We believe that the psychological mechanism that we have labeled the IIM-a is responsible for this (Bleiberg, Fonagy, and Target 1997; Fonagy 2000). Other workers have independently come to very similar theoretical conclusions (Blair 1995; Corcoran 2000). Darwin considered sympathy to be the core moral emotion as it involved the automatic experiencing of the other's distress, which gives rise to altruistic attempts to offer comfort or relief (O'Connell 1998).

Neurophysiological studies support the distinction. The purely cognitive task of identifying belief states in the other has been associated with activation of medial prefrontal foci around BA8 using SPECT (single-photon emission computed tomography) (Baron-Cohen et al. 1994), PET (Blair, Jones, Clark, and Smith 1997; Goel et al. 1995) and fMRI (Gallagher et al. 2000). The infant's understanding of his own emotional responses (by definition, a precursor of empathy) itself arises out of a complex process of early mirroring between caregiver and child, which leads to the creation of a second-order representation of the child's emotional state (Gergely and Watson 1996, 1999). This model is detailed in chapter 4. Innate emotional responses to facially expressed emotion, particularly fear or sad expressions, underpin the acquisition of empathy and morality, or the moral emotions (Blair et al. 1997). The amygdala (AM) and orbitofrontal areas have been implicated as mediators of these capacities (Anderson, Bechara, Damasio, Tranel, and Damasio 1999; Blair, Morris, Frith, Perrett, and Dolan 1999).

The distinction might be most effectively illustrated by taking an extreme clinical example: antisocial personality disorder (ASPD). Some severely antisocial psychopathic individuals have been generally regarded as lacking an adult moral sense—hence the term "moral imbecility" (Hare and Cox 1987). These individuals arguably cannot feel a sense of right and wrong, guilt or remorse, because the neural mechanisms (IIM-a) underlying these experiences are impaired, and they can feel neither empathy nor sympathy (Blair et al. 1997; Damasio 1994a).

We suggest that the ability to predict and experience the emotions of others might be mediated by the functional connection of the two interpersonal interpretive centers in the brain. Normally, evaluation of the social significance (meaning) of internal states in self and other is possible through linking the representations of epistemic states of the mind in the medial prefrontal cortex (IIM-c) with the emotional control centers (IIM-a) in the orbital frontal cortex (OFC) and temporal lobe. It could be argued that these functional connections are impaired in individuals with antisocial personality disorder, some of whom have no IIM-a function (cannot feel empathy at all), but most of whom may simply have poor connections between the IIM-a and IIM-c systems (do not feel context-appropriate empathy).

Extreme ASPD (high psychopathy) individuals do not respond autonomically to distressed faces. They seem to be insensitive to the distinction between moral transgressions that result in harm to someone and conventional transgressions that are socially disruptive but do not harm an individual. Responsiveness to distress is necessary for the acquisition of this distinction. This might be lost on two levels, at least. Some have suggested that this response is ensured by the AM, and the impairment of this structure accounts for the limited morality of the ASPD individuals (Blair et al. 1999). Others have suggested that early damage to the OFC is associated with severely impaired and immature moral judgment, and evidence of OFC lesions is associated with loss of autonomic responsiveness to social stimuli (Anderson et al. 1999).

We suggest that some individuals with limited capacity for empathy will show limited AM responses to the depiction of distress in children's faces, while others will show no AM deficit but demonstrate limited OFC activation. Those with AM impairment are likely to have failed to acquire a proper understanding of their own emotional responses that directly led to a failure of empathy. Those with insensitive caregivers—perhaps disorganized early attachments—would not have acquired the second-order representation of emotional states, and this level of incapacity manifests in OFC dysfunction. A third level of failure may occur as a consequence of a disconnection between the medial frontal and the orbital frontal areas (IIM-a and IIM-c), whereby the individual might experience affect in relation to an other's distress but this is inappropriately or inadequately linked to a representation of the belief and intentional state of that person. This latter pattern of functional disconnection might be most likely to arise as a function of severe social adversity at later stages of development.

CLINICAL IMPLICATIONS

What are the clinical implications of a reconciliation of environmentalism and nativism? As the Nobel Laureate Eric Kandel speculated, it is quite plausible for us to consider therapeutic, and particularly preventive, interventions as being effective because they alter the mechanisms of genetic expression (Kandel 1998, 1999). Changes in the social environment brought about through psychosocial intervention may result in alterations of specific gene expression. Knowledge of these mechanisms would help us sharpen our intervention strategies and may prompt us to advance new modes of prevention or treatment intervention. We would suggest that at least some psychosocial treatments, like psychoanalysis, or preventive efforts, like affect training—for example, the PATHS Program (Kusche and Greenberg 2001)—work because they enhance the functioning of the IIM and moderate gene expression. Of course, by enhancing mentalization, social adaptation in general might also be enhanced. In either case, we maintain that attachment-related early social experiences of other minds are necessary for this to take place because the normal functioning of interpersonal interpretive processes requires simultaneous access to epistemic and affective information. Most probably, social experience in an attachment context in developmental periods of neural plasticity enhances connections between what we assume to be the anatomically separate but functionally normally integrated affective and cognitive structures. This is why effective psychotherapy, particularly with individuals whose capacity for mental representations of internal states is vulnerable, must focus on affect as well as cognition, be delivered in an interpersonal context that permits the development of attachment relationships, and meet a criterion for coherence that is consistent with the requirement of repetition of stimuli in the generation of neural networks (e.g., Rumelhart and McClelland 1986) and the switching-on of specific genes (Kandel 1998, 1999).

Perhaps, further into the future, we may envision the measurement of the outcome of psychosocial interventions by tracking changes in the expression of specific genes in specific sites relevant for the development of psychopathology (the brain, endocrine organs, etc.). More realistically, suitability for specific types of treatment may be determined in terms of genetic variability. In the meantime, we can measure the impact of interventions on measures that might tap into the IIM (the RF scale, the "reading the mind in the eyes" test).

CONCLUSIONS

Though what is proposed here may sound radical, when closely scrutinized it actually contains very little that is new. We suggest that psychoanalysis needs to look to the cognitive neurosciences to find its intellectual fulfillment. Current theorization in neuroscience is sadly devoid of considerations of emotional life and relationality even around topics such as social development, where the subject matter directly concerns the child's subjectivity. Happily, there are a number of energetic initiatives underway that pursue this path for knowledge acquisition (e.g., Solms 1997a, 1997b), and a new journal, *Neuro-Psychoanalysis*, offers a ready forum for these developments.

The evidence clearly shows that it is naive to assume that the child's genotypic destiny is fulfilled in a hermetically sealed brain, somehow isolated from the social environment within which ontogeny occurs and the sound adaptation to which is the organizing purpose of the whole system. Subjectivity, the understanding of the individual response, will be an essential piece in putting together the microbiological puzzle of genetic expression. Psychoanalysis, with its focus on the representation of subjectivity and how this emerges from early development, might have much to contribute to the understanding of how individual differences in the quality of functioning of basic mental mechanisms arise. We are suggesting that infant attachment functions —in part at least—to facilitate the development of an interpersonal interpretive capacity. The quality of the early relationship plays a major role in determining the robustness of that capacity, but attachment security per se is less relevant to later development. The interpretive capacity, in turn, plays a key role in the processing of social experience. The level of functioning of the IIM will be reflected in an individual's ability to function in close interpersonal relationships without recourse to strategies for amplifying the distinction between self and other representations. The unfolding of disturbance over time is conditioned by the interpretive capacity—we speculate that the expression of pathogenic genotypes is made more likely by the poor functioning of a mechanism designed to differentiate the psychological states of self and other.

This is a function of immense importance, as the laborious move from genotype to phenotype is conditioned in this way. A full understanding of the interaction between individual mentalized representations of life experience and the expression of genetic dispositions is the task of the developmental psychopathology of the next decades. Eric Kandel (1998) cites François Jacob (1998), who wrote in *Of Flies, Mice and Men*: "The century that is ending has been preoccupied with nucleic acids and proteins. The next one will concentrate on *memory and desire*. Will it be able to answer the questions they pose?" (Jacob 1998, p. 152).

PART II

DEVELOPMENTAL PERSPECTIVES

In Part II, we present a comprehensive picture of the development of a psychological sense of self, beginning with infancy and ending with adolescence. In chapter 4 we introduce the social biofeedback view of mirroring, a precise account of the mechanisms through which infants learn to identify and control affect states through interaction with primary caregivers—moving from coregulation to being self-regulating agents. The social biofeedback view of mirroring is a fundamental extension of psychoanalytic theory; it is important not just as an account of normal development but as a basis for explaining later vulnerability to psychosocial stress and psychopathology. (This is made evident in the case material in chapter 7.) Chapter 5 moves on to delineate five distinct aspects of the self: physical, social, teleological, intentional, and representational—which is also autobiographical. The notion of the intentional stance—and its relation to the teleological stance—borrowed from the philosophy of mind is particularly important to our point of view, as it spells out how we learn to fathom ourselves through fathoming others. We make the case here for the central importance of intersubjectivity once it unfolds in early development. However, we criticize currently popular arguments that intersubjectivity is present from the start and argue instead that it emerges within the attachment relationship together with the capacity for mentalization. Chapter 6 continues the developmental sequence: it highlights the dialectic between "psychic equivalence" (that mental reality must map onto physical reality) and "pretend" (that mental and physical reality are completely separate from each other)—two modes of childhood experience that become integrated through "playing with reality," leading to the appreciation that the mind only partially reflects external reality. Chapter 7 is a clinical illustration of the usefulness of these concepts to the understanding of a young boy whose disturbed relationship with his mother resulted in the distortion of these developmental processes. Chapter 8 focuses on the processes underpinning normal and pathological stresses in adolescence and presents case material illustrating serious psychopathology.

4

The Social Biofeedback Theory
of Affect-Mirroring: The Development
of Emotional Self-Awareness
and Self-Control in Infancy

In many ways this chapter forms the core of our thinking about the role of affects in self-development—a theoretical and conceptual problem that we tackle more fully in chapter 5. We start this chapter by placing the construct of emotions within the framework of the development of intentionality and mentalization, the concepts that lie at the core of our theoretical and clinical work. We then focus on the nature of the developmental processes involved in the emergence of understanding of emotions in self and other. The development of emotions during the first year of life is outlined and placed in the context of one of the organizing concepts of this book: the infant's sensitivity to contingencies between his actions and their perceived environmental effects. We describe the social biofeedback theory of emotional development, which we see as the key to understanding the link between early experience and later vulnerability to psychosocial stress. We also point briefly to a number of pathological modes of early infant–caregiver interaction that could give rise to later psychological disturbance and the vulnerability of the self as agent. Chapter 5 then attempts to integrate the particular view of emotional development described in this chapter within our more general theoretical approach to the early development of self and agency.

EMOTIONAL DEVELOPMENT
FROM A THEORY-OF-MIND PERSPECTIVE

During the last decade philosophers (Dennett 1987; Fodor 1987, 1992) and cognitive developmentalists (Astington, Harris, and Olson 1988; Baron-Cohen et al. 1993; Hirschfeld and Gelman 1994; Perner 1991; Wellman 1990; Whiten 1991) have focused on the nature and developmental origins of our capacity to attribute causal mental states to others. Dennett (1987) has argued that applying such a mentalistic interpretational strategy, which he calls the "intentional stance," is an evolutionary adaptation that is highly successful in predicting the behavior of other agents. Thus, the currently dominant cognitive developmental view holds that even young children are so-called belief–desire psychologists who attribute intentional mental states—such as goals, emotions, desires, and beliefs—to others as the causes of their actions.

Researchers take different views, however, when they address the question of how children identify and attribute mind states to others or to themselves. Simulation theorists (e.g., Goldman 1993; P. L. Harris 1991, 1992) assume that humans have direct introspective access to their own mental states, while they have to infer those of others indirectly through imagining themselves in their place and then attributing the simulated mental experience to the other. In contrast, others (Dennett 1987; Gopnik 1993; Gopnik and Wellman 1994) argue that direct perceptual access to mind states is illusory, and they propose that the identification of mental states is equally inferential in the case of self and other.

When do children take the intentional stance and start to infer mind states in other agents? While the attribution of apparently more complex intentional states, such as false beliefs, generally appear only at around 3–4 years of age (see chapter 5 for a comprehensive developmental account of the emergence of this ability—Perner 1991; Wellman 1990; Wimmer and Perner 1983), many (e.g., Bretherton 1991a; Stern 1985; Tomasello 1999) believe that certain new behaviors emerging during the last quarter of the first year, such as pointing and gaze alteration (E. Bates 1979; Bretherton and Bates 1979; Murphy and Messer

1977) or social referencing (Campos and Stenberg 1981; Klinnert, Campos, Sorce, Emde, and Svejda 1983), imply the appearance of a rudimentary ability on the infant's part to attribute at least some kinds of mind states—such as attention states or emotions—to other agents. In a series of habituation studies, Gergely, Csibra, and their colleagues (Csibra, Gergely, Brockbank, Bíró, and Koós 1999; Gergely et al. 1995) have provided evidence that 9- and 12-month-old infants can, indeed, interpret an agent's behavior as goal-directed and rational and can predict its future action toward the goal in a new situation on that basis. However, 6-month-olds showed no signs yet of such an understanding of intentional behavior, which is in line with the general assumption that the earliest time in development when infants may be able to take the "intentional stance" toward other agents is around the end of the first year (Tomasello 1995, 1999).

The "theory-of-mind" perspective is clearly relevant when we consider the origins of the infant's ability to understand and attribute emotional states to others. While much of the discussion in the theory-of-mind literature has concentrated on beliefs and desires, it should be clear that emotions also belong to the types of intentional mental states that we attribute to other minds to explain and predict their behavior. In fact, emotions share many of the representational properties that characterize intentional mental states. The "intentionality" of mental states such as beliefs and desires refers to their "aboutness" (Brentano 1874; Dennett and Haugeland 1987)—thus, a belief is "about" an actual or possible state of affairs in the world, whereas a desire is "about" a future state of affairs. Clearly, in that sense emotions are also mental attitudes that are "about" some state of affairs (as when Peter is angry about having lost his wallet[1]) and attributing that information to a person can certainly help to explain or predict his behavior.

---

[1] That emotions belong to the class of intentional mental states is also shown by the fact that emotion terms, similarly to other "intentional idioms," express propositional attitudes and are characterized by the semantic property of "referential opacity" (Dennett and Haugeland 1987; Quine 1960). This property refers to the fact that certain logical operations, such as substitutability of terms with

However, when attributing an emotion to someone, one also attributes dispositional information that is related more to the attitude itself than to the intentional object that the attitude is about. Attributing "anger about having lost his wallet" to Peter allows one to generate a set of predictions about his future behavior that are only incidentally related to what his anger is about—for example, predicting that Peter is likely to kick the dog if he sees it. The dispositional information that emotions express specifies that under certain circumstances a person who is in the given dispositional emotion state is likely to behave in certain ways rather than in others. In other words, it specifies a set of potential states of affairs that can be propositionally described in terms of a set of "if–then" conditional statements. When we attribute an emotion state to someone, we must be able to generate at least some of these conditional states of affairs in our mind, otherwise we would not be able to infer anything about the person's future behavior.[2]

Therefore, from a theory-of-mind perspective the central questions of the psychology of emotional development would be the following: (*a*) How do infants come to know about the dispositional content of emotions? (*b*) How do they identify what an emotion state is about? (*c*) When do they start to attribute either kinds of information to other minds to support reasoning about behavior? (*d*) How do they learn the conditions under which the attribution of emotions to others—or, for that matter, to themselves—is justified?

In the latter regard, we should note that emotions differ in interesting ways from other intentional mental states such as beliefs and desires. First, emotions may be easier to infer in another person, because they tend to be accompanied by sali-

---

identical referents, break down in the case of expressions involving intentional relations such as "*x* believes that *p*" or "*y* desires that *q*." Thus, while the statement "Oedipus was angry about Laius's comments" is true, it does not follow that "Oedipus was angry about his father's comments" is also true, even though "Laius" and "Oedipus's father" refer to the same individual.

[2] In fact, apart from their dispositional content, we often exploit other types of knowledge as well when we reason about emotions—for example, knowledge about the typical causes of emotions or about the typical consequences of acting emotionally (Watson 1995).

.

ent—and, in the case of basic emotions, possibly universal—expressive facial displays (Ekman 1992; Ekman, Friesen, and Ellsworth 1972; Izard 1977). Also, having an emotion seems to involve specific and differential changes in physiological arousal (at least, in the case of some basic emotions—see Ekman, Levenson, and Friesen 1983), as well as a characteristic subjective feeling state, which, it can be argued, makes correct self-attribution relatively easy. Furthermore, there is evidence suggesting that there may be a set of basic emotions that is universal and innate (Ekman 1992; Ekman et al. 1972; Izard 1977, 1978). On the basis of these considerations it seems plausible to ask whether emotions are among—if not the—earliest mental states that infants attribute to minds (cf. Meltzoff and Gopnik 1993).

IMITATION-BASED ATTRIBUTION OF EMOTIONAL STATES: THE MELTZOFF–GOPNIK HYPOTHESIS

Meltzoff and Gopnik (1993) proposed that innate mechanisms allow the infant to attribute emotional states to others from the beginning of life. Their theory is based on Meltzoff's extended work (Meltzoff and Moore 1977, 1989) demonstrating an innate ability and inclination in newborn babies to imitate certain facial gestures of adults—such as tongue protrusion and mouth opening—and maybe also the components of some of the basic facial emotion expressions (Field, Woodson, Cohen, Garcia, and Greenberg 1983). Additionally, their model assumes the existence of an innate set of primary emotions that are expressed by prewired facial muscular action patterns (Ekman 1992b; Ekman et al. 1972; Izard 1977, 1978).

Based on Ekman et al.'s (1983) findings with adults, Meltzoff and Gopnik suggest that there are prewired bidirectional connections between facial emotion expressions and corresponding differential physiological emotion states, which are active from birth. Thus, they embrace a basic assumption of differential emotions theory (Izard 1977; Izard and Malatesta 1987; Malatesta and Izard 1984), according to which "there is an innate expression-to-feeling concordance in the young infant" (Malatesta et al. 1989, p. 6). They hypothesize that when the infant imitates the adult's facial emotion expression, he automatically activates, through these prewired connections, the corresponding bodily emotion state in himself. In their words, "imitation of behavior provides the bridge that allows the internal mental state of another to 'cross over' to and become one's own experienced mental state" (Meltzoff and Gopnik 1993, p. 358). According to Meltzoff and Gopnik, the imitation-generated emotion state is then introspectively accessed, and the felt affect is attributed to the other's mind.

However, there is no direct evidence to support the assumption that discrete innate emotion displays automatically activate emotion-specific conscious feeling states in early infancy. In fact, several researchers explicitly reject this possibility, arguing that affect states are likely to be undifferentiated during the first few months of life and that the appearance of differentiated conscious feeling states is the consequence of cognitive development (e.g., Sroufe 1979). Lewis and Michaelson (1983) argue that, during the earliest phases of infancy, internal states and expressive behaviors are not yet coordinated and that conscious feeling states that are linked to discrete expressive displays emerge only later due to the influence of socialization and cognitive growth (see also Kagan 1992; Lewis and Brooks 1978).

In addition to embracing the—as yet unsupported—innatist assumption of an initial linkage between emotion expressions and specific feeling states, the Meltzoff–Gopnik model must make a further nativist assumption to account for the ensuing attribution of the imitation-generated emotion state to the other's mind. Without that, the proposed imitation-mediated emotional contagion process would generate an emotion state in the infant that would match the adult's expressed affect, but the process would stop there, and no mental-state attribution would occur. Accordingly, Meltzoff and Gopnik go on to argue that "one fundamental assumption of mentalism—that external, visible behaviors are mapped onto phenomenologically mental states—is apparently given innately" (1993, p. 340). This assumption of "primary intersubjectivity" is extensively scrutinized in chapter 5.

But even if one were to accept the innatist set of assumptions of the Meltzoff–Gopnik model, there would still remain a question concerning the nature of the imitation-generated affect state that seems crucial from the point of view of the theory-of-mind approach to emotional development. Apart from experiencing a differential phenomenological quality, is it proposed that the baby becomes aware of the dispositional content of the emotion state as well—not to mention its aboutness? It is not clear whether Meltzoff and Gopnik (1993) conceive of the dispositional content of emotions as also genetically specified, but it is clear that without making that strong innatist assumption, attributing pure—uninterpreted—physiological feeling states to the other would not serve the vital evolutionary function of the "intentional stance": it would not help the infant in *predicting* the other's behavior.

Finally, a central assumption of the Meltzoff–Gopnik model is the proposition that from the beginning of life infants have direct introspective access to their internal emotion states. However, the viability of the classical Cartesian position, according to which the mental states of the self are accessed directly through (infallible) introspection while those of the other have to be inferred on the basis of indirect evidence, has been a matter of lively debate in the theory-of-mind literature. (See chapter 5 for a detailed criticism of this Cartesian assumption.) In fact, Gopnik (1993) herself argued forcefully that in development, understanding of mind states in the other and in the self appears simultaneously and is based on similar inferential processes in both cases. (See also Dennett 1987, chapter 4.) In contrast, for the case of emotions, the Meltzoff–Gopnik (1993) model implies innately given direct introspective access to the affective states of the self. Below we argue, however, that emotions should not be considered a special case in this respect. We propose an alternative view, according to which the infant in his initial state is not yet sensitive to the groups of internal-state cues that are indicative of discrete emotion categories.

In sum, it seems that the Meltzoff–Gopnik model, while intellectually intriguing and based on some important insights, is heavily burdened with innatist assumptions, some of which, we believe, might be avoided in accounting for the developmental lines leading to the understanding and attribution of emotions in infancy. In what follows, we outline an alternative approach to conceptualizing early emotional development, which, while perhaps more parsimonious, is, admittedly, equally speculative.

INITIAL SENSITIVITY
TO INTERNAL VERSUS EXTERNAL STIMULI

We believe that there is no compelling reason to assume that the dispositional contents of emotion states are available to the infant at birth. This is, of course, not to deny the potential presence of innate primary emotions, which can be conceptualized as complex prewired behavioral organizations activated under specific input conditions. Such emotion programs are likely to contain information about the goal—such as removal of obstacle—and the specific action tendencies—for example, approach and attack—characteristic of the given emotion (anger), which could be used to support at least some predictions about likely actions. However, we assume that this information is represented in an implicit form as procedural knowledge, and as such it is at first cognitively inaccessible to the infant.

Instead, we propose that the dispositional content of emotions is learned first by observing the affect-expressive displays of others and associating them with the situations and behavioral outcomes that accompany these emotion expressions. Of course, if Meltzoff and Gopnik are right in assuming that the infant has direct introspective access to his innate primary emotion states, such perceptual learning could be based on monitoring the emotional states of the self as well as those of others.

In assuming that the infant's initial state is characterized by direct introspective access to internal states, Meltzoff and Gopnik (1993) follow the tradition of a long line of developmental theorists. For example, Freud and other psychoanalysts (e.g., Mahler et al. 1975) have long held the view that the infant is initially more sensitive to internal than to external stimuli. Bruner, Olver, and Greenfield (1966) also proposed that the infant moves from an initial reliance on internal, proprioceptive cues to a reliance on exteroceptive cues (see also Birch and Lefford 1967; Gholson 1980; for a review, see Rovee-Collier 1987).

However, as Colombo, Mitchell, Coldren, and Atwater (1990) have pointed out, there are practically no empirical data in the infant learning literature to support this classical assumption directly. In contrast, in a series of experiments designed to test the assumption, these authors have demonstrated that 3-month-olds show discrimination learning on the basis of exteroceptive as well as interoceptive cues.[3] Moreover, in 6- and 9-month-olds they actually found dominance of the exteroceptive over the interoceptive cues in learning.

Therefore, it seems to us that it might be worthwhile to explore the consequences of abandoning the classical assumption concerning the presumed dominance of internal stimuli in the initial state of the infant. In fact, we hypothesize that at the beginning of life *the perceptual system is set with a bias to attend to and explore the external world and builds representations primarily on the basis of exteroceptive stimuli.* In this view, then, the set of internal—visceral as well as proprioceptive—cues that are activated when being in and expressing an emotion state are, at first, not perceived consciously by the infant, or, at least, are not grouped together categorically in such a manner that they could be perceptually accessed as a distinctive emotion state.[4]

This raises the question: How, on the basis of this theory, does the infant develop awareness of and come to represent the sets of internal-state cues as indicating categorically distinct

---

[3] Note furthermore that one cannot rule out the possibility that the position cues in Colombo et al.'s (1990) study, which were based on eye fixation, might have been computed on the basis of the position of the nose, which is, in fact, an *exteroceptive* cue, see Bower (1974).

[4] As will become apparent, our proposal does not necessarily imply—while being compatible with—the more radical view that at the beginning of life infants are lacking any kind of awareness of their internal states. It is possible that the infant has some awareness of the component stimuli that belong to the groups of internal-state cues that are indicative of categorical emotions, but only as part of the "blooming, buzzing confusion" (W. James, 1890) of internal sense impressions he may experience. Such state cues may also contribute to the overall—positive or negative—hedonic quality of the infant's awareness. Our—less radical—suggestion is (a) that the groups of internal-state cues that are indicative of dispositional emotion states are initially not perceptually accessible as distinct feeling states, and (b) that the infant's perceptual system is at the start set with a bias to actively explore and categorize external rather than internal stimuli.

emotion states? We propose that the species-specific human propensity for the facial and vocal reflection of the infant's emotion-expressive displays during affect-regulative interactions plays a crucial role in this developmental process. Below we identify a number of significant developmental consequences of the instinctive human inclination to expose infants to affect-reflective behavioral displays during emotion-regulative interactions. We also argue that all of these consequences are mediated by the same underlying mechanism—namely, contingency detection and maximizing. Before describing our model, however, let us briefly review the available empirical evidence on the role and nature of affect-regulative interactions during emotional development in the first year of life.

EMOTIONAL DEVELOPMENT DURING THE FIRST YEAR OF LIFE

During the last thirty years we have witnessed the accumulation of a large body of compelling evidence in developmental psychology that has radically changed our conceptualization of the initial state of the infant. While not so long ago the standard view held that at the beginning of life infants are basically passive, undifferentiated, diffuse organisms surrounded by a stimulus barrier (e.g., Mahler et al. 1975), it is now generally accepted that they are equipped from the start with remarkably rich perceptual, learning, and representational capacities and specific preparedness for the structure of the physical and social world around them (Bower 1974; Emde 1988; Gergely 1992; Meltzoff 1990; Stern 1985).

This change of perspective has certainly also characterized recent research on early emotional development (Ekman 1992a; Ekman and Oster 1979; Izard 1977; Izard and Malatesta 1987; Malatesta et al. 1989; Tronick and Cohn 1989), which assumes a strong biosocial preparedness for emotion expression and emotional communication in infancy. Following Darwin's (1872) early insight, recent cross-cultural research on facial emotion expressions (Ekman 1992b; Ekman et al. 1972; Izard 1977,

1978) has indicated that there is a set of innate basic emotions—including, at least, enjoyment, anger, fear, sadness, disgust, and surprise—that are expressed by the same facial muscular action patterns across cultures and are universally recognized. Young infants have been reported to make nearly all the muscle movements that are used by adults to express the primary emotions (Ekman and Oster 1979; Oster 1978), and the facial expressions of interest, joy, disgust, surprise, and distress have been identified in young babies (Izard 1978). Furthermore, the facial muscular actions involved in the expression of at least some of the universal emotions have been shown in adults to generate specific and differential physiological arousal patterns characteristic of the given emotion (Ekman et al. 1983).

Based on findings such as these, numerous psychologists embraced the view that basic emotions are innate dynamic behavioral organizations with adaptive functions, characterized by specific facial display patterns that are connected through prewired activation channels to differential physiological response structures (Ekman 1992b; Ekman and Oster 1979; Izard 1977, 1978; Izard and Malatesta 1987; Malatesta et al. 1989; Meltzoff and Gopnik 1993).

Furthermore, the currently dominant biosocial view of emotional development holds that mother and infant form an affective communication system from the beginning of life (Beebe, Jaffe, and Lachmann 1992; Bowlby 1969; Brazelton, Kowslowski, and Main 1974; Hobson 1993; Sander 1970; Stern 1977, 1985; Trevarthen 1979; Tronick and Cohn 1989) in which the mother plays a vital interactive role in modulating the infant's affective states. While young infants do have some rudimentary means of affective self-regulation—such as turning away from overarousing stimuli or thumb-sucking (Demos 1986; Malatesta et al. 1989)—there is agreement that the quality of maternal interactions exerts a strong regulative influence on the infant's affective state changes (Field 1994; Malatesta and Izard 1984, 1989; Tronick, Ricks, and Cohn 1982). Mothers are generally rather efficient in reading their infants' emotion displays, and sensitive mothers tend to attune their own affective responses to modulate their infants' emotional states (Malatesta et al. 1989; Tronick and Cohn 1989). There is also some evidence that infants can perceptually differentiate at least some facial emotion expressions early in life (Field et al. 1983; Malatesta and Izard 1984), though whether the basis of this discrimination is the full expressive pattern seems questionable before 4 months of age (see C. Nelson 1987). Studies using the still-face procedure (Tronick, Als, Adamson, Wise, and Brazelton 1978) or delayed-feedback techniques (Murray and Trevarthen 1985; see also Nadel, Carchon, Kervella, Marcelli, and Reserbat-Plantey 1999; Bigelow and DeCoste, in press) suggest that young infants are sensitive to the contingency structure of face-to-face interaction and, at least after 3 months of age, are actively searching to reestablish such a pattern of communication when being abruptly deprived of it. By using time-based microanalytic methods (e.g., Gottman 1981) to examine the structure of face-to-face interactions, several researchers provided evidence for the early existence of bidirectional influence of behavior and mutual regulation of affective communication between mothers and infants (Beebe, Jaffe, Feldstein, Mays, and Alson 1985; Beebe and Lachmann 1988; Cohn and Tronick 1988; Tronick, Als, and Brazelton 1977; Tronick and Cohn 1989). By the age of 6 months, infants' emotional expressions are already well organized and are systematically related to environmental events (Weinberg and Tronick 1996). There is evidence that imitative matching activity is frequent during mother–infant interactions (Uzgiris, Benson, Kruper, and Vasek 1989), and mother–infant pairs have been shown to increase their degree of coordination in terms of matching and synchrony with infant age (Tronick and Cohn 1989). Maternal imitative behavior has been shown to evoke more smiling and vocalization than nonimitative responses in 3½-month-old babies (Field, Guy, and Umbel 1985).

A number of infant researchers (e.g., Beebe and Lachmann 1988; Papousek and Papousek 1987, 1989; Stern 1985; Trevarthen 1979; Tronick et al. 1982) have proposed that *facial and vocal mirroring of affective behavior* may be a central feature of parental affect-regulative interactions during the first year. In line with this view, it has been reported (Malatesta, Culver, Tesman, and Shepard 1989; Malatesta and Izard 1984) that mothers react with differential facial attunements to infants' emotion expressions, and are more likely to imitate their baby's categorical emotion displays than their more "random" facial movements—such as twitches or half-smiles. Infants' expressions of sadness and anger have been observed to produce affective responses of sadness and anger in their mothers (Tronick 1989), and maternal reactions to negative affect include mock expressions of negative affect (Malatesta and Izard 1984).

Research on the facial and vocal interaction between depressed mothers and their infants (Bettes 1988; Cohn, Matias, Tronick, Connell, and Lyons-Ruth 1986; Tronick 1989) has shown that there is a decrease in the number of contingent affective interactions as well as more intrusiveness and more negative affect expression on the part of the mother. Furthermore, such infants' affective and regulatory reactions as well as their later security of attachment have been found to be related to the affect and behavior of their depressed mothers (Field 1994; Field et al. 1988; Murray 1992; Pickens and Field 1993; Tronick 1989).

In general, such findings seem to support the view of psychoanalytic theorists who have long identified the maternal mirroring function as an important causal factor in early emotional and personality development (e.g., Bion 1962a, 1962b; Jacobson 1964; P. F. Kernberg 1984; Kohut 1971, 1977; Mahler and McDevitt 1982; Mahler et al. 1975; Winnicott 1967). However, the exact nature of the causal mechanism mediating such effects has not yet been identified.

In sum, the reviewed findings indicate that infants during their first year of life (a) show an innate tendency to express their emotion states automatically, (b) are sensitive to the contingency structure of face-to-face affective communication, (c) can discriminate discrete facial patterns of emotion expression, (d) are, to a large extent, dependent on their parent's affect-regulative interactions as a means of emotional self-regulation, and (e) the quality of their affective states and their emerging self-regulative reactions are strongly influenced by the characteristics of their parents' affective communicative behavior.

Toward the end of the first year, however, one can witness the emergence of a set of qualitatively new communicative behavioral competencies that seem to indicate a new level of emotional awareness and control as well as the beginning of understanding, attributing, and reasoning about emotional states. One of the first signs of voluntary control over emotion expressions is shown by the behavior of avoidant (A-type) infants in the Strange Situation (Ainsworth et al. 1978) at 1 year of age. These babies seem to suppress the automatic expression of separation-induced negative affect, whose presence is indicated by an increase in heart rate (Sroufe and Waters 1977b) as well as in cortisol level (Spangler and Grossmann 1993). There is also evidence (Demos 1986; Malatesta et al. 1989) of some degree of affect modulation through control of facial musculature emerging during the second year of life.

Another early form of instrumental self-regulation of affective behavior is indicated by the emergence of social referencing by the end of the first year (e.g., Campos and Stenberg 1981; Klinnert et al. 1983). At this time infants who find themselves in an ambiguous situation and cannot decide among several behavioral alternatives—such as whether or not to crawl across a visual cliff to their mother—tend to examine their parent's facial emotion display and use the emotional information expressed to modulate their own behavior. The exact mechanism underlying social referencing is as yet unclear. A number of different interpretations have been proposed. Some would prefer to explain the phenomenon as a simple case of operant conditioning (Barresi and Moore 1996; Gewirtz and Pelaez-Nogueras 1992; Moore and Corkum 1994), while others argue that it is one of the first signs of the infant's emerging theory of mind as it involves inferring and attributing a mind state to the parent (Bretherton 1991a; Stern 1985). It seems also possible that the infant, who is by now well-trained in emotion-regulative mirroring interactions, is actively seeking out a clarifying affect-mirroring cue from the parent that will strengthen and bring one of his current conflicting emotion states to dominance, thereby resolving his indecision. This would be an interesting case of active instrumental use of parental emotional communication for self-regulative purposes.

Social referencing appears simultaneously with other novel forms of intentional communication involving the voluntary manipulation of the other's attentional state (Bretherton and Bates 1979; Bates, Benigni, Bretherton, Camaioni, and Volterra 1979;

Carpenter, Nagell, and Tomasello 1998; Moore and Corkum 1994; Murphy and Messer 1977; Tomasello 1995, 1999). These include pointing and gaze-following as well as protodeclarative gestures such as object-showing.

The emerging ability at the end of the first year to reason about behavior on the basis of an attributed emotion state is demonstrated by a study by Spelke, Phillips, and Woodward (1995), who showed that while 8-month-olds were not yet able to infer a person's next behavior on the basis of her gaze direction and facial emotion expression, 12-month-old infants could already do so. Thus, 1-year-old babies are not only able to discriminate discrete emotion expressions of others, but are also able to make inferences on the basis of the dispositional content of the emotion displayed.

It seems, therefore, that by the end of the first year infants can already do something more than simply "be in" an emotion state and react in an affective way to other people's emotion displays: they are able to attribute emotions to others and use that information to reason about their behavior. This seems to imply that infants are already able to represent the dispositional content of at least some basic-emotion states in a cognitively accessible form. We wish to argue that this level of representation of emotions is qualitatively different from the primary-level, implicit, procedural representations of prewired automatisms of the basic emotions.

LEVELS OF REPRESENTATIONS OF SELF-STATES: AUTOMATIC VERSUS CONTROLLED PROCESSES

There are a number of dichotomies in cognitive theory, such as the procedural/declarative, implicit/explicit, unconscious/conscious, or automatic/controlled distinctions (e.g., Karmiloff-Smith 1992; Shiffrin and Schneider 1977), that refer to qualitatively different levels of information representation in humans. *Automatized processes* refer to prewired or overlearned structures of behavioral organization in which information is represented implicitly, embedded in procedures, and is unavailable to other representational systems of the mind. Such automatisms are inflexible and perceptually driven, and they operate outside consciousness. In contrast, *deliberative or controlled processes* refer to voluntary and conscious operations that are flexible and modifiable, can be governed by higher-order cognitive goals, and can override automatisms.

In this framework, the infant's primary emotions can be conceived of as prewired, stimulus-driven, dynamic behavioral automatisms over which he has no control at first. Affect regulation is carried out mainly by the caregiver who, reading the infant's automatic emotion expressions, reacts to them with appropriate affect-modulating interactions. In this view, emotional self-control will become possible with the establishment of *secondary control structures* that (a) monitor, detect, and evaluate the primary-level dynamic affective-state changes of the organism, and (b) can inhibit or modify the emotional reaction if the anticipated automatic affective response would jeopardize higher-order cognitive plans.

Therefore, a precondition for the voluntary control and self-regulation of primary affective states is that the level of deliberative processes be informed about the ongoing dispositional state changes of the organism that take place at the level of automatized processes. Within this framework, consciously felt emotions can be conceived of as *signals* that inform the level of deliberative processes about the automatic affective state changes of the organism.

As the secondary representations of primary affect states become established, they will be subject to a process of representational elaboration as a result of the learning processes linking emotion expressions with types of situations and characteristic behavioral outcomes. At this point, the dispositional content of emotions, which comes to be encoded in the secondary representational structures, becomes cognitively accessible and can serve as the basis for action prediction when the emotion state is attributed to the self or the other.

As we develop below our account of the various functions served by parental mirroring of affects, we propose that mirroring also plays an important causal role in the establishment of secondary emotion representations by the end of the first year of life.

THE SOCIAL BIOFEEDBACK MODEL OF PARENTAL AFFECT-MIRRORING

Earlier we hypothesized that the internal-state cues that are activated when being in an emotion state are initially not perceived consciously or, at least, do not form a categorical group that could be perceptually accessed as a distinctive emotion state. Now we wish to propose that the repetitive presentation of an external reflection of the infant's affect-expressive displays serves a vital "teaching" function that results in gradual sensitization to the relevant internal-state cues as well as to the identification of the correct set of internal stimuli that correspond to the distinctive emotion category that the baby is in. As a result of this process the infant will eventually come to develop an awareness of the distinctive internal cues that are indicative of categorical emotion states and will become able to detect and represent his particular dispositional emotion states.

One may, of course, ask in what way the presentation of an external emotion display that is contingent on the baby's on-line internal affect state would lead to the sensitization to and recognition of the internal state that was not consciously accessible before. Furthermore, is there any evidence that would indicate that such externally induced sensitization to internal states is possible?

In fact, we can point to at least one intriguing example of such a process, which shows a high degree of family resemblance to the current proposal, namely *biofeedback training procedures* (e.g., Dicara 1970; Miller 1969, 1978). In such studies continuous measurements are made of the ongoing state changes of some internal stimulus state to which the subject initially has no direct perceptual access, such as blood pressure. The internal-state changes are mapped onto an *external* stimulus equivalent directly observable to the subject, the state of which covaries with that of the internal stimulus. Repeated exposure to such an externalized representation of the internal state eventually results in *sensitization to*—and in certain cases subsequent *control over*—the internal state.

We hypothesize that the psychological mechanism involved in affect-mirroring is the same process as that demonstrated in biofeedback training procedures. Our proposal is that parental affect-mirroring provides a kind of *natural social biofeedback training* for the infant that plays a crucial role in emotional development, and that the underlying learning mechanism that mediates the influence of both affect-mirroring and biofeedback training is that of *contingency detection and contingency maximizing* (see Gergely and Watson 1996, 1999; see also Lewicka 1988; Watson 1972, 1979, 1985, 1994). Before developing this hypothesis in detail, let us, therefore, briefly summarize what is known about the mechanism of contingency detection and its role in infant development.

THE CONTINGENCY-DETECTION MODULE: CONTINGENCY ANALYSIS AND MAXIMIZING IN INFANCY

Numerous studies have demonstrated that young infants are highly sensitive to the contingent relations between their physical responses and consequent stimulus events (e.g., Bahrick and Watson 1985; Field 1979; Lewis, Allessandri, and Sullivan 1990; Lewis and Brooks-Gunn 1979; Papousek and Papousek 1974; Rochat and Morgan 1995; Watson 1972, 1994). For example, Watson (1972) has shown that 2-month-olds increase their rate of leg kicking when it results in a contingent event (the movement of a mobile), but not when they experience a similar but noncontingent event. In fact, the detection of causal control over the mobile's movement proved positively arousing for these infants. After some experience with the contingency, they started to smile and coo at the contingent mobile. In a similar paradigm, Lewis and colleagues (1990) also demonstrated that when 2-

month-olds detect that their previously experienced contingent control over a stimulus event no longer holds, they express frustration and distress.

How do young infants perceive response–stimulus contingencies so efficiently? Based on Watson's extensive studies (Watson 1979, 1985, 1994), Gergely and Watson (1999) have recently proposed the existence of an innate *contingency-detection module* that analyses the probability structure of contingent relations between responses and stimulus events. Watson (1979, 1994) has provided evidence that the infant's contingency-detection device applies two independent mechanisms for analyzing the conditional probability structure of contingent response–stimulus events: one looks forward in time, registering the conditional probability of an upcoming stimulus event as a function of an emitted response, called the "sufficiency index," while the other tests backward in time, monitoring the relative likelihood that a given stimulus event was preceded by a given response, called the "necessity index." The two separate indices estimate two aspects of the contingency relation that can vary independently of each other, providing a scale of different magnitudes of contingent relatedness.

To illustrate: imagine that the infant's right leg is attached by a string to a mobile, which moves whenever the baby kicks with his leg. Thus, the conditional probability of the infant's response resulting in the stimulus event is 1.0 (sufficiency index). If the mobile always moves when the infant kicks but never in the absence of a kick (which makes the "necessity index" also 1.0), the infant is in perfect contingent control over the mobile's movements. Imagine, however, that half of the mobile's movements are induced by the wind or by the experimenter, who has another string attached to the mobile. In this case, checking backward in time for the presence of a leg kick preceding the mobile's movement will produce only a conditional probability of 0.5 (necessity index), while the sufficiency index will remain perfect at 1.0. Thus, even though the infant's response continues to be fully effective in bringing about the stimulus event, his overall degree of control over the mobile's movements is reduced. Such a situation is, in fact, rather typical of the baby's relationship to his social environment: even the most responsive parent will not be able to pick up the baby (stimulus event) every time the infant cries (response) (thus reducing sufficiency), and there will be occasions when she picks the baby up even though he was not crying (which reduces necessity).

We need one more piece of information about the workings of the contingency-detection module before we can turn back to the question of affect-mirroring. Watson (1979) argued that whenever the two indices of contingent control are unequal, it is always possible that the infant has failed to detect the true degree of control he has over the stimulus event. Imagine, for example, that the response class that the infant is monitoring is "kicking with either leg." Let us assume, however, that the mobile is tied to the baby's right leg only and so it moves whenever the infant kicks with his right leg but does not move otherwise. Given that the infant kicks equally frequently with either leg, he would find that a leg kick results in mobile movement only half of the time, setting the sufficiency index at 0.5. The necessity index, however, will be 1.0, since every mobile movement is preceded by a (right-) leg kick.

Therefore, whenever the necessity index is higher than the sufficiency index, it is always possible that the response class monitored is too wide, and by reducing it the infant may discover that he is exerting more control over the stimulus event than previously estimated. In our example, if the infant goes on to reduce the response class examined to that of "kicking with the right leg," he will raise the sufficiency index higher, and the two indices will match, indicating perfect control over the mobile's movements. In general, then, whenever the necessity index is higher than the sufficiency index, it is a good strategy for the infant to *reduce* the response class examined in order to discover the maximal degree of contingent control he actually has over the stimulus event. (This works in the opposite direction as well: when the sufficiency index is higher than the necessity index, it is necessary to expand the response class examined to maximize the contingency.)

Watson (1979) argues that the infant may, in fact, be able to apply such a fancy contingency-maximizing strategy by actively experimenting with reducing or extending the response category examined as a function of the unequal degree of contingent control indicated by the sufficiency versus the necessity index. His finding that the rate of responding is highest when both the sufficiency and the necessity index are reasonably high and equal is in line with this hypothesis. (For further details of the contingency-detection and -maximizing model and the supporting evidence, see Gergely and Watson 1996; Watson 1972, 1979, 1994.)

Up to now we have described the workings of the contingency-detection module only in relation to temporal contingency. However, though much of the evidence for this mechanism has come from studying purely temporal contingencies, there are, in fact, three separate and independent bases of contingency: *temporal*, *sensory relational* (relative intensity), and *spatial* (similarity of spatial distribution or pattern) (Watson 1984). This is especially relevant when we consider the case of affect-mirroring (see below), as such parental displays are contingently related to the infant's emotion-expressive behavior not only in terms of temporal contingency, but also in terms of relative intensity and similarity of pattern. (See also Stern's 1984, 1985, views on "affect attunement," which we critically discuss below.)

Correspondingly, Gergely and Watson (1999) argue that the contingency-detection module is an analytic device that at its input end monitors for and then registers *all the three parameters of contingency* in parallel and computes as its output an overall value indicating the estimated degree of *causal relatedness* between responses and stimuli. There is converging evidence that infants use all three informational bases in contingency detection. (For a review, see Gergely and Watson 1999, pp. 103–107.)

THE DEVELOPMENTAL FUNCTIONS
OF CONTINGENCY DETECTION

Differentiation of the Self

Watson (1994, 1995) proposed that one of the primary functions of the contingency-detection mechanism is *self-detection*. One's motor actions produce stimuli that are necessarily perfectly response-contingent (e.g., watching one's hands as one is moving them), while the perception of stimuli emanating from the external world typically show a lesser degree of response-contingency. Therefore, the detection of the degree of contingency between efferent (motor) activation patterns and consequently perceived stimuli may serve as the original criterion for distinguishing the self from the external world.

In a seminal study Bahrick and Watson (1985; see also Rochat and Morgan 1995; Schmuckler 1996) have demonstrated that infants can use their perception of perfect contingency between their physical actions and the consequent feedback for self-detection and self-orientation as early as at 3 months of age. In a series of experiments 5- and 3-month-old infants were seated on a high chair in front of two monitors in such a way that they could freely move their legs. One monitor presented a live image of the subject's moving legs, providing a visual stimulus that was *perfectly contingent* with the infant's responses. The other monitor presented a previously recorded image of the infant's moving legs, which was, therefore, *not contingent* with the baby's present movements. Five-month-olds clearly differentiated between the two displays, looking significantly more at the *noncontingent* image. A number of other preferential looking studies (Lewis and Brooks-Gunn 1979; Papousek and Papousek 1974; Rochat and Morgan 1995; Schmuckler 1996) in which the live image of the self was contrasted with the moving but noncontingent image of another baby also indicate that 4- to 5-month-old infants differentiate self from other on the basis of response–stimulus contingencies and prefer to fixate *away* from the self.

Interestingly, Bahrick and Watson (1985) found that for 3-month-olds the distribution of preference was significantly bimodal: one subgroup preferred the perfectly contingent image, whereas the other preferred the noncontingent image. Field (1979) also reported a preferential visual orientation in her sample of 3-month-olds toward the perfectly contingent self-image as opposed to a noncontingent image. Piaget's (1936) observation that during the first months of life cyclic repetitions of actions on the self, which he called "primary circular reactions," dominate also suggests an initial phase of preoccupation with perfect response–stimulus contingencies. Based on such data, Watson (1994, 1995) proposed that during the first two to three months the contingency-detection module is genetically set to seek out and explore perfectly response-contingent stimulation. Watson hypothesizes that this initial attention bias serves the evolutionary function of developing *a primary representation of the bodily self* as a distinct object in the environment by identifying those stimuli that are the necessary sensory consequences of the body's motor actions and over which the infant exercises perfect control. Referring to the results of connectionist simulations teaching a computer net to guide a mechanical arm in accurate reaching for objects (Jordan and Rumelhart 1991), Watson (1995) suggests that an initial phase of self-seeking behavior may be a necessary preparatory stage for the later capacity to cope with the environment.

Orientation toward Social Objects

Watson (1994) further hypothesized that at around 3 months, due to maturational factors, the preferred target value of the contingency-detection mechanism is "switched" to *high but imperfect degrees of (social) contingencies* typically provided by the reactions of attachment figures attuned to the infants' affective–communicative displays. In support of this hypothesis, in further studies Watson (1979, 1985) demonstrated that when tested on a range of different degrees of contingencies, 4- to 6-month-olds were most motivated to engage moderately high contingencies while failing with very low or near-perfect contingency magnitudes. The hypothesized "switch" at 3 months resulting in an attention bias toward high but imperfect contingencies also accounts for the avoidance of the perfectly contingent self-image after 3 months in Bahrick and Watson's (1985) older group of 5-month-olds and the other subgroup of their 3-month-olds (whose contingency "switch" has already been reset). This maturational change functions to orient the infant after 3 months of age away from self-exploration (perfect contingencies) and toward *the exploration and representation of the social world* as presented by the (necessarily less-than-perfectly response-contingent) parental environment.

CONTINGENCY DETECTION AS THE MECHANISM UNDERLYING BIOFEEDBACK TRAINING AND PARENTAL AFFECT-MIRRORING

We propose that one of the functions of the contingency-detection mechanism outlined above is to mediate the sensitization to internal-state cues that is brought about as a result of biofeedback training (Dicara 1970; Miller 1969, 1978). In biofeedback, subjects are instructed to try to monitor for an internal target state—say, blood pressure—whose state changes are contingently related to the presence or absence of an externally presented stimulus equivalent. Changes in the target state will result in a set of consequent changes in the subject's internal (interoceptive and proprioceptive) states and will possibly induce peripheral, externally perceptible state changes as well. This set of internal and external stimulus cues will exhibit contingent variation not only with the internal target state that is causing them, but also with the external feedback stimulus that covaries with the internal target state. Let us assume that whenever the external feedback cue is on, the subject will carry out a contingency analysis backward in time (the necessity index) scanning for the presence of internal and behavioral responses that were present before the onset of the "teaching" stimulus—that is, the external biofeedback cue. Furthermore, the subject will also monitor for the contingent effects of the sampled set of internal- and external-state cues forward in time (the sufficiency index), testing to what degree they predict the appearance of the external biofeedback stimulus. By gradually expanding or reducing the set of state cues considered to be associated with the target state as a function of the direction of inequality between the necessity versus the sufficiency indices of contingent control (contingency maximizing), the subject will eventually identify the set of internal and external-state cues that show the highest degree of contingent variation with the biofeedback cue and, by association, with the internal target state as well. As a result, the subject will eventually become sensitive to and learn to group together those (internal and external) state cues whose combined presence is indicative of the change in the internal target state and so will become able to detect and attribute the presence of the internal state to himself.

Similarly, we hypothesize that the developmental process leading to sensitization to and categorization of emotion state cues in the self as a function of parental affect-mirroring is also mediated by the contingency-detection module. The onset of an emotion state in the baby will result in two types of automatic stimulus consequences: (*a*) It will induce a set of internal physiological state changes. (*b*) It will trigger the expressive behavioral display of the emotion category. The activation of the emotion-expressive display behaviors will produce a further set of internal (proprioceptive) stimuli that show contingent variation with the internal target state.

Some of these stimulus cues, when considered in isolation, will have a relatively low degree of predictive validity in relation to the target state as they may be evoked by the presence of other internal states as well. However, there is evidence (Ekman 1992b; Ekman et al. 1983; Izard and Malatesta 1987) indicating that there is a set of basic-emotion states that induce the activation of distinctive patterns of internal-state cues as well as a distinctive configuration of expressive behavioral cues. Therefore, the predictive validity of these cues when combined as a group is highly indicative of the presence of the underlying emotion state. However, as we hypothesized earlier, infants are initially unaware of the categorical sets of internal-state cues in question. Therefore, to achieve the capacity to detect and attribute their internal emotion states to themselves, they must become sensitive to and categorize together the relevant group of internal-state cues that covary with the internal dispositional state. It is this learning process that, according to the present hypothesis, is made possible by the parent's intuitive provision of a state-contingent external biofeedback cue in the form of the empathic reflection of the infant's state-expressive emotion displays.

In this view, the parent who—unlike the infant—is able to read and interpret the baby's affect-expressive facial, vocal, or postural emotion displays will produce affect-modulating interactive behaviors that will include the repeated production of an external reflection of the affect-expressive displays of the baby. This interactive process can be conceived of as a case of intuitive instructed learning in which the "teacher" role is played by the repeated presentation of the parent's affect-reflective emotion expression that is contingent on the presence of the dispositional emotion state in the infant.[5]

Thus, we assume that perceiving the parent's affect-mirroring emotion expression, the baby will start to apply the contingency-detection algorithm backward in time (the necessity index) to identify which of his internal and behavioral responses preceded the onset of the parent's affect-mirroring display. The infant will also examine the contingent consequences of the sampled group

---

[5] Among his numerous insightful suggestions to psychologists, Dennett (1991) outlines a somewhat similar biofeedback training procedure designed to "raise consciousness" in blindsight patients. It is well known that, as a result of brain injury in the occipital cortex, blindsight patients (Weiskrantz 1986) lose conscious awareness of part of their visual field, but they can nevertheless report about the presence and certain features of visual stimuli in their scotoma above chance level when asked to guess. However, they can make use of the nonconscious visual information in this way only when prompted when to guess. Dennett's suggestion is to try to train blindsight patients to "guess when to guess" by providing them with an external biofeedback cue that indicates to them when they are in an (unconscious) informational state that allows for successful guessing. Dennett wonders (1991, p. 332) whether by initially relying on such a "biofeedback crutch," blindsight patients may eventually come to learn to guess when to guess successfully. Were this the case, he speculates, then such patients may also develop a sense of being conscious about being informed. As he puts it: the patient "doesn't just come to be informed about the motion of the light; he *realizes* he's come to be informed; . . . he has a second-order thought to the effect that he's just had a first-order thought" (pp. 332–333).

of internal and behavioral cues forward in time (the sufficiency index) to identify the degree of predictive power they have over the parental target behavior. Following a strategy of contingency maximizing (Watson 1979), the baby's learning mechanism will compare the registered degree of contingent control experienced when testing forward versus backward in time and will then expand or reduce the set of cues considered to contribute to the contingent control over the external parental feedback, as a function of the direction of inequality between the necessity versus the sufficiency indices. This process will zero in on the set of internal and behavioral cues whose combined predictive validity shows the highest degree of contingent control over the parent's affect-mirroring display. Furthermore, since the latter covaries with the infant's internal dispositional emotion state as attributed by the parent, the set of internal and behavioral cues categorized together in the process of the contingency analysis will also be indicative of the emotion state of the infant.

PARENTAL AFFECT-MIRRORING
AND THE ON-LINE REGULATION OF EMOTION STATES

The standard view concerning the function of parental affect-mirroring behaviors is that they are involved in the on-line state regulation of the infant achieved by parental ministrations. This statement may sound uncontroversial—nevertheless, it may be worthwhile to consider a few observations that could induce doubt in its validity. One may argue, for example, that just because empathic emotion-mirroring behaviors occur during affect-modulating interactions, one cannot be certain that they play an actual causal role in bringing about the desired state change in the infant. After all, affect-mirroring is embedded in a set of other parental behaviors (such as physical contact, tender holding, vocal stimulation, reorienting from obnoxious stimuli), which seem to be clearly instrumental in bringing about the modification of the infant's state. Furthermore, it may also seem paradoxical to some that the parental display of a *negative* affect, even though it reflects the to-be-regulated emotion display of the infant, would, in fact, lead to a decrease—rather than an escalation—in the negative emotion state of the baby. On the basis of such arguments one could in fact reasonably claim that the parent's affect-mirroring displays may play no direct causal role in the affect regulation of the infant. Instead, they could be viewed simply as by-products of the parent's emotional recognition of and empathic identification with the baby's affective state, which would, in turn, lead to the actually effective affect-regulative activities such as holding.

Nevertheless, in our view the parent's affect-mirroring display behaviors during state-regulative interactions do, indeed, play a significant role in bringing about the modification of the infant's emotion state. We shall argue that there are several ways in which the contingency-detection and maximizing process involved in interpreting the emotion-reflective displays of parents contributes to the affect-regulative influence of parental interactions with the infant.

First, observations of soothing interactions indicate that parental affect-mirroring does not accompany the infant's ongoing negative emotion displays in a continuous manner. Rather, the parent is more likely to "join in" for brief periods with short bouts of empathic emotion-reflective displays and then to take "time-outs" or breaks before returning again to mirroring. (During the time-outs the caregiver may, of course, continue to engage in other, nonreflective soothing activities, such as holding, caressing, and talking to the baby.) This cyclic character of the distribution of mirroring acts over time may be a natural consequence of the nature of empathic identification with another person's emotion state: empathic emotion expressions tend to be brief communicative acts or gestures rather than more continuous state-expressions. However, the ensuing on-and-off temporal structure of mirroring interactions has interesting consequences when we consider it from the point of view of contingency analysis.

Let us assume that the infant's contingency-detection system is testing backward in time (the necessity index) for the conditional probability of the baby's emotional state cues preceding the appearance of the parent's mirroring display. Clearly, this will provide a very high contingency value on the necessity index, as the attuned parent will tend to produce empathic mirroring displays only when the baby is actively expressing the negative emotion in question. However, when the baby is testing forward in time (the sufficiency index) to see with what probability his emotion responses result in the onset of the parent's mirroring display, he will register only a moderate degree of contingent control in the sufficiency index, as during "time-outs" his emotional displays are not going to be followed by empathic affect reflections on the part of the parent. Overall, therefore, assuming an attuned and empathic parent, the sufficiency index will show a lower degree of contingent control than will the necessity index due to the cyclic distribution of empathic emotion-mirroring displays over time.

According to the contingency-maximizing hypothesis (Watson 1979), finding that the necessity index is higher than the sufficiency index will induce the infant to *reduce* the response class to see whether he can bring the two indices closer to matching and thereby to discover the true degree of contingent control he has over the parental mirroring display. As a result, the infant will decrease the set of and/or the frequency and intensity of emotion responses he is producing. The net effect, therefore, of the infant's attempt at identifying the maximal degree of contingent control he has over the mirroring display is the *reduction in the frequency and intensity of negative emotion expression*, which thus leads to the regulation (diminishing) of the negative affect state.

A further source of affect regulation that results from the infant's contingency analysis is the resulting experience of *causal efficacy* in controlling and bringing about the parental affect-mirroring display. As we have seen, there is evidence (Watson 1972, 1994) indicating that the detection of a high level of contingent control is positively arousing for infants—resulting in positive social responses such as smiling—and that they are motivated to modify their behavior in order to discover the actual degree of their contingent control (Watson 1979). Therefore, the detection of contingent control over the parent's affect-mirroring display will induce positive affect in the infant, which, through reciprocal inhibition, can be expected to decrease his negative affect state further.

An interesting additional feature of the complex contingency-detection and -maximizing process described above is that the infant will experience the ensuing emotional state regulation as an *active causal agent.* Apart from experiencing causal efficacy in bringing about an externalized version of his internal affective state in the form of the adult's emotion-reflective displays, the infant will simultaneously register the ensuing positive modification of his negative affect state as well. Therefore, it can be hypothesized that successful emotion-regulative interactions involving parental affect-mirroring may provide experiential basis for the establishment of a *sense of self as self-regulating agent.*[6] In other words, it is suggested that affect-regulative mirroring interactions may provide the original proto-situation in which infants can learn that by externalizing their internal emotion states they can achieve successful regulation of their affective impulses. While at this stage the parent is vitally instrumental in this process as the medium of externalization, later in pretend play the child will already be able to produce an externalized version of his internal states without parental mediation. (This point is further elaborated in the description of the case of "Mat" in chapter 7.)

---

[6] From this point of view, it may be worthwhile to contrast emotion-regulative interactions involving parental affect-mirroring with other, often equally effective, parental styles of emotion-regulation, such as, for example, the practice that can be called "disruption-soothing." This type of affect-regulation involves the abrupt induction of some intensive alternative emotion in the infant that is incompatible with the to-be-regulated negative affect—for example, by throwing the baby up in the air or by tickling him. Since in such emotion-regulative events the infant has no contingent control over the state transformation he is going through, it is likely that his experience will be a passive one of externally induced affect-modulation. A further interesting difference between disruption-soothing versus soothing-by-mirroring has to do with the perceived locus of causal control over the state transformation that the infant is experiencing. In soothing-by-mirroring the infant perceives internal causal control as he experiences active causal efficacy and agency in having contingent control over the ensuing state regulation. In contrast, in disruption-soothing the infant will locate the locus of causal control over his state transformation in an external agent or event. One may speculate that being systematically exposed to one versus the other type of parental soothing styles in infancy may contribute to the establishment of the individual differences in cognitive causal attribution styles (internal vs. external control) documented in the locus-of-control literature (Rotter 1966).

THE REPRESENTATIONAL CONSEQUENCES OF PARENTAL AFFECT-MIRRORING: THE "MARKEDNESS" HYPOTHESIS

Let us turn now to a somewhat different question concerning the nature of parental affect-mirroring interactions. As we have said, one of the most intriguing and apparently paradoxical aspects of parental affect-mirroring during state-regulative interactions is the fact that when the baby is in a negative state, the parent presents a reflection of a *negative* emotion display while success-fully soothing the infant. How does the baby interpret the nega-tive affect-expression of the parent, and how is it possible that the presentation of a negative emotion display is instrumental in modulating the infant's emotion state in a positive direction?

Previously, we have argued that the infant first learns about the dispositional content of emotion expressive displays by ob-serving the behavioral consequences of affect expressions in others. Assuming that the infant has in this way already come to represent the dispositional content of a given affect expression, the presentation of a corresponding emotion-reflective display by the parent during affect-regulative interactions may pose a po-tential danger of misattribution. Clearly, the parent's affect-reflecting display expresses an emotion state whose category is recognizable to the infant, but how does the baby know that this expression refers to his *own* state and not to that of the parent? Misattributing the expressed emotion to the parent would be especially problematic in the case of affect-regulative interac-tions in which the parent's affect-reflective display expresses the infant's *negative* emotion state—say, his fear or anger. Were the infant to misattribute the expressed negative affect to the par-ent, his own negative emotion state would, instead of becoming regulated, be likely to escalate, as the sight of a fearful or angry parent is clearly cause for alarm (and, if occurring systemati-cally, of possible trauma—see Main and Hesse 1990, and also the case vignette in chapter 7).

Thus, the question arises: How does the baby come to know that the dispositional state expressed by the external emotion display he seems to be controlling belongs to himself rather than to the parent, who is, after all, expressing it? In other words, how does the baby come to understand that the parent's affect-mirroring display is characterized by a *special kind of referential property* insofar as it is a reflection of the infant's state rather than that of the parent? We argue that this attribution problem is solved by a specific perceptual feature of the parent's affect-expressive displays, which we refer to as their "markedness."

In his seminal paper on the mother's mirroring function, Winnicott suggests that infants, when looking at their mother who is looking at them, see *themselves* in her face. This is so, says Winnicott, because when "the mother is looking at the baby . . . *what she looks like is related to what she sees there*" (1967, p. 131, emphasis in original). Winnicott's insight, however, leaves implicit the complex structural nature of the way the mother's face is related to that of the baby. In what follows we take a closer look at the structure of affect-regulative mirroring interactions in an attempt to specify those aspects of the mirroring stimuli that allow the infant to *interpret the mirroring face as a reflection of his own state.*

First of all, we should recognize that looking at the mirroring expression of the parent's face is qualitatively different from looking at one's reflection in a mirror. Recognizing himself in the mirror is no easy task for the baby; in fact, that cognitive feat is not achieved before the end of the second year of life (Gallup and Suarez 1986; Gergely 1994, 2001a; Lewis and Brooks-Gunn 1979). Note, furthermore, that, unlike the parent's affect-reflecting emotion displays, the mirror image is perfectly contingent both with the infant's visual features and with his behavior. Therefore, it can be argued that the processes that enable the infant to interpret the parental affect-mirroring displays as referring to the self are different from those involved in the understanding of the reflective properties of mirrors.

In fact, when we look at the structural relation between the stimulus features of the parent's mirroring expression and those of the infant's state-expressive behavior, it becomes clear that the term "mirroring" is a seriously misleading one. First of all, let us note that no matter how well attuned the parent is to the baby's state, her mirroring facial and vocal behavior will never perfectly match the temporal, spatial, and sensory intensity parameters of the infant's behavioral expressions. This is a crucial difference, as there is evidence to suggest that the infant is extremely sensitive to the distinction between perfect and high but imperfect degrees of response–stimulus contingencies, and he uses this information very early in life to categorize stimuli as belonging to the self or to a social object, respectively (Bahrick and Watson 1985; Watson 1979, 1994). This is important because it makes it clear that the simple recognition of the high— but necessarily imperfect—degree of correspondence between the infant's own state-expressive behaviors and the adult's affect-mirroring displays will not be sufficient for the baby to interpret the parent's expressive display as referring to himself.

Second, we should also realize that if the mother, in her attempt to mirror the baby's affect display as authentically as she can, were to produce her normal, realistic expression of the corresponding emotion, the chances of misattribution would dramatically increase, as the infant would identify the mother's affect expression as a realistic emotion display and would attribute the corresponding dispositional emotion state to her.

Therefore, to avoid the misattribution of the reflected emotion to the parent, it is proposed (see Gergely 1995a, 1995b, 2000) that mothers are instinctually driven to saliently *mark* their affect-mirroring displays to make them perceptually differentiable from their realistic emotion expressions. Marking is typically achieved by producing *an exaggerated version* of the parent's realistic emotion expression,[7] similarly to the marked

---

[7] Of course, the idea of a separate register or marked communicative code for expressions directed to young children is not new. It has been described in the realm of verbal communication as "infant-directed speech" or "motherese" (Ferguson 1964; Fernald 1991, 1992; Snow 1972), and it is characterized by phonological and syntactic modifications and prosodic cues such as elevated pitch and exaggerated pitch modulation. While several aspects of the distinctive prosodic patterns of child-directed speech have been suggested to facilitate early linguistic development (e.g., by highlighting word boundaries), researchers have also identified a number of primary, prelinguistic functions associated with infant-directed speech such as directing the infant's attention, modulating arousal and affect, or communicating emotions and intentions (Fernald 1991, 1992; Stern, Spieker, Barnett, and Mackain 1983). In fact, there is evidence (Fernald 1991) for the cross-cultural universality of exaggerated intonation contour in infant-directed speech as well as for an innate preference for exaggerated prosody (Cooper and Aslin 1990). Fernald (1992) argues that the exaggerated prosody of infant-directed speech is an evolutionary adaptation to the

"as-if" manner of emotion display that is characteristically produced in pretend play. The marked affect-display, remains, nevertheless, sufficiently similar to the parent's normative emotion
expression for the infant to recognize the dispositional content of
the emotion. However, it is hypothesized that due to the markedness of the display the attribution of the perceived emotion to the
parent will be inhibited. We shall call this process *referential
decoupling*,[8] referring to the fact that in the interpretation of the
marked affect-display the referential connection between the
emotion expression and the corresponding dispositional state of
the agent producing the display will be *suspended*: the perceived
emotion display will be "decoupled" from its referent.

However, while due to its markedness the parental emotion
display may become "decoupled" from its referent, it still needs
to be interpreted by the infant from a referential point of view as
expressing *someone's* emotion. We suggest that this process of
referential anchoring is determined by the *high degree of contingent relation* between the parent's affect-reflecting display and
the infant's emotion-expressive behavior. The infant's contin-

---

infant's perceptual and physiological system with signal-enhancing as well as
direct state-modulating properties.

The current proposal is that the universal tendency to use exaggerated
expressive patterns in infant-directed interactions will be present in affect-
mirroring displays as well. We suggest that apart from exaggerating the intonational vocal pattern of their affect-expressive displays, caretakers will also
exaggerate the visual facial features of the emotion display. In fact, Fernald
(1992) reports that mothers of deaf children intuitively exaggerate the visual
features of their facial communicative expressions. As an automatic consequence, emotion-mirroring facial and vocal parental expressions will be marked
as perceptually different from the corresponding realistic affect expressions of
parents. Therefore, the "markedness" of affect-mirroring expressions and its
representational consequences (see below) can be conceived of as a further and
separate evolutionary function of the universal parental inclination to address
infants with exaggerated expressive patterns of communication.

[8] The terms "referential decoupling" and "referential anchoring" were first
introduced by Alan Leslie (1987, 1994) to characterize the representational
properties of communicative expressions produced in pretend play. The potential functional and representational relationship between the markedness of
affect-mirroring expressions, on the one hand, and the markedness of expressions in the "pretend" mode of communication, on the other, is illustrated by the
case vignette of "Mat" in chapter 7.

gency-detection system will register the temporal contingency and cross-modal similarity of pattern between the parent's expression and his own on-going affective behavior. The perception of this contingent relation will provide the basis for the referential interpretation and grounding of the decoupled emotion display. As a result, the infant will *referentially anchor* the marked mirroring stimulus as expressing his *own* self-state.

In this view, then, over time infants are likely to experience emotion displays of others in *two different forms*: in their *realistic* and in their *marked* versions. We hypothesize that the baby will come to represent these two forms as qualitatively different versions of the emotion expression not only because of their marked differences in terms of perceptual features, but also because of two further distinguishing characteristics:

1. The situational features and behavioral outcomes that will become associated with the realistic emotion expression—such as with the sight of an angry mother—will be qualitatively different from those that are characteristic of the corresponding marked display—that is, the sight of an anger-reflecting mother. In other words, the *dispositional outcomes* associated with the realistic emotion will not hold for the case of the marked expression: instead of the negative behavioral and emotional consequences typically accompanying a realistic anger display, when faced with a marked anger-reflecting display the infant will be likely to experience positive outcomes in the form of successful affect regulation.

2. The realistic and the marked emotion displays of others will also become differentiated in terms of their *different contingency relation* to the infant's ongoing activity. Realistic emotion expressions are likely to be much less under the infant's contingent control than are the marked emotion-reflective displays. A realistic expression of, say, fear on the mother's face is more likely to be contingent on some external event or to be induced by some intrapsychic stimulus in the mother than to be under the control of a particular behavior of the infant. The marked affect-reflective version of the emotion display is, however, under the contingent

behavioral control of the baby, as it is produced as a response to the infant's corresponding emotion expression during affect-regulative mirroring interactions.

We hypothesize that in normal development the behavioral transformations distinguishing the marked displays from the realistic ones will become established as a *generalized communicative code* associated with (a) referential decoupling of the expressed content from the agent producing the display, (b) referentially anchoring the expressed content in an agent other than the one displaying the emotion,[9] and (c) suspension of the dispositional consequences of the realistic version of the expressed content (Gergely 1995a, 1995b, 2000). These features will become the central characteristics of the "*as-if*" *mode of communication* as it first emerges in the ability to comprehend and produce pretend play during the second year of life (see Fonagy and Target 1996; Leslie 1987, 1994).

The markedness of the affect-mirroring display is likely to have a further interesting effect as well. Since the mirroring display is differentiated from the corresponding realistic emotion expression by its perceptual markedness, its differential dispositional consequences, and its high degree of contingency with the baby's affective behavior, we hypothesize that the infant will construct a *separate representation* for it. Due to its contingent association with the infant's automatic affective reactions registered during the affect-regulative interactions, this representation will retain its associative link to the baby's primary-level affective states. Therefore, the separately represented marked emotion display will come to function as a *secondary representational structure,* which will become activated through associative routes whenever the set of internal-state cues corresponding to

---

[9] Note that in the original proto-situation of affect-regulative interactions the marked emotion is anchored in the infant as a result of the experience of contingent control; later, however—for example, in the use of the marked code in pretend play—the expressed content may be anchored in another—possibly imaginary—agent with whom the person producing the marked behavior identifies (see Leslie 1987, 1994).

the given dispositional emotion state are activated in the infant. Henceforth, the onset of an emotion state will result in the automatic activation of this "proto-symbolic" secondary emotion representation in the baby's awareness, allowing him to attribute the dispositional emotion state to himself.

In sum, it can be argued that the instinctive inclination of parents to expose their infants to marked affect-reflective behavioral displays during emotion-regulative interactions results in three significant developmental consequences: (*a*) The infant will come to detect and group together the sets of internal-state cues that are indicative of his categorically distinct dispositional emotion states. (*b*) He will establish secondary representations associated with his primary-level procedural affect states providing the cognitive means for accessing and attributing emotion states to the self. (*c*) He will acquire a generalized communicative code of "marked" expressions characterized by the representational functions of referential decoupling, anchoring, and suspension of realistic consequences.

"AFFECT ATTUNEMENT" FROM THE POINT OF VIEW OF THE SOCIAL BIOFEEDBACK THEORY

Stern (1984, 1985; Stern, Hofer, Haft, and Dore 1985) has also proposed a theory concerning the role of parental affect-reflective behaviors in early socio-emotional development. Similarly to our position, Stern believes that interactions involving emotion-reflective parental displays have a significant influence on self-development and affective self-regulation. His views on the developmental functions and mediating mechanisms involved in affect-reflective parental interactions, however, differ from ours in several important respects.

Stern's theory focuses on a specific type of affect-reflective interaction that he calls "affect attunements," which he demonstrated to occur regularly in normal mother–infant interactions between the ages of 9 and 12 months (Stern et al. 1985). He noted that during free play mothers periodically reflect some aspect of their infant's actions by providing a partial match of the baby's behavior in another modality. For example, he describes an 8½-month-old boy who is reaching for a toy just beyond reach. As he is stretching his body in an obvious voluntary effort to achieve his goal, "his mother says 'uuuuuh . . . uuuuuh!' with a crescendo of vocal effort. The mother's accelerating vocal-respiratory effort matched the infant's accelerating physical effort" (Stern et al. 1985, p. 250).

Stern makes several interesting points concerning the nature of such acts of behavioral attunement. Among other things, he emphasizes the fact that they are not simple acts of imitation, as they involve only a partial match of the amodal (temporal, intensity, and shape) characteristics of the infant's target act rendered in a different modality. He also points out that "during the first half year of life it is our impression—as yet untested—that imitations predominate over attunements. The reverse is true after nine months" (Stern 1984, p. 11).

Stern proposes that the reason why at around 9 months the mother—nonconsciously—chooses to "attune" to, rather than simply provide an imitative replica of, the infant's behavior is that she intends to refer to the internal affect state of the infant rather than to his surface behavior. In Stern's view, the matched amodal characteristics correspond to the abstract representational forms of affects that accompany the external behavioral act. Thus, the suggested function of such affect attunements is that of "interpersonal communion": "to share" or "to participate in" the internal affective experience of the infant. Of course, for the infant to interpret affect attunements as indicating parental sharing of his internal mental state, he must be (*a*) aware of his affect state, and he (*b*) must understand that the parent also experiences internal mental states, which (*c*) can be either shared or different from the particular mental state of the infant. Stern argues for this view by pointing out a purported correlation between the emerging dominance of parental attunements— over imitations—starting at 9 months on the one hand, and the emergence of the infant's "naive theory of interfaceable minds" (Bretherton and Bates 1979) during the same period on the other.

Before contrasting Stern's ideas with ours, let us point out some aspects of his proposal that seem questionable to us.

1.   Central to Stern's argument is the contention that at around 9 months there is a shift in the mother's reflective behaviors from intramodal faithful imitations to cross-modal attunements of amodal properties rendered in a different modality. However, it should be pointed out that in the technical sense, all imitative behaviors are—at least partially—cross-modal: if a tongue protrusion is faithfully imitated with a tongue protrusion, the infant experiences an intermodal (motor-visual) correspondence between his own behavior and the imitative act of the parent. It is also well known that even newborn infants are able to appreciate cross-modal correspondence, as shown by phenomena such as neonatal imitation (Kaye and Bower 1994, 1979; Meltzoff and Moore 1977, 1989; Stern 1985). Obviously, then, what Stern has in mind is not so much the question of intra- vs. intersensory modality but, rather, the fact that the attunement behavior, while showing a partial match in terms of amodal properties, is an act that is different from the target behavior of the infant.

2.   Whether Stern's impression about a qualitative shift at around 9 months from imitations to attunements can be empirically substantiated remains to be seen. Certainly, mothers do engage in attunement behaviors even much earlier (as in the prototypical theme-variation games described by Watson 1972). However, even if we assume with Stern that there is a statistical tendency to engage in more attunements than imitations after 9 months, there seems to be a more mundane reason for this than Stern's account in terms of the emerging mentalism of the infant. At the end of the first year, infants become more mobile, and the previously dominant face-to-face interactions are superseded by object-oriented joint activities (Stern 1985; Trevarthen and Hubley 1978). This imposes a pragmatic constraint on the mother's choice of behavior when she intends to reflect the infant's target act in a way that is accessible to the infant; for example, if the baby is visually orienting toward a toy that he is reaching for rather than toward the parent, the mother may be forced to attune to the baby's motor effort vocally.

3.   While the momentous changes in the infant's competence after the age of 9 months—such as joint attention, pointing, gaze-following, or social referencing—have been interpreted by some researchers as indicating the emergence of understanding of intentional mind states (Bretherton 1991a; Bretherton and Bates 1979; Stern 1985), others have resisted this temptation and proposed nonmentalistic interpretations for the same phenomena (Barresi and Moore 1996; Gergely et al. 1995; Gewirtz and Pelaez-Nogueras 1992; Moore and Corkum 1994). For example, as one of us has argued in detail elsewhere (Csibra and Gergely 1998; Gergely and Csibra 1997), the emerging new competencies at the end of the first year can be understood in terms of a "naive theory of rational action," which is an as yet nonmentalistic teleological interpretational system. Furthermore, while the 9-month-old may not have an appreciation of mind states as yet, mothers certainly attribute intentionality and mentalizing to their infant even at a much earlier age (as shown by the work on cognitive scaffolding by Bruner, Stern, and others: see, e.g., Bruner 1983; Reznick 1999; Stern 1985; Wood, Bruner, and Ross 1976). In terms of Stern's hypothesis that the function of attunements is to signal the sharing of attributed internal affect states, this would predict that caregivers engage in affect attunements even before their infant is 9 months of age.

In our minds, the above arguments raise enough doubts concerning Stern's interpretation of the function and nature of affect attunements that it may be worthwhile to explore an alternative approach to this intriguing developmental phenomenon. Our contingency-based social biofeedback model of affect-reflective parental behaviors provides such an alternative.

Note first of all that the three amodal features—time, intensity, and shape—identified by Stern as the abstract stimulus properties matched in affect attunements correspond to the three sources of contingency monitored by the contingency-detection module (Gergely and Watson 1999). Therefore, even if an attunement behavior is presented only on a single occasion, the combined value of the three contingency parameters can be sufficient to indicate a highly-but-imperfectly contingent external stimulus that is controlled by the infant's preceding behavior. In other words, the contingency-detection device will categorize the parent's attunement behavior as a causal consequence of the infant's on-going activity, resulting in a momentary sense of causal efficacy and the concomitant induction of positive arousal. The ensuing fleeting sense of causal control and instrumentality will become associated with the particular act in which the infant is engaged while being attuned to. This leads to our first proposal concerning the developmental function of reflective attunements: by momentarily attuning to them, the parent can selectively reinforce those affective, voluntary, or playful acts of the infant that she would like to see continued or repeated in the future. In other words, reflective attunements are an efficient tool of early nonverbal socialization whereby the parent can selectively reinforce and shape the infant's emerging voluntary, goal-oriented, or playful social activities.

In a somewhat more speculative vein, we would also like to propose that selective attunements might serve an additional sensitizing and representation-building function as well. Recall that our model, unlike Stern's, assumes that infants initially lack awareness of their internal affective and proprioceptive states that accompany their behaviors. By providing a partial rendering of some of the amodal features of the target act in a different behavioral format, the attunement behavior presents the infant with a nonidentical but highly contingent externalized version of his procedural behavioral routine. As a result, the infant will form a representation of the reflected amodal features that will become associated, due to their high degree of perceived contingency, with the nonconscious, primary, procedural representation of his on-going activity. In this way, reflective attunements contribute to the establishment of secondary representations of primary procedural states, which will be more cognitively accessible and more subject to conscious awareness.

This hypothesized secondary representation-building process can be conceived of as a special case of what Annette Karmiloff-Smith (1992) has called "representational redescription." She has argued that the human mind has the capacity to access and re-represent in a more explicit and cognitively accessible form the implicitly represented structural information embedded in nonconscious, automatic procedural routines. While Karmiloff-

Smith's theory postulates an innate endogenous epistemic drive that carries out such a process of "self-discovery" of one's own mind, our social biofeedback model identifies the contingent reflective externalizations provided by social partners as the informational basis for re-representing the amodal internal structure of nonconscious primary representations.

But do affect attunements serve the function of interpersonal communion or internal state sharing as well, as suggested by Stern? Our guess is that initially this may not yet be the case, especially insofar as the infant has not yet been sensitized to his internal categorical affect states as a result of the social biofeedback training provided by affect-reflective interactions. We do agree, however, that communicating the sharing of internal states may become a secondary function of attunement behaviors later in life. In verbal behavior, paraphrasing often serves the function of informing the other that the underlying meaning of his surface utterance has been correctly encoded. Nonverbal reflective attunements are also likely to come to serve a similar communicative function later in life.

MELTZOFF AND GOPNIK'S "LIKE ME" HYPOTHESIS

Meltzoff and Gopnik (1993; Gopnik and Meltzoff 1997; Meltzoff 1990) have proposed that imitative interactions between caregivers and infants can provide a basis that could lead babies to pay special attention to fellow human beings. This arises in specific regard to the times that the caregivers imitate their infants as opposed to when the babies imitate the caregivers. Meltzoff and Gopnik propose that an infant may use his innate cross-modal capacity to map the caregiver's visual movements onto the proprioceptive feelings of his own movements, which the parent is imitating. The caregiver's movements become attractive (attention capturing) because they are perceived (via the mapping) to be very much like the baby's own. For example, Meltzoff (1990) used a preferential interaction paradigm in which 14-month-old infants were faced with two adult models, one of whom imitated the child's object-related behaviors as best as she could, whereas the other always performed a temporally contingent but dissimilar (spatially noncontingent) action. The infants looked and smiled more at the adult who mimicked them than at the one whose actions were only temporally contingent with theirs. Meltzoff and Gopnik hypothesize that it is the infants' "like me" experience that explains their preferential attention and smiling to the mimicking adult model over the only temporally contingent one.

Since our contingency-based social biofeedback theory also generates specific predictions for the infant's attraction to parental "mirroring" acts, we would like to make explicit two important differences between our position and that of Meltzoff and Gopnik. First, Meltzoff and Gopnik (1993) assume that infants have direct introspective access to their internal "feeling states" from the beginning of life. In contrast, we are assuming that initially many of the infants' state transitions are outside their perceptual awareness. We assume this to be so both for the visceral and for the physiological state cues that accompany basic-emotion states and for many of the proprioceptive consequences of facial muscular movement. Indeed, a central aspect of our model is that these internal-state cues of the infant only become liminal after a period of biofeedback sensitization brought about as a result of parental mirroring interactions. This difference in assumption about what is and what is not "felt" by the infant is not likely to be resolvable empirically, however. The reason for this pessimism is that we, and very probably Meltzoff and Gopnik as well, are using the term "felt" in the sense of a state of conscious awareness. For example, we do not contend that the infant has no functional use of proprioceptive feedback from facial muscle movement prior to social mirroring experiences. What we contend is that while such feedback exists and is used in various motor control systems, it does not enter conscious awareness. For us as adults, many motor events—such as eye movement, head rotation, chest diaphragm expansion, and even limb motion—are subliminal until we attend to them. But it is not easy to think of how to measure such a distinction in relation to the subjective experience of an infant.

The second point of difference between our model and Meltzoff and Gopnik's "like me" hypothesis about the attractiveness of social mirroring is far more assessable empirically. The "like me" hypothesis would seem to predict clearly that the more closely the mirroring act reproduces the infant's behavior, the more attractive it will be for the baby. In contrast, we assume (see Bahrick and Watson 1985; Watson 1994) that after the age of about 3 months, the target setting of the contingency-detection mechanism of the normal human infant is switched toward seeking out high but imperfect degrees of contingency. This predicts a preference for high but imperfectly contingent mirroring displays over perfectly contingent ones, whereas the opposite prediction follows from the "like me" hypothesis.

Our explanation for the looking pattern in Meltzoff's (1990) study is that the mimicking model provides a high but nevertheless only imperfectly contingent action that is preferred as such over the simply temporally contingent model, which produces a much lower degree of contingency. We agree with Meltzoff and Gopnik that the infants appear to use the spatial—or, in their words, structural—information in differentiating between the two models. Somewhat tautologically, however, we propose that the preference for the temporal plus spatial (the mimicking adult) over the merely temporal (the alternative model) contingency simply indicates that the imitating model provided a contingency magnitude that was closer to the target criterion of best—high-but-not-perfect—contingency of the contingency-detection mechanism than was the alternative model.

THE "NEARLY, BUT CLEARLY NOT, LIKE ME" HYPOTHESIS

In contrast to Meltzoff and Gopnik's "like me" hypothesis, however, we predict that if given a choice between a perfectly contingent and the highly but only imperfectly contingent imitative display used by Meltzoff, after the age of 3 months the infant would preferentially attend to the latter. In other words, we predict that the infant would be attracted to the "nearly, but clearly not, like me" versus the "like me" display because, rather than preferentially orienting toward a self-like (perfect) contingency, he is committed to engaging contingencies that are specifically not self-based (i.e., not perfect).

To test this hypothesis, one of us has carried out a study that has specifically contrasted the effect on young children's behavior of the availability of perfect as against imitative feedback of their manual activity (see Magyar and Gergely 1998). We tested 32 children between 18 and 36 months of age, who sat in front of two TV monitors each displaying the moving image of a schematic hand. The subjects moved a small metal bowl (with a computer mouse hidden inside) freely on the surface of the table in front of them. On one of the screens they saw the perfectly response-contingent movements of the schematic hand, generated by a computer program controlled by the subjects' manual manipulation of the bowl. The second screen displayed a highly but imperfectly response-contingent image of the schematic hand, which was generated by the imitative efforts of a human experimenter. This person attempted to copy the subject's manual behavior faithfully by moving a mouse under the visual guidance of the subject-generated movements of the schematic hand (the perfect feedback display) viewed on a separate monitor in another room. This procedure was used in an attempt to provide the normal lag and imperfection of a human act of direct imitation. We found that the children attended more to the imitation-based (highly but imperfectly) contingent image than to the perfectly contingent one ($p < 0.04$). This, then, provides support for our hypothesis that children are selectively attracted to response-contingent stimuli that are "nearly, but clearly not, like them" rather than being "just like them."

IMPLICATIONS FOR DEVELOPMENTAL PSYCHOPATHOLOGY AND THERAPEUTIC INTERVENTIONS

Having presented our social biofeedback model of affect-mirroring within the framework of a theory of normal emotional development, we shall discuss some clinical implications of our model with the aim of integrating it with current psychodynamic approaches to mirroring developed in object-relations theory and attachment theory.

Our social biofeedback model of affect-mirroring postulates a complex biosocial system in which the infant is instinctually driven to express the dynamic changes in his internal affect states behaviorally, while the mother is instinctually driven to reflect the infant's state-expressive behaviors in a marked form. This system serves two major developmental functions: the mirroring environment (a) contributes to the on-line homeostatic regulation of the infant's dynamic affective state changes and (b) provides a kind of "teaching" or "scaffolding" environment that results in the internalization of the maternal affect-regulative function through the establishment of secondary representations of the infant's primary emotion states. In fact, it can be argued that this theory is close in spirit to certain psychodynamic characterizations of the developmental functions of the infant's maternal environment as formulated in attachment theory (Bowlby 1969), object-relations theory (Bion 1962a; Winnicott 1965), self psychology (Kohut 1971, 1977), or analytically oriented developmental theory (Stern 1985).

These diverse approaches share a strong emphasis on the vital causal role played in the infant's early psychic development by the mother's biologically determined ability and inclination to read, modulate, and reflect back the infant's state-expressive behaviors. These theories also agree that such maternal ministrations, apart from providing on-line need satisfaction and state regulation for the baby, also contribute significantly to psychic structure-building and to the emergence of emotional self-awareness and control. In fact, a number of these theories have explicitly identified the mother's ability to adaptively "mirror," "echo," or "match" the infant's affective states as a significant and central mechanism underlying the early development of the self (Bion 1962a, 1962b; P. F. Kernberg 1984; Kohut 1971, 1977; Mahler and McDevitt 1982; Mahler et al. 1975; Stern 1985; Winnicott 1967). However, no specific models have been advanced to characterize the psychological processes through which affect-mirroring achieves the various developmental functions that have been attributed to it. Therefore, we wish to suggest that our social biofeedback model can be interpreted as specifying an underlying psychological mechanism that mediates—at least some of—the developmental effects of the affect-reflective maternal environment as discussed, for example, in Winnicott's model of the mother's holding function (Winnicott 1965), Kohut's model of the maternal mirroring function (Kohut 1971, 1977), or Bion's model of maternal containment (Bion 1962a, 1962b).

For example, both Winnicott and Kohut emphasize the importance of the infant's early experience of omnipotence for healthy self-development that is afforded by maternal attunement to and mirroring of the infant's need states. This clinical insight may be related to the workings of the contingency-detection mechanism proposed in our social biofeedback model. In this view, the sense of infantile omnipotence may be interpreted as corresponding to the sense of causal efficacy and control that is generated by the contingency-detection mechanism during adaptive mirroring interactions.

Another example is contained in certain features of Bion's influential notion of the maternal "container" function (Bion 1962a, 1962b). According to Bion, the mother "contains" and re-presents in a modified form the negative contents that the infant projects into her. He suggests that "the mother, with her capacity for reverie, transforms the unpleasant sensations . . . and provides relief for the infant who then reintrojects the mitigated and modified emotional experience" (Grinberg, Sor, and De Bianchedi 1977, p. 57). Bion (1962a) also emphasizes that maternal containment, transformation, and re-presentation of the baby's negative internal states is a necessary prerequisite for the infant to become able to reflect upon and process his experience, or in Bion's words, to think his own thoughts and feel his own feelings. In terms of our social biofeedback model, these ideas can be interpreted as referring to the mother's ability to modulate the infant's negative affect by producing contingent and marked emotion-reflective displays on the one hand, and to the ensuing establishment of the secondary representations of the infant's primary emotion states through the introjection of the marked and decoupled affect-reflective maternal expressions on the other.

Until now our discussion of the nature of parental affect-mirroring has concentrated on the case of adaptive and successful emotion-regulative interactions and their consequences for normal development. However, based on our model, we can also specify some of the processes that may result in pathological development of emotions in deviant parental mirroring environments.

NORMAL VERSUS PATHOLOGICAL CONSEQUENCES OF AFFECT-MIRRORING

According to our model, adaptive affect-reflective interactions result in the following consequences in normal development: (*a*) Due to the markedness of the mirroring display, the expressed affect will be decoupled from the parent. (*b*) As a result of the high degree of contingency between the infant's emotion state and the marked affect-mirroring display, the expressed emotion will be referentially anchored as belonging to the baby. (*c*) The infant will establish a separate representation for the marked emotion-expression of the parent that will be associatively linked to his implicit procedural primary emotion state. (*d*) Due to its similarity to—and categorical identity with—the parent's corresponding realistic emotion display, the internalized marked emotion representation will "inherit" the dispositional information already associated with the parent's realistic emotion expression. In this way, the infant will not only acquire a secondary, cognitively accessible representation of his primary emotion state, but will also become able to attribute to himself the dispositional information associated with that emotion, resulting in an ability to represent and predict his likely behavior when being in that state.

Given these consequences for normal development, our social biofeedback model of affect-mirroring can also identify certain structural types of deviant mirroring styles that may result in pathological outcomes. In particular, the selective lack of either markedness or category congruence may produce *deviant mirroring styles* that, if they become dominant in the infant's experience, may to lead to characteristic pathological consequences.

Deviant Affect-Mirroring Styles

1. *Lack of markedness.* Let us first take the case of affect-mirroring that is *categorically congruent but lacks perceptual marking.* (A case illustration of this kind of deviant affect-mirroring is provided in chapter 7.) Mothers who, due to their own unresolved intrapsychic conflicts, are unable to contain and become overwhelmed by their infant's negative affect-expressions can be expected to show this structural pattern of mirroring. Borderline patients or parents showing the "preoccupied" (E) profile in Mary Main's Adult Attachment Interview[10] (George et al. 1985; Main and Goldwyn 1991) are likely candidates for exhibiting unmarked affective responses of this kind. (See also Fonagy, Steele, et al. 1995.)

Such parents react to their infant's negative affect-expression by producing the same—categorically congruent—emotion-expression, but in an *unmarked, realistic* manner. According to our hypothesis, the dominance of this kind of deviant mirroring style is likely to lead to the following consequences: (*a*) Since the mirroring affect-display is not marked, it is not going to be decoupled from the caregiver and will be attributed to the parent as her real emotion. (*b*) As the unmarked emotion display is not decoupled, it will also not become anchored to the infant. Consequently, the secondary representation of the baby's primary emotion state will not be established, leading to a corresponding deficiency in self-perception and self-control of affect. (*c*) Since the infant will attribute the mirrored affect to the parent, he will experience his own negative affect "out there" as belonging to the other, rather than to himself. (*d*) Instead of regulating the in-

---

[10] Patrick, Hobson, Castle, Howard, and Maughan (1994) provided evidence indicating a strong correlation between borderline pathology and "E" classification on the AAI, and this was confirmed in a larger study with personality-disordered controls (Fonagy, Leigh, et al. 1996).

fant's negative affect, the perception of a corresponding realistic negative emotion in the parent will escalate the baby's negative state, leading to traumatization rather than containment (Main and Hesse 1990).

This constellation corresponds to the clinical characterization of *projective identification* as a pathological defensive mechanism characteristic of borderline personality disorder (Kernberg 1976; Klein 1946; Sandler 1987; H. Segal 1964). Therefore, it can be hypothesized that sustained experience with *categorically congruent but unmarked affect-mirroring* in infancy might play an important causal role in the establishment of projective identification as the dominant form of emotional experience in borderline personality development.

2. *Lack of category congruence.* A second type of deviant mirroring structure might be produced by the dominance of *marked, but incongruent, categorically distorted parental mirroring.* Over-controlling parental attitude and/or defensively distorted parental perception of the infant's affect may produce a mirroring style of this sort. Think of an infant whose erotically colored excitement about physical contact induces anxiety and defensive anger in the mother due to her intrapsychic conflicts in relation to bodily tenderness. The mother might project her defensive emotional reaction onto the infant, as a result of which she will distortedly perceive the baby's libidinal excitement as aggression. She may then proceed to modulate this thus (mis)perceived affect in her baby by properly marked mirroring of an *aggressive* display.

According to the present hypothesis, marked but categorically distorted affect-mirroring of this kind, when dominant in the infant's experience, may lead to the following consequences: (a) Due to the markedness of the mirrored affect, it will be decoupled from the parent. (b) As the mirroring display shows a sufficiently high degree of contingency with the infant's—miscategorized—affect state, he will referentially anchor the mirrored affect-display to his primary emotion state. (c) However, since the category of the mirrored affect is incongruent with the actual affect state of the infant, he will establish a *distorted secondary representation* of his primary emotion state. As a result, the infant will attribute dispositional information to himself that is incongruent with his actual (primary) emotion state, leading to a distorted perception of his self-state.

Thus, one may speculate that marked, but categorically distorted, incongruent mirroring of affects might be causally related to pathologically *distorted self-representations*, which may, for example, underlie sexual pathologies in which libidinal excitement is perceived as aggression.

This type of deviant mirroring provides a link between our model and Winnicott's concept of the false self. According to Winnicott (1960a), impingements from the environment may arise out of the caregiver's difficulty in understanding the infant's thoughts or feelings, substituting her gestures instead of representing his own intentional state to the baby, invalidating the gestures, and obstructing his illusion of omnipotence. When this continues despite persistence by the infant, Winnicott suggests that a number of reactions can arise: the self may be overwhelmed, it may become anxious anticipating further impingement, it may come to experience itself only when it acts in opposition to impingements, and, finally, it can acquiesce and hide its own gestures, undermining its own ability. In this latter case, Winnicott assumed, the self ends up mimicking its caretaking environment, resigned to the deficiency, setting aside creative gestures, and perhaps even forgetting they ever existed. Winnicott suggested that the infant compliantly relates to the caregiver's gestures as if they were his own, and this compliant stance lies at the root of the false-self-structure. It follows from Winnicott's view of the hallmarks of the true self that the false self is revealed by a lack of spontaneity or originality. It also follows from his understanding of how false-self-structure originates that such individuals later seek out external impingements to recreate the experience of compliant relating and, with it, a sense of realness about their own existence. Winnicott also identified the kind of self that appears to be real but is built on identification with early objects and thus lacks something uniquely its own.

Winnicott described how the false self may sometimes set itself up as real and generally convey this impression to others, but it does so mechanically, lacking genuine links between internal states and actions. A self whose own constitutional state has not been recognized is an empty self. The emptiness reflects the activation of secondary representations that lack the corresponding connections to affective activation within the constitutional self. Emotional experience will be meaningless, and the individual might look for powerful others to merge with or extraneously caused (drug-induced) physical experiences of arousal to fill the vacuum with borrowed strength or ideals. Only when the person is challenged by the need to act spontaneously as a whole person, particularly in intense relationships, will the limitations become evident.

The false self is thought to serve to hide, and thus protect, the true self. The true self is the constitutional state that was largely unrepresented by parental mirroring. Thus it may emerge only in the course of extreme states of emotional arousal, when the internalized but nonreferential expression can no longer serve to mask emotional upheaval—for example, in the course of physical or psychological illness. Symptom formation may express the true self because historically this was how the emerging self found that it could exist without being overwhelmed by the environment, having creative gestures replaced or ignored.

In distinguishing between deprivation and privation, Winnicott (1960a) brought a critical concept to an understanding of the influence of the environment, which is closely related to the current formulation of two styles of affect-mirroring. Privation is experienced at a stage where the infant does not have an awareness of maternal care; deprivation can occur only once the infant becomes aware both of his own needs and of the object and is able to perceive environmental maladjustment. Privation occurs when mirroring is marked but distorted, undermining the infant's awareness of his own experience. Deprivation occurs when mirroring is unmarked and the caregiver's congruent affect is foisted on the infant without modulation.

This distinction is crucial to our understanding of antisocial behavior where, in Winnicott's formulation, a certain degree of integration within the self has already taken place but deprivation is sufficiently severe and chronic for the representation of the good-enough environment to be compromised (Winnicott 1967). In these cases there is no active discouragement of the expression of the true self; rather, the child cannot cope with the failure or withdrawal of ego support, and an antisocial tendency develops to protect his sense of self. Capacity for concern is limited because the self is reorganized at a more primitive level. Within Winnicott's model, the capacity for concern is achieved only toward the end of the second year of life, when constructive and creative experiences of reparation lead the child to feel responsibility. Once concern has been established, the individual can use constructive elements of aggression in the service of work and play.

The perception of the self in the mind of the other becomes the representation of the child's experience, the representation of the representational world. Consistent with Winnicott's observations, the child who fails to develop a representation of an intentional self is likely to incorporate in his image of himself the representation of the other, sometimes mental, sometimes physical. The picture of the self will then be "false": distorted, as the child's experience of himself is overly influenced by his early perceptions of what others think and feel, and strangely out of touch with what he himself or others are currently experiencing. This may be why many neglected or maltreated children show apparent failures of object permanence, leading to primitive separation anxiety or feelings of merger with the object. In reality, they continue existentially to depend on the physical presence of the other, both for self-sustaining auxiliary reflective function—continuing to seek and find their intentionality in the mind of the other—and, more subtly, as a vehicle for the externalization of parts of the self-representation that are experienced as alien and incongruent with the self. This alien other is still internalized as part of the self-structure, but without the appropriate links and associations that would enable the self-representation to function coherently.

This state of affairs places a massive burden on those with severe personality disorder. In order for the self to be coherent, the alien and unassimilable parts require externalization: that is, they need to be seen as part of the other where they can be hated, denigrated, and often destroyed. The physical other who performs this function must remain present for this complex process to operate. The borderline child or adult cannot feel that he is a self unless he has the other—often the therapist—present to frighten and intimidate, to seduce and excite, to humiliate and reduce to helplessness. The other's departure signals the return of these "exterojects" and the destruction of the coherence the child achieves by such projection.

The alien self is present in all of us, because transient neglect is part of ordinary caregiving; it is pernicious when later experiences of trauma in the family or the peer group force the child to dissociate from pain by using the alien self to identify with the aggressor. Hence the vacuous self comes to be colonized by the image of the aggressor, and the child comes to experience himself as evil and monstrous. In later chapters we elaborate on how this, in turn, leads to three important changes: (a) a repudiation of mentalization in an attachment context, (b) disruption of the psychological self by the emergence of the other within the self, and (c) vital dependence on the physical presence of the other as a vehicle for externalization. A further twist to this sequence can be added when later brutalization within an attachment relationship generates intense shame. Coupled with a history of neglect in infancy and a consequent weakness in the capacity for mentalization, this becomes a potent trigger for violence because of the intensity of the humiliation experienced when trauma cannot be attenuated via mentalization. Unmentalized shame is then experienced as the destruction of the self—we have called it "ego-destructive shame." The concept of "ego-destructive shame" plays a key role in our discussions of violence in adolescence and adulthood. (See chapters 8–10.)

AFFECT-MIRRORING
AS A MECHANISM OF THERAPEUTIC INTERVENTION

There is no particular reason to believe that affect-mirroring and its consequent effects on psychic structure-building would be restricted to the initial stages of development only. Contingency detection is likely to be a pervasive information-processing mechanism active over the life span, and empathic affect-reflective gestures are characteristic of adult communication as well as of parent–infant interactions. In fact, emotional mirroring can be identified as a potentially central mechanism of therapeutic change in child psychotherapy, and it has been demonstrated to characterize face-to-face patient–therapist interactions in adult psychotherapy as well (Krause 1997).

In fact, it is tempting to suggest that the social biofeedback model of affect-mirroring specifies an important mediating mechanism underlying the therapeutic influence of so-called mirroring interpretations in psychotherapy. Chapter 6 extends the social biofeedback model to the theory-of-mind perspective in the context of an assumed model of the development of psychic reality. Briefly, we propose the existence of two levels of representational functioning in normal development, which we call the "psychic equivalence" and the "pretend" modes of mentalizing. "Psychic equivalence" (derived from Freud's original concept of psychic reality—see Freud 1900a, 1950 [1895]) refers to the more primitive level of mental functioning where the feelings and fantasies are experienced as reality and not as mental states representing reality. The "pretend" mode, on the other hand, involves an awareness of the representational, mentalistic nature of experiences, which is made possible by "decoupling" the mental representations involved from external reality. In the "pretend" mode traumatic memories, threatening emotional impulses, or unacceptable fantasies can be safely activated and dealt with as their connection to reality has been suspended (see also Freud 1920g; Gergely 1995a; Gergely and Watson 1996). The "pretend" mode has to be clearly marked, and the lack of correspondence to actual reality is frequently exaggerated (cf. Fónagy and Fonagy 1995). We also suggest that as a precondition for the establishment of the "pretend" mode, the child needs to experience his feelings and thoughts being repeatedly reflected in a marked manner by another person. The child needs an adult or older child who will "play along," so that the child sees his fantasy or idea represented in the adult's mind, reintrojects this, and uses it as a representation of his own thinking. (See also our case illustration in chapter 7.)

In chapter 6 we consider the psychoanalytic psychotherapy of a 4-year-old girl, "Rebecca." While she had already achieved the general ability to use the "pretend" mode of mentalizing, there remained in her mind an "island of psychic equivalence" related to the traumatic feelings and fantasies involving her unknown father and the recent death of a grandfather. This local arrest of the development of the "pretend" mode of mental functioning was related to her mother's inability to tolerate and reflect in a marked manner the child's expressions of frustration and aggressive fantasies about her absent father, as the mother herself also tended to be stuck—in this area—in a mode of psychic equivalence. During analysis it proved to be possible to integrate this "island of psychic equivalence" into the "pretend" mode of mentalizing by providing marked mirroring interpretations about the child's feelings and thoughts within the framework of play therapy.

It seems to us that our social biofeedback model of affect-mirroring can be fruitfully applied to the above case as the psychological mechanism mediating both the developmental arrest resulting in the "island of psychic equivalence" and the therapeutic intervention leading to its integration into the "pretend" mode of functioning. Thus, it can be suggested that the little girl's mother is likely to have either systematically avoided affect-reflective interactions in relation to the child's expressed emotions concerning her absent father, or engaged in unmarked, realistic re-presentations of the child's intense negative affects. This is likely to have intensified the child's traumatic negative emotional reactions even more, as well as leading to the absence of secondary marked emotion representations in this content area. However, since the little girl had already acquired the marked "pretend" mode of mentalizing in other areas of thought, the generalized communicative code of marked expressions as indicative of decoupling and as suggestive of self-reference was available for her. As a result, through the application of marked mirroring interpretations of her traumatic feelings and fantasies in the framework of reality-decoupled play therapy, it became possible to establish the secondary marked representational structures that could raise the "island of psychic equivalence" into the safer and more tolerable "pretend" mode of emotional experience.

CONCLUSION

Parental mirroring of the infant's emotion expressions seems to be a uniquely human instinctual propensity that has long been considered in both academic and psychoanalytic developmental psychology as playing a central role in early psychological development. However, the various developmental functions associated with parental affect-reflective interactions have, with few exceptions, been based on clinical reconstruction and insight rather than direct evidence, and the underlying psychological mechanisms mediating the hypothesized developmental effects remained mostly unspecified. In contrast, in this chapter we have advanced a new theory of the nature of parental affect-mirroring during early emotion-regulative interactions, which provides a specific model of the psychological processes involved and identifies the set of developmental functions that are served by these processes.

Our social biofeedback model of parental affect-mirroring is specifically based on two sources of empirical evidence: it builds on the infant learning literature concerning contingency detection and maximization on the one hand, and on adult biofeedback training studies on the other. Our central proposal has been that by reflecting in a "marked," exaggerated form the infant's emotion expressive displays, the caregiver provides a kind of natural biofeedback sensitization training to the infant whose effects are mediated by the baby's sophisticated ability to detect and analyze response–event contingency relations. We have identified four separate developmental functions that are served by parental mirroring of affects:

1. *The sensitization function:* As a result of the biofeedback training, the infant will become able to detect and group together the sets of internal-state cues that are indicative of his categorically distinct dispositional emotion states.

2. *The representation-building function:* By setting up separate representations for the parent's "marked" emotion-reflective displays that are contingent with the infant's emotion-expressive

behaviors, the baby establishes secondary representations that become associated with his primary, nonconscious, procedural affect states. These secondary representational structures will provide the cognitive means for accessing and attributing emotion states to the self that will form the basis for the infant's emerging ability to control as well as to reason about his dispositional emotion states.

3. *The state-regulation function:* During empathic parental mirroring of the baby's negative affect expressions, the infant's contingency-detection device registers the high degree of contingent control of the baby's emotion expressions over the caregiver's mirroring displays. This generates a sense of causal efficacy and positive arousal that, through reciprocal inhibition, leads to a decrease of the infant's negative affect state. Furthermore, as a by-product of the infant's attempts to identify the maximal degree of contingent control he has over the parent's affect-reflective displays during soothing interactions, the baby will modify—in fact, reduce—his negative emotion-expressive behaviors, thereby also contributing to the soothing effect.

4. *The communicative and mentalizing function:* By internalizing the "marked" secondary representations associated with primary self-states, the infant will acquire a generalized communicative code of "marked" expressions characterized by the representational functions of referential decoupling, referential anchoring, and suspension of realistic consequences. This creates a new "pretend" mode of mentalizing and communicating about affective states that will provide the young child with powerful representational means of emotional self-regulation and expression.

5

The Development of an Understanding
of Self and Agency

The aim of this chapter is to present the most important discoveries from developmental research over the last twenty years that in our view pertain directly to the psychoanalytic understanding of self-development and have clear clinical implications for the treatment of individuals whose primary disturbance is rooted in disorganized self-representation and affect dysregulation. We wish to distinguish the model of self-development and affect regulation proposed in this volume from other contemporary developmentally grounded psychoanalytic views. We trace the development of mentalization from infancy and engage in the developmental debate about exactly when the intentional stance is achieved. In our view many recent contributions have overstated the case for early intersubjective processes in self-development. We argue that intersubjectivity is an emergent phenomenon whose establishment is a function of early interactive processes within an attachment context. In chapter 3 we laid the foundations for a model of self-development rooted in interpersonal understanding; in this chapter this model is elaborated, and five stages in the development of the self as agent are distinguished. The chapter also lays the crucial groundwork for the explorations of borderline personality disorder in terms of an early nonmentalistic perception of causality in social actions— the teleological stance. Finally, the chapter gives a relatively comprehensive summary of the developmental literature concerning the development of an understanding of self and others as intentional mental agents.

INTRODUCTION: EARLY UNDERSTANDING OF THE SELF AS AGENT FROM THE POINT OF VIEW OF THEORY-OF-MIND DEVELOPMENT

For a long time, the study of the "self as a mental agent" was a neglected topic. Historically, it has received much less attention than the other major aspect of self-knowledge that William James (1890) classically termed the "empirical self" or "Me" and which in current terminology is often called the "conceptual" or "categorical" self-concept or representation (Harter 1999; Lewis and Brooks-Gunn 1979; Neisser 1988). The "categorical self" refers to the representation of the collection of those features and properties that the person believes to be true of himself (blue-eyed, handsome, good in math, poor soccer player, etc.) and that he has mostly inferred from the self-directed reactions of his social environment. (For a recent review, see Harter 1999.)

The historical bias toward studying the social construction of the categorical self-concept rather than the Jamesian "subjective self" or "I" can be explained by the traditionally strong conceptual influence of the Cartesian doctrine of "first-person authority," which claims that one has direct and infallible introspective access to one's own intentional mind states. The influence of Cartesian doctrine has encouraged the belief that the conscious apprehension of our mind states through introspection is a basic, direct, and probably prewired ability of our mind, leading to the conviction that knowledge of the self as a mental agent is an innately given rather than a developing or constructed capacity. As we shall see (especially in our discussion of currently popular views of initial-state "intersubjectivity"), the Cartesian doctrine still seems to have its sway among many developmental researchers. However, current philosophy of mind, cognitive neuroscience, and developmental theory have seriously challenged the Cartesian view of the mind (Damasio 1994a; Dennett

1991; Gopnik 1993; Wegner and Wheatley 1999). At the same time, recent philosophical (D. Davidson 1980; Searle 1983), cognitive, and neuropsychological (C. D. Frith 1992; Jeannerod 1999; Pacherie 1997; Prinz 1997) models of the representation of intentional action indicate that the representation of intentional mind states has a rather complex internal structure whose conscious access may be absent or only partial and may depend on a variety of factors (Dienes and Perner 1999). This, together with the demonstrations from current theory-of-mind research documenting an intriguingly complex developmental unfolding of the understanding of different types of intentional mind states—such as desires, intentions, and beliefs (Bartsch and Wellman 1995; Perner 1991)—strongly indicates that the mature understanding of the self as a mental agent is also likely to be the product of rather complex developmental processes. The aim of this chapter, therefore, is to trace in the light of these new theoretical and empirical advances the different stages of the development of self-knowledge from the early understanding of physical and social agency in infancy to the more mature understanding of the self as a mental agent in early childhood.

We can differentiate five levels of agency of the self, of which the developing human infant acquires a progressive understanding: physical, social, teleological, intentional, and representational. (These were briefly introduced in chapter 3.) At the level of physical description, actions enter into two types of causal relations: they are related to bodies that provide their causal source of energy, and they have a causal impact on the environment, bringing about states of affairs that did not exist before. Understanding the *self as a "physical agent,"* therefore, minimally involves some appreciation of these causal relations: the self as a physical entity with force that is the source of action and the self as an agent whose actions bring about changes in their proximal environment (Leslie 1994). Furthermore, starting from birth, human infants engage in species-specific interactions with their caregivers (Meltzoff and Moore 1977; Stern 1985; Trevarthen 1979). In such exchanges the infant's displays have effects in the form of the behavioral reactions and emotion displays they induce in their parents. Early understanding of the *self as a "social agent"* involves, therefore, at least the representation of the causal effects at a distance that species-specific communicative displays can bring about in the social environment (Neisser 1988). However, the types of causal relations that connect actions to their agents on the one hand and to the world on the other go beyond the level of physical description, and, correspondingly, adults and young children come to understand much more about both of these relations as they develop. Thus, at around 8–9 months of age (Tomasello 1999), infants come to differentiate actions from their outcomes and represent actions as means that function to bring about goal states. At this level the *self is understood as a "teleological agent"* (Csibra and Gergely 1998; Leslie 1994) who can choose among alternative actions the one that is most efficient in bringing about a goal given the constraints of a particular situation. Sometimes during the second year infants seem to develop an already mentalistic understanding of agency: they start to construe the *self as an "intentional agent"* whose actions are caused by prior intentional mental states such as desires (Wellman and Phillips 2000). At this point, they also understand that actions can change mental as well as physical properties of the world: for example, they clearly understand that a declarative pointing gesture functions to change the attentional state of another agent (Corkum and Moore 1995). At around 3 to 4 years of age this understanding of agency in terms of mental causation also comes to include the representation of epistemic mind states—such as beliefs (Wimmer and Perner 1983). At this stage, the young child already shows an understanding of the *self as a "representational agent"* whose actions are caused by intentional mental states (desires and beliefs) that are construed as representational in nature (Perner 1991; Wellman 1990). Related advances at this stage, such as the ability to understand the "causal self-referentiality" of intentional mind states (Pacherie 1997; Perner 2000b; Searle 1983) and the representational capacity to relate the memories of the self's intentional activities and experiences into a coherent causal-temporal organization (Povinelli and Eddy 1995), leads to the establishment of the—temporally— "extended" or "proper" self (W. James, 1890)—in other words, to an understanding of the *"autobiographical self."* As this brief preview indicates, the development of an understanding of self and agency is a highly complex and currently much researched field of study.

EARLY DEVELOPMENT OF THE SELF
AS A "PHYSICAL AGENT"

Traditionally, it was believed (Freud 1911b; Piaget 1936) that the newborn baby's world is basically solipsistic and that infants are at first unable to differentiate between stimuli that belong to the self and those that belong to the environment. Such a differentiation, however, seems to be a prerequisite for the development of a sense of physical agency, which involves representing the causal relationships between actions and the physical self on the one hand, and actions and the external world on the other. Contemporary research has challenged the traditional belief in an initial undifferentiated state, uncovering a number of objective information sources and corresponding innate detection mechanisms that provide for the direct perception of the "ecological self" (Butterworth 1995; Neisser 1988) as a differentiated objective entity moving in space among other physical objects. Following Gibson's (1966) ecological perspective, a series of studies demonstrated that young infants can detect and differentiate the bodily self in relation to the environment on the basis of invariance patterns in the flow of visual information that accompanies self-movement in space. For example, Lee and Aronson (1974) demonstrated that when tested in a "moving room" (whose walls approach or recede), babies compensated for visually specified—but nonexistent—loss of balance by adjusting their body posture, resulting in swaying, staggering, or even falling. Follow-up studies by Butterworth and colleagues (Butterworth and Cicchetti 1978; Butterworth and Hicks 1977) have shown that even 2-month-olds can use visual feedback to control their head posture, showing compensatory head movements when perceiving visually specified instability in the moving room. Young infants also modify the position of their heads and/or blink when perceiving an object approaching on a collision course (Dunkeld and Bower 1980; Pettersen, Yonas, and Fisch 1980).

As discussed in some detail in chapter 4, a number of studies have demonstrated that young infants are highly sensitive to the contingent relations between their physical responses and consequent stimulus events (e.g., Bahrick and Watson 1985; Field 1979; Lewis et al. 1990; Lewis and Brooks-Gunn 1979; Papousek and Papousek 1974; Rochat and Morgan 1995; Watson 1972, 1994). As we have argued (see also Gergely and Watson 1999), the evidence supports the view that infants possess an innate contingency-detection module for analyzing the degree of contingent relatedness between motor responses, and consequent sensory events. Bahrick and Watson (1985) demonstrated that before 3 months of age infants show a preferential bias to attend to and explore perfect contingencies. Based on findings such as these, Watson (1994) hypothesized that the primary function of the contingency analyzer is that of self-detection: by identifying those sensory stimuli that are perfectly contingent with one's motor responses the module constructs a primary representation of the physical self as a distinct object in the environment. (See chapter 4 for details.)

After 3 months of age infants start to turn their attention toward the less-than-perfectly contingent effects of their actions on the external world (Watson 1994). Piaget (1936) reported that from about the age of 4 months infants tend to repeat motor actions that result in salient changes in the external environment ("secondary circular reactions") in order to "make interesting things last." Habituation studies with 5- to 6-month-olds (Leslie 1984; Woodward 1998) suggest that by this age infants discriminate grasping hands from other—inanimate—physical objects, attributing to them special causal powers such as transporting objects through space.

In sum, there is converging evidence that innate information-processing devices enable infants during the first six months of life to represent their bodily self as a differentiated object in space that can initiate action and exert causal influence on its environment. While such a representation of the self as a physical agent certainly involves sensitivity to the causal relations that relate agents to actions on the one hand and actions to outcomes on the other, this understanding is still restricted in important ways at this stage. For example, awareness that actions have a causal power in bringing about salient outcomes does not yet involve a differentiation between goals and behavioral means (Piaget 1936). This is shown by the fact that while infants younger than 6–8 months would repeat acts that had previously resulted in a salient outcome, they would not modify their action in response to relevant changes in the situation—for example, they would not make a detour around a newly inserted obstacle to reach an object. The ability to differentiate between goals and means is, however, a prerequisite for understanding intentional goal-directed action within a teleological framework (Csibra and Gergely 1998; Gergely et al. 1995; Tomasello 1995, 1999). This involves the ability to choose from multiple alternatives, whichever action realizes a goal state in the most efficient manner, given the changing constraints of reality. Infants start to organize their behavior in relation to goal states in this rational manner only at around 8–9 months of age (Piaget 1936; Tomasello 1999; Willatts 1999), when they also begin to interpret and predict other agents' goal-directed actions within the same teleological interpretive framework (Csibra and Gergely 1998; Csibra et al. 1999).

Apart from an early understanding of their causal power over the physical environment through action involving direct contact, infants also show an early sensitivity to their causal influence over objects at a distance, as in Watson's (1972) mobile studies—a sensitivity mediated by the contingency-detection module (discussed in detail in chapter 4; see also Gergely and Watson 1999). The natural domain of such causal efficacy at a distance is that of social interactions, so in the next section we consider the origins of understanding the self as a "social agent."

EARLY UNDERSTANDING OF THE SELF AS A "SOCIAL AGENT"

A large body of evidence indicates that from the beginning of life infants discriminate and actively orient toward people (Stern 1985). They show a very early sensitivity to facial patterns (Fantz 1963; Morton and Johnson 1991), they habituate to their mothers' voice *in utero* and recognize it after birth (DeCasper and Fifer 1980), and they show neonatal imitation of facial gestures (Meltzoff and Moore 1977, 1989). Young infants engage in interactions with their caregivers that are characterized by a "protoconversational" turn-taking structure (Beebe et al. 1985; Brazelton et al. 1974; Brazelton and Tronick 1980; Stern 1985; Trevarthen 1979; Tronick 1989). The currently dominant biosocial view of emotional development holds that mother and infant form an affective communication system from the beginning of life (Bowlby 1969; Brazelton et al. 1974; Hobson 1993; Sander 1970; Stern 1977, 1985; Trevarthen 1979; Tronick 1989) in which the mother plays a vital interactive role in modulating the infant's affective states. During their interactions, caregivers often engage in facial and vocal mirroring of their baby's displays of emotion in order to regulate the infant's affects (Gergely and Watson 1996, 1999; Malatesta and Izard 1984; Papousek and Papousek 1987; Stern 1985).

Infants, therefore, seem to show an initial species-specific sensitivity to human facial/vocal and behavioral displays and an innate propensity to engage in affective interactions with caregivers. But how do they understand such affective social interactions and their own causal role in them as social agents? There is a large spectrum of different theoretical views on this intriguing question.

1. First of all, there is what we shall call the "*strong intersubjectivist*" *position*, which assumes (*a*) that human infants are born with innate mechanisms to identify and attribute mental states such as intentions and feelings to the other's mind during early contingent social interactions, (*b*) that from the beginning of life there is a relatively rich set of differentiated mental states of the self such as emotions, intentions, motives, and goals that are introspectively accessible to the infant, and (*c*) that such subjective mental states of the self can be recognized as being similar to corresponding mental states of the other and, as such, are experienced as "being shared" with her (e.g., Braten 1988, 1992; for a recent collection of papers on intersubjectivity, see Braten 1998; Stern 1995; Trevarthen 1979, 1993).

For example, Trevarthen (1979) claims that the richly structured early affective interactive exchanges observable between mothers and infants imply what he calls "primary intersubjectivity." A well-known study by Murray and Trevarthen (1985) using 6- to 12-month-old infants as subjects is often cited as providing empirical support for this position. In an ingenious paradigm infants were observed while interacting with their mother's live image through a TV monitor. After a certain period, the TV image was switched to a noncontingent image recorded earlier of the mother engaged in interaction with her baby. These very young infants were reported to have detected the subtle change in the contingency structure of the interaction and reacted with displays of dissatisfaction and negative affect to the loss of maternal contingency. Trevarthen (1993) therefore proposes that infants are born with a dialogic mind, with an innate sense of "the virtual other" (see also Braten 1988) and can interpret the other's affectively attuned interactions in terms of a rich set of underlying motives, feelings, intentions, and goals. Stern also suggests that "from a very early age, the infant perceives intentions in the self and the other, that he 'sees past' the specific overt behaviors in order to read in them the intentions that organize these behaviors" (1995, p. 420). As shown in chapter 4, Meltzoff and Gopnik (see 1993; Meltzoff and Moore 1997, 1998) also embrace the primary intersubjectivity assumption when they speculate that the innate "active intermodal mapping" mechanism that mediates neonatal imitation also functions as a mechanism for attributing intentional, motivational, and feeling states to the other during early imitative interactions.

In contrast to advocates of the "strong intersubjectivist" position, a number of researchers believe that the phenomena of early affective and imitative social interactions can be parsimoniously explained without assuming "primary intersubjectivity" (e.g., Gergely and Watson 1996, 1999; R. Thompson 1998; Tomasello 1999). In this view, if attentiveness and reactivity to human facial patterns and affective displays are innate, an early sensitivity to the contingency structure of interactive behavioral exchanges and an innate propensity to imitate human facial gestures provide sufficient basis to explain the structured two-way affective interactions of early infancy as well as the infant's affective/behavioral reactions to experimentally induced perturbations of the flow of contingent exchanges—for example, the "still-face" procedure (Tronick et al. 1978) or the delayed-feedback procedure of the Murray and Trevarthen (1985) paradigm.

First, as described above, there is a good deal of evidence to indicate that while young infants are positively aroused when they find that they have a high degree of control over whether a stimulus event happens (Lewis et al. 1990; Watson 1972), loss of previously experienced contingency results in frustration and expressions of distress, even when the stimulus is not a human person (Lewis et al. 1990). Thus, sensitivity to loss of contingent control would seem sufficient to explain the Murray and Trevarthen's (1985) finding discussed above. (For attributing a central role for social contingency perception in infancy, see also Bigelow, 2001; Bigelow and DeCoste, in press; Muir and Hains 1999; Nadel and Tremblay-Leveau 1999; Rochat and Striano 1999; Tomasello 1999.)

Furthermore, it has proved difficult to replicate the findings of Murray and Trevarthen—whose original study was based on four 2-month-old infants only—with infants under 3 months of age in studies using methodologically improved designs. Nadel, Carchon, Kervella, Marcelli, and Reserbat-Plantey (1999) did replicate the effect in 2-month-olds, but Rochat, Neisser, and Marian (1998) failed to do so in two studies using 2- to 3-month-old infants and Bigelow and DeCoste (in press) found the effect in 4- and 6-month-olds but also failed to replicate it with a group of 2-month-olds.

It is interesting to consider this pattern of findings in the light of Watson's (1994) hypothesis that a maturational "switch" takes place at around the age of 3 months in the preferred target value of the contingency-detection module. As we have seen, a significant proportion of 3-month-olds in the Bahrick and Watson (1985) study seemed preoccupied with their perfectly contingent self-image (see also Field 1979), whereas 5-month-olds preferred to avoid the perfectly contingent display, looking more at the noncontingent image. Further studies by Watson suggest that this tendency is due to an avoidance of perfect contingencies rather than to a preference for noncontingency. Watson (1979,

1985) aimed to identify the preferred degree of contingency after 3 months of age. He examined 4- to 6-month-olds' reactions to different magnitudes of response–stimulus contingencies in the range from slightly greater than 0 to slightly less than 1 (in terms of conditional probability). He found that at this age infants have great difficulty with contingency magnitudes that are less than 0.5. At the same time, they also failed to engage contingencies that approached a magnitude of 1. In contrast, the infants were very motivated to engage high-but-imperfect contingencies.

As discussed in chapter 4, Watson (Gergely and Watson 1999; Watson 1994) therefore hypothesized that at around 3 months the target value of the contingency analyzer in normal infants is "switched" to a preference for *high-but-imperfect contingencies* that are characteristic of the infant-directed reactive behaviors of well-attuned social objects. This maturational change functions to orient the infant after 3 months of age away from self-exploration (perfect contingencies) and toward *the exploration and representation of the social world*. These assumptions raise the possibility that before 3 months of age the degree of contingency provided by parental interactions may not be high enough for its disappearance to be detected by the infant when the parent continues to display similar interactive but noncontingent behavior. This, then, may explain the difficulty found in several studies of replicating the Murray and Trevarthen (1985) finding under 3 months of age (cf. Bigelow, 2001). Some recent findings provide further support for the position that infants around 3 months of age are in a transitional period in which sensitivity to high-but-imperfect social contingencies begins to emerge. Even though in the Bigelow and DeCoste (in press) study the 2-month-olds as a group did not distinguish between contingent and noncontingent displays, approximately half of the infants did show a decrease in visual attention to the noncontingent display when they were examined individually. Furthermore, Legerstee and Varghese (2001), using a similar paradigm, reported that a subgroup of their sample of 3-month-olds whose mothers were warm, sensitive, and attuned to the infants' cues in their interactions reacted with more visual attention, smiling, and melodic vocalizations to the contingent than to the noncontingent displays. Infants of mothers who scored low on these measures, however, showed no such differentiation between the two types of displays. It seems likely that the mothers in the attuned, highly responsive group provided degrees of contingent reactivity that were high enough for their 3-month-old infants to detect, and so the sudden loss of contingency in the non-contingent display became discriminable for these babies. This finding also supports the argument, more fully explicated in chapter 3, that the level of sensitivity manifested by the caregiver influences the rate at which the child acquires the capacity to exert control over its internal states.

The second objection to the "strong intersubjectivist" position concerns its assumption that innate mechanisms identify and attribute intentional and emotional states to the minds of others. Two types of prewired architecture for accessing subjective mental states of others can be imagined to accomplish this task: (a) direct perception through innately specified triggering displays, and (b) inferential access to the other's subjective states through motor simulation.

Some researchers have indeed claimed that newborn infants can differentiate among a set of discrete basic-emotion expressions (Field et al. 1983; Haviland and Lelwica 1987; Izard and Malatesta 1987) such as happiness, surprise, or sadness. However, later research (C. Nelson 1987) has questioned whether the babies are really differentiating between emotions or, rather, between some other non-emotion-specific perceptual features. For example, Caron, Caron, and Myers (1985) demonstrated that 4- to 7-month-olds could differentiate between toothy and non-toothy emotion expressions, but they could not differentiate between angry and happy expressions if both of them showed teeth. Caron, Caron, and MacLean (1988) also showed that 4-month-olds could not discriminate happy from sad dynamic facial/vocal expressions, and 5-month-olds failed to do so with happy and angry displays. Such findings suggest that even if one accepts the notion that there is a set of universal, prewired, discrete facial emotion expressions (Ekman 1992b; Izard 1991; Malatesta and Izard 1984), there seems to be no compelling evidence that infants can discriminate between such emotion-expressive facial patterns in others before 5 to 6 months of age.

Apart from facial emotion expressions, some innatist thinkers have proposed that certain types of behavioral cues, such as self-propelled movement or direction of movement, automatically trigger attribution of intentionality or goal to other agents (Leslie 1994; Premack 1990; Premack and Premack 1995). However, recent habituation studies (Csibra et al. 1999) and elicited gaze-following studies (Johnson, Slaughter, and Carey 1998) have demonstrated that while such cues may be informative, they are neither necessary nor sufficient for triggering goal attribution even in 9- and 12-month-old infants.

The alternative to the idea that infants perceive emotions directly through innate releasers is the suggestion that they can infer the other's intentions and feelings by generating and experiencing them through motor simulation. As we have seen, Meltzoff and his colleagues (Meltzoff and Gopnik 1993; Meltzoff and Moore 1989) have proposed such a mechanism in their "active intermodal mapping" account of neonatal imitation. Their use of this mechanism to explain not only the fact of infantile imitation *per se* but also the assumed fact of attributing subjective mental states to the other requires some further strong innatist assumptions about the extent to which infants are able to differentiate between intentional and emotional self-states on the one hand, and about the introspective accessibility of such differentiated mental states on the other. Thus, the "strong intersubjectivist" view implies (*a*) that imitation of the other's expressive displays induces corresponding emotional and intentional self-states (the Correspondence Assumption), (*b*) that the self-states generated by motor simulation are directly accessible to the infant through introspection (the Primary Access and Self-Awareness Assumption), and (*c*) that the infant attributes subjective internal states to the other's mind by consulting his own felt subjective state, which is generated by his imitation (the Other Mind Assumption).

There is very little evidence to support any of these assumptions, however. For example, do infants experience the same types of emotion states the expression of which they observe in their mothers during early affective interactions? Even though proponents of differential emotions theory (Izard 1991; Malatesta and Izard 1984) claim that—using the MAX (Izard 1979) or the AFFEX (Izard, Dougherty, and Hembree 1983) coding systems—expressions of emotions such as fear, anger, or sadness can be objectively differentiated in early infancy, others (Oster, Hegley, and Nagel 1992) using a different coding system, the Baby-FACS (Oster and Rosenstein, in press), dispute this claim and argue that young babies' negative expressions show only undifferentiated distress at first. Camras (1992) pointed out that the conditions that induce particular emotion expressions in young babies are often idiosyncratic and unexpected, as in the case of a 1-month-old who expressed sadness when eating a sour vitamin. Recently, Camras (2000) reviewed a number of further empirical phenomena that raise problems for the view that babies' expressions of emotion are linked to internal feelings like those that adults experience and that these expressions will be prompted by the same kinds of stimuli as those to which adults react.

In fact, many emotion researchers believe that babies are not yet able to differentiate emotions and/or do not yet have conscious access to them during the first few months: they argue that these abilities are the consequence of early self-organizing dynamic systems processes (Fogel et al. 1992; Lewis and Granic 2000) or early socialization of emotions during affective interactions (Gergely and Watson 1996, 1999; Sroufe 1979, 1996), as well as cognitive development (Barrett and Campos 1987; Kagan 1992; Lewis and Brooks 1978; Lewis and Michaelson 1983).

There are two alternative theoretical approaches, both compatible with the above criticisms of the "strong intersubjectivist" view: (a) one that can be called the "weak intersubjectivist" position, and (b) one that we will call the "no starting-state intersubjectivism" position.

2. The *"weak intersubjectivist" position* (see Tomasello 1999) accepts that the existence of early affective and imitative interactions reflects a specifically human biological adaptation to "identifying" with other persons as "like me." In Tomasello's simulation theory the human propensity for "identification" plays a crucial role in the developing understanding of other minds insofar as the infant comes to understand—and attribute subjective states to—the other through analogy to the internally

experienced subjective mental states of the self. However, Tomasello emphasizes that "in attempting to understand other persons human infants apply what they already experience of themselves— . . . [but] this experience of the self changes in early development, especially with regard to self-agency" (1999, p. 70). Thus, Tomasello differs significantly from proponents of the "strong intersubjectivist" position in that he believes that before 9 months of age infants do not yet have a differentiated understanding of their own subjective internal states such as intentions or goals, and so they cannot understand such intentional states in others either. As he puts it: "Some researchers, especially Trevarthen, believe that these early interactions are 'intersubjective', but in my view they cannot be intersubjective until infants understand others as subjects of experience— which they will not do until nine months of age" (p. 59).

Some of Meltzoff's writings seem also to be best interpreted within the "weak intersubjectivist" framework. For example, Meltzoff and Moore suggest that "infants progress from conceptions of others as entities with whom one can share actions to persons with whom one can share goals and intentions" (1998, p. 49). They also state that "newborns are not isolated from others at birth, but . . . do not yet understand the internal feelings and mental states of others in the way a 2-year-old does" (p. 49). Thus, although these views of "weak intersubjectivity" assume an innate mechanism for identification with other humans, this mechanism can only result in attributing subjective mental states to the other if the corresponding subjective states have already been established and can be consciously accessed in the self.

3.   Our third theoretical alternative, the *"no starting-state intersubjectivism" position*, raises a further objection to the functions that proponents of initial-state intersubjectivity tend to attribute to early affective/communicative and imitative exchanges. It is often assumed that infants and caregivers engage in such interactions in order to "share or participate in" each other's subjective affective and intentional states or to "discover" the subjective world of intentions and feelings of the other (Meltzoff and Gopnik 1993; Stern 1985; Trevarthen 1979). These assumed functions

presuppose, of course, the infant's innate ability to attribute subjective mental states to the other from the beginning of life.

There are, however, plausible alternative evolutionary functions for such early interactions that do not require the assumption of this ability: (a) The infant's innate readiness to engage in affective interactions with caregivers may function to establish and maintain proximity to the attachment figure (Bowlby 1969), as the infant's reactivity is highly reinforcing to the caregiver. (b) Infants' innate propensity to engage parents in affective interchanges contributes to affective self-regulation in two ways: the baby experiences and maintains positive arousal through the direct affect-regulative influence of interaction with the parent and, if contingent control over the parent's behaviors is detected (see above), the baby also experiences feelings of causal efficacy. (c) Finally, innate social reactivity may have the evolutionary function of creating a facilitating learning environment—in the form of the infant-directed affect-expressive and mirroring displays of the parent—in which learning about the dispositional displays of others, sensitization to intentional and affective self-states, and the establishment of secondary representations for primary emotion states of the self are optimized (cf. Fonagy 2000; Gergely, Koós, and Watson, in press; Gergely and Watson 1996, 1999). This argument was vigorously advanced in chapter 3 of the present volume. To state the argument explicated in detail in that chapter more generally, we believe that a strong case can be made for the early interactions between infant and caregiver as having a primary biological function of facilitating the development of the mental mechanisms essential for the establishment of a sense of subjectivity and the interpersonal interpretive processes that underpin self-agency. At the heart of this argument is the view that subjectivity in the infant cannot be assumed but, rather, must be considered as acquired in the process of interaction.

For example, Gergely and Watson (1996, 1999; Gergely, Koós, and Watson, in press) have proposed that instead of providing a vehicle for intersubjective communication between minds, early contingent affect-regulative interactions serve—among a number of other functions—to establish one important *precondition* for *later* intersubjectivity: namely, the introspective accessibility of differentiated emotional and intentional states of the self. Contrary to the classical Cartesian view, the "social biofeedback theory of parental affect-mirroring" outlined in chapter 4 assumes that infants initially lack introspective awareness of differential basic-emotion states. It is suggested that the perceptual system is set with a bias to attending to and exploring the external world and that it builds representations primarily based on stimuli received from the outside. Babies become sensitive to the distinctive internal patterns of physiological and visceral stimulation that accompany discrete emotion expressions through the application of the contingency-detection mechanism to the contingent relation between the automatic emotion expressions of the infant on the one hand, and the caregiver's consequent affect-reflective facial/vocal displays on the other.

The clinical relevance of this is considerable. If the mirroring of internal states is dysfunctional, internal states will be unlabelled, confusing, and experienced as unsymbolized and therefore difficult to regulate. The case of "Emma" described in chapter 10 might be an example of this phenomenon. As we shall see in chapter 6, the interactive origins of the sense of subjective self-states can account for substantial differences between the ways children interpret their subjective experiences and ultimately perhaps even clinical conditions that are strongly linked to distorted interpretations of internal states such as certain types of panic disorders.

To conclude—there is no compelling evidence to support the intersubjectivist notion that structured affective mother–infant interactions during the first months of life involve an ability on the part of young infants to access their own differentiated mental states introspectively or that they are able to attribute corresponding subjective intentional and feeling states to the other's mind. Of course, this is not to deny that during such attuned or imitative interactions mother and infant may experience similar subjective states. However, in our view such "affect sharing" can, at best, be called "objective intersubjectivity," because although the subjective states of parent and infant may become aligned due to empathic parental mirroring or infantile imitation of parental affect expressions, this does not imply that the young infant is aware of sharing the subjective state with the other, or, for that matter, that the other experiences a subjective state at all.

How, then, can we characterize young infants' experience of their social agency during early affect-regulative interactions with their caregivers? We have seen that after 3 months of age infants begin to be most interested in interactions where the degree of contingency of stimuli on their responses is high but imperfect (Watson 1994). Since attuned and imitative interactions with the caregiver provide such rich—but imperfect—contingencies, we can assume that infants' discovery of their high degree of contingent control over their caregivers' reactions positively arouses them and gives them feelings of causal efficacy. They are also likely to experience the pleasurable changes in their affective states that the parent's affect-modulating soothing interactions bring about (and become associated with—see Gergely and Watson 1996, 1999) . Since such attuned interactions often involve affect-mirroring, infants may come to associate the control they have over their parent's mirroring displays with the ensuing positive change in their affect state, leading to an experience of the self as a self-regulating-agent (Gergely and Watson 1996, 1999; Gergely et al. in press). Whether at this stage infants experience more differentiated, discrete emotions or intentions and goals with specific contents is currently uncertain, but clearly the evidence available at the present time does not call for such an assumption.

At what point in infancy does "true" intersubjective understanding of other minds begin, then? One clear sign of understanding the other's subjective feeling state while differentiating it from one's own comes with the appearance of mature empathic reactions at some point during the second part of the second year (Hoffman 2000; R. Thompson 1998). Understanding others' intentional mental states, such as their attention, desire, or intention, also becomes dominant during the second year of life (Bartsch and Wellman 1995; Corkum and Moore 1995; Wellman 1990), though these abilities first start to emerge between 9 and 12 months of age when the set of so-called joint-attention skills first appears (Carpenter et al. 1998; Tomasello 1999). Some of these skills—such as protodeclarative pointing, a communicative gesture whose goal is to modify the other's mental state of attention—seem to imply an ability to attribute at least some type of intentional mental states to others, whereas others—such as protoimperative pointing or imitative learning—may be explained in a still nonmentalistic teleological interpretive framework (see below; see also Gergely and Csibra 2000).

An important theoretical question, then, concerns the way in which the innate propensity of human infants to engage in affective and imitative interactions with caregivers during the first 6 to 9 months of life may be related to the later emergence of the intersubjective mentalistic stance starting at around 1 year of age. We have reviewed three positions: (*a*) The "strong intersubjectivist" view (Trevarthen 1979) holds that such early affective communicative exchanges are examples of an already fully functioning mind-reading capacity present from birth. (*b*) The "weak intersubjectivist" position considers such early affective interactions as evidence for the presence of a human specific innate mechanism specialized to "identify" with the subjective perspective of other human persons. This view holds, however, that the simulation of differentiated intentional mind states of others by this mechanism becomes possible only at around 9 months of age. This is so because certain types of intentional mind states of the self do not become differentiated and introspectively accessible to serve as the basis for attributing corresponding subjective states to others until this age is reached (Tomasello 1999). (*c*) Finally, we considered the "no starting-state intersubjectivism" view. This position holds that early affect-regulative and imitative interactions serve a number of important evolutionary functions (such as proximity maintenance and affect regulation), but that these functions do not involve, on the infant's part, the ability to read and attribute subjective mental states to others. However, it is hypothesized that one of these evolutionary functions has a relationship to the later emerging intersubjective mentalistic stance in that it helps to establish one of its preconditions: the cognitive accessibility of the infant's own discrete emotional and intentional mind states (Gergely and Watson 1996, 1999). In this view, early affect-regulative mirroring interaction with the caregiver provides an environment in which, through the processes of contingency detection and social biofeedback, sensitization to internal states and secondary representation-building can take place, leading to the establishment of cognitively accessible representations of the subjective mental states of the self. However, the emergence of a truly mentalistic intersubjective stance during the second year is viewed as a result of the maturation of representational abilities (theory of mind), which make the causal mentalistic interpretation of actions in terms of intentional mind states possible both for the other and for the self.

UNDERSTANDING SELF AND OTHER AS "TELEOLOGICAL AGENTS": THE NINE-MONTH SOCIAL-COGNITIVE REVOLUTION

A large body of evidence indicates that by 9 months of age infants develop a qualitatively new level of understanding of goal-directed action (e.g., Csibra et al. 1999; Piaget 1936; Tomasello 1999; Uzgiris and Hunt 1975; Willatts 1999). This has been aptly referred to as the 9-month social-cognitive revolution (Rochat and Striano 1999; Tomasello 1999). This new capacity involves the ability to differentiate goals from the means that bring them about, to modify an action to suit a new situation, and to choose the means that bring about the goal in the most efficient manner from the available options. Piaget (1936) described the first appearance of such intentional coordinated means–end behaviors between 7 and 9 months of age (Stage IV). Before this stage, infants would repeat previously successful action schemes to recreate salient effects; however, they would fail to adjust and vary their actions to fit the requirements of changing circumstances. For example, when an obstacle was placed between the infant and the goal object, 4- to 6-month-olds would either simply give up or start acting on the obstacle itself, seemingly becoming oblivious of the goal object, whereas 8-month-olds would already proceed to remove the obstacle in a deliberate manner in order to reach for and grasp the desired object (Piaget 1936; Willatts 1999).

Recently, Gergely, Csibra, and their colleagues (Csibra et al. 1999; Gergely and Csibra 1998; Gergely et al. 1995; see also Woodward and Sommerville, 2000) have demonstrated in a series of visual habituation studies that at the same time as they become capable of means–end coordination in producing intentional goal-directed actions, infants also start to interpret the actions of others as goal-directed and rational. For example, 9- and 12-month-olds—but not 6-month-olds—were shown to interpret the behavior of an abstract computer-animated figure as goal-directed and could infer its novel action in a new situation. Infants were habituated to an event in which a small circle repeatedly approached a large circle by "jumping over" a rectangle separating them. In the test phase, when the "obstacle" was removed, infants looked longer if the small circle repeated its familiar jumping action—which, given the absence of the "obstacle," was no longer seen as a "sensible" goal approach—than when it took a novel more efficient straight-line route (rational approach). No such looking-time differences were found, however, in a control condition that differed only in that there was no "obstacle" in the habituation phase to start with—and so the small circle approached the large one in a nonrational manner by jumping over nothing. This suggests that infants attributed the end state (contacting the large circle) as the goal of the action only if the action (the jumping approach) was evaluated as a rational or efficient means to bring about the outcome state given the constraints of the situation (i.e., the presence of the "obstacle").

On the basis of these results, Gergely and Csibra (1997; Csibra and Gergely 1998) proposed that by 9 months of age infants come to interpret goal-directed spatial behavior in terms of a *"teleological stance"* or a *"naive theory of rational action."* Teleological explanations differ from causal ones in two respects: (a) The explanatory element referred to is in a different *temporal* relation to the to-be-explained action. Teleological interpretations refer to the outcome that *follows* the action, whereas causal explanations point at some necessary condition that is *prior* to the event. (b) They use different *criteria* of acceptance. Causal explanations single out a prior condition that *necessi-*

tates the action providing its generative source. In contrast, reference to the outcome state is accepted as a teleological explanation (reason) for a behavior when it *justifies* it—that is, when, given the constraints of reality, the behavior can be seen as a sensible way to bring about the goal state.

The teleological interpretive system represents goal-directed action by establishing an explanatory relation among three representational elements: the action (A), the goal state (G), and the relevant constraints of physical reality (RC)—in the above case, the presence or absence of an obstacle. Such teleological representations are based on the *"principle of rational action,"* which assumes that agents pursue their goals in the most rational or efficient manner available to them given the constraints of physical reality. Gergely and Csibra have shown that, relying on the principle of rational action, 1-year-olds can infer any one of the three representational elements (A, G, or RC) given perceptual information about the other two. (See Csibra et al. 1999; Csibra, Bíró, Koós, and Gergely, 2002; Gergely and Csibra 1998, 2000.)

Adults tend to describe the goal-directed jumping action in mentalistic terms such as "it *wants* to get to the other circle and *thinks* that the obstacle is impenetrable, so it jumps over it" (cf. Heider and Simmel 1944). However, it is possible to make a viable teleological interpretation without such mentalistic attributions. The interpretation works even if it makes reference only to the relevant states of current reality, such as the presence of an obstacle, that constrain the goal approach and to future reality—the goal state of contacting the large circle—as represented by the infant himself. Thus, infants could construct a viable teleological action interpretation or prediction without attributing prior desires and beliefs to the actor's mind. Gergely and Csibra (1997; Csibra and Gergely 1998) hypothesize, therefore, that in its initial form the infant's "teleological stance" generates reality-based representations for goal-directed actions that are neither mentalistic nor causal.[1]

---

[1] The representational requirements of the "teleological stance" correspond to those of the second level of Leslie's modularist theory of Agency (ToMM/System 1), which represents the actional properties of agents in terms of "teleological causality" (Leslie 1995). In Leslie's view, however, teleological interpretation of action is triggered by innately specified stimulus cues such as self-propelled

In chapter 9 we construct a developmental psychopathology model that has the notion of the teleological stance at its core. To anticipate these discussions, we shall argue that individuals whose use of the intentional stance is only partially accessible or is blocked by either biological deficits or social experiences beyond the normal range frequently revert to the teleological stance in their interpretations of interpersonal behavior, particularly in the attachment context. It is important to note that such a dominance of the teleological construal of social reality is thought to be more likely in those individuals for whom the building blocks of the intentional stance, such as the second-order representations of primary constitutional self-states, were not firmly established in the first place.

The 9-month social-cognitive revolution also manifests itself in the emergence of a set of qualitatively new communicative behaviors: goal-directed coordinated activities between infants and parents involving joint attention to objects or situations (Carpenter et al. 1998; Corkum and Moore 1995; Tomasello 1995; Trevarthen and Hubley 1978). At this stage infants start to follow the adult's gaze reliably (gaze following), actively attend to the adult's facial and vocal attitude expressions about unfamiliar objects or situations to modify their own behavior (social referencing), and act on objects in the way adults are acting on them (imitative learning). They also begin to use communicative gestures themselves (such as pointing or object showing) in order to direct adults' attention and behavior to objects or situations (imperative and declarative gestures). Carpenter et al. (1998) have demonstrated that this series of "joint-attention skills" (including protoimperative and protodeclarative gestures, imitative learning, cooperative learning, and intentional teaching),

---

movement (Leslie 1994) that identify the actor as a physical agent with internal "force." In the alternative modularist approaches of Premack (1990) and Baron-Cohen (1994) self-propulsion directly triggers the categorization of the actor as an intentional agent. In contrast to these proposals, Csibra et al. (1999) provided evidence indicating that movement cues of agency or animacy are neither necessary nor sufficient for teleological interpretation to occur. In their view, goal attribution is based on the applicability of the principle of rational action rather than the perception of innately specified stimulus cues, and a teleological interpretation is set up as a result of the perception of justifiable adjustment of behavior as a function of situational constraints.

emerges in a coordinated fashion between the ages of 9 and 15 months in human infants.

On the basis of this evidence, Tomasello (1995, 1999) has developed an alternative theory to capture the nature of infants' emerging capacity to interpret rational goal-directed action, proposing that at around 9 months of age infants start using a qualitatively new interpretational system to understand other persons. He calls this the *"intentional stance."* Tomasello (1999) argues that the set of joint-attention skills emerging at the end of the first year—as well as infants' performance in the Csibra–Gergely type of habituation tasks)—are different behavioral manifestations of the same underlying new understanding of other persons as intentional agents.

According to Tomasello (1999), the emergence of the intentional stance depends on two factors. First, it presupposes the ability to differentiate goal states from the means leading to them (Piaget 1936) as well as the related capacity to choose the most rational or efficient action from the set of alternatives available in a given situation to realize the goal (cf. Gergely et al. 1995). In Tomasello's view, as soon as infants can represent their goals separately from their action schemes and start to show flexible means–end coordination, they immediately also become able to interpret other agents' goal-directed behavior in terms of intentions and rational choice of means. This inference is made possible by the second component of Tomasello's theory: he assumes that infants are born with the ability to "identify" with other humans who are "just like them" and attribute subjective intentional states to them through analogy to their own self-experience. Therefore, the simultaneous emergence by 9 months of means–end coordination in action production on the one hand, and the ability to understand intentional goal-directed action in others on the other, is explained by the fact that infants become able to simulate the intentional actions of others in terms of goal attribution and rational choice of means only when they themselves have achieved a differentiated and coordinated representation of their own intentional actions in terms of goals and available means.

When comparing Gergely and Csibra's "teleological stance" account with Tomasello's "intentional stance" account of the 9-

month social-cognitive revolution, we can identify three—clearly related—theoretical issues that differentiate the two approaches. These concern (a) the role of simulation, (b) the mechanisms for understanding self versus other as goal-directed agents, and (c) the issue of mentalism.

1. *The role of simulation in understanding others as goal-directed agents—full simulation versus default simulation.* Simulationist theories of understanding intentional action tend to assume that mental states such as desires or intentions are attributed to others to the extent that the other's behavior is perceived as "just like me." An often cited example is Meltzoff's (1995) important demonstration that 18-month-olds infer and reenact an underlying intention when observing a human model's failed attempts at realizing it, but they do not do so if the same acts are performed by a robot—which does not behave in a "just like me" manner. However, in habituation studies that involve no imitation, Gergely and Csibra (1998; Csibra and Gergely 1998; Csibra et al. 2002) demonstrated that already at 12 months infants can infer the goal of an incomplete action, even when the actor is not human but a computer-animated 2D disk with no facial features or biomechanical movement characteristics. In fact, Csibra and colleagues (1999) showed goal attribution as early as 9 months of age even when the actor's (again a 2D disk) behavior was lacking *all* animacy or agency cues such as self-propelled, irregular, and biomechanical movement that could be expected to trigger a "just like me" judgment. These findings suggest, therefore, that early goal attribution may, in fact, *not* be restricted to humans or animate agents. (See also Johnson et al. 1998.) Why is it, then, that Meltzoff's 18-month-old subjects did not imitate the inanimate robot whose behavior could have suggested goal-directedness? Csibra and colleagues (1999) suggested that this may be because it is imitation rather than goal attribution that is restricted to human action only. In fact, Legerstee (1991) provided evidence suggesting that when presented with analogous actions performed by humans versus inanimate objects, infants imitate only the human model.

The above findings suggest that early goal attribution may be a rather general process that is—at least initially—not restricted to the domain of persons or animate agents whose surface behavior warrants a "just like me" judgment. This, in turn, suggests that simulation through analogy to the self may not be the only—or, for that matter, the most central—mechanism through which interpretation of goal-directed intentional actions of others is mediated.

In contrast to Tomasello's "intentional stance," Gergely and Csibra's "teleological stance" is not based primarily on simulation. Rather, the infant's "naive theory of rational action" is seen as directly applicable to goal-directed actions, whether these are performed by the other or by the self. A central component of the theory is the principle of rational action that drives the process of evaluating whether the observed action constitutes an efficient means of bringing about the end state in the particular situation. This judgment is made in the light of the infant's available knowledge about situational constraints—such as the impenetrability of a solid obstacle—and about biological and dispositional constraints that characterize the actor. To illustrate this latter point: while a straight-line approach to a goal may be judged as the most efficient means for a human actor, a hopping approach may be seen as more appropriate in the case of a kangaroo, assuming that the infant knows that kangaroos have an overriding disposition to hop. Thus, relevant information about the agent can influence the evaluation of rational goal-directed action even if such properties do not correspond to those of the self.

Nevertheless, simulation also plays an important role in Gergely and Csibra's teleological model; we can call this "default simulation." If no previous knowledge or current perceptual evidence is available about the dispositional constraints of the agent, the infant will simulate the agent by default as being similar to—and so being subject to the same constraints on possible action as—the self. However, simulation is only a default option to fall back on when lacking relevant information about the other. In fact, Csibra and Gergely (1998) have recently demonstrated that perceptual information about the agent's dispositions can indeed modify the infant's expectations about what particular goal approach the agent will follow.

2. *Understanding the self versus the other.* A corollary to Tomasello's simulationist account is his view that before infants can understand the other's behavior as intentional and goal-directed, they must first achieve means–end differentiation of action schemes and their effects in relation to their own actions primarily on the basis of introspective evidence—such as feelings of intentional effort (Piaget 1936; Tomasello 1999). For Tomasello, this is a representational precondition for simulating the other's behavior as goal-directed and intentional. Whether understanding intentional action is, indeed, achieved first in relation to the self rather than the other is difficult to ascertain, however. This is because the behavioral evidence suggesting such understanding emerges more or less simultaneously—somewhere between the ages of 7 and 9 months—both in producing and interpreting goal-directed intentional acts. Tomasello (1999) accounts for this simultaneity of emergence by proposing that as soon as means–end differentiation is achieved in relation to the self's own actions, it is *immediately* applied through simulation to understanding intentional actions of other agents as well.

There is no developmental asynchrony that would indicate that understanding intentional action depends primarily on accessing self-states. The literature on the ability of adults to rely on internal information in making conscious agency judgments about perceived actions indicates a dominance of exteroceptive—for example, visual—information over internal cues (Jeannerod 1997; Pacherie 1997). We know even less about the degree of introspective accessibility of internal correlates of intentional action in infancy, though again there is evidence from 6- and 9-month-olds indicating the dominance of exteroceptive—visual—cues over proprioceptive—head orientation—cues in discriminative learning (Colombo et al. 1990). Gergely and Watson (1996, 1999) have, therefore, argued that learning on the basis of exteroceptive stimuli may, in fact, have primacy in infancy, and sensitivity to internal cues correlated with differential emotional and intentional states may develop as a function of contingency detection and "social biofeedback" processes (see above).

Such considerations, together with the apparent simultaneity of the emergence of understanding of intentional action in the self and in others, are, therefore, compatible with the view that the development of self-knowledge does not enjoy primacy in the 9-month revolution. In this vein, Gergely and Csibra's (1997) theory of the infant's teleological stance holds that the inferential principle of rational action brings about a qualitatively new level of understanding of goal-directed action simultaneously in the other and in the self. (See also Dennett 1987, and Gopnik 1993, for arguments against the Cartesian notion of the primacy of "first-person authority" in understanding agency.)

3. *The origins of mentalism.* For Tomasello (1995, 1999) the 9-month-old's intentional stance marks the first appearance of understanding that the actions of other agents—as well as of the self—are driven by causal *mental* states such as desires and intentions. Tomasello's evidence for this claim is twofold: (a) He emphasizes the important fact that at least some of the joint-attention skills emerging between the ages of 9 and 15 months (see Carpenter et al. 1998), such as *protodeclarative gestures*, seem to involve understanding—and influencing—another agent's intentional *mental* state, such as her attention. (See also Leslie and Happé 1989.) (b) Tomasello's simulationist view implies that 9-month-olds start to represent the causal conditions of the other's goal-directed actions by making reference to their own internally experienced subjective mental states —attention, intention—through which they simulate the mental causes of the other's observable behavior. This is made possible by the hypothesized human-specific evolutionary adaptation to "identify" with the subjective perspective of other persons who are perceived as "just like me." For Tomasello, the coordinated emergence of the set of joint-attention skills at the end of the first year is underpinned by this propensity for mental simulation.

In support of this view, Tomasello (1999) argues that the reason why primates do not seem to acquire joint-attention skills in their natural environment is not because they cannot achieve differentiated representations of means and goals in relation to their own actions. (They clearly do—see Tomasello and Call's excellent 1997 review on primate cognition.) Rather, what they are lacking is the human-specific biological adaptation to "identify" with the subjective perspective of other agents—that is, they lack the ability mentally to simulate the subjective experience of others.

In contrast, Gergely and Csibra (1997; Csibra and Gergely 1998) argue that the teleological stance mediating the 9-month-old's understanding of goal-directed rational action can be parsimoniously modeled without attributing an ability to represent causal intentional *mental* states yet. In their view (see Csibra and Gergely 1998; Gergely and Csibra 2000) the requirements for a "purely" teleological interpretational system are less severe than are those for later theory of mind, because teleological understanding does not require representation of propositional attitude states—such as beliefs and desires (Fodor 1992; Leslie 1987, 1994) or comprehension of the representational nature of intentional mind states (Perner 1991). Thus, the teleological system is *ontologically more restricted* as its explanatory elements involve only the interpreter's *own* representations of— present and future—reality states, and it is *computationally simpler* as it does not involve the inference and attribution of intentional mental states to the other. It can also work without understanding the causal conditions of belief fixation (Leslie 1995) such as the fact that perception leads to knowledge. These differences may, in fact, help to explain the remarkably early appearance of such interpretations by 9 months of age.

Of course, nothing in Gergely and Csibra's habituation results directly necessitates this "lean" nonmentalistic interpretation. For example, Kelemen (1999) suggested that infants' early competence on such tasks may already reflect the attribution of mental states such as desires or intentions to the actors. How could one empirically differentiate between these views? Kelemen's mentalistic construal of teleological reasoning suggests that the infant's understanding of teleological relations and that of intentional mind states are not independent but are aspects of the same underlying innate ability to attribute causal mental states to agents. This view predicts that the two types of ability must be either present or absent concurrently in any organism or species. Therefore, a dissociation between the ability for teleological interpretation on the one hand and understanding causal intentional mind states on the other would represent potential counterevidence for this position.

In contrast, the "independent teleology" position maintained by Gergely and Csibra (2000; Csibra and Gergely 1998) holds that the teleological stance is a biological adaptation that may have evolved independently from theory of mind to interpret and represent goal-directed and rational spatial behavior. The wide-ranging presence of goal-directed organization of behavior among numerous species (including rats—see Tolman, Ritchie, and Kalish 1946) in the evolutionary environment may have exerted selective pressure for the evolution of a mechanism specialized for the discrimination and prediction of goal-directed action. In this view, the mentalistic "theory-of-mind" stance represents a further biological adaptation that leads to the ontological enrichment of the teleological stance by including, apart from representations of—current and future—states of reality, the mental representations of *fictional* or *counterfactual* states as well in the form of mentally represented propositional attitude relations (Fodor 1992; Leslie 1987, 1994).

Therefore, the teleological stance may be a useful interpretational strategy only in the—restricted—domain of intentional actions that are driven by causal mental states that represent aspects of actual reality truthfully. This is so because in such cases teleological interpretation of action can be based directly on reality without taking into consideration the actor's mental representations of that reality. The teleological stance would, however, break down in cases of intentional action where the actor's causal mind states represent fictional or counterfactual realities such as in pretense or false-belief-based action. This predicts the possibility of dissociation within an organism or a species that could exhibit an intact—reality-based—teleological reasoning capacity, while lacking a mentalistic understanding of intentional action.

The clinical usefulness of the present propositions rests on the assumption that teleological thinking does not necessarily entail knowledge of the intentional stance or mentalization. In chapters 9–11 we review clinical evidence that is consistent with the assumption that some individuals with profound disorders of character are unable to make use of the intentional stance in attachment contexts but can and do think teleologically, to the great detriment of their social relations.

Below we consider two types of dissociative[2] evidence that seem to favor the "independent teleology" position (see Gergely and Csibra 2000).

Dissociation 1:
Intact Teleological Understanding,
but Impaired Theory of Mind in Children with Autism

Children with autism perform poorly in tests that require them to attribute intentional mind states—such as false beliefs—to others (Baron-Cohen, Leslie, and Frith 1985; Leslie and Thaiss 1992). According to the "theory-of-mind deficit" account, childhood autism is a primary cognitive dysfunction, caused by a genetic defect of the innate "theory-of-mind" module that enables the representation of intentional mental states. Therefore, if teleological interpretations always involve representing intentional mind states, children with autism should be equally impaired in tests that require teleological reasoning, like those used in the Csibra–Gergely type of infant habituation studies (Csibra et al. 1999; Gergely et al. 1995). In contrast, the "independent teleology" position predicts that children with autism may have an intact reality-based "teleological stance" to interpret goal-directed actions, while, due to their pervasive metarepresentational deficit (Leslie 1994), they may be unable ontologically to enrich their teleology to form a "proper" theory of mind.

For example, a study by Abell, Happé, and Frith (2001) provides evidence for this dissociation. Children with autism and matched controls were presented with three types of computer-animated events involving abstract figures—such as triangles—to elicit verbal descriptions for these events. In their Random

---

[2] The term "dissociative" is used here in the logical rather than the psychiatric context.

Animations condition the triangles did not interact but moved around purposelessly and independently of each other—floating in space; bouncing off the sides. Their Goal-directed sequences involved one of the triangles reacting to the other's behavior—such as, following, chasing, or fighting. In their Theory-of-mind sequences one character reacted to the other's mental state—for example, seducing, hiding and surprising, coaxing, or mocking. Normal adults predominantly used physicalist action descriptions for the Random sequences, teleological interactive descriptions for the Goal-directed events, and mentalistic descriptions for the Theory-of-mind sequences. Interestingly, while high-functioning children with autism were not as good at providing accurate mentalistic descriptions for the Theory-of-mind sequences as were the matched controls, there was no difference in their ability to provide physicalist or teleological descriptions. Thus, their performance indicates a dissociation between their intact capacity to interpret goal-directed interactions teleologically, on the one hand, and their impaired theory of mind, on the other.

Aldridge, Stone, Sweeney, and Bower (2000) have reported an intriguing replication in children with autism of Meltzoff's (1995) task in which 18-month-old normal infants were shown to infer and reenact the goal-directed action that an adult model intended to perform after witnessing three failed attempts by the model to realize the intended act (see above). Aldridge and colleagues found that while children with autism were much worse than the controls at imitating adult gestures—such as tongue protrusion—that were not goal-directed, they nevertheless had no difficulties with reenacting the intended (but not actually observed) goal-directed actions implied by the model's failed attempts. Aldridge and coworkers argue that this finding demonstrates that children with autism infer and attribute a mentally represented intention to the actor's mind—a result that they portray as paradoxical given the theory-of-mind deficit account of childhood autism. Meltzoff offered a more cautious view, suggesting that his 18-month-old "infants may think that human acts have goals without yet ascribing underlying mental states in the mind" (1995, p. 848). This, in fact, corresponds precisely to the assumptions of the teleological stance (Gergely and Csibra

1997). The Aldridge et al. demonstration can therefore be seen as further evidence for the proposition that autistic children's ability to interpret actions as goal-directed—which does not necessarily require assumptions about others' states of mind—is not affected by their lack of capacity to infer intentional mental states in others.

Dissociation 2:
Differential Emergence of Teleologically—
but not Mentalistically—Based Joint-Attention Skills
in Apes as a Function of Human Enculturation

As we have seen, Tomasello (1999) argues that nonhuman primates lack the human-specific evolutionary adaptation to "identify" with the internal experience of others who behave "just like them." As a result, even though they achieve means–end coordination of their own goal-directed actions in a way similar to 9-month-old humans, they nevertheless cannot use these self-representations to simulate the causal intentional mind states that drive the goal-directed actions of other agents. This inability to take the intentional stance may explain why nonhuman primates do not normally develop the series of communicative joint-attention skills that emerge in human infants between the ages of 9 and 15 months (Carpenter et al. 1998), which are thought to depend on the ability to take the intentional stance.

In his review on the effects of human enculturation on apes, Tomasello (1999; Call and Tomasello 1996) takes a position that is partly at odds with this theoretical view. He reports that two "joint-attention skills" do emerge in chimpanzees who have been raised by humans. These skills are protoimperative pointing at objects in order to get them and acquiring novel object-directed actions through imitative learning. However, chimpanzees who have been brought up by humans do not seem to acquire the other skills in the set of joint-attention behaviors—such as protodeclarative gestures or intentional teaching. But if, as Tomasello hypothesizes, the human-specific innate capacity to simulate the other's intentional states through "identification" is, indeed, a prerequisite for *all* of these joint-attention skills, then how is it that apes that are raised by humans can develop even this partial understanding of intentionality?

If we accept the view that nonhuman primates lack the innate capacity to represent intentional mind states but nevertheless can adopt the nonmentalistic teleological stance to interpret goal-directed actions, it becomes possible to explain why chimpanzees brought up by humans develop this particular subset —that is, protoimperatives and imitative learning—of the "joint-attention skills." The crucial difference between these skills and, say, protodeclarative communication or intentional teaching is that they consist of goal-directed activities whose goals involve visible changes of external reality. In contrast, a protodeclarative communication aims to induce or modify a *nonvisible intentional mind state* of the other. Significantly, children with autism are also able to produce and understand protoimperative pointing gestures that are goal-directed acts that can be teleologically interpreted, but they fail to understand or produce protodeclarative pointing, which requires a mentalistic construal of goals (see Baron-Cohen 1991).

The nonmentalistic teleological interpretational system common to both humans and apes enables apes to parse and represent protoimperative communicative acts or new instrumental actions modeled to them in imitative learning situations in terms of their visible outcomes—as goals-of-action—differentiated from the means that bring those goal states about. In addition, an upbringing by humans can teach them—through modeling, shaping, selective rewarding, and so on—specifically to attend to and imitatively produce the particular means modeled, and so to overcome their naturally dominant tendency to selectively attend to the salient outcome state only—as evidenced in emulation. However, enculturation *cannot* teach them to represent goals-of-action that are *nonvisible and mental* such as inducing, sharing, or modifying an intentional mind state of the other—because they lack the theory-of-mind capacity to represent intentional mental states.

To conclude—we have reviewed two types of dissociative evidence in support of the view that the nonmentalistic teleological stance may have evolved independently of the human-specific ability to represent and attribute intentional mind states such as intentions to others. This teleological interpretational system can parsimoniously account for the 9-month social-cognitive revolution in human infants that involves the emergence of qualitatively new abilities to produce goal-directed rational actions and to interpret such actions in others. There is evidence to suggest that the teleological stance is present not only in normal human infants by 9 months of age, but also in non-human primates and in children with autism. Both of the latter seem, however, to lack the mentalistic intentional stance, which is likely to be an additional human-specific adaptation that has evolved to enable us to understand and communicate with other minds.

UNDERSTANDING THE SELF AND OTHER AS "INTENTIONAL MENTAL AGENTS"

The next qualitative step in human development is the emerging ability to attribute "prior intentions" (Searle 1983) to the other and the self to explain or predict future goal-directed actions. By 2 years of age infants show the first signs of understanding that the other can have a prior intention or desire before or without actually acting on it and can attribute such prior intentions to others from evidence other than observing the goal-directed action itself. This clearly implies the capacity to represent *intentional mental states* (mentalism), and the ability to predict goal-directed action from inferred prior intentions implies the capacity to think in terms of *mental causation.*

Evidence for the appearance of such a *mentalistic* understanding of causal intentions by the second year comes from a number of sources. (For a recent review, see Wellman and Phillips 2000.) For example, Bartsch and Wellman (1995) demonstrated that 2-year-olds spontaneously use verbal references to their own or another person's specific desires—using mostly the word "want"—even when the desire-based action has not yet been performed or when the action executed did not fulfill the attributed desire. Verbal references to desires or intentions at this age also clearly demonstrate that 2-year-olds can differentiate between their own and other people's subjective desire states. Repacholi and Gopnik (1997) demonstrated that when 18-month-olds were asked to give the experimenter something to eat, they provided her with the particular food item—broccoli vs. goldfish crackers—that she had previously expressed a liking for—by saying "yuck" or "yummy" when first facing the food item. Thus, they modulated their own goal-directed action—to give food to the experimenter—by considering the specific content of the desire they had attributed to the other previously, based on an earlier and different action, even when that desire was different from their own preference. In contrast, 14-month-olds gave the experimenter the item they themselves liked, basing their choice on their own preference without being able to consider the other's relevant prior intention.

Mature empathic reactions of concern leading to pro-social acts also appear during the second year (Hoffman 2000; R. Thompson 1998; Zahn-Waxler and Radke-Yarrow 1990). Infants of this age can attribute a subjective emotion state to the other and differentiate this state from their own felt emotion as shown by the capacity to devise a goal-directed pro-social act aimed at modifying the emotion state of the other.

From the age of 2 years on, young children also start to show some sensitivity to the causal connections that exist between different types of intentional mental states. For example, they can infer that a desire that is unfulfilled by a given action triggers sadness or frustration rather than joy and will generate further alternative goal-directed action. (See Wellman and Phillips 2000.)

Such demonstrations, therefore, clearly imply that by 2 years of age infants possess a rudimentary concept of desire as an intentional mental state that represents—is "about"—a hypothetical state of the world—the goal state—that has the power to cause instrumental action and that has causal connections to other types of mental states. This representational system amounts to a "naive theory of mind" (Fodor 1992; Leslie 1987, 1994; Leslie and Keeble 1987), which holds that goal-directed actions are caused by intentional mental states that represent states of affairs in the world and that are systematically connected to each other causally.

The ability to represent agents in terms of relatively enduring causal intentional mental states that can be divorced from particular goal-directed actions also establishes new conditions for how children will predict and interpret behavior. As a result of repeated experiences with similar types of goal-directed actions of significant others—such as caregivers or siblings—in comparable situations, children will begin to attribute *generalized intentions or attitudes* to them: these become stable characteristics of their representations of these others. Such generalized and enduring intentional properties of particular persons will come to function as further constraining factors, in addition to situational and dispositional constraints, when the principle of rational action is applied to predict or interpret their behavior. At this point, a new principle of reasoning of naive theory of mind, which we can call the "principle of mental coherence" (cf. Dennett 1987), comes into play: this is the assumption that a rational agent's causal intentions are not contradictory. The child has to be able to make this assumption if he is to produce well-formed action predictions: if an agent's intentions involve contradictory goals, it is impossible to infer a rational course of action. In developmental psychopathology parents whose behavior toward their children is abusive and dissociative provide inferential grounds to attribute contradictory generalized intentions to them. In cases where this happens, it has been hypothesized that this will lead to a dysfunctional theory of mind and consequent pathological patterns of self-development involving disorganization and splitting (see Fonagy, Target, and Gergely 2000; Gergely 2000; Gergely, Koós, and Watson, in press). The developmental distortions of the capacity to attribute generalized intentions or attitudes are manifest in a range of clinical features of borderline disorder, particularly in the predominance of split representations of self and others (see chapter 9) and the common failure to represent the distinction between external reality and internal representations of that reality (see chapter 10).

Development of the Self-Concept during the Second Year

The ability of the 2-year-old to adopt this mentalistic intentional stance, representing agents in terms of generalized and enduring intentional properties, also brings about a new level of self-understanding. As Tomasello (1993, 1999) argues (in keeping with the long tradition of social constructivism in self-development—see, e.g., Baldwin 1902; Cooley 1912; Fonagy and Target 1997; Mead 1934), the intentional actions and attitudes repeatedly expressed toward the young child by caregivers and peers lead the child to infer and attribute generalized intentional properties to himself in an attempt to rationalize his social partners' behavior. This is how the establishment of a "categorical" self-concept or representation—the Jamesian "Me"—originates (Harter 1999; Lewis and Brooks-Gunn 1979). Apart from the directly perceivable features of the "empirical" self, this self-representation includes generalized intentional properties that are socially inferred. For example, in developmental psychopathology unrealistically negative self-attributions are seen to arise from the child's attempts to rationalize the abusive or seriously neglectful treatment that he has received from attachment figures (Allen 1995, 2001; Cicchetti and Toth 1994; Fonagy and Target 1997; Fonagy, Target, and Gergely 2000). The case of "Emma" (chapter 10) may be a helpful illustration. Cared for by a suicidal mother with bipolar disorder and a paranoid psychotic father, she internalized a picture of herself as mad and unpredictable and could behave accordingly. These internalizations into the self-structure were, however, distinct and separate from her representation of herself as a competent and helpful person who could sort out the problems of others with their difficulties in thinking and feeling. Clinically, the challenge is that the mad and sometimes abusive caregiving figure is internalized into the same representational system as the representation of the constitutional self, and thus both are felt to be parts of the Jamesian "Me."

The developmental origins of the cognitive concept or representation of the self as an objective entity with enduring properties has also been tied to the end of the second year by the results of extended research on early *self-recognition in the mirror* (Amsterdam 1972; Gallup 1991; Gallup and Suarez 1986; Lewis and Brooks-Gunn 1979; Parker, Mitchell, and Boccia 1994). The fact that between 18 and 24 months of age—but not before—infants can recognize in the mirror an inadvertently placed rouge mark on their nose or forehead as belonging to themselves (as shown by the fact that they attempt to remove it from their own body rather than from the mirror image) indicates that, based on previous experience with their mirror image, infants have inferred and attributed to their self-representation the directly not perceivable visual features of their faces. The implications of this finding for the representational nature of the self-concept at this age, however, have been a subject of controversy (see Parker et al. 1994). While for some (e.g., Bertenthal and Fisher 1978; Menzel, Savage-Rumbaugh, and Lawson 1985) mirror self-recognition can be accounted for in terms of increased perceptuomotor skills, at the other extreme Gallup and his followers (e.g., Gallup and Suarez 1986) argue that this capacity implies self-awareness and the achievement of a representational self-concept that is inherently linked to understanding intentional mind states of others. This strong mentalistic interpretation of mirror self-recognition has, however, been challenged by numerous researchers on a number of grounds (e.g., Gergely 1994; R. W. Mitchell 1993; Povinelli 1995; Povinelli and Simon 1998)—for example, by observing the fact that mirror self-recognition is present in chimpanzees (Gallup 1970) as well as in children with autism (Dawson and McKissick 1984), both of whom seem to lack a theory of mind (Baron-Cohen et al. 1985; Call and Tomasello 1999).

Howe and Courage (1993, 1997) have argued that the appearance of the cognitive self-concept at 2 years of age, as evidenced by mirror self-recognition, is a precondition for—and marks the lower bound of—autobiographical memory for personally experienced events. In their view, the well-known phenomenon of infantile amnesia can be attributed to the lack of a cognitive self-concept before 2 years of age. They propose that the organization of personal event memories into an integrated and coherent memory structure that allows for later autobiographical recall is made possible by the establishment of the cognitive concept of the self as a representation of an objective entity with temporal and causal continuity. This provides a common conceptual schema in terms of which the particular memory traces of personal experiences become encoded. In the next—final—section we review some intriguing new findings about the development of the self-concept, which suggest that mirror self-recognition may indicate only a limited understanding of the self that is tied to the present (the "present self"—see Povinelli 1995). The construction of a temporally "extended self" underlying autobiographical memory in which past events experienced by the self are causally integrated with the present self into a unified self-concept (the "proper self"—see W. James, 1890) seems to require some further developments in representational capacities: it appears to be achieved only at around 4 to 5 years of age.

UNDERSTANDING SELF AND OTHER AS "REPRESENTATIONAL AGENTS" AND THE DEVELOPMENT OF THE "AUTOBIOGRAPHICAL SELF"

A mature understanding of mental agency—that is, naive theory of mind—involves a number of factors (see Fodor 1992; Leslie 1987), including the ability to attribute and represent different types of intentional mind states (such as desires and beliefs), understanding how they are causally related, comprehending the representational nature of such mental states (Perner 1991), and knowing both that they have causal potential to generate action and that they themselves are caused by perceptual experiences, verbal testimony, or inference (i.e., their properties of "causal self-referentiality"—Campbell 1997; Perner 2000a; Searle 1983). The reasons for the fact that these different aspects of knowledge about the mind surface at different ages in young children have been the subject of heated controversy and theorizing for the last twenty years or so (e.g., Astington et al. 1988; Baron-Cohen, Tager-Flusberg, and Cohen 2000; Carruthers 1996; Davis and Stone 1995; Lewis and Mitchell 1994; Whiten 1991). Three major positions, outlined in brief already in chapter 1, have been identified concerning the nature of the underlying cognitive mechanisms that lead to the development of mature theory of mind by about 4 years of age. These are (*a*) the innate modularist approach (Fodor 1992; Leslie 1987, 1995), (*b*) the simulationist view (Gordon 1995; P. L. Harris 1991, 1992), and (*c*) the theory–theory position (Gopnik and Wellman 1992, 1994; Perner 1991). In chapter 1 we contrasted these formulations from the standpoint of the account they might give of the integration of attachment processes with the development of theory of mind. Here we shall not attempt to review and evaluate the relative merits of these theories. Rather, we shall simply concentrate on characterizing some of the qualitatively novel aspects of understanding self and other as representational agents that seem to arise between 3 and 4 years of age.

One of the central issues is the question of why it is that, while a mentalistic understanding of desires seems to be present by 2 years of age, the representational understanding of belief, as diagnosed by the ability to comprehend false-belief-based actions, is delayed until 3 to 4 years of age. Wimmer and Perner (1983) were the first to demonstrate that 3-year-olds who witness a person leaving an object in container A before leaving the room and who see the object being transferred to container B in that person's absence make the—reality-based—error of predicting that she will search in container B—where the object actually is—rather than in container A—where she left the object—when she comes back. By the age of 4 or 5, children no longer commit this error: they tend to predict correctly that the person will look in container A, because they are able to attribute a false belief to her.

A number of theoretical positions have been put forward to explain this late occurrence of understanding false beliefs. Modularists like Leslie (1987, 1994) and Fodor (1992) argue that the metarepresentational system necessary to represent propositional attitude concepts such as desire, pretense, or belief is fully in place by the end of the second year (as evidenced by the capacity to produce and understand pretend play—see Leslie 1987). In Leslie's view, attributing false beliefs is delayed because of performance limitations in attending to and learning about the causal conditions of belief fixation—for example, that perception leads to knowledge (see Leslie and Roth 1993). In contrast,

Perner and others (e.g., Gopnik and Wellman 1992, 1994; Perner 1991, 2000b) argue that before 4 years of age children do not yet understand intentional mind states "as representations": that is, as mental states that are "about" some—real or hypothetical—state of affairs and that can be evaluated as true or false in relation to such a state of affairs (Perner 2000b). Perner also argues that understanding beliefs "as representations" is also a necessary requirement for understanding that actions are *mentally caused by representations* of reality rather than by reality itself.

One kind of—newly emerging—evidence on which Perner and others (see Mitchell and Riggs 2000; Perner and Lang 1999) rely in arguing that understanding intentional states as mental representations with causal power over behavior is arrived at only around 3 to 5 years of age comes from intriguing correlations that have been discovered between understanding false-belief-based action (theory of mind) on the one hand and showing mature self-control abilities in executive function tasks and mastery of counterfactual reasoning tasks on the other. To explain the correlated dramatic improvement in these rather different task domains at around 4 years of age, Perner (2000a) argues that they all require an understanding of the fact that the intentional mental states they involve have the property of *"causal self-referentiality"*—a notion taken over from philosophy of mind (see Campbell 1997; Searle 1983). Briefly, this notion suggests that to understand a mental intentional state properly, say, an intention to act, we must be aware not only that the intention represents some state of affairs, but also that it specifies—represents in its content—that the intended action be caused by the intention to act (Perner 2000b, p. 300). (This forms the representational basis for our awareness or sense of agency as well as ownership of action.) Similarly, in order to be recalled as an item in autobiographical memory, the memory representation of a specific event that a person has experienced must not only specify the event itself but must also represent the fact that the memory has been caused by that event (memory for causal source of knowledge).

Perner (2000b) reviews evidence from theory-of-mind research indicating that children before 4 to 5 years of age are notoriously bad at identifying the causal sources of their beliefs (such as whether they have seen, were told about, or inferred what is in a box—see, e.g., Gopnik and Graf 1988; Wimmer, Hogrefe, and Perner 1988; Wimmer, Hogrefe, and Sodian 1988). Executive function tasks, such as the Wisconsin card sorting task, in which failure in 3-year-olds and in children with autism (see Hughes and Russell 1993; J. Russell 1996) correlates with failure on theory-of-mind tasks, involve the need to inhibit a natural response tendency in favor of an adaptive response. It is suggested (see Pacherie 1997; Perner 2000b; J. Russell 1996, 1997) that self-awareness of the causal power of the mental disposition that results in the natural response is a necessary prerequisite before this natural response can be inhibited. It has also been hypothesized that difficulties in self-monitoring of intentions underlie the co-occurrence of self-control difficulties—and mistaken attributions of one's own intentional contents to external sources—and theory-of-mind problems in schizophrenia (C. D. Frith 1992) on the one hand, and the co-occurrence of executive function problems and theory-of-mind difficulties in children with autism on the other (Carruthers and Smith 1996; Pacherie 1997; J. Russell 1996, 1997).

The Emergence of the Autobiographical Self

Perner also argues that infantile amnesia (the lack of genuine memories of personally experienced events that occurred prior to about 3 to 4 years of age—see K. Nelson 1992, 1993; Perner 1990, 1991) is due to young children's inability to "encode personally experienced events *as personally experienced*" (Perner 2000b, p. 306)—that is, in terms of their causal informational source "as having been seen." At around 4 to 5 years of age, as the ability to represent the informational source as well as the content of knowledge emerges in theory-of-mind tasks, the autobiographic organization of memories as personally experienced events is also established.

An ingenious recent series of studies by Povinelli and his colleagues has confirmed that children below 4 to 5 years of age find it extremely difficult to integrate self-related experiences into a coherent causal-temporal organization around a self-concept extended in time (Povinelli and Eddy 1995; Povinelli, Landau, and Perilloux 1996; Povinelli, Landry, Theall, Clark, and Castille 1999; Povinelli and Simon 1998). The previously widely held belief that mirror self-recognition by 2 years of age signals the construction of a stable cognitive concept of the self (see Gallup and Suarez 1986; Howe and Courage 1993; Lewis and Brooks-Gunn 1979) has been challenged by Povinelli's demonstrations that recognition of the self on a briefly delayed video feedback is absent before 4 to 5 years of age. In one study (Povinelli and Simon 1998) children were videotaped while playing a game with an experimenter who covertly placed a large sticker on the child's head during the game. Three minutes later, when the videotape was played back to the children, 3-year-olds failed to reach up to remove the sticker (visible on the videotape) from their head, even though they generally managed to "recognize" their video image as themselves verbally by saying "it's me" or their proper name when asked who the child was on the video. (However, when asked where the sticker was, they tended to reply that "it's on *his* head" instead of their own!) They nevertheless did reach up to remove the sticker when presented with a mirror. In contrast, 4- to 5-year-olds could relate the delayed video feedback to their current self: they removed the sticker when presented with the videotape.

Perner explains this finding by arguing that "3-year-olds seem to lack an understanding of the causal link between recorded events and what they see on the video record" (2000b, p. 302). However, in a series of control studies Povinelli et al. (1999) demonstrated that 3-year-olds do understand the equivalence between delayed video images and the real world, as they are able to witness an object being hidden on video and then successfully locate it. In Povinelli's theory (Povinelli and Eddy 1995; Povinelli and Simon 1998; Povinelli et al. 1999) the concept of an *"autobiographical self"* emerges at around 4 years as a function of changes in the child's representational capacities. First, at the end of the second year infants develop the ability to hold a single representation or model of the world in mind (see also Olson and Campbell 1993; Perner 1991), which they can compare to presently perceived aspects of reality. This underlies the ability to recognize the self in the mirror between 18 and 24 months: the single mental representation of the self's actions and physical features—the "present self"—is compared to the mirror image with which an equivalence relation is assumed. At around 4 years, however, "children become able to hold in mind multiple representations or models of the world simultaneously" (Povinelli and Simon 1998, p. 189). This enables them to establish temporal and causal relations among memories of previously encoded experiences of the self and, in particular, to causally "evaluate the relevance of previous states of the self to the present self" (p. 189). Thus, 4- to 5-year-olds can draw a causal inference that if a few minutes ago a sticker was placed on their head (as revealed by the videotape), their present state is likely to be affected by this past event, so that the sticker is probably still on their head. The ability to relate multiple representations underlies, therefore, the establishment of an abstract historical-causal self-concept (the "autobiographical stance"), which integrates memories of previously unrelated states of the self into an organized, coherent, and unified autobiographical self-representation. The therapeutic implications of the profound restriction on individuals with severe self-pathology to manipulate multiple representations of the self are taken up again in chapter 10.

IMPLICATIONS FOR DEVELOPMENTAL PSYCHOPATHOLOGY

In this chapter we have traced the complex and intricate development of the young child's emerging understanding of the self and others as agents in the environment starting from birth to about 5 years of age. Our discussion focused on the ways in which the young child develops a representational understanding of the causal relations—both physical and mental—between persons and their actions and between actions and consequent changes in the environment. We found it useful to distinguish among five different levels of the development of understanding agency and selfhood:

1. *the self as a "physical agent,"* which involves the differentiated representation of the body as a separate and dynamic entity that can cause physical changes in the environment;

2. *the self as a "social agent,"* which represents the species-specific affective-communicative interactions—as well as their subjective emotional-intentional correlates—in which infants and caregivers engage from birth on;

3. *the self as a "teleological agent,"* which refers to the qualitatively new but still nonmentalistic understanding of goal-directed rational action emerging at around 9 months of age and underlying the so-called "9-month social-cognitive revolution";

4. *the self as an "intentional mental agent,"* which emerges during the second year and involves an already mentalistic understanding of some causal intentional mind states such as desires and intentions that are represented as existing prior to and separately from the actions they generate;

5. *the self as a "representational agent" and the emergence of the "autobiographical self"* around 4 to 5 years of age, which involves the ability to comprehend the "representational" and "causally self-referential" properties of intentional mind states, leading, among other things, to the establishment of an abstract, temporally extended, historical-causal concept of the "autobiographical self."

Contingency detection may have a key role to play in several forms of psychopathology that involve the malformation of the self as agent. We envision a spectrum of disturbances all involving abnormal sensitivities to contingencies. At one extreme might be cases where, for primarily biological reasons, a lack of sensitivity to anything other than perfect contingencies might entirely undermine the possibility of social development. Watson has hypothesized (Gergely 2001b; Gergely et al. in press; Gergely and Watson 1999; Watson 1994) that the etiology of *childhood autism* may be related to a genetically based malfunctioning of the "switching mechanism" of the contingency-detection module. According to this hypothesis, in autistic individuals the contingency analyzer gets "stuck" forever in its original setting of preferentially seeking out and processing perfectly self-contingent stimuli. As a result, children with autism continue to invest in perfect contingencies—generated by stereotypic self-stimulation or repetitive object-manipulation—throughout their lives, while showing a lack of interest in the less-than-perfect contingencies provided by their social environment. (See Gergely 2001b; for some preliminary supporting evidence, see Gergely, Magyar, and Balázs 1999; Gergely and Watson 1999, pp. 125–130.) From such a primary deficit in contingency detection one can derive a range of the focal symptoms associated with childhood autism, such as the preponderance of behavioral stereotypies and rhythmicities, intolerance to variation in routines, difficulties in inhibiting prepotent or habitual responses involved in executive function deficits, aversion to social objects, and even the lack of sensitivity to the social cues that drive mindreading skills. (For details, see Gergely 2001b; Gergely and Watson 1999.)

Throughout this volume we suggest that in less severe cases, attachment environments that involve dysfunctional patterns of contingencies between actions of the self and the response of the other may lead to a distorted functioning of contingency detection. This, in turn, might undermine the normal development of self-agency by depriving the individual of some key building blocks for the development of this structure. As we have indicated above, inadequacies of the structuralization of the self might arise out of a biologically determined predisposition to fail to engage less-than-perfect social contingencies in an interpersonal context. Alternatively, the normal development of the self may become undermined as a result of the caregiver's inadequate provision of adaptive contingent responsiveness. For example, abusive caregivers or preoccupied, dissociating caregivers who are unresolved in relation to trauma periodically show a severe reduction of contingent responsivity—during abusive episodes or periods of parental dissociation. During such recurring episodes, the child repeatedly experiences periods of drastic loss in the contingent effectivity of his affective and communicative responses (Koós and Gergely 2001).

This may lead to disorganization in self-development characterized by a tendency for dissociation accompanied by preoccupation with self-generated perfect contingencies in the attachment context. In support of this view, we have preliminary evidence indicating an early association between disorganized infant attachment and an abnormal preference for perfect contingencies (Koós and Gergely 2001; Koós et al. 2000).

In our view, then, both the maladaptive features of the caregiver's contingent responsiveness and the infant's inadequate sensitivity to social contingencies may determine the establishment of an abnormal focus on perfect contingencies and a pathological development of self-agency. In either case, the most pertinent observation is one of early vulnerability, which stems from the poor establishment of agentive self-structure.

Taking the perspective of the developmental psychopathologist, these distinctions might help us to understand some key features of later disturbance, particularly personality disorders. It is clear that, associated with certain extreme social dysfunctions—such as childhood maltreatment, environmental trauma of various kinds—an individual's capacity to behave with any degree of flexibility comes to be compromised. Some of these dysfunctions of interpersonal behavior might be understood as reflecting an intensified need on the part of the individual to demand closer-to-perfect contingent responses from individuals with whom they have emotionally loaded relationships. It is as if these relationships triggered the need to rediscover the self in the response of the other (see chapters 3 and 4) and therefore reactivated the need for high levels of contingent responsiveness. In later chapters we describe ways in which we think this need is unconsciously experienced and how we understand the pathological solutions that come to be enacted in later attachment relationships.

In the chapters that follow we attempt to integrate the developmental concepts and research reviewed in the last three chapters with a clinical model for the development of subjectivity (see chapter 6) and its distortions in childhood (see chapters 7 and 10) and adult personality disorders (see chapters 8 and 9). In this chapter we hope we have laid the groundwork for the developmental models of severe personality problems described in the chapters that follow. We hope that we have established some of the characteristics of prementalistic functioning that we believe to be relevant to our developmental understanding of personality disorder. In general, we believe that many common symptoms and problems identified in these patients are "revealed" by absence of mentalistic functioning in the self as agent. Features such as impulsivity, emotion dysregulation, and the predominance of primitive defenses can be seen either as an adaptation of processes that anteceded mentalization or as attempts of the mind to adapt to the limited range of capacities available to it, or some combination of these two possibilities.

6

"Playing with Reality": Developmental Research and a Psychoanalytic Model for the Development of Subjectivity

This chapter concerns changes in the child's perception of psychic reality during normal development, culminating in the major shift in the child's understanding of minds (theory of mind) at the oedipal stage, which we equate with the qualitative shift in the development of mentalization whereby the self becomes a representational agent (see chapter 5). We integrate empirical studies of this transition with material from the analysis of a 4-year-old girl. We propose a psychoanalytic model of the development of an awareness of mental states, which conceives of the very young child as using two modes for representing internal states or—using psychoanalytic terminology—psychic reality; we have called these "psychic equivalent" and "pretend" modes, which differ primarily in the assumed relationship between internal and external realities. We argue that the integration of the dual modes into a singular reflective mode is normally completed by about the age of 4, with the mentalization of affect leading the mentalization of belief states or cognitions: the child first understands that people have different feelings, then that they may have different thoughts about the same external reality. We link Freud's classic notion of psychic reality and current psychoanalytic formulations of symbolization. This chapter describes normal psychological growth in childhood; the next offers a further clinical example, which applies the model outlined in this chapter and chapter 4 to a young child. Chapter 8 concerns the changes that occur in adolescence, and the following two chapters, using the same developmental model, consider failures of these crucial cognitive transitions as seen in adult personality disorder.

THE CONCEPT OF PSYCHIC REALITY

Most psychoanalysts use the term "psychic reality" informally, to mean subjective experience influenced by unconscious processes (Michels 1984). Thus in the psychic reality of the patient, the analyst may be alternately represented as destructive and cruel or perfect and omnipotent in the transference. Freud's original concept was of "thought-reality," which he distinguished from "external reality." The import of this distinction was that internal experience could in certain circumstances be treated as though it were as real as the external world, and Freud was particularly interested in how the ego judges the "quality" of thought and the impact on this ego function of emotional cathexis and language: *"Thus thought accompanied by a cathexis of the indications of thought-reality or of the indications of speech is the highest, securest form of cognitive thought process"* (1895, p. 374, emphasis in original). In this chapter we investigate how the individual experiences and evaluates his "thought-reality" at different stages of development and how, all being well, he comes to exercise the highest form of cognitive process, a sort of reality testing of internal states (Hartmann 1956), in both oneself and others.

Freud went on to use the concept of psychic reality to explain how neurotic phenomena provoked by childhood trauma—seduction—could be indistinguishable from cases where the supposedly pathogenic events had never taken place (Freud 1900a). The events could be "real" psychologically, and the individual might react to wishful fantasies in the way that they or others would respond to actual events. Freud wrote: "What lie behind the sense of guilt of neurotics are always *psychical* realities and never *factual* ones. What characterizes neurotics is that they prefer psychical to factual reality, and react just as seriously to thoughts as normal people do to realities" (1912–13, p. 159). This sense of equivalence is also suggested by Laplanche and Pontalis's definition of psychic reality as "whatever in the subject's psyche presents a consistency and resistance comparable to those displayed by material reality" (Laplanche and Pontalis 1973, p. 363). Freud thought that psychic reality poses a danger when there is imperfect discrimination ("reality testing," Brenner 1955) between stimuli from the outer world and stimuli that arise as products of unconscious processes. Although the neurotic adult knows whether experiences originate internally or externally, he gives more weight to certain internal experiences than he does to his knowledge of the outside world. An obsessional person, for instance, "knows" that the door is locked but still checks several times, because for him the internal image of an unsecured house has much more meaning and power than the external images provided by his senses. Because "psychic reality" now has a variety of connotations, we use the term "psychic equivalence" to denote domination by psychic reality in Freud's sense.

THE IMPORTANCE OF A DEVELOPMENTAL PERSPECTIVE

Ambiguity in the term "psychic reality" may be due to insufficient utilization of a developmental perspective in psychoanalysis. Arlow (1984) underscores the qualitative differences in the perception of physical and human—psychological—realities. We may infer from his paper that a robust sense of this psychological reality will lag behind the acquisition of a clear portrayal of the physical world, both developmentally and in terms of complexity. What may underlie this difference is the relative opaqueness of our mental world (Brentano 1874); in fact, the concept of psychic reality begs a whole range of questions concerning the nature of subjective experience with which, as we have said, Freud was grappling from the time of the 1895 "Project" (Freud 1950 [1895]). How do we know our minds? Is psychic reality directly experienced, as perhaps is the case for pain and other sensations, or are thoughts, beliefs, desires, and intentions—mental states—perhaps constructions of our minds, built up over the early years of development? If a developmental process underlies the evolution of psychic reality, what is its nature, and how does the child's subjective experience of reality differ from that of the adult? Do psychoanalytic clinical data shed light on this evolution? Can we learn from philosophers of mind or observational studies in developmental psychology about the way psychic reality evolves?

A number of philosophers of mind assume that the experience of mental states is intrinsic, psychic reality is a "given" (e.g., Searle 1983), and awareness of others' mental states is arrived at by simulating the mental states of others (Goldman 1992; Gordon 1986, 1992). The model that we propose places Freud's notion of psychic reality in a developmental perspective. We have already presented empirical evidence and developmental observations in the previous three chapters to support the view that our understanding of the mental world is not a given, is radically different in the young child, and crucially depends for its healthy development on interaction with other people who are sufficiently benign and reflective. (For a philosophical demonstration of this basic position see Cavell 1991.) In chapter 3 we made a claim—one that may be perceived as risky from the point of view of cognitive science but is far less so from a psychoanalytic perspective—that one of the key evolutionary functions of early object relations for humans was to equip the very young child with an environment where the processing capacity for the understanding of mental states in others and the self can fully develop. The social nature of thought is thus part of the very essence of subjectivity.

EMPIRICAL OBSERVATIONS CONCERNING THE DEVELOPMENT OF PSYCHIC REALITY

In chapter 4 we considered evidence that demonstrates that from the first months of life a child is intensely concerned about the social world (e.g., Stern 1985, 1994; Trevarthen 1980). However, it is also evident that the way in which a child of 3 or 4 years experiences interpersonal reality—and his role within it— is qualitatively different from the way that an older child or adult experiences it. One instance of this critical difference is in the understanding that children have of the mind, in their theory of mind (e.g., Baron-Cohen 1995; Mayes and Cohen 1992). The ability to attribute intentional mental states—goals, desires, and beliefs—to oneself or others as an explanation for actions is not fully developed until around 4 years of age (Wellman 1990). However, most developmental psychologists believe that precursors of this capacity—pointing and looking, or checking back for the caregiver's reaction to strange situations—imply awareness of other people's minds in the first year of life (Butterworth, Harris, Leslie, and Wellman 1991; Klinnert et al. 1983; see also Stern 1985). Gergely's experimental paradigms, described in chapters 4 and 5, appear to show that babies of 8 to 9 months attribute purpose to events. Soon after the end of the first year children show, implicitly, a partial awareness of the difference between internal representations and reality. Reddy (1991) offers amusing examples of the 1-year-old's awareness of the appearance/reality distinction from his observations of children "mucking about" and demonstrating in their delight that they did not really imagine that their mother would allow them to keep the whole chocolate bar for themselves, or to walk across the road without holding hands, and so on.

As shown in chapter 5, by the age of 3 years many important building blocks for understanding the nature of psychic reality are in place (e.g., Wellman 1990). For instance, children can distinguish between dream images, thoughts, and real things, they start pretend games, and they easily appreciate someone else's intention to pretend—for example, that Daddy is a dog. Nevertheless, the 2- or 3-year-old's awareness of his inner world is markedly different from that of a child in his fifth year. We wish to propose that the very small child's sense of psychic reality has a dual character. The child generally operates in "psychic equivalence" mode, where ideas are not felt to be representations but, rather, direct replicas of reality, and consequently always true. At other times, however, the child uses a "pretend" mode in which ideas are felt to be representational but their correspondence with reality is not examined. We will look at the evidence for these in turn.

The "Psychic Equivalence" Mode of Experiencing Psychic Reality

When a 3-year-old is given a sponge that has been painted and shaped to look like a rock, his answers to the questions of what the object looks like and what it actually is tend to be identical (Flavell, Green, and Flavell 1986). The child is shown and allowed to feel the object.

Q: "What does it look like?"
A: "It looks like a rock."
Q: "What is it?"
A: "It's a rock."

The child is prompted to squeeze the object.

Q: "What do you think it is?"
A: "It's a sponge."
Q: "What does it look like?"
A: "It looks like a sponge."

The child equates appearance and reality. Very young children behave as though their own and others' thoughts faithfully mirror the real world.

Philosophers of the nineteenth and early twentieth centuries pointed out that once a person can imagine false beliefs, the assumption of equivalence between appearance and reality becomes untenable (Brentano 1874; B. Russell 1905). Conversely, without understanding that the same physical reality can generate alternative ideas, small children are unlikely to appreciate that their beliefs may vary, be false, and differ from those of another person. The ability to imagine different perspectives is therefore a crucial indicator of the child's assumptions about the status of his thoughts: how his psychic reality corresponds to the external world.

We will give one example of many experimental studies of this indicator: Perner and his colleagues (Perner et al. 1987) showed a series of 3-year-old children a familiar candy box. Each child expected the box to be filled with candy but was shown that it contained pencils. Each was then asked what they thought their friend waiting outside would think the box had in it, to which they confidently replied that the other person would think that it contained pencils. Here, their current psychic reality, which reflected physical reality, dominated their representation of the psychic reality of the other, and they appeared not to understand that the other person's belief might be false. They continued to make this error when they saw the other person respond with surprise and when they were explicitly told what the other person thought (Moses and Flavell 1990; Wellman 1990). The mind of the other could not yet be represented as a separate entity, with a potentially different point of view. Equally, the children were unable to recall that they themselves had ever thought the box had candy in it. They firmly believed that they knew it had pencils inside from the beginning, while freely admitting other kinds of difficulty or mistake. It seems that, if the young child believes something, it must be so; if it is so, then someone else will see it in the same way; if it was so before, he must have seen it that way before.

Young children's sense of the psychic reality of their own and others' feelings and desires, as opposed to beliefs, seems to be more advanced. Children in their second year learn, at least superficially, to acknowledge that some wishes may not be fulfilled (Astington and Gopnik 1991). By the third year they can appreciate that their own feelings might not correspond to those of other people. "Do you want me to look both ways? I don't wanna look both ways!" (Wellman and Banerjee 1991). They are more ready to say that they think of something that someone else thought was undesirable ("yucky") as desirable ("yummy") than they are to recognize an alternative belief as to whether a box is full of candy or pencils (Flavell, Flavell, Green, and Moses 1990). These and other findings are consistent with the psychoanalytic emphasis, pointing to the developmental lead that emotions and desires have over beliefs and the developmental push that we may expect from the child's unfolding awareness of the diversity of desire.

The young child's need to maintain the equivalence between psychic and physical reality is clearest when the external world requires an adjustment of his internal representation. It follows that when a child is offered an external representation, a symbol, of his mental state, his performance of such tasks should improve. This turns out to be the case. When Mitchell and Lacohé (1991) gave children a drawing of the chocolate they had expected to be in the candy box in the belief-change task, they were better able to answer questions concerning both their own and others' beliefs. Having access to a token of their belief created an identity for it independent of current physical reality. In the absence of a representation—or symbol—of their earlier representation, these 3-year-old children were unable to keep it in mind.

So how does the 3-year-old understand his mind? What is the nature of his psychic reality? The very young child does not yet have the capacity to appreciate the *merely representational* nature of ideas and feelings. Older children know that what they think or believe about something does not necessarily reflect reality. The young child, who is not yet able to mentalize, to reflect on thoughts and feelings, as it were, from outside, is forced to believe that his thoughts and beliefs inevitably and correctly mirror the real world.

Britton has considered the relationship between belief and knowledge in Kleinian terms. It is important to clarify the difference between our position and his related ideas. He describes mature mentalization as an "epistemic attitude" in which a person can believe but know that he does not know; Britton contrasts this with a more psychotic frame of mind: "The contrary assumption that belief is knowledge is the basis of delusion and characterizes the paranoid-schizoid position. Emancipation from the equation of belief with knowledge is an aspect of working through the depressive position" (1995, p. 22). We suggest that although the very young child does in a sense believe that belief is knowledge, his attitude differs from that of the psychotic in that the child is more inclined to fit "mind-to-world" than "world-to-mind" (Searle 1983), and in this way is more like a weather-vane than like a psychotic person. When working with young children and other patients who are still functioning in this mode of psychic experience, it is external reality, not the contents of the child's mind, that is immensely and sometimes terrifyingly compelling; the child's thoughts and beliefs seem very vulnerable and evanescent by contrast. We return to this point later, when discussing play.

The "Pretend" Mode of Experiencing Psychic Reality

Thus far, we have only looked at one side of this story, which may have led readers to feel that we, together with developmental psychologists, are only looking at the less interesting side of the real child, at cognition rather than imagination. We maintain that we need to understand the form and limitations of the child's thinking, partly in order to understand the great importance of imagination in his life at this age, and partly in order to adopt appropriate techniques with young children and with older patients who continue to show these limitations.

A child can pretend that a chair is a tank and yet not expect it to shoot real shells, and there have been experimental demonstrations that small children can keep alternative or changing beliefs in mind if they are doing a task in play rather than for real.[1] Vygotsky wrote: "in play the child is always above his average age, above his daily behavior; in play it is as though he were a head taller than himself" (1978, p. 102). In the world of play it becomes possible partially to free representations from their referents and allow these freed representations to be modified, creating a more flexible mode of thought that encourages the emergence of latent mental structures (Marans et al. 1991). Playfulness enables ways of functioning that are rarely used,

---

[1] Gopnik and Slaughter (1991) created a "pretend version" of the belief-change task. They asked children to pretend that an empty glass had a chocolate drink in it; the glass was then "pretend emptied" by the adult, and the child was asked to pretend that the glass was now full of lemonade. Almost no 3-year-olds had any difficulty in remembering that the original imagined content was chocolate.

developmentally surpassed, or only just being formed to occupy center stage. Thus playing or pretending at times reveals surprising competencies, while at other times it offers opportunities for regression and the expression of unconscious concerns. When small children are asked to visualize something that does not exist, they readily understand the phrase, "make a picture in your head." They use the metaphor of the head as a container in which imaginary situations or objects may be created and examined. When playing, even the young child has a mentalizing model of psychic experience and sees his mind as representing ideas, desires, and other feelings. However, it seems to be necessary for children of this age to prevent correspondence between the "pretend world" and external reality in the "pretend" modes of thinking. Not surprisingly, the difference between the equivalent and pretend mode has to be clearly marked, and the lack of correspondence to actual reality is frequently exaggerated (Fónagy and Fonagy 1995). If this is not ensured, it quickly becomes clear just how threatening the isomorphism of internal and external realities can become for the child, who has limited awareness of the implications and realistic dangers of many events. Although the child strictly separates the two realities in his thinking, his affective investment in his play may directly reflect the extent to which his phantasy incorporates a disguised piece of "serious" reality, such as the relationship between his parents or the imagined consequences of acting on dangerous wishes.

Two examples from normal development may illustrate the potency of thought for the small child. A 4-year-old boy was read a ghost story by his mother. Although the story was not expected to be particularly frightening, he was visibly shaken by it. The mother quickly offered reassurance: "Don't worry, Simon, it didn't really happen." The child, clearly feeling misunderstood, protested in reply: "But when you read it, it did really happen to me!" A further example is provided by the father of a 3-year-old boy, whose son asked him to find a Batman outfit on his trip abroad. The father had great difficulty, but eventually he found a fancy-dress shop and bought an expensive costume. Unfortunately, the costume was so realistic that the boy was frightened when he saw himself in the mirror, refused to wear it again, and went back to using his mother's skirt as his Batman cloak. Similarly, the common observation that children of 2 or 3 spend much time together "scene-setting," negotiating the roles and rules of their pretend games, sometimes leaving little opportunity for entering into the game itself, underlines the importance of a clear division between "playing" and "reality" for children of this age.

When adults think about children playing, they often think of it using their own, rather than the child's, perspective on psychic reality. It is easy to assume that because a child at play can reflect on states of mind including false beliefs, he is able to do this outside his play. The small child playing can think about thoughts as thoughts because these are clearly and deliberately stripped of their connection to the real world of people and even things. It is also easy to overlook the fact that the child may only be able to reflect on thoughts and feelings about real-life events during play if an adult is there to provide a necessary frame and insulate him from the compelling character of external reality. Winnicott recognized the vital mediating role children need from adults in order to play. He pointed out that our attitude toward play "must include recognition that playing is always liable to become frightening. Games and their organization must be looked at as part of an attempt to forestall the frightening aspect of playing. The precariousness of play belongs to the fact that it is always on the theoretical line between the subjective and that which is objectively perceived" (1971, pp. 58–59). The very young child's understanding of minds may be developmentally advanced in play because of the segregation of this from external reality, and the avoidance of the sense of encroachment of reality on thought, which the child would otherwise experience.

The Integration of Dual Modes of Experience: Learning to Mentalize

In the fourth and fifth year, the "psychic equivalence" and "pretend" modes normally become increasingly integrated, and a reflective or mentalizing mode of psychic reality is established (Gopnik 1993). Children begin to acknowledge that things may not be what they appear to be, that another person may perceive external reality differently, that beliefs may be held with different degrees of certainty, and that they felt differently in the past about something (Baron-Cohen et al. 1985). With this new way of thinking about his experience, the child not only shows an understanding that his own and his object's behavior make sense in terms of mental states, but also learns to recognize that these states are representations, which may be fallible and may change because they are based on but one of a range of possible perspectives.

We must emphasize the crucial importance of this cognitive integration and acquisition of the capacity to mentalize: (*a*) It brings with it the possibility of continuity in the experience of the psychological self (Fonagy, Moran, and Target 1993). The child can fit his thinking to the world without feeling as though he has to change himself in order to change his mind (literally has to "change his mind"), losing continuity with the self that thought before. (*b*) It enables the child to see people's actions as meaningful through the attribution of thoughts and feelings. This means that their actions become predictable, which in turn reduces moment-to-moment dependency on others. This is an important component of the process of individuation. The child of around 4 or 5 years is frequently able to understand what the mother is doing and why, without her needing constantly to bear his limited perspective in mind ("I can't do that now because I am worried about granny's illness," etc.). This allows both child and caregiver to attain increasing mental and physical independence, needing to refer far less to each other in order to allow the child to borrow the mother's understanding. (*c*) It allows for a distinction between inner and outer truth, enabling the child to understand that the fact that someone is behaving in a particular way does not mean that things *are* like that. While this may not be important in all contexts, we believe that it becomes critical in cases of maltreatment or trauma, allowing the child to survive psychologically and relieving the pressure to relive the experience in concrete ways. Once the child can mentalize, he has available a crucial attenuating function for psychic experience. (*d*) Without a clear representation of the mental state of the other, communication must be profoundly limited. The philosopher Grice (1975) formulated the overriding principle of conversation as one of collaboration, whereby the effective speaker needs constantly to bear in mind the other person's point of view. The absence or underdevelopment of the capacity to mentalize can have a limiting effect on the possibility of doing analytic work, and there are implications for technique when undertaking analysis of such persons. (*e*) Finally and most importantly, mentalizing can help an individual to achieve a higher level of intersubjectivity, in terms of deeper experiences with others and ultimately a life experienced as more meaningful.

We think that it is the successful connecting of internal and external that allows belief to be endowed with meaning that is emotionally alive but is manageable and therefore does not have to be defended against. A partial failure to achieve this integration can lead to neurotic states. In more profound and pervasive failures of integration, reality may be experienced as emotionally meaningless. In such cases other people and the self are related to as things, and the relating itself occurs at a very concrete level. It must not be forgotten, however, that achievement of the capacity to mentalize also has the potential massively to increase conflict, when fantasies such as oedipal wishes become stable representations that can be set against external reality. As Winnicott (1971) wrote:

> It is assumed here that the task of reality acceptance is never completed, that no human being is free from the strain of relating inner and outer reality, and that relief from this strain is provided by an intermediate area of experience (cf. Riviere, 1936) which is not challenged (arts, religion, etc.). This intermediate area is in direct continuity with the play area of the small child who is "lost" in play." [p. 15]

THE ROLE OF THE OTHER IN DEVELOPING THE CAPACITY TO MENTALIZE

Most developmentalists regard the development of mentalizing capacity as simply maturational. Many psychoanalytic theories of development have assumed that the self develops transcendentally, from within the individual. In his paper on narcissism (Freud 1914c), Freud argued that there was "an original libidinal cathexis of the ego, from which some is later given off to objects, but which fundamentally persists and is related to the object-cathexis much as the body of an amoeba is related to the pseudopodia which it puts out" (p. 75). For Freud, in infancy and early childhood others in the external world are extensions of the self. While this may be an accurate description of the phenomenology, for us it seems more accurate to see the self as originally an extension of experience of the other. Its development is an interpersonal process requiring interaction with the minds of others, as described in relation to earlier infancy. In this chapter, we argue that the involvement of the caregiver, and to a lesser extent of older siblings, is crucial in helping the child of 3 or 4 years to accept the two realities, internal and external, without needing to split his ego functioning to maintain dual modes of thinking.

In order to achieve the integration of a nonmentalizing reality-oriented and mentalizing nonreality-connected mode, to create fully mentalized psychic reality, the child needs repeated experience of three things: his current mental states, these states represented—thought about—in the object's mind, and the frame represented by the adult's normally externally reality-oriented perspective. We believe that the "frame" provided by the parent, or by other children, is an essential part of this model. The child needs an adult or older child who will "play along," so that the child can see his fantasy or idea represented in the adult's mind, reintroject this, and use it as a representation of his own thinking. When the omniscient and omnipotent parent playfully pretends with the child that a banana is a telephone, the child is able simultaneously to equate the apparent and the real while clarifying the distinction between pretend and serious mode. He becomes able to "know about" his idea or wish, alongside experiencing it. By entering into the child's world in a playful way, the child sees the adult adopting an "as-if" attitude to his intentional state. The frame is present so that he knows that his thoughts or feelings are not "for real," yet he perceives them outside, in the parent's mind. Linking his internal state to a perception of that state outside offers a representation—a symbol—of the internal state: it corresponds to, yet it is not equivalent to, the state. The playful attitude of the parent is crucial. The child's mental state must be represented sufficiently clearly and accurately for the child to recognize it, yet sufficiently playfully for the child not to be overwhelmed by its realness. In this way he can ultimately use the parent's representation of his internal reality as the seed for his own symbolic thought, his representation of his own representations.

If the adult's attitude precludes the duality of holding the frame of external reality while offering mirroring or reflection, the child's transition toward integration and mentalization may be jeopardized. He may not feel free—secure—to explore the adult's mind and find himself in it, or what he finds there may be a distorted, spoiled picture of his mental state, which the child cannot safely use to represent his experience. If, on the other hand, the caregiver can frequently provide links between reality and fantasy in a way that includes an accepting, recognizable reflection of the child's mental states, then he affords the child a basis for organizing and comparing numerous experiences bridging the psychic equivalence and pretend modes. Gradually, the child comes to be able to maintain a mentalizing stance himself, having internalized the process through repeated interactions with the caregiver and probably also with other children. The essence of the process is not simply play, but play that breaks away from psychic equivalence while retaining contact with reality. In other words, the child, using the parent's mind, is able to *play with reality.*

We suggest that it is no coincidence that the child makes, or fails to make, this cognitive transition at the time traditionally associated with oedipal conflict. A number of writers have recently suggested that successful working-through of the oedipal situation involves the sort of opening-up of thinking into a triangular space which we and others suggest can occur through play with reality. Following Hanna Segal's (1957) work on symbol formation and Bion's (1970) abstract exploration of the oedipal triangle as a model, Ogden (1985) conceives of the pretend mode of functioning as developed out of the triangularity of the symbol, the symbolized, and the interpreting subject. Britton (1989, 1994) has done much to explore the source and significance of this triangularity, in the context of applying depressive-position thinking to the mourning involved in resolving the oedipal situation. He argues that not only does the acceptance of internal triangular relationships provide space for thinking and the possibility of looking at dyadic relationships from the perspective of a third, but it consolidates the depressive position and provides a "stabilizing structure" (Britton 1994). He emphasizes that an important aspect of the triangular oedipal situation is that it enables the child to conceive of being observed and, by implication, being thought about: "This provides us with a capacity for seeing ourselves in interaction with others and for entertaining another point of view whilst retaining our own, for reflecting on ourselves whilst being ourselves" (Britton 1989, p. 87). We suggest that this capacity is specifically fostered by the support of adults or sometimes of other children for the child's play, providing a safe internal context in which to reflect; the child can trust the other person to know about reality.

Although we have emphasized the transition that normally occurs around 4 years of age, we must emphasize that the ability to represent mental states is not acquired all at once; rather, it is a developmental achievement, which, like all mental capacities, may be present to a greater or lesser extent in any individual at any one time. The tendency of the empirical data we have referred to is to suggest that in some sense the function does not exist until the child "passes" a task in an experimental situation. (Experimentalists are usually, of course, as aware as anyone else that no capacity emerges suddenly into the mind and that all that the experimental task can imply is that from that moment the child is likely to be able to perform that function *in that situation.*) The experimentalist frame of reference is concerned with demonstrable causes and effects. Observers of child behavior, whether clinical or social psychological (e.g., Dunn 1994), are interpreting the child's behavior with a developmental end-point in mind and can thus see components of a function in the process of coming together. The weakness of this interpretive tradition is the unavoidable tendency to ascribe to the child the full capacity, on the basis of what must be partial evidence. Our formulation is linked to the current Kleinian view that there is continuing oscillation or equilibrium (Bion 1963) between the paranoid-schizoid and depressive positions in the face of new experience. Even after integration has taken place, emotional factors can impede the availability of the capacity for mentalization in specific areas. Steiner (1992) explores the defenses operating at different levels within the two basic Kleinian positions, and his discussion of the differentiation within the depressive position is relevant to the transition we have written about in this chapter. At the risk of oversimplifying Steiner's subtle distinctions, we suggest that the "normal splitting" he describes in the depressive position, at the level of "fear of loss of the object," may be thought of—at least in the young child—as including operating with a dual mode of psychic reality. The mode of psychic equivalence might then be seen as operating through (relatively benign) projective identification, which he describes as a key mechanism in reducing this fear of loss. The more mature depressive position, as described by Steiner, involves "experience of loss of the object," relinquishing (the phantasy of) control of the object, and allowing separation and mourning to take place. While in this paper Steiner does not link the process to the resolution of the oedipal situation, we speculate that, in normal development, accepting the loss of the illusion of exclusive possession and allowing the emergence of a triangular relationship may be a major turning point that offers the opportunity to function at the higher level within the depressive position, and that this is crucially connected with accepting that ideas are merely ideas.

We would like now to illustrate these ideas with material from an analysis during which a young child overcame her resistance to this developmental progress and was thus enabled to link her two modes of understanding psychic reality and to find a greater integration of inner and outer.

FRAGMENT FROM THE PSYCHOANALYTIC
TREATMENT OF AN UNDER-FIVE:
"REBECCA"

Rebecca[2] was a pretty little girl, charming and precocious, even when clearly depressed. When she was 4 years old, her mother brought her to the Anna Freud Centre because over the past year she had developed a variety of problems, including recurrent nightmares, daytime terrors often but not always associated with separation, demanding clinginess, and other indications of her anxiety, such as hyperactivity, aggressiveness, and fear of loneliness and death. At times her anxiety led her to be destructive, disobedient, and aggressive and a bit of a bully at school as well as with her mother. In her assessment she was willing to talk about her nightmares and her fear of spiders and snails.

She went on to enact a scene of a Daddy doll cuddling Mommy doll, which she concluded by banging the Daddy figure's head on the skirting-board, announcing that he was killed, and taking him off the scene. In this way she quickly communicated her murderous fantasy about why her father had been absent from her life. Rebecca was the only child of an unmarried young woman who had given birth to her at 18, having had two previous terminations. The mother was ambitious and impatient to pursue a career. Rebecca's father was a casual partner of the mother; he apparently totally withdrew from her soon after her pregnancy was confirmed. Rebecca had never met her father, although she had a photograph of him, which she frequently looked at. She had often said that she wanted to meet him, but by the time of the referral these demands had abated. In her interview with me, Rebecca's mother became immediately tearful when the issue of her feelings about the father of this child was raised. She made it clear that she felt quite unable to address this subject with her daughter.

Rebecca had been brought up in a complicated environment, partly with her grandparents and partly with her mother, who

---

[2] The case is narrated in the first person; the analyst was Peter Fonagy. Peter Fonagy would like to acknowledge his indebtedness to Rose Edgcumbe, who supervised the case.

worked as a child-minder. The household included her mother's occasional partners and other children from her grandfather's previous marriages. In her fourth year, her charismatic grandfather died. Rebecca's mother's bereavement reaction signaled the onset of Rebecca's symptoms.

There were difficulties in the initial phase of Rebecca's treatment. She insisted that her mother should stay in the room, yet she was clearly inhibited by her presence, her play subdued and repetitive. She drew stereotyped figures, each drawing having to be shown to mother, and her defensive exclusion of me was clear. I decided to tackle her anxiety directly, that a relationship with me would exclude her Mommy, which might make Mommy become angry and love her less. Although this allowed her to let her mother leave the room, her anxiety had not abated entirely. Being alone with me made her immensely anxious. She defended against the anxiety by taking command of the environment. She ordered me, in an agitated way, to rearrange the positions of the chairs, her play table, and even my big desk, and then she charged me with the task of controlling the lights, to help her to "organize the show." It was daylight, so it was clear that the lights stood for another aspect of the environment that she needed desperately to bring under her control. I felt that she was moving the external furniture, both to make the unfamiliar territory of the consulting-room as much hers as mine and to prevent us from moving forward in our dialogue about her state of mind. I said that she felt worried she would be moved around by me, like she moved the furniture about. But while she moved the furniture, she didn't have to think about her worries. Later, I added that it was terribly hard for her that our time together began and ended so abruptly, just as the light came on for such brief moments.

This refocusing on her psychic reality was helpful. Rebecca's pattern of play then changed. She started playing with Plasticene (modeling clay), her declared intention being to "make a Plasticene world." My role was to "make the Plasticene soft," while she molded the figures. This was the first time that Rebecca played with me cooperatively. She symbolically conveyed her need for me to make pliable the harsh and fixed ideas in her mind, which she was not able to manipulate. She confirmed the generality of my feeling about the role she put me into by claiming that she had made a "Plasticene world blanket," which would cover everyone and everything, and she placed all the figures in her toy box under the flat piece of Plasticene she made. The task was difficult; even though she flattened a size-able piece of Plasticene, it could not cover all the figures properly. Despite her careful positioning, some were "left out in the cold." Noticing her anxiety about this, I commented that I thought it might be troubling her that someone might be shut out of our little world. She confirmed that the source of her anxiety might have, at least in part, been the exclusiveness of my relationship with her, by rolling up the "world blanket" so that there was room for only two of the figures under it; all the others were put back into the box with great care. I noticed that the last to be tentatively picked up were the Mommy and Granny dolls. I said: "Many children are frightened about coming up here and leaving their Mommy downstairs. Sometimes they are frightened about what might happen to their Mommies, and sometimes about what might happen to them." She then went on to play with the Plasticene on her own, rolling a piece into the shape of a snake, and placing it round a doll's head, like a crown. She commented that all the other figures were frightened of the little girl doll, because she had the big snake. I said that the big snake was like the worries inside her head, which were scaring her when her mother wasn't there to protect her, now but also at night. She looked up at me and smiled slightly for the first time and said that the people were only pretending to be frightened of the snake. I said that I was sure that people often told her that she should not feel frightened because there was nothing there really to be afraid of, but the two of us knew that her worries felt terribly real. She said: "You mean, like the pirates?" I said: "Perhaps when you can't see Mommy, you are frightened that she might be taken away by pirates?" To my surprise, she said, "She is." Only subsequently did I understand that in her night-mares and daytime terrors, her mother or her grandmother were abducted by pirates. My acceptance of the reality of her anxieties and other emotions was critical in freeing her mind from the grip of the worry-snakes.

At this time Rebecca began to play more complex games, and her oedipal anxieties, distorted by the circumstances of her childhood, came to the fore. She played royal families: the king and queen doll had a daughter. The daughter doll was abandoned when the king and queen dolls cuddled, but later she was inserted between the king and queen doll. The sexualization of this theme was made more explicit by the whole scene being transferred to the couch and everyone jumping about until the daughter doll fell off. Then there was a street fire, which filled the house with smoke and burned down the whole street. I said: "I know some little girls who are very frightened of being so excited, because their thoughts make them feel hot and muddled and then everything goes wrong." She said: "I think I am one of those girls."

Much of Rebecca's treatment consisted of a single game, with apparently infinite variations. In the game, she is a somewhat older girl, Hannah, who has a father, which was the analyst's role. Hannah and her father "Peter" had many adventures, most of which involved visiting Hannah's friend, "pretend Rebecca,"[3] who lived in the same house as real Rebecca but who—in the game—had a father "Jeff" as well as a mother. Jeff was a pathetic, incompetent figure who frequently got things wrong, and on such occasions would often be unceremoniously dismissed, mostly by mother and sometimes by her. Hannah would sensitively intercede with pretend Rebecca and Rebecca's mother on Jeff's behalf: "You don't understand him!" she berated pretend Rebecca on one occasion, "He is only upset because you told him off for making a mess." I, as Hannah's father, was encouraged to do the same: "Let's pretend that Rebecca does not understand. You pretend to tell her (pretend Rebecca) that she is not being nice to him." I said she (Rebecca) perhaps did not want to understand because it was frightening to think that her anger could be so powerful that it could send a big man like Jeff away and she was very frightened of feeling angry.

---

[3] Pretend Rebecca was an imaginary friend. She shared the patient's first name but was definitely not identical with the narrator (the patient or real Rebecca). Both patient and analyst talked to her, and the patient, mostly as Hannah, spoke for her.

Rebecca's rage with her mother for not providing her with a father also quickly surfaced in these interchanges, as did her shame and frustration about failing to hold on to him herself. For instance, on one occasion, Hannah berated her mother for not looking after the family dog, which then went missing and Hannah's Daddy had to go out to find it and therefore could not be there to play with Hannah. Rebecca, playing Hannah, quite angry and flushed, remonstrated with the chair where the imaginary mother was sitting: "It's all your fault that Daddy isn't in!" I reflected that Hannah was very, very upset, and that perhaps she felt that Hannah's mother had let the dog go deliberately. Hannah confirmed my suspicion and, still in role, added: "She didn't want us to be playing making breakfast." Later on in the game, it turned out that Hannah had lost the dog herself but was embarrassed to admit it. I was able to address Hannah's anger from a slightly different viewpoint: "Perhaps Hannah got so angry with her Mom because she felt ashamed of losing the dog and spoiling the chance to play with Daddy." Rebecca agreed that she probably must have done.

Gradually, the terrifying fantasy that her father had died in an overwhelmingly exciting sexual union with her mother was enacted, and I was able to interpret her terror that he (as Jeff) might run away because he was so frightened of both her and her mother's violent rage and voracious, man-consuming sexual appetites. All this is par for the analytic course and clearly illustrates aspects of this child's psychic reality. Here, we want to focus on a specific feature of the work with her: the importance of the subtle distinctions between pretense and reality in Rebecca's games and what was learned about the nature of her problems through playing with reality.

The confusion of identities was a recurrent theme. When Hannah stayed at Rebecca's overnight, her father came to find her in Rebecca's bedroom but, unbeknownst to him, Hannah and Rebecca had changed places in the bunk beds. Looking for Hannah and finding Rebecca, he would be surprised. Depending on the context, there was much to interpret in this game. On one occasion, when both Hannah and pretend Rebecca seemed particularly excited about whom Hannah's father was going to find, I could point to both Hannah's and pretend Rebecca's wish to be found, as father's special person. The oedipal wish to be found by the father, defensively displaced to a pretend child, was self-evident. However, this scenario occurred so often that clearly there were many other determinants: the transference gratification of externalizing her confusion onto the adult analyst, representing in the transference the muddled character of her internal world with its confusions of identities; the split in her self- and object-representations between an idealized Hannah, who had control over her father, and the impoverished Rebecca, struggling to maintain her self-esteem with her delinquent, uncaring paternal figure. No single interpretation seemed crucially important, and the game continued. The scenario offered by Rebecca, marked by the experience of surprise, seemed above all to create a rich opportunity to speculate about what everybody in the story was thinking. For example, pretend Rebecca's father would be incessantly quizzed by pretend Rebecca: "What did you think when you found Hannah? Did you think I had gone?" At other times when Jeff could not be found, patient and analyst would spend considerable time trying to work out why he was not there and what pretend Rebecca thought about it.

Trickiest to tackle was the narrator's (Rebecca's) experience that, during the games, she, as Hannah or the pretend Rebecca, experienced me as her father, in all the roles I was assigned. There was no instance when Hannah or pretend Rebecca addressed me in any way other than as Daddy. When I spoke as an analyst, Rebecca immediately switched out of the game. When Rebecca needed slight limit-setting, to be dissuaded from leaning too far when looking out of the window, the Hannah game would come to an abrupt halt unless I intervened as the pretend father. I noticed in the countertransference how hard it felt to address my actual role vis-à-vis real Rebecca, as narrator. It seemed impossible to make any observation on why Rebecca might be playing this game. There seemed to be no room for interpretation in this domain, because Rebecca and I were dealing with her experience of an actuality. For Rebecca, and probably for all children at her stage of development, the transference was, at the moment she felt it, not a fantasy but a subjective experience as real as that of a physical object. On one occasion, when Jeff had disappeared, Rebecca was almost in tears. I said, "It is terribly hard for little girls who have never had a father at home to think about fathers who might suddenly disappear, without a clue as to where they might be." I was thus addressing the narrator's, rather than pretend Rebecca's, sadness that her father had gone. Here, Rebecca immediately stopped the game. The next session, Rebecca cheerfully announced that she had met her father and described him as tall, bearded, and bald. I said that yesterday I had muddled and somehow spoiled there being a real father, but Rebecca knew how important it was for them to have him here, and she was helping by bringing another picture of him. For the first time, she cried and eventually said, "You look just like a Daddy, but I know you are my therapist." In this way Rebecca made me recognize the sadness involved in giving up the momentary illusion of the equivalence of thought and reality.

Very gradually I interpreted what was evident from the first time we played this game: Rebecca's unbearable disappointment at realizing that her wish for her grandfather or the analyst to be her real father did not make it true. In the role plays she could explore her confusion about why her father refused to acknowledge paternity and why her mother, who clearly felt guilty and angry, could not discuss the matter with her, and how real it felt to her that if she demanded to see her father, her mother would send her away in anger, as she had the father.

The following vignette illustrates some aspects of the change in the nature of the material. In one session, Rebecca was excited about going to see the musical "Oliver." She claimed that she was only going for the songs, because they were funny, then added "Oliver was lost, very sad you know," and nodded emphatically. I said that I supposed Rebecca wanted to concentrate on the funny parts, because she, like Oliver, so often felt lost and alone. Rebecca then asked, "Do you know that babies are very sad without daddies?" She then asked me to play the giraffe game, with a shadow-puppet daddy giraffe and baby giraffe. The daddy giraffe was expected to teach baby giraffe about jumping, walking, and eating from trees. Although the phallic narcissistic aspects of this game were evident, I only took her enjoyment of this game up in the context of it making her sadness better to feel that the giraffe baby had such a clever giraffe daddy, because she was so sad that she did not have a real Daddy to teach her and that I was not really a proper Daddy to her either. She turned to face me, and, looking at me in a somewhat school-marmish way, she said, "You are just a shadow Daddy."

Psychoanalytic Conceptualization

Most psychoanalytic formulations of therapeutic action share two principal propositions (e.g., Abrams 1987, 1990)—namely, that pathology is associated with the persistence of develop-mentally primitive mental structures, and that psychoanalysis exerts its mutative influence through a process of reorganization and integration of repudiated unconscious mental structures with developmentally higher-order conscious ones. To take one example, Rebecca's fantasy about the mother having driven away or killed the father, wherein the mother is seen as a terrifying monster, was a primitive idea amplified by the projec-tion of Rebecca's own considerable aggression. Rebecca had got stuck with this developmentally primitive, unconscious picture, unmodulated by higher-level thinking. Her analysis helped her to reintegrate the repudiated and threatening phantasies rooted in her father's absence from her life, amplified by oedipal and more regressive omnipotent phantasies, structured to protect her injured narcissism. From a modern Kleinian perspective (e.g., Spillius 1994), one might add that the projective identifica-tion of Rebecca's terrifying envy and rage with the mother (characteristic of the developmentally primitive paranoid-schiz-oid mode of thought), together with her total dependence on her single and rather unpredictable parent, led to a persistent split in her representation of objects and in her own immature ego. Thus, although she was in many ways functioning well, Rebecca was prevented from developing a more integrated view of the mother characteristic of the experience of objects in the depres-sive position (Klein 1935, 1940).

These ways of thinking about Rebecca's difficulties are helpful in understanding aspects of the analytic material. However, it is clear that in most traditional psychoanalytic accounts meta-phors referring to developmental arrest or changes in psychic structures as accounts of pathology and therapeutic action turn out, upon closer scrutiny, to be relatively empty and circular, given the lack of specificity about the ways in which the young child's inner experience differs from that of an older one and how the former places the child at risk of disturbance and the latter may come to the rescue in the context of the psychoanalytic encounter.

Rebecca and Her Analysis: Play and the Self

What do the empirical findings and our model of cognitive development have to say about Rebecca's difficulties and their treatment? Rebecca's behavior was fully symbolic and could not be regarded as "concrete" in any general sense. She initiated pretend play with her analyst and readily accepted the analyst's establishment of the analytic situation as one where pretend play was welcome. She could label and talk about her feelings, dreams, and fantasies and distinguish these from physical reality. She was spontaneous and rarely resorted to clichés that might have raised doubts about her genuine awareness of her inner world. Nevertheless, her mentalizing capacity was in some important respects flawed, and certain changes that took place in the course of therapy resembled those described in empirical studies of the development of the psychic reality of the child between the ages of 3 and 5 years.

While Rebecca would probably have been able to conceive of a sponge that looks like a rock, when it came to accepting that her analyst was both a therapist and someone who looked like a daddy, she retreated from the kind of integration of appearance and reality required by her experience of the transference. Rebecca could *pretend* that her analyst was pretend Rebecca's father and know it was not real. What real Rebecca did not know while playing was that she was playing with an analyst who only felt like a father. For her, the analyst looking and acting like a father was, for that moment, the reality. To question this spoiled the game and led to a devastating sense of loss. This happened through the developmental analogue of the preference for psychic reality over factual reality described by Freud (1912–13) as being characteristic of neurotics. Rebecca was developmentally ready to see the distinction and could use it in circumstances that were less emotionally salient, but she was prevented from fully experiencing it in this context by her intense desire for a real father, for the actualization of the father figure in the transference. At the moment she felt it, the transference was, for Rebecca, and probably for all children at her stage of development, not a fantasy, but a subjective experience as real as that of a physical object. This can, of course, be equally true for many patients at certain times in their analysis, but Rebecca's analysis was, at least initially, completely dominated by the mode of psychic equivalence, where there was no "potential space" (Winnicott 1971) in which the narrator's experience of the analyst as a father could be looked at and understood. Only by playing with reality in analysis, permitting Rebecca to observe the analyst's mental representation of her playing, was she able to develop a tentatively held image of her own desires for a father and see these as wishes that were part of phantasy rather than the outside world. The wishes could then be brought into Rebecca's thinking about external reality.

We suggest that Rebecca could not afford to "play" that she had a father because her mother reacted too severely to this fantasy. The reflection in herself of Rebecca's sadness about her absent father was too real. This may have been the principal reason for Rebecca's initial inability to play that she had a father and for the compulsive, addictive quality of this play when it became possible. Normally the young child tends to adopt a defensive strategy of dealing with unacceptable ideas in the realm of pretense and phantasy, where they can be played with, all connections to actuality removed. Perhaps this is a way in which play can be said to have a vital role in the development of mastery (Freud 1920g)—the reworking of a passive experience into an active one (Drucker 1975). In "pretend" mode ideas cannot threaten; they have lost their equivalence to what is real. However, Rebecca's attempt to decouple phantasy from reality, inner from outer, may have been undermined not just by the intensity of her desires—and her unwillingness to give up the idea of their actuality, but also by her mother's inability to take Rebecca's ideas and feelings into her subjective reality.

Her mother could not tolerate a genuine awareness of Rebecca's frustration and unhappiness because she herself also tended to be stuck (in this area) in a mode of psychic equivalence. The phantasy father, Rebecca's exploration of the idea of a father, was too real and intolerable for her mother. The idea could not be played with or genuinely entertained as a wish. Rebecca arrived at the analytic situation troubled by the "realness" of her psychic reality. Her normal developmental progression was arrested because the intensity of her feelings forced an idea from the pretend but unreal world of fantasy into the part of her mind where mental contents corresponded to physical realities. In these circumstances, we suggest, the pretend mode may be given up by the child in this area, and the idea is forced into the mode of psychic equivalence: it becomes as "real" for the child as it threatened to be for the mother.

The young child, attempting to make the developmental step between a nonrepresentational and a representational mode of psychic reality, is in a highly vulnerable state. The integration of the pretend (representational but unreal) and the actual (nonrepresentational but real) confronts the child with particular difficulties when a representation, made actual, signals danger. While the worlds of pretend and reality are separate, the child's psychic reality can include fantasy representations that would be highly conflictual if their truth or falsity were to be examined in conjunction with the world outside. The fantasy of the sexual possession of the parent of the opposite sex is safe as long as it is held in the pretend mode of psychic reality, where concerns with possibility or impossibility, or relation to physical reality, are absent. Pretend desire, even if conscious, arouses no conflict. Only when the representational mode of pretense comes gradually to be integrated with the experience of psychic reality corresponding to external reality—where the thought suddenly becomes real—do terrifying conflicts arise through the increasingly clear image of the feelings of the other, in seeing the child's wish. Resolution of this dilemma normally arises through the radical restriction of such dangerous fantasies, through the establishment of the repression barrier, first to a pretend mode and later to an unconscious mode of thought.

Internal and external circumstances can conspire to make such a progression difficult, as was the case for Rebecca. Before the two modes of functioning are fully integrated, representations from the pretend mode may become so intensively and actively stimulated that they encroach upon the child's mental world in its mode of psychic equivalence. The absence and unknowability of Rebecca's father may have been such a circumstance. Her belief that her charismatic grandfather was her father acquired the qualities of a fact, making his death a trauma of far greater intensity than it might otherwise have been. The penetration of the psychic barrier between real and pretend, the feeling of actualization that comes to characterize worrying thoughts, the difficulty in discriminating between possibility and certainty, all serve to magnify the small child's anxiety. The acknowledgment of the reality of these experiences for the child is the only therapeutic starting point and a major source of reassurance as it begins the move toward a representational level.

Because Rebecca had no "other" to pretend and reflect with, she was, in a sense, obliged to keep an idea in her mind (the image of her father) that was isomorphic with reality. Rebecca must have found some comfort in the solution that "believing is having." The hurt and shame of being fatherless could not be tolerated and was avoided by retaining this "psychotic island" (Rosenfeld 1971) within her subjective experience. According to Rosenfeld's notion, there is a part of the patient's thinking where the equivalence of subjective experience and physical reality has been retained, but in such a way that subjective experience is projected onto and distorts actual reality, which then, in turn, becomes a source of terrifying anxiety.

Rebecca's metaphor of the snake, which placed her worries outside herself, was a characteristic example of the thought as a concrete physical object. She needed the adult to soften her ideas so that she could herself shape them and create a psychic world that was no longer either pure fantasy or hard reality, but which could cover her entire range of experiences, just as she wished that the "world blanket" would cover all the objects in her internal world. Many might see the image of the snake as a phallic, dangerous, but highly prized possession, perhaps representing the analysis or just the devoted attention of a male adult. The "world blanket" also may have been a protection against anxiety, which increased as her sexual wishes and hopes became more transparent. This view of the material is quite compatible with the perspective we offer, in that we suggest that the reason the sexual wishes were so worrying was that they were experienced in the mode of psychic equivalence. They felt too real to be fantasies. It needed the analyst to recognize that they could be pretend and yet feel real.

As always, then, there was a price to pay, and the comfort of keeping an idea of her father alive could only be short-lived. Her unconscious phantasies of sexual destructiveness and annihilation came with this idea, entering into the real world of psychic equivalence, making them even more real and terrifying. All children have such fantasies, but normally the ideas may be "metabolized" (to borrow Bion's terminology) through play, licensed and supported by the parents, and without consequence. A father sits down during a mock battle, only to be told, "You are the monster—you have to stand up so that I can kill you!" If the father dutifully stands up, he is helping his child to metabolize and work through the murderous phantasy. If he stays sitting down—or especially if he responds to the phantasy with disapproval, anger, sadness, or fear, reinforcing the child's sense that it might become too real—the murderous thoughts remain unmetabolized. They may pass back from the pretend mode to the mode of psychic equivalence, and an opportunity for the child to see his idea as an idea is lost. Rebecca's mother's depression following the death of her own father may well have made it intolerable for her to contemplate Rebecca's feelings of loss at the time that she felt them, and her reaction of real sadness reinstated a mode of psychic equivalence in relation to those thoughts.

The acute separation anxiety that brought Rebecca to analysis in the first place may also be understood as indicating a lack of continuity in the experience of the psychological self. In previous chapters we have described (see also Fonagy, Moran, and Target 1993; Fonagy and Target 1995) a dialectical theory of early self-development, drawing on work by Winnicott and Bion, according to which the infant finds an image of himself, in his mother's mind, as an individual with thoughts and feelings. Winnicott (e.g., 1967) stressed that it is vital for the infant to see a reflection of his *own* state (albeit processed to make it more containable—Bion 1962a, 1962b), not of the *mother's* own fixed preoccupations or defensive maneuvers, when he looks to her for images of himself. Rebecca's mother was, apparently, depressed and angry when Rebecca was born. The baby had not been planned, and the father abandoned the mother in response to news of the pregnancy. Rebecca's mother felt the baby to be a disastrous threat to her independence, destroying her hopes for the future. We suggest that the infant Rebecca, in searching for her mother's picture of her and her states of mind, may have been confronted with the picture of a wrecker, a ruthless invader who steals what is most precious: a pirate, in Rebecca's later frightened image. This idea of the pirate, like the ideas about her father's disappearance, became all too real for Rebecca by becoming part of the world of "psychic equivalence" rather than of play and phantasy.

Rebecca may have clung to her mother not only because of the fear of the destructiveness felt to threaten both of them, but also because the only time Rebecca could get away from the negative "pirate" image of herself, internalized from the early mother, was, paradoxically, when she was with her real, external mother of the present. When with her mother, she could externalize the alien, frightening image of the pirate and retain a clearer, uncontaminated image of herself. When she battled with her mother, as she frequently did, this introjected image no longer obscured Rebecca's self-representation, and she felt obvious relief. The price of this strategy was that Rebecca needed to stay physically close to the object if she was to avoid the image of the pirate emerging as the core experience of herself, as it did in her daytime terrors and nightmares.

So Rebecca's thoughts, about the dangerousness of her own and her mother's aggression and sexuality, seem partly to have blocked the development and integration of the girl's psychic reality and forced her to retain a part of her mind in which thought and actuality were treated as the same. This protected her from anxiety related to her mother's actual angry and rejecting response to her, but it deprived her of another form of protection, which would have followed integration of the two modes of thinking. With this integration, the capacity to mentalize, to see ideas as merely ideas and not facts, to play with different points of view, there comes the capacity to test ideas against reality and therefore to moderate their impact. Insulated from knowledge of what could or could not "really" happen in relation to her anxiety-provoking ideas, Rebecca's terror of her thoughts and feelings in this area was magnified as these repeatedly surfaced, to be experienced as "real."

The same phenomenon emerged in the transference, where the analyst could be either Rebecca's analyst or her father, but never the analyst representing the father. When he drew her attention to the dual reality that he looked like a Daddy but was actually a therapist, Rebecca responded by making the father more real—someone she had really met who really looked like the analyst. However, we can also see how important it was that the analyst could play with Rebecca's ideas and recognize that they were part of her internal world and not external reality. The loss involved in giving up the fulfillment of a wish was balanced, over the course of the analysis, by the reassurance of finding that her fears were fears rather than facts and that, although they could not be mastered by Rebecca alone, they could be played with and made safer in the "potential space" between two minds. Psychoanalysis is in many respects a "pretend" experience. Play is essential to it, just as it is essential to our psychoanalytic model of the developing mind. Analyst and patient discuss fantasies, feelings, and ideas that they "know" at the same time to be false. Klauber (1987) wrote beautifully about this in his paper on transference as an illusion. This refocusing of the role of the analyst highlights the role played by the adult in the child's construction of his own mind and the development of a representation of it (effectively a metarepresentation).

Rebecca was able to arrive at an integration represented by the analyst/father, real as a subjective experience but at the same time known to be a mere idea. In her role play, Rebecca moved the experience of her thoughts and feelings to a developmentally higher level, where these became increasingly differentiated. She repeatedly explored the boundaries of her self-experience, looking at herself from within (as pretend Rebecca) and without (as Hannah) while also constantly monitoring whether she was recognized and understood by the other in the specific role that she herself assigned. Her play allowed her to adopt numerous perspectives, each one offering a test of her imagined place in relation to the object, each self-representation clearly separate and distinct from the internal picture of the object. She adopted the point of view of the third, observing a relationship between herself and the object and thus greatly strengthening the coherence and stability of her representation of herself as she related to others. In this way, she could relinquish the wish reinforced by psychic equivalence and exchange it for the defenses that mentalizing offers to the child. This happens gradually, in ordinary family life or in analysis, not just by addressing particular thoughts but also by addressing thoughts in general. In Rebecca's game, what was important was not simply playing with the idea of an absent father, but setting up a structure where the thoughts and feelings of each person could be imagined and considered. In time, and with much analytic work she became far clearer about the analyst's role. When the analyst mistakenly addressed her shadow game with the daddy giraffe as a consolation for her Oliver Twist feelings of abandonment, she was able to set the analyst right and indicate that she knew that the experience that it created was like a shadow—real yet at the same time illusory.

The background to Rebecca's problems was a state of confusion and ignorance about the actual circumstances of her family, resulting from the mother's unwillingness to contemplate them, which made thinking about the possible feelings of those around her more frightening than usual and made it impossible for her to work her anxieties out without help. In the absence of an adult at home who could help her bridge the gap between inner and outer, she needed another adult, the analyst, to provide the necessary frame for play and reflection.

Thus the analyst's play with the child has an important development—enhancing function. Not only is it his sole route to engaging the child's representational system, but it is also a developmental opportunity for the child to gain better understanding of the nature of mental states. In Rebecca's play, all the characters (eight in all) felt, thought, believed and wished, and their shared world—the consulting-room—brought into sharp contrast their different perceptions, their sometimes painfully incongruent experiences of the world. Naturally their (interpersonal and intrapsychic) conflicts, worries, relationships provided a rich source of material for interpretation as well as insight into Rebecca's perceptions and feelings about the transference as well as the general state of her psychic functioning. But there was something else. Rebecca used her play with the analyst to test out her ideas about how her own mind and the minds of others functioned. When she repeated again and again the scenario where the analyst (as Hannah's father) was startled to find Rebecca where Hannah had been expected, she not only enjoyed the fantasy of a surprise reunion with her father, or the reversal of the normal dominance of grown-up over child, but she also practiced, in a safer context than her home environment normally provided, the experience of the fallibility of adults' beliefs and rejoiced in her awareness of the reestablishment of her existence in the adult's mind.

A DEVELOPMENTAL MODEL OF EARLY OBJECT RELATIONSHIPS AND THE EVOLUTION OF PSYCHIC REALITY

As described above, the caregiver produces intentionality through complex linguistic and interactional processes, primarily through behaving toward the baby and child in such a way that it leads him eventually to postulate that his own behavior may be best understood in terms of ideas and beliefs, feelings and wishes that determine his actions and the reactions of others to him. Unconsciously and pervasively, with her behavior the caregiver ascribes a mental state to the child that is ultimately perceived by the child and internalized, permitting the development of a core sense of mental selfhood. Prototypically in playfulness, the adult adopts the child's mental stance and represents it to him in relation to a third object, held symbolically in mind by both. We assume that this, by and large, is a mundane process, in the sense of happening every day through-out early life, preconscious to both infant and caregiver, inaccessible to reflection or modification. Caregivers, however, differ in their ways of carrying out this most natural of human functions. Some may be alert to the earliest suggestions of intentionality, others may need stronger indications before perceiving the child's mental state and responding to it. Using Vygotsky's (1966) framework, we may conceive of this as the strength of the scaffolding provided for the "artificial development" of the child's understanding of his own mind. We may assume, as do most cognitivists working in this area, that the development of a theory of mind is canalized, in Waddington's (1966) use of the term, but the canal is dug not by biology, but by infant–parent interaction.

We suggest that the symbiotic relation of caregiver and infant structures the emergence of the psychological self, the "I" of intentional ascriptions. Knowledge of minds and the intentional stance arise out of a phase when the mental worlds of child and caregiver overlap. This intersubjective state does not necessarily imply the experience or even phantasy of fusion between the child and caregiver, yet both the child and the mother are in a state of primary preoccupation, building intimate knowledge of the other parallel to their knowledge of themselves. The developing child's perception of mental states in himself and others thus depends on his sense of the *psychic reality* of his caregiver. Understanding the nature of the mental world cannot be done alone—it requires understanding of the self in the eye of the other.

We suggest that where the parent is unable to incorporate and think about a piece of reality and cannot then enable the child to do so safely through playing with the frightening ideas, this reality remains to be experienced in the mode of psychic equivalence. Neither child nor parent can "metabolize" the thoughts, and the "unthinkable" thoughts are passed on from one generation to the next. On an everyday scale, Rebecca's mother could not help her with the unacceptable reality of her fatherless situation. On a massive scale, traumas such as Holocaust experiences may be passed on, or not, depending on the parents' capacity to allow the trauma to be part of shared reality, which can be thought and talked about, not only relived as a continuing and fixed reality.

Once the child can mentalize, he has available a crucial attenuating function for psychic experience. He is able to manipulate mental representations to defensively bar or modify perceptions of reality. The neurotic child fails to achieve a full integration of the "actual" and "pretend" modes into a representational framework, and certain ideas retain the immediacy of external reality. Before the integration of the two modes is achieved, the child is vulnerable to all kinds of appearances, particularly in relation to adults around them. By mentalizing, attributing ideas and feelings to himself and to others, the child makes his human world more explicable to himself. Until he is able to step beyond appearance and grasp the distinction between this and the mental state that might underpin it, he remains vulnerable to the immediate emotional reaction of his object. Inconsistency or hostility in the object's behavior may then be taken at face value as showing something bad about him. In contrast, if the child is able to attribute a withdrawn, unhappy mother's apparently rejecting behavior to her emotional state—of depression, or anger about some external circumstances—rather than to himself as bad and unstimulating, the child may be protected from lasting injury to his view of himself.

Our acceptance of a dialectical perspective of self-development shifts the traditional psychoanalytic emphasis from the internalization of the containing object to the internalization of the thinking self from within the containing object. This is what makes such concepts as thinking inherently intersubjective. Shared experience is part of the "very logic" (Sellars 1963, p. 189) of mental-state concepts. All analytic work with young children contains an element of this developmental process, and some patients' treatment may be almost entirely focused on the elaboration of the self as a mental or psychological entity. The reflective aspect of the analytic process is understanding and not simply empathy (the accurate mirroring of mental state). In order to move the child from the mode of psychic equivalence to the mentalizing mode, analytic reflection, of whatever orientation, cannot just "copy" the child's internal state—it has to move beyond it and go a step further, offering a different, yet experientially appropriate, re-presentation. The analyst's mind acts as scaffolding (Vygotsky 1966) designed to enhance the development of representation in the child's psychic reality by being constantly one step ahead of the child's experience of his mental self. Thus child psychoanalysis is more than just the removal of obstacles to mentalization. It is the exercise of a developmental universal in pure form. The analyst must begin by acknowledging the compelling reality of the child's experience, entering into the pretend world, and only gradually showing him, through contact with his mental experience, that it is a set of representations that can be shared, played with, and changed.

7

Marked Affect-Mirroring and the Development of Affect-Regulative Use of Pretend Play

Chapter 6 proposed a psychoanalytic model for the development of full subjectivity, closely linked to the quality of interaction between parent and child. A clinical illustration was offered to show that, for internal reality to be experienced as truly representational rather than as either totally real or totally unreal, the object's mirroring of the child's internal reality, preferably in a playful manner, was a prerequisite. In this chapter, the psychological underpinnings of the processes involved in playful mirroring interactions between child and caregiver are elaborated in the context of a further case report. It is argued that the specific features of interactions that effect a change in the quality of internal representation involve the caregiver creating "marked externalizations" of the child's internal states with the key qualities of separating or decoupling internal experience from physical reality, offering a sense of control over the experience and potentially modifying the content of the experience in the direction of increased pleasure or wish fulfillment. Marked parental mirroring in the context of pretend play or empathic pro-social actions offer early opportunities for the infant to encode features of markedness of expressions (signaling "nonconsequentiality" and decoupling from physical reality), content modifications (leading to reduction of unpleasure and wish fulfillment), and the enhancement of agentive aspects (which exert control and mastery over affective experience). Such interactions may provide important experiential preconditions that facilitate the emergence of the active use of these features for emotional self-regulation by the infants themselves.

We argue that the absence of parental mirroring can lead to a developmental arrest at the level of psychic equivalence. The absence of "markedness" in the caregiver's response can lead to affective dysregulation, which ultimately results in a fear of externalization on the part of the child: he becomes reluctant to enter social interactions where mirroring would be expected from the caregiver. This discourages the child from seeking social experiences that might correct this developmental deviation. We present a case of a 4-year-old child where therapeutic intervention appeared to have the power to supplement the child's psychosocial deprivation. A cognitive analysis of the treatment is used as a springboard for understanding a facet of what might be effective in the psychoanalytic therapeutic process for adolescents and adults as well.

INTRODUCTION

In previous chapters we have proposed two closely related developmental theories about the relationship between understanding the representational nature of minds and affect regulation—the theory of psychic equivalence and the pretend mode of mentalizing on the one hand (chapter 6), and the social biofeedback theory of parental affect-mirroring on the other (chapter 4). From a historical point of view, both of these theories can be seen as present-day elaborations within the framework of theory-of-mind development of Freud's original proposals about the nature of psychic reality (Freud 1900a, 1950 [1895]) and about the role of pretend play in affective life (Freud 1920g).

The first theory, put forward in chapter 6, distinguishes between two basic types of representational functioning: the "psychic equivalence" and the "pretend" modes of representing internal experience, which antedate the full development of the capacity for mentalization (see also Fonagy 1995b; Fonagy and Target 1996; Target and Fonagy 1996). "Psychic equivalence" refers to the more primitive level of mental functioning, where internal mind states such as thoughts, fantasies, and feelings are confused with and experienced as reality and not as representations of reality. In contrast, the "pretend" mode of mentalizing involves an awareness of the representational nature of internal mind states: by separating or "decoupling" (Leslie 1987) the mental representations from reality, the child can differentiate thoughts and fantasies from actual reality, although on his own he can create no useful connection between this representation and physical reality. The theory holds that the development of mentalization is a function of the quality of early attachment experiences, as the integration of the "pretend" and "equivalence" modes occurs principally in the course of repeated experiences of interactions with a playful caregiver who reflects the child's feelings and thoughts in a "marked" manner. The theory also considers the role that these two levels of mental functioning play in the development of normal and psychopathological forms of affect regulation and self-organization and uses the Gergely–Watson social biofeedback model of the development of emotional self-awareness (see chapter 4).

The second theory, originally developed by Gergely and Watson (1996) and described here in chapter 4, proposes a specific, contingency-based psychological mechanism (the "social biofeedback model of parental affect-mirroring") that explains how empathic affect-regulative mirroring interactions within the attachment context contribute ontogenetically to the establishment of second-order representations of affect states and their adaptive use in more mature forms of affective self-regulation. The theory also outlines specific hypotheses about how a lack or deviant forms of early affect-regulative mirroring interactions by attachment figures may be involved in the etiology of affective and dissociative disorders and pathologies of the self (see chapters 4 and 5).

In this chapter, we present a clinical case that illustrates the explanatory relevance of these two theories for our understanding of the ontogenesis of certain pathologies of the self that involve deficits in mentalization and affect regulation. The case vignette also sheds some light on how these theories can lead to an understanding of the psychological processes through which psychotherapeutic interventions may induce corrective change in representational functioning in such patients. Before turning to the case material, however, we shall first take a closer look at an important key concept that plays a crucial role in both of our theories and that also looms large in the case study to be discussed: namely, the concept of *"marked externalizations"* of affectively charged internal mental contents. We briefly discuss the characteristics and functional properties of the construct and identify its different forms—such as pretend play, fiction, art, fantasy, daydreaming, or imagination—encountered in mature representational functioning. Finally, we discuss the representational and experiential prerequisites for the unfolding ability to use marked externalizations for affective self-regulation and outline our central developmental hypotheses about the role that contingent affect-regulative mirroring interactions play in the development of this ability.

"MARKED EXTERNALIZATIONS"
AND AFFECTIVE SELF-REGULATION

Humans have evolved a unique mental capacity for representing the intentionality—that is, "aboutness"—of symbols, such as language, pictorial representations, conventional gestures, and so on. This ability is widely used by humans to externalize their mental contents (such as their beliefs, desires, intentions, and emotions) in order to communicate with each other—that is, to exchange culturally relevant information with other members of their species that fosters survival. However, throughout this book we have emphasized that apart from communicating knowledge, this vital representational ability also serves a rather different evolutionary function: people often externalize their affectively charged mental contents in order to *regulate*—maintain, modify, reduce, or intensify—*their affective states.* Evidently, one can externalize both positive and negative affective impulses in the service of emotion regulation (cf. Stern 1985).

Nonetheless, historically at least, clinicians have been particularly interested in their patients' tendency to use different forms of externalizations to "get rid of" or modify their *negative* affect states. These states could arise from painful memories of traumatic life events, from—conscious or unconscious—mental representations of (real or fantasized) interpersonal conflicts and interactions, or from socially unacceptable desires that generate painful feelings of anxiety, helplessness, guilt, shame, anger, fear, rage, and so on.

The clinical meaning of the term "externalization," however, is rather broad, as it includes phenomena such as projection, projective identification, enactment, and acting out. In all these instances, the internal experience that is being externalized for affect-regulative purposes appears to be perceived by the individual as being part of actual external reality and as not belonging to the self. We would like to distinguish cases of externalizations that involve a defensive distortion of reality perception from cases such as pretend play, symbolic drawing and painting, theater and drama, listening to fairy tales, creating art, fantasizing, or daydreaming, where the affect-regulative function of externalization is fulfilled without undermining reality testing. In such cases the externalized affective content is clearly understood to be "not for real": it is conceptualized as being "decoupled" from reality (Leslie 1987), as being (only) a *representation* of reality (Perner 1991) that belongs to a *fictional* world instead of the real one. We use the terms "marked externalizations" and "symbolic externalizations" to refer only to the latter types of expressions of internal contents, where the subject always maintains some level of awareness and understanding of the representational nature of the externalized symbolic form.

When interpreting such externalized expressions, their representation needs to become somehow "tagged" or "marked" as being only a "representation" of reality in order to avoid confusion with actual reality. Earlier we have argued that in the cases of pretend play as well as of the affect-reflective parental mirroring displays discussed in chapters 4 and 6, the negative emotional contents of the child's mind are externalized in a perceptually clearly "marked" form that signals that the externalization is "not for real." Take the case of pretend play: here *markedness* is conveyed by a series of salient perceptual features that distinguish a pretend action or pretend emotion expression from a realistic one. Knowing looks, slightly tilted head, high pitch and slowed down, exaggerated intonation contour, schematic, abbreviated, or only partial execution of action schemes, and the use of invisible imaginary objects all clearly and saliently mark for the child that the pretend expression is categorically different from its realistic equivalent—that it is "not for real." We have argued (see chapter 4) that in the case of adaptive parental affect-mirroring interactions, the affect-reflective emotion display is also modified by the same kinds of transformations of the corresponding realistic emotion display resulting in a saliently different, marked form of emotion expression. As a result, while the affective content of the mirroring display will be recognized by the child, it will not be attributed to the parent as her real emotion: it will be interpreted as "not for real." This reality-decoupled interpretation is further reinforced by the experienced "*nonconsequentiality*" of marked expressions and actions, both in pretense and in empathic mirroring: the normally experienced typical consequences that would be expected to follow the realistic, unmarked form of the same expression do not ensue when the perceived display or action is performed in a "marked" pretend mode. We have hypothesized (see chapter 4 and Gergely and Watson 1996) that the perception of markedness activates the young child's metarepresentational system (Leslie 1987), which allows for the "decoupling" of the expression from its referents in actual reality. The ensuing understanding of the marked pretense or affect-mirroring display as referring to a fictional world and, as such, as having no realistic consequences contributes crucially to affect regulation. The child feels safe in the "decoupled," fictional world of representational reenactment in which no realistic negative outcomes can occur (Gergely and Watson 1996).

Freud's (1920g) famous analysis of the "*fort–da*" pretend game of his 18-month-old grandson highlights some further important features of the use of marked externalizations that foster affective coping with negative affect. He observed his grandson playing out repeatedly the very same event, which involved throwing a bobbin of thread over the curtain of his crib, saying "*fort*"

[away] as the object disappeared from sight and then retrieving it, saying *"da"* [back]. According to Freud's interpretation, in the first event of the pretend episode (*"fort"*) the child was externalizing the separations from his mother that inevitably occurred in the course of their daily lives. The second part of the sequence (*"da"*), however, corresponded to a wishful imaginary undoing of these painful separations. The externalized pretend version differed from the internally represented traumatic event encoded in memory in that during the reenactment the child was an *active agent who was in control* over the unfolding of the pretend episode, whereas during the actual event as represented in his memory he was a helpless subject, passively experiencing the traumatizing separation event. This resulted in an emotionally corrective experience insofar as the perception of the qualitatively transformed, marked externalization of the originally traumatic event generates positive affects of agency and reunion that counteract the negative emotions associated with the original event memory. This type of self-controlled modified reenactment within the safe "pretend mode" of a fictional representational world provides, therefore, an effective way of helping to cope with the painful memory of the traumatic event.

Up to now we have discussed two types of phenomena exemplifying what we called "marked externalizations": empathic parental affect-mirroring and pretend play. In both cases the marked expressions of the child's internal affective contents are, indeed, "externalized": they are perceived by the child as external events "out there" in the world. (The same is true, of course, in the case of "symbolic externalizations" using external media of expression such as drawings, paintings, sculptures, or protagonists in a play.) However, there are also other ways of expressing one's internal affective contents for self-regulative purposes that involve purely mentally generated subjective "internal events" that are perceived only introspectively, as in daydreaming, fantasizing, and imagination. (Pretend play and discussions with an imaginary partner exemplify a truly "mixed" form of externalization and internal imagery.)

In chapter 11 on mentalized affectivity dealing with forms of affect regulation in adult patients, we develop the concept of "inward expression of affects" that involves self-reflective and introspective apprehension and awareness of one's own emotions as those are expressed and represented to oneself in one's mind. We wish to argue that these "inner forms of self-reflective emotional experiences" belong to the same category of "marked" and "symbolic externalizations" as pretend play and empathic affect-mirroring, except for the fact that they use an internal—rather than external—medium of representation for the affect-regulative expression of primary emotional experiences. The three features that we identified as contributing to the emotionally corrective affect-regulative experience in marked externalizations—perceptual markedness, transformation of the role of the experiencer from passive subject into active agent, and content modification—can also be found in daydreaming, fantasy, and imagination. In fact, these "internal expressions" are also perceived (in the "mind's eye") as decoupled and representational in nature (markedness). As such, they are not confused with the actual emotional experience they inwardly express: the introspecting subject remains aware that these internal affect expressions are "not for real." In the same vein, inward expressions of emotionally charged event memories or fantasies can be actively controlled by the subject and their contents can be modified willfully, just as in the case of externally represented pretend play.

From a developmental point of view, we hypothesize that marked externalizations of internal affective contents using an external medium of expression precede and pave the way for the development of forms of purely "inward expressions" of affect states in the service of affective self-regulation. In particular, it is noteworthy that in empathic parental affect-mirroring the act of externalization, the perceptual marking of the expression, and the partial modification of its content (as in the case of partial mirroring or presenting "mixed emotions"—cf. Fónagy and Fonagy 1995) are all carried out by the mirroring adult, not by the infant. In this case, even the infant's sense of control and agency over the ensuing affect-regulative experience is generated automatically by the detection of the high degree of contingent relatedness between the baby's emotion expressions and the mirroring display. Therefore, we suggest that repeated experience with affect-regulative parental mirroring may provide infants with an early proto-form of marked externalizations at an age when they are as yet unable on their own to generate marked externalizations of their internal affective states. Thus, we believe that early opportunities to encode the markedness (signaling "nonconsequentiality" and decoupling from physical reality), the content modifications (leading to reduction of unpleasure and wish fulfillment), and the agentive aspects of parental mirroring displays (exerting control and mastery), together with the establishment of an association between these features and the ensuing affect-regulative experience, may provide important experiential preconditions that facilitate the emergence of the active use of these features for emotional self-regulation by the infants themselves (as in pretend play or empathic pro-social actions appearing during the second year of life—see chapter 5).

BIOLOGICAL AND SOCIAL DETERMINANTS OF THE AFFECT-REGULATIVE USE OF "MARKED EXTERNALIZATIONS"

From the representational point of view, all of these different—external and internal—forms of intentional self-expressions are *metarepresentational* in nature (Leslie 1987): they presuppose the availability of *second-order representations* (Dennett 1991; Dennett and Haugeland 1987) and the ability to "decouple" representations from reality (Leslie 1987, 1994). It is precisely for that reason that all these different forms of self-expressions of primary affective contents have the potential to be used for affective self-regulation: they can be experienced as "not for real" and as "nonconsequential," they provide an experience of safety and agency through the exertion of control, and they can generate corrective emotional "rewriting" of the negative affect memory by reexperiencing it in the marked "as-if" mode with a modified emotional content.

From this view it follows that lacking second-order representations to express internal affective states or lacking the metarepresentational capacity for referential decoupling can be expected to lead to an impoverished or nonexistent understanding of intentional mental states—such as beliefs and desires—in the self and others. Such a primary deficit in theory of mind is the central feature of the debilitating condition of "mindblindness" (Baron-Cohen 1995) that is characteristic of the disorder of childhood autism. A further predictable consequence that we wish to emphasize here is the lack of *affective impulse control* that is also highly typical of children with autism (see Hobson 1993). The mental capacity to represent second-order representations and the related ability for referential decoupling may well turn out to be innate adaptations of the human mind (Fodor 1992; Leslie 1987, 1994) that may be genetically impaired in childhood autism (Baron-Cohen et al. 1985; U. Frith 1989).

However, even if the innate representational abilities necessary for theory of mind were intact, our view is that certain types of dysfunctional early attachment environments may still result in a delayed or impoverished unfolding of the capacity to mentalize and/or in an acquired inhibition of its adaptive use for affective self-regulation. The case for a partially psychosocial model of the development of mentalization was made in chapter 3 against the background of behavior-genetics research. There are several causal pathways through which deviant patterns of affective reactivity within the attachment context may lead to acquired deficits or developmental arrests in the unfolding of the functional use of early mentalization capacities.

1.   As hypothesized in chapter 4 (see also Gergely and Watson 1996), through processes of social biofeedback, the infant-attuned affect-mirroring environment may play an important role in establishing differentiated emotion representations through sensitization to emotion-specific patterns of internal-state cues. Furthermore, already during the preverbal stage adaptive affect-mirroring may provide an early opportunity for establishing second-order representations of primary affect states in the form of internalized representations of the marked mirroring displays that the infant comes to associate with the contingent internal affect state. Serious absence of such adaptive mirroring within the attachment context may, therefore, result in undifferentiated internal affective states, in impoverished awareness of emotional self-states, and in a tendency to confuse internal mind states

with external reality. In other words, it may lead to a *developmental arrest at the level of "psychic equivalence" functioning* where mental states and reality states remain confused and undifferentiated.

2. Deviant mirroring exchanges that involve externalization of the infant's negative affects in the form of unmarked and realistic negative emotional reactions of the caregiver may lead to escalation rather than modulation in the baby's negative affect state. This can establish a strong association between externalizations of negative internal contents and consequent dysequilibration and traumatization. Such an attachment environment can lead to a *generalized avoidance of externalization as a means of self-regulation*, resulting in serious problems of impulse control. Furthermore, learning about the significance of perceptual cues of markedness as signaling referential decoupling and nonconsequentiality (i.e., acquiring the generalized communicative code of the pretend mode as indicating decoupling from reality) may become seriously delayed and impoverished. This would lead to a kind of "blindness to markedness," leading to a tendency to confuse pretense with reality.

CLINICAL ILLUSTRATION: "MAT"

Mat was brought to psychotherapy by his mother at 4.1 years of age with a series of behavioral and impulse-control problems. In his mother's view the most serious of these was failure to achieve toilet training by 4 years of age and the child's strong tendency to withhold his feces. Mat would obstipate for several days, would refuse to pass stool sitting on the toilet, and would oblige only if given a diaper. His mother also complained bitterly about Mat's uncontrollable emotional outbursts, frequent tantrums, and externalizing violent behavior, both at the day-care center and at home. He often attacked smaller children at the day-care center, and he tortured his dog at home. He was also described as being obstinate, oppositional, and controlling ("giving orders") in his relationship with his mother. Mat's mother complained that he was always asking "silly questions," which indicated serious castration anxiety, fantasies of physical intrusion, a phobic fear of babies, and an anxious interest in Cesarean births.

Mat was a sickly child, with a history of illnesses (croup, a form of acute respiratory distress in children, pneumonia, allergies) and hospitalizations. Following the pediatrician's advice, his mother stayed at home with him for the first three years of his life. He started to go to day-care only shortly before starting therapy and only for the morning hours. Mat showed an anxious, ambivalent attachment attitude to his mother, clinging to her yet avoiding her gaze at the same time. He exhibited strong separation anxiety when left in day-care or when entering my room for therapy.[1]

Mat's mother was a stiff, poker-faced woman with flat emotionality who, nevertheless, did not hesitate to convey to me her exasperation, dissatisfaction, and often openly hostile feelings (including anger and disgust) toward her son. She was rather dismissive of her child, whom she described as hopelessly spoiled and worthless. She was cold, intrusive, and overcontrolling in her interactions with Mat. She told me that she often "lost her head," shouting at him and beating him up. They lived in a closely symbiotic relationship that was dominated by aggression, rage, and often escalating negative affects. She struck me as being remarkably incapable of feeling empathy or attunement to her child's mental states, and as being in general quite unable to cope with her son's negative emotions. When faced with Mat's negative affective displays, she often reacted with complementary and realistic negative emotions herself, which typically led to an escalation of the child's negative state.

A good example of this is her description of the recurring pattern of interaction in relation to Mat's willful refusal to open his bowels. When left in the nursery by his mother, Mat would refuse to pass stool, but when he was picked up by her in the afternoon, he could hardly withhold it on the way home. At home she would make him sit on the toilet and would sit down next to him herself. He would, however, refuse to pass stool (even though often in pain), and they would be sitting there like this

---

[1] The therapist was György Gergely.

"for hours." She would get more and more angry with him and would plead with him to do it, reinforcing her pleas by threatening him with punishments and by making promises. Eventually, she would become deeply resentful, put diapers on Mat, place him in his crib, and attempt to leave the room. Facing the prospect of separation, however, Mat would then promptly soil his diapers. This would outrage his mother, because she would need to come back and change him. At this point she would often shout at him and hit him in her rage.

I had the strong impression that Mat's mother was quite incapable of attending to and reading the dispositional displays that would allow her to identify her child's mental states. This was corroborated by the almost incredible story about Mat's older sister that Mat's mother shared with me in a rather casual tone of voice. Mat's sister was born practically blind, but this fact went unnoticed by her parents for several years. They found out about her condition only when at around the age of 3 or 4 years she was taken to a routine medical checkup in her nursery school. Both parents had apparently missed the girl's almost total inability to see them clearly unless very close and directly facing them. This made me wonder about the seriousness of this dismissive mother's insensitivity to and lack of monitoring of the dispositional facial cues of her children.

For a long time Mat showed seriously regressive functioning during therapy sessions. When he arrived, he would be extremely frightened, crying and clinging to his mother and trying to stop her from going out to the waiting-room. Mat was clumsy and somewhat dirty and smelly; he breathed heavily, continually salivated slightly, and was easily frightened of small sounds. He would disregard my presence and avoid eye contact with me, and he would not react verbally or otherwise to my attempts at making contact with him. He only spoke to me when giving orders. Here, we will concentrate on two pathological features of Mat's behavior that became increasingly apparent during the early phases of the therapy.

One was Mat's inadequate and sometimes bizarre use of language. He did not obey the implicit pragmatic rules (Grice 1975) underlying normal communicative exchanges: he would very often not respond to verbal inquiries but would sometimes repeat the question in a monotonous, echolalic fashion. When speaking, he would sometimes mix up the first-, second-, and third-person pronouns in his sentences. His interpretations were concretistic and literal, and he often used words with obscure, idiosyncratic meanings and interpreted expressions independently of their context of use.

The second strikingly dysfunctional feature was the fact that Mat seemed *incapable of either producing or understanding symbolic play and pretense.* His play activities consisted solely of repetitive, stereotypic actions using mainly wooden building blocks to make towers and roads. He was fascinated with toy cars, which he pushed back and forth between the wooden structures. However, for the most part he avoided using figurative toys such as dolls, and he did not engage in any pretend activities. My efforts at engaging him in symbolic play were generally futile. In fact, Mat showed a clear aversion to human or animal toy figures and would turn away from them or throw them away when they were offered to him. According to his mother, he never played with figurative toys at home either: he was only interested in computer games and in building blocks. He never had a transitional object. His paintings were composed of diffuse lines and smeared paint, without any discernible figurative content.

It also soon became clear that Mat had serious difficulties with interpreting pretend activities and communications and had trouble understanding the marked, exaggerated pretend mode of expressions. For example, while he was painting, I pointed at the orange-colored water in his cup and said: "Look, it's just like orange juice!" He looked up with fright and said: "But you cannot drink that!" "Of course I can," I replied jokingly, with a marked pretend intonation and raising the cup to my mouth, obviously pretending to drink the "orange juice." Mat became even more frightened (apparently believing that I was actually drinking the painting water) and shouted: "Don't do that, it cannot be drunk!" On another occasion I took out a puppet figure of a fox and asked Mat if he wanted to play with the puppet. He said immediately that he didn't. But I proceeded to animate the puppet, making it walk around while speaking with a "foxy" marked intonation. Mat looked at the fox with intense fear, as if it had really come alive. Then, nearly crying, he begged me to stop, almost shouting that he didn't like puppets. A final example: in one session, Mat and I played a board game in which one could win small treasure chests when arriving at certain positions. Without following the rules of the game, Mat always put his pieces on the winning positions and collected all the treasure chests, while I received nothing. I pretended to cry (in a clearly marked manner), complaining that I didn't get any treasure. Mat looked at me with fright, shouting: "Don't do that! Only babies cry! You are not a baby!"

Both Mat's inability to understand or produce pretend play and his dysfunctions of language use described above are core features of the symptomatology of childhood autism. Other features of Mat's pathology, such as his difficulties with impulse control, his tendency for tantrums, his perseverative, repetitive, and stereotypic object-manipulative activities with nonfigurative objects, his lack of eye contact, and his obsessive interest in vehicles, were also suggestive of a possible autistic disorder. Children with autism seem to lack the metarepresentational ability for "decoupling" (Baron-Cohen et al. 1985; Leslie 1994) that is argued to be a representational prerequisite both for understanding intentional mental states in others such as false beliefs and for understanding pretense (Leslie 1987). In normal development, children start to understand and produce pretend play by the end of the second year (Harris and Kavanaugh 1993), and they pass the so-called false-belief theory-of-mind tasks (Wimmer and Perner 1983) by 4 years of age (see chapter 5). Children with autism, however, tend to fail on these tasks even at a significantly higher mental age than 4 years. The related ability to distinguish appearance from reality (understanding that something looks like X, but is really Y) also emerges at around 4 years of age (Flavell et al. 1987). I tested Mat on two versions of the standard false-belief tasks as well as on a standard appearance–reality task at 4.6 and at 5.0 years (an age at which normal children already pass these tasks). He failed each time, showing a clear lack of understanding of false beliefs as well as of the appearance–reality distinction.

While this provided potentially supporting evidence for the possibility that Mat was, in fact, autistic, this early suspicion was clearly refuted by later developments in the therapy, when his previously dormant ability to understand and use pretend play started to emerge. In the light of these developments, it became clear that his pervasive difficulties with understanding and producing symbolic play and pretense were not due to a genetically based lack of metarepresentational competence, but had a psychosocial origin. We believe that Mat was arrested in his development functioning at the level of "psychic equivalence" (cf. Fonagy and Target 1996 and chapter 6) because of the deviant and traumatizing affect-mirroring environment that his mother provided him with. But before expanding this hypothesis, let us briefly describe two disturbing episodes from Mat's therapy that, we believe, illustrate well our hypothesis that Mat's mental functioning was arrested at the level of psychic equivalence.

Traumatizing "Reality-Play": Functioning at the Level of Psychic Equivalence

At the beginning stages of the therapy there were, in fact, two occasions when it proved possible to engage Mat in "playing" using figurative, symbolic toys that depicted human persons. However, on both occasions Mat showed a clear lack of understanding of the "as-if" nature of the situation, confusing play with reality and experiencing the aggressive and anxious fantasies externalized in the play as actual reality of (re)traumatizing intensity. As a result, during these play episodes he became more and more excited, fearful, aggressive, and anxiety-ridden. These negative affects escalated to such traumatic intensity that for weeks to come Mat avoided the toys and even the corner of the room where these play episodes had taken place.

During the first episode, I called Mat's attention to a toy bathroom at the corner of the room. In it there was a bathtub, a toilet, and—for some accidental reason—an oven. There was also a large chunk of playdough at hand and two (a smaller and a larger) naked baby dolls. Mat first took one of the dolls and put it in the bathtub. Then he took it out and made it sit on the toilet to make it poop. I called his attention to the chunk of playdough and told him he could make poop out of it if he wanted to. Mat tore off a piece excitedly and placed it in the toilet under the doll. He then found a toy spatula, showed it to me, and asked me what it was for. I told him, but he refused my explanation with a definite "no." He started to use the spatula to cut pieces off the chunk of playdough and said: "This is for putting the big poop into them!" He then took the doll from the toilet and stuck the "poop" he had cut off with the spatula to its bottom. He took another piece of playdough, one end of which looked elongated and "spiky." "This is the big spiky poop!" he said excitedly and, wheezing heavily, he stuck it to the bottom of the other doll. "Is the first one done yet?"—I asked. "No, no, he needs to poop a lot, he is going to stay there until Spring!"—Mat said. Then he took the small doll off the toilet and put the big doll on instead to make it poop as well. He started to squeeze the small doll with its bottom forward into the oven, shouting: "We will cook his bottom!" He then took the "cooked" small doll out of the oven and tried to squeeze in the large one, but didn't quite succeed. So he put it into the bathtub instead. "Is he taking a bath?"—I asked. "No, he is dead!"—he answered. "How did he die?" "From the fire and the water, from the fire and the water!!!"—he shouted in uncontrollable excitement, his whole body shaking. Then he put the other doll back into the oven: "We'll cook his bottom, too, and so he will die as well!" "Who are these children?—I asked him. "Johnny and Mat"—he said (Johnny was his friend at the nursery).

At the beginning of the second episode some two months later, I called Mat's attention to a large painted Russian doll that could be taken apart to reveal a smaller doll inside, which again could be taken apart to reveal an even smaller doll, and so on. Mat was very interested; he put the dolls back and then took them apart again. He then said: "I've seen a lot of babies on TV; they were all crippled: they didn't have hands, and legs, and ears, and they didn't have a weenie!" He laughed in excitement and ran to the dolls placed on a shelf to look for one with a penis. He found one, ran with it to the corner of the room where the toy bathroom was with the oven that was used in the first traumatizing "reality-play." He opened the oven, looking for the small doll that he had "cooked to death" in it two months earlier. He took the doll with the penis and started to shout: "I'm giving him an injection into his weenie, and into his bottom, and into his arm," and so on. He used a sharp pencil as his needle and injected the different parts of the doll with increasing excitement. "Did you also get an injection?"—I asked him. "Yes, into my arm"—he said. He then ordered me to inject the doll's bottom while he was wildly poking his pencil into its penis. Then he shouted out: "Let's cut up his stomach and take out the baby!" He continued to give shots to the doll, more and more wildly, until the pencil broke. "Now we'll put a nail into his weenie! . . . Nailed baby!!!"—he cried. "We'll heat him up! . . . We'll give him a cold shower!!!"—he shouted as he was pressing a toy pretzel (the "cold shower") as hard as he could into the doll's nailed penis.

Moving to the Pretend Mode of Functioning:
The Discovery of the Affect-Regulative Potentials
of Markedness and Pretend Play

After about six months Mat's behavior and metacommunication started to show signs of qualitative improvement. He was much less disorganized, his speech cleared up and showed much less confusion and fewer idiosyncratic elements, he held and even initiated eye contact, and he seemed to start to enjoy coming to the sessions. These changes coincided with a remarkable play episode in which he seemed to have "discovered" the meaning of the marked "as-if" mode of expressions and the affect-regulative potentials of the pretend mode of functioning. This episode clearly changed the course of the therapy.

We were playing the board game mentioned before in which small treasure chests could be won. Disregarding both me and the rules of the game, Mat threw his dice and collected as many treasure chests as he could again and again, while I got nothing. This was the occasion when I pretended to cry a little, with a clearly marked, exaggerated "as-if" intonation. Mat became very frightened and told me to stop because only babies cry, and I was not a baby. I stopped immediately and tried to calm Mat by explaining gently that I wasn't really sad and wasn't really crying—that I was just pretending to cry. Mat looked at me attentively and for a long time, as if slowly understanding (maybe for the first time) what was meant by these words. He seemed to calm down and continued to play. At the next session he came in with a broad smile on his face and announced immediately that he wanted to play the board game again. When it was my turn, Mat looked at me smiling and told me that he remembered that last time I was sad, but now I didn't need to be sad any more because he would let me go directly to the position where I can get the treasure chests. Then he pointed at the bolted door of the tower on the board game that was guarded by a dragon and said: "This is where we need to go in and save the woman!" "Aren't you afraid of the dragon?"—I asked him. "No, together we shall kill it!"—Mat said, smiling. Then he again asked me whether I was sad. I answered that indeed I was feeling a bit sad, and I pretended to cry a little. He watched me "crying" with fascination and then consoled me by helping me win some more treasure. He then went directly to the tower, killed the dragon, and saved the "woman."

When we finished playing, Mat found another board game: a game somewhat like checkers. He asked me how to play it, and I told him that if he stepped over my piece, I would "die" and would have to take my piece off the board. Mat then stepped over my piece and took it off the board, watching me carefully and asking whether I was sad to have died. Guessing what he expected me to do, I pretended to cry a little. Mat smiled broadly and told me: "Don't be sad, but step over me, and then I shall die!" "And you won't be sad?"—I asked. "No, because I *like* to die!"—he answered cheerfully.

We went on playing these two games repeatedly for a few months. We developed several variations on the same theme: one of us would get into some kind of trouble, pretend to be sad and cry or even die, until the other invariably came to the rescue. The themes always had to do with dying and coming alive, getting into trouble and being saved, getting wounded and being cured, becoming sad and being cheered up. Mat enjoyed these games enormously. It was as if he had discovered a whole new world: the world of "as-if" reality.

During our last session we played a new board game in which we were hunters in the jungle. "You are the Mother-hunter, and I am the Father-hunter," Mat said. As usual, we got into all sorts of trouble again and again, but each was invariably saved by the other. At the end of the hour I wanted to escort Mat to the waiting-room (we had to pass through two doors and go up a staircase). Mat said: "No, stay here, I'll go on my own." I followed him from a distance and saw how he met his surprised mother on his own, smiling broadly and telling her: "When I grow up, I'll be a hunter, and I'll shoot a rabbit!" His mother never brought him to therapy again.

DISCUSSION

We believe that Mat's case illustrates well our theory of the role of markedness as a vehicle of affective self-regulation, both in affect-mirroring interactions and in imaginary pretend play. It also helps us illustrate our hypothesis that adaptive mirroring of negative affects may play an important role in the young child's transition in representational functioning from the level of psychic equivalence to a level of mentalizing where pretend play is possible. Finally, it sheds light on how a certain type of deviant parental mirroring environment, in which the negative affective displays of the child result in contingent but unmarked and realistic negative emotional reactions of the caregiver, may lead to a developmental arrest at the level of psychic equivalence functioning. In our discussion we shall restrict our attention to only these aspects of Mat's case.

Mat's mother had a dismissive, but at the same time intrusive and overcontrolling personality. She also seemed to lack the ability adaptively to mirror and thereby to modulate the negative affect states of her child. Their emotional life was dominated by negative affect that tended to escalate rather than subside as a result of their affective interactions. Mat's expressions of negative feelings tended to result in contingent and realistic negative affective reactions by her mother, leading to an increase in Mat's negative affect state, which sometimes reached traumatizing intensity. An example of such deviant affect-mirroring interactions (lacking markedness) is the recurring episode in which the obstinately withholding boy would sit on the toilet "for hours" while his mother, sitting next to him, tried to persuade him to defecate. One can assume that Mat was experiencing a variety of growing negative feelings, such as abdominal pain, anxiety, anger, and anticipatory fear, and he displayed at least some of these feelings. His obstinate refusal to produce feces and his negative affect displays induced growing frustration, anger, hatred, and, eventually, rage in his mother. This gruesome interchange predictably culminated in violence and traumatization when Mat's mother "lost her head" and beat Mat.

In adaptive affect-regulative interactions involving marked parental mirroring of negative affects, the child's experience is that the contingent externalization of his negative emotion states (in the form of the parent's marked mirroring displays) results in a positive soothing effect (Gergely and Watson 1996, 1999). Such interactions establish an association between externalizing one's negative affects and consequent affect regulation. We hypothesized that such affect-regulative mirroring interactions may, therefore, provide a proto-form and experiential prerequisite for the child's later ability to actively use marked forms of externalizations of his negative states in pretend play and in imagination in an effort to achieve successful self-regulation. We believe that Mat was deprived of such crucial experiences of emotion-regulative interactions in which markedness, externalization of negative affects, and consequent affect regulation could have become associated. Instead, his traumatizing interactions with his mother, in which she mirrored his negative states in an unmarked, realistic manner, leading to escalation (rather than modulation) of his painful affects, led to an association that related contingent externalization of negative internal states to anticipated traumatization. This then led to a phobic avoidance of possibilities for symbolic externalization of internal states in the forms of imagination, symbolic play, or figurative drawing and painting.

The lack of adaptive mirroring interactions involving markedness also resulted in a decreased ability to recognize the functional significance of markedness as a generalized communicative code indicating decoupling from reality. As a result, Mat was initially quite incapable of differentiating pretense from reality and would experience the marked symbolic externalizations of negative affects as being real rather than as being only representations of reality. In other words, Mat was arrested at the level of psychic equivalence functioning where feelings, thoughts, fantasies, and pretend activities were all experienced at a single level as being parts of reality. For example, when he used the spatula for scooping feces, he could not simultaneously understand that the proper function of a spatula in reality is entirely different: the imaginary function became reality itself.

However, Mat was not imprisoned forever in a mental world of psychic equivalence. The therapeutic breakthrough involving the "pretending to cry" episode indicates that corrective emotional and representational experience involving adaptive mirroring of negative affects was possible and therapeutic. His first reaction to the therapist's marked and playful expression of sadness and crying was at the level of psychic equivalence: he showed an initial confusion of pretense with reality and consequently became frightened. However, the conspicuous lack of negative consequences, the repeated presentation of a clearly marked emotion display, and the calming verbal explanation that "this is not for real" could activate the child's dormant representational capacities that, eventually and with practice, led to an adaptive understanding of the functional use of markedness and the pretend mode of mentalizing. Mat, perhaps for the first time, could experience that marked externalizations of negative affective states do not necessarily culminate in trauma but can lead to positive emotions of sharing, empathy, and soothing. He discovered that "he likes to die" as long as he is in the pretend mode with a self-regulating other.

CONCLUSION

Mat's case illustrated two central points about the role of marked externalizations in emotional self-regulation: (a) It exemplified how the sustained lack of early emotion-regulative experiences involving marked affect-mirroring with the primary attachment figure may result in a developmental arrest at the level of psychic equivalence functioning. (b) It showed that in child psycho-therapy, the sensitive use of marked externalizations of negative affects by the therapist may lead to corrective emotional and representational experience, helping the child to move from the level of psychic equivalence to the adaptive use of the pretend mode of mental functioning in the service of affect regulation.

It seems clear in Mat's case that his metarepresentational capacities were not genetically impaired, but their use for affec-tive self-regulation was seriously undeveloped or inhibited by his experience with the deviant style of affective reactivity of his mother, which lacked markedness and resulted in a traumatic escalation of Mat's negative affect states. However, we do not know how general this acquired representational dysfunction was in Mat's case. It is possible that the boy's phobic avoidance of symbolic externalizations was restricted to the specific attach-ment context involving his mother and to situations involving separation from his mother (as in the nursery or in the thera-peutic setting). We could not rule out the possibility that Mat may have had different and possibly more adaptive emotional interactions with other attachment figures in his life—such as his father or grandmother—where he, in fact, could already have attained the pretend mode of mental functioning.

As discussed in chapter 1 (see also Cicchetti and Rogosch 1997; Rutter 1987; E. E. Werner 1990), the existence of at least one congenial attachment context fostering representational development may be sufficient to establish relatively mature mentalizing or reflective functioning. High reflective function, in turn, has been shown to correlate with the capacity successfully to metabolize and cope with the potentially dangerous affective consequences of traumatization (Allen 2001; Fonagy, Steele, et al. 1994). If Mat had already established the capacity to use the pretend mode in some alternative attachment context, then the therapist's success may have involved no more than lifting the domain-specific inhibition of Mat's otherwise functioning ability to use marked and symbolic externalizations for self-regulation (for a similar example, see the case of Rebecca discussed in chapter 6).

But what if a child has no reasonable attachment relationships at all and comes to experience marked affect-mirroring and affect-regulative symbolic externalizations only in psychotherapy? This, in fact, may have been so in Mat's case. To what degree can such therapeutic experiences functionally substitute for the effects of secure attachment in bringing about the unfolding of mentalization capacities—thereby transforming psychic equivalence into the pretend mode of mental functioning? We hope that future clinical research will shed more light on this important question.

A further related issue concerns the treatment of adolescents and adult patients who show a pathological fixation of mental functioning at the level of psychic equivalence. Can, for example, our developmental model and its application to child psychotherapy shed new light on the nature of therapeutic change that the psychoanalytic treatment of adult borderline patients can achieve? In chapters 9–11 we take up this issue in greater detail. Here it will be sufficient to point out that even though psychoanalytic psychotherapy of adult patients applies different—and more age-appropriate—methods from those used in child psychotherapy (such as free association and verbal interpretations instead of evocative pretend play), these techniques nevertheless seem to exploit the same underlying psychological mechanisms—markedness, contingency detection, and social biofeedback—that are operative in parental affect-mirroring and symbolic play. For example, the formal features of the psychoanalytic setting as well as the rules of conduct specified in the analytic contract can be interpreted as establishing salient features of markedness that clearly distinguish the use of language in the analytic discourse from its everyday use in communicative exchanges. The primary normative function of everyday linguistic communication is the efficient exchange of novel and relevant information between members of the language community that fosters survival. The implicit pragmatic rules of verbal communication specified in the so-called Gricean maxims (such as "Be relevant" or "Be succinct"—Grice 1975), to which we automatically adhere in everyday communication, serve to optimize precisely this function (see Sperber and Wilson 1995). In psychoanalysis and psychoanalytic therapy, however, this primary function of language use is explicitly de-emphasized: the patient—as well as the therapist—is effectively "unplugged" from the normative constraints of linguistic communication by suspending the Gricean maxims and replacing them with the rule of "free association." In classical psychoanalysis, lying on the couch, lack of eye contact, and the consequent deprivation from on-line metacommunicative feedback from the therapist during verbal exchanges also serve to suspend the application of the pragmatic rules that govern everyday communication. These normative rules are similarly suspended as regards the analyst: she can choose to remain silent, is free to provide no informative answers to the patient's inquiries, or can turn the question back, asking about the underlying motives of the patient rather than dealing with his consciously intended meaning. The analyst is also sanctioned to provide interpretations that do not refer to the literal meaning of the patient's verbal communication but to its inferred underlying affective content.

Note that these highly specialized psychoanalytic rules of verbal exchange serve to make the *externalization of internal affective contents* the primary function of language use within the therapeutic context. The darkened room, the relaxed and safe atmosphere, and the patient's lying on the couch all serve the purpose of focusing the patient's attention on his internal mental contents, which are to be externalized within the safe, reality-decoupled "as-if" world of the analytic situation. The differential features and rules of the psychoanalytic setting function to "mark" the externalized verbal expressions of internal affective contents as "being not for real" and as being "nonconsequential."

The therapist's "hovering attention" is a specialized state of attunement the aim of which is to identify the patient's internal affect states in order to mirror them back to the patient in the form of marked interpretations and reactions. Through the transference the developmental setting of the original attachment context is recreated and the dysfunctional forms of parental affective reactions are reexperienced in the reality-decoupled safe environment of the analytic situation. At the same time, the analyst provides corrective emotional and representational experience for the patient through emotion-regulative marked externalizations of the patient's affects in the form of mirroring interpretations or expressions. Similarly to the processes of social biofeedback in parental affect-mirroring, these contingent and marked externalizations serve the multiple functions of (a) sensitizing the patient to his internal affective states, (b) establishing second-order representations for these states by providing verbal labels for them, and (c) adaptively transforming their affective content by externalizing them in a modified interpretive perspective.

The central therapeutic aim of psychoanalysis is therefore to foster the capacity for "mentalization of affectivity" in the patient—a topic that we address in greater detail in chapter 11. Through sensitization to and establishing second-order representations for his internal affective states, the patient becomes able to apprehend and reflect on his subjective affective contents as mentalized representational states, with minimal risk of these being confused with external reality. Through the processes of social biofeedback, the therapist's marked externalizations of the patient's internal affective contents help to establish a new introspective capacity in the patient for the "inward expression of affects." This comes about through the internalization of the newly experienced safe forms of affect-regulative marked externalizations provided by the therapist's mirroring interpretations. This way the patient gradually learns new mental skills of affective self-regulation: he becomes able to express internally, apprehend, and modify his emotional impulses by "mirroring himself" through generating marked forms of inward expressions of internal affective contents. In chapter 11 we provide clinical case illustrations for the different levels of mentalization of affectivity that we can encounter in adult patients with affective disorders of varying severities.

8

Developmental Issues
in Normal Adolescence
and Adolescent Breakdown

In previous chapters we have considered the development of mentalization up to about the age of 5 years, when the autobiographical self first emerges (see chapter 5). While certain developmental disorders are already apparent at this age, many do not emerge until adolescence or later. This chapter adds a further stage to our description of the development of reflective function, considering the implications of the cognitive developments associated with adolescence for the ontogeny of mentalization. The key question addressed in this chapter concerns the increased frequency of various kinds of mental disorder at this developmental stage, the worsening of preexisting conditions, and the emergence of new conditions specifically linked to adolescence, as well as the onset of many that are lifelong problems but whose onset is linked with this age. That is, we attempt to answer the deceptively simple question of why breakdown occurs relatively often in adolescence. We suggest that this might be understood partly in terms of the vicissitudes of reflective function during this developmental phase. The chapter begins with a summary of the view of self-development advocated in this book, which pulls together the threads of the argument so far.

INTRODUCTION

One explanation of the rise in psychopathology in adolescence was provided by the Laufers: "The break in the developmental process of adolescence is the pathology, because the outcome of such a break must be a distorted relationship to oneself as a sexual being, a passive relationship to the parent of the same sex, and the giving up of the wish or the ability to leave infantile sexuality behind" (Laufer and Laufer 1984, pp. ix–x).

We all recall the heat of sexuality in adolescence, but is it generally the cause of the breakdown, or is the breakdown the result of earlier developmental disturbances, its form colored by the intensification of sexual feelings? We think that the latter is more likely. An example of the clues that suggest that we need to look beyond a hormonal upheaval is that while puberty arrives earlier and earlier, not all adolescent disorders are occurring at an earlier age. Thus, although eating disorders have been developing at younger ages, criminal activity and suicide have not (D. J. Smith 1995). This suggests that the prevalence reflects social more than physical—sexual—pressures. The picture of "adolescent turmoil" was replaced in the 1980s and 1990s by a model in which there is a sequence of bodily changes, any of which might trigger emotional upheaval. Which biological events might do so could be quite idiosyncratic, depending to a degree on what particular changes represent to the adolescent (Paikoff and Brooks-Gunn 1991).

In this chapter, we focus on the interaction of two maturational processes, which may be quite central to a number of different kinds of pathology in adolescence. The first is the leap to formal operations thinking and the consequent intensification of pressure for interpersonal understanding. This is normally thought of in biological terms, but in our frame of reference the development of symbolic thought is intertwined throughout childhood with emotional growth in the context of attachment. This is where we make a link to the second process: the pressure toward separation from the external and internally represented parents, which, we suggest, can reveal developmental failures or weaknesses that were established much earlier in life, but which it may have been possible to conceal at this earlier stage. More specifically, we try to describe how some affective disturbances in adolescence can be thought about in terms of an inadequate consolidation of symbolic capacity.

Thus, we believe that one thing that drives—but can also derail—the achievement of separateness is freshly enhanced cognitive complexity, which means that the adolescent is faced with the task of integrating a far more complicated set of thoughts about his own and others' feelings and motivations. As a result, there is a developmental hypersensitivity to mental states, which may overwhelm the adolescent's capacity to cope with thoughts and feelings except through bodily symptoms or physical action. Although such adolescents may seem able to talk and think about mental states quite fluently, more abstract ideas about mental states create a considerable strain on the adolescent's system. This can lead to an apparently dramatic breakdown in mentalization, withdrawal from the social world, and the intensification of anxiety and enactments. The extent to which these changes lead to long-term difficulty may depend not only on the inherent strength of the adolescent's psychic structures, but also on the capacity of the environment to support the adolescent's weakened mentalizing function. Naturally, this is further complicated by the fact that the adolescent may undermine the capacity of institutions to support him.

THEORY OF SELF-DEVELOPMENT

The theory of self-development on which our ideas about adolescence are based has been described in the preceding chapters. Here we briefly summarize the propositions within the theory that will be central in our discussion of adolescent psychopathology:

1. The psychological self is rooted in the attribution of mental states to self and other (chapters 1 and 3);

2. This capacity emerges through interaction with the caregiver, in the context of an attachment relationship, via a process of mirroring (see chapter 4). Internal experience acquires a

second-order representation through the internalization of the mirroring actions of the caregiver (chapter 5).

3. The rudimentary early experience of the internal world consists of two alternating modes—a mode of "psychic equivalence" (where internal = external) and a mode of "pretend" (where internal is forever separated from external) (chapter 6).

4. Safe, playful interaction with caregivers leads to the integration of these modes, creating mentalization (chapter 6).

5. In the case of chronically insensitive or misattuned caregiving, a fault is created in the construction of the self, whereby the infant is forced to internalize the representation of the object's state of mind as a core part of himself (chapter 7).

6. In early development this "alien self" is dealt with by externalization; as mentalization develops, it can be increasingly woven into the self, creating an illusion of cohesion (this is discussed more fully in part III, chapters 9 and 10).

7. The disorganization of the self disorganizes attachment relationships by creating a constant need for projective identification (for the externalization of the alien self) in any attachment relationship (part III, chapter 10).

SEPARATION AS THE PRIMARY TASK OF ADOLESCENCE

So how can this model help us to understand normal and abnormal development in adolescence? Margaret Mahler (Mahler et al. 1975) saw separation–individuation as a gradual distancing from the mother, whereby the transition from dependency to independent functioning went on throughout the life-cycle as a more or less continuous process of distancing from the introject of the lost symbiotic mother. Peter Blos (1979) extended Mahler's model and identified the critical change in adolescence as the loosening of infantile object ties. He emphasized that individuation could be seen as a process or as an achievement, but both were integral components of the adolescent process. Mahler's model, and its extension in the work of Peter Blos, are clearly related to our formulation. Mahler's symbiotic mother is functionally equivalent to our notion of an alien self.[1] Greater separation in adolescence means that the alien self, or symbiotic mother, can no longer be externalized in interaction with the caregiver. The enactments and manipulations necessary to project the alien self into the parent have to become more dramatic as separation increases. This (for example, fighting with the parents) might have been mistaken for striving to achieve an independent identity. Until a partner can be found with whom the adolescent can reestablish a symbiotic relationship, there is a hiatus in externalization, which creates enormous pressure for adolescents whose alien self cannot be integrated.

Erikson sees the attainment of self-identity as a precondition of true engagement (Erikson 1968). This overriding emphasis on individuation neglects its dialectic counterpart, attachment (Blatt and Behrends 1987; Blatt and Blass 1990). Real separateness implies an ability to recognize both difference *and* similarity, and it is paradoxically the latter rather than the former that may be a true mark of autonomy. The challenge to identity in adolescence comes from accepting not difference, but similarity. The adolescent with a secure sense of connection and likeness to the caregiver can tolerate physical separation, whereas one who has projected parts of the self and needs to perceive the caregiver as completely different feels that he has lost his identity if he is separated from her. Thus, an exaggerated claim to be different may be seen as a defensive response to pressure for separation, which threatens the return of projected parts of the self.

Internal coherence and mental separation of self and object, then, require the physical presence of the other. Otherwise, the adolescent fears that the residual core self will be swamped, he will lose contact with it, and his sense of identity will be lost.

---

[1] With the exception that, in agreement with Stern, we do not see symbiosis as a normal stage, but the "symbiotic mother" as a very common deviation from normal development.

Physical separateness is, in our view, the smaller of two developmental challenges that face each child in adolescence. The second arises out of the enhanced awareness of emotional and cognitive complexity, most pivotally in the context of attachment relationships. In adolescence, emotional development reaches "a new developmental tier" (Fischer et al. 1990) with the capacity for abstract thinking. Both the appreciation and the expression of affect take on a new dimension and thus many new meanings. For example, rather than attributing basic emotional states, adolescents start to contemplate adultlike scripts for emotions. Feelings such as jealousy or resentment become elaborated into scenarios. This new capacity for abstraction and elaboration is tenuously maintained and quickly reversed by emotional stresses generated by the developmental process. These stresses are often internal—for example, due to conflict or unfamiliar and intense emotional states—but they may also arise from overwhelming external situations such as parental mental illness.

Building on Piaget's concept of reversibility, A. E. Thompson (1985, 1986) considers affect "irreversible" when the child cannot imagine other reactions to the object, or feelings other than the one he currently feels. Reversibility gradually emerges between middle childhood and early adolescence. Slowly the child wonders what it might take *not* to feel as he does, or to change the feeling state of the object. With formal operations fully deployed, the child begins to think of general principles rather than aspects of the specific situation that can explain or change emotions. However, while advances in the capacity for abstract thought enable the adolescent to take a step back and to monitor himself and others, this does not necessarily feel like a good thing. For the adolescent, as *experiencer* of affect in himself and others, the world is suddenly much more complicated and confusing. Thus, he needs at times to withdraw from interactions, or from mentalization in general, to take a rest from the ramifications of alternative motivations.

For example, the child of a depressed mother may at the age of 3 years feel that his mother lies in bed because he is bad or boring or unlovable. At 5, this child may have come to realize that the mother's behavior reflects a state of mind, depression, which does not necessarily relate to her feelings about him; it is something in her own head. At 7, the child may have produced a contextual explanation: "Mom is depressed because her Mom died, then Dad left, and we've got hardly any money, and she hasn't got friends." However, from perhaps 11 on many disturbing new possibilities enter the picture, hinging on the fact that emotional states need not be as they are and people have choices about how they respond to them. Interestingly, this may lead the child back to a more sophisticated version of his first assumptions—"Why doesn't Mom get up and do something if she feels so terrible? If she wasn't getting something out of lying in bed, she wouldn't keep doing it for so long. OK, she feels terrible, but she *could* get up and come to my parent–teacher evening. If she really loved me, she would." Later, the adolescent formulation might be in terms of depression being a result of loss of love, or conflict, or the parents' marriage, or, more egocentrically, the parents' disappointment in him. These new ways of thinking about people's feelings and behavior, as well as about his own feelings and behavior, can be overwhelming, and the adolescent needs to absorb the implications. There may also be a reaction against mentalizing. Some adolescents may engage in arcade games, surfing the Internet, and so on; others may develop a passion for stereotyped soap-operas and romantic novels, in which emotions are again presented as simple and intense. They may also retreat into apparently mind-numbing music.

The entire developmental process is fluid and dynamic, with enhanced cognitive capacity generating enriched mentalizing, which, in turn, leads to anxiety and/or preoccupation. As this state undermines abstract thought, the adolescent may—in addition to sometimes switching off into really mindless activity—regress in apparent relief to a thoughtless, socially insensitive state. Thus, the parents become infuriated that the adolescent, who is obviously capable of keeping other people in mind and imagining the effect of his actions, behaves as though he were oblivious, selfish, and willfully inconsiderate.

In the second section we describe two cases that illustrate, in their different ways and degrees of impairment of mentalization, what we see as the dual challenge of adolescence: the potentially disastrous consequences of the drive for separateness in an adverse attachment context and regression in the face of the leap forward in mentalizing.

CLINICAL ILLUSTRATION: "TONY"

Tony was 15 years old when he was referred to a residential adolescent psychiatric unit. His parents, his teachers, and his psychiatrist had become very concerned about explicit violent threats that he had made to his parents, peers, and women teachers. He was admitted after threatening another boy with a knife. He was a sullen, stocky boy who did not talk to staff or peers on the unit, usually glaring and snarling at them if they tried to engage him.

Tony was the only son of a failed businessman and a former teacher. His unpredictable violent outbursts had worsened six months before admission, at which point his parents had asked for him to be taken into the care of the social services. His history is far from unusual for a violent adolescent, except for the remarkably close relationship that Tony had with his outwardly loving and affectionate mother. As a baby he was said to have been valued beyond measure, after a long period when his parents had thought they could not have a child. His mother abandoned her promising career in educational administration to spend all her time looking after little Tony. The relationship between them was so intense that the father often felt jealous and resentful, even though he, too, had been delighted to have a son. The mother insisted for some years on sharing their bedroom with Tony, excluding the father; until Tony was 10 years old, she would not go out at night with the father because she did not want to leave Tony with anyone else.

Tony's father was never violent toward him. He was, however, abusive to his wife. His frustration in his business dealings and his sense of being neglected by Tony's mother led him to become increasingly aggressive, screaming and threatening. He occasionally hit the mother, to which she responded with hysterical rage of her own and intimate discussions with her son about the father's behavior. As you might expect, Tony was frequently the focus of the father's rage. Her wish to protect and indulge Tony was treated with derision and threats to leave her. Tony often witnessed these confrontations, and as a young boy he was reported to have tried to shield her; when he was older, he threatened to kill his father if he did not leave his mother alone.

Meanwhile, Tony was doing badly. He was encopretic until he was 10; at elementary school he made poor educational progress, and he was teased and bullied. Once at secondary school, he increasingly became the bully, terrorizing the playground with his unpredictable violent outbursts and too difficult for teachers to contain in class.

When Tony was admitted to the adolescent unit, everyone was frightened of him. He refused to give a history to the admitting psychiatrist and barely talked to the nurses or other residents. No one wanted to share a room with him. The young men in particular shunned and ridiculed him, and he was defended only by a girl, Elaine, who, like him, was surly and isolated. After Elaine stood up for Tony, they formed a wordless friendship based on hatred of the others. The only person he talked to a little was a young trainee psychologist who was assigned to carry out his psychological testing. She found that he could hardly read and had minimal mathematical skills, and she realized that she needed to help him navigate the minefield of mortification represented by aptitude and attainment tests. In doing so, Tony began to express how he had hated school and everyone there, and how he had desperately tried, on his own, to learn to read better but had then given up in shame and frustration. Because he seemed able to talk to her to some degree, the team decided to offer him some sessions with her to see whether some therapeutic relationship might be possible.

In the first meeting with the psychologist, Tony described his rage with his father, adding that he would like to murder him. He was filled with anger and talked venomously about other young people who, he felt, had been set against him and were all ridiculing him behind his back. He was enraged by the rather minimal rules of the unit and said that he refused to fit in with the stupid ward timetable for meals, meetings, and so on. The psychologist gently suggested that if he felt he was hated so much, it was not surprising he preferred to do things alone, but he also seemed to be lonely. He talked about how he had never been able to make friends. The psychologist reported Tony's wish to kill his father to the staff team, but as he seemed to be settling in, he was kept on the open unit under closer observation.

His next session was in the afternoon, two days later. That morning Elaine had seriously slashed her wrists and had been taken out of the unit on a stretcher. Tony came to his session clearly agitated, blaming the staff for failing to protect Elaine. His anger quickly engulfed the interview-room, and he became menacing. He grabbed the psychologist's keys from the table, locked the interview-room door from the inside, and shoved the keys down his shirt and into his pants. His excitement was obvious as he taunted the psychologist that she had to get the keys back. She asked him to give them back to her and then sit down and talk about how he felt and what had happened, but it was clear that he was very excited by feeling he had her at his mercy and he was not going to give up that position willingly. He pushed her and repeatedly said that she would have to reach into his pants to get her keys. She pressed the alarm button and explained to him that this meant staff would come and be available outside the door to help; however, it would be much better if he would return the keys and continue the session without needing to bring other people in. He unfastened his pants as though to give her the keys, but then exposed himself to her and got more excited, pushing her against a window away from the panic button and trying to take her clothes off. Two male members of staff came into the room.

Tony was grabbed and dragged away with his pants round his knees, through the main unit room where the other residents and staff were gathering for tea. When interviewed, Tony aggressively claimed that the psychologist had "had it coming to her," but he also wanted to make sure that she would see him for the planned sessions. He was told that this would not happen because he would be moved that day to the high-security adult unit—a place dreaded by all the young people in the unit. He was also given a forcible injection and placed in extended "time out" while the transfer was arranged.

Tony broke his window and abseiled out of the unit. The police were unable to find him for 24 hours, when they were called to his parents' home by his mother. Tony had broken in during the night and had stabbed his father to death. He was committed for an indefinite period to a maximum-security psychiatric hospital.

Tony had not been neglected. He had not been beaten by his parents (although he was extensively bullied at school), and the murder was triggered by an incident that occurred in a relatively caring setting. We would like to suggest (as we have argued more fully elsewhere—Fonagy and Target 1995) that, although Tony was not neglected *physically*, at the level of emotional experience and development of self-organization he was. Neither his mother, with her excessive devotion—which seemed to serve her own needs not to separate—nor his father, with his anger and jealousy, was actually able to relate to Tony as himself. They could not relate to his real feelings and experiences, and this absence of recognition by the attachment figures generated a vulnerability to conduct disorder and violence.

Excessive closeness, like excessive distance, undermines the psychological self. In vain does the infant try to find representations corresponding to his internal state in the expression of the caregiver. The self remains incompletely organized, and internal reality continues to be experienced in the "psychic equivalence" mode. It is thus vulnerable to the introjection of later malign experience.

Tony was not a bright boy. He was cruelly teased by his peers for being slow, clumsy, odd-looking, and unkempt. Such teasing may seem minor to the adults surrounding the child and even to other children, who are capable of adopting a mentalizing perspective. But bullying is experienced as literally lethal to those children who cannot distinguish a feeling of humiliation from obliteration. A similar sense of ego-destructive shame accompanied Tony's experience of thinly veiled violence at home. In witnessing the arguments, overly identified with the mother, he felt abused himself and powerless to prevent his or his mother's suffering. This aroused the same sense of helpless shameful humiliation from which he could escape only through identification with the aggression. In the context of the incomplete self-organization that is the residue of disorganized attachment, identification with the aggressor can never be successful. It is the dissociated, alien part of the self that accommodates to aggression and comes to be colored by a climate of violence, be that at school, at home, or perhaps in the culture at large.

The tragic consequence for Tony, as for other children whose experience of relative neglect is followed by brutalization, is that a part of the self has become a destroyer of the rest. Given the very real sense of internal persecution, tingeing all of Tony's relationships with paranoia, the coherence of the self could only be restored by externalization. In disorganized attachment generally, the externalization may be of something that is not destructive, and the result may simply be a controlling style of interaction. Where this disorganization has been followed at some point by brutalization, violence to self or other is likely. The alien self is so persecutory that its projection is a much more urgent and constant task. Any threat to self-esteem triggers this externalization, which can, in turn trigger an attack in the hope of destroying the alien other.

Let us revisit the sequence of events that culminated in Tony's murder of his father. Notwithstanding his surly behavior, Tony was relieved to be in the adolescent unit. He then found two women who, he felt, understood him. Feeling understood brought forward inarticulate but intense affection and hopefulness. Their consideration toward him aroused feelings of love and need to be loved, which he could not titrate—either internally or externally—appropriately to the situation. Often when we consider the deficit in affect regulation in these cases, we focus on the difficulty in containing *negative* affects, forgetting that the same difficulty applies to *positive* feelings when they are aroused. Losing the hope of love, he felt humiliated, and this experience in turn triggered his aggression. His sexual assault on the psychologist was at one level an act of self-protection. He arrived feeling threatened and frightened by Elaine's disappearance, and the only way he could express his love and need was by first externalizing his alien self, filled with fear and helplessness, into the psychologist. While holding her hostage, his affection and gratitude could be (clumsily) shown. Once the discontinuity in his self-representation had been dealt with, he was almost able to express affection. Sadly, it could only be done while maintaining this threatening posture. He destroyed the possibility of being accepted by his desperate defensive maneuver—the psychologist who had been able to see him and to show understanding was now bringing further humiliation on him. She responded to his taunting by calling for help: understandable and probably necessary, but for him a double loss. We can imagine that Tony may have felt that she first lost sight of his gentler and more loving side, then saw only the menacing posture, apparently relating to that (as in psychic equivalence) as the only reality. To destroy the vision of him in her mind as evil, he would have felt that she had to be attacked.

The rest of the story demonstrates with tragic inevitability what can so often happen when institutions—always prone to mindlessness, even with the best of intentions—attempt to contain a person struggling to achieve mentalizing. The incident created some panic and much guilt about having exposed a trainee to this danger, and all the participants responded by belatedly showing their support for her, meting out an excessive, ego-destructive punishment. No one, in the rather chaotic aftermath of the incident, communicated an understanding of Tony's actions and the feelings of loss and love contained in them. He was alone with the memory of his complete humiliation in front of his peers, the irreversible loss of his hopes of closeness, and the terror of an environment far more mindless than the one he was already finding excruciating.

We can speculate about how this state of mind led to murder. Tony probably experienced Elaine's serious suicide attempt as a repetition of his father's attack on his mother and his failure to save her. With these feelings left uncontained, he chose the following night to take his ultimate revenge. He had to reestablish his sense of self, which humiliation had threatened with annihilation. The unit and the father came to be fused, and their destruction generated the illusion that he could attain identity.

These feelings were not far from his conscious awareness. When visited by the adolescent-unit psychologist in the maximum-security hospital, Tony was able to talk about his hope for (an idealized) union with his mother now that his father was out of the way. Perhaps a deeper, unconscious hope, however, was for a separation from her, which his act of murder clearly achieved. Just as the unit's authority probably represented the father, so the possibility of understanding and closeness perhaps reminded him of the maddening seductiveness of intimacy with his mother. He may have hoped that, separated from her, he might rediscover a coherent sense of self, even a genuinely understanding attachment relationship. Sadly, he found instead a place where mentalization tended to be eroded still further.

Discussion

In what senses was Tony's predicament characteristic of adolescence? Tony's violence, always present, became increasingly lethal from the time he reached puberty. His "symbiotic relationship" with his mother had disguised the extent to which he used her as a vehicle for his experience of his own mental states. His father, in a far more destructive way, performed the same function in enabling him to externalize his hatred and revulsion and place himself in the role of protector. Longer periods away from his parents made this difficult to sustain. His enactments had to become increasingly dramatic to achieve the changes in affect in his parents necessary for his self to feel coherent. As in a conversation, the voices must get louder as the speakers move farther apart. Paradoxically, this resulted in an even greater separation: his placement in the care of social services, creating the claustrophobic anxiety described by John Steiner (1993) and before that by Herbert Rosenfeld (1987). The terror was that the alien part of the self would be trapped forever, with no possibility for externalization. This drove Tony to the desperation so characteristic of violent adolescents.

CLINICAL ILLUSTRATION: "GLEN"

Glen[2] started his analysis in a profoundly dissociated state. Although he was 15, he had the appearance of a 10-year-old and behaved like a child half that age. He just sat in a chair, withdrawn, angry, and depressed, huddled up in a tentlike coat that was far too big for his small stature; sometimes he hid his face in his hands, occasionally looking at me through a gap he made between his fingers. There was immense hostility in the room, and a sense of uncontained confusion. There were sessions when he was able to talk, and at these times the infantile nature of his mental functioning was revealed in a stark and disturbing way. Glen's clinical diagnosis would have been obsessive-compulsive disorder, together with a major depression. Such labels cannot, however, adequately convey the word and thought magic that had overtaken his life. His life was organized around rituals from the moment he got up and had to tidy his room in a particular order—sometimes repeatedly if he felt he might have got the order wrong—to the moment he got into bed, when he had to place his pillows at certain angles to the room and to his body. On the surface, he wished to avoid "bad luck," but it was easy to see that underneath was a dread of intrusive ideas, concretized as alien beings, spiders, and bacteria. He was terrorized by the continuously intrusive thought that the creature from the film *Alien* was in the fireplace or in the garden. He was also oppressed by his aggressive fantasies and his constant dread that any spontaneous action on his part might bring harm to someone else.

There was little in Glen's background to justify his state of mind. His father was an authoritarian man who certainly lacked empathy but who was also rather concerned about his son and felt helpless in the face of his odd behavior. His mother also seemed to be a caring person, even if also depressed; she denied the pervasive nature of Glen's disturbance and described her

---

[2] Glen was treated by Peter Fonagy, whose report this is.

relationship with Glen's father as deeply troubled. The trigger for Glen's difficulties may have been his mother's chronic illness and consequent surgery. It was difficult to know how to understand Glen's difficulties; he seemed relatively bright, and in some ways even talented, but embattled in a constant struggle against a regressive pull in order to contain intense destructive fantasies. His symptoms had been intensifying rapidly before his referral for treatment, and he was terrified that he was going mad.

I was at a loss as to how to help Glen. I did interpretive work with little success; I focused on his fear of me confusing him and causing him to become mad, his terror of my aggression toward him and of his toward me, his sense that his parents had abandoned him with me, having given up on him, his hopelessness about himself and me, his isolation outside the treatment, which he showed me concretely inside the room, his fear that talking would break his tenuous control over his mind, and so on. None of these interpretations had any apparent effect; I was not getting through to him. I became angry and found it quite hard to resist the temptation to give up on him. I blamed others: the diagnostic team for not screening him adequately, his parents for not recognizing his difficulties, but above all Glen for remaining inaccessible and making me so helpless.

About two and a half months into the treatment, around the Christmas break, I decided to change tack. I abandoned some of my formal interpretive style with him and became livelier, almost trying to persuade him out of his passive–aggressive stance. I started making jokes and humored him about his feelings of anger with me and his wish to kill me so I would stop bothering him "once and for all." I imitated his behavior, showing him rather than telling him how he appeared to me. I chatted to him about my messy room and how I thought he disliked it but didn't want to say so in case I would be offended. On a wet morning we talked about him being cross about getting wet, just so he could come and be bored by me for 50 minutes. I talked to him about his wonderful feeling of liberation when it came to the Christmas break from analysis. On another occasion, when he mentioned a teacher of his who was bald, he inadvertently glanced at me, and

I said to him how pleased he must feel that he had hair and I didn't, and how ridiculous he thought I looked.

Happily, this change of strategy began to bear fruit. Slowly he became visibly more relaxed, his posture changed, he took his coat off. He also opened up verbally and told me about what turned out to be crucial anxieties, particularly about work. He shared his worries about not being able to do his homework, his wish to be appreciated by his teachers, and the dread that he might disappoint them. I was able to interpret what must have been a dominant feature of the transference all along, the terrible feeling of disappointing me if he let himself care what I thought and felt about him.

The atmosphere changed. Glen started looking at me, and there were fewer periods of long silence. He began to talk about his thoughts and feelings when he had been withdrawn. He had imagined that he was throwing knives into my body or just missing me, loving the feeling of control and torture. He gave me room to interpret that his fear of my power over him could be related to his wish to control and frighten me; that he wished to destroy people because he was so afraid of them, but his anger was so clear that it frightened him and made him feel terribly guilty. He was increasingly grateful for my interpretations and almost seemed pleased to see me. By the end of the six-month period a therapeutic alliance had developed where I was seen as both useful and, on the whole, benign. The major transference theme, however, remained the same—that I could not contain and tolerate his rage and mad thoughts; the tiniest and most subtle shift in my stance could lead to immense anxiety and could trigger withdrawal from me. I felt that our work had begun.

Over the next year he made increasingly good use of the analysis and improved symptomatically in ways that both he and his parents clearly noticed. For example, the rituals ceased to preoccupy him, and his obsessional work patterns gave way to a far more relaxed but still organized attitude. There were several key points. The first was our joint recognition of the significance of his early period at school, when he had been regarded as a slow learner and offered remedial teaching. He had found the experience humiliating, not least because of the exceptionally high performance of his older brother and his father's thinly disguised mockery. As we recognized that his obsessional work patterns reflected his conflict over wishing to avoid educational humiliation on the one hand, and his anger with both his parents, his brother, and his teachers for mocking him on the other, his attitude toward his work changed. He stopped forcing himself to do the same piece of work half a dozen times; instead, he decided to work only a certain number of hours after he came home from school, and he stopped worrying about work accumulating.

His self-esteem took a boost when his fear of his sadism entered the material. This was triggered by a school visit to the film *Schindler's List,* which he had wanted to avoid. He was greatly disturbed by the film and eventually disclosed that he had fantasized being the Camp Commandant who was using Jewish workers for target practice. This quickly led to the elaboration of these fantasies and to a shameful disclosure that he constantly fantasized about attacking people and killing them in painful ways. We talked at some length about his enjoyment of the fantasy of torturing me, and he described the various ways he had thought of causing me pain, particularly enjoying the idea of my begging for mercy. Interestingly, this linked with Glen's neurotic concern about his father's moods. He was worried that his father shut himself off in his study, particularly after he had been subjected to playful teasing by his family. He feared that his father might commit suicide, and he dreaded both being blamed and blaming himself. Historical material emerged about his experience of his father's sensitivity and current and past thoughts about the fragility of his parents' marriage. Eventually it transpired that his concern was far greater about his mother's depression than about his father's. It seemed that his mother terrified him by retiring to bed, sometimes as early as 6 p.m., leaving the children to look after themselves. His fears about my fragility suddenly made more sense to both of us, and he told me how reassured he had been when he realized "that you can take a joke." He became increasingly relaxed in the sessions: he would sit slouched in the chair, play games at my expense, mock my room, mimic my habits, and comment on my baldness and my monotonous clothes. In the transference I seemed to become a predepressed mother, and he visibly enjoyed this. Other clinicians working at the center noted the change in him: unbeknown to me, he was walking down the stairs whistling.

About twelve months into the treatment he began to trust me with his sexual secrets. It transpired that he had reached sexual maturation and had started masturbating to ejaculation. He was excited by pictures of naked women. He felt deeply ashamed about this and wondered if I would refuse to see him after he disclosed his practices. Part of the fear of the Alien was clearly linked to a split-off aspect of his sadistic sexual wishes. His aggression permeated his sexuality. The excitement of guns, pain in others, and sexual pleasure appeared to be confused in his mind. My acceptance of these fantasies led to an immense sense of relief, and he started thinking about asking girls out.

An extract from a session may illustrate his progress. I had canceled the previous Friday's session, and he came on Monday depressed, having had a "bad weekend." He told me about a school fireworks party where he wandered around feeling lonely; also, he told me about feeling overwhelmed by the amount of homework he had to do; and he ended by saying he was "really pissed off." I made an attempt to link his loneliness and his sense of being overwhelmed to the canceled session, and he responded that he knew I would say that, and he scathingly wondered why it took a trained analyst to spot that he was feeling depressed. He claimed that he had actually enjoyed Friday, particularly not having to get up early, but immediately went on to talk about the school party and his father's pathetic attempts at cheering him up. But the real problem was that he didn't have any friends. I said that I thought my canceling the session must have felt to him as if I too wasn't really his friend, and the analysis was no more than a pathetic attempt at trying to cheer him up. He talked in a sad way about walking about at the party, finding no one to talk to, and then, in a derogatory way, about boys rushing around squirting each other with water pistols; even fireworks weren't as good as they used to be. He thought his father had

had a good time talking to other parents. He had listened for a while but decided that they, too, were stupid.

I took up his disappointment with me and the pain of being excluded: that he wasn't good enough, just like the fireworks. He went back to talking about work. He was really worried, he said, about his work not being good enough, about being perfection-istic and then getting behind. Then he mentioned the clown at the party, who had followed him about; he was quite distressed as he described trying to get away from him and all the revelry going on around him. I said that I thought he felt mocked by the party, just like he felt mocked by my claimed interest in him and by his father's attempt to cheer him up. None of these felt genuine, and he was feeling really pissed off by the thought that I had been mocking him secretly all along. He agreed; he said he felt ridiculous and had not wanted to come to see me this morning. There was a long tirade about his pet-hate subject—photography. He complained that he should have shot a roll of film this weekend and described his struggles to get some work done for his project. He gave a clue about the nature of his inhibition about taking pictures when he mentioned his feeling that his photography teacher only liked taking pictures of girls. I suggested that maybe he was frightened that I would mock or ridicule his interest in girls, yet perhaps he wouldn't mind taking pictures of girls if he had the opportunity. The tirade about the photography teacher continued with increased ferocity—he was a "real lecherous bastard," he only gave adequate teaching to girls, yet he was fat and ugly. They called him "Fat Sam the blow-job man." I said that I thought it was very hard for him because he felt so guilty about not really being able to set aside his interest in pictures of girls, and that every other task, includ-ing the analysis, seemed overwhelming.

He went on to describe his struggle with himself over not wanting to masturbate during the weekend until he had finished his homework; ultimately he lost the struggle and gave in, but he felt terrible about it. But that wasn't the same as the teacher—"He should be able to control his interest, he's sixty, for goodness sake," that's why he hated him. I said that perhaps he had wondered if I had not canceled Friday's session because I was not able to put my work with him above my interest in girls. He laughed and said that perhaps he would call me Sam from now on. But he added that he found it very disturbing to think of adults having sexual interests; then he talked of his father being away a lot recently. I said tentatively that perhaps there was something about his parents' sexuality that disturbed him.

He was relieved and replied: "I'm glad you mentioned it first." Over the weekend he had overheard his parents arguing about sex; it seemed to him that his mother didn't want to have sex with his father any more. He was worried that they would start fighting or that his mother would leave. He said that he hated his father, that he could be a real shit sometimes. I said that I understood how upsetting and confusing overhearing his parents' conversation must have been, that perhaps he just wanted to walk away from it like he did from his father's excited discussions at the party, because it made him hate a part of himself so much. I wanted to add that sometimes he was afraid of growing up, in case he would grow into a man like his father, but he said: "Do you think I'll turn into a little shit like my father when I grow up?"

I said that I thought that what he was describing was a terrible trap he felt he was in, between feeling like a little boy who was isolated and abandoned, who could be ridiculed because he only had a water pistol not a proper penis, or feeling he would grow up and be like Fat Sam, whose sexuality was a subject of ridicule as well as resentment and hatred. There seemed no alternative, no possibility of being just an ordinary man. He said rather sadly that he didn't think he'd ever have a girl friend, that nobody would want him. I added that that was part of it, but he was also frightened that somebody might. He said that was very true. The session ended with Glen leaving much cheered but adding, on his way out: "I still haven't forgiven you for last Friday, though."

Glen's analysis was completed in three and a half years. During this time anxieties about performance in exams, masturbation, and other aspects of sexuality emerged, as would be developmentally expected. His obsessional rituals either stopped or they no longer bothered him. His exam performance was very good, and he was offered places in a number of universities. He continued in psychotherapy for a further year and has made good progress since ending.

Discussion

Glen's problems resolved quickly, not just through addressing his unconscious conflicts but through being given space to play with feelings and ideas. The analytic setting allowed him once again to bring together his two modes of experiencing inner reality. He had withdrawn from the complexity of interpersonal relations into his tentlike coat, apparently unable to think. Yet his difficulty was rooted in a hyperactivity of mentalizing brought forth by his developmental leap. The leap had thrown him back into a mode of psychic equivalence that made the contents of his mind terrifying to him but could be alleviated by the analyst's scaffolding. Glen had known that thoughts were only thoughts and feelings were only feelings, but the preoccupation with the complexity of his own and his parents' feelings, which he had discovered in adolescence, defeated him, and he took refuge in a mental state that does not recognize the nature of psychic reality. Just like the 2-year-old who escapes into pretend in order to avoid the terror that psychic equivalence generates, so Glen, like many adolescents, retreated into a state of dissociation. His obsessionality was a more direct expression of psychic equivalence; however, it was not characterological, and it disappeared simultaneously with the return of mentalization.

There are many differences between the cases of Tony and Glen, but one feature in particular concerns us here. While both Tony and Glen experienced a regression to a dual mode of mental functioning, only in Tony's case did this reveal a destructive and hostile alien self. Both were immensely vulnerable to humiliation and shame because of the return of psychic equivalence. Only in Tony, who had been far more brutalized by earlier experiences, did this shame become ego-destructive. The power of externalization (projective identification) was intense in both patients, and this may indeed be a feature in most adolescent analyses given the pressures for separateness to which we referred above. In Glen's case the externalization of his alien self left a more mature and intact structure, which needed little by way of external support. The challenge of trying to treat someone like Tony is that not only is the therapist required to accept the externalization without which the patient is unable to relate, but that having become what the patient needs her to be, she is required to provide scaffolding and support, recognition of the patient's true (even loving) self. To do this while reflecting the terror that the patient needs to see outside and fending off physical assault is more than can be asked of most therapists.

So how can we cope with regressed adolescent patients? The patients we are considering experience very deep anxieties about the self being overwhelmed, because the parent is no longer there to have an archaic image of herself projected back onto her. Technique has to take account of this. Accepting projections, often initially without interpretation, may be particularly important. One is likely to be made into a good, bad, valued, and hated figure, to be transported at magical speeds and unpredictably through a massive intrapsychic terrain. There is a constant search for alternative figures to serve as hosts for the alien self, which gives rise to the apparent "promiscuity" of these adolescents. Sadly, most people are not accepting of their projections, and experiences of profound rejection tend to dog these young people.

One technical difficulty is likely to be that the more real something feels to the patient, the more it is to talk about, because it feels like a primitive, concrete experience that can only be managed in physical ways. The things that feel real can be apparently trivial experiences, particularly in the transference, which can feel entirely unbearable, and if the analyst approaches those things, there can be dramatic ruptures to the alliance. There may be bizarre demands for concrete solutions, which it is tempting to interpret in terms of more ordinary transference.

Analytic help needs to be offered in a way that is consistent with the developmental challenges of this stage, facilitating the forward movement toward an autonomous identity. This occurs through a process that is analogous to playing with a young child, helping the adolescent to represent and manage his mental states psychologically rather than physically. This has to take place alongside the patient's efforts to re-find an external vehicle, through the transference, for intolerable aspects of his earliest relationships.

PART III

CLINICAL PERSPECTIVES

In part III, we extend our analysis of case material from children and adolescents to adults, illustrating the theoretical and developmental views we have introduced. We have two chapters on serious character pathology, focusing on cases of borderline personality disorder, demonstrating how this pathology has its source in the failure of mentalization and in problems with sustaining the intentional stance. We also propose the notion of an alien self to account for intolerable disturbances in the sense of identity in these patients, the vulnerability to self-harm, and the fact that attachment is both desperately needed and rapidly unbearable, including in the therapeutic relationship. In chapter 11, we broaden our focus to include four case studies of adults, ranging from relatively mild to severe psychopathology. In this chapter, we describe the processing of affects through mentalization—what we term "mentalized affectivity." Finally, the clinical material shows what mentalized affectivity is and how it can be enhanced in and by psychotherapy.

9

The Roots
of Borderline Personality Disorder
in Disorganized Attachment

THE ATTACHMENT SYSTEM AND THE DISTORTION
OF INTERPERSONAL RELATIONSHIPS
IN PERSONALITY DISORDER

There have been many attempts in the past to illuminate the symptomatology of borderline personality disorder using attachment theory. Implicitly or explicitly, Bowlby's suggestion that early experience with the caregiver serves to organize later attachment relationships has been used in explanations of psychopathology in BPD. For example, it has been suggested that the borderline person's experiences of interpersonal attack, neglect, and threats of abandonment may account for a perception of current relationships as attacking and neglectful (Benjamin 1993). Others have suggested that borderline individuals are specifically characterized by a fearful and preoccupied attachment style reflecting "an emotional template of intimacy anxiety/anger" (Dutton, Saunders, Starzomski, and Bartholomew 1994). In studies of AAI narratives of borderline patients, the classification of "preoccupied" is most frequently assigned (Fonagy et al. 1996) and, within this, the "confused," "fearful," and "overwhelmed" subclassification appears to be most common (Patrick et al. 1994). Not surprisingly, such patients also tend to be unresolved with regard to their experience of trauma or abuse.

Past attempts at linking work on attachment with theories of borderline pathology have stressed the common characteristic shared by the ambivalently attached/preoccupied and borderline groups "to check for proximity, signaling to establish contact by pleading or other calls for attention or help, and clinging behaviors" (Gunderson 1996). Gunderson highlights the theme of intolerance of aloneness and terror of abandonment in such patients, which has been claimed to account for many of the clinical features observed in this group of patients. Consistent with this view is the lack of stable representation of the other and the use of the therapist as a transitional object, an extension of the patient, who lacks separate identity and feelings (Modell 1963). Transitional relatedness in these patients is marked by histories of using transitional objects (Morris, Gunderson, and Zanarini 1986) as well as bringing such objects to hospital more frequently than patients with other psychiatric disorders (Cardasis, Hochman, and Silk 1997).

However, directly applied, normative observations of attachment in infancy are probably insufficient to provide an account of the behavior of borderline patients. There is no doubt that borderline individuals are insecure in their attachment, but for several reasons descriptions of insecure attachment from infancy or adulthood provide an inadequate clinical account: (a) Anxious attachment is very common; in working-class samples the majority of children are anxiously attached (Broussard 1995). (b) Anxious patterns of attachment in infancy correspond to relatively stable adult strategies (Main et al. 1985), yet the hallmark of the disordered attachments of borderline individuals is the absence of stability (Higgitt and Fonagy 1992). (c) While the angry protests of the resistant infant may seem to provide a challenging analogy for the pervasively aggressive stance in interpersonal relationships of the borderline individual (Dutton et al. 1994), the clinical presentation of borderline patients frequently includes a violent attack on the patient's own body or that of another human being. It is likely that the propensity for such violence must include an additional component, which predisposes such individuals to act upon bodies rather than upon minds, and indeed it is this very inadequacy in their capacity to represent aggression-related attachment ideation mentally that may place them at risk of violent acts in the context of intimate interpersonal relationships (Fonagy and Target 1995b).

There is some evidence of a specific link between childhood maltreatment—particularly childhood sexual abuse—and borderline personality disorder (Paris, Zweig-Frank, and Guzder 1993). As children, such individuals frequently had caregivers who were themselves within the so-called borderline spectrum of severe personality disorder (Shachnow et al. 1997). Many writers have criticized the term "borderline" as too imprecise, but most continue to find it useful. It may be helpful to clarify the clinical phenomena that we shall be discussing. There are two main psychoanalytic uses of the term, one rooted in psychiatry (e.g., Kernberg 1987) and the other rooted in psychoanalytic clinical practice. Here we are concerned with the second of these meanings; furthermore, the model described here is intended to explain borderline phenomena in many patients, not simply those who fulfill diagnostic criteria of borderline personality disorder. Although we refer to borderline patients, we are therefore not referring to the diagnostic group. Our aim is to elucidate the mental functioning of a larger group of patients whose thinking and affective experience become massively disorganized in the clinical setting as well as elsewhere. Clinical descriptions of borderline phenomena (e.g., Rey 1979) are of individuals who regress dramatically in psychoanalytic treatment, showing psychotic-like phenomena, and who evoke intense feelings in the analyst. These feelings, in combination with the patient's intense emotional lability, create a troubled and troublesome analytic process. Their journey through analysis is marked by transference and often countertransference enactments, with periods of intense dependence punctuated by ruptures of the treatment process. Analysis tends to be prolonged and limited in its results. This chapter is intended to be integrative, in that we aim to account for the experience of borderline patients within the analytic relationship by providing not so much a new clinical description, but more a developmental perspective on the ego mechanisms underlying these phenomena. We also offer some technical suggestions that seem to us to follow from an understanding of the developmental roots of these patients' difficulties.

We have proposed that some personality-disordered individuals are those victims of childhood abuse who coped by refusing to conceive of their attachment figure's thoughts and thus avoided having to think about their caregiver's wish to harm them (Fonagy, Leigh, et al. 1996). There is accumulating evidence that maltreatment impairs the child's reflective capacities and sense of self. Schneider-Rosen and Cicchetti (1984, 1991) noted that abused toddlers showed less positive affect on recognizing themselves in the mirror than did controls. Beeghly and Cicchetti (1994) showed that these toddlers had a specific deficit in the use of internal-state words and that such language tended to be context-bound. Our Menninger study of maltreated 5- to 8-year-olds found specific deficits in tasks requiring mentalization, particularly among those referred for sexual or physical abuse. These results suggest that maltreatment may cause children to withdraw from the mental world. Continuing defensively to disrupt their capacity to depict mental states in themselves and in others leaves them operating on inaccurate, schematic impressions of thoughts and feelings. They are then immensely vulnerable in intimate relationships. There are two propositions here: (a) individuals who experience early trauma may defensively inhibit their capacity to mentalize; and (b) some characteristics of personality disorder may be rooted in this inhibition.

In this chapter, we consider a limited set of symptoms and personality characteristics found in BPD in the light of these propositions: (a) disorganized and dysfunctional self-organization and consequent problems in affect regulation and emotional self-control (including feelings of emptiness, lack of a stable sense of self, emotional instability, and impulsivity); (b) dysfunctional and distorting "social-reality-testing" abilities: the dominance of defensive modes of functioning in intimate relationships and in the analytic transference characterized by splitting and projective identification; (c) vulnerability to trauma, serious difficulties in maintaining intimate attachment relations, proneness to provoke abandonment, and consequent suicidality. We will show how the developmental theory we have advanced in previous chapters can shed light on the symptomatology of BPD.

ATTACHMENT EXPERIENCES AS DETERMINANTS OF CAPACITIES FOR SOCIAL COGNITION

To deepen our understanding of the relation of attachment and BPD, let us consider the question of how the transgenerational transmission of attachment may be mediated. Genetics may seem to provide an obvious explanation. However, the early findings of an ongoing twin study in our laboratory have yielded no evidence of differential levels of concordance of attachment classification between identical and nonidentical twins (Fonagy, Fearon, and Target 1999). Attachment theorists have assumed that securely attached adults are more sensitive to their children's needs, thus fostering an expectation in the infant that dysregulation will be rapidly and effectively met (Belsky et al. 1995; De Wolff and van IJzendoorn 1997). Disappointingly, standard measures of caregiver sensitivity do not appear to explain transgenerational consistencies in attachment classification at all well (van IJzendoorn 1995).

An alternative account of the crucial mediator of attachment security is provided by Mary Main (1991) and Inge Bretherton (1991a), who independently drew attention to Daniel Dennett's concept of the "intentional stance," which has been a core construct in this monograph as well (see chapters 3–5). As we have described, Dennett (1987) theorized that humans have evolved a mentalistic interpretational system that he calls the "intentional stance," whose function is efficiently to predict and explain other people's actions by inferring and attributing causal intentional mind states (such as beliefs, intentions, and desires) to them. This system implies an understanding that behavior can be caused by representational mental states that can be either true or false in relation to actual reality. Since intentional mind states (such as beliefs) are not directly visible, they need to be inferred from a variety of behavioral and situational cues that the interpreter needs to monitor constantly. The ability to mentalize, which can be seen as the central mechanism of "social *(or mental) reality testing*," is therefore a developmental achievement that unfolds through the gradual sensitization to and learning about the mental significance of relevant expressive, behavioral, verbal, and situational cues that indicate the presence of mind states in persons. The ability to mentalize affords the child a measure of protection: for example, a child who is confronted with an unresponsive, depressed mother is protected from confusion and a negative view of himself if he is able to hypothesize that her sadness is due to a loss.

As we have seen, current evidence indicates that normally developing children only construct a relatively mature naive theory of mind at around 3 to 4 years of age. This is well illustrated by the false-belief task first developed by Wimmer and Perner (1983) and described in detail in chapter 5. Such studies indicate that although at the age of 3 years the great majority of children fail in tasks that require them to predict another person's action based on a false belief attributed to his mind, by 4 years of age they have usually mastered this ability. In Wimmer and Perner's experiment, 4-year-old children showed sensitivity to the situational cues that enabled them to infer that the experimenter would continue to act on the basis of an outdated false belief about reality. So by 4 years of age children can understand that actions are caused by mental representations of reality rather than by reality itself (as they see it). By this time, they have also learned the significance of the relevant mindcue—that seeing leads to knowing—that would have sanctioned them to attribute a change in belief to the other's mind.

The securely attached child perceives in the caregiver's reflective stance an image of himself as desiring and believing. He sees that the caregiver represents him as an *intentional being*, and this representation is internalized to form the self. If the caregiver's reflective capacity has enabled her accurately to picture the child's intentional stance, then the child will have the opportunity to "find himself in the other" as a mentalizing individual. At the core of our selves is the representation of how we were seen. Our reflective capacity is thus a transgenerational acquisition. We think of others in terms of desires and beliefs because— and to the extent that—we were thought of as intentional beings.

Only following this process of internalization can the development of awareness of mental states in oneself be generalized to others, including the caregiver.

ATTACHMENT AND THE NORMAL DEVELOPMENT OF THE SELF

Attachment is involved in the development of reflective function at three levels:

1. We assume that the internalization of second-order representations of internal states (self-states) depends upon the sensitive reflection of the caregiver, as discussed in chapter 4. The child's concept of affect is not arrived at by introspection; rather, the caregiver's emotional expression, congruent with the child's state, is internalized and becomes its "representation" (Gergely and Watson 1996; Target and Fonagy 1996). These self-states become the building blocks with which a reflective internal working model can be constructed. The combination of the representation of self-experience and the representation of the reaction of the caregiver elaborates the child's teleological model of the mind and ultimately enables him to interpret and understand affective displays in others as well as arriving at the regulation and control of his own emotions.

2. The gradual move from a teleological to an intentional stance is intrinsically linked to the child's experience of safety in exploring the caregiver's mind to disentangle the feelings and thoughts that might account for the caregiver's behavior. The secure infant feels safe in making attributions of mental states to account for this behavior. In contrast, the avoidant child shuns the mental state of the other to some degree, while the resistant child focuses on his own state of distress, to the exclusion of close intersubjective exchanges. Disorganized infants may represent a special category; hypervigilant of the caregiver's behavior, they use all cues available for prediction and may be acutely sensitized to intentional states, and thus they may be more

ready to construct a mentalized account of the caregiver's behavior. In such children mentalization may be evident, but it does not have the central and effective role in self-organization that characterizes securely attached children. There may be a number of linked reasons for this: (*a*) the caregiver of the disorganized infant is less likely to be reliably contingent in responding to the infant's self-state, and further to show systematic biases in her perception and reflection of his state; (*b*) the mental state of the caregiver evokes intense anxiety, either through frightening behavior, suggesting malevolence toward the child, or behavior suggesting fear, which may include fear of the child himself; (*c*) the child needs to use disproportionate resources to understand the parent's behavior, at the expense of reflecting on self-states. These factors combine, perhaps, to make disorganized infants keen readers of the caregiver's mind under certain circumstances, but (we suggest) poor readers of their own mental states.

3. The caregiver makes a further important contribution, perhaps most important at a somewhat later stage. Prototypically, while playing with the child, the caregiver simultaneously engages the child's internal world while retaining an external reality-based perspective (Fonagy and Target 1996; Target and Fonagy 1996). The child is moved from a subjective world of psychic equivalence—where internal experience and external reality are assumed to be equivalent—to a mentalized internal world where subjective experiences are recognized as but one version of external reality, a "representation of reality." This is analogous to psychoanalytic discussions of the cognitive impact of the oedipal triad, where the shared reality of two people is suddenly experienced from the point of view of the third (Britton 1998). The parents' engagement in the child's internal world moves him beyond the conception of his mind as a replica of the external world.

These three components—the second-order representation of affect and the intentional representation of the caregiver and of the self—equip the child to confront a sometimes harsh social reality. The robust establishment of reflective function is protective; fragile reflective function predicts a vulnerability to later trauma. Secure attachment and reflective function are overlapping constructs, and the vulnerability associated with insecure attachment lies primarily in the child's diffidence in conceiving of the world in terms of psychic rather than physical reality. Given trauma of sufficient intensity, even a secure bond may sometimes crumble, yet in the absence of psychosocial pressures, reflective function may offer only marginal developmental advantage. To understand severe personality disorder, it is important that we are attuned to the limited capacity of the patient to use the language of mental states for self-organization as well as social understanding.

A TRANSGENERATIONAL MODEL
OF PERSONALITY DISORDER

The social inheritance aspect of BPD may be an important clue in our understanding of the disorder. Studies by our group (Fonagy et al. 1996) as well as others (Patrick et al. 1994) have demonstrated considerable distortions of attachment representation in personality-disordered, particularly borderline, individuals. In our study, individuals with BPD diagnosis had predominantly *preoccupied* attachments, associated with unresolved experiences of trauma and a striking reduction in reflective capacity. In a further study we compared our patient group to a matched group of forensic psychiatric referrals. In the latter group, *dismissing* patterns of attachment predominated, unresolved trauma was less evident (although the prevalence of trauma was comparable), and reflective capacity was even lower (Levinson and Fonagy, unpublished manuscript, UCL).

We shall argue that the dysfunctional and distorted understanding of other minds (and of the mind of the self) characteristic of some personality-disordered individuals is the result of adverse traumatic experiences with attachment figures (often involving physical maltreatment and/or sexual abuse) during the early formation of attachment representations. We recognize, however, that explicit maltreatment is not an inevitable part of

BPD pathology. Early neglect may sensitize individuals to later attachment trauma, and psychological abuse associated with persistent neglect of the young child's sense of subjectivity might be harder to recognize than frank maltreatment. The pathological consequences of early attachment trauma are mediated by the distorting effect that such a deviant attachment context exerts on the normal unfolding of mindreading abilities.

THE IMPACT OF MALTREATMENT ON REFLECTIVE FUNCTION

One serious consequence of parental neglect, maltreatment, and abuse is the lack of a sensitive and infant-attuned emotional-intentional mirroring environment that we hypothesized to be necessary for the establishment of secondary representations for the infant's self-states. Lacking such secondary representations, the affective impulses of the "constitutional self" remain relatively inaccessible and nonconscious, resulting in feelings of emptiness and disorganization and in a deficient ability for impulse control. There is accumulating evidence that maltreatment impairs the child's reflective capacities and sense of self (Beeghly and Cicchetti 1994; Schneider-Rosen and Cicchetti 1984, 1991). This situation can, and probably often does, induce a severe and vicious developmental cycle. Poor comprehension of mental states associated with maltreatment amplifies distress, activating the attachment system. The need for proximity thus persists and perhaps even increases as a consequence of the distress caused by abuse. Mental proximity becomes unbearably painful, and the need for closeness is expressed at a physical level. Thus, the child may paradoxically be driven physically closer to the abuser. This ability to adapt to, modify, or avoid the perpetrator's behavior is likely to be constrained by limited mentalizing skills, and exposure to further abuse is likely. The paradox of proximity seeking at the physical level concurrent with psychological avoidance lies at the root of the disorganized attachment so consistently seen in abused children.

Why should the family environment of maltreatment undermine reflective function? (*a*) Recognition of the mental state of the other can be dangerous to the developing self. The child who recognizes the hatred or murderousness implied by the parent's acts of abuse is forced to see himself as worthless or unlovable. (*b*) The meaning of intentional states may be denied or distorted; abusive parents commonly claim beliefs or feelings at odds with their behavior. (*c*) The attachment context and the public world, where reflective function is common, are kept rigidly separate. (*d*) Last, the dysfunction may occur, not because of the maltreatment itself, but because of the family atmosphere that surrounds it. Authoritarian parenting, commonly associated with maltreatment, is also known to retard the development of mentalization (Astington 1996). These youngsters and their mothers find it difficult to take a playful stance (Alessandri 1992), so the social scaffolding needed for the development of mentalization may be absent. A mentalizing stance is also unlikely to develop in a child who generally feels treated as an uncared-for physical object.

Stating this more generally, we would argue that exploring the infant-directed intentions and emotional attitudes inferable from the abuser's actions can result in seriously dysfunctional consequences for the developing self. On the one hand, the persecutory intentions attributed to the abusive attachment figure represent continuous danger to the self and an acute lack of feelings of attachment security. On the other hand, the child, in an attempt to rationalize the persecutory intentions of the caregiver, often ends up attributing seriously negative properties of worthlessness, unwantedness, ugliness, and so forth to his own self-image. We have proposed (Fonagy 1991) that the characteristic defensive reaction of coping with these consequences by the general inhibition of the tendency to mentalize about the abusive caregiver's intentions is most likely to occur if the capacity to mentalize was poorly established in early infancy. The child is more likely to develop a tendency to avoid contemplating the mental states of the abuser if thinking has remained somewhat teleological and the internal world is more likely to be represented in the mode of psychic equivalence (see chapters 5 and 6). In the long run, the selective exclusion of internal-state representations vis-à-vis the maltreating caregiver results in a deficit in mentalization capacities, at least, in object relations that are related or similar to the abusive attachment context. We see this as the result of a reversible inhibition of a natural biological tendency to try to read the mind states of the attachment figure; the child's tendency to stop monitoring and learning about the relevant cues that support mental-state attributions, however, leads gradually to an increasingly impoverished understanding of other minds. This, then, creates a deficit-like state that is a great deal more difficult to reverse, even given more favorable social circumstances.

PERSONALITY DISORDER
AND DEFICIT IN MENTALIZING

Are some characteristics of personality disorder rooted in a deficit of mentalization? It may be tempting to argue that some problems of violence and borderline states can be explained as dismissive and preoccupied forms of nonmentalizing self-organizations, respectively. This would be oversimplistic. In both instances there are variations across situations or types of relationships. The delinquent adolescent is, for example, aware of the mental states of others in his gang and the borderline individual is at times hypersensitive to the emotional states of mental-health professionals and family members.

Following the principles of Kurt Fischer's "dynamic skills theory" of development (Fischer et al. 1990), we assume that maltreatment is associated with a "fractionation" or splitting of reflective function across tasks and domains. During the earlier stages of Piagetian development, just as the understanding of conservation of liquid does not as yet generalize to conservation of area, reflective capacity in one domain of interpersonal interaction may not at first generalize to others. In normal development, there would be some degree of integration and generalization of a mentalizing model of behavior. In severe personality disorder, however, development goes awry—the normal coordination of previously separate skills does not come about.

Teleological models of behavior persist in all of us and develop in sophistication, as in many circumstances they provide useful predictions and adequate explanations. For example, if on a wet day one observes one's friend crossing the road, one might, taking the intentional stance, infer that he does not wish to get wet (desire state) and he thinks there is still a shop on that side that sells umbrellas (belief state). (It actually closed two weeks ago—I snigger with appropriate Schadenfreude.) However, the same action could also be interpreted as rational within the teleological framework. One could conclude that one's friend has crossed the road in order to be able to walk faster (visible outcome) because there are too many people on this side (visible constraint). Clearly, the application of the teleological stance can become problematic in the context of attachment relationships. Assume that X is a close friend. Adopting the teleological stance may be helpful in avoiding imputing the desire to X that he wanted to avoid me and the belief state that he thinks I did not see him or that he thinks that I think that he did not see me.

The mentalizing inferences of the intentional stance are no more likely to be correct than the physicalistic ones of the teleological mode. However, mentalizing models are uniquely valuable in complex interpersonal situations, involving for instance conflict, deception, or irrationality. Unfortunately, nonreflective internal working models come to dominate the behavior of personality-disordered individuals in emotionally charged or intimate relationships, and any interpersonal situation that calls forth relationship representations that derive from the primary attachment relationships. These individuals can be disadvantaged because (a) their caregivers did not facilitate mentalizing capacity within a secure attachment relationship (vulnerability), (b) they have subsequently acquired an emotional disincentive for taking the perspective of others who are hostile as well as nonreflective (trauma), (c) subsequent relationships are jeopardized by the lack of a mental-state attributional model of the original trauma and subsequent experiences (lack of resilience), and (d) they may divide mentalizing resources unevenly between their external and internal worlds, becoming hypervigilant toward others but uncomprehending of their own states (uneven adaptation).

DISORGANIZED ATTACHMENT
AND PERSONALITY DISORDER

Why should emotionally charged interactions trigger a "regression" to nonmentalistic thinking? We have suggested that reflective function and its attachment context are at the root of self-organization. There is overwhelming pressure on the child to develop a representation for internal states. As we saw in chapter 4, within the biopsychosocial attachment system the child seeks out aspects of the environment that are contingently related to his self-expressions. The child's emerging self-representation will map onto what could be called a primary or "constitutional self" (the child's actual internal states). In the case of disorganized attachment, however, the self-representation will not be true to this. Winnicott (1967, p. 33) warned us that a child who fails to find his current state mirrored is likely to internalize the mother's actual state as part of his own self-structure. Evidence is accumulating that caregivers of disorganized infants frequently respond to the infant's distress by hostile–helpless (Lyons-Ruth, Bronfman, and Parsons 1999), dissociated or disorganized, frightened or frightening (Jacobovitz, Hazen, and Riggs 1997; Schuengel 1997; Schuengel, Bakermans-Kranenburg, and van IJzendoorn 1999) behavior. It is as if the infant's emotional expression triggers a temporary failure on the part of the caretaker to perceive the child as an intentional person, and she responds with massive withdrawal, communication errors, role confusion, or negative–intrusive or frightening behavior. Consequently, these children come to experience their own arousal as a danger signal for abandonment, which triggers teleological, nonmentalizing functioning; it brings forth an image of the parent who withdraws from the child in a state of anxiety or rage, to which the child reacts with a complementary dissociative response (Liotti 1999). Thus the internal experience of such individuals remains unlabelled and chaotic, and the uncontained affect generates further dysregulation. Rather than internalizing a coherent self-representation from the caregiver, the child incorporates a representation of the other into his nascent self-structure (Fonagy and Target 1995a). When confronted with a frightened or frightening caregiver, the infant takes in as part of himself the mother's feeling of rage, hatred, or fear and her image of him as frightening or unmanageable.

As this image undermines self-organization, often it needs to be externalized for the child to achieve a coherent self-representation. The disorganized attachment behavior of the infant (Main and Solomon 1990) and its sequelae, bossy and controlling interactions with the parent, may be understood as a rudimentary attempt to blot out the unacceptable aspects of the self-representation. Research shows that the disoriented disorganized behavior of the infant is gradually replaced, over the first 5–7 years of life, by brittle behavioral strategies that seek to control the parent, through either punitive acts or age-inappropriate care-giving behavior (Cassidy and Marvin 1992; Main and Cassidy 1988). Such attempts at manipulating the behavior of the caregiver (George and Solomon 1998; Solomon, George, and Dejong 1995; Wartner, Grossmann, Fremmer-Bombrik, and Suess 1994) permit the externalization of parts of the self and limit further intrusion into the self-representation. Similar patterns are reported in observations of peer interactions (Jacobovitz and Hazen 1999). There is further evidence that the parents of such children experience the child as taking control of the relationship and, consequently, experience themselves as increasingly immobilized and helpless and failing to provide care-giving (George and Solomon 1996; Solomon and George 1996). The descriptions by mothers of disorganized children are often quite remarkable; they see the child as a replica of themselves and experience themselves as merging with the child. We assume that these experiences are explained by the child externalizing aspects of his self-representation that relate, not to the internalization of the mother's representation of the self, but to the representation of the mother within the self. The tendency for such children to show precocious care-giving behavior (West and George, in press) is also consistent with the idea that the representation of the mother is internalized into the self.

In line with Lyons-Ruth's diathesis model (Lyons-Ruth, Bronfman, and Atwood 1999; Lyons-Ruth and Jacobovitz 1999), we conceive of the flawed self-organization that follows disorganized attachment as a vulnerability. In particular, the poorly constructed self-structure of such children sensitizes them to later trauma. We believe that there is a biological drive to construct a secondary representation of the constitutional self through internalizing the infant-directed reactions of attachment figures. This was discussed in some detail in chapter 4. We argued that when a contingent affect-mirroring environment is provided, the internalized self-representations will map onto the primary, procedural self-states of the constitutional self. The biologically driven internalization of the self-directed attitudes of the attachment figure into the self-structure takes place, however, even when the caregiver is nonreflective, neglectful, or abusive. In such cases, the internalized other will remain alien and unconnected to the structures of the constitutional self. Furthermore, in seriously abusive and maltreating environments the internalized alien part of the self will be persecutory and will represent a continuous danger of self-harm and consequent lack of feelings of attachment security. The absence of adequate second-order (symbolic) representations of self-states creates a continuous and intense desire for understanding what is experienced as internal chaos. The child's self-development is delayed, and he remains on the look-out for an object that, once internalized, would be capable of bringing about an integration of self-states. Disastrously, in the case of some children maltreated later in development, this will not be a neutral other but, rather, a torturing one. Once internalized and lodged within the self-representation, this hostile "alien" representation will have to be expelled not only because it does not match the constitutional self, but also because it is persecutory. The consequences for interpersonal relationships and for affect regulation are then disastrous (Carlson and Sroufe 1995). The fact that the internalized alien is not grounded in or bound to the actual self-states of the constitutional self, together with the further fact that it represents a persecutory threat to the self, motivates a strong defensive tendency to externalize the alien part of the self by projecting it onto others. As long as the internalized torturing alien is projected onto the other, the self achieves a temporary (and illusory) sense of control and feeling of security. The price to pay for this fleeting sense of self-organization and control is great, however.

The mechanism described here may be a prototypical example of the psychoanalytic notion of projective identification or, more specifically, what Elizabeth Spillius (1994) has termed "evocatory projective identification." Simply put, disorganized attachment gives rise to a disorganized self. The individual, when alone, feels unsafe and vulnerable because of the proximity of a torturing and destructive representation from which he cannot escape because it is experienced from within the self. Unless his relationships permit externalization, he feels almost literally at risk of disappearance, psychological merging, and the dissolution of all relationship boundaries (Gunderson 1984).

SYMPTOMATOLOGY OF BORDERLINE PERSONALITY DISORDER

Several lines of evidence suggest that borderline patients are seriously deficient in social (or mental) reality testing. In particular, their ability to monitor and interpret correctly the relevant mind-state cues available in intimate attachment relationships seems inhibited, undeveloped, or distorted. When attributing mental states, they often disregard or bypass such cues, and, instead, they identify the mind states of others in a distorted way through defensive splitting and projective identification. Nor do they do much better when it comes to understanding their own mind states: they often report feelings of emptiness or chaotic and undifferentiated self-states. Their emotional instability, their proneness for acting out and for externalizing violent impulses, all indicate a rather low degree of awareness of self-states and a consequent lack of self-control.

Let us briefly review some common symptomatology of borderline states from the point of view of the model we have outlined.

1. The *unstable sense of self* of many such patients is a consequence of the absence of reflective capacity and of accurate second-order representations of internal states (feelings, beliefs, wishes, ideas). A stable sense of self is illusorily achieved when

the alien self is externalized onto the other and controlled therein. The individual, then, is an active agent who is in control, despite the fragility of the self. The heavy price paid is that by forcing the other to behave as if he or she were part of his internal representation, the potential for a "real" relationship has been lost, and the patient is actually preparing the way for abandonment. The projective and persecutory construction of the other's mind in intimate relationships represents a coercive, aggressive, and distorting communicative attitude that is usually greatly resented by the partner. As a result, there is a serious realistic risk of abandonment in such relationships. The eventual abandonment also means a return of the projected hostile and torturing alien into the self, together with the consequent feelings of danger, terror, and disorganization.

2. The *impulsivity* of such patients may also be due to a lack of awareness of their own emotional states associated with the absence of symbolic representations of emotions. Borderline patients often find themselves in states of emotional arousal that are beyond self-control, since mentalization is an essential component of affect regulation. Other affects are often brought forth to protect the self, and apparently uncontrollable rage may express, as well as obscure, the experience of fragmentation. Impulsivity may also be due to the dominance of prementalistic physical action-centered strategies, particularly in threatening relationships. It is only when behavior is construed as intentional that one can conceive of influencing it through changing the other's state of mind. Talking about it only makes sense if the behavior of the other has been explained in terms of wishes and beliefs. If, on the other hand, it is interpreted solely in terms of its observable consequence, a kind of "*learned mentalistic helplessness*" sets in. The obvious way then to intervene will be through physical action. This may include words that sound like an attempt at changing the other person's intentions but are, in fact, intimidation—efforts to force the other person into a different course of action. Only a physical end-state is seen. This may be represented in terms of that person's body. The patient may physically threaten, hit, damage, or even kill; alternatively, he may tease, excite, even seduce.

Such patients bring many memories of having been treated in such ways. A young man confessed to his father that he had accidentally broken a lamp. The father reassured him that it was OK since he didn't do it on purpose. The father later saw that the lamp the child had broken was his favorite, and he beat his son so hard that he fractured his arm as the child raised it to protect himself. The father's mind is working in a nonmentalizing (teleological) mode in these examples. It is what the child has done (visible outcome), rather than his intention (mental state), that drives the father's action.

In this context the distinction between the two apparently overlapping modes of representing intentional action is particularly helpful. It will be remembered that following Jeannerod (1994) an "*intention-in-action*" was defined as a representation with a content that specifies the particular bodily action in relation to its goal state and is the proximal cause of the motor behavior. It is a representational state that does not simply trigger the action but also functions to monitor and guide it, allowing for an on-line comparison between perceptual feedback about the outcome state achieved and the goal state as specified in the representation. Their content can become the subject of consciousness especially if their execution is blocked, which might make them appear as if they were mentalized representations, but in essence they are nonconscious actions carried out automatically. In contrast, "*prior intentions*" are representations that are present prior to the motor action (and the concomitant intention-in-action). They can be active and consciously experienced even when the intended action does not get executed. Prior intentions contain a representation of the self in relation to the desired goal state (future reality) and can generate particular intention-in-actions when conditions in the external world allow the self to execute a viable action to fulfill the goal. Prior intentions need not represent the specific goal state aimed at but just the general motivational state prior to the action. Impulsivity in BPD may be thus seen as representations of intentional actions generated by the "teleological stance" corresponding to the level of representations of intention-in-actions. The principle of rational action still guides impulsive acts but as a function of available evidence about the "*pragmatic*" aspects of a goal object, about the specific situational constraints on action, and about the dispositional constraints characteristic of the actor. Thus, for example, prior intention is not attributed to the other, and the consequences of the action are not predicted, commonly leading to sizable interpersonal conflicts and other social disasters.

3. *Emotional instability and irritability* require us to think about the representation of reality in borderline patients. Interpersonal schemata are notably rigid in borderline patients because they cannot imagine that the other could have a construction of reality that is different from the one they experience as compelling. If the behavior of the other and knowledge of reality do not fit, we normally try to understand the behavior in mentalizing terms. For example, "He mistook my $20 for a $10 bill (false belief)—that is why he only gave me $5 change." If this and other possibilities do not readily occur to one, and alternatives cannot easily be compared, an oversimplified construction is uncritically accepted: "He was cheating me!" Especially for individuals who had nonreflective, coercive caregiving, this frequently leads to paranoid constructions of the other's desire state.[1] Mentalization acts as a buffer: when actions of others are unexpected, this buffer function allows one to create auxiliary hypotheses about beliefs, which forestall automatic threatening conclusions.

Once again, we see the traumatized individual doubly disadvantaged. Internal working models constructed on the basis of abuse assume that malevolence is not improbable; being unable to generate auxiliary hypotheses, particularly under stress, makes the experience of danger even more compelling. Psychic equivalence makes it real. Normally, access to the mentalization buffer allows one to play with reality (Target and Fonagy 1996). Understanding is known to be fallible. But if there is only one way of seeing things, an attempt by a third party, such as a therapist, to persuade the patient that he is wrong might be perceived as an attempt to drive him crazy.

---

[1] The striking facet of such constructions is that they tend to be self-related. The individual with a self-representation constructed around an abusive caregiver is constantly on the alert to externalize this persecutory self-representation. He needs enemies to prevent the destructiveness within.

4. A brief word about *suicidality*. Clinicians are familiar with the enormous fear of physical abandonment in borderline patients (Gunderson 1996). This, perhaps more than any other aspect, alerts clinicians to the disorganized attachment models with which such patients are forced to live. When the other is needed for self-coherence, abandonment means reinternalizing the intolerable, alien self-image and consequent destruction of the self. Suicide represents the fantasized destruction of this alien other within the self. Suicide attempts are often aimed at forestalling the possibility of abandonment; they seem a last-ditch attempt at reestablishing a relationship. The child's experience may have been that only something extreme would bring about changes in the adult's behavior, and that their caregivers used similarly coercive measures to influence their own behavior. The strong tendency for suicide so often triggered by abandonment in borderline patients can also be understood to represent a fantasized destruction of the internalized hostile alien, a final attempt to liberate the constitutional self from its torturer.

Whereas suicide and self-harm are common manifestations of disorganized attachment in women, in men with similar pathology it is violence against the other that is more common. Such a person can only maintain a relationship if this enables him to externalize alien parts of the self. The relationship that violent men are forced to establish is one where their significant other can act as a vehicle for intolerable self-states. They control their relationship through crude manipulation in order to engender the self-image that they feel desperate to disown. They resort to violence at times when the independent mental existence of the other threatens this process of externalization. At these times, dramatic and radical action is taken because the individual is terrorized by the possibility that the coherence of self achieved through control and manipulation will be destroyed by the return of what has been externalized. The act of violence at such moments performs a dual function: (*a*) to recreate and reexperience the alien self within the other, and (*b*) to destroy it in the unconscious hope that it will then be destroyed forever. Perceiving the terror in the eyes of their victim, they are once again reassured, and the relationship regains its paramount importance in their psychic organization. Thus their pleas for forgiveness and unreserved contrition are genuine, in the sense that their need for a relationship where this externalization is possible is undoubtedly absolute.

5. *Splitting*, the partial representation of the other (or the self) is a common obstacle to adequate communication with such patients. Understanding the other in mental terms initially requires integrating assumed intentions in a coherent manner. The hopelessness of this task in the face of the contradictory attitudes of an abuser is seen as one of the causes of the mentalizing deficit. The emergent solution for the child, given the imperative to arrive at coherent representations, is to split the representation of the other into several coherent subsets of intentions (Gergely 1997, 2000)—primarily, into an idealized and a persecutory identity. In the absence of reflective function, the individual finds it impossible to use both representations simultaneously. Splitting enables the individual to create mentalized images of others, but these are inaccurate and oversimplified and allow for only an illusion of mentalized interpersonal interchange.

As splitting is generally agreed to be the prototypical defense of borderline personality disorder, it seems appropriate to expand on this idea further. In naive theory of mind, predicting another person's actions from his beliefs and desires is driven by a basic principle of "rational action" (Gergely et al. 1995). This principle assumes that human agents tend to pursue a course of action to fulfill their desires that seems most rational or efficient, given their beliefs about the situation. This is supplemented by a further assumption that we can call the principle of "mental coherence" (Dennett 1987; Gergely 2000). This additional principle assumes that the intentions, beliefs, and desires of rational human beings are not contradictory or ambivalent. Clearly, if this assumption is seriously violated, it becomes impossible to identify and predict a rational course of action that would satisfy the simultaneously present contradictory intentions of the other. In such a case, the other's behavior becomes unpredictable by the child through mentalization, and feelings of anxiety, helplessness, and insecurity are generated.

Gergely (2000) proposed that the maltreatment attachment context represents precisely such a dilemma for young children. By about 2 years of age infants become able to derive generalized intentions and attitudes that characterize the mind of the attachment figure. The caregiver who generates attachment disorganization (Lyons-Ruth and Jacobovitz 1999; Schuengel et al. 1999), however, typically provides contradictory information regarding her infant-directed mental attitudes: sometimes she abuses the child, while at other times she seems to deny this and even behaves in a caring fashion. By inferring the corresponding persecutory and benevolent intentions and attributing them to the caregiver's mind, the child faces the impossible task of anticipating the other's behavior from contradictory or ambivalent intentions. As a defense against the ensuing uncertainty, anxiety, and helplessness, the child splits the identity of the abuser into separate minds with noncontradictory (persecutory versus benevolent) sets of intentions. As a result, predicting action through mentalization becomes possible again, since within the separate and split identities of the other the principle of mental coherence can be maintained. In this way the feelings of helplessness and anxiety triggered by the inability to predict the other's behavior through mentalization are avoided. The great price to be paid for this defensive construction of social experience is, of course, the ensuing distortion of reality and the generation of mistaken and maladaptive responses when actions are anticipated incorrectly based on the split representations of the other's mind.

6. The second prototypical borderline defense is held to be *projective identification* (Ogden 1979; Spillius 1992). We have argued that in the normal development of mindreading there are two mechanisms by which attribution of mental states to the other is accomplished: (*a*) by monitoring the relevant behavioral and situational cues to infer the mind states of the other, or, if such cues are not available or not recognized, one can (*b*) resort to "default simulation": attributing mental states to the other through analogy to the self. Above we argued that in an abusive attachment context the child often develops a defensive inhibition to mentalizing about the caregiver's intentions. This may, in

turn, result in a general deficiency of attention processes in monitoring for and reading the relevant behavioral and situational cues that would allow the child to infer the other's mental states. As a result, the child will automatically resort to interpreting the other's mind through "default simulation" even when the relevant informative cues are, in principle, available. Now the question is: what contents of his own mind will the child use to "default simulate" the other's mental experience? We have seen that as a result of abusive caregiving, the young child internalizes the representation of the hostile and alien other into his self-structure. We have also argued that due to the danger that its persecutory aspects represent to the self, and due to its lack of groundedness in the actual self-states of the constitutional self, a defensive tendency to expel this internalized alien through projection onto others will be established. Now if the other's mental states cannot be identified through cue-reading as a result of the defensive inhibition of mentalizing about the abuser's mind, when resorting to "default simulation," the to-be-expelled alien part of the self-representation will be readily available to provide the informational basis for simulating the other. Thus, borderline patients will show a tendency to "default simulate" the other's mental state automatically by projecting onto him the internalized persecutory representation of the abusive caregiver. This is why the defense mechanism of "projective identification" becomes so prominent in the manner in which borderline patients construct distorted representations of the mental states of others in intimate relationships and in the analytic transference.

7. A further common experience of such patients is the feeling of *emptiness* that accompanies much of their lives. The emptiness is a direct consequence of the absence of secondary representations of self-states, certainly at the conscious level, and of the shallowness with which other people and relationships are experienced. The abandonment of mentalization creates a deep sense of isolation. To experience being with another, the person has to be there as a mind; to feel the continuity between past and present, it is mental states that provide the link; emptiness and, at an extreme, dissociation is the best description such

individuals can give of the absence of meaning that the failure of mentalization creates.

SOME QUALIFICATIONS
OF THE MODEL PROPOSED

A number of qualifications are in order.

1. Abnormalities of parenting represent but one route to difficulties with mentalization. Biological vulnerabilities, such as attention deficits, are also likely to limit the child's opportunities for evolving reflective capacity. We should be aware that, as in most aspects of development, there is a subtle bidirectional causal process inherent in such biological vulnerabilities. Vulnerabilities provoke situations of interpersonal conflict as well as placing limitations on the child's capacities. Thus biological factors can limit mentalizing potential but may also act through generating environments where mentalization is unlikely to be fully established.

2. Many of us working with borderline patients willingly attest to their at times apparently acute sensitivity to mind states, certainly for the purposes of manipulation and control. Does this imply that mentalization is not a core dysfunction? The likely solution to this puzzle is that patients with severe personality disorders do develop a certain level of nonconscious mindreading skills. Clements and Perner (1994) show that children just before the age of 3 years have an intuitive understanding of false belief, which they are unable to communicate verbally but can demonstrate in their nonverbal reactions, such as eye movements. It is conceivable that, at a stage when such nonconscious mindreading skills begin to evolve, the implications of the child trying to infer the intentions behind their caregivers' reactions are so negative that they are forced to fall back on the strategy of influencing the other by action rather than by words. However, they retain access, at a nonconscious level, to mental states but repudiate consciousness of it. Reflective function does not

permanently disappear: borderline patients are not "mind blind": rather, they are not "mind conscious." They pick up on cues that influence the behavioral system, but this does not surface in terms of conscious inferences. The developmental deficit is: (*a*) restricted to specific internal working models (or relationship patterns); (*b*) likely to be activated in specific attachment contexts; and (*c*) may pertain more to reflective self-function (reflection on self-states) than to envisioning the mental world of the other.

3. Not all parents of individuals with problems related to mentalization are borderline. Some parents, in our experience at least, are highly reflective individuals, who have, however, significant problems related to their children and sometimes to a specific child. Lack of sensitivity to intentional states is not a global variable affecting all situations. It must be assessed in relation to a specific child–caregiver relationship.

PSYCHOTHERAPY AND MENTALIZING

Psychotherapy, in all its incarnations, is about the rekindling of mentalization. Whether we look at Marcia Linehan's dialectic behavior therapy protocol (Linehan 1993), John Clarkin's and Otto Kernberg's recommendations for psychoanalytic psychotherapy (Clarkin, Kernberg, and Yeomans 1999; Kernberg and Clarkin 1993), or Anthony Ryle's cognitive analytic therapy (Ryle 1997), they all: (*a*) aim to establish an attachment relationship with the patient, (*b*) aim to use this to create an interpersonal context where understanding of mental states becomes a focus, and (*c*) attempt (mostly implicitly) to recreate a situation where the self is recognized as intentional and real by the therapist, and this recognition is clearly perceived by the patient.

The core of psychological therapy with individuals with severe personality disorder is the enhancement of reflective processes. The therapist must help the patient to understand and label emotional states with a view to strengthening the secondary representational system. Often this is achieved not just by interpretations of moment-to-moment changes in the patient's emotional stance but by focusing the patient's attention on the therapist's experience. The patient comes in looking somewhat timid. The therapist says: "You see me as frightening." The therapist avoids describing complex mental states and rarely refers to the patient's conflicts or to his ambivalence (conscious or unconscious). Change is generated in these patients by brief, specific interpretation. The inevitable destructiveness of these patients in relation to the therapeutic enterprise is rarely adequately dealt with by confrontation or interpretations of their aggressive intent. Rather, comments are often more helpfully aimed at the emotional antecedents of enactments—the emotions that cause confusion and disorganization.

As we have seen, gaps in mentalization engender impulsivity, and the intensification of the therapeutic relationship frequently highlights the patient's difficulties in creating a distance between internal and external reality. The therapist's task is in some way analogous to that of the parents who create a frame for pretend play—except in this case it is thoughts and feelings that need to become accessible through the creation of such a transitional area. The therapist must get used to working with precursors of mentalization. The task is the elaboration of teleological models into intentional ones. Integrating or trying to bridge the dissociated mode of the patient's functioning where nothing feels real (certainly not words or ideas) with moments when words and ideas carry unbelievable potency and destructiveness can seem an awesome task. Yet progress is only conceivable by being able to become part of the patient's pretend world, trying to make it real while at the same time avoiding entanglement with the equation of thoughts and reality.

Should the psychoanalytic therapist work in the transference with borderline patients? The answer is No and Yes. No—in the sense that the transference of early relationship patterns onto current relationships, while ever-present, is rarely helpful to highlight. Without mentalization, transference is not displacement but is experienced as real. The therapist is the abuser—no as–if about it. When such transference interpretations are made, the patient is often thrown into a pretend mode, and gradually patient and therapist may elaborate a world that, however detailed and complex, has little experiential contact with reality. Thus a more productive line is the simple acknowledgment of affect in the here-and-now while conveying, in words, tone, and posture, that the therapist is able to cope with the patient's emotional state. Yes—in that the transference, using the term in its broadest sense, is helpful as a concrete demonstration of alternative perspectives. The contrast between the patient's perception of the therapist as she or he is imagined and as she or he is may help to place quotation marks around the transference experience.

The most complicated challenge arising out of treating such patients relates to externalizations of unbearable self-states. Some therapists split the transference by creating alternative foci for the patient's feelings—a pharmacotherapist and a psychotherapist, individual and group treatments. Others attempt to control enactments by making therapy contractually dependent. Sometimes neither of these is possible, at other times neither is sufficient. Often, having modest aims is the most helpful device. With patients like these, insight will not prevent enactment: the therapeutic aim is simply the gradual encouragement of mentalization. Rather than interpreting enactments, the therapist tries to deal with their antecedents and consequences. She needs to be equally permissive about her own tendency to enact in the countertransference. Within this model, it is necessary to accept that in order for the patient to stay in mental proximity, the therapist must occasionally allow herself to become the vehicle for the alien part within his self. If she is to be of any use to him, she has to become what he needs her to be. Yet if she becomes that person fully, she can be of no help to him. She aims for a state of equipoise between these two positions—allowing herself to do as required yet trying to retain in her mind as clear and coherent an image of the state of his mind as she is able to achieve.

What are the hallmarks of a successful therapy with an individual with severe borderline features? While we do not believe that any theory, including the present one, gets anywhere close to explaining the patient's problems, we do believe that it is important to have a theoretically coherent approach. Such patients require that we are predictable, and our models of them can then come to form the core of their self-representations. A stable, coherent image is hard to maintain should the therapist swap theoretical approaches at an alarming rate. Mentalization can only be acquired in the context of an attachment relationship. And this means that the therapy must embody a secure base. Attachment is inseparable from a focus on the mental state of the other. There can be no bond without understanding, even if understanding is possible without a bond. In our experience these treatments always take considerable time, and consistency over such prolonged periods is often hard to maintain. The patient is terrified of and actively fights mental closeness, even when physical proximity appears to be his overarching goal. Retaining such proximity while under persistent attack is neither comfortable nor likely to be achieved unless one leaves one's narcissism at the door.

If the therapist is able to maintain a mental proximity to the patient without allowing herself to be overwhelmed by the alien other, then her mentalistic, elaborative stance can ultimately enable the patient to find himself in the therapist's mind as a thinking, feeling being and to integrate this image as part of his sense of himself. There is a gradual transformation of a non-reflective mode of experiencing the internal world that forces the equation of the internal and external to one where the internal world is treated with more circumspection and respect, separate and qualitatively different from physical reality. Even if work were to stop here, much would have been achieved in terms of making behavior understandable, meaningful, and predictable. The internalization of the therapist's concern with mental states enhances the patient's capacity for similar concern toward his own experience. Respect for minds generates respect for self, respect for other, and ultimately respect for the human community. It is this respect that drives and organizes the therapeutic endeavor and speaks with greatest clarity to our psychological heritage.

10

Psychic Reality in Borderline States

This chapter is a contribution toward understanding the difficulties of severely borderline patients as they are uncovered within the psychoanalytic process. We consider how the pattern of behavior and relationship—including the transference relationship—characteristics of borderline patients may be understood in terms of an inadequate integration of the two early modes of experiencing psychic reality, as elaborated in this chapter and summarized below. Specifically, we suggest that the borderline patient's failure to mentalize adequately is compounded by the persistence of an undifferentiated mode of representing external and internal experience. It is rooted in a childlike understanding of mental states, where feelings and ideas are construed as direct (or equivalent) representations of reality with consequent exaggeration of their importance and extension of their implications. The persistence of this mode of functioning is a self-perpetuating consequence of the failure of mentalization. The experience of unconscious as well as conscious feelings and ideas as equivalent to physical reality inhibits individuals' capacity to suspend the immediacy of their experience and create the psychological space to "play with reality."

In this way, borderline individuals are forced to accept a mental environment where ideas are too terrifying to think about and feelings too intense to experience. In the long term they defensively forgo mentalization and show an intolerance of alternative perspectives. The extensive failure of mentalization only occurs, however, in individuals whose psychic reality— whose mental experience of themselves—was not properly established in infancy. In place of some representations of their internal states, these individuals experience a disturbing sense of otherness, historically the internalization of the infantile perception of the mother, in place of the mother's image of the infant's self-states. This may be combined with a retreat into compelling fantasy, which can only be minimally integrated with perceptions and experiences of reality. However, we see these deficits as partial and most likely to be seen when feelings and thoughts related to attachment are aroused.

In this chapter we expand on the theory of borderline pathology outlined in chapter 9 using the framework of dysfunctions of psychic reality in addition to attachment disorganization to help us to understand two severe cases of borderline personality disorder, both of whom underwent successful five-times-weekly psychoanalytic treatment. Self-harm played a more central role in the first of the cases to be considered, whereas violence toward others was more significant in the second case, creating an interesting contrast; the theoretical and technical considerations are, however, surprisingly similar.

INTRODUCTION:
THE NORMAL DEVELOPMENT OF PSYCHIC REALITY

In chapter 6, we used both clinical and research evidence to show that the normal experience of psychic reality is not an inherent property of the mind but, rather, a developmental achievement. We see the child's development as normally moving from an experience of psychic reality where mental states are not depicted as representations to an increasingly complex view of the internal world, which has as its hallmark the capacity to mentalize. Initially, the child's experience of the mind is as if it were a recording device, with exact correspondence between internal state and external reality. We have used the term "*psy-*

chic equivalence" to denote this mode of functioning in order to emphasize that for the young child mental events are equivalent, in terms of power, causality, and implications, to events in the physical world. Equating internal and external is inevitably a two-way process. Not only will the small child feel compelled to equate appearance with reality (how it seems is how it is), but also thoughts and feelings—distorted by phantasy—will be projected onto external reality in a manner unmodulated by awareness that the experience of the external world might have been distorted in this way.

Perhaps because it can be terrifying for thoughts and feelings to be experienced as concretely "real," the infant develops an alternative way of construing mental states. In *"pretend mode,"* the child experiences feelings and ideas as totally representational, or symbolic: as having no implication for the world outside. Only gradually, and through the close participation of another mind that can simultaneously hold together the child's pretend and serious perspectives, does the integration of these two modes give rise to a psychic reality in which feelings and ideas are known to be internal yet in close relationship with what is outside (Dunn 1996).

The notion of an increasingly symbolic and reflexive awareness of mental states is assumed by many psychoanalytic formulations of self-development (see review in chapter 6). More recently, it has also come to be at the core of conceptual and empirical work in cognitive and developmental psychology (see review in chapter 5). Our formulation differs from most developmentalists in considering reflective function to be a developmental achievement that is never fully acquired—that is, maintained across situations—and to have roots in the earliest attachment relationships, not just in the verbal, toddler stage. Also, our emphasis, along with that of other psychoanalytic authors, is on the self-organizing quality of mentalizing, and the implications that individual differences in this capacity have for later pathology.

We have suggested that the emergence of mentalizing is deeply embedded in the child's primary-object relationships, first in the mirroring relationship with the caregiver. This is conceived somewhat differently from the traditional psychoanalytic concepts of mirroring proposed by Kohut (1977), Bion (1962a), and Winnicott (1967). It is much more akin to the model recently described by Gergely and Watson (1996) and presented in chapters 4 and 5. We suggest that the infant only gradually realizes that he has feelings and thoughts and slowly becomes able to distinguish these. This happens mainly through learning that his internal experiences are meaningfully related to by the parent, through her expressions and other responses. These habitual reactions to his emotional expressions focus the infant's attention on his internal experiences, giving them a shape, so that they become meaningful and increasingly manageable. Primary representations of experience are organized into secondary representations of these states of mind and body (Fonagy and Target 1997). The experience of affect is the bud from which eventually mentalization can grow, but only in the context of at least one continuing, safe attachment relationship.

The parent who cannot think about the child's mental experience deprives him of a core self-structure that he needs to build a viable sense of himself. For the infant, repeated internalization of the mother's processed image of his thoughts and feelings provides "containment" (Bion 1962a); Joyce McDougall has observed that "a nursling, through its cries, bodily gestures and somato-psychic reactions to stress, gives nonverbal communications that only a mother is able to interpret. She functions, in this respect, as her baby's thinking system, and finds an adequate response to her infant's distress" (McDougall 1989, p. 169). This "adequate" response involves not only interpreting the baby's physical expressions, but also giving him back a manageable version of what he is communicating (Winnicott 1967). The absence or distortion of this mirroring function early in life may lead to a desperate search for alternative ways of containing psychological experience and the mental world. These ways may, for example, come to involve various forms of self-harm or aggression toward others.

Why should such failure of attunement occur? Many factors may make the mother unresponsive to the baby's communication of need; most commonly perhaps, distress mobilizes unacceptable anxiety. Reactions such as these disrupt the mother's capacity to reflect on the baby's feelings and arouse her habitual defenses against unmanageable affect. A. Stein (1994) demonstrated that mothers with current diagnoses of bulimia nervosa had specific difficulties in responding accurately to 6-month-old babies, particularly in the feeding situation. They were very intolerant of messiness and insisted on controlling the infant's access to the food. As a consequence, they consistently misread the child's cries, and this tendency was also seen in play with toys. One of the most distressing observations during feeding was that cries of frustration and hunger were misread as rejection of the offered food, leading to serious failure to thrive in some cases. In the secure relationship, the sensitivity—and, we might add, availability—of the caregiver (Belsky et al. 1995) ensures that the infant is able to find out what he feels and hence increasingly to feel understood. This allows him to internalize the experience of containment and develop a representational system for internal states.

Within a secure or containing relationship, the baby's affective signals are interpreted by the parent, who is able to reflect on the mental states underlying the baby's distress. For this reflection to help the baby, it must involve a subtle combination of mirroring and the communication of a contrasting affect. The nature of the object's mirroring may be most easily understood in the context of our description of the parent's pretend play with the child: in order to contain the child's anxiety, the mother's mirroring expression will display a complex affect, which combines fear with a conflicting emotion, such as irony. At one level, this communicates that there is nothing "truly" to worry about, but, more importantly, the parent's reaction, which is the same yet not the same as the baby's experience, creates the possibility of generating a second-order (symbolic) representation of the anxiety. This is the beginning of symbolization. In another paper, we have discussed how in language (Fónagy and Fonagy 1995) speakers frequently, quite unconsciously, combine two patterns of intonation, each characteristic of a different emotion. The listener is affected by both, even when only one of the affects expressed is consciously perceived. We believe that the infant is soothed (or contained) through much the same process.

There may be many reasons for the failure of attunement between infant and parent, some rooted in the parent's pathology, others in constitutional factors, trauma, and other experiences. Whatever the reason, if the parent is unable to respond in the way described above, what will be internalized by the child will tend to be the parent's own experience or defenses; the infant's distress is either avoided or mirrored without first being "metabolized." In extreme cases, the child may be pushed toward the highly maladaptive defense of inhibiting mentalization. Even in less extreme cases, parent–child relationships in which mirroring has been inadequate may lay the groundwork for subsequent distortions of personality development in one of two ways. These correspond to the two modes of experiencing psychic reality that we described in chapter 6. The mother may echo the child's state without modulation, as in the mode of psychic equivalence, concretizing or panicking at the child's distress. Alternatively, she may avoid reflection on the child's affect through a process akin to dissociation, which effectively places the mother in a pretend mode, unrelated to external reality, including the child. The mother may then ignore the child's distress, or translate it into illness, tiredness, and so on. Both strip the child's communication of meaning that he can recognize and use. It may also lead to a currency between mother and child of interpretation of feelings in physical terms, so that the physical state is the "real" thing. Lynne Murray (1992), in her work with mothers suffering from puerperal depression, has provided some vivid illustrations of such mothers offering an alternative reality, marked by the exaggeration associated with pretense but not related to the infant's experience. Psychoanalytic observers of this type of interaction would rapidly identify the operation of massive denial and even manic defense. The infant has not been able to find a recognizable version of his mental states in another person's mind, and the opportunity to acquire a symbolic representation of those states has been lost.

As shown more fully in chapters 4 and 5, normally the child achieves control over affect partly through this kind of symbolization. The representation of his feelings is increasingly associated with the modulation included in her reflection of his emotional state. The reflection is clearly related to the original state but is not the same. The infant will match the mother's modulated reaction to his own feelings and slowly learns that symbolic play with affect has the potential to bind his emotional and physiological reactions. Clinically this means that the child who has not received recognizable but modified images of his affective states may later have trouble in differentiating reality from fantasy and physical from psychic reality. This may restrict him to an instrumental or functional (manipulative), rather than signal (communicative) use of affect. (See chapter 5 for the stages of development of agency.)

In chapter 9 we described the way in which this instrumental use of affect is a key aspect of the tendency of borderline patients to express and cope with thoughts and feelings through physical action, against their own bodies or in relation to other people. Central in this chapter is the limitation imposed by the delayed or absent secondary (or metacognitive) representation of affect on the development of the child's psychic reality. We assume that the integration of the two primitive modes of experiencing mind (equivalence and pretense) requires precursors of mentalization. Play *with* reality, rather than *apart from* reality, will be possible only if the conceptual capacity for representing experience as a version of reality is present. Such integration normally begins in the second year of life and is partially completed by the fifth or sixth year.

Common observations of the young child, toddlers, and even 3- and 4-year-olds readily confirm that, as far as the boundaries of the psychological self are concerned, a young child readily assumes that his object's desires are the same as his own. A boy of 4, in a considerable temper, warned his mother that he no longer wanted to sleep in her bed, or have a birthday party, or even wished for a Megazord (a prized model from "The Power Rangers"). Maybe somewhat more infantile than usual because of his emotional arousal, nevertheless this boy assumed that his mother's desires were identical to his, and her sense of loss at these deprivations would be as great as his. A borderline child treated by George Moran at the Anna Freud Centre offered food to the analyst when George asked whether he was hungry. Clinicians often note the difficulty such children frequently have with personal pronouns as a consequence of this confusion. A borderline 4-year-old treated at the same clinic by Jack Novick was congratulated on his birthday the following day; he replied, "that's my birthday too!" In brief, awareness of the physical separateness of bodies, and even of mental states, does not immediately bring with it the capacity to attribute a mental state appropriately or even to identify a particular person.

The mental boundaries of the self probably remain permeable throughout development and perhaps even in adulthood. Sandler (1992) stressed the importance of primary identification as underpinning empathic gestures (for example, correcting one's stance when seeing someone else slip). Normally these experiences are circumscribed, preconscious, and limited to the earlier stages of perception. Nevertheless their very existence underscores the importance of intersubjective states that underpin the development of self-knowledge. At the core of the mature child's self is the other at the moment of reflection. Metacognitions—the mental representations of mental representations—are object images congruent with internal states, yet clearly not identical with them. They share elements of the child's self sufficiently coherent and stable for the formation of a symbolic link and for the child to construct further self-representations on it in the physical absence of the object.

THE ROLE OF TRAUMA
IN PREVENTING THE INTEGRATION
OF THE TWO MODES OF PSYCHIC REALITY

As shown in chapter 9, trauma plays a significant role in the psychogenesis of borderline states (e.g., Johnson et al. 1999). We suggest that when perpetrated by an attachment figure, trauma interferes with the developmental process described above. Evidence of this can be seen in severely abused children in one or more of the following ways: (a) the persistence of a psychic equivalence mode of experiencing internal reality; (b) the propensity to continue to shift into a pretend mode (e.g., through dissociation), (c) a partial inability to reflect on one's own mental states and those of one's objects. We are suggesting that these ways of thinking persist into adulthood and play an important role in borderline phenomena.

The maltreated child cannot afford the luxury of seeing the parent's expression as indicating only a psychic reality, as "nonconsequential," since the parent's feelings can carry terrifying repercussions. Normally, between the ages of 2 and 4 years the child will increasingly notice discrepancies between his internal states and the world outside, or other people's states of mind. However, the child who is surrounded by threat or actual trauma will have little opportunity to develop an awareness of any distinction between inner and outer; his focus on the outside world and its physical and emotional dangers needs to be maintained so closely that there is little room for the idea of a separate, internal world. In normal circumstances, a parent will be able to protect the child from some of the frightening force of reality, not so much by concealing events and feelings, but by conveying to the child that there is more than one way of seeing things. Perhaps the child has seen the parent being angry, even frightening; if the parent is able to recognize the child's experience but also is able to communicate that that fear is unjustified, the child is safe. However, in cases of maltreatment, the child is not safe, and any reassuring communication of containment will be false. It will also further undermine the child's capacity to trust inner reality. Thus, abuse inevitably reinforces a lack of integration between the two infantile modes of experience of mental states. It reinforces a psychic equivalent mode of functioning, because it forces the child to attend primarily to the physical world, to mistrust any opportunities for playfulness, and to be suspicious of the internal world in general, because the object's internal world is incomprehensible, terrifying, or deceptive. It also reinforces a pretend mode because it may be the only way available to the child to sever connection between internal states and an intolerable external reality.

Parents who cannot enter a mentalizing mode with their child (where pretend and real can coexist) are by no means always overtly abusive, neglecting, or mentally ill. A wide range of people share the type of early experience associated with insecure attachment. Although frequently found in childhoods that are traumatic, it is by no means restricted to these. This may be one of the reasons why many characteristics of children who have experienced severe maltreatment may also be found in those whose childhoods have apparently been relatively benign. The parent may have been unable to reveal herself enough to the child, preventing him from finding himself within her mind. We speculate that the capacity on the parent's part to adopt a playfully empathic attitude may be essential for the child to experience his projections as contained. Instead, the parent may be emotionally inaccessible to the child, preventing him from creating an image of his internal world in the parent's mind, which would then have been available for internalization to form the core sense of himself. Some parents may in addition unconsciously reveal states of mind (hatred, disgust) that, if pervasive, constitute psychological abuse, because the child has to recoil from the implied image of himself. The most disturbing aspect for the child might be to contemplate the cruelty or hatred the caregiver feels toward him. He can have no protection from this, other than barring ideas about feelings and thoughts in others and in himself from his consciousness. The maltreated child can thus grow up to fear minds and to repudiate awareness of feelings or motives, with the persistence of psychic equivalence as the inevitable by-product of this process.

Furthermore, as Main and Hesse (1992) have pointed out, it is as disruptive for the parent to be experienced as frightened as for her to be seen as frightening. There may be at least two processes in operation here: (*a*) Because at this early stage the infant perceives the object as part of the self, the child will tend to assume that his own mental state is dangerous or even catastrophic, because it is associated with frightening behavior from the parent. For instance, a baby might bite the mother's breast in excited pleasure and find a reaction of anger and rejection. If such experiences were frequent, then they could be expected to have a disorganizing effect on the baby's understanding of his own states of mind; excited pleasure becomes equated with anger and rejection. (*b*) The child may perceive the caregiver's image of him as a frightening, unmanageable person—for instance, a reminder of an abusive figure from the mother's own history—and this may be internalized as an unacceptable and confusing part of the child's self-image. (In chapter

6 we discussed the role that this process may have played in the case of Rebecca.)

Trauma may also disrupt the representation of feelings or thoughts by creating a propensity for shifting into the infantile mode of pretend. Some traumatized children grow up with an apparent hypersensitivity to mental states, needing to guess immediately what those around them feel and think in order to preempt further trauma. As part of this, a pseudo-knowledge of minds can develop, which is superficial and may be very selective, scanning for particular danger signals and avoiding reflection on meanings or connections. What seems to result is a keenness to identify psychological states in others, but these states are essentially meaningless to the patient, a common but heavily devalued currency. "Expertise" in the psychological world of the other develops at the expense of knowledge of the patient's own mind. This thinking, which in research we have called "hyperactive mentalizing," occurs in the pretend mode, without firm ties to internal and external experience that is felt to be real.

An example may be helpful. "Sandra" is a 35-year-old woman with a twenty-year history of self-mutilation and suicidal gestures and a background of psychological abuse from the grandmother who brought her up.[1] In the first part of her analysis, Sandra was endlessly preoccupied with analyzing the motives behind the reportedly cruel and paranoid behavior of her grandmother and her psychiatrist. The events described, whether from childhood or yesterday, had a hackneyed quality, like a soap opera. The motives that Sandra attributed to the offending characters were unconvincing and quite interchangeable. They were also often transparently projected. Sandra habitually twisted her reflective function, deflecting attention from her own mental states and distorting or negating those of other people. Her systematic abuse of mentalization protected her from actual insight or intimacy. Her reflective capacity seemed to have been hijacked into the pretend mode of experience, in which psychological events, like her relationships, were idealized but emptied of emotional depth. An illustration of this was that, after a night of self-cutting and getting her 9-year-old son to help her write a

---

[1] Mary Target was her fourth analyst.

suicide note, Sandra came to her session excitedly trying to understand the stinginess of her brother's new wife and only mentioning in passing her own outbursts of the previous day.

More commonly, mindless or cruel treatment of a child leads to the rejection of mentalization (Fonagy, Steele, Steele, and Target 1997). This should be thought about not simply as a deficit, but as an *adaptation* that has helped the child to attain some distance from a traumatizing situation (see chapter 7 for a clear example). Although restriction of mentalization was originally adaptive, there is a clear and powerful link between this restricted capacity and vulnerability to later trauma. The inability to reflect upon the mental state of the perpetrator, as well as the reaction of the self, may prevent the child from resolving the original traumatic experience or coping with subsequent assault. Conversely, mentalizing is an important component of the self-righting capacity of individuals who are able to withstand early adversity (Fonagy, Steele, et al. 1994). There is a mutual developmental relationship between trauma and mentalizing; trauma may undermine the child's willingness to play with feelings and ideas (felt as too real) in relation to external events, but, at the same time, the lack of a full mentalizing mode of internal organization will create a propensity for the continuous repetition of the trauma, in the absence of the modulation that a representational view of psychic reality would bring.

THE RIGIDITY OF RELATIONSHIP PATTERNS AND THE PETRIFICATION OF SYSTEMS OF REPRESENTATION

As described in chapter 9, one of the most characteristic features of borderline psychopathology is the instability and tempestuousness of relationships. These show a rapidly accelerating tempo, where intimacy immediately follows acquaintance, and there are numerous crises, often featuring dependence, masochism, and dominance. In fact, we may say, paraphrasing Winnicott, that in some sense "there is no such thing as a borderline person, there is only the borderline couple—the borderline person and her object." However, these patients tend to lack a realistic sense of the psychic reality of the other person. What is represented is an association between a self-state and the state in a "virtual other" that is not consistently plausible. For example, Sandra talked extensively about friends, but the feelings and thoughts attributed to them were often improbable and inconsistent with their actions. In the narrative, these people felt two-dimensional, and as the patient incorporated the analyst into the cast of characters, the analyst strongly felt a shallowness and artificiality in the way she was represented. This was not like the elaboration of distortions as transferences developed; rather, it felt like being a joker in a card game, which could stand for any other card but had no actual identity or continuity.

While all psychoanalytic treatment is likely to develop a capacity for reflective function in the patient (and in the analyst), work with borderline patients suggests that the stunting or twisting of this capacity may be a key to their pathology. Treatment then needs to be intensively—though not necessarily directly—focused on its development. We suggest that some aspects of borderline pathology arise from the inadequate integration of early forms of the representation of internal experience, which would normally form the basis of a mentalizing mode of experiencing psychic reality. Perhaps the single most important indicator of this is the quality of rigidity that imbues the internal representational world, the experience of the self, and relationships with others.

Borderline patients persist in particular patterns of relating with a tenacity far beyond that associated with habitual defenses. These individuals, like other patients, organize the analytic relationship to conform to their unconscious expectations, but for borderline patients these expectations have the full force of reality and there is no sense of alternative perspectives. At moments when external reality does not fit with the tenaciously held active schema, there is emptiness and confusion.

Just as behavior and interpersonal relations are rigidly restricted, so is internal experience; of the total spectrum of experiences, only some are registered and felt, leading to a discontinuity in self-experience. Because of the lack of flexibility of the representational system for mental states, the individual cannot evoke psychic experiences other than by enactment and provocation. Subjective states, such as anxiety, may be known mainly through creating them in another person. Many have explained the manipulative aspects of eating disorders and other forms of self-harm (e.g., Bruch 1982; T. Main 1957) in terms of the projection or projective identification of intolerable parts of the self, or as part of communication. Here our emphasis is somewhat different. It is the creation of an internal experience akin to reflection, normally intrapsychic, that is established through interpersonal interaction. *Not being able to feel themselves from within, they are forced to experience the self from without.* Sandra, at various times of crisis, said she knew that she had been overwhelmed with anxiety because her son had called the police, or her analyst had talked to her psychiatrist. These reactions made sense of what she had felt to be a "mental mess," and she was then somewhat more able to deal with it appropriately.

An important aspect of such rigidity is the persistence of psychic equivalence as a predominant mode of experiencing psychic reality. Much of the apparent inflexibility of such patients may be understood in terms of the increased weight they give to psychic reality. When mental experience cannot be conceived of in a symbolic way, thoughts and feelings have a direct and sometimes devastating impact that can only be avoided through drastic and primitive defensive moves.

Early in his analysis, one male patient reported a very acrimonious argument between himself and a shop assistant about the change he was given. "*I knew* I gave her five pounds, but the stupid woman only gave me 30 pence change, when she should have given me 80. She kept saying that she gave me 80 pence, but I knew that she had kept 50." What was interesting from an analytic standpoint in his account was not simply his obvious sense of omnipotence in relation to her (i.e., "he knew") and the sense of betrayal by the analyst in the transference, but his inability to contemplate any other point of view. Reflecting on this episode some years into his analysis, he said: "I just could not see any possibility, other than I was right; it's not that I did not want to see it, it simply did not exist."

A borderline young man treated by Peter Fonagy and described more fully in an earlier paper (Fonagy 1991) was prone to long periods of silence during an early phase of his analysis. The silences were impenetrable and, for some time, unexplained. On one occasion, the trigger was a two-minute delay in the analyst's arrival for the session, which led to over a week of silence. Interpreting the silence as punishing the analyst, communicating frustration, or a sense of being excluded or not understood failed to break the deadlock. Eventually it transpired that on this and many other occasions the analyst's lateness created an image of being with someone uncaring and unreliable to the point of being mad. "You are just an unprofessional, uncaring bastard, and you know it." At those times, the analyst was experienced as someone totally unsafe to be with, and questioning this perception carried no meaning.

While there is little that was unusual about this transference image, it was held with enormous tenacity, impervious to any consideration of other times that had been experienced equally definitively as showing an opposite reality. Each view replaced the other completely, and each was seen as so clear that it was not even worth discussing. The analyst saw that as based in a lack of ability to "play with reality"; the patient was mesmerized by an idea and unable to experience it as psychic rather than physical reality. The analyst had to accept the distortion. Attempting to evoke the patient's complete picture of the analyst was inevitably perceived as an attack on the patient's sanity. While often not consciously aware of this, we respect it by entering the patient's reality and accepting the role of the "unprofessional, uncaring bastard," or whatever it may be.

We now describe work with a patient whose difficulties illustrate many of the theoretical points we have been putting forward. We then discuss more specifically some aspects of the failure to achieve full mentalization in adults with severe personality disorder and the way in which, using borderline disorder as an example, such states may be understood in terms of the persistence of primitive modes of understanding psychic experience.

DYSFUNCTIONAL PSYCHIC REALITY
IN SELF-DESTRUCTIVENESS—
CLINICAL EXAMPLE: "EMMA"

Emma[2] at 19 was a slightly overweight, highly intelligent young woman, looking younger than her years. She was referred to us at the Anna Freud Centre from another center because her diabetes had been hopelessly out of control since she was first diagnosed diabetic at the age of 12. She openly admitted to manipulating her insulin to control her weight. She had been hospitalized with keto-acidosis eight times during the previous year. After her last admission her diabetologist, who is renowned for his antipsychoanalytic sentiment, agreed to the psychoanalytic referral with the comment: "We might as well let somebody else watch her kill herself."

When Emma was assessed, her main concern was about her imminent failure in her Arts Foundation Course, for which she found herself unable to submit the necessary course-work. She was living on her own in a tiny single room and spending her money on drugs, alcohol, and vast quantities of "bad" food. She smoked cannabis and heroin, drank excessively, and binged on potatochips, chocolate, cheese, and cakes. She would "burn off" the carbohydrates by omitting insulin and abusing alcohol. The alcohol would also anesthetize her, as would the cannabis. The most dramatic expression of aggression was in the lacerations she inflicted on herself with a razor blade. She described the triggers for such acts as a "sinister little voice" inside her head, tempting and daring her to self-mutilate: "You know you'll feel better. Do it! Do it! Do it!" She openly discussed her suicidal intent and readily agreed with me when I suggested that a part of her had lost all hope for herself.

Her family had been torn apart by psychiatric and physical illness. In her early years she was cared for by her mother, who had been diagnosed at various times as both schizophrenic and

---

[2] The patient was treated by Peter Fonagy, and this is his report. The treatment was part of the Anna Freud Centre's Brittle Diabetes Research Programme headed by the late George Moran, who provided much direction and inspiration to the thinking about this case.

manic-depressive. During her mother's psychotic episodes, and later during her physical illness, Emma was looked after by her three older sisters, the family's neighbors, or whoever happened to be around at the time. From her accounts it seems clear that despite being the youngest, her role in the family was a pivotal one. As the youngest child, she was the person around whom the family rallied and whose survival justified the continued existence of the family unit. Soon after she turned 10 the burden she had assumed as peacemaker in family arguments became even heavier when her brother and sisters as well as her mother began approaching her for advice. It was apparent in the way she described the interminable family conversations, sometimes reaching far into the night, that even as a relatively young girl she had a capacity to create in her mind a little space where she was able to deal with other people's confusions in a rational, even if not yet mature, way. She referred to this in a disparaging way as being a "rubbish bin" for other people's troubles. Yet she also recalled feeling valued and appreciated. Thus, she had some capacity to mentalize, even if this could only be achieved at substantial cost, by needing those around her to represent the confused and unthinking parts of herself.

Emma's father's psychiatric disturbance was probably as severe as her mother's. Emma recalls a very early memory of her father screaming through the house, turning all the children out of their beds, and making them stand outside in the garden so that the "evil spirits" would not possess their souls. She also recalls violent battles between her parents, when they would set about each other with ferocious intensity. Her father left the home when Emma was 6 years old, and his departure was both sudden and unexplained. He continued to live in the same provincial English town and kept up superficial contact with the children. He was, however, out of work and in and out of psychiatric hospitals and offered the family little by way of physical or psychological support.

Emma spoke warmly about her mother, as someone who was trying to do her best in very difficult circumstances. What united the family was their war of attrition with Social Services, who repeatedly threatened to take the children into care, particularly at times when their mother's illness became acute. There clearly was a desperate bond between the mother and the children. Emma recalls pretending to a social worker that her mother was out shopping when in fact her brother and sister were holding her down and trying to stop her from cutting her wrists. When mother was hospitalized, the children would go and visit her regularly, despite the fact that the hospital was far away.

Her mother became ill with a rapidly disseminating cancer when Emma was 8. She underwent a radical mastectomy and a further operation on her neck. Finally, in the last stages of the illness, Emma's mother took her own life.

Emma emphatically did not want to come into treatment. Her reasons for this were both complex and telling. Having treatment was escaping—"not facing the music." She should be able to battle it out on her own. I said to her that I understood how hard it must be for her to contemplate receiving help when so many of her good feelings about herself were to do with being the one who could help her sisters and her mother. At this point she began to weep and told me that she had heard, at the Bulimics Anonymous group she had once attended, that I knew about diabetics. I said that perhaps she was concerned that I might *think* that I knew about *her*, whereas she knew that nobody could really know about the impossibility of her situation. She went on to say that none of the people at the hospital understood what she was going through. "They all think I am a naughty child, wanting to get attention, and when ignoring me doesn't work, they just don't know how to deal with me. But I really don't care about what they do, they are no use to me." I said that perhaps she felt worried about the prospect of psychoanalysis because it might be a situation in which she would mind whether she was ignored or not. She said that she could not imagine that coming to see someone every day would do anything except make the person an addict, as food and heroin did, "except that food and heroin are up to me and in psychoanalysis you are in control." I suggested that she might be far more worried about being out of control than she knew. Furthermore, if she could force the doctors at the hospital to lose their tempers with her, she might also be able to force an analyst to lose control.

Many months into the analysis she told me how important this interview had been for her, in that she felt I was aware of her need to create madness and confusion in me, in the treatment. In the first months of the analysis her anxieties about the destructiveness of her thoughts and fantasies often caused her to be silent, sometimes to remain so for entire sessions. She would attend punctually, despite a long and complex journey, but then she would just lie on the couch, make a few apparently superficial comments about the journey or about the room or even about the weather, and then lapse into a state of self-imposed quarantine.

At no stage did one have the feeling, however, that she did not wish to communicate. I attended carefully to her body movements and from time to time commented on what I thought these said about her current mental state (and this, in an unremarkable nutshell, is the essence of our technique): the constant availability and active offering of the analyst's mind so that within it she may discover her own self. For example, on one occasion, when she greeted me at the beginning of the session but then said nothing else, I noticed how she took out her bus pass and pressed it against her fingers until it was bent almost double under the pressure, then she released it, allowing it to snap back into its normal shape. She repeated the movement exactly five times. I said that perhaps she wanted me to know what an effort it felt to have to come and see me five times a week. Realizing that I must have been reacting to what she was doing with her bus pass, she tucked it away into her purse. The action was incomplete and the bus pass disappeared only half-way, so that the part with her photograph on it was still sticking out, as if peering over the edge. I said that I understood that a frightened part was always on the look-out to make sure that nothing had been revealed inadvertently, but that there was another part of her that wanted me to understand her, and no matter how hard the frightened part might try to ensure that everything was carefully tucked away, this other more communicative part of her would leave a nice clear trail for me to follow. She then said indignantly: "What do you mean, communicative? I could no more communicate to you than I could talk to Medusa." I said: "You know, even Medusa could be confronted with the help of a mirror." She turned away so that I would not be able to see her face, but I could tell that she was smiling.

The moment when she decided that she wanted to talk was rather dramatic and illustrates both the nature of her pathology and the clinical approach that we take in dealing with borderline patients. I had been told, not by her but by the physician treating her, that she was about to undergo a fundoscopy to check for diabetic retinopathy. Fundoscopy involves instilling a mydriatic into the eye to dilate the pupil and causes a temporary blurring of vision. She came into the session directly after her investigation and uncharacteristically avoided looking at me and lay on the couch, burying her head in the cushion. The silence lasted for at least ten minutes. Eventually I noticed that her index finger was tracing small grooves almost imperceptibly in the texture of the couch. Fascinated, I thought the grooves she was tracing looked like rivers and their tributaries and also like the small blood vessels that are involved in diabetic retinopathy. It then struck me that Emma was tracing two rivers that sometimes seemed to be joined up by their tributaries but sometimes drifted sharply away from one another. When I was reasonably confident of the pattern, I wondered aloud if she didn't suddenly feel that she might lose me, even if she did not quite understand why she feared this. In response she buried her face even deeper in the cushion. I said that we both realized how terrified she was of losing her sight, but that perhaps there was also a part of her that felt that if she could not keep an eye on things, the analysis might break up, and everything would become blurred. She remained silent but drove her fingernail deeper and deeper into the couch. Eventually she was violently criss-crossing over what had been the river pattern. I said that I knew that somewhere she felt deeply ashamed about what was happening to her body and was very angry with the analysis and with me for just standing by and watching it happen. She then broke her silence. She said, almost shouting: "If you are so fucking clever, why don't you stop me from doing this before I go blind?" Reflecting on Emma's sense of helplessness and the helplessness she engendered in me, I remarked: "I think you would like me to stop you from feeling the sadness and the rage that drive you to do this to yourself. I think you are frightened that if we come together to see the feelings that lead you to hurt yourself, it will become so unbearable that we will both be destroyed." Emma was quite still for a moment and then said: "I suppose it would not do if I asked what it is that you want to know?"

This point in Emma's analysis, and in that of numerous other such self-harming and self-destructive patients whom we have treated, represented a spoken or unspoken realization on the part of these patients that they are more frightened of their mental experience, their emotions and phantasies, than of the immediate physical pain or the long-term consequences of their self-destructive actions, such as Emma's mismanagement of her diabetes.

The central theme of Emma's analysis concerned the externalization—which to her was real—of her confusion and madness. Because she was operating in a mode of psychic equivalence, she felt as though these aspects of her experience really had left her mind, and the calmness that was left felt like her real self. The person who had been in turmoil, who was insanely ravaging her own body, was not she. Frequently, in her free association and dreams, she described the image of a bubble or a vessel stuck in outer space. She elaborated such images mostly in tranquil terms. For example, she referred to watching lights flicker from her space capsule, imagining that each was a light from a person too far away to seem human. However, whenever she seemed to feel that she had had a good analytic experience, anxiety would tend to overwhelm the sense of calmness. The reality of our relationship as analyst and patient seemed to make it impossible for her to maintain the conviction of madness and disturbance being somewhere else. On one occasion, I commented on her fear that if she abandoned her seclusion, the alternative was madness. Responding, characteristically seeing her mental state in me, as if it was I who was terrified, she said: "Don't worry, its important to let things float a bit."

For example she fantasized that my garden was the only ordered, well-kept one in the area, in the middle of a veritable jungle of weeds and overgrown grass of the neighboring gardens. When I pointed out how frightening it must be to feel surrounded by the menace of such chaos, she shrugged: "Well, that's your problem, isn't it?"

Her self-esteem and grandiosity were noticeably enhanced when she inflicted pain and damage on herself through gross diabetic mismanagement. She flaunted her ill-treatment of her-self constantly and conveyed her capacity calmly to damage or kill herself. She imagined me to be "pleading" with her to take care of herself, like her relatives and the staff of the medical (endocrine) unit, who had spared little effort to keep her alive. On one occasion she entered the consulting-room and told me that she had just tested her blood sugar. It was so high, she boasted, that it no longer registered on the glucometer. She gave off a pungent odor of ketones, like nail-varnish remover. I replied that she seemed to feel so triumphant over pain and the fear of death that there was nothing I could offer that could compare. She said, "When you are diabetic, you have to have something to feel good about." This seemed to show that experiencing her psychic reality in a mode of psychic equivalence enabled her to feel that she had destroyed parts of her mind externalized into the body, as well as triumphing over death.

In the analysis she created a shallow, half-hearted concern for her objects and for me in the transference. I was aware of being kept at a distance from something she felt was highly dangerous. I was also aware of the tendency to let myself drift into a state of near-complete inattentiveness. I understood this countertransference to derive from my reluctance to allow myself to experience her terror in the face of relating to the part of her mind representing her mentally ill parents of the past. Likewise, externalized in the transference, she reacted to me with tenta-tiveness for fear that I was unstable and could respond at any moment with mad rage.

One day, when it was possible to smell her ketotic state several meters from the waiting-room and I could discern from her slurred speech and general vagueness that she was pro-foundly unwell, her conscious thoughts seemed to be taken up with my state of health. Her fantasy was that I was suffering continuously from a cold because I worked too hard. She was confident that work was my way of avoiding depression. When I put it to her that I thought she was telling me how hard she felt she had to work to protect us from *her* sadness, she responded facetiously: "Well, one does what one can."

At this stage it seemed to be necessary for the analysis to represent that part of Emma's mind which she endeavored to keep safe and tranquil and isolated; the pressure on me to mold my responses to her expectations was intense, because perceiving any unexpected feelings and thoughts from me, and hence having to see me as a real person with a separate reality, constantly threatened to confuse and overwhelm her.

Her careful monitoring of my well-being (again, a characteristic hypervigilance) was a key feature of this transference. She faced an insoluble dilemma in needing me to be mad but being terrified by the perception of my madness—that is, finding her madness within me. These aspects were particularly vividly illustrated by the following episode: about two years into Emma's analysis, I was involved in a small bicycle accident, which led to quite significant bruising on my forehead as well as a sizeable cut above my right eye, which required stitches. The total effect, which included an extremely bloodshot eye, was as unattractive as it was dramatic. Equally striking was Emma's capacity to scotomize my injury. When I collected Emma from the waiting-room she avoided even glancing at me. She went through the session mostly in silence. The only way of knowing that something was amiss was that the atmosphere of the session had a dreaminess about it in which it was almost impossible to sustain any kind of alertness or concentration. This gave a sense of Emma's state of mind as it tried to grapple with her fantasies about the injury through striving for a state of almost complete dissociation. We would understand this on a very pathological form of a pretend mode of experiencing psychic reality: Emma was desperately trying to create a state of mind that had no connection with external reality, in which her thoughts and imaginings had no power. At the end of the session she walked out of the room without looking at me, and she again seemed to take no notice of my face at the beginning of next day's session.

In this session, unusually, Emma reported a dream in which *a number of horses had broken out of their stables. They were blind and threatened to trample all over her.* She woke up just before the horses were upon her. The dream seemed to be vaguely connected to Peter Shaffer's play, *Equus*. In her associations it was difficult to tell when she was recounting the dream and when she was giving a highly distorted account of the play. In Emma's version of the play, the boy, who was in a hospital for the violently insane, developed hysterical blindness after he had flown into a rage and blinded a horse. The focus of her account, however, was the insanity of the psychiatrist treating the boy, who was, according to her, the villain of the piece.

I said I thought that Emma was terrified in case somehow her anger might break out of the stables she created for it and make everyone in our "analytic hospital" violent and mad. She responded that the night before she had been so anxious about not being able to see that she could not take her insulin. She found that the pain of hyperglycemia distracted her. Nevertheless, she still had to smoke heroin to get to sleep. She went on to wonder why people talked of "blind rage." I said that it was so painful for her to see the manifestations of violence that being blind was almost preferable. And yesterday, when she had noticed my facial injury, she had suddenly felt that she was in terrible danger because she was evidently unable to keep the violence out of the room.

She now became extremely anxious and asked repeatedly what injury I was talking about. I replied that I understood how frightening it was for her to feel that there had been violence, because it made her feel both as if she might inadvertently have caused it and also as if it were happening to her. She shouted that I was talking nonsense, like the psychiatrist in the play. How could I expect her to be able to see things if I could not make my meanings clear to her? I said that these thoughts were particularly frightening because if she found that I was mad, I might terrify her and drive her insane.

She was silent for a while. Then slowly and very deliberately she said: "I must have seen your eyes yesterday because I have not been able to get a picture out of my mind since then. The first time I remember visiting my mother in hospital, I could not recognize her because one of the other patients had hit her and given her a black eye." She recalled feeling terrified of her mother and responsible for her injury.

The infantile perception of the mother was part of Emma's self-representation and contained her own unintegrated aggressive wishes. It could only be dealt with as part of her body, not as a mental representation that could be thought about consciously or unconsciously. In a less damaged patient it may have been repudiated and thus avoided—but this would assume a capacity to mentalize, which was not, at this stage, within Emma's capabilities. The fusion of self with the nonreflective mother constituted an overwhelming threat to the fragile, sane part of her self-representation that she, and all those around her, clearly valued. To conserve this limited self-representational structure, the representation of mother's mental state within the self was externalized into her body, where it could be attacked and perhaps destroyed. Emma's insane acts of self-destruction paradoxically helped her to deny the presence of her mother within her mind and were associated with relief and hope because within her immature mode of responding to mental states, dominated by psychic equivalence, these acts signaled the restored integrity of her self-representation. Although she enacted destructive wishes on her body, she experienced these acts as safe, inconsequential, and even desirable, because the body upon which they were perpetrated was alien and deliberately excluded from her sense of self.

It was only when conflicts surrounding the emotional investment in the object representation of her mother as a separate being (outside the self-representation) could become the focus of the analysis that her fear of loss of love and its relation to her self-injury could be clarified. In her material, as in her actions, physical closeness to death (in keto-acidosis) represented the only possible way of achieving mental closeness to her mother as the object who had *her* in mind. As she improved, she increasingly feared that the ghost of her mother was in the consulting-room. To illustrate, we will now describe a Monday session.

She began the session by reporting a dream about *a bomb threat*; she described the intense fear she felt and the conflict over whether to stay in the building. In her associations she told me that she felt terrific physically, now that she had stopped eating animal products, and that when she was keto-acidotic, she felt vital and somehow real. She said she had loads of life left in her. I replied: "You seem to feel alive and real when you are on the edge of a disaster and your life is actually in danger." I added that it was at such times that she seemed to feel I was most worried about her. She said: "How did you know that I did not take my insulin last night?"

She said angrily that she felt that there was this evil inside her, that perhaps it could only be exorcized by some "physical means," not by talking alone. She then had an image of injecting insulin into an empty shell. This was followed by a long lecture on the way that confidence can affect your appearance. She was particularly struck by French women who, by wearing appropriate clothes, were able to make themselves almost beautiful. She wondered vaguely if there was such a thing as real beauty. I responded: "You seem frightened that I might recognize something good in you, that I might be taken in and find you appealing as a person."

Her voice dropped an octave. "You despise me, don't you? You must do." She then went on the attack. When she deliberately cut her leg the other day she was terrified because she had not felt a thing. Dr. Y had looked into her eye at the clinic and had shaken his head. He, too, must be wondering what the analysis was achieving. For two years she had been coming, and things were, if anything, worse now than they had ever been. She couldn't afford another year of not getting better. I said: "You are frightened that you are too ill ever to feel loved."

She paused and then spoke of her Bible reading in the evenings. The previous night she had read the passage on the judgment of Solomon in which King Solomon was confronted by two women who both claimed to be the mother of the same baby. She emphasized with horror that the wrong mother had the live baby and the innocent mother had the dead baby, again emphasizing that it was the wrong one. Despite reading the passage again and again, Emma could not see why, if Solomon was wise, he had said that they should cut the baby in half and divide it between the mothers. I remarked: "You feel that 'something is wrong,' that the part of you that can be cared about is dead, and you are terrified in case you may stop me from being able to see the difference between what is alive and what is dead. Then you will be in the care of an analyst who is not capable of keeping his patients alive." I held back the more important interpretation, that she could not understand why splitting the baby in two would be of concern, as in her phantasy the unity of her body did not contain her mental existence and thus made no sense to her as the focus of the object's concern.

She became anxious and said that today she had thought of her mother for the first time in a long while. She had looked into the mirror and had felt for a moment that she was going crazy because she had seen her mother. She then went on to tell me how her mother had been so sad that she went to see a psychiatrist shortly before she died, but by then it was too late; how nobody had told her that she had cancer. She ended by saying: "The poor woman, you know she stole from a shop and the local papers were going to report it. It must have been terribly humiliating for her." I said: "I think it is very important to you to try to hide, from me and from yourself, how ashamed and humiliated you feel because it seems as if nobody could want to look after your body, and it feels as if you've stolen whatever affection you get."

In response Emma showed genuine emotion almost for the first time in the analysis. She said: "I just can't listen to my body, I want to ignore it. My mind gets in the way, I can't bear to hear what it is saying to me. It's just no use for anything, it's worthless." I said: "I think you feel terrified by how much you need me to listen to you and talk to you. You would prefer to kill that part of yourself that needs to be liked and loved."

Emma said that it hurt terribly when her senses were awake, particularly her sense of smell, which she could experience when she was not acidotic. Understanding in analysis was like taking insulin. Getting nearer to being better made her feel how hopeless everything was. I responded: "If you come back to life, you feel my reason for caring for you will be gone. If you are near death, I think you also feel you are near to me and somehow close to your mother."

Toward the end of this session she revealed an important memory about her mother's double incontinence before her death and the shame and humiliation she had felt on her mother's behalf. She also remembered hating to go into the room to see her because of the smell. At the very end of the session she surprised me with her reflectiveness; she said: "I suppose now I make myself smell because I am frightened you don't want to see me."

This material enabled us to understand better Emma's extreme mismanagement of diabetes. Continuing to live by adhering to her medical regimen induced anxiety and terror because it brought her in contact with her desperate infantile need to be loved and understood by a frequently psychotic mother. To cope with the terror, the separate existence of the mother was denied, foreclosing the opportunity for her achievement of full mentalization. Yet retaining only primitive modes of experience of psychic reality brought with it actual grave physical danger. Experience, particularly traumatic experience, could be lived but not thought about.

The need to keep the object close through provocation and aggression recreated in the transference the guilt and helplessness that Emma must have felt about her intermittently crazy and dying mother. She needed to know whether I was able to remain close to her despite her furious attacks upon herself and upon me when I became the vehicle of the mad other within the self. Equally, in her attacks on her own body Emma was her suicidal mother experienced within the self. In her symptoms, she was the destroyer of her remote and mentally inaccessible mother's body, as well as the victim of its destruction.

Emma felt that she could be safe only as long as she made sure that she kept a small part of her mind clear, separate from her dangerous and chaotic feelings and ideas. Her active self-representation was separate, physically distant from the source of danger, the alien other externalized into her body. The affectional tie to the mother, which could not be mentally represented (and therefore felt), could only be recreated in enactment.

Her interactions with her chaotic and crazy parents resulted in heavily invested but confusing internalizations, which she could not easily integrate. Consequently she tried to disavow these aspects of self-structure and presented herself to herself as vulnerable but free of confusion. Because of the fragmented nature of her self-representations, she could only interact with the object in superficial and inconsequential ways. The repudiated aspects of herself, which derived from the introjections of mad family members into the self, expressed themselves in her crazy ill-treatment of her body and in fantasies of her destructive influence on others, particularly the analyst in the transference.

Her body offered a favored locus for such an expression because it appeared to be possible for her to exclude it from her self-representation. Her partial representation of herself implied that, experientially at least, what was happening to her body was happening to that disavowed part of herself in which was located her experience of confusion and senseless ill-treatment that only gained mental representation outside the subjective domain of her mind. It gradually emerged that her resistance against analysis contained within it her terror that in letting down the barriers to her haven she would be confronted by the mad and unpredictable reactions of her objects. Notwithstanding her symptomatic misuse of her body, Emma's irresolvable problem was that her internalizations of her mad objects were inseparably interwoven with mental representations that constituted her sense of her own mental existence.

The intensity of the psychoanalytic encounter gave Emma the opportunity to extend her self-representation on the basis of differentiated perceptions of the chaotic responses of her objects. The process was a long and painstaking one. Its critical component was that Emma gradually became able to reintegrate within her self-representation the dangerous images from which she sought refuge in the pain of keto-acidosis. To give up the relative safety of her encapsulated identity, separated from the chaos that surrounded it, meant experiencing in the transference a terrifying sense of fusion with me as a psychotic object. This occurred repeatedly, and sessions such as the one in which the *Equus* dream emerged were but particularly dramatic examples of a long-term process that, in our view, was critical in bringing about her improvement.

Emma was not easy to treat, but in six years she made substantial gains and was no longer brittle diabetic or self-harming, although she remains deeply confused about relationships and her own role in them. She is a reasonably successful art student and now has a boyfriend who is a competent sculptor and is very encouraging of her work. Emma has finished her treatment. Her bingeing and almost delusional disregard for insulin have ceased. Her periods of improved control were, for a time, still punctuated by episodes of acute self-destructiveness. At her discharge from the clinic she was symptom-free, and we hope that her treatment will have ultimately been comparatively successful.

Separation and Separateness

Let us begin by considering the dysfunction in Emma's psychic reality and its implications for key aspects of her psychopathology: her dependency, her self-harming, and her reaction to the analysis.

Emma's major difficulty was at the level of *metarepresentations* (see chapter 4). Emma, like other borderline patients, had only partial pictures of her own mental experience (her representational world). The mental processes that underpin psychic reality were dysfunctional as a consequence of early trauma. She therefore had no clear vision of herself; she experienced herself as an empty shell into which insulin was injected, as a vehicle stuck in outer space, remote from the "terra firma" of her primary representations, and consequently she had little control over her feelings and thoughts, and her identity rapidly shifted between any incompatible images. An essential source of psychic organization—reflective capacity—was absent.

A striking aspect of the analyst's relationship with Emma was her clear dependency on him as a physical presence. Her attendance was remarkable, particularly within a lifestyle totally lacking in self-discipline. It is tempting to understand this as an indication of a bond or at least as part of an idealized identificatory process. We believe that her dependence may have been more primitive than these possibilities suggest. Emma required the continued physical presence of the other principally not for her protection (Bowlby 1988) but because, without an external mirror, she was incapable of becoming aware of herself as something more than a physical being, as a thinker, as a container of feelings and desires, as an intentional human being. Our core sense of self depends on the coherence and clarity with which we were able to perceive ourselves as intentional beings in the minds of attachment figures. Emma's incoherent sense of herself required the continued physical presence of another in whose voice, face, and behavior she could identify herself as a person. As the analyst disappeared at the end of the session or at the time of a break, she no longer had access to this image. She felt literally lost in the ferment of her feelings and ideas over which she had such poor control. Her capacity to mentalize was tenuous, and in the analyst's absence she felt abandoned to an experience of her mental world, which felt mad and overwhelming. Again and again the analyst's simple mentalization of her feelings visibly calmed her. In this context her need was not for the recapitulation of a failed developmental experience (Kohut 1984) but, rather, a solution to a current problem—the addressing of a deviant developmental process. Emma's need was not for the provision of a general holding environment (Winnicott 1962) but for the creation of an interpersonal situation where her potential for reflective function could be specifically and safely exercised.

As Edith Jacobson (1964) noted, the internalization of the representation of another before the boundaries of the self are fully formed undermines the creation of a coherent sense of self because the infant is forced to internalize the other as a core part of his self. Now, not only is the creation of an integrated psychic reality compromised because of the weakness of the core self, but the individual has to contend with an alien being lodged within the self-structure: the thoughts and feelings associated with the introjected mother rather than the experiences of the child himself feel real.

The suggestion here is that the child, experiencing the internal world in the mode of psychic equivalence, frequently solves this problem by externalizing these alien aspects of the self-representation back onto the real object. While this may lead to great conflict or ambivalence in the external relationship (oppositional behavior, aggression to protect the self from the object, etc.), it works in that the individual can experience himself in a more authentic way, as long as there are other parts of the self-representation that are not seriously distorted and can be drawn on to create a coherent if impoverished inner world.

This may be a relatively stable structure throughout childhood, or as long as the *physical* presence of the object can be ensured. This was the case for Emma, whose psychological problems were clearly linked with the physical loss of the maternal object. The onset of her symptoms might be understood as having been triggered by the loss of an ambivalent relationship (Freud 1917e [1915]). We believe that the analytic material suggests that the crisis for Emma was a result of the loss of somebody who was required to embody aspects of the self that could not be accommodated. The loss of this person thus precipitated a sense of loss of the self; this loss could, then, only be dealt with by finding another object into which these aspects could be externalized. This becomes a critical problem for adolescents with this form of disorganization of the self—an issue that was addressed in detail in chapter 8.

The Use of the Body as a Channel for Unprocessed Mental States

The absence of an object that could contain her feelings forced Emma to create interpersonal experiences with physical objects rather than with people. Even more important, there was a constant pressure for the currency of the relationship between analyst and analysand, as between the primary caregiver and the infant, to become physical—the real thing, as opposed to a thought, a feeling, or an idea. Emma would communicate anxiety by becoming ketotic. Her bodily states of "highs" and "lows" conveyed her mood far better than did her verbalizations. This is a manifestation of a mind functioning within a psychic equivalence mode, in the absence of mentalization. Thus, she enacted with her body in the session, created real anxiety, real anger, and real confusion, rather than being able to describe these as current internal states. The focus of her disturbance on her body is characteristic of these patients, as this indeed is the only part of the internal world that they can feel in control of. Many of the feelings and ideas that Emma was unable to represent as thoughts and feelings were experienced in relation to her body. Her awareness of there being something wrong with her as well as her efforts at self-improvement were focused on the body, which, she felt, achieved a degree of lethal perfection. She was able to maintain her diabetes at the edge of ketotic coma and, at the same time, maintain her weight within the range she considered ideal.

Clinical experience provides ample evidence for the often deeply distorted attitudes of borderline patients to their bodies.

Why should developmental failures in the psychological self have a significant impact on physical identity and adjustment?

1.   When psychic reality is poorly integrated, the body takes on an excessively central role for the continuity of the sense of self. This may become critical in adolescence, when changes in body shape and function signify a far greater change in identity for these individuals than for those whose psychological self-representation is developmentally more advanced. Some adolescents (such as early-onset anorexics) experience existential anxieties in relation to puberty: as if they have ceased to exist—have become different people. There is psychic equivalence between the experience of body shape and its concrete parameters; to be thinner is felt to be superior and *is* therefore superior.

2.   The persistence of psychic equivalence contributes to specific physical states acquiring exaggerated significance in relation to the self. Mental states, unable to achieve representation as ideas or feelings, come to be represented in the bodily domain. Physical attributes such as weight come to reflect states such as internal well-being, control, sense of self-worth, and so on, far beyond the normal tendency for this to happen in adolescence. For Emma, getting thinner could make her feel not just better about herself but a different person. Serious eating disorders show us how concretely the body shape can be felt to represent aspects of personality. Emma looked at her body, and her perception was distorted not because she looked fat, but because she felt that there were unacceptable things inside her that could be controlled, by manipulating her diet and insulin, or even got rid of (from the mind via the body) by inducing hyperglycemic states of confusion or coma.

3.   A further complication is that not only were Emma's own states of mind and self-experience experienced as externalized into the body, but so also was the alien part of her self-representation. This gave a further reason for punishing it. For Emma, this alien object was the psychotic part of her mother. She looked into the mirror and saw her mother. The destructive

attack on the other experienced as in one's own body perhaps gives an additional feeling of well-being and integrity of the self, which can be seen in some of these abnormal states, such as self-cutting or starvation. Hurting the body helps, we would suggest, by leaving the mind feeling more coherent and bounded, belonging more clearly to the self while the body is sacrificed. The object cannot be genuinely attacked mentally because it resides within the mental self. The body, however, because of its separateness from the self-representation, can be readily converted into a vehicle for the introjected other part of the self.

We are suggesting that self-harm, in particular, can be used to create a sense of reflection that would normally be intrapsychic but has to be established for some people through external relationships or through visible attacks on their bodies. Not having a clear sense of themselves from within, they need to find a sense of the self through getting other people to react to them, and through treating themselves as objects, literally rather than metaphorically, because the self is experienced as a physical being without psychological meaning.

Implications for the Analytic Process

What may be crucial here is the sense of psychic equivalence in the relationship between a state of mind and a physical reality. In this sense, it is wrong to think of a representational process mediating these forms of pathology: the body is not symbolic of a state of mind in the mother; it is at that moment experienced as equivalent to the mother's state of mind and is reacted to accordingly. The interpretation of the symbolic meaning of the state of the body for the individual has been found, in our work with brittle diabetics, rarely to be effective (Fonagy, Moran, and Target 1993b; Moran 1984). It is the split-off part of the self (the alien object) that interpretive work may assist in restoring to and then distinguishing from the self-representation. As in the analysis of Emma, this will often mean that the alien other comes to be experienced in the transference: the analyst becomes the mad mother with the damaged eye. Once the analyst, through mentalizing this experience repeatedly, has helped Emma to understand that this mad mother is actually part of herself, she could at the same time own and distance herself from it. She came to be able to resist damaging her own eyesight in the service of this externalization. Only after this disentangling had been achieved could the complexity of mental states, such as conflicts and defenses, begin to be considered therapeutically.

Unfortunately, balancing the therapeutic effect of the relationship with the analyst was also a countertherapeutic tendency inherent to such analytic relationships. Whereas with many patients it is possible to interpret the pressure toward role-responsiveness, patients such as Emma are invested in the externalization in a much more malignant way. They are not just trying to push the analyst into representing part of themselves but (because of the predominance of psychic equivalence) to be the disavowed part of the self-representation. If the analyst were to reject the function of Emma's psychotic mother, about whom she could feel concern, that would have left her with having to contain it within herself, which she could only do by externalizing it into her body. On the other hand, if he did accept the role of the mad doctor, as she said, how could he possibly help her?

The physical other who performs this function must remain present for this complex process to operate. Emma could not feel that she was herself unless she had her analyst there to intimidate and reduce to helplessness. His departure would signal the return of those "exterojects" and the destruction of the coherence she achieved by projection. The analyst was thus faced with a seemingly impossible challenge. For the relationship to serve a function and to be tolerable, the analyst has to become what the patient wishes him to be. To be an analyst and help the patient overcome such primitive modes of relating, the analyst must be anything but what is projected onto him. Unless he is able to adopt an attitude analogous to that of the parent engaged in pretend play with a child, constantly juggling responses to these opposing pressures, the analysis is doomed to become a rigid stereotypic repetition of pathological exchanges.

There are further complications in working with patients whose psychic reality remains at an archaic level, predominantly of psychic equivalence. Emma's observation of her analyst's injury led her to reexperience, rather than to remember, the real violence of her childhood. At moments when she could experience the mad part of herself as in her body, Emma succeeded in achieving a calm detachment that totally precluded the need for analysis, while (at a physical level) a fierce battle raged for her life. She needed the contact with the analyst for the reasons that we have mentioned, but she genuinely saw no reason for her to be analyzed. Her attitudes were understandable in terms of the belief that wanting to be a particular type of person made it true for others and true for herself as well. This clearly involved a split way of experiencing internal reality. There was an imperfect integration between the child's two modes of representing ideas and feelings.

Implications for Technique

The focus of technique in such cases is thus no longer on making conscious what had been unconscious. Emma improved symptomatically, in terms of her diabetes, her depressions, and her relationships, but it would be even more inappropriate for the analyst to be focusing on changing these symptoms with a borderline individual than it is with neurotic patients. We believe that the appropriate technical priority is the analyst's survival, with a coherent identity, or, more specifically, the preservation of a clear picture of the patient's mental state in the analyst's mind. The analyst's survival ensured that Emma did not succeed in destroying the perception of herself as a person. He needed to hold on to a sense of himself and of her experience, so that she could slowly discover this apperception of herself in his mind, to gain a foothold for her own representation of her thoughts and feelings.

A major hurdle can lie in overcoming the countertransference resistance to a full recognition of the depth of the patient's disturbance. The source of the resistance is partly narcissistic—a reluctance to see oneself as one is being seen. Allowing the real possibility of being psychotic, relinquishing the need to assert one's sanity as a way of reassuring oneself, or interpreting the patient's need to take over and totally possess as an aggressive attack, all serve to give patients space to think for themselves, but naturally at the expense of the analyst's capacity to do so. Analytic capacity is called for not in deciphering unconscious motivation, but in being able to reflect on one's own very uncomfortable experience sufficiently to be able to resist the pull of this psychic equivalence mode, to retain a mentalizing stance.

Clinicians may confront the discrepancy between their perception of themselves and that of the patient (Kernberg 1995). The patient's rigid commitment to a false belief might prompt one to say: "Either I am mad or a liar, or you are mistaken." We feel that it is important to appreciate that the status of psychic reality for such individuals involves a direct correspondence between their beliefs and reality. The possibility of false belief or doubt is inaccessible. Only one version of reality can be true; the possibility of viable alternatives implies terrifying and deeply resisted mentalization and must be obliterated.

In normal child development, it is prototypically through engaging playfully with an adult simultaneously entertaining two realities that the child becomes able to adopt the parent's perspective on the play (see also Emde, Kubicek, and Oppenheim 1997). Ultimately, this allows the child to integrate the psychic equivalence and pretend modes of representing psychic reality and, having made this step, to develop a reflective mentalizing capacity. The analyst's stance toward the patient is not a playful one; we think that this would be an inappropriate extension of the developmental metaphor. However, there is an analogy with play. What we believe the analyst needs to try to do is to provide an alternative perspective on the patient's state of mind while all the time supporting her in retaining her sense of her own experience, a way of presenting the same yet not the same. This is the idea that underpins Winnicott's notion of object presentation (Winnicott 1960). This is a functional, but not a developmental, equivalent of an absence of environmental impingement, in Winnicott's sense.

A patient at the opposite end of the dichotomy of externally versus internally focused aggression, a violent man, was very upset by a rather clumsy interpretation made by his analyst (Peter Fonagy). Aiming to be empathic, the analyst had referred to the pain the patient had felt about a canceled session. The patient jumped up, shoved a fist under the analyst's nose, and said, "I'll show you what pain is, you little shit!" Without thinking, the analyst said, "You know, as I get older I can't see things so clearly when they are too close to my eyes," and with that he gently moved the clenched fist away from his face. To the analyst's relief and surprise, the patient immediately calmed down and smiled. On reflection, it seems clear what might have been critical in this exchange: the analyst's awareness of the patient's pain, while accurate, reached the patient in a mode of psychic equivalence, making his distress frighteningly real. The same interpretation to Emma might have reached her in pretend mode and led to immediate acceptance and meaningless integration with her false self-representation. The analyst's intuitive playful response forced this patient to experience the world through his somewhat long-sighted perspective and thus to see him as a real person, allowing the patient to enter his mental world. Let us examine at greater length another female case whose problems with dysfunctional psychic reality found expression in significant externalizing as well as internalizing behavior problems.

DYSFUNCTIONAL PSYCHIC REALITY IN INTERPERSONAL VIOLENCE: "HENRIETTA"

Henrietta[3] was in her mid-thirties when she referred herself to a forensic psychiatrist colleague for counseling. Strangely, the referral on to me mentioned nothing about a forensic history but described repeated suicide attempts, unstable but intense relationships, and abuse of her medication. The referral did not prepare me, however, for the paranoid, almost psychotic, but in fact dissociated episodes with hallucinations and some thought disorder that were to be so striking in my work with her.

Two facts make Henrietta's history unusual from a psychoanalytic standpoint. The first is that she was a murderer—not of her internal objects, her self-representation, her thinking and

---

[3] The analyst was Peter Fonagy, and this is his account.

feeling or other parts of her and her object's mind, although she was undoubtedly guilty of all these, but of her boyfriend. She had stabbed him in the course of a violent quarrel. She pleaded self-defense and that the stabbing was accidental. She was charged with manslaughter and was freed with a suspended sentence. About four years into the analysis she confessed to me that the stabbing had not, in fact, been an accident. While not premeditated, it had certainly been intentional. She had felt driven by violent, blinding rage. By that time, four years into the analysis, I was familiar with Henrietta's vicious, explosive attacks of rage. I was not really surprised by her revelation.

The second fact was her experience of abuse. She described having first been sexually abused by her alcoholic father, then as a teenager by a teacher in her boarding school. Both experiences included intercourse. Her father also beat Henrietta for various misdemeanors at least once a week and more severely, usually for "answering back," at least once a month. The abuse by her father remained a secret between them until his death shortly before the start of her treatment. The relationship with the teacher became public, and the man concerned was dismissed.

Why would someone like Henrietta come into analysis? She seemed never to have had an understanding relationship. She said she wanted to get help with the terrifying dreams that had started with the death of her father. She came to the first interview in a strident mood, demanding a brief period of counseling. She did not know that I was a psychoanalyst, and, on noticing the couch some time into the interview, she said, "So, this is where you fuck your patients?" A feeling of fear washed over me. Rather than reacting directly to her combative intrusive manner, I was aware of the vulnerability and enormous anxiety behind her need to strike out and hurt. I said, aiming to be reassuring, "You must feel quite brave that you dared to come and see me." She said, continuing her contemptuous tone, "You shrinks are abusers. It's just a power trip." I said, now more confident of my countertransference response, "I think it is your *own* power to destroy and abuse that frightens you about therapy. You feel much more confident about being able to cope with me." She stopped short and asked me what I meant by "therapy."

She started once a week, but over eighteen months built up to four times a week. She would have come five times, but her work was no longer in London. She missed almost no sessions. Her commitment to the analytic process was humbling and strengthened my belief in the pervasiveness of the wish to be heard and recognized. However, what happened between Henrietta and myself might not generally be regarded as analysis. My interventions were rarely experienced as interpretations. I am certain that she had little sense of insight, at least during the early years. Let us illustrate what happened at that time.

She arrived on time to the session, sat in a chair, and said she felt upset, and she looked at me challengingly without speaking further. I said, "I don't understand. You need to tell me what upset *is* for you at the moment." She said that she had had another dream about her father, which had upset her. In the dream, *he had asked her to put her head up his backside and she did not want to do it.* She was ready to follow through with a string of obscene images depicting the sexual life between her father and herself. I interrupted: "I think you are upset because you are frightened that I will make you bury your head in messy thoughts here." She stopped in her tracks, told me in a rapid sequence I could hardly follow that she was lost, that her mother didn't understand, she wasn't trying to hurt anybody, that the death was an accident, that she tried to resuscitate him, to give him the kiss of life, but failed, and now I was trying to kill her. There was a gradual acceleration of tempo and intensification of affect. By the end I was in the room with an apparently angry yet basically terrified person. It was unclear what these feelings were about. She seemed terrified by violence—her own or mine. She expected to be killed by a raging jealous object or to kill an invading, threatening one. I said, trying to calm her by stepping outside the fray: "It seems that you feel driven by a terror that you might lose me in this violence. You feel you constantly have to resuscitate me, to breathe life into me just to keep me alive for yourself." She was silent. Eventually she responded, somewhat more calmly, that she was frightened of being a person. She preferred being empty; people only attacked you if they knew you were somebody. I said, "I agree. I think you feel safer with me when you feel empty. It feels even safer if you feel you have emptied me too." Her terror that I might kill her and the even greater fear that she might kill me, intentionally or accidentally, overrode all other concerns.

This brief vignette raises several issues. The analyst did not presume to know what "upset" meant for Henrietta at this time. Most patients would have been aware that the analyst was not going to know what was upsetting them, but for a patient working in psychic equivalence mode, the analyst already knows what she knows (perhaps better than she does) and does not need to be told. After the intervention, Henrietta immediately shifted into a kind of pretend mode when she started to talk about the dream images. Unlike the situation with a neurotic patient, for whom the exploration of a sexual fantasy might be very therapeutic, for a patient like Henrietta it seemed vital to interrupt this retreat into something that was represented as unreal. The analyst's task was then to find something that was felt to be real, though obscure, within that image. The analyst therefore focused on the anxiety about the confusion with which having to talk about her thoughts and feelings evidently confronted her. That in itself provoked more anxiety than it contained. Suddenly, the fantasies became real: she shifted into a psychic equivalence mode and seemed almost to feel that her life was in danger. This panic escalated until somebody else contained it. Somebody was going to get killed. The aim of this sort of cathartic outburst is not mainly, we suggest, a wish to be contained or to work through an experience but, rather, an emptying of the self which quite consciously feels like preempting an imminent attack. The countertransference response is often a sense of emptiness, which is seen as the result of an attempt to relieve anxiety by reducing both people to an equally unthinking state, rather than a primarily destructive attack on the analyst's thinking.

Psychoanalysts often write about the concreteness of thought, broadly building on Freud's distinction between word and thing representations. Mostly, these concern concreteness of meaning, whereas with Henrietta it was the reality of the thought processes themselves that created such an obstacle. For Henrietta, her thoughts sometimes did not feel owned by her mind but were, rather, experienced as if spoken and thus made externally real. We see this as one possible consequence of equating inner experience with outer reality.

It took me some time to realize that in these conversations there was often a third presence. There was a voice inside her head—someone who, she felt, was she, but not she at the same time, an alien aspect of her often dissociated state. Her thoughts seemed to possess an immediacy that was difficult to appreciate fully. Fleeting ideas or images were experienced as disembodied voices, sometimes friendly but mostly persecutory and vicious. While clearly not hallucinations, her thoughts were also not felt to be coming from her own mind. Her "associations" at these times were responses to what she "heard" as much as a dialogue with me. This posed an interesting challenge for my work in the transference. Eventually, I began to address this voice more directly.

In one session Henrietta came in confused, obviously more than usually so. She sat down on the couch and looked at me quizzically, as if asking, "What is going to happen next?" I said, equally puzzled: "You don't know what to say to me, and I don't know what to say to you." This prompted her to launch into a long and puzzling narrative about dancers who "gave their blood" in training and practice, went to endless auditions, but found no work. She said she was upset about the injustice of it all. But then, as though she were responding to someone else—almost as if she were aware of the transference meaning of what she had been saying—she said in quite a different voice, "You are going to have to stop this treatment, aren't you?" Thinking of the concrete reality of her internal experience and wanting to acknowledge how completely compelling it felt to her, I said, "I think that you are being *told* that I will reject you, no matter how hard you try here. You *want* me to understand your distress but you are not being allowed to tell me about it. It all feels so real that you must feel terribly confused." She buried her head in the pillow and started to sob violently: "I am so confused. I feel so bad. I am told I am fine, but I feel hopeless. Please tell me what is wrong with me." I replied with the intention to enter into her mental world, but at the same time to insert the analyst's voice as another perspective that could eventually become therapeutic: "You feel that because I ask you to come here for only 50 minutes on a particular day, I can't possibly understand what your needs really are. I think you have a *voice* inside your head telling you 'you are fine.' And it sometimes sounds like my voice." She calmed down a bit, and then she seemed to suffer something like an allergic response to contact with the analyst. She suddenly said, as if unaware of the contradictions, "I don't need help. I am fine. I am sick. I want to throw up." Then a pause. "I want to throw up when people get too close. You get taken over. You must understand me. You don't understand me. Do you understand me?" I said, trying to identify the source of anxiety, "You are terrified of what I *do* understand. It must be so sickening that I have to throw you out." She said, still sobbing, "It's the sex. It's so wrong. I am so frightened you might *mis*understand. I am trying so hard to make something happen this time." I said, regarding the reference to sex as defensive, aiming to distract us from the immediate source of her anxiety: "You hope for something good to happen here, but you are also frightened because you hear a voice telling you to spoil it by confusing and misleading me."

There are many analytic understandings to explain what was happening between us: the wish to create a perverted analytic intercourse filled with sexual excitement, which hid her guilt and vulnerability; the wish to make me into a pathetic dancer to her tune and observe me "giving my blood" in a futile attempt to save her; the regressive infantile omnipotence of the triumph of chaos over understanding; the self, defensively split between a pleading vulnerable identity and an omnipotent, invulnerable dictator; and so on. All these and more were true. The additional understanding that I had to hold on to over these early years was somewhat different. Alongside her craving for anything that might give a sense of order to her psychic chaos, she desperately fought the truth of *any* idea, not for its specific contents, but because of the intolerable sickness engendered by the closeness of two human minds. There was something that felt sickening and disgusting about genuine feelings and ideas; there was an abhorrence of communication and reflection. She had tried to repudiate her capacity to conceive of mental states, in herself and in me, leaving her with rigid, schematic representations.

Analysis was an obscene seduction because thinking about mental states was *an incestuous act,* experienced as the intrusion of an object into a space far too small to contain it. Her adaptation to trauma entailed the disavowal of feelings and intentions, in herself and in all others close to her. The primary thoroughfare for sharing psychic reality—symbolic thought—was blocked. Instead, the thoughts were experienced as literally, externally real and unchangeable, thinking was felt as words that have been spoken and cannot be taken back. Talking of thoughts as though they were voices was a way of depicting the sense that they were perceived rather than conceived by her. The transference could not be referred to as an "as-if" experience; at this stage perhaps the analyst needs to work partly within the frame of reference of psychic equivalence, notwithstanding the immense countertransference resistance against entering that frame of reference with somebody whose thoughts were terrifyingly violent and confused. It was the analyst's task to make the capacity for the representation of her internal states safe. This is what a parent needs to be able to do with a small child, but to identify with the perspective of a violent, uncontrolled adult is far more threatening and disturbing than doing the same with a child, even a child with similar feelings.

Ideally, the parent accepts the child's experience when the child is in a mode of psychic equivalence, but at the same time behaves in a way that implies that the parent does not have the same experience. A small child may be too frightened to sleep because the dressing gown hanging behind the door seems to be a man waiting to jump out. This is real to the child at those times, and the feeling of terror is correspondingly compelling. The parent does not simply tell the child that the dressing gown is not a man, or that it is silly to be frightened, but removes the dressing gown in a way that recognizes the reality of the frightening idea, but without showing fear.[4] Thus, the parent both

---

[4] This may come close to a psychoanalytic account of the effectiveness of behavioral treatments involving exposure, which appear on the surface to involve little by way of cognition or interpretation but in reality entail the same communication of the simultaneous acknowledgment of psychic reality and an alternative perspective signaling safety.

enters into and provides the possibility of distance from the child's perception, introducing a different perspective. This is parallel to the introduction of alternative perspectives through playing and pretending with the child, but this time in a serious frame of mind. This is what the analyst is engaged in with borderline patients. Henrietta's analyst respected the reality of her terror of closeness, but in doing so also introduced the idea that the terror was based on belief rather than fact. No technical innovation is implied here. This is the very ordinary thing that analysts do, particularly when working in the transference. Individuals with borderline pathology have such a powerful predisposition to distortion that the analyst cannot assume that the mere act of interpretation will convey this idea without specifically and repeatedly addressing alternative perspectives.

In the sessions with Henrietta, the affect was intense. The terror and the distress were real: a desperate hunger for understanding was only matched by her desire to empty her mind. The countertransference was brimming with discomfort and confusion. She acted dangerously, regularly threatened to kill herself, and got into violent quarrels with both friends and strangers for which I was made to feel culpable. She frightened me with the threat of litigation for negligence and gave me a letter of complaint that she drafted for my professional association, where my "incompetence" was carefully documented: any change of appointment, cancellation, lateness, confusion about times, misremembering of names—all were listed and dated. I was criticized for speaking and then ridiculed for my silences. At other times I was made to feel her savior. The fluidity of her psychic reality meant that much of the time I could not know what I was doing, beyond the basic effort to appreciate what her psychic equivalence exposed me to, and then to attempt to communicate that awareness to her.

The kind of dramatic splitting reflected in Henrietta's understanding of her analyst's intentions is, of course, a hallmark of the paranoid-schizoid position in general, and of borderline states in particular. Elsewhere (Fonagy, Target, and Gergely 2000) we have speculated, following Gergely (2000), that the mechanism of splitting is a developmental by-product of the infant's need to create a coherent image of the mental state of the other, which in the immature mind generates coherent but limited subsets of intentional states, primarily an idealized and a persecutory identity.

My ability to orientate to Henrietta's psychic reality was further reduced by what I came to refer to as the "gaps" in the analytic dialogue. There were periods of minutes where my sense of there being any meaning simply disappeared. Usually, these occurred in periods of silence. In contrast to patients whose silence implies thoughtfulness, or others for whom it indicates withholding or resistance, or yet others whose silence is a communication in the transference, Henrietta's silences communicated nothing. On the first few occasions, I blundered into the silences and tried to attribute meaning to them: "My words frightened you, and you feel you need to cut me out," or "You feel rejected, so you are now rejecting me." Mostly, these suggestions would get no response, and when this occasionally was not the case, Henrietta responded as if I had woken her from a state of reverie: "What did you just say?" I gradually noticed that these episodes extended beyond the silence. Henrietta would sometimes start to speak with some feeling, but when I made a comment, she would be quite unable to respond, sometimes even apparently not hearing. For example, on one occasion she described her father's funeral with a clarity that almost made me feel that I was there. Later, when she mentioned not being able to cry, I mentioned that she had cried at the funeral; to my surprise, she responded, "What funeral? Don't you remember I never went to my father's funeral?"

These encounters with dissociation in the analytic setting are probably not unusual with this group of patients. Henrietta's moments of self-seclusion seemed to be attempts at escaping from the intensity of the feelings evoked by mental closeness to the analyst. However, while clearly defensive, these gaps in the narrative could not, at least at the time, be interpreted. The experiences had no meaning for Henrietta, and she was unable to reflect on them. They appear, to that extent, to be analogous to the play of a 2-year-old child, which cannot yet admit playmates and takes place within a subjective world radically severed from the world outside. We could say that Henrietta *imag-ined* that she was at her father's funeral, but at that moment she had no awareness of an act of imagination. The suspension of mentalization, triggered by the threats that attachment rela-tionships bring, throws into relief the persistence of the infantile mode of experiencing psychic reality, which we have called the "pretend mode." Perhaps a key part of dissociation as a phenom-enon is the reemergence of the pretend mode—the mode in which the very young child fully enters a separate psychic world and cannot simultaneously maintain contact with ordinary reality.

The Alien Self

The lack of a stable sense of self is a central difficulty for borderline patients. We have written elsewhere about the role of reflective function in self-organization (Fonagy and Target 1997). The patient lacks an authentic, organic self-image built around internalized representations of self-states. The absence or weak-ness of such a self-image leaves the child, and later the adult, with affect that remains unlabelled and confusing—uncontained (Bion 1962a). The absence of a reflective object for the child's experience creates a vacuum within the self, where internal reality remains nameless, sometimes dreaded. This will create a desperation for meaning and a willingness to take in reflections from the other that do not map onto anything within the child's own experience. We suggest that this leads to the internalization of representations of the parent's state, rather than of a usable version of the child's own experience. This creates what we term an "alien experience within the self," based on representations of the other within the self. This may be close to what Britton (1998) described in similar terms, on the basis of clinical work with patients such as these. Once internalized, the alien pres-ence interferes with the relationship between thought and iden-tity: ideas or feelings that do not seem to belong to the self are experienced. The alien self destroys the sense of coherence of self, which can only be restored by constant and intense projection. Understanding this process is vital clinically, because—in contrast to the neurotic case—the projection is motivated not by superego pressures but by the need to establish a basic continuity of self-experience.

With Henrietta, dreams were like small oases in a cruel desert of enactments and manipulations, which all but destroyed the possibility of reflectiveness. The dreams were vivid and varied, but I gradually noticed a consistent theme. There was always something within something else, and the thing within was absolutely dependent—almost parasitic—upon the thing without. For example, there was a dream about *a lizard with a fly buzzing inside its stomach.* She had a particularly unpleasant recurrent dream that *a beetle's larva was growing inside her brain.* She had a whole series of dreams where she dreamt that *she was dreaming another dream.* I came to believe that in patients incapable of reflectiveness, dreams still provide a valuable window. Perhaps dreams are, in part, residues of a nascent reflective capacity where the dreamer tries unconsciously to depict the structural constellation within his mind (the state that precludes intentional reflection).

In these Russian-doll constellations, Henrietta perhaps represented an inner world in which a self contained another self or, in fact, a representation of the other. This could be internalized in early infancy when the mother's reflective function too often failed the infant. The infant, trying to find *herself* in the mother's mind may find—as Winnicott (1967, p. 32) so accurately put it— the mother instead. The image of the mother would come to colonize the self. This alien other probably exists in seed form in all our self-representations. It may come into its own when later trauma calls it forth as part of a defensive maneuver: identifying with the state of mind of the abuser, in an attempt to restore a feeling of control. The alien other within the self, fostered by maltreatment, is unmasked by the absence of reflective function. Normally, parts of the self-representation that are not rooted in the internalized mirroring of self-states are nevertheless integrated into a singular, fairly coherent self-structure by the capacity for mentalization. This process preconsciously works to lend a coherence and psychological meaning to one's life, actions, and identity. Henrietta lacked the capacity to understand the experience of the buzzing fly inside her self-representation, or to metabolize the feelings and ideas that she experienced as having been placed there, like a larva in her brain. Henrietta could learn little about herself through interpretations of this kind, yet the mental language of the analyst's communications strengthened her reflective capacities, which in turn strengthened the integrity of the self. Let us illustrate what we mean by elaborating on her experience of having been abused and of her own violence.

Henrietta's mother, probably herself a "survivor," had suffered a prolonged postnatal depression after the birth of her second child when Henrietta was 2 years old. She withdrew almost completely from both Henrietta and her father, and eventually she left the family. This probably exacerbated the father's already considerable drug problems, and he began to seek solace at first from cuddling and finally from vaginally and then anally penetrating his daughter. This had apparently begun when she was about 7 years old and had gone on for at least four years. Henrietta recalled initially welcoming his attention (even encouraging it) and gradually, when "the pain" started, going blank, which helped him get inside her. She described imagining herself as one of her dolls. This meant that she blocked any awareness of thoughts and feelings in herself and the other. It was impossible for her to understand how her father could mean to hurt her as part of what grew out of an act of affection. The disavowal of mental states gave her distance from what he might have felt, as well as from her own feelings. As she turned away these, she was forced to rely on the nonreflective organization within the self—the alien other.

The alien other is not entirely a creation of trauma. It is an infantile structure internalized in place of, yet also within, parts of the self. Henrietta's mother of infancy could probably not satisfy her baby's need for reflection of her distress and her needs. (Her daughter's dependency may have been an unbearable reminder of her *own* experience of helplessness—by all accounts she did better with her son.) We suggest that Henrietta, neglected or unrecognized as a small child, internalized a blank image of absence *as the representation of her state of distress.* This state was reactivated in the acute distress of seduction and,

later, when these experiences were relived in analysis. Reflectiveness temporarily abandoned and the self–other boundary destroyed, the abusing father's cruelty was then internalized into
the alien self-representation through a process that may be
related to the mechanism whereby the victim identifies with the
aggressor. Thus, the alien part of the self became *torturing* as
well as vacuous. Her experience of abuse at boarding school,
after the age of 11, presumably reinforced this pathological self-
organization.

Finding others to be a vehicle for this torturing part of her
self-representation became vital. Her experience of self-coherence depended on finding someone willing to abuse her. The
teacher was perhaps the first. A series of severely sadomasochistic relationships showed that he was certainly not the last. The
transference was a lived instance. In contrast to the "role-
responsiveness" model of transference–countertransference (Joseph 1985; Sandler 1976), where an aspect of the self–other
relationship is externalized, a self–self transference evolved, in
which the analyst became a temporary home to the alien aspect
of Henrietta's self-representation. These instances of evocatory
projective identification (Spillius 1992) are pervasive for two
reasons: (*a*) as we have already mentioned, the normal binding
of alien aspects of the self by mentalization does not occur,
and therefore these aspects are more likely to be externalized.
(*b*) Even more critically, once these experiences are created, they
are actually far more compelling for these individuals, because
they are experienced in a mode of psychic equivalence. Let us
give a relatively mild example.

One day Henrietta came in late, complaining that she could
no longer park her car for free. The change in parking regulations was somehow my fault. It was also my fault that she could
not afford the parking fees, and I was going to be away again the
following week. In fact, her lack of progress was entirely down to
me. She had heard of a senior Kleinian colleague who was
renowned for her abilities to deal with difficult patients. She
wished she had been referred to her. *I* was a disaster. She would
have gone on, but, as far as I was concerned, she had said
enough. I said, perhaps attempting to imitate the colleague
whose reputation I envy and failing to recognize the obvious

manipulativeness: "You are trying to destroy my ability to help you, to think about you clearly." This was a misunderstanding. I think she had no intention to destroy me but, rather, a wish to bring forth a critical, irritated reaction. She was silent for a while and then said, "You see. I was right. You can't cope. You are too young, too inexperienced." I found myself saying, "You see, you are frightened! You may have destroyed me, but without me you can't cope and you feel lost." She got up, said, "For me, you and this analysis are dead," and walked out of the session.

Of course, as soon as she left, I knew I had misunderstood. I had become the vehicle for her alien self by becoming critical and irritated, and I had abandoned my analytic self with some capacity to communicate understanding. This was confirmed in the next session, when she came in, feeling a lot better, full of apologies, hoping that I was not too angry with her, reassuring me left, right, and center about how helpful I was being and that she would surely have killed herself by now were it not for my remarkable commitment and skills. I said, "I think you hope that I will believe you, because that will confirm your picture of me as conceited and stupid. What you said yesterday was far closer to what you need to feel about me." She said, contemptuously, "Don't you realize it makes no difference what you think? You mean nothing to me. Nothing!" I said, "I think you are right. But being able to make me into someone who means nothing to you makes you feel in control, and that makes all the difference." She thought for a moment and then said, "You are just clever with words, like my teacher X (the abuser). You are evil. You care nothing about your patients." I said, "If you can make it so that you can see me as evil, then you can kill me, and then you will be free." She fell silent, but the sense was that we both knew that this was the truth.

Not that stating the truth ever necessarily made Henrietta feel better—it made her sad and sometimes suicidal. What seemed to be helpful were those few precious moments (like this last session) when I could become what she needed me to be, yet retain my capacity to hold her in mind with her fears and anxieties and enable her to see this in my words and actions.

Like Emma and other patients with borderline features, Henrietta absolutely required my physical presence. While such dependency might appear as classical secure-base behavior, I never felt that I was able to offer her much by way of safety or protection. Rather, I was required as an assurance of her existence. Her mind was unable to sustain an experience of continuity as an agent. Only in relation to her impression of the impact of her thoughts and feelings on me could she experience these as enduring and stable. As we have said before, this process should not be seen as an attempt to recapitulate a developmental experience that was, in Henrietta's case, deeply distorted. More simply, her terror of abandonment reflected an intrapsychic state of affairs where she was not confident of being able to locate her intentional states once separated from her object.

Over its fourth year, her analysis began to take on a tragic quality, and the dramatic outbursts receded. She was functioning better, but the sessions had come to be dominated by expressions of bitterness. Hatred for her father had begun to emerge, together with a heart-felt dislike of me. The transference could now become sexualized, and at times, when she was angry with me, she explicitly asked me to molest her. She came in one Thursday evening and recounted a particularly ghastly episode of allowing herself to be used and abused by "an old friend" who regularly visited her as his needs dictated. My mind was filled with bizarre and perverse associations. I said that I suspected that it was particularly important to feel that she could control me by exciting me or worrying me, and I suspected that she had felt the same vital sense of control in relation to her "old friend."

She responded that she hadn't been going to tell me but that she had had a dream about me where *I had offered her my penis, suggesting that she should take it in her mouth. She was revolted by it because it was smelly and dirty. She was frightened because she knew I was going to beat her unless she submitted.* She paused, waiting for me to say something. I remained silent. She said that she thought that I was probably extremely clean since I always wore well-ironed white shirts. But in the dream *my shirt was deep red.* She added, speaking particularly calmly, that red was the color of anger.

I said that I understood very well how important it was for her to feel that she was in control, because she was terrified that I would be angry because of what she had done with her friend.

The dream was like an appeasement. If she sensed that I was repelled, it was better for me to be dead. I added that red was also the color of blood. Her body shook as if an electric current had passed through it. "I think that is why I had to kill him," she said. "I couldn't bear him thinking I was disgusting." The tragic story unfolded. She had regularly allowed herself to be mal-treated by her boyfriend. Normally, she had felt "cleansed" by the experience, particularly by his shame about his own actions. But on the final occasion she saw contempt in his eyes. She screamed and shouted at him. He ridiculed and disparaged her. She picked up the knife, and as he moved toward her, still mocking and sneering, she stabbed him. And with it she hoped to have killed her self-hatred and humiliation.

My work with Henrietta has now ended. She improved enormously in terms of both structural and symptomatic criteria—yet horror and despair were never far away, right until the end.

Psychic Equivalence and Violent Enactment

Why is the brutalization of attachment so potent a trigger for violence? We believe that the brutalization of affectional bonds serves to partially deactivate the attachment system in specific contexts and suggests that the malign nature of brutalization experiences is rooted in the intensity of the humiliation associated with them. The absence of the capacity for mentalization and the reemergence of psychic equivalence make individuals with a history of psychological neglect exceptionally vulnerable to brutalization in these contexts. The attacks cannot be attenuated by mentalization of the pain engendered by the dehumanization of attachment. Unmentalized shame is not an "as-if" experience. It is tantamount to the destruction of the self. It would not be an exaggeration to label this emotion "*ego-destructive shame*" (Gilligan 1997). The coherence of the self-representation—identity itself—is under attack. The ability to mentalize would mitigate this process, permitting the individual to continue to conceive of himself as a meaningful intentional subjectivity in spite of the lack of recognition from the attachment figure at that moment. The more robust the capacity for mentalization, the more easily the person may see what lies behind the attack, its meaning, and not mistake it for the possibility of a real destruction of the ego. The intensity of the humiliation might be the immediate cause of the inhibition of mentalization following abuse: all things felt to be internal (subjectivity) become experiences to be resisted. In describing her experience of brutalization, Henrietta reported finding the very act of thinking unbearable: "I stopped thinking" . . . "I went numb" . . . "I could not bear to think."

Why should the brutalization of affectional bonds, whether in the context of relationships with parents or with intimate peers, be associated with such an intense and destructive sense of self-disgust verging on self-hatred? Once again, there is a paradox: the shame concerns being treated as a physical object in the very context where special personal recognition is expected. Overwhelming mental pain is associated with experiencing a discrepancy between the representation of an actual self, based on how one is being treated and the representation of the ideal shape of the self (Joffe and Sandler 1967). The expectation of being seen and understood as a feeling and thinking person, which is created by the attachment context, clashes violently with the brutalized person's objectification and dehumanization. Shame is a higher-order derivative of this basic affect of pain. Unbearable shame is generated through the incongruity of having one's humanity negated, exactly when one is legitimately expecting to be cherished. Violence or the threat of violence to the body kills the soul because it is the ultimate way of communicating the absence of love by the person inflicting the violence, from whom understanding is expected. As Freud (1914c) taught us, the self is sustained by the love of the object, so it can become self-love; the sign of a self starved of love is shame, just as cold is the indication of an absence of heat (Gilligan 1997). And, just like cold, shame, while painful as an acute experience, is, when it is intense and severe, experienced as a feeling of numbness or deadness.

The state of humiliation can only be erased through selective but deep disavowal of the subjectivities of both the object and the self. A prisoner who was incarcerated for aggravated assault recalled his alcoholic father urinating on him and on his sister regularly when he returned home late at night from drinking. He reported that his terror of his father coming home at a certain point changed into an explicit wish to maim and disfigure him. At that point, he said, "The fucking bastard stopped existing for me." In many criminals a similar dramatic reconfiguration of the self seems to take place. There is a turning point when the normal barrier against intentionally injuring another human is penetrated. From this point, the person appears to feel no remorse for violent acts performed on others. A state that might be mistaken for psychopathy sets in. The word "functional" might be inserted before psychopathy since the disappearance of interpersonal sensibility is thought to be defensive, temporary, and reversible. It should not, therefore, be considered a deficit but, rather, an adaptation. So far we have talked about the predisposition to violent crime. This must be distinguished from the act of violence itself. While the predisposition involves the destruction of interpersonal awareness in a specific context, I would suggest that the act of violence itself represents the perverted restoration of a rudimentary mentalizing function.

There is a traditional psychoanalytic assumption that violence is an act of madness—the ego's abandonment of logical thought in favor of primitive and profoundly destructive impulses. The act of violence, whether impulsive or calculated, is rarely one of blind rage. Rather, it is a desperate attempt to protect the fragile self against the onslaught of shame, often innocently triggered by an other. The experience of humiliation, which the individual tries to contain within the alien part of the self, comes to represent an existential threat and is therefore abruptly externalized. Once outside and perceived as part of the representation of the victim in the perpetrator's mind, it is seen as possible to destroy once and for all. In this sense violence is a gesture of hope, a wish for a new beginning, even if in reality it is usually just a tragic end.

We suggest that it is important, in understanding borderline states, to grasp the sense of psychic equivalence between a state of mind and a physical reality. Henrietta's victim did not symbolize an attitude or a mental state—he was killed because he *was*, at that moment, the embodiment of her shame, and destroying him was also felt to destroy the unbearable mental state. Small children are generally not physically capable of dealing with their intolerable feelings in this way, but adults who experience their internal worlds in such ways can be dangerous to themselves and others.

Henrietta resorted to violence to destroy a mental state—a mental state that was hers and yet did not feel like hers. At the moment of the murder, her object turned from feeling her shame to shaming her—a feeling she was desperate to disown. She had tried to disown it, but when it threatened to return, murder seemed the only solution. She felt a terror that the coherence of her self would be destroyed. The act of violence was felt to destroy both her shame and this terror. Her unconscious hope seemed to be that they would then be gone forever.

The lack of a capacity to mentalize reveals the alien self as much as it creates it. It also reveals a mode of thinking where feelings and thoughts feel real and only one version of reality is possible. The impact of her boyfriend's affect could not be reinterpreted or put into context through mentalization. Her primitive experience of psychic reality, which equated external with internal, made her into a joke and threatened the actual destruction of her sense of self. Psychic equivalence makes humiliation a matter of life and death. The killing that ensued was not lacking in empathy, an act of "blind rage." It seemed essential that she saw his reaction and, within that, something that she would otherwise have had to experience as part of herself. His struggle and suffering were vital features of the experience as she later went over it in analysis. At the moment of murder Henrietta felt alive, coherent, and real, out of reach of the deadly rejections, insults, and taunts, and momentarily for once experiencing self-respect. She described having felt a strange but deep tranquility.

Henrietta needed her abusers—the analyst in countertransference enactments and a series of others who, through their maltreatment of her, helped her temporarily reduce the unbearable sense of diffused identity. The other who performs this function must remain present for this complex process to operate. Henrietta could not feel that she was herself unless she had her analyst or someone else to frighten and humiliate. Alternatively, she would attempt to provoke the analyst to become rejecting and contemptuous. However, having succeeded in provoking such reactions, she felt attacked by the immediacy and reality of her perceptions, which were too compelling to be juxtaposed with other experiences with the object. Nor is escape from the object a solution—with the departure of the other person the "exterojects" would return, destroying the coherence she achieved by projection.

The seemingly impossible challenge presented by patients such as Henrietta and Emma is, we believe, rooted in this aspect of the transference. For the relationship to serve a function and to be tolerable, the analyst has to become what the patient wishes him to be. But at these moments he is likely to be too terrifying to be able to offer help that can be accepted. To be an analyst and help the patient overcome such primitive modes of relating, the analyst must be anything but what is projected onto him. Unless he is able to juggle responses to these opposing pressures, the analysis is doomed to become a rigid repetition of pathological exchanges.

Part of the difficulty undoubtedly arises out of the pressure we inevitably feel as clinicians to enact that which is projected onto us. We are pushed to be as our patients wish us to be because we sense that without this, prolonged contact with us might be intolerable. This, of course, happens to a degree in any transference situation, but it is vital to appreciate the difference introduced when the patient is experiencing events primarily in the mode of psychic equivalence. If ordinary transference experiences are illusions, the experience of borderline patients is felt as a delusion it seems unquestionably real. Because, as analysts, we try extremely hard not to react as expected to provocation, we unwittingly push borderline patients to become even more difficult. All such patients get under our skin and eventually discover what will make us react with anger, what will cause us to neglect or reject them or to feel excited by them, in all instances temporarily losing our therapeutic balance.

Implications for Technique:
Between the Psychic Equivalence
and the Pretend Mode

As with Emma, we believe that with Henrietta an appropriate technical priority was the survival of the analyst's picture of the patient's mental state in his mind. It was vital that Henrietta did not succeed in destroying the perception of herself as a person, which she needed if she were gradually to discover this image of herself in his mind, to gain a foothold for her own representation of her thoughts and feelings.

This description might create the impression that patients such as Henrietta cannot respond to psychoanalysis; interpretation necessarily involves some openness to an alternative perspective. In the adult mind, however, repudiation of mentalization is in reality never absolute. It is likely to be greatest at moments of particular stress and/or in attachment relationships; hence the patient has some experience of mentalizing in other contexts that can begin to be built on. The analyst preconsciously assesses how much openness there might be and aims progressively to enlarge that space, if only very slowly. There are wide, moment-to-moment variations in the capacity available, and interventions need to be titrated against the current potential.[5]

Anthony Bateman (1997) described the same phenomenon sensitively in the context of Rosenfeld's (1964) distinction between thick-skinned and thin-skinned narcissists. Extending Rosenfeld's description, Bateman argued that narcissists alternate between the thick-skinned (derogatory and grandiose) and thin-skinned (vulnerable and self-loathing) states. Bateman shows that interpretive work can only be done with such patients at the dangerous moments when they are in movement from one state to the other. We think what Bateman describes is the successful externalization of the alien self (derogatory or self-hating). The externalization of the persecutory object within the self leaves the patient able to listen and even experience concern.

---

[5] We are indebted to Dr. Efrain Bleiberg for this observation.

The analyst needs to be in a dual functioning mode, to infer and create a coherent representation of the patient's true self, separate from but concurrently with any countertransference enactment. However, this is where analysis often fails, because as soon as the patient hears anything other than what he projected, he must once again be on the alert. He might be risking the return of his laboriously ejected introject.

One risk of treatment for these patients is that the analyst will present the patient with more than he is able to absorb, overwhelming the residual capacity truly to understand. This might result either in an overflow into action or, perhaps, in the development of a false "analytic" attitude, which we have called "hyperactive mentalizing." In contrast, a lack of ambition to expand the patient's experience of psychic reality, as in some supportive psychotherapy, misses the opportunity of increasing affect regulation, and, as intense attachment to the analyst develops, so the need to create their feelings in action is likely to escalate, and serious suicide attempts may be the result.

In this context, there is the further danger also touched on in connection with Emma's case of crediting the patient's material with more meaning than it really contains. Henrietta, like many other similar patients, brought much pseudo-symbolic communication, especially in the early phases of her treatment. Her words referred to internal states, yet after a while it became clear that their meaning had little in common with the way other patients might have described feelings or fantasies. Normal interpretive dialogue seemed mostly useless; in Henrietta's case it created an endless stream of words without leading to real change. Analysis of borderline patients can switch into a pretend mode in which words are exchanged but meaning and therefore psychic change are elusive; patients' verbalizations of mental state are, of necessity, "pseudo-insights," as they cannot link to the patient's primary level of internal experience. The progress of such an analysis might resemble that of a car whose wheels are spinning in sand. The overestimation of the patient's mental capacity, the assumption that her psychic reality is experienced like that of the analyst, can lead to a fruitless search after truth. Mentalization can exist separately from the actual affective experience but this is worth little, certainly in a therapeutic context.

Interpretations in the classical sense have no place in the early phases with such patients. Some enactment on the part of the analyst is inevitable; a realistic aim is for him to retain sufficient insight to be able to continue to reflect on his experience to the patient. Henrietta's analyst had to teach her about an inner world, principally by opening his mind to her experience. "Deep" interpretations felt like taunts, intrusions, distractions, or seductions. The appropriate focus seemed to be the exploration of triggers for feelings, small changes in mental states, highlighting differences in perceptions of the same event and bringing awareness of the intricate relationships between action and feeling, as in the analyst's response to her nonverbal gestures in the early phase of the treatment. Such interpretive work as there was had to have a strict focus on the consulting-room and on the feelings and attitudes of patient and analyst. (Note that if the term "transference" is used in this context, it is being used somewhat differently from the traditional definition—see Sandler, Dare, and Holder 1992.) The patient's actions in relation to the analyst—such as the terrifying para-suicidal behavior that was the backdrop to Henrietta's treatment—are not seen by us as unconsciously intended communications, but as desperate reactions to intolerable intimacy. The analyst's task is to elaborate on the emotional states that might have triggered the enactment. The difficulty is the preservation of the "as-if" nature of the therapeutic exercise in the face of the powerful, intrusive projections that the analyst also has to accept. Sometimes there is a place for humor or playfulness in the struggle with psychic equivalent modes of functioning, but naturally this requires much delicacy and judgment of the patient's likely experience of this approach.

The psychotherapist's mentalistic elaborative stance enables the patient ultimately to find himself in the therapist's mind and integrate this image as part of his sense of himself. In successful treatment, the patient gradually comes to accept that feelings can safely be felt and ideas may safely be thought about. There is a gradual shift to experience of the internal world as separate and qualitatively different from external reality (Fonagy and Target 1996). This is part of a maturational process that was, we suggest, defensively abandoned by these patients in an attempt to avoid overwhelming conflict.

Through all these devices, the analyst adopts a nonpragmatic elaborative, mentalistic stance, which places a demand on the patient to focus on the mental state of a benevolent other. This stance in itself enhances or disinhibits the patient's biological propensity for reflection and self-reflection. Perhaps more important, he is able to find himself in the mind of the therapist as a thinking and feeling being—the representation that never fully developed in early childhood and was probably further undermined by subsequent painful interpersonal experience. In this way, the patient's core self-structure is strengthened and sufficient control is acquired over mental representations of internal states so that psychotherapeutic work proper can begin. Even if work were to stop here, much would have been achieved in terms of making behaviors understandable, meaningful, and predictable. The internalization of the analyst's concern with mental states enhances the patient's capacity for similar concern toward her own experience.

11

Mentalized Affectivity
in the Clinical Setting

In this chapter, we focus on the idea of mentalized affectivity, which will allow us to elaborate on a form of affect regulation that is particularly relevant for adults. As introduced in chapter 2, mentalized affectivity is a sophisticated kind of affect regulation that denotes how affects are experienced through the lens of self-reflexivity. It would be mistaken to assume that all adults are capable of such affectivity; yet neither is it a rarified achievement. As we demonstrate in this chapter, mentalized affectivity is a concept that can be enhanced by psychotherapy and thus pertains to a phenomenon that is especially relevant to the clinical realm. In the first section of this chapter we begin with a description of mentalized affectivity as a concept, in the second we delineate three elements of mentalized affectivity, and in the third we turn to four clinical examples to illustrate its importance.

THE CONCEPT OF MENTALIZED AFFECTIVITY

Affects are mental states that can be subjectively or unconsciously experienced. Affect regulation is a process of crafting mental states in accordance with a sense of agency. It occurs at different levels—from something like homeostatic regulation, which occurs without awareness, to self-regulation through our relations with others, in which awareness is critical. It is fair to assume that the more familiar one is with one's subjective experience, the more effective regulation can be. Correspondingly, the more advanced one is with affect regulation, the closer it is to self-regulation. Mentalized affectivity transcends being a state or a process; in its ultimate form, it bears a close relation to character style. It is important to appreciate, however, that not all forms of mentalization have to do with affective experience.

Mentalized affectivity is predicated upon familiarity as well as a sense of comfort with one's own subjective experience. Indeed, such affectivity presumes an agent who is self-reflective. What distinguishes mentalized affectivity from other points of view— like the one where cognition is applied to determine and alter affective experience—is that the agent remains within or recaptures the affective state. As anyone engaged in psychotherapy recognizes, there is a profound difference between abstract self-understanding and the kind of insight that is mediated by live affective experience.

Through mentalized affectivity, one acquires a more complex understanding of one's own affective experience. This will often mean that affects are rendered into new and/or subtler shapes; however, it does not necessarily require that affects are transformed in nature. It is possible that mentalized affectivity directs us to appreciate new meanings in the same affects, not simply to create new affects. Affectivity of this sort has the aim of promoting positive affect, but it should also help us to be able to accept and cope with negative affect. In its essence, mentalized affectivity designates the human need to fathom and reinterpret one's affects and is particularly exemplified through the internal expression of affects. As we have argued throughout this book, mentalization denotes interest in one's mind in general. The term "affectivity" denotes interest in one's own affects—that is, in a specific domain of one's mind. The term "mentalized affectivity" describes how affect regulation is transformed by mentalization.

THE ELEMENTS OF MENTALIZED AFFECTIVITY

Having characterized mentalized affectivity broadly, let us address its composition in a more specific way. This will provide a deeper understanding of the concept, and it will also serve as a basis for how the concept might be operationalized for the purposes of research. There are three elements of mentalized affectivity: identifying, modulating, and expressing affects. Each of the three elements has a basic and more complex form. As we imagine it, identifying affects is the prelude to modulating them. It is not impossible to change what one feels without knowing what it is; however, it is most plausible that regulating/modulating one's affect will depend upon having some awareness of the affect itself. Similarly, expressing one's affects is contingent here upon modulation; on our account, though, it is also important to realize that affects can be expressed inwardly as well as outwardly.

Let us take a closer look at each of the three individual elements. In its most basic form, identifying affects will mean naming the basic emotion that one feels. There are some patients who, one might begin to notice, characteristically avoid naming their affects or in some cases omit the names of specific affects. The process of understanding what this means must commence with the attempt to clarify whether the patient is just somewhat uncomfortable with or is actually in ignorance about the affect in question. Indeed, one can glimpse how readily the matter of naming affects can be complicated and is not necessarily a straightforward matter of knowing what state one is in. Someone can be confused about what he feels—that is, whether it is one affect or another or some combination of both. In instances where one feels a combination of affects, it can be worth while to sort out the relative degrees of each affect.

The complex aspect of identifying affects is exemplified by cases in which there are links—sometimes hidden ones—between affects. An example would be of someone who, whenever he feels angry, undergoes a shift to becoming anxious. Some such links may be predictable, like oscillation between anger and sadness when one is disappointed in love. Other links can be more unusual, as in the patient who, whenever she becomes angry, quickly moves to explain it away by focusing sympathetic and even warm attention on the motivation of the agent who had caused her to be angry. Thus, beyond the task of naming affects, identifying affects can include the process of discerning the relation among distinct affects.

In its basic form, modulating affects will mean that the affect is altered in some way. This can entail modifications in intensity or duration, or it can refer to more subtle adjustments, where the affect is refined. Modulation can mean that the affect is sustained as well as adjusted upward or downward. One of us has a highly narcissistic patient (see "Scott," below), who, just after hearing that a woman on whom he had a crush was getting engaged, announced that he was "feeling pretty good." Upon further exploration, he claimed not that he had not been sad about this news, but that his sadness had subsided. This seems like a case in which modulation might serve to sustain the affect in order for the patient to experience it fully, rather than either increase or decrease it. It is easy to imagine examples in which someone clings persistently to negative affects—let us say anger or resentment—in a way that colors too much of his experience. This would mean that modulation points to the value of adjusting the negative affect downward.

The complex form of affectivity concerns the revaluing of affects. This is a crucial moment within the process of affectivity, as it brings out that one does not necessarily adopt new affects as much as one reinterprets the meaning of the same affects. So through revaluing affects one comes to have a greater sense of the complexity of one's affective experience. This might be illustrated with a case in which one comes to understand how one's predisposition to experience an affect in a certain way extends from early interactions and experiences. Modulating the affect through revaluation would mean taking one's own experience and history into account. This is shown more specifically in the example of a patient (see "Rob," below) who revalues his experience of the ending of a relationship: he does so by coming to terms with how his parents' divorce influenced his experience, leading him to regard himself more as a victim rather than an agent in what transpired.

The third element of affectivity is the expression of affects. At the most rudimentary level, we can distinguish between the choice to restrain expression or to let it flow. Although one might readily presume that expression means the outward manifestation of the affect in the world, this is not necessarily the case. In our view, it is important not to ignore the sense in which affects can be expressed inwardly. Insofar as sociobiological accounts regard emotions as manifest in facial expression and as action responses that aid survival, it is legitimate to question what the idea of expressing one's affects inwardly could mean. Here we would emphasize that the concealment of emotional responses can be a useful and beneficial strategy for an organism. Expressing one's affects inwardly, then, can be understood as a strategy to resort to in a situation in which expressing one's affects outwardly is undesirable. The inward expression of affects is predicated upon the existence of a representational system that gives us an option other than outward expression.

There are important implications for psychotherapy here. One might understand psychotherapy as experimenting with the inward expression of affects through expressing them within an atmosphere that is contained and safe compared to the real world. As we have described in chapter 6—"Playing with Reality"—psychotherapy can be understood as relying on a kind of pretend mode of functioning in which the therapist acts as a playful parent and thus serves to promote fantasy and imagination in the way that a patient regulates his affects. Indeed, it is often an indication of progress in psychotherapy to observe that a patient has begun to express his affects inwardly. This entails no slight to value and importance of outward expression; the key matter is whether an agent is able to make a choice that is genuinely in his self-interest.

The inward expression of affects is especially consistent with self-reflexivity. Recall that as we have outlined the concept of mentalized affectivity, it entails reflecting on one's affects while one remains within an affective state, rather than from a position of distance. In moving to express the affect, it can be sufficient to let one feel the affect anew without having it emerge in the world. For example, a patient realized how angry he was at his wife because she blamed him for her pregnancy, although he believed at the time that his wife was feeling too vulnerable to hear this from him. The point is that it was helpful for him to experience his anger at a deeper level than he had done, but it was equally important to confirm the choice not to convey his affect directly to his wife. We want to stress here how this account differs from one in which one recognizes one's anger from an intellectual standpoint. Mentalized affectivity goes further in pushing us to own our affects; being able to express affects inwardly adds an option in situations where outward expression is not desirable.

Expressing affects takes on greater complexity as a form of communication. Especially in those instances where the affect is expressed outwardly, we can distinguish between an expression that occurs without regard for others and one that occurs within the context of a dialogue with others. Communicating affects means that the expression is offered with the expectation of how it will be received by others. One wants the other person(s) not just to know what one feels, but also to understand and perhaps respond to this feeling. For instance, a patient expressed annoyance at a break, inquiring whether he was right that last year's break had lasted for a shorter time. This goes beyond a statement of how the patient feels; it includes the expectation of a response. Thus, there is something more self-conscious about communicating affects that reflects an investment in intimate and social relationships. We should recall here that the development of a communicative aspect of affects was stressed in chapter 4, "The Social Biofeedback Theory of Affect-Mirroring." Affect-mirroring is a basis for later communication in language.

Although delineating the elements of mentalized affectivity gives us a better sense of what the concept involves, so far we still have remained at an abstract level. We have had some occasion to refer to case material; however, the value of mentalized affectivity as a concept will be enriched considerably by an elaboration of its clinical manifestations. In the next section we look at four different cases that highlight diverse aspects of such affectivity.

CLINICAL EXAMPLES

In this section, we present four cases from our clinical work.[1] The presentations are guided by our interest in the concept of affectivity; inevitably, this involves the inclusion of material that goes beyond the idea of affectivity. It is not our intention, however, to offer full case presentations. Thus, interesting aspects of these cases are raised without being fully explored. The case material reveals a range of affectivity—from very little affectivity (and the disastrous consequences of this) to a case in which affectivity has started to emerge within the treatment, and another case in which the patient came to the treatment with considerable affectivity. We also occasionally contend with affectivity as it pertains to the clinician. Any form of psychotherapy has, in our view, the aim of altering the patient's relation to his own affects, and affectivity represents this possibility. Even for those who possess affectivity, though, it is a continuing struggle.

"TERESA"

Teresa is an African–American woman in her late thirties who grew up in New York; in fact, she once told me that she had never been outside Manhattan. She is quite disturbed and has been in and out of hospitals, diagnosed at different times over the last twenty years as schizophrenic, bipolar, and borderline. She was not psychotic during the two-and-half years during which she was treated. She was disheveled and occasionally smelled badly (to the extent that the patient who followed her once complained that the chair smelled like urine). She was also not very responsive at first, and I often wondered how I could help her, especially as she would reject and even ridicule whatever I said.

---

[1] Written in the first person; the clinician was Elliot L. Jurist.

There was, nonetheless, something likable about Teresa: she had a lively wit, and occasionally she would make comments about other therapists or patients at the clinic that were mean-spirited but funny and devastatingly accurate. It interested me that she seemed to be able to observe others in a way that she could not observe herself. However, her observations of others never included positive affect and at times seemed to me to be based on misinterpretations, which led her to act in ways that had unfortunate consequences for her. During the course of working together I came to appreciate how her intuitions about others could be used in the treatment—serving as an affirmation of her interest in the human mind, even if it was not her own mind.[2]

At first glance, it might seem strange to claim that a patient with strong borderline tendencies should be able to read others' minds, given the discussion of borderline personality disorder in chapter 9 ("The Roots of Borderline Personality Disorder in Disorganized Attachment"), which stresses that underlying such pathology is precisely one of defective mindreading. However, we can distinguish between the capacity to be able to relate to and accept another as an other, which Teresa clearly lacked, and the fleeting, sometimes profoundly astute insights that borderlines like Teresa often exhibit. In using Teresa's comments on others as a way of indirectly encouraging her to talk about herself, therefore, we are not weakening our support for a philosophy-of-mind point of view.

Teresa originally came to therapy because she was ordered to in connection with her court battles to regain custody of her children. She had four children, all of whom had been taken away by the Bureau of Child Welfare (now ACS) for neglect and abuse—including a bizarre allegation that she had performed oral sex on her 8-year-old son. Teresa had been physically and possibly also sexually abused herself.

Teresa did not like to talk about her past. She had a husband, with whom she had had two of the children, but they were no

---

[2] Joseph (1989) has pointed out that with patients who are not interested in understanding themselves, one can still work with their wish to be understood. My point is related—that as a prelude to the desire for self-understanding, one can work with the patient's interest in understanding others.

longer together. Whenever Teresa saw him, she would become agitated afterward, denouncing him violently in our sessions—although she refused to tell me anything about the encounters. Teresa rarely spoke about her mother; she said that she did not like to see her mother because "all she does is nag me." When I inquired about what her mother would nag her about, she said: "and now you're going to nag me?" Teresa also had a sister with whom she had no contact. Her father had deserted the family when she was 9 years old. She did recall one incident shortly before her father left, when she was sitting at the kitchen table doing homework, and he came home drunk and responded to a question she asked him by smashing her in the head so hard that she fell out of the chair. Teresa grew edgy and defensive in narrating this incident and went on to claim boastfully that many other things happened to her, but they did not bother her or have any other effect on her. I gathered that from an early age Teresa had been on her own.

The affect that was most prominent in our sessions was her rage. Primarily she raged against the court system—against the judges, lawyers (both the DAs and her own lawyers), and court officers—but also against the mental health system, including me as its representative. The sessions were repetitive and varied little in content. This atmosphere went on for a long time before I started to observe a change, not in the content of the sessions, but in that she started to miss fewer of them—from coming for two out of every four sessions to coming almost every week.

One day she came in, freshly enraged by her encounter with a court-appointed psychiatrist as part on the ongoing evaluation of her suitability as the mother of her youngest daughter. She began by telling me that the psychiatrist was "all white, alright." When I asked her to elaborate, she said in a huff: "His hair was white, his coat was white, his eyebrows were white . . . he was all white." She then told me about a revealing moment in their interaction. In the course of his interview, the psychiatrist posed the standard question: "Do you have thoughts of harming yourself?" Teresa's response was: "No, but I have thoughts of harming you!" As she narrated the story, I felt a rush of feelings—in which I was able to discern simultaneous feelings of starting to laugh and starting to cry.

Let me try to be as precise as possible about my internal reaction, as it felt unfamiliar and utterly strange. The feeling was distinct from experiencing a mixture of opposing things together—expressed, for example, in the notion of a "bittersweet feeling" or in the way that, in extreme circumstances, pleasure and pain can converge. There was something unalloyed and contradictory about what I felt, which, it is fair to suspect, might have been influenced by the patient's desire to rid herself of intolerable feelings and, therefore, embodied something of her unintegrated inner world. Having one's own psyche filled in this way from another exemplifies "projective identification." On reflection, I was able to analyze my experience as follows: I was laughing because of how brazen Teresa was and because I was amused by her (fleeting) sense of having triumphed over the psychiatrist. In a way, she had called his bluff: as he wanted to know how she felt, she was going to comply and tell him the unadorned truth. I was crying, of course, because in drawing attention to her own capacity for violence, she was dooming herself to be judged unfit as a mother. The psychiatrist, who met with her for an hour, judged her to be incompetent, and in his report he questioned whether she would ever be fit to be a mother.

Teresa's behavior was hostile to the psychiatrist, and it is hardly consoling that her avowal of homicidal ideation might be construed as intending to answer the question about suicidal thoughts in the negative. Her behavior was blatantly self-destructive: it is hard to imagine her saying anything that would be as damaging to her own case. It is helpful to strive to look at things through Teresa's eyes. Teresa was a woman who was incredibly sensitive to slights and tended to misread the intentions of others to her as malevolent. Thus, I would conjecture that she perceived the context—and, in particular, the psychiatrist's query and, indeed, his very personhood—as an affront. (His pure and total whiteness exacerbated her experience of being judged and condemned.) When the psychiatrist raised the specter of self-harm, she felt harmed and then responded in a kind of self-defense. Her words ostensively deny suicidal intent, but on a deeper level this was an enactment in which she performed her own suicide directly in front of the psychiatrist.

I would like to describe one other incident that occurred in Teresa's treatment. We had been meeting for almost two years when, one day, she came in and sat down. After a few minutes of silence, she said sharply: "Man, look at you! Don't you know anything . . . you're going to catch cold, if you walk around like that." (I realized that she was looking at my leg where, between the top of my socks and my trousers, about two inches of flesh was exposed.) She continued: "Now listen to me . . . if you catch cold, this is what you should do: you make yourself some tea; then you take a teaspoon of honey and lemon. You drink that, and you'll be all better." She shook her head, grinning and triumphant: "You ought to listen to me. I know what I'm talking about." This little interaction was notable as it contains a rare instance of positive affect expressed by Teresa. Teresa meant well, regardless of something bossy and scolding about her tone and her quirky perception of reality, revealed in her loose associations. The affective quality to her language rendered the literal exchange of words to be less relevant. One could discern, I think, a wish on Teresa's part to express concern for my welfare.

This interaction was moving because of her expression of empathy and care, suggesting that, after two years, she felt less oppositional and, perhaps, was offering a reciprocating gesture that she felt cared for by me. But the truth is that I did not often have the feeling that I was helping her. Very little of what I actually said seemed to matter; what did matter, I believe, was that I listened to her—being listened to, without being judged, was an experience conspicuously absent from her past history or present reality. (Notice the repetition of the word "listen" in the patient's expression of her concern for me.)

From what I could tell, Teresa lived an extremely isolated life. Her best friend—the only friend she ever spoke about—a homeless woman, who could usually be found in one of three or four locations, would disappear for stretches of time. Thus, it was significant that she was able to form enough of a bond with me to move from coming halfheartedly and under duress to coming by choice. Her rage remained obdurate throughout the treatment. Teresa felt wronged in a profound sense, and, in immersing herself in fighting alone in the court system, managed to find a willing conspirator in making her feel wrong—not necessarily without justice, but certainly without compassion.

Instances of positive affect remained rare and too charged to be openly acknowledged. We had some touching moments, however, when she would make me laugh or smile, and while she would not overtly reveal it, I could tell that this pleased her and could even witness her attempt to suppress her own positive reaction. If I tried to draw attention to our shared pleasure, she would brutally reject it. The treatment ended abruptly after a problem with her Medicaid coverage and my subsequent departure from the clinic. Thus our work would remain incomplete.

A year or so later, however, I saw Teresa on the street. She was preoccupied, looking through a garbage can, and did not look up. I wanted to greet her, but I also did not want to intrude; I decided that if she saw me, I would say hello. Quickly, the moment passed. As I walked away, I felt an overwhelming feeling of sadness.

Discussion

The range of affects that Teresa displayed was limited and repetitive. Her rage was explosive, and at times, frightening.[3] Her reaction to the court psychiatrist was disturbing because it revealed how seriously she misread the intentions of others. Her hostility here is best understood as an attempt to fend off what felt to her like hostility being directed at her. This is suggestive, perhaps, of traumatic reenactment as well as an eruption of primary process.

Teresa showed little evidence of being able to identify or distinguish affects. Not surprisingly, this had implications for

---

[3] Narcissistic rage, in Kohut's sense (Kohut 1972), is relevant here, as this patient's damaged self-esteem leaves her feeling vulnerable, requiring her to keep others at a distance and at times erupting with aggression. I describe an incident that occurred with Teresa, in which she got out of her chair and threatened to hit me, in my review article of John Steiner's *Psychic Retreats* (Jurist 1997).

whether she was able to regulate her affects. Her rage flared up and automatically poured out; it loomed ominously in her psychic functioning. Teresa must have felt tremendous fear in the situation of having to defend herself as a mother, yet her rage contaminated the experience of this or any other affects. Her rage seemed not so much like a hyperbolic form of anger, but a monolithic, domineering presence.

As my experience of starting to laugh and cry together suggests, Teresa's projective identification both masked and unveiled a confused, disorganized inner world. It provided a window into her fragmented sense of agency. Problems in her sense of agency emerged clearly in the episode with the court psychiatrist: although her wish to be deemed a worthy mother was strong, her behavior ensured that she would be assessed as unworthy.

The consequences of Teresa not being able to regulate her affects were dramatic. Her negative affects overwhelmed her. It is equally pertinent that even where she felt positive affect (to me), there was a tinge of some aggression as well. It did not feel safe for Teresa to feel positive affect; indeed, she worked at curtailing it, rather than risk expressing it. In this interaction with me, we can witness Teresa's struggle to be able to tolerate positive affect.

One would be hard pressed to find evidence that Teresa possessed mentalized affectivity. Indeed, it is interesting how much I felt my own affect regulation to be undermined—for example, in my response to her story about the court psychiatrist and especially in my response to meeting her on the street after the treatment had ended. Teresa was a difficult patient to whom one's own countertransference reactions were powerful; yet, these reactions provide one of the only clues to infer what she was experiencing.

Teresa showed hints of developing a connection to her therapist. This was a promising sign, in my opinion, of some potential to develop a measure of mentalized affectivity in a long-term, ongoing treatment. Whenever a patient exhibits a sense of humor, there is hope, and Teresa had a delightful if wicked sense of humor. Without mentalized affectivity, Teresa is bound to run into and repeat problems in her life. Her treatment was interrupted, and, therefore, we can only imagine whether and to what degree she might have acquired mentalized affectivity.

"BENNIE"

Bennie is a Jewish man in his early fifties. He grew up in a working-class family just outside New York. He was an excellent student and won a scholarship to attend an elite university, where he majored in history. Bennie fell apart during his junior year and has never recovered the same level of functioning. He once showed me his college transcript, which provides dramatic evidence of the manifestation of his illness: during his freshman year, he received grades of Bs mostly and a few Cs; during his sophomore year, he received mostly Bs again, with one A and one C; during the Fall semester of his junior year, he failed every course. He made a few attempts to enroll again before dropping out permanently.

Bennie's decompensation is consistent with the classic symptoms of schizophrenia. Over the years, he has had numerous breakdowns and hospitalizations. He spent almost a decade living on the streets and in SRO's (single rooms), refusing medication and relishing his choice to live within a delusional world. Bennie can be extremely articulate about this time of his life, as when he describes his identification with Native Americans, which led him to wander through Riverside Park "on a sacred quest for meaning," immersing himself in observing tiny details of plant and animal life, indifferent only, he is aware, to the presence of other human beings. Bennie recalls this time as a period when he was fully alive, and he becomes defensive in the face of being reminded of his suffering—for example, occasions when he was beaten up on the streets.

About eleven years ago, Bennie moved into a social service hotel. He has a social worker there, and he also attends a vocational group once a week. He has had several psychologists over the years, whom, for the most part, he remembers fondly.

He has seen numerous psychiatrists whom he recalls more ambivalently. He likes his current psychiatrist very much and sees her once a month. He is diligent about taking his medication for his current diagnosis of schizoaffective disorder. About ten years ago, he had to be brought to the emergency room because he was screaming "kill the Jews, kill the Jews" while thinking about his father in his room; he was released the following day.

I have been seeing Bennie twice a week for the last nine years. He never misses his appointments, and he takes psychotherapy seriously—often bringing in a list of topics he wants to talk about. We have a good working relationship. He is no longer actively delusional, although he does have peculiar compulsive habits—like finding himself eating in restaurants in rhythm with conversations at other tables, or like watching his clock until 6:05 because "605" was the street address of the house where he grew up. Bennie frequently has ideas of reference; interestingly, when we work together on examining these, he can distinguish among their plausibility and will jokingly rate them in percentage to their relation to reality—usually with a fair degree of accuracy. Humor has emerged to be a crucial component in my work with Bennie. It is a way for him to tolerate shared moments without feeling threatened. Moments of humor stand in lieu of, but might be seen as a promise for, a more abiding sense of closeness to others.

Bennie's daily life is uneventful. He works two mornings a week as an English-language tutor. He hangs out in the lobby of his building. He has a favorite restaurant in his neighborhood, where he eats almost all his meals; he has some social contact with other tenants in his building, and he also has a few college friends with whom he keeps up. His parents have moved far away, to be near a sister who is married and who has a daughter who is in medical school. Minute details of interactions with others often become the focus of our sessions. Bennie can be profoundly affected by a friendly glance from the storekeeper at the Korean grocery.

In general, Bennie is hypersensitive to others. However, he is not always astute in his understanding of others' intentions. The behavior of others can swiftly become the basis of elaborate fantasies, some of which have a distinctly paranoid flavor. He will imagine someone looking at him on the bus and then invent tales of who the person is and what he/she thinks of him. Bennie tends to keep his distance from others; yet, he is also dependent in the relationships he has—especially the group of mental-health workers on whom he relies to sustain him. He is both afraid of real contact with others and craves it.

Occasionally, Bennie is able to be deeply in touch with his unconscious life through his dreams. He has narrated dreams that last for 25 minutes, leaving me overwhelmed and confused by the sheer intensity of the imagery. He tends to be more interested in narrating the dreams than he is in interpreting them. He does have a rare capacity to be in touch with psychotic parts of himself and to bring them into the treatment.

It is difficult to know to what extent Bennie's reports about his relationship to his parents and his early life in general are reliable. He regards his mother as intrusive and domineering, and his father, who died at 89 years of age after many years of incapacitating illness, as unresponsive and occasionally cold and even hostile. In phone calls prior to his father's death, Bennie was disturbed by his father's response to him and had seemingly little appreciation for the extent of his father's infirmity. Bennie chose not to go to his father's funeral, but he did journey to be with his family a few weeks after that. His reactions to his father's death have mostly featured his disappointment with his father, and he has only expressed overt grief on one occasion. Bennie is fragile and has strong guilt feelings about being a disappointment to his parents, so I have not pushed him to deal with this loss.

Bennie understands that he must be vigilant about not allowing himself to act on the basis of his thoughts. Sometimes he becomes grave and still, pondering his mind, which regularly manufactures false or at least unreliable beliefs. Although I have confidence that he can identify signs of becoming actively psychotic and that we might have a chance to intervene to stop further decompensation, it is harder to know what constitutes success in the treatment. Many mental-health professionals would scoff at the notion of a successful outcome for a schizophrenic in psychotherapy. Other mental-health professionals would be inclined to emphasize that staying the course and monitoring Bennie from getting worse is itself a positive outcome and not to be minimized. Indeed, Bennie's positive symptoms have been well-controlled by the combination of psychotherapy and psychopharmacology, although his negative symptoms—not getting out of bed, not keeping himself and his room clean, not finishing projects he begins—remain a problem. I have been struck by Bennie's need for self-understanding, and this has been a guiding light throughout the treatment.

Bennie continues to battle his devastating illness. A measure of his success can be marked by his current work as a tutor in reading at a public library, for which he has received heartfelt thanks from a number of his students. Yet, Bennie's well-being has its vicissitudes, and he seems to be sitting on a well of sadness. Like most other people, he benefits from exploration of his personal history and dynamics. In his case, though, the project of self-understanding must contend with the enormous power and force of his disorder.

Discussion

Bennie is a patient who has a serious mental illness. The illness interferes with his perception of reality, and, thus, Bennie's reading of the intentions of others can often be dangerously mistaken. In particular, Bennie can be quite paranoid in the way he construes what appear to be innocuous interactions. With such a patient, it is not possible to expect a high degree of affectivity.

Bennie does exhibit a range of affects. He is able to identify affects like fear, sadness, and anger. Moreover, he is able to identify, distinguish, and express positive affects as well. Bennie has activities that he enjoys, like listening to music and drawing. He can be warm and concerned for others—he notices and expresses sympathy if I have a cold, and he dotes on his 3-year-old nephew. He has intervened to get help for others in the social services building in which he lives. Yet, it is difficult for him to sustain positive affects in relationships.

Although Bennie has a range of affects, he has difficulty modulating them. Let me offer an example: during a visit with his nephew at a restaurant, he was pleased to engage in a game of hide and seek using a menu, but when the nephew fell asleep shortly thereafter, Bennie's interpretation was that it must have been because he was bored with Bennie's company. His anxiety about being disregarded is played out with a young child—without any appreciation that the child's sleepiness might have an independent cause. When I tried to draw attention to other possible interpretations of the nephew's behavior, Bennie could appreciate that he was jumping to a conclusion. Yet, it is clear that he would not have come to this point by himself.

What about Bennie's reaction to a major life experience, such as his father's death? It does not appear that he is passing through some of the common, expected stages of grief. In one sense, he uncompromisingly refuses to revise or minimize the extent of his negative feelings about his father. Yet, there is some kind of failure in regulation that is revealed in how he thinks about his father—as well as his widowed mother. Bennie is at a loss about what to do about his father's death. He reports having moments where something about his father flashes through his mind, but he is not inclined to use this as a basis of reflection about what his father meant to him.

Bennie feels a deep, deep sadness about the trajectory of his life. He is aware of having a mind that does not work right. At this point in his life, he is remarkably adept at remaining free of trouble. I try to be with him in his moments of sadness without unrealistically raising expectations of a better tomorrow. The work that we do together has implications for mentalized affectivity. In reviewing his ideas of reference, Bennie can sometimes distance himself from some of his assumptions that he is inclined to make by himself. This often leads him to distinguish his affects better and to be able to modulate them. It is significant that this does not happen when Bennie is alone. However, he would have resisted such a mutual effort during the first five to six years of the treatment.

In conclusion, I would like to return to Bennie's sense of humor. When he laughs, it sounds like the clanking of a rusty machine. Bennie can tolerate mutual positive affect through humor. As I have already suggested, humor serves to join us in intimate moments and as a fleeting marker of greater satisfaction. Bennie feels closer to me than to anyone else in his life. Indeed, it is not all inadvertent that Bennie's closest relationships are with mental-health professionals; relations with others have been much more conflicted and confusing. Our work together enables Bennie to experience genuine moments of connection and to sustain his commitment to finding a meaningful life for himself. With some help, Bennie has moments in which he exhibits the capacity to reflect on his affects. Although it is perhaps idealistic to hope that he might attain mentalized affectivity more fully, the battle to seek it is surely worth fighting.

"SCOTT"

Scott is a 40-year-old man who was raised in a middle-class family and grew up in various places in the Midwest and in Arizona. His early life was characterized by numerous moves, which left him with few friends and lonely. In high school, he started to truant and to drink and do drugs. In his early twenties, he moved to New Mexico to become a painter and to work in an art gallery. At this time, he drank and smoked heavily and did lots of drugs. Scott was married for three years, neglecting his wife until eventually she left him to return to her parents' home. Scott had many casual relationships and a few more serious ones during these years. As his life in the fast lane became increasingly self-destructive, Scott turned to therapy for help. He spent three years in therapy at that time, which helped him to stop abusing substances and led to his decision to move to New York.

Scott has little contact with his family. He has not seen his parents in seven years; he receives letters from his mother a few times a year, including Christmas. His father, a fairly successful businessman, was tough and bullying and disdained his son's artistic leanings. He himself had not gone to college, and he thought it was a waste of time for others. Scott describes his mother in generic terms: as a typical 1950s' housewife, passive and conventional. Scott has a younger sister, who is gay and who has been in a committed relationship for many years; Scott has not seen his sister in four years.

Scott was particularly close to his paternal grandmother. When he was 6 years old, he was sent to live with her for two years—ostensively because the air in Arizona would be better for his health. (He had a respiratory problem of unknown severity.) Scott now suspects, however, that he might have been sent away because his mother felt overwhelmed with dealing with him. This insight is based upon some key memories where Scott recalls beseeching her to play with him as she ironed or cleaned, and she reacted by getting fed up, fleeing to the bedroom, and shutting the door behind her.

Although Scott felt loved by his grandmother, he had a dawning awareness that she was disturbed. He came to see that she was unreliable as a storyteller, making up that she owned property that he would inherit and that she was friendly with famous people whom they saw on television. She used multiple names, which, Scott later ascertained, had to do with the fact that she had been married six times. She also tried to influence Scott against his mother. Later in life, she traveled around for years, staying with acquaintances all over the country without having her own home. This grandmother died alienated from Scott as well as from Scott's parents.

Scott had some success in the art world in New Mexico, but he also had some failures, and in his mid-thirties he decided that what he really wanted to do was to get an education. At the time he entered treatment with me, he had attempted to attend college numerous times without having completed a semester.

Scott has been in treatment for five years. During that time, he has won two scholarships and several awards, and he has spent a year abroad. He has also returned to painting. Interestingly, he formed a relationship with a woman while he was away. When he returned to treatment after the year abroad, he rejected the possibility of trying to remain in a long-distance relationship.

Scott has ambitious career plans, including organizing an art exhibition at a major museum. At the same time, he has had to struggle not to allow incompletes to mount up—jeopardizing his achievement. In the context of discussing this situation, he told the following story: he had turned in a paper for an English class to complete a course, which was an accomplishment and also a great relief. The following week he was reading in the library, and he became aware of someone walking by him, and he heard a voice. He looked up to see that it was his English professor, who was talking to him, telling him that the paper was excellent and that he had enjoyed reading it. Scott realized that he did not comprehend what was said until later, and he was unable to respond directly, mumbling something that was incoherent.

As Scott sat and thought about the incident, he became aware that, at the moment he perceived that the person near him was his professor, he was anticipating criticism—that he would be told that the paper was terrible and that the professor was disappointed in his efforts. His sense of confusion during the interaction was produced, according to Scott, by the conflict between the imagined voice in his head and the real external voice. He averred that this conflict had to do with difficulty in believing in his own success—even though he had worked hard and deserved it. Moreover, the internal voice reminded him of his domineering father, who never believed in his success and who derided his interest in education. It is interesting how the professor's praise manages to be blocked, in effect preventing an experience of positive affect. As Scott reflected about the incident after it had occurred and before talking about it in therapy, he was consumed with worry that he had insulted the professor by not responding appropriately; he also felt vaguely upset at himself. In our session, Scott was able to allow himself gratification with some prompting and to express pride that his work was praised.

This incident shows Scott's internal world prohibiting the experience of positive affect—the intermingling between (imagined) negative affect and (actual) positive affect paralyzed him. Scott was also able to make sense of some of his emotions. Still, when he is by himself, he stays with feeling bad. With help in the session, he moves to amend this, resulting in some regret about what happened but primarily a sense that he ought to feel good. The patient's tendency toward negative affect is entrenched enough to prevent him from having positive affect at first, but not so entrenched that it must be excluded at all cost. The interaction, which he reports as a kind of bystander to himself, is altered so that he understands the incident and then re-experiences it.

There has been an interesting change in Scott's relationship to his own affects over the course of the therapy. At the beginning of the treatment, it was as striking as it was perplexing that he would omit reports of feelings and at times mislabel his feelings—like the opening moment of a session (already mentioned in the section on "The Elements of Mentalized Affectivity" in this chapter), after he had just learned that a woman on whom he had a crush for several months was getting engaged, when he announced: "I've been feeling pretty good. . . ." Although it is helpful to aid Scott in identifying his feelings, being too direct in doing so can actually backfire.

A few years into the treatment, Scott continues to struggle to be able to experience his own affects. For instance, he returned from an appointment with a doctor who, after a number of tests, told him that a chronic urological problem he has is due to a congenital problem with his kidney. Scott was told that he might require surgery—with two options: a more serious operation or a newer, less painful, but also more uncertain high-tech procedure. I asked Scott what he thought about the situation. He responded: "Well, I don't feel too worried. . . . I mean, I hope that I won't end up having kidney failure. I would hate to have to go to dialysis, which is time-consuming and would get in the way of my work."

Despite the ostensive denial of feeling worried, Scott went on to make it fairly evident by jumping to a worst-case scenario—that, naturally, he was quite concerned. From experience I was aware that Scott's impulse not to acknowledge what he feels could have the undesirable effect of rendering his feelings more extreme. However, I was also concerned that too active an interpretation about his affect state might make him defensive and disputatious. Scott had something at stake in talking about his affect state without specifying it—as if to ward off falling into the state without hope of getting out of it. With some help, though, he was able to move in this direction—that is, to feel appropriately worried, mindful of both his personal history and the immediate circumstances.

Scott and I have had success in working on his relation to his affects, particularly through his interest in art. Art serves the complex function of allowing him to distance himself from and at the same time to process his affects. There is one painting in which he has developed a strong interest, which depicts a scene from Homer's *Odyssey*. The context is Odysseus' famous encounter with the Cyclops, Polyphemos, who savagely gobbles up a few of Odysseus' men. The scene reveals Odysseus at his best and worst: he restrains himself from acting, devising a resourceful way to save his men and himself, but then he jeopardizes all of their survival by indulging in his omnipotence. He devises the resourceful plan of getting Polyphemos drunk and then blinding him with a huge, sharpened pole. This enables Odysseus and his men to crawl out of Polyphemos' cave by tying themselves to the underbelly of sheep; when the blinded Cyclops searches for them, touching the backs of the sheep, they escape undetected. After they have successfully escaped and are about to depart, however, Odysseus yells out to Polyphemos, taunting him that his name is "Nobody." This provokes Polyphemos into tossing a massive boulder, which comes close to shipwrecking the boat and dooming their survival. The painting that Scott is working on represents the precise moment when Odysseus boasts to the Cyclops.

Our interpretation of the painting has been ongoing and from multiple angles. First of all, Scott's father, whom he experienced as bullying and uncivilized, resembles the dangerous Cyclops. This resemblance was confirmed through a quite extraordinary fact that came out in interpreting Scott's relationship to the painting: like the one-eyed Cyclops, Scott's father is blind in one eye—having suffered an accident as a young man. The oedipal theme is prominent, as Scott identifies with Odysseus who asserts himself with phallic aggression against Polyphemos. The blinding of Polyphemos, like Oedipus's self-blinding, is a kind of symbolic castration. However, we have also pondered the importance of the (pre-oedipal) theme of omnipotence suggested by the painting.[4] The painting resonates with Scott, we discovered to-gether, precisely because it gives expression to the danger he associates with strong affect.

Through the external representation of art, Scott has found a way to observe his inner conflicts. Indeed, it is hard to imagine that he would be able to deal with these issues as comfortably without this distance. It is interesting that his intellectuality provides a means for him to be in touch with deep emotional issues. Scott has articulated the insight that he might have learned that it is better not to feel, since feeling is linked to aggression that gets out of control. It is rather interesting that Odysseus acts uncharacteristically here: he is usually depicted as someone who gets what he wants through restraint and adhering to a course of moderation. Ironically enough, then, we might conclude that the painting provides not merely a diagnosis, but the path for a cure for Scott.

Discussion

The absence of affect was a notable part of the early phases of Scott's therapy.[5] Not only did he omit affects where one would expect them, but often he did not describe them as part of his experience at all. At times, he would seem to mislabel his feelings. Not surprisingly, he had very little overt response in his transference to me. I recall that Scott would pause to hear me speak and then continue as if it were merely an interruption of his own line of thinking. This changed, particularly during breaks for vacations, when Scott reported physical illnesses that

---

[4] The oscillation of narcissistic self-esteem is conveyed in the contrast of extremes between "Polyphemos," which means "much-famed" in Greek, and "Nobody," the false name Odysseus gives to himself (the Greek word "*Oudos*" here is a play on Odysseus' real name). In the treatment, Scott's narcissism came up in the context of his reading and his awareness of his own narcissistic tendencies.

[5] Scott reminded me of the alexithymic patients whom Krystal (1988) describes who often abuse substances as a way of distancing themselves from painful affects. Also, like the patients Krystal describes, Scott would report one-sentence dreams—without any ability to provide associations.

we could understand in terms of the treatment as protection against pain.

It was quite important that the treatment resumed after Scott's year abroad: he became more vulnerable, manifested in a new interest in examining the past—like when he had been sent away and then returned home to his family. Although Scott still did not openly display his affects, I could observe a shift—which can be conveyed in the difference between his posture of "I've been feeling pretty good" in the face of a narcissistic rejection and an implicit recognition of his sadness of the narcissistic rejection in feeling alone and confused after being sent away from home at the age of 6 years.

Scott has trouble identifying his affects, but he is growing to be more interested in making sense of his affective experience. Given his difficulty in identifying and distinguishing affects, it is predictable that he also struggles with regulating them. This is nicely illustrated in Scott's reaction to his kidney disorder, where he is estranged from his anxieties and takes them in an extreme direction— before modulating them with the help of my input. We also see that Scott is more comfortable exploring his affects with the distance that aesthetic objects provide.

There also has been evolution in the transference. He registers what I say to a greater degree. The value of therapy for him is conveyed in the way he divides his life into a before and an after. Scott does not express positive affect about therapy or me; this is consistent with someone who would need to block positive affect, as he does in the incident with his English professor. Not only has he never asked me a question about myself, he has shown very few signs of having such curiosity. Yet, Scott is now able to express negative transference reactions to me—like being bothered by interruptions with vacations and occasionally being annoyed by something I've said.

Scott is now clearly more alive in the way he lives. After many years of living precariously—with periods of being down and out—he has had some genuine success. His education represents a triumph over the discouragement he received at home. It is still difficult for him to accept what he feels inside himself. Yet, mentalized affectivity has emerged within the course of therapy. With some help, Scott is able to reflect upon the incident with the English professor, moving from focusing on his fear of having insulted the professor to pondering his own need to interfere with a pleasurable experience. Something similar occurs with Scott's reflection about his kidney disorder. Although these instances of affectivity occur in sessions, he is doing more of the work by himself.

A promising example of Scott's emergent affectivity can be seen in his choice not to engage in fruitless confrontations during the course of his daily life. The first few years of therapy were filled with such antagonistic encounters with others. I recall that in our very first session he described an unpleasant encounter with a security guard, who was talking on the telephone instead of doing his job—checking the bags of students exiting the library. Scott made an audible comment about his resentment at having to wait around; the result, of course, was that the security guard took his time, they exchanged angry words, and he ended up being delayed still further. Let us compare this to a recent incident: Scott was crossing the street as a taxi was letting a passenger off, blocking his way. He tossed the driver a dirty look, which prompted the driver to get out of his taxi and start yelling at Scott. Scott had an impulse to return fire with fire, but he decided it was not worth the effort and walked away.

Although Scott is still responsible for initiating the conflict in the second incident, he restrains himself from exacerbating it. Moreover, we can see this as a moment in which initially Scott displays his feeling of disgust at the driver outwardly; then he shifts and makes the choice to express his affects internally. In Scott's narration of this incident, he was aware that he remained upset at that moment, but he felt good about having opted to act in accordance with a deeper sense of his own purpose. Here Scott displays mentalized affectivity in precisely the manner that the *Odyssey* entertains in the scene of Odysseus deriding Polyphemos. Like Odysseus, whom Homer describes as "*polytropos*" (he is, literally, the man of "many ways"), Scott has options about how he will respond. Reflecting upon readings of the *Odyssey* has made Scott aware of the danger he associates with the expression of affects. His fascination with the *Odyssey*, which I happen to share, has been a meeting place in our relationship. Although Scott does not exteriorize his transference to me, my responsiveness to interpreting a work of great emotional import has helped him to feel more secure and begin to thrive. The change in his affectivity that we glimpse over time is central to his therapeutic progress.

"ROB"

Rob is a bright and sensitive young man in his mid-twenties who grew up in a Wasp (White Anglo-Saxon Protestant) family from the South. His family was close when he was young. Rob got along with his younger sister, even though she is extroverted and he is introverted. Rob has always been particularly close to his mother: he remembers coming home from school and sitting down with her as she attentively listened to him describe his day while he enjoyed milk and cookies.

Rob began therapy because he was depressed after splitting up with his girl friend of five years. Their relationship had started during his freshman year in college—the same year, it turns out, that his parents announced that they were getting divorced. His parents informed him of this by flying out together to visit him and discussing their decision. Rob had had no idea that his parents were having trouble. The family dynamic mixed sensitive parenting with a strong undercurrent of suppressing all conflict.

At first, Rob was somewhat resistant to my suggestion that he might be reexperiencing the pain of his parents' divorce through the current breakup with his girl friend. But as he gained more distance from the end of the relationship and formed a connection to me, he began to realize that he had avoided dealing with his reactions to his parents' divorce. More specifically, Rob recalled how in college he threw himself into activity—his work, politics, and sports. He had not had much experience with women up to that point, but he soon commenced his first serious relationship (with the woman with whom he broke up just before entering treatment). A couple of years into the treatment, Rob started to become interested in how his depression at the end of a relationship reactivated older feelings about his parents' divorce. Not only could he see that he had much stronger feelings about the divorce than he realized at the time, but he came to be in touch with his anger with his father, whom he saw as the one responsible for breaking up the family.

As his involvement in therapy deepened, Rob and I explored new and different angles of his past. His understanding of what had happened in the relationship underwent a shift: he began to see the outcome less as a matter of his girl friend leaving him, and more as a matter of their interests diverging and the inherent difficulty of sustaining a relationship that began in college. Rob was able to acknowledge aspects of his own dissatisfaction in the relationship. He also became aware of some differences between his parents' divorce, which occurred without warning and without his input, and the breakup of the relationship, which, at least to some degree, reflected his own choice. Rob developed a complex interpretation here, starting from his flight into a relationship in the face of his parents' divorce, which enabled him not to feel hopeless about relationships and to be a little less involved with his family in the aftermath of his parents' divorce but also served to distance him from the range of feelings he had about it. Rob gave voice, too, to the frustratingly symbiotic quality of this relationship. Finally, he had insights about how the divorce, while looming largely in his late-adolescent experience, itself reenacted much earlier developmental issues. The divorce had an aspect of being an oedipal victory for him, since he had always been close to his mother and she turned to him more during and after the divorce, and also because it brought heightened conflict with his father. Yet, the divorce evoked intense anxiety because Rob felt that he was prematurely on his own and would have to fend for himself with less support.

There was and there remains real sadness about the breakup of his family: Rob wept in a session as he realized that leaving home for him coincided with there being no more home left. Over the next year, Rob moved from feeling despair about relationships and from isolating himself to being sad from time to time, but ready to move ahead in his life. He became involved in a new relationship. Our work has focused more on his tendency to drift into how he thinks he should feel rather than staying with how he really feels.

Since the divorce, Rob's mother has not become involved in a new relationship, and she remains very much involved in her children's lives. Rob's father remarried a few years ago with a younger woman; his father has made an effort to maintain a relationship with him, but Rob feels that it is perfunctory. Rob does not like his stepmother and resents that she controls his father, although he is also critical of his father for allowing her to do so.

During a family gathering, which concluded a long weekend together, Rob's father made an announcement in front of Rob and his younger sister (as well as their grandmother and some cousins) that startled Rob: his wife and he planned to adopt a baby. Rob was aware that they were contemplating having a child, but figured the matter had been resolved when his step-mother did not get pregnant. Rob had a negative reaction to the way the issue of adopting a child was raised—just at the conclu-sion of the gathering, as if to ensure that there would be no discussion, making him feel doubly left out. In therapy, we focused on the possibility of Rob disclosing his feelings to his father. He wrote his father a letter; his father answered promptly with an email—not responding to what Rob said, but affirming the value of talking and openly exchanging their opinions.

No heart-to-heart talk ensued. Rob felt that his father was obliged to be the one to follow up. Neither Rob nor his father made the time to initiate a serious conversation on the next occasion when they got together. Rob began to think that per-haps they had cooled to the idea of adoption, but several months later he received a phone call from his father, explaining that, on short notice, they were leaving to pick up a baby girl to adopt. Rob felt angry and betrayed. He understands that part of his reaction is irrational: that at some level he knew this might happen, that his father is perfectly entitled to choose to have a new family, and that this need not exclude him. The inception of this new family, however, has meant that Rob is facing anew the demise of his old family. Rob acknowledged his anxiety of both being rejected by his father and being left with his mother.

This experience repeated elements of his parents' divorce: that the announcement was precipitous and especially that his father voiced the right sentiments, but failed to follow through. Rob's negative reaction to his father was exacerbated shortly thereafter when his father phoned after the baby was at home but did not have time to talk, and mentioned in an off-hand way that he had thought Rob would not be at home, and he had planned to leave a message. The situation is actually even more complicated by the fact that Rob's mother has made no effort to conceal her resentments about her former husband from Rob or his sister.

Rob has had moments of sadness in therapy about this situation, but he has also muted his emotional reaction and initially withheld the extent of his true feelings. A week or so after finding out about the adoption, Rob left for a (scheduled) vacation. His girl friend was not able to go with him, so he planned to go away by himself—a first for him. The trip itself went fine, but on the way home, he suffered from a phobic reaction while flying. He was anxious and distracted during the two takeoffs, ruminating about what could go wrong. It was crucial, according to his report of what he was feeling at the time, that his fate was completely out of his hands.

Rob had had a flying phobia before, although this time was worse. We had been successful in reducing his fear of flying, especially after linking his fear to his freshman year in college, when his parents got divorced. Rob realized that prior to this he had suffered no fear of flying. Just as he felt that his life was out of his control in an airplane, so he felt that the life of his family was out of his control when his parents announced their intention to divorce.

Rob could see that the return of the phobia seemed to be precipitated by the painful reminder of the past that his father's new family rekindled. His struggle to achieve autonomy is conveyed in his attempt to go away by himself, only to have a recurrence of his phobia on the flight home—as he was returning to face negative affects that he had pushed aside during his trip.

Discussion

Rob exhibits a wide range of affects. The influence of his family style, which minimizes affects, is also evident. This interferes with his regulation of affects. On occasion, the regulation does not work, and his sadness slips into depression, his anxiety into phobia. In spite of a tendency to intellectualize what he feels, Rob's affect regulation should not be overly pathologized. He is high-functioning in his work life, and he is well adjusted socially. It is evident that Rob brings to therapy a capacity for mentalized affectivity and is able to put it to good effect in the treatment. Rob's affectivity is revealed in his reassessment(s) of what he felt about his parents' divorce, allowing him to experience his own feelings in a more open and complex way. He has come to see that he had opted not to experience negative affects fully in connection with an important event from the past and that this has continued to influence his relationship in the present, and he embraces the ongoing task of reinterpretation.

Rob's recognition that he had warded off feelings of depression about the divorce has spurred his movement into new affective experiences. He is able to move from feeling morose to feeling sad in a way that is accompanied by an affirmative sense of self-understanding.[6] His sadness pertains to the demise of both his parents' and his own (first) relationship, but he has also come to appreciate that while he had no control over what happened with his parents, the end of his own relationship was neither out of his control nor opposed to his real wishes. As he has come to accept what he felt, so his sense of agency has been enhanced. An overall sense of gloom has lessened.

---

[6] Sadness is an affect, of course, that can be regarded as a developmental achievement. Melanie Klein's depressive position, for instance, occurs when a child is able to see the mother as a whole object—that is, as differentiated from himself—and thus experiences her absence as a loss. The distinction between sadness and depression is, I think, important to uphold—marking the difference between the normal and the pathological, but also highlighting that not all negative affects are equally undesirable. It can feel good to be sad, while the same cannot be said about being depressed (although it might feel comfortable, because it is familiar). The work of Samuel Beckett is preoccupied with discerning the boundary between sadness and depression.

Rob's capacity for mentalized affectivity has room for growth. He has a tendency to suppress his feelings—a good example of this is revealed in his reaction to his father's new family. Rob knows that he was displeased with this development, and he is able to communicate this to a certain extent. However, there is something restrained about his reaction, reflecting his wish to sound reasonable and to edit his real feelings. Rob's tendency not to allow his affects to be expressed freely has produced countertransference responses on my part where I am aware of putting more affect into my voice, as if to provide examples of immediate affective reactions and to compensate for his low-key responses. This has been an issue in his relationship with his current girl friend: she has complained that he is not demonstrative enough.

Although Rob is someone who struggles to allow himself to express his affects, this should not be construed as exclusively meaning that he needs to learn to express them outwardly. The inward expression of affects is equally important. For example, Rob has started to become progressively more aware of his anger toward his father. Apart from whether and how he chooses to communicate this to his father, it has been crucial for Rob to allow himself to feel his resentment and to begin to separate himself from his family's style of downplaying all affective responses. In glimpsing that his father may not be willing to respond to his attempts to communicate with him, Rob's expression of his affects inwardly serves as a valuable affirmation of his own experience of the new family situation.

The mentalized affectivity that Rob does exhibit in coming to terms with his parents' divorce and the impact it had on his life has come under stress with the fresh reminder that his own nuclear family dissolved as his father begins to constitute a new family. This does not contradict the suggestion that he possesses mentalized affectivity; rather, it highlights that circumstances can temporarily undermine affectivity or at least make it difficult to sustain. Indeed, mentalized affectivity can break down at the moment when the impact of a strong affect is felt. Normally, mentalized affectivity requires gaining some perspective, which, in the heat of the moment, can be beyond the capacity of most of us. It is certainly possible to acquire mentalized affectivity in situations where one has previously lacked it, but it would imprudent to fail to heed how much of a struggle it is to maintain it consistently. In drawing attention to Rob's ability to reflect on and craft his affects, I am acknowledging the sense in which affects are chosen; it should be clear, however, that I am not disputing the sense in which Rob feels that affects happen to him. My point is simply to emphasize that we can influence what we feel and, in addition, that psychotherapy can serve to develop and enhance mentalized affectivity.

CONCLUSION

These four cases present a spectrum from severe to mild psychopathology, and correspondingly affectivity is better where the psychopathology is less severe. The first two examples are cases of severe mental illness: Teresa and Bennie have extensive psychiatric histories and major mental disorders, and they have had numerous hospitalizations over the years. Teresa's range of affect display is more limited than is Bennie's, and she lives a much more isolated life. Bennie has chosen to remain in therapy for a longer time; he has a strong bond with his therapist and is able to have moments of mentalized affectivity within the clinical setting. For both Teresa and Bennie, humor has been a way of establishing a connection with their therapist—the least dangerous way of sharing positive affect.

Scott has a character disorder as well as a history of substance abuse. He has been able to free himself from the latter, and, after a number of years in treatment, his life has started to change significantly for the better. The quality of his relationships is improving. He has begun to channel his considerable intellectual abilities in a productive direction. His ambitions are being realized, although grandiose fantasies continue to obtrude. In the case of Scott, we witness the development of mentalized affectivity within the course of the treatment itself.

Rob's psychopathology is relatively mild. Despite the phobia and his unresolved feelings about his parents' divorce, he is high-functioning. He continues to have academic success; he has a job in which he has been given increased responsibility; he has numerous friends—both acquaintances and close relationships; and he is working hard at figuring out whether problems in his relationship can be resolved. He brings a high level of mentalized affectivity with him to the treatment, but the treatment has also served to deepen it.

The concept of mentalized affectivity describes a clinical phenomenon that pertains to the mediation of affective experience through self-reflexivity. This is a compelling concept because at the heart of psychotherapy is the aim of changing one's relation to one's own affects. Mentalized affectivity, which includes the elements of identifying, modulating, and expressing affects, helps us to understand how one's relation to one's own affects can be changed. Ultimately, the justification for such a concept must be found in empirical research. Our hope in this chapter is to demonstrate that there is a need for such a concept, and that undertaking further research on this subject would be worth while.

Epilogue

Research on the social development of infants has probably been the most influential advance in empirical science for psychoanalysis. The work of Daniel Stern (1985, 1994) and Robert Emde (1997, 1980a, 1980b, 1981, 1988, 1992) established infant research at the center of psychoanalytic theorization. The work reported in this volume has built on the achievement of these and other pioneers of infant research to produce a psychoanalytic model that, we hope, is of relevance to clinicians.

There have been some cogent objections to the impact of infancy research on psychoanalysis. For example, Wolff (1996) warned of the epistemological dangers in extrapolating from infant research to the behavior of adult patients. Others point to what such perspectives omit from the traditional psychoanalytic approach (e.g., Fajardo 1993; Green 2000). We welcome this dialogue and to an extent agree with these cautions—particularly that new ideas should not be felt to devalue the truth of the old, that the baby should always be taken safely out before dealing with the bath water. Nevertheless, we sense that many clinicians would join us in seeing the findings of psychoanalytically oriented empirical studies of early development as being of clear relevance to clinical understanding and technique. The general body of psychoanalytic opinion warmly welcomes infant research. For example, Joseph Lichtenberg wrote: "Seen through

modifications of theory and technique, the findings of psychoanalytically oriented empirical studies of early development have
and will have, I believe, a cumulative effect far greater than we
have as yet appreciated" (1995, p. 275).

MENTAL MODELS AND PROCEDURES

Developmental research has helped to revise some developmental propositions of psychoanalysis that turned out to be naive.
For instance, there has been a shift in emphasis in psychoanalytic practice from a focus on the retrieval of forgotten experience
to one where the creation of a meaningful narrative is regarded
as mutative (e.g., Spence 1982, 1984). The interactional and
interpersonal aspects of clinical work have become recognized as
crucial, giving insight into the more primitive aspects of interaction seen in psychoanalysis (e.g., S. A. Mitchell 1997). While
we do not assume that formative experiences underlying these
aspects have been retained in a way that allowed them to be
recalled, analogies continually emerge between aspects of parent–infant interaction and the analyst–patient relationship.

Implicit in the understanding of these analogies is the idea
that procedures, or patterns of actions rather than individual
experiences, are retained from infant–caregiver interactions and
that these procedures come to organize later behavior (Clyman
1991). The procedures are organized as mental models (Johnson-
Laird and Byrne 1991, 1993). They should not be conceived of as
pictures; they are better thought of as intricately interlinked
sequences of events. Nevertheless, taken together, groups of
procedures amount to a representation of a relationship, forever
confined to the unconscious (phenomenologically rather than
dynamically speaking) and observable only through an individual's manner or style of relating, rather than through the ideas or
memories described. The goal of therapy, then, is the observation
of patterns of interaction and the identification and correction of
maladaptive models, principally through strengthening an overarching mental capacity to activate alternative models of interaction selectively; in language influenced by cognitive science,

this capacity may be labeled "mentalization" or "reflective function."

THE OBJECT AT THE CORE OF THE SELF

Our concern in this book has been with individual differences in self-representational capacities and consequent differences in affect (Bleiberg 1984, 1994) and mentalization. At one extreme clinically we encountered individuals whose self-representation was so fragmented as to appear almost nonexistent, or so distorted that it seemed completely out of touch with real emotional experience. Bleiberg (Bleiberg et al. 1997) has described severely personality-disordered children who experienced a sense of almost total alienation from their core self. These children present significant disturbances of social and emotional development, including marked impairment of peer relationships, affect regulation, frustration tolerance, and impulse control, as well as poor self-esteem and poor self-image. Some of them, designated as Cluster A, show a more fragile reality contact and thought organization, particularly when faced with lack of structure. Idiosyncratic, magical thinking pervades their lives, but it acquires greater intensity in emotionally charged contexts. Shy and friendless, they retreat to a world of bizarre fantasies, haunted by ideas of reference, suspiciousness, and extreme discomfort in social situations. Their ability to "make sense" of human exchanges and empathize with others is strikingly limited. They are equally impoverished in their capacity to communicate, which is hampered by the oddness of their speech and the constriction or inappropriateness of their affect. Descriptively, they generally resemble a range of DSM-IV's diagnoses that include schizotypal, schizoid, and milder forms of pervasive developmental disorder. They also resemble the children described by Cohen and colleagues as suffering from "multiplex developmental disorder" (Cohen, Towbin, Mayes, and Volkmar 1994).

In contrast, a second group of youngsters, designated as Cluster B, shows intense, dramatic affect and hunger for social response. Clinginess and a vulnerability to separations, hyperactivity, and temper tantrums are common features of their early development. By school age, they meet diagnostic criteria for an Axis I diagnosis; more commonly, attention-deficit hyperactivity disorder, conduct disorder, separation anxiety disorder, or mood disorder. Many of these children appear anxious, moody, irritable, and explosive. Minor upsets or frustrations trigger intense affective storms—episodes of uncontrolled emotion, which are wholly out of proportion to the apparent precipitant. This affective lability mirrors the kaleidoscopic quality of these children's sense of self and others. One moment they feel elated and expansive, blissfully connected in perfect love and harmony with an idealized partner; the next moment they plunge into bitter disappointment and rage, coupled with self-loathing and despair.

Self-centeredness is a striking characteristic of these children. They need constant attention and respond with rage to rejection or indifference. Alternating between idealization and devaluation, they seductively and manipulatively strive to coerce others to provide them with a stream of emotional supplies. By the time they reach adolescence, drugs, food, or promiscuous sex have become common strategies to block feelings of subjective dyscontrol, fragmentation, and loneliness. Self-mutilation and suicidal gestures are common among girls, while aggression, coupled with hidden fears of rejection, is more typical of boys. This cluster of patients has been linked to early manifestations of "dramatic" personality disorders (in the adult personality disorder classification of DSM-IV, these would be the Cluster B disorders).

In spite of the heterogeneity—and the obvious need for systematic studies to determine the validity and reliability of particular clinical and developmental clusters—these youngsters seem to share a crucial characteristic: some pervasively—Cluster A—and others intermittently—Cluster B—seem to lack the capacity to be aware of their own and other people's mental states.

We conceive of such children as showing an extreme version of the strategy of insecure infants. Confronted with a frightened or frightening caregiver, they adapt via a wholesale internalization of the caregiver's reaction to them. This leaves at the core of their self-structure the representation of the object rather than of the self. Not only is the child then out of touch with his affect, but he also experiences the self-representation as foreign to his internal experience, yet very much a part of himself. Internal coherence later becomes impossible to achieve without first externalizing this alien part of the self-representation. We have suggested that this is why young children, classified in infancy as disorganized in their attachment, have been shown to behave in an unusually controlling way toward their parents. The object must be consistently controlled in order that it can remain an effective vehicle for the alien part of the self.

The mechanism we have described in this book is a type of projective identification, although that construct is perhaps too broad to convey exactly what we intend here. One hallmark of the special category of projective identification we are describing is the desperation felt by the individual to be able to get rid of the unwanted aspects of the self. The alien part must be externalized for the child to feel a sense of being in touch with the real, experiencing self. The closer to the core of the self such an alien object resides, the greater the need for the physical presence of the other, to permit this externalization. For the child who was disorganized as an infant, the object who was internalized as part of the self-representation is the most likely vehicle for this projective process. Thus, even brief separations may feel like an impossible challenge. Often, in young children, the difficulty is compounded by the continuing need of the child for a mirroring object. They continue to attempt to find themselves in the other, at the same time as externalizing onto the other their alien self-representation. This is very often a self-perpetuating pattern, where the child struggles to rid himself of parts of himself and actualize them in the parent, at the same time desperately needing the parent to reflect and strengthen the feeble but true core. If the parent or later attachment figure is able to accept the projection and yet retain some capacity for reflective functioning, then the course of the child's development may be changed. In our experience, relatively few parents are able to change in this way. Commonly, quite a vicious transactional cycle develops, where the relative strength of the true self weakens and the corresponding need for externalization increases; the contact between parent and child then becomes a struggle that is often described as a sadomasochistic relationship, though we would see this as misleading in that it suggests perverse erotic gratification as the driving force.

SOME SPECULATIONS
ABOUT PATHOLOGICAL DEVELOPMENT

As we have said, a fundamental need of every infant is to find his own mind, or intentional state, in the mind of the object. For the infant, internalization of this image performs the function of "containment," which Winnicott has written of as "giving back to the baby the baby's own self" (Winnicott 1967, p. 33) . Failure of this function leads to a desperate search for alternative ways of containing thoughts and the intense feelings they engender. The search for alternative ways of mental containment may, we have suggested, give rise to many pathological solutions, including taking the mind of the other, with its distorted, absent, or malign picture of the child, as part of the child's own sense of identity.

With development, and exacerbated by the apparently sado-masochistic patterns described above, this picture can become the germ of a persecutory object that is lodged in the self but is alien and unassimilable. There will be a desperate wish for separation in the hope of establishing an autonomous identity or existence. However, sadly, this identity is centered around a mental state that cannot reflect the changing emotional and cognitive states of the individual because it is based on an archaic representation of the other rather than on the thinking and feeling self as seen by the other.

As for children, so for adults whose search for mirroring or containment has failed, the striving for separation will only produce a movement toward fusion. The more the person attempts to become himself, the closer he moves toward becoming his object, because the latter is part of the self-structure. This may account for the familiar oscillation of borderline patients between the struggle for independence and the terrifying wish for extreme closeness and fantasized union. Developmentally, a crisis may be expected to arise in late adolescence and early adulthood, when the external demand for separateness becomes irresistible. Self-destructive and (in the extreme) suicidal behavior may then be perceived as the only feasible solution to an insoluble dilemma: the freeing of the self from the other through the destruction of the other within the self.

In some people, for whom separateness is a chronic problem, we have assumed that the experience of selfhood can only be achieved through finding a physical other onto whom the other within the self can be projected. Thus, many will find leaving home very difficult and only sustainable by finding an alternative, comparable figure onto whom the other within the self may be projected. If the other person dies or leaves, a pathological mourning process may be initiated, whereby the person feels compelled to maintain a live picture of the other in order to shore up the integrity of the self.

Another possible outcome of poor development of the psychological self is that the body may be used to contain and enact mental states. In these cases the child's own body comes to serve the function of second-order representation of feelings, ideas, and wishes. Violence toward the body of the self (e.g., self-cutting) or that of the other (apparently unprovoked aggression or "mindless violence") may be a way of "controlling" mental states that are invested in bodily states (e.g., the mother seen as part of one's own body) or destroying "ideas" experienced as being within the body of the other.

In both physical violence and self-destructive acts, a number of factors combine. (*a*) In these acts the individual functions in a nonmentalizing mode of psychic equivalence. There is both an intolerance of alternative perspectives—that is, these have to be destroyed—and a belief that by destroying the person representing the idea, the persecuting idea itself will be eradicated from the person's own mind. (*b*) In both externally and internally directed aggression, there are indications of the persistence of a pretend mode of functioning, in that at one level the individual perceives his acts as inconsequential, except in obliterating the intolerable thoughts. External reality can be ignored: the overdose can be conceived as getting rid of certain thoughts belonging to another, yet leaving the body unharmed. (c) The absence of mentalizing removes key restraints on action against both the self and the other. Even when someone can intellectually conceive of the impact of his or her actions on another person, this may be felt as meaningless, empty of emotional conviction (Blair 1995). Linked to this may be a reason why women more commonly self-harm, whereas men are more often aggressive toward others. We would suggest that for women, the image of the mother (most often the primary caregiver in early life) resides more easily in their own body, whereas for men it is easier to externalize this and the thoughts it represents onto others.

In extreme cases, where the child has found no alternative relationship in which his thoughts and feelings are perceived and reflected, his own potential for reflective capacity will not be fulfilled. In cases of abusive, hostile, or simply totally vacuous relationships with the caregiver, the infant may deliberately turn away from the object; the contemplation of the object's mind is overwhelming as it harbors frankly hostile intentions toward the infant's self. This may lead to a widespread avoidance of mental states, which further reduces the chance of identifying and establishing intimate links with an understanding object.

As studies of resilient children suggest, even a single secure/understanding relationship may be sufficient for the development of reflective processes and may "save" the child. We do not anticipate that trauma outside the context of a close attachment would pervasively stunt the development of mentalization. It is because reflective function evolves in the context of intense interpersonal relationships that the fear of the mind of another can have such devastating consequences on the emergence of social understanding.

If the traumatized child has had no social support of sufficient strength and intensity for an attachment bond and then reflectiveness to develop, then the experience of later trauma or abuse will probably not be reflected on or resolved. Naturally, the unresolved experience of abuse diminishes the likelihood of meaningful relationships, which, in a self-perpetuating way, makes it more difficult to reach a satisfactory resolution of the disturbing experience through reflective processes. In fact, a pattern may be established whereby suspicion and distrust generalize and lead to a turning away from the mental state of most important others and to an apparent "decoupling" of thinking about people, leaving the person bereft. The "neediness" of people with borderline personality disorders seems to be a step in this direction; no sooner do they become involved with another person than the malfunctioning of their mentalizing capacity leads them into confusion and chaos within the relationship. They may regress to the intersubjective state of earlier mental representation, no longer able to differentiate their own mental representations from those of others and either of these from external reality. As these processes combine, they may become terrorized by their own thoughts about the other—particularly their aggressive impulses and fantasies—experienced (via projection) as *in* the other; these become crippling, and most commonly they reject or arrange to be rejected by their object. Psychoanalysis or psychotherapy can break the vicious cycle by reinforcing reflective capacity.

PSYCHOTHERAPY AND MENTALIZING

Acceptance of this model does not imply a change in psychotherapeutic practice, or that these ideas are relevant to most forms of later pathology. Many patients with neurotic problems have relatively good reflective capacities, founded (we would suggest) on adequate early attachment relationships and on adequate mentalizing capacities in at least one caregiver. In these cases, we see traditional psychoanalytic understanding and the interpretation of current unconscious conflicts as very powerful and able to produce substantial, lasting change. It does, however, call for a reappraisal of the relative importance of aspects of technique in cases showing the kinds of early developmental failure that we have tried to describe. This means that certain more supportive techniques may shift from the status of parameter to mutative components, at least in the early stages of what is likely to be a prolonged analysis.

In these cases of severe character and developmental pathology the focus on reflective function in psychopathology brings with it an implication concerning the role of insight. Insight is an unlikely goal early on, given the profound limitations on listening to and understanding interpretations shown by these patients. In some less severe cases, the therapist may be impressed by the patient's apparent receptiveness to interpretations and may only become suspicious in the long term when the apparent building of insight fails to lead to significant change. Patients such as these acquire insight within what we would see as a pretend mode, where reflection is possible as long as it is kept separate from everyday reality. In other words, the patient plays at being in analysis but is unable to integrate it with genuine feeling or meaning.

What are the analyst's goals when understanding is unattainable at first and is in fact perceived as a serious threat? We aim to enhance certain psychic processes. To do this, the analyst needs, of course, to create an environment within which thinking about feelings and ideas can be experienced as safe, perhaps for the first time. There is then the opportunity for the patient to find himself as a thinking and feeling person within the analyst's mind. The analyst presents a picture to the patient that is related to the patient's experience at that moment but is also sufficiently different for the patient to learn the possibility of alternative perspectives. There is a constant and sometimes overwhelming pressure on the analyst to accept the patient's externalization, and this she must do, in a way, for a refusal to do so brings about the experience of the self as destroyed by the return of the alien other. Yet by becoming this other person, the analyst would have obliterated her capacity to think about the patient. The situation is made more difficult because unlike talking to more neurotic patients about the transference, the simple presentation of the dilemma to the patient has little effect.

The analyst's task is primarily to remain in touch with the patient's mental state, despite the patient's dramatic enactments, to address and challenge the patient's mental capacities by verbalizing internal states, differentiating feelings, breaking down unmanageable anxiety-provoking experiences into simpler, more manageable entities, helping the development of an "as-if" attitude where ideas can begin to be thought about as ideas rather than as reality, yet retaining their links to the internal world, and so on. We think of these interventions as "small interpretations," generally pertaining to aspects of the mental world that are neither unconscious nor overly complex. In neurotic patients, such feelings and thoughts would require no elaboration on the part of the analyst, yet without such background work the analysis of severely disturbed people is, we suggest, bound to fail, ending prematurely or turning into an impasse.

Psychoanalysis inevitably deals with individuals whose past experience has left them vulnerable to current stress and to the repetition of adverse early experiences. The treatment of people such as those we have focused on in this chapter involves an elaborative, mentalistic stance. This enhances the development of reflective self-function and may in the long run enhance the psychic resilience of individuals in a generic way, providing them with improved control over their system of representation of relationships. It can equip them with a kind of self-righting capacity where, through being able to make their representational models more flexible, they can be reviewed and changed. Such gradual and constant adjustments facilitate the development of an internal world where the behavior of others may be experienced as understandable, meaningful, predictable, and human. This reduces the need for the splitting of frightening and incoherent mental representations of mental states, and new experiences of other minds can more readily be integrated into the framework of past relationship representations.

The abused or traumatized child, evading or entangled in the mental world, never acquires adequate regulatory control over the representational world of internal working models. Unhelpful models of relationship patterns emerge frequently, and the internal world of the child and adult comes to be dominated by negative affect. Caught in a vicious cycle of paranoid anxiety and exaggerated defensive maneuvers, the person becomes inextricably entangled in an internal world dominated by dangerous, evil, mindless objects. He has abandoned the very process that could extract him from his predicament—the capacity to reflect on why people do things, what goes on in their minds.

Over a long period, frequent and diverse interpretations about the patient's perception of himself, the analyst, and their analytic relationship may enable him to attempt to create a mental representation both of himself and of his analyst, as thinking and feeling, together and independently. This can then form the core of a sense of himself with a capacity to represent ideas and meanings and create the basis for the bond that ultimately permits new possibilities of separation and intimacy.

References

Abel, T., and Kandel, E. (1998). Positive and negative regulatory mechanisms that mediate long-term memory storage. *Brain Research Reviews, 26*, 360–378.

Abell, F., Happe, F., and Frith, U. (2000). Do triangles play tricks? Attribution of mental states to animated shapes in normal and abnormal development. *Cognitive Development, 15*, 1–16.

Abrams, S. (1987). The psychoanalytic process: A schematic model. *International Journal of Psycho-Analysis, 68*, 441–452.

Abrams, S. (1990). The psychoanalytic process: The developmental and the integrative. *Psychoanalytic Quarterly, 59*, 650–677.

Adolphs, R., Tranel, D., Damasio, H., and Damasio, A. R. (1995). Fear and the human amygdala. *Journal of Neuroscience, 15* (9), 5879–5891.

Ainsworth, M. D. S. (1985). Attachments across the lifespan. *Bulletin of the New York Academy of Medicine, 61*, 792–812.

Ainsworth, M. D. S., Bell, S. M., and Stayton, D. J. (1971). Attachment and exploratory behavior of one year olds. In: H. R. Schaffer (Ed.), *The Origins of Human Social Relations*. New York: Academic Press.

Ainsworth, M. D. S., Blehar, M. C., Waters, E., and Wall, S. (1978). *Patterns of Attachment: A Psychological Study of the Strange Situation*. Hillsdale, NJ: Lawrence Erlbaum.

Aldridge, M. A., Stone, K. R., Sweeney, M. H., and Bower, T. G. R. (2000). Preverbal children with autism understand the intentions of others. *Developmental Science, 3* (3), 294–301.

Alessandri, S. M. (1992). Mother–child interactional correlates of maltreated and nonmaltreated children's play behavior. *Development and Psychopathology, 4,* 257–270.

Alexander, J. F., and Parsons, B. V. (1982). *Functional Family Therapy.* Monterey, CA: Brooks/Cole.

Alexander, M. P., Stuss, D. T., and Benson, D. F. (1979). Capgras syndrome: A reduplicative phenomenon. *Neurology, 29* (3), 334–339.

Allen, J. G. (1995). *Coping with Trauma: A Guide to Self-Understanding.* Washington, DC: American Psychiatric Press.

Allen, J. G. (2001). *Interpersonal Trauma and Serious Mental Disorder.* Chichester, U.K.: John Wiley.

Allen, J. G., Huntoon, J., Fultz, J., Stein, H. B., Fonagy, P., and Evans, R. B. (2000). *Adult Attachment Styles and Current Attachment Figures: Assessment of Women in Inpatient Treatment for Trauma-Related Psychiatric Disorders.* Topeka, KS: Menninger Clinic.

Amsterdam, B. (1972). Mirror self-image reactions before age two. *Developmental Psychobiology, 5,* 297–305.

Anderson, S., Bechara, A., Damasio, H., Tranel, D., and Damasio, A. (1999). Impairment of social and moral behavior related to early damage in human prefrontal cortex. *Natural Neuroscience, 2* (11), 1032–1037.

Appleton, M., and Reddy, V. (1996). Teaching three-year-olds to pass false-belief tests: A conversational approach. *Social Development, 5,* 275-291.

Arlow, J. A. (1984). The concept of psychic reality and related problems. *Journal of the American Psychoanalytic Association, 32,* 521–535.

Arsenio, W., and Lover, A. (1995). Children's conceptions of sociomoral affect: Happy victimizers, mixed emotions, and other expectancies. In: M. Killen and D. Hart (Eds.), *Morality in Everyday Life* (pp. 87–130). Cambridge, U.K.: Cambridge University Press.

Astington, J. (1996). What is theoretical about the child's theory of mind?: A Vygotskian view of its development. In: P. Carruthers and P. K. Smith (Eds.), *Theories of Theories of Mind* (pp. 184–199). Cambridge, U.K.: Cambridge University Press.

Astington, J., and Gopnik, A. (1991). Developing understanding of desire and intention. In: A. Whiten (Ed.), *Natural Theories of Mind: The Evolution, Development and Simulation of Second-Order Mental Representations* (pp. 39–50). Oxford: Basil Blackwell.

Astington, J., Harris, P., and Olson, D. (1988). *Developing Theories of Mind.* New York: Cambridge University Press.

Astington, J., and Jenkins, J. M. (1995). Theory of mind development and social understanding. *Cognition and Emotion, 9,* 151–165.

Auerbach, J. S. (1993). The origins of narcissism and narcissistic personality disorder: A theoretical and empirical reformulation. In: J. M. Masling and R. F. Bornstein (Eds.), *Psychoanalytic Perspectives on Psychopathology* (pp. 43–110). Washington, DC: American Psychological Association.

Auerbach, J. S., and Blatt, S. J. (1996). Self-representation in severe psychopathology: The role of reflexive self-awareness. *Psychoanalytic Psychology, 13*, 297–341.

Averill, J. (1994). In the eyes of the beholder. In: P. Ekman and R. Davidson (Eds.), *The Nature of Emotion*. Oxford: Oxford University Press.

Axelrod, R. (1984). *The Evolution of Cooperation*. New York: Basic Books.

Bahrick, L. R., and Watson, J. S. (1985). Detection of intermodal proprioceptive–visual contingency as a potential basis of self-perception in infancy. *Developmental Psychology, 21*, 963–973.

Baldwin, J. M. (1902). *Social and Ethical Interpretations in Mental Development* (3rd ed.). New York: Macmillan.

Ball, D., Hill, L., Freeman, B., Eley, T. C., Strelau, J., Riemann, R., Spinath, F. M., Angleitner, A., and Plomin, R. (1997). The serotonin transporter gene and peer-rated neuroticism. *Neuroreport, 8* (5), 1301–1304.

Bandura, A. (1977). *Social Learning Theory*. Englewood Cliffs, NJ: Prentice-Hall.

Barasalou, L. W. (1991). *Cognitive Psychology: An Overview for Cognitive Scientists*. Hillsdale, NJ: Lawrence Erlbaum.

Barnes, J. (Ed.) (1984). *The Complete Works of Aristotle: Rhetoric*. Princeton, NJ: Princeton University Press.

Baron-Cohen, S. (1991). Precursors to a theory of mind: Understanding attention in others. In: A. Whiten (Ed.), *Natural Theories of Mind: The Evolution, Development and Simulation of Second-Order Mental Representations*. Oxford: Basil Blackwell.

Baron-Cohen, S. (1994). How to build a baby that can read minds: Cognitive mechanisms in mind reading. *Current Psychology of Cognition, 13*, 513–552.

Baron-Cohen, S. (1995). *Mindblindness: An Essay on Autism and Theory of Mind*. Cambridge, MA: Bradford, MIT Press.

Baron-Cohen, S. (2000). Autism: Deficits in folk psychology exist alongside superiority in folk physics. In: S. Baron-Cohen, H. Tager-Flusberg, and D. J. Cohen (Eds.), *Understanding Other Minds: Perspectives from Autism and Developmental Cognitive Neuroscience* (2nd ed., pp. 59–82). Oxford: Oxford University Press.

Baron-Cohen, S., Leslie, A. M., and Frith, U. (1985). Does the autistic child have a "theory of mind"? *Cognition, 21*, 37–46.

Baron-Cohen, S., Ring, H., Moriarty, J., Schmitz, B., Costa, D., and Ell, P. (1994). Recognition of mental state terms. Clinical findings in children with autism and a functional neuroimaging study of normal adults. *British Journal of Psychiatry, 165* (5), 640–649.

Baron-Cohen, S., and Swettenham, J. (1996). The relationship between SAM and ToMM: Two hypotheses. In: P. Carruthers and P. K. Smith (Eds.), *Theories of Theories of Mind* (pp. 158–168). Cambridge, U.K.: Cambridge University Press.

Baron-Cohen, S., Tager-Flusberg, H., and Cohen, D. J. (1993). *Understanding Other Minds: Perspectives from Autism.* Oxford: Oxford University Press.

Baron-Cohen, S., Tager-Flusberg, H., and Cohen, D. J. (Eds.) (2000). *Understanding Other Minds: Perspectives from Autism and Developmental Cognitive Neuroscience.* Oxford: Oxford University Press.

Barresi, J., and Moore, C. (1996). Intentional relations and social understanding. *Behavioral and Brain Sciences, 19,* 107–154.

Barrett, K., and Campos, J. (1987). Perspectives on emotional development: II. A functionalist approach to emotions. In: J. D. Osofsky (Ed.), *Handbook of Infant Development* (2nd ed., pp. 555–578). New York: John Wiley.

Bartholomew, K., and Horowitz, L. M. (1991). Attachment styles among young adults: A test of a four-category model. *Journal of Personality and Social Psychology, 61,* 226–244.

Bartsch, K., and Wellman, H. M. (1989). Young children's attribution of action to beliefs and desires. *Child Development, 60,* 946–964.

Bartsch, K., and Wellman, H. M. (1995). *Children Talk about the Mind.* Oxford: Oxford University Press.

Bateman, A. (1998). Thick- and thin-skinned organisations and enactment in borderline and narcissistic disorders. *International Journal of Psycho-Analysis, 79,* 13–25.

Bateman, A., and Fonagy, P. (1999). The effectiveness of partial hospitalization in the treatment of borderline personality disorder—a randomized controlled trial. *American Journal of Psychiatry, 156,* 1563–1569.

Bateman, A., and Fonagy, P. (2001). Treatment of borderline personality disorder with psychoanalytically oriented partial hospitalization: An 18-month follow-up. *American Journal of Psychiatry, 158* (1), 36–42.

Bates, E. (1979). Intentions, conventions and symbols. In: E. Bates, L. Benigni, L. Camaioni, and V. Volterra (Eds.), *The Emergence of Symbols: Cognition and Communication in Infancy* (pp. 69–140). New York: Academic Press.

Bates, E., Benigni, L., Bretherton, I., Camaioni, L., and Volterra, V. (1979). Cognition and communication from 9–13 months: Correlational findings. In: E. Bates, L. Benigni, L. Camaioni, and V. Volterra (Eds.), *The Emergence of Symbols: Cognition and Communication in Infancy.* New York: Academic Press.

Bates, J., Maslin, C., and Frankel, K. (1985). Attachment security, mother–child interactions, and temperament as predictors of behavior problem ratings at age three years. *Growing Points in Attachment Theory and Research,* ed. by I. Bretherton and E. Waters. *Monographs of the Society for Research in Child Development, 50* (Serial 209, 1–2), 167–193.

Beck, A. T. (1967). *Depression: Clinical, Experimental, and Theoretical Aspects.* New York: Harper and Row.

Beck, A. T. (1976). *Cognitive Therapy and the Emotional Disorders.* New York: International Universities Press.

Beebe, B., Jaffe, J., Feldstein, S., Mays, K., and Alson, D. (1985). Interpersonal timing: The application of an adult dialogue model to mother–infant vocal and kinesic interactions. In: T. M. Field and N. A. Fox (Eds.), *Social Perception in Infants* (pp. 217–247). Norwood, NJ: Ablex.

Beebe, B., Jaffe, J., and Lachmann, F. M. (1992). A dyadic systems view of communication. In: N. Skolnick and S. Warshaw (Eds.), *Relational Perspectives in Psychoanalysis* (pp. 61–82). Hillsdale, NJ: Analytic Press.

Beebe, B., and Lachmann, F. M. (1988). The contribution of mother–infant mutual influence to the origins of self- and object-representations. *Psychoanalytic Psychology, 5* (4), 305–337.

Beebe, B., Lachmann, F., and Jaffe, J. (1997). Mother–infant interaction structures and presymbolic self- and object-representations. *Psychoanalytic Dialogues, 7,* 113–182.

Beeghly, M., and Cicchetti, D. (1994). Child maltreatment, attachment, and the self system: Emergence of an internal state lexicon in toddlers at high social risk. *Development and Psychopathology, 6,* 5–30.

Belsky, J. (1984). The determinants of parenting: A process model. *Child Development, 55,* 83–96.

Belsky, J., Garduque, L., and Hrncir, E. (1984). Assessing performance, competence and executive capacity in infant play: Relations to home environment and security of attachment. *Developmental Psychology, 20,* 406–417.

Belsky, J., and Isabella, R. (1988). Maternal, infant, and social–contextual determinants of attachment security. In: J. Belsky and T.

Nezworski (Eds.), *Clinical Implications of Attachment* (pp. 41–94). Hillsdale, NJ: Lawrence Erlbaum.

Belsky, J., Rosenberger, K., and Crnic, C. (1995). The origins of attachment security: "Classical" and contextual determinants. In: S. Goldberg, R. Muir, and J. Kerr (Eds.), *John Bowlby's Attachment Theory: Historical, Clinical and Social Significance* (pp. 153–184). Hillsdale, NJ: Analytic Press.

Benjamin, L. S. (1993). *Interpersonal Diagnosis and Treatment of Personality Disorder.* New York: Guilford Press.

Bennett, A. J., Lesch, K. P., Heils, A., Long, J., Lorenz, J., Shoaf, S. E., Champoux, M., Suomi, S. J., Linnoila, M., and Higley, J. D. (2002). Early experience and serotonin transporter gene variation interact to influence primate CNS function. *Molecular Psychiatry, 7,* 118–122.

Bergman, A. (1999). *Ours, Yours, Mine: Mutuality and the Emergence of the Separate Self.* New York: Jason Aronson.

Bertenthal, B., and Fisher, K. (1978). Development of self-recognition in the infant. *Developmental Psychology, 14,* 44–50.

Bettes, B. A. (1988). Maternal depression and motherese: Temporal and intonational features. *Child Development, 59,* 1089–1096.

Bidell, T. R., and Fischer, K. W. (1994). Developmental transitions in children's early on-line planning. In: M. M. Haith, J. B. Benson, R. J. Roberts, and B. F. Pennington (Eds.), *Development of Future-Oriented Processes.* Chicago, IL: University of Chicago Press.

Bifulco, A., Brown, G., and Harris, T. (1987). Childhood loss of parent, lack of adequate parental care and adult depression: A replication. *Journal of Affective Disorders, 12,* 115–128.

Bigelow, A. E. (2001). Discovering self through other: Infant's preference for social contingency. *Contingency Perception and Attachment in Infancy,* ed. by J. Allen, P. Fonagy, and G. Gergely. *Bulletin of the Menninger Clinic, Special Issue, 65* (pp. 335–346).

Bigelow, A. E., and DeCoste, C. (in press). Infants' sensitivity to contingency in social interactions with familiar and unfamiliar partners. *Infancy.*

Bion, W. R. (1959). Attacks on linking. *International Journal of Psycho-Analysis, 40,* 308–315.

Bion, W. R. (1962a). *Learning from Experience.* London: Heinemann.

Bion, W. R. (1962b). A theory of thinking. *International Journal of Psycho-Analysis, 43,* 306–310. Also in: *Second Thoughts.* London: Heinemann, 1967.

Bion, W. R. (1963). *Elements of Psycho-Analysis.* London: Heinemann.

Bion, W. R. (1970). *Attention and Interpretation.* London: Tavistock.

Birch, H., and Lefford, A. (1967). Visual differentiation, intersensory integration, and voluntary control. *Monographs of the Society for Research in Child Development, 32.*

Blair, R. (1995). A cognitive developmental approach to morality: Investigating the psychopath. *Cognition, 57,* 1–29.

Blair, R., Jones, L., Clark, F., and Smith, M. (1997). The psychopathic individual: A lack of responsiveness to distress cues? *Psychophysiology, 34* (2), 192–198.

Blair, R., Morris, J., Frith, C., Perrett, D., and Dolan, R. (1999). Dissociable neural responses to facial expressions of sadness and anger. *Brain, 122* (5), 883–893.

Blatt, S. J., and Behrends, R. S. (1987). Internalization, separation–individuation, and the nature of therapeutic action. *International Journal of Psycho-Analysis, 68,* 279–297.

Blatt, S. J., and Blass, R. B. (1990). Attachment and separateness: A dialectical model of the products and processes of development throughout the life cycle. *Psychoanalytic Study of the Child, 45,* 107–127.

Bleiberg, E. (1984). Narcissistic disorders in children. *Bulletin of the Menninger Clinic, 48,* 501–517.

Bleiberg, E. (1994). Borderline disorders in children and adolescents: The concept, the diagnosis, and the controversies. *Bulletin of the Menninger Clinic, 58,* 169–196.

Bleiberg, E., Fonagy, P., and Target, M. (1997). Child psychoanalysis: Critical overview and a proposed reconsideration. *Psychiatric Clinics of North America, 6,* 1–38.

Blos, P. (1979). *The Adolescent Passage.* New York: International Universities Press.

Blum, K., Noble, E. P., Sheridan, P. J., Montgomery, A., Ritchie, T., Jagadeeswaran, P., Nogami, H., Briggs, A. H., and Cohn, J. B. (1990). Allelic association of human dopamine D2 receptor gene in alcoholism. *Journal of the American Medical Association, 263,* 2055–2060.

Bogdan, R. J. (1997). *Interpreting Minds.* Cambridge, MA: MIT Press.

Bogdan, R. J. (2001). *Minding Minds.* Cambridge, MA: MIT Press.

Bohman, M. (1996). Predisposition to criminality. Swedish adoption studies in retrospect. In: M. Rutter (Ed.), *Genetics of Criminal and Antisocial Behavior.* Chichester, U.K.: John Wiley.

Bolton, D., and Hill, J. (1996). *Mind, Meaning and Mental Disorder.* Oxford: Oxford University Press.

Botterill, G. (1996). Folk psychology and theoretical status. In: P. Carruthers and P. K. Smith (Eds.), *Theories of Theories of Mind* (pp. 105–118). Cambridge, U.K.: Cambridge University Press.

Bower, T. G. R. (1974). *Development in Infancy.* San Francisco, CA: W.H. Freeman, 1982.

Bowlby, J. (1958). The nature of the child's tie to his mother. *International Journal of Psycho-Analysis, 39*, 350–373.

Bowlby, J. (1969). *Attachment and Loss, Vol. 1. Attachment.* London: Hogarth Press and the Institute of Psycho-Analysis.

Bowlby, J. (1973). *Attachment and Loss, Vol. 2. Separation: Anxiety and Anger.* London: Hogarth Press and Institute of Psycho-Analysis.

Bowlby, J. (1980). *Attachment and Loss, Vol. 3. Loss: Sadness and Depression.* London: Hogarth Press and Institute of Psycho-Analysis.

Bowlby, J. (1988). *A Secure Base: Clinical Applications of Attachment Theory.* London: Routledge.

Bowlby, J. (1991). *Charles Darwin: A New Life.* New York: Norton.

Bracken, B. A. (Ed.) (1996). *Handbook of Self-Concept: Developmental, Social and Clinical Considerations.* New York: John Wiley.

Braten, S. (1988). Dialogic mind: The infant and the adult in proto-conversation. In: M. Carvallo (Ed.), *Nature, Cognition and System, Vol. 1* (pp. 187–205). Dordrecht: Kluwer Academic.

Braten, S. (1992). The virtual other in infants' minds and social feelings. In: H. Wold (Ed.), *The Dialogical Alternative* (pp. 77–97). Oslo: Scandinavian University Press.

Braten, S. (1998). *Intersubjective Communication and Emotion in Early Ontogeny.* Cambridge, U.K.: Cambridge University Press.

Brazelton, T., Kowslowski, B., and Main, M. (1974). The origins of reciprocity: The early mother–infant interaction. In: M. Lewis and L. Rosenblum (Eds.), *The Effect of the Infant on Its Caregivers* (pp. 49–76). New York: John Wiley.

Brazelton, T. B., and Tronick, E. (1980). Preverbal communication between mothers and infants. In: D. R. Olson (Ed.), *The Social Foundations of Language and Thought* (pp. 299–315). New York: Norton.

Brazzelli, M., Colombo, N., Della Sala, S., and Spinnler, H. (1994). Spared and impaired cognitive abilities after bilateral frontal damage. *Cortex, 30* (1), 27–51.

Brenner, C. (1955). *An Elementary Textbook of Psychoanalysis.* New York: International Universities Press.

Brentano, F. (1874). *Psychology from an Empirical Standpoint.* London: Routledge, 1973.

Bretherton, I. (1991a). Intentional communication and the development of an understanding of mind. In: D. Frye and C. Moore (Eds.), *Children's Theories of Mind: Mental States and Social Understanding* (pp. 271–289). Hillsdale, NJ: Lawrence Erlbaum.

Bretherton, I. (1991b). Pouring new wine into old bottles: The social self as internal working model. In: M. R. Gunnar and L. A. Sroufe (Eds.), *Self Processes and Development: Minnesota Symposia on Child Psychology, Vol. 23* (pp. 1–41). Hillsdale, NJ: Lawrence Erlbaum.

Bretherton, I., and Bates, E. (1979). The emergence of intentional communication. In: I. C. Uzgiris (Ed.), *Social Interaction and Communication during Infancy*. San Francisco, CA: Jossey-Bass.

Bretherton, I., Bates, E., Benigni, L., Camaioni, L., and Volterra, V. (1979). Relationships between cognition, communication, and quality of attachment. In: E. Bates, L. Benigni, I. Bretherton, L. Camaioni, and V. Volterra (Eds.), *The Emergence of Symbols: Cognition and Communication in Infancy* (pp. 223–269). New York: Academic Press.

Bretherton, I., and Munholland, K. A. (1999). Internal working models in attachment relationships: A construct revisited. In: J. Cassidy and P. R. Shaver (Eds.), *Handbook of Attachment: Theory, Research and Clinical Applications* (pp. 89–114). New York: Guilford Press.

Bretherton, I., Ridgeway, D., and Cassidy, J. (1990). Assessing internal working models of the attachment relationship: An attachment story completion task. In: M. T. Greenberg, D. Cicchetti, and E. M. Cummings (Eds.), *Attachment in the Preschool Years: Theory, Research and Intervention* (pp. 273–308). Chicago, IL: University of Chicago Press.

Brierley, M. (1937). Affects in theory and practice. In: *Trends in Psycho-Analysis*. London: Hogarth Press, 1951.

Britton, R. (1989). The missing link: Parental sexuality in the Oedipus complex. In: R. Britton, M. Feldman, E. O'Shaughnessy, and J. Steiner (Eds.), *The Oedipus Complex Today: Clinical Implications* (pp. 83–102). London: Karnac.

Britton, R. (1994). The blindness of the seeing eye: Inverse symmetry as a defence against reality. *Psychoanalytic Inquiry, 14*, 365–378.

Britton, R. (1995). Psychic reality and unconscious belief. *International Journal of Psycho-Analysis, 76*, 19–23.

Britton, R. (1998). *Belief and Imagination*. London: Routledge.

Bronfenbrenner, U. (1979). *The Ecology of Human Development: Experiments by Nature and Design*. Cambridge, MA: Harvard University Press.

Broussard, E. R. (1995). Infant attachment in a sample of adolescent mothers. *Child Psychiatry and Human Development, 25*, 211–219.

Brown, J. R., Donelan-McCall, N., and Dunn, J. (1996). Why talk about mental states? The significance of children's conversations with friends, siblings, and mothers. *Child Development, 67*, 836–849.

Brownell, C. A., and Kopp, C. B. (1991). Common threads, diverse solutions: Concluding commentary. *Developmental Review, 11*, 288–303.

Bruch, H. (1982). Anorexia nervosa: Therapy and theory. *American Journal of Psychiatry, 139* (12), 1531–1538.

Bruner, J. (1983). *Child's Talk: Learning to Use Language.* Oxford: Oxford University Press.

Bruner, J., Olver, P., and Greenfield, P. M. (1966). *Studies on Cognitive Growth.* New York: John Wiley.

Busch, F. (1995). Do actions speak louder than words? A query into an enigma in analytic theory and technique. *Journal of the American Psychoanalytic Association, 43*, 61–82.

Butterworth, G. (1995). An ecological perspective on the origins of the self. In: J. Bermudez, A. Marcel, and N. Eilan (Eds.), *The Body and the Self.* Cambridge, MA: MIT Press.

Butterworth, G., and Cicchetti, D. (1978). Visual calibration of posture in normal and motor retarded Down's syndrome infants. *Perception, 6*, 255–262.

Butterworth, G., Harris, P., Leslie, A., and Wellman, H. (1991). *Perspectives on the Child's Theory of Mind.* Oxford: Oxford University Press/ British Psychological Society.

Butterworth, G., and Hicks, L. (1977). Visual proprioception and postural stability in infancy: A developmental study. *Perception, 6*, 255–262.

Cadoret, R. J., Leve, L. D., and Devor, E. (1997). Genetics of aggressive and violent behavior. *Psychological Clinics of North America, 20*, 301–322.

Call, J., and Tomasello, M. (1996). The effect of humans on the cognitive development of apes. In: A. E. Russon, K. A. Bard, and S. T. Parker (Eds.), *Reaching into Thought* (pp. 371–403). Cambridge, U.K.: Cambridge University Press.

Call, J., and Tomasello, M. (1999). A nonverbal theory of mind test: The performance of children and apes. *Child Development, 70*, 381–395.

Campbell, J. (1997). The structure of time in autobiographical memory. *European Journal of Philosophy, 5*, 105–118.

Campos, J., and Stenberg, C. R. (1981). Perception, appraisal and emotion: The onset of social referencing. In: M. E. Lamb and L. R. Sherrod (Eds.), *Infant Social Cognition* (pp. 273–314). Hillsdale, NJ: Lawrence Erlbaum.

Camras, L. A. (1992). Expressive development and basic emotions. *Cognition and Emotion, 6*, 269–283.

Camras, L. A. (2000). Surprise! Facial expressions can be coordinative motor structures. In: M. D. Lewis and I. Granic (Eds.), *Emotion,*

Development, and Self-Organization: Dynamic Systems Approaches to Emotional Development (pp. 100–124). Cambridge, U.K.: Cambridge University Press.

Cardasis, W., Hochman, J. A., and Silk, K. R. (1997). Transitional objects and borderline personality disorder. *American Journal of Psychiatry, 154,* 250–255.

Carlson, E., and Sroufe, L. A. (1995). Contribution of attachment theory to developmental psychopathology. In: D. Cicchetti and D. J. Cohen (Eds.), *Developmental Psychopathology, Vol. 1. Theory and Methods* (pp. 581–617). New York: John Wiley.

Carlson, V., Cicchetti, D., Barnett, D., and Braunwald, K. (1989). Disorganized/disoriented attachment relationships in maltreated infants. *Developmental Psychology, 25,* 525–531.

Caron, A. J., Caron, R. F., and Myers, R. S. (1985). Do infants see facial expressions in static faces? *Child Development, 56,* 1552–1560.

Caron, R. F., Caron, A. J., and MacLean, D. J. (1988). Infant discrimination of naturalistic emotional expressions: The role of face and voice. *Child Development, 59,* 604–616.

Carpenter, M., Nagell, K., and Tomasello, M. (1998). Social cognition, joint attention, and communicative competence from 9 to 15 months of age. *Monographs of the Society for Research in Child Development, 63.*

Carruthers, P. (1996). *Language, Thought and Consciousness. An Essay in Philosophical Psychology.* Cambridge, U.K.: Cambridge University Press.

Carruthers, P., and Smith, P. K. (Eds.) (1996). *Theories of Theories of Mind.* Cambridge, U.K.: Cambridge University Press.

Cassam, Q. (Ed.) (1994). *Self-Knowledge.* Oxford: Oxford University Press.

Cassidy, J. (1988). Child–mother attachment and the self in six-year-olds. *Child Development, 59,* 121–134.

Cassidy, J. (1994). Emotion regulation: Influences of attachment relationships. *The Development of Attachment Regulation,* ed. by N. A. Fox. *Monograph of the Society for Research in Child Development* (Serial 240), 228–249.

Cassidy, J., Kirsh, S. J., Scolton, K. L., and Parke, R. D. (1996). Attachment and representations of peer relationships. *Developmental Psychology, 32,* 892–904.

Cassidy, J., and Marvin, R. S. (1992). Attachment organization in preschool children: Coding guidelines. Seattle, WA: MacArthur Working Group on Attachment, unpublished coding manual.

Cassidy, J., Marvin, R. S., and The MacArthur Working Group on

Attachment. (1989). Attachment organization in three- and four-year-olds: Coding guidelines. University of Illinois, Urbana, IL, unpublished scoring manual.

Castellanos, F. X., Lau, E., Tayebi, N., Lee, P., Long, R. E., Giedd, J. N., Sharp, W., Marsh, W. L., Walter, J. M., Hamburger, S. D., Ginns, E. I., Rappoport, J. R., and Sidransky, E. (1998). Lack of an association between a dopamine-4 receptor polymorphism and attention deficit hyperactivity disorder: Genetic and brain morphometric analyses. *Molecular Psychiatry, 3*, 431–434.

Cavell, M. (1988). Interpretation, psychoanalysis and the philosophy of mind. *Journal of the American Psychoanalytic Association, 36*, 859–879.

Cavell, M. (1991). The subject of mind. *International Journal of Psycho-Analysis, 72*, 141–154.

Cavell, M. (1994). *The Psychoanalytic Mind*. Cambridge, MA: Harvard University Press.

Cavell, M. (2000). Reasons, causes, and the domain of the first-person. In: J. Sandler, R. Michels, and P. Fonagy (Eds.), *Changing Ideas in a Changing World: The Revolution in Psychoanalysis. Essays in Honour of Arnold Cooper*. New York: Karnac.

Channon, S., and Crawford, S. (1999). Problem-solving in real-life-type situations: The effects of anterior and posterior lesions on performance. *Neuropsychologia, 37* (7), 757–770.

Channon, S., and Crawford, S. (2000). The effects of anterior lesions on performance on a story comprehension test: Left anterior impairment on a theory of mind-type task. *Neuropsychologia, 38* (7), 1006–1017.

Chess, L. K., and Thomas, C. G. (1979). *Childhood Pathology and Later Adjustment*. New York: John Wiley.

Chew, S. J., Vicario, D. S. T., and Nottebohm, F. (1996). Quantal duration of auditory memories. *Science, 274*, 1909–1914.

Chisolm, K. (1998). A three year follow-up of attachment and indiscriminate friendliness in children adopted from Russian orphanages. *Child Development, 69*, 1092–1106.

Churchland, P. S. (1986). *Neurophilosophy*. Cambridge, MA: MIT Press.

Cicchetti, D. (1987). Developmental psychopathology in infancy: Illustration from the study of maltreated youngsters. *Journal of Consulting and Clinical Psychology, 55*, 837–845.

Cicchetti, D., and Cohen, D. J. (1995). Perspectives on developmental psychopathology. In: D. Cicchetti and D. J. Cohen (Eds.), *Developmental Psychopathology, Vol. 1. Theory and Methods* (pp. 3–23). New York: John Wiley.

Cicchetti, D., and Rogosch, F. A. (1997). The role of self-organization in the promotion of resilience in maltreated children. *Development and Psychopathology, 9,* 797–815.

Cicchetti, D., and Toth, S. L. (Eds.) (1994). *Rochester Symposium on Developmental Psychopathology, Vol. 5. Disorders and Dysfunctions of the Self.* Rochester, NY: University of Rochester Press.

Clarkin, J. F., Kernberg, O. F., and Yeomans, F. (1999). *Transference-Focused Psychotherapy for Borderline Personality Disorder Patients.* New York: Guilford Press.

Clarkin, J. F., and Lenzenweger, M. F. (1996). *Major Theories of Personality Disorder.* New York: Guilford Press.

Clements, W. A., and Perner, J. (1994). Implicit understanding of belief. *Cognitive Development, 9,* 377–395.

Clyman, R. B. (1991). The procedural organization of emotions: A contribution from cognitive science to the psychoanalytic theory of therapeutic action. *Journal of the American Psychoanalytic Association, 39* (Supplement), 349–382.

Cohen, D. J., Towbin, K. E., Mayes, L., and Volkmar, F. (1994). Developmental psychopathology of multiplex developmental disorder. In: S. L. Friedman and H. C. Haywood (Eds.), *Developmental Follow-Up: Concepts, Domains and Methods* (pp. 155–182). New York: Academic Press.

Cohn, J. F., Matias, R., Tronick, E. Z., Connell, D., and Lyons-Ruth, K. (1986). Face-to-face interactions of depressed mothers and their infants. In: E. Z. Tronick and T. Field (Eds.), *Maternal Depression and Infant Disturbance* (pp. 31–45). San Francisco, CA: Jossey-Bass.

Cohn, J. F., and Tronick, E. Z. (1988). Mother–infant interaction: Influence is bidirectional and unrelated to periodic cycles in either partner's behavior. *Developmental Psychology, 24,* 386–392.

Collins, N., and Read, S. J. (1990). Adult attachment, working models and relationship quality in dating couples. *Journal of Personality and Social Psychology, 58,* 633–644.

Collins, N., and Read, S. J. (1994). Representations of attachment: The structure and function of working models. In: K. Bartholomew and D. Perlman (Eds.), *Advances in Personal Relationships, Vol. 5. Attachment Process in Adulthood* (pp. 53–90). London: Jessica Kingsley.

Colombo, J., Mitchell, D. W., Coldren, J. T., and Atwater, J. D. (1990). Discrimination learning during the first year: Stimulus and positional cues. *Journal of Experimental Psychology: Learning, Memory, and Cognition, 16,* 98–109.

Comings, D. E. (1997). Why different rules are required for polygenic inheritance: Lessons from studies of the DRD2 gene. *Alcohol, 16*, 61–70.

Comings, D. E., Comings, B. G., Muhleman, D., Dietz, G., Shah-bahrami, B., Tast, D., Knell, E., Kocsis, P., Baumgarten, R., and Kovacs, B. W. (1991). The dopamine D2 receptor locus as a modifying gene in neuropsychiatric disorders. *Journal of the American Medical Association, 266*, 1793–1800.

Comings, D. E., Gonzalez, N., Wu, S., Gade, R., Muhleman, D., Saucier, G., Johnson, P., Verde, R., Rosenthal, R. J., Lesieur, H. R., Rugle, L. J., Miller, W. B., and MacMurray, J. P. (1999). Studies of the 48 bp repeat polymorphism of the DRD4 gene in impulsive, compulsive, addictive behaviors: Tourette syndrome, ADHD, pathological gambling, and substance abuse. *American Journal of Medical Genetics, 88*, 358–368.

Comings, D. E., Muhleman, D., and Gysin, R. (1996). Dopamine D2 receptor (DRD2) gene and susceptibility to posttraumatic stress disorder: A study and replication. *Biological Psychiatry, 40*, 1793–1800.

Conger, R. D., Ge, X., Elder, G. H., Lorenz, F. O., and Simons, R. (1994). Economic stress, coercive family process, and developmental problems of adolescents. *Child Development, 65*, 541–561.

Cooley, C. H. (1912). *Human Nature and the Social Order*. Revised edition New York: Shocken Books, 1964.

Cooper, R. P., and Aslin, R. N. (1990). Preference for infant-directed speech in the first month after birth. *Child Development, 61*, 1587–1595.

Corcoran, R. (2000). In: S. Baron-Cohen, D. Cohen, and H. Tager-Flusberg (Eds.), *Understanding Other Minds: Perspectives from Developmental Cognitive Neuroscience* (pp. 358–391). Oxford: Oxford University Press.

Corkum, V., and Moore, C. (1995). Development of joint visual attention in infants. In: C. Moore and P. Dunham (Eds.), *Joint Attention: Its Origins and Role in Development* (pp. 61–83). New York: Lawrence Erlbaum.

Craik, F. I. M., Moroz, T. M., Moscovitch, M., Stuss, D. T., Winocur, G., and Tulving, E. (1999). In search of the self: A positron emission tomography study. *Psychological Science, 10*, 26–34.

Crittenden, P. M. (1988). Relationships at risk. In: J. Belsky and T. Nezworski (Eds.), *Clinical Implications of Attachment* (pp. 136–174). Hillsdale, NJ: Lawrence Erlbaum.

Crittenden, P. M. (1990). Internal representational models of attachment relationships. *Infant Mental Health Journal, 11*, 259–277.

Crittenden, P. M. (1992). Quality of attachment in the preschool years. *Development and Psychopathology, 4*, 209–241.

Crittenden, P. M. (1994). Peering into the black box: An exploratory treatise on the development of self in young children. In: D. Cicchetti and S. L. Toth (Eds.), *Rochester Symposium on Developmental Psychopathology, Vol. 5. Disorders and Dysfunctions of the Self* (pp. 79–148). Rochester, NY: University of Rochester Press.

Crittenden, P. M., and DiLalla, D. (1988). Compulsive compliance: The development of an inhibitory coping strategy in infancy. *Journal of Abnormal Child Psychology, 16*, 585–599.

Csibra, G., Bíró, S., Koós, O., and Gergely, G. (2002). One-year-old infants use teleological representations of actions productively. Submitted.

Csibra, G., and Gergely, G. (1998). The teleological origins of mentalistic action explanations: A developmental hypothesis. *Developmental Science, 1* (2), 255–259.

Csibra, G., Gergely, G., Brockbank, M., Bíró, S., and Koós, O. (1999). Twelve-month-olds can infer a goal for an incomplete action. Paper presented at the Eleventh Biennial Conference on Infant Studies (ICIS), Atlanta, Georgia.

Currie, G. (1995). Imagination and simulation: Aesthetics meets cognitive science. In: A. Stone and M. Davies (Eds.), *Mental Simulation: Evaluations and Applications* (pp. 99–127). Oxford: Basil Blackwell.

Damasio, A. (1994a). *Descartes' Error: Emotion, Reason and the Human Brain.* London: Macmillan.

Damasio, A. R. (1994b). Descartes' error and the future of human life. *Scientific American, 271* (4), 144.

Damasio, A. (1999). *The Feeling of What Happens: Body and Emotion in the Making of Consciousness.* New York: Harcourt Brace.

Darwin, C. (1872). *The Expression of Emotions in Man and Animals.* New York: Philosophical Library.

Davidson, D. (1980). *Actions, Reasons, and Causes. Essays on Action and Events.* Oxford: Clarendon Press.

Davidson, R. (1992). Prolegomenon to the structure of emotion: Gleanings from neuropsychology. *Cognition and Emotion, 6*, 245–268.

Davis, M., and Stone, T. (Eds.) (1995). *Folk Psychology: The Theory of Mind Debate.* Oxford: Blackwell.

Dawson, G., and McKissick, F. C. (1984). Self-recognition in autistic children. *Journal of Autism and Developmental Disorders, 9*, 247–260.

Deary, I. J., Battersby, S., Whiteman, M. C., Connor, J. M., Fowkes, F. G., and Harmar, A. (1999). Neuroticism and polymorphisms in the serotonin transporter gene. *Psychological Medicine, 29* (3), 735–739.

Deater-Deckard, K., Fulker, D. W., and Plomin, R. (1999). A genetic study of the family environment in the transition to early adolescence. *Journal of Child Psychology and Psychiatry and Allied Disciplines, 40,* 769–795.

DeCasper, A. J., and Fifer, W. P. (1980). Of human bonding: Newborns prefer their mothers' voices. *Science, 208,* 1174–1176.

Demos, V. (1986). Crying in early infancy: An illustration of the motivational function of affect. In: T. B. Brazelton and M. W. Yogman (Eds.), *Affective Development in Infancy* (pp. 39–73). Norwood, NJ: Ablex.

Denham, S. A., Zoller, D., and Couchoud, E. A. (1994). Socialization of preschoolers' emotion understanding. *Developmental Psychology, 30,* 928–936.

Dennett, D. (1978). *Brainstorms: Philosophical Essays on Mind and Psychology.* Montgomery, VT: Bradford.

Dennett, D. (1983). Styles of mental representation. *Proceedings of the Aristotelian Society* (pp. 213–226). London: Aristotelian Society.

Dennett, D. (1987). *The Intentional Stance.* Cambridge, MA: MIT Press.

Dennett, D. (1988). Precis of "The intentional stance" with peer commentary. *The Behavioral and Brain Sciences, 11,* 495–546.

Dennett, D. (1991). *Consciousness Explained.* Boston: Little Brown.

Dennett, D., and Haugeland, J. C. (1987). Intentionality. In: R. L. Gregory (Ed.), *The Oxford Companion to the Mind.* Oxford: Oxford University Press.

DeSousa, R. (1987). *The Rationality of Emotion.* Cambridge, U.K.: MIT Press.

De Wolff, M. S., and van IJzendoorn, M. H. (1997). Sensitivity and attachment: A meta-analysis on parental antecedents of infant attachment. *Child Development, 68,* 571–591.

Dias, M. G., and Harris, P. L. (1990). The influence of the imagination on reasoning by young children. *British Journal of Developmental Psychology, 8,* 305–318.

Dicara, L. V. (1970). Learning in the autonomic nervous system. *Scientific American, 222,* 30–39.

Dienes, Z., and Perner, J. (1999). A theory of implicit and explicit knowledge. *Behavioral and Brain Sciences, 22* (5), 735–808.

Dobzhansky, T. (1972). Genetics and the diversity of behavior. *American Psychology, 27,* 523–530.

Dodge, K. (1990). Developmental psychopathology in children of depressed mothers. *Developmental Psychology, 26,* 3–6.

Drucker, J. (1975). Toddler play: Some comments on its functions in the developmental process. *Psychoanalysis and Contemporary Science, 4*, 479–527.

Dunkeld, J., and Bower, T. G. (1980). Infant response to impending optical collision. *Perception, 9*, 549–554.

Dunn, J. (1994). Changing minds and changing relationships. In: C. Lewis and P. Mitchell (Eds.), *Children's Early Understanding of Mind: Origins and Development* (pp. 297–310). Hove, Sussex, U.K.: Lawrence Erlbaum.

Dunn, J. (1996). The Emanuel Miller Memorial Lecture 1995. Children's relationships: Bridging the divide between cognitive and social development. *Journal of Child Psychology and Psychiatry and Allied Disciplines, 37*, 507–518.

Dunn, J., and Brown, J. (1993). Early conversations about causality: Content, pragmatics, and developmental change. *British Journal of Developmental Psychology, 11*, 107–123.

Dunn, J., Brown, J., and Beardsall, L. (1991). Family talk about feeling states and children's later understanding of others' emotions. *Developmental Psychology, 27*, 448–455.

Dunn, J., Brown, J., Slomkowski, C., Telsa, C., and Youngblade, L. (1991). Young children's understanding of other people's feelings and beliefs: Individual differences and their antecedents. *Child Development, 62*, 1352–1366.

Dunn, J., and McGuire, S. (1994). Young children's non-shared experiences: A summary of studies in Cambridge and Colorado. In: E. M. Hetherington, D. Reiss, and R. Plomin (Eds.), *Separate Social Worlds of Siblings*. Hillsdale, NJ: Lawrence Erlbaum.

Dutton, D. G., Saunders, K., Starzomski, A., and Bartholomew, K. (1994). Intimacy-anger and insecure attachments as precursors of abuse in intimate relationships. *Journal of Applied Social Psychology, 24*, 1367–1386.

Eaves, L. J., Silberg, J. L., Meyer, J. M., Maes, H. H., Simonoff, E., Pickles, A., Rutter, M., Neale, M. C., Reynolds, C. A., Erikson, M. T., Heath, A. C., Loeber, R., Truett, K. R., and Hewitt, J. K. (1997). Genetics and developmental psychopathology: 2. The main effects of genes and environment on behavioral problems in the Virginia Twin Study of Adolescent Behavioral Development. *Journal of Child Psychology and Psychiatry and Allied Disciplines, 38* (8), 965–980.

Ebstein, R. P., Gritsenko, I., Nemanov, L., Frisch, A., Osher, Y., and Belmaker, R. H. (1997). No association between the serotonin transporter gene regulatory region polymorphism and the Tridimensional Personality Questionnaire (TPQ) temperament of harm avoidance. *Molecular Psychiatry, 2* (3), 224–226.

Edelman, G. (1992). *Bright Air, Brilliant Fire.* New York: Basic Books.

Egeland, B., and Farber, E. A. (1984). Infant–mother attachment: Factors related to its development and change over time. *Child Development, 55,* 753–771.

Eisenberg, N., and Fabes, R. (Eds.) (1992). *Emotion and Its Regulation in Early Development.* San Francisco, CA: Jossey-Bass.

Ekman, P. (1992a). An argument for basic emotions. *Cognition and Emotion, 6* (3–4), 169–200.

Ekman, P. (1992b). Facial expressions of emotion: New findings, new questions. *Psychological Science, 3* (1), 34–38.

Ekman, P., and Davidson, R. (Eds.) (1994). *The Nature of Emotion: Fundamental Questions.* Oxford: Oxford University Press.

Ekman, P., Friesen, W. V., and Ellsworth, P. (1972). *Emotion in the Human Face.* New York: Pergamon Press.

Ekman, P., Levenson, R., and Friesen, W. V. (1983). Autonomic nervous system activity distinguishes between emotions. *Science, 221,* 1208–1210.

Ekman, P., and Oster, H. (1979). Facial expressions of emotions. *Annual Review of Psychology, 30,* 527–554.

Elicker, J., Englund, M., and Sroufe, L. A. (1992). Predicting peer competence and peer relationships in childhood from early parent–child relationships. In: R. Parke and G. Ladd (Eds.), *Family–Peer Relationships: Modes of Linkage* (pp. 77–106). Hillsdale, NJ: Lawrence Erlbaum.

Elman, J. L., Bates, A. E., Johnson, M. H., Karmiloff-Smith, A., Parisi, D., and Plunkett, K. (1996). *Rethinking Innateness: A Connectionist Perspective on Development.* Cambridge, MA: MIT Press.

Emde, R. (1980a). Toward a psychoanalytic theory of affect: Part 1. The organizational model and its propositions. In: S. I. Greenspan and G. H. Pollock (Eds.), *The Course of Life: Infancy and Early Childhood* (pp. 63–83). Washington, DC: DHSS.

Emde, R. (1980b). Toward a psychoanalytic theory of affect: Part 2. Emerging models of emotional development in infancy. In: S. I. Greenspan and G. H. Pollock (Eds.), *The Course of Life: Infancy and Early Childhood* (pp. 85–112). Washington, DC: DHSS.

Emde, R. (1981). Changing models of infancy and the nature of early development: Remodeling the foundation. *Journal of the American Psychoanalytic Association, 29,* 179–219.

Emde, R. (1983). Pre-representational self and its affective core. *Psychoanalytic Study of the Child, 38,* 165–192.

Emde, R. (1988). Development terminable and interminable: 1. Innate and motivational factors from infancy. *International Journal of Psycho-Analysis, 69,* 23–42.

Emde, R. (1992). Individual meaning and increasing complexity: Contributions of Sigmund Freud and Reni Spitz to Developmental Psychology. *Developmental Psychology, 28,* 347–359.

Emde, R., and Fonagy, P. (1997). An emerging culture for psychoanalytic research? Editorial. *International Journal of Psycho-Analysis, 78,* 643–651.

Emde, R., Kubicek, L., and Oppenheim, D. (1997). Imaginative reality observed during early language development. *International Journal of Psycho-Analysis, 78* (1), 115–133.

Erikson, E. H. (1968). *Identity, Youth and Crisis.* New York: Norton.

Evans, J. D., and Wheeler, D. E. (2000). Expression profiles during honeybee cast determination. *Genome Biology, 2,* e1–e6.

Fairbairn, W. R. D. (1952). *An Object-Relations Theory of the Personality.* New York: Basic Books, 1954.

Fajardo, B. (1993). Conditions for the relevance of infant research to clinical psychoanalysis. *International Journal of Psycho-Analysis, 74,* 975–992.

Fantz, R. (1963). Pattern vision in newborn infants. *Science, 140,* 296–297.

Faraone, S. V., Biederman, J., Weiffenbach, B., Keith, T., Chu, M. P., Weaver, A., Spencer, T. J., Wilens, T. E., Frazier, J., Cleves, M., and Sakai, J. (1999). Dopamine D4 gene 7-repeat allele and attention deficit hyperactivity disorder. *American Journal of Psychiatry, 156,* 768–770.

Ferguson, C. A. (1964). Baby talk in six languages. *American Anthropologist, 66,* 103–114.

Fernald, A. (1991). Prosody in speech to children: Prelinguistic and linguistic functions. In: R. Vasta (Ed.), *Annals of Child Development, Vol. 8* (pp. 43–80). London: Jessica Kingsley.

Fernald, A. (1992). Human maternal vocalizations to infants as biologically relevant signals: An evolutionary perspective. In: L. C. J. H. Barkow and J. Tooby (Eds.), *The Adapted Mind: Evolutionary Psychology and the Generation of Culture* (pp. 391–428). Oxford: Oxford University Press.

Field, T. (1979). Differential behavioral and cardiac responses of 3-month-old infants to a mirror and peer. *Infant Behavior and Development, 2,* 179–184.

Field, T. (1994). The effects of mother's physical and emotional unavailability on emotion regulation. *Monographs of the Society for Research in Child Development, 59* (2–3).

Field, T., Guy, L., and Umbel, V. (1985). Infants' responses to mothers' imitative behaviors. *Infant Mental Health Journal, 6,* 40–44.

Field, T., Healy, B., Goldstein, S., Perry, S., Bendell, D., Schanberg, S.,

Zimmerman, E., and Kuhn, C. (1988). Infants of depressed mothers show "depressed" behavior even with nondepressed adults. *Child Development, 59,* 1569–1579.

Field, T., Woodson, R., Cohen, D., Garcia, R., and Greenberg, R. (1983). Discrimination and imitation of facial expressions by term and preterm neonates. *Infant Behavior and Development, 6,* 485–490.

Fischer, K. W., and Ayoub, C. (1994). Affective splitting and dissociation in normal and maltreated children: Developmental pathways for self in relationships. In: D. Cicchetti and S. L. Toth (Eds.), *Rochester Symposium on Developmental Psychopathology, Vol. 5. Disorders and Dysfunctions of the Self* (pp. 149–222). Rochester, NY: University of Rochester Press.

Fischer, K. W., and Farrar, M. J. (1987). Generalisations about generalisation: How a theory of skill development explains both generality and specificity. *International Journal of Psychology, 22,* 643–677.

Fischer, K. W., Kenny, S. L., and Pipp, S. L. (1990). How cognitive processes and environmental conditions organize discontinuities in the development of abstractions. In: C. N. Alexander, E. J. Langer, and R. M. Oetzel (Eds.), *Higher Stages of Development* (pp. 162–187). New York: Oxford University Press.

Fischer, K. W., Knight, C. C., and Van Parys, M. (1993). Analyzing diversity in developmental pathways: Methods and concepts. In: W. Edelstein and R. Case (Eds.), *Constructivists Approaches to Development. Contributions to Human Development, Vol. 23* (pp. 33–56). Basel, Switzerland: S. Karger.

Fischer, K. W., and Pipp, S. L. (1984). Development of the structures of unconscious thought. In: K. Bowers and D. Meichenbaum (Eds.), *The Unconscious Reconsidered* (pp. 88–148). New York: John Wiley.

Flavell, J. (1982). On cognitive development. *Child Development, 53,* 1–10.

Flavell, J., Flavell, E. R., and Green, F. L. (1987). Young children's knowledge about the apparent–real and pretend–real distinction. *Developmental Psychology, 23,* 816–822.

Flavell, J., Flavell, E. R., Green, F. L., and Moses, L. J. (1990). Young children's understanding of fact beliefs versus value beliefs. *Child Development, 61,* 915–928.

Flavell, J., Green, F. L., and Flavell, E. R. (1986). Development of knowledge about the appearance–reality distinction. *Monographs of the Society for Research in Child Development, 51* (Serial 212, 1).

Flory, J. D., Manuck, S. B., Ferrell, R. E., Dent, K. M., Peters, D. G., and Muldoon, M. F. (1999). Neuroticism is not associated with the serotonin transporter (5-HTTLPR) polymorphism. *Molecular Psychiatry, 4* (1), 93–96.

Fodor, J. A. (1987). *Psychosemantics*. Cambridge, MA: MIT Press.

Fodor, J. A. (1992). A theory of the child's theory of mind. *Cognition, 44*, 283–296.

Fogel, A. (1993). *Developing through Relationships: Origins of Communication, Self, and Culture*. Chicago, IL: Chicago University Press.

Fogel, A., Nwokah, E., Dedo, J. Y., Messinger, D., Dickson, K. L., and Holt, S. A. (1992). Social process theory of emotion: A dynamic systems approach. *Social Development, 2*, 122–142.

Fónagy, I., and Fónagy, J. (1987). Analysis of complex (integrated) melodic patterns. In: R. Channon and L. Shockey (Eds.), *In Honour of Ilse Lehiste* (pp. 75–98). Dordrecht: Foris.

Fónagy, I., and Fonagy, P. (1995). Communication with pretend actions in language, literature and psychoanalysis. *Psychoanalysis and Contemporary Thought, 18*, 363–418.

Fonagy, P. (1989). On tolerating mental states: Theory of mind in borderline patients. *Bulletin of the Anna Freud Centre, 12*, 91–115.

Fonagy, P. (1991). Thinking about thinking: Some clinical and theoretical considerations in the treatment of a borderline patient. *International Journal of Psycho-Analysis, 72*, 1–18.

Fonagy, P. (1995a). Mental representations from an intergenerational cognitive science perspective. *Infant Mental Health Journal, 15*, 57–68.

Fonagy, P. (1995b). Playing with reality: The development of psychic reality and its malfunction in borderline patients. *International Journal of Psycho-Analysis, 76*, 39–44.

Fonagy, P. (1997). Attachment and theory of mind: Overlapping constructs? *Association for Child Psychology and Psychiatry, Occasional Papers, 14*, 31–40.

Fonagy, P. (1998). Moments of change in psychoanalytic theory: Discussion of a new theory of psychic change. *Infant Mental Health Journal, 19*, 163–171.

Fonagy, P. (2000). The development of psychopathology from infancy to adulthood: The mysterious unfolding of disturbance in time. Paper presented at the Seventh Congress of the World Association for Infant Mental Health, Montreal.

Fonagy, P. (2001). *Attachment Theory and Psychoanalysis*. New York: Other Press.

Fonagy, P., Edgcumbe, R., Moran, G. S., Kennedy, H., and Target, M. (1993). The roles of mental representations and mental processes in therapeutic action. *Psychoanalytic Study of the Child, 48*, 9–48.

Fonagy, P., Fearon, P., and Target, M. (1999). How can children in the same family have different attachment classifications? Paper presented at the Society for Research in Child Development Biennial Meeting, Albuquerque, New Mexico.

Fonagy, P., Leigh, T., Kennedy, R., Mattoon, G., Steele, H., Target, M., Steele, M., and Higgitt, A. (1995). Attachment, borderline states and the representation of emotions and cognitions in self and other. In: D. Cicchetti and S. S. Toth (Eds.), *Rochester Symposium on Developmental Psychopathology: Cognition and Emotion, Vol. 6* (pp. 371–414). Rochester, NY: University of Rochester Press.

Fonagy, P., Leigh, T., Steele, M., Steele, H., Kennedy, R., Mattoon, G., Target, M., and Gerber, A. (1996). The relation of attachment status, psychiatric classification, and response to psychotherapy. *Journal of Consulting and Clinical Psychology, 64*, 22–31.

Fonagy, P., Moran, G., and Target, M. (1993). Aggression and the psychological self. *International Journal of Psycho-Analysis, 74*, 471–485.

Fonagy, P., Redfern, S., and Charman, T. (1997). The relationship between belief–desire reasoning and a projective measure of attachment security (SAT). *British Journal of Developmental Psychology, 15*, 51–61.

Fonagy, P., Steele, H., Moran, G., Steele, M., and Higgitt, A. (1991). The capacity for understanding mental states: The reflective self in parent and child and its significance for security of attachment. *Infant Mental Health Journal, 13*, 200–217.

Fonagy, P., Steele, H., and Steele, M. (1991). Maternal representations of attachment during pregnancy predict the organization of infant–mother attachment at one year of age. *Child Development, 62*, 891–905.

Fonagy, P., Steele, M., Moran, G. S., Steele, H., and Higgitt, A. (1992). The integration of psychoanalytic theory and work on attachment: The issue of intergenerational psychic processes. In: D. Stern and M. Ammaniti (Eds.), *Attaccamento e Psiconalisis* (pp. 19–30). Bari: Laterza.

Fonagy, P., Steele, M., Steele, H., Higgitt, A., and Target, M. (1994). Theory and practice of resilience. *Journal of Child Psychology and Psychiatry and Allied Disciplines, 35*, 231–257.

Fonagy, P., Steele, H., Steele, M., and Holder, J. (1997). Children securely attached in infancy perform better in belief–desire reasoning task at age five. University College London, unpublished manuscript.

Fonagy, P., Steele, M., Steele, H., Leigh, T., Kennedy, R., Mattoon, G., and Target, M. (1995). Attachment, the reflective self, and borderline states: The predictive specificity of the Adult Attachment Interview and pathological emotional development. In: S. Goldberg, R. Muir, and J. Kerr (Eds.), *Attachment Theory: Social, Developmental and Clinical Perspectives* (pp. 233–278). New York: Analytic Press.

Fonagy, P., Steele, M., Steele, H., and Target, M. (1997). *Reflective-Functioning Manual, Version 4.1, for Application to Adult Attachment Interviews*. London: University College London.

Fonagy, P., Stein, H., and White, R. (2001). Dopamine receptor polymorphism and susceptibility to sexual, physical and psychological abuse: Preliminary results of a longitudinal study of maltreatment. Paper presented at the Tenth Biannual Meeting of the Society for Research in Child Development, Minneapolis, MI.

Fonagy, P., and Target, M. (1995). Understanding the violent patient: The use of the body and the role of the father. *International Journal of Psycho-Analysis, 76*, 487–502.

Fonagy, P., and Target, M. (1996). Playing with reality: I. Theory of mind and the normal development of psychic reality. *International Journal of Psycho-Analysis, 77*, 217–233.

Fonagy, P., and Target, M. (1997). Attachment and reflective function: Their role in self-organization. *Development and Psychopathology, 9*, 679–700.

Fonagy, P., Target, M., Cottrell, D., Phillips, J., and Kurtz, Z. (2000). *A Review of the Outcomes of All Treatments of Psychiatric Disorder in Childhood* (MCH 17–33). London: National Health Service Executive.

Fonagy, P., Target, M., and Gergely, G. (2000). Attachment and borderline personality disorder: A theory and some evidence. *Psychiatric Clinics of North America, 23*, 103–122.

Fonagy, P., Target, M., Steele, H., and Steele, M. (1998). *Reflective-Functioning Manual, Version 5.0, for Application to Adult Attachment Interviews*. London: University College London.

Fox, N. (Ed.) (1994). *The Development of Emotion Regulation*. Chicago, IL: Chicago University Press.

Fox, R. A., Platz, D. L., and Bentley, K. S. (1995). Maternal factors related to parenting practices, developmental expectations, and perceptions of child behavior problems. *Journal of Genetic Psychology, 156*, 431–441.

Freud, A. (1981). *A Psychoanalytic View of Developmental Psychopathology*. New York: International Universities Press.

Freud, S. (1900a). *The Interpretation of Dreams*. In: J. Strachey (Ed.), *The Standard Edition of the Complete Psychological Works of Sigmund Freud (S.E.), Vols. 4–5*. London: Hogarth Press.

Freud, S. (1911b). Formulations on the two principles of mental functioning. In: J. Strachey (Ed.), *S.E., Vol. 12* (pp. 213–216). London: Hogarth Press.

Freud, S. (1912–13). *Totem and Taboo.* In: J. Strachey (Ed.), *S.E., Vol. 13* London: Hogarth Press.

Freud, S. (1914c). On narcissism: An introduction. In: J. Strachey (Ed.), *S.E., Vol. 14* (pp. 67–104). London: Hogarth Press.

Freud, S. (1915e). The unconscious. In: J. Strachey (Ed.), *S.E., Vol. 14* (pp. 161–216). London: Hogarth Press.

Freud, S. (1917e [1915]). Mourning and melancholia. In: J. Strachey (Ed.), *S.E., Vol. 14* (pp. 237–258). London: Hogarth Press.

Freud, S. (1920g). *Beyond the Pleasure Principle.* In: J. Strachey (Ed.), *S.E., Vol. 18* (pp. 1–64). London: Hogarth Press.

Freud, S. (1926d [1925]). *Inhibitions, Symptoms and Anxiety.* In: J. Strachey (Ed.), *S.E., Vol. 20* (pp. 77–172). London: Hogarth Press.

Freud, S. (1950 [1895]). A project for a scientific psychology. In: J. Strachey (Ed.), *S.E., Vol. 1* (pp. 281–397). London: Hogarth Press.

Frith, C. D. (1992). *The Cognitive Neuropsychology of Schizophrenia.* Hillsdale, NJ: Lawrence Erlbaum.

Frith, U. (1989). *Autism: Explaining the Enigma.* Oxford: Blackwell.

Frosch, A. (1995). The preconceptual organization of emotion. *Journal of the American Psychoanalytic Association, 43,* 423–447.

Gaensbauer, T. (1982). The differentiation of discrete affects. *Psychoanalytic Study of the Child, 37,* 29–66.

Gallagher, H. L., Happe, F., Brunswick, N., Fletcher, P. C., Frith, U., and Frith, C. D. (2000). Reading the mind in cartoons and stories: An fMRI study of "theory of mind" in verbal and nonverbal tasks. *Neuropsychologia, 38* (1), 11–21.

Gallup, G. G., Jr. (1970). Chimpanzees: Self-recognition. *Science, 167,* 86–87.

Gallup, G. G., Jr. (1991). Towards a comparative psychology of self-awareness: Species limitations and cognitive consequences. In: G. R. Goethals and J. Strauss (Eds.), *The Self: An Interdisciplinary Approach* (pp. 121–135). New York: Springer-Verlag.

Gallup, G. G., Jr., and Suarez, S. D. (1986). Self-awareness and the emergence of mind in humans and other primates. In: J. Suls and A. G. Greenwald (Eds.), *Psychological Perspectives on the Self, Vol. 3* (pp. 3–26). Hillsdale, NJ: Lawrence Erlbaum.

Garber, J., and Dodge, K. A. (Eds.) (1991). *The Development of Emotion Regulation and Dysregulation* (pp. 3-11). New York: Cambridge University Press.

Garmezy, N., Masten, A. S., and Tellegen, A. (1984). The study of stress and competence in children: A building block for developmental psychopathology. *Child Development, 55,* 97–111.

Ge, X., Conger, R. D., Cadoret, R., Neiderhiser, J., and Yates, W. (1996). The developmental interface between nature and nurture: A mutual influence model of child antisocial behavior and parent behavior. *Developmental Psychology, 32,* 574–589.

Gelernter, J., Goldman, D., and Risch, N. (1993). The A1 allele at the D2 dopamine receptor gene and alcoholism: A reappraisal. *Journal of the American Medical Association, 269,* 1673–1677.

Gelernter, J., Kranzler, H., Coccaro, E. F., Siever, L. J., and New, A. S. (1998). Serotonin transporter protein gene polymorphism and personality measures in African American and European American subjects. *American Journal of Psychiatry, 155* (10), 1332–1338.

Gelernter, J., Southwick, S., Goodson, S., Morgan, A., Nagy, L., and Charney, D. S. (1999). No association between D2 dopamine receptor (DRD2) "A" system alleles, or DRD2 haplotypes, and posttraumatic stress disorder. *Biological Psychiatry, 45,* 620–625.

George, C., Kaplan, N., and Main, M. (1985). The Adult Attachment Interview. Berkeley, CA: University of California at Berkeley, Department of Psychology, unpublished manuscript.

George, C., and Solomon, J. (1996). Representational models of relationships: Links between caregiving and attachment. In: C. George and J. Solomon (Eds.), *Defining the Caregiving System (Infant Mental Health Journal, 17)* (pp. 198–216). New York: John Wiley.

George, C., and Solomon, J. (1998). Attachment disorganization at age six: Differences in doll play between punitive and caregiving children. Paper presented at the International Society for the Study of Behavioral Development, Bern, Switzerland.

Gergely, G. (1992). Developmental reconstructions: Infancy from the point of view of psychoanalysis and developmental psychology. *Psychoanalysis and Contemporary Thought, 15,* 3–55.

Gergely, G. (1994). From self-recognition to theory of mind. In: S. T. Parker, R. W. Mitchell, and M. L. Boccia (Eds.), *Self-Awareness in Animals and Humans: Developmental Perspectives* (pp. 51–61). Cambridge, U.K.: Cambridge University Press.

Gergely, G. (1995a). The role of parental mirroring of affects in early psychic structuration. Paper presented at the Fifth IPA Conference on Psychoanalytic Research, London.

Gergely, G. (1995b). The social construction of self-awareness and first-person authority. Paper presented at the Twelfth SRCD Conference, Indianapolis, IN.

Gergely, G. (1997). Margaret Mahler's developmental theory reconsidered in the light of current empirical research on infant development. Paper presented at the Mahler Centennial Conference, Sopron, Hungary.

Gergely, G. (2000). Reapproaching Mahler: New perspectives on normal autism, normal symbiosis, splitting and libidinal object constancy from cognitive developmental theory. *Journal of the American Psychoanalytic Association, 48* (4), 1197–1228.

Gergely, G. (2001a). The development of understanding of self and agency. In: U. Goshwami (Ed.), *Handbook of Childhood Cognitive Development.* Oxford: Blackwell.

Gergely, G. (2001b). The obscure object of desire: "Nearly, but clearly not, like me": Contingency preference in normal children versus children with autism. *Contingency Perception and Attachment in Infancy,* ed. by J. Allen, P. Fonagy, and G. Gergely. *Bulletin of the Menninger Clinic, Special Issue,* 411–426.

Gergely, G., and Csibra, G. (1996). Understanding rational actions in infancy: Teleological interpretations without mental attribution. Paper presented at the Symposium on Early Perception of Social Contingencies, Tenth Biennial International Conference on Infant Studies, Providence, RI.

Gergely, G., and Csibra, G. (1997). Teleological reasoning in infancy: The infant's naive theory of rational action. A reply to Premack and Premack. *Cognition, 63,* 227–233.

Gergely, G., and Csibra, G. (1998). La interpretacion teleologica de la conducta: La teoria infantil de la accion racional [The teleological interpretation of behavior: The infant's theory of rational action]. *Infancia y Aprendizaje, 84,* 45–65.

Gergely, G., and Csibra, G. (2000). The teleological origins of naive theory of mind in infancy. Paper presented at the Symposium on Origins of Theory of Mind: Studies with Human Infants and Primates, Twelfth Biennial International Conference on Infant Studies (ICIS), Brighton, U.K.

Gergely, G., Koós, O., and Watson, J. S. (in press). Contingency perception and the role of contingent parental reactivity in early socioemotional development: Some implications for developmental psychopathology. In: J. Nadel and J. Decety (Eds.), *Imitation, Action et Intentionnalité.* Paris: Presses Universitaires de France.

Gergely, G., Magyar, J., and Balázs, A. C. (1999). Childhood autism as "blindness" to less-than-perfect contingencies (poster). Paper presented at the Biennial Conference of the International Society for Research in Childhood and Adolescent Psychopathology (ISRCAP), Barcelona.

Gergely, G., Nadasdy, Z., Csibra, G., and Bíró, S. (1995). Taking the intentional stance at 12 months of age. *Cognition, 56*, 165–193.

Gergely, G., and Watson, J. (1996). The social biofeedback model of parental affect-mirroring. *International Journal of Psycho-Analysis, 77*, 1181–1212.

Gergely, G., and Watson, J. (1999). Early social–emotional development: Contingency perception and the social biofeedback model. In: P. Rochat (Ed.), *Early Social Cognition: Understanding Others in the First Months of Life* (pp. 101–137). Hillsdale, NJ: Lawrence Erlbaum.

Gewirtz, J., and Pelaez-Nogueras, M. (1992). Social referencing as a learned process. In: S. Feinman (Ed.), *Social Referencing and the Social Construction of Reality in Infancy* (pp. 151–173). New York: Plenum Press.

Gholson, B. (1980). *The Cognitive-Developmental Basis of Human Learning: Studies in Hypothesis Testing.* New York: Academic Press.

Gibson, J. J. (1966). *The Senses Considered as Perceptual Systems.* Boston, MA: Houghton-Mifflin.

Gilligan, J. (1997). *Violence: Our Deadliest Epidemic and Its Causes.* New York: Grosset/Putnam.

Goel, V., Grafman, N., Sadato, M., and Hallett, M. (1995). Modeling other minds. *Neuroreport, 6*, 1741–1746.

Goldman, A. (1989). Interpretation psychologized. *Mind and Language, 4*, 161–185.

Goldman, A. (1992). In defense of simulation theory. *Mind and Language, 7* (1–2), 104–119.

Goldman, A. (1993). *Philosophical Applications of Cognitive Science.* Boulder, CO: Westview Press.

Golinkoff, R. (1986). "I beg your pardon?": The preverbal negotiation of failed messages. *Journal of Child Language, 13*, 455–476.

Gopnik, A. (1993). How we know our minds: The illusion of first-person knowledge of intentionality. *Behavioral and Brain Sciences, 16*, 1–14, 29–113.

Gopnik, A. (1996). Theories and modules: Creation myths, developmental realities, and Neurath's boat. In: P. Carruthers and P. K. Smith (Eds.), *Theories of Theories of Mind* (pp. 169–183). Cambridge, U.K.: Cambridge University Press.

Gopnik, A., and Astington, J. W. (1988). Children's understanding of representational change and its relation to the understanding of false belief and the appearance–reality distinction. *Child Development, 59*, 26–37.

Gopnik, A., and Graf, P. (1988). Knowing how you know: Young children's ability to identify and remember the sources of their beliefs. *Child Development, 59,* 1366–1371.

Gopnik, A., and Meltzoff, A. (1997). *Words, Thoughts, and Theories.* Cambridge, MA: MIT Press.

Gopnik, A., and Slaughter, V. (1991). Young children's understanding of changes in their mental states. *Child Development, 62,* 98–110.

Gopnik, A., and Wellman, H. M. (1992). Why the child's theory of mind really is a theory. *Mind and Language, 7,* 145–171.

Gopnik, A., and Wellman, H. M. (1994). The theory theory. In: L. A. Hirschfeld and S. A. Gelman (Eds.), *Mapping the Mind: Domain Specificity in Cognition and Culture* (pp. 257–293). New York: Cambridge University Press.

Gordon, R. M. (1986). Folk psychology as simulation. *Mind and Language, 1,* 158–171.

Gordon, R. M. (1992). Simulation theory: Objections and misconceptions. *Mind and Language, 7,* 11–34.

Gordon, R. M. (1995). Simulation without introspection or inference from me to you. In: T. Stone and M. Davies (Eds.), *Mental Simulation: Evaluations and Applications* (pp. 101–119). Oxford: Blackwell.

Gosling, J. C. B., and Taylor, C. C. W. (1982). *The Greeks on Pleasure.* Oxford: Clarendon Press.

Gottman, J. M. (1981). *Time-Series Analysis: A Comprehensive Introduction for Social Scientists.* Cambridge, U.K.: Cambridge University Press.

Gould, S. J. (1987). *An Urchin in the Storm.* New York: Norton.

Gove, F. (1983). Patterns and organizations of behavior and affective expression during the second year of life. Minneapolis, MN: University of Minnesota, unpublished doctoral dissertation.

Green, A. (1975). The analyst, symbolization and absence in the analytic setting: On changes in analytic practice and analytic experience. *International Journal of Psycho-Analysis, 56,* 1–22.

Green, A. (1999). *The Fabric of Affect in the Psychoanalytic Discourse.* London: Routledge.

Green, A. (2000). Science and science fiction in infant research. In: J. Sandler, A.-M. Sandler, and R. Davies (Eds.), *Clinical and Observational Psychoanalytic Research: Roots of a Controversy* (pp. 41–73). London: Karnac.

Greenberg, B. D., Li, Q., Lucas, F. R., Hu, S., Sirota, L. A., Benjamin, J., Lesch, K. P., Hamer, D., and Murphy, D. L. (2000). Association between the serotonin transporter promoter polymorphism and personality traits in a primarily female population sample. *American Journal of Medical Genetics, 96* (2), 202–216.

Greenspan, P. (1988). *Emotions and Reasons: An Inquiry into Emotional Justification.* New York: Routledge.

Grice, H. P. (1975). Logic and conversation. In: R. Cole and J. Morgan (Eds.), *Syntax and Semantics: Speech Acts* (pp. 41–58). New York: Academic Press.

Griffiths, P. (1997). *What Emotions Really Are.* Chicago, IL: Chicago University Press.

Grinberg, L., Sor, D., and De Bianchedi, E. T. (1977). *Introduction to the Work of Bion.* New York: Jason Aronson.

Gross, J. J. (1998). The emerging field of emotion regulation. *Review of General Psychology, 2,* 271–299.

Gross, J. J. (1999). Emotion regulation: Past, present and future. *Cognition and Emotion, 13,* 551–573.

Grossmann, K., Grossmann, K. E., Spangler, G., Suess, G., and Unzner, L. (1985). Maternal sensitivity and newborn orienting responses as related to quality of attachment in Northern Germany. *Growing Points in Attachment Theory and Research,* ed. by I. Bretherton and E. Waters. *Monographs of the Society for Research in Child Development, 50* (Serial 209, 1–2), 233–256.

Grossmann, K. E., Grossmann, K., and Schwan, A. (1986). Capturing the wider view of attachment: A reanalysis of Ainsworth's Strange Situation. In: C. E. Izard and P. B. Read (Eds.), *Measuring Emotions in Infants and Children, Vol. 2* (pp. 124–171). New York: Cambridge University Press.

Guardia, J., Catafau, A. M., Batile, F., Martin, J. C., Segura, L., Gonzalvo, B., Prat, G., Carrio, I., and Casas, M. (2000). Striatal dopaminergic D_2 receptor density measured by [^{123}I]Iodobenzamide SPECT in the prediction of treatment outcome of alcohol-dependent patients. *American Journal of Psychiatry, 157,* 127–129.

Gunderson, J. G. (1984). *Borderline Personality Disorder.* Washington, DC: American Psychiatric Press.

Gunderson, J. G. (1996). The borderline patient's intolerance of aloneness: Insecure attachments and therapist availability. *American Journal of Psychiatry, 153* (6), 752–758.

Gustavsson, J. P., Nothen, M. M., Jonsson, E. G., Neidt, H., Forslund, K., Rylander, G., Mattila-Evenden, M., Sedvall, G. C., Propping, P., and Asberg, M. (1999). No association between serotonin transporter gene polymorphisms and personality traits. *American Journal of Medical Genetics, 88* (4), 430–436.

Hamilton, C. (1994). Continuity and discontinuity of attachment from infancy through adolescence. Los Angeles, CA: University of California–Los Angeles, unpublished doctoral dissertation.

Hamilton, S. P., Heiman, G. A., Haghighi, F., Mick, S., Klein, D. F., Hodge, S. E., Weissman, M. M., Fyer, A. J., and Knowles, J. A. (1999). Lack of genetic linkage or association between a functional serotonin transporter polymorphism and panic disorder. *Psychiatric Genetics, 9* (1), 1–6.

Hamilton, W. D. (1964). The genetic evolution of social behavior. *Journal of Theoretical Biology, 7,* 1–52.

Hare, R. D., and Cox, D. N. (1987). Clinical and empirical conceptions of psychopathy, and the selection of subjects for research. In: R. D. Hare and D. Schalling (Eds.), *Psychopathic Behavior: Approaches to Research* (pp. 1–21). Toronto, Ontario: John Wiley.

Harris, J. R. (1998). *The Nurture Assumption: Why Children Turn out the Way They Do: Parents Matter Less Than You Think and Peers Matter More.* New York: Free Press.

Harris, P. L. (1991). The work of the imagination. In: A. Whiten (Ed.), *Natural Theories of Mind* (pp. 283–304). Oxford: Blackwell.

Harris, P. L. (1992). From simulation to folk psychology: The case for development. *Mind and Language, 7,* 120–144.

Harris, P. L. (1996). Desires, beliefs, and language. In: P. Carruthers and P. K. Smith (Eds.), *Theories of Theories of Mind* (pp. 200–221). Cambridge, U.K.: Cambridge University Press.

Harris, P. L., and Kavanaugh, R. D. (1993). Young children's understanding of pretence. *Monographs of the Society for Research in Child Development, 58* (Serial 237, 1).

Harris, P. L., Kavanaugh, R. D., and Meredith, M. (1994). Young children's comprehension of pretend episodes: The integration of successive actions. *Child Development, 65,* 16–30.

Hart, D., and Killen, M. (1995). Introduction: Perspectives on morality in everyday life. In: M. Killen and D. Hart (Eds.), *Morality in Everyday Life* (pp. 1–22). Cambridge, U.K.: Cambridge University Press.

Harter, S. (1999). *The Construction of the Self: A Developmental Perspective.* New York: Guilford Press.

Harter, S., Marold, D. B., Whitesell, N. R., and Cobbs, G. (1996). A model of the effects of parent and peer support on adolescent false self behavior. *Child Development, 67.*

Hartmann, H. (1956). Notes on the reality principle, *Essays on Ego Psychology* (pp. 268–296). New York: International Universities Press.

Haviland, J. M., and Lelwica, M. (1987). The induced affect response: 10-week-old infants' responses to three emotional expressions. *Developmental Psychology, 23,* 97–104.

Heider, F., and Simmel, M. (1944). An experimental study of apparent behavior. *American Journal of Psychology, 57,* 243–259.

Heils, A., Teufel, A., Petri, S., Stober, G., Riederer, P., Bengel, B., and Lesch, K. P. (1996). Allelic variation of human serotonin transporter gene expression. *Journal of Neurochemistry, 6,* 2621–2624.

Heinz, A., Higley, J. D., Gorey, J. G., Saunders, R. C., Jones, D. W., Hommer, D., Zajicek, J., Suomi, S. J., Weinberger, D. R., and Linnoila, M. (1998). In vivo association between alcohol intoxication, aggression and serotonin transporter availability in non-human primates. *American Journal of Psychiatry, 155,* 1023–1028.

Herbst, J. H., Zonderman, A. B., McCrae, R. R., and Costa, P. T., Jr. (2000). Do the dimensions of the temperament and character inventory map a simple genetic architecture? Evidence from molecular genetics and factor analysis. *American Journal of Psychiatry, 157* (8), 1285–1290.

Herrera, C., and Dunn, J. (1997). Early experiences with family conflict: Implications for arguments with a close friend. *Developmental Psychology, 33,* 869–881.

Hewitt, J. K., Silberg, J. L., Rutter, M., Simonoff, E., Meyer, J. M., Maes, H., Pickles, A., Neale, M. C., Loeber, R., Erickson, M. T., Kendler, K. S., Heath, A. C., Truett, K. R., Reynolds, C. A., and Eaves, L. J. (1997). Genetics and developmental psychopathology: 1. Phenotypic assessment in the Virginia Twin Study of Adolescent Behavioral Development. *Journal of Child Psychology and Psychiatry and Allied Disciplines, 38* (8), 943–963.

Higgitt, A., and Fonagy, P. (1992). The psychotherapeutic treatment of borderline and narcissistic personality disorder. *British Journal of Psychiatry, 161,* 23–43.

Higley, J. D., Hasert, M. L., Suomi, S. J., and Linnoila, M. (1991). A new non-human primate model of alcohol abuse: Effects of early experience, personality and stress on alcohol consumption. *Proceedings of the National Academy of Sciences USA, 88,* 7261–7265.

Higley, J. D., Hommer, D., Lucas, K., Shoaf, S. E., Suomi, S. J., and Linnoila, M. (in press). CNS serotonin metabolism rate predicts innate tolerance, high alcohol consumption and aggression during intoxication in rhesus monkeys. *Archives of General Psychiatry.*

Higley, J. D., King, S. T., Hasert, M. F., Champoux, M., Suomi, S. J., and Linnoila, M. (1996). Stability of individual differences in serotonin function and its relationship to severe aggression and competent social behavior in rhesus macaque females. *Neuropsychopharmacology, 14,* 67–76.

Higley, J. D., Suomi, S. J., and Linnoila, M. (1996). A non-human primate model of Type II alcoholism? Part 2: Diminished social competence and excessive aggression correlates with low CSF 5-HIAA concentrations. *Alcoholism: Clinical and Experimental Research, 20,* 643–650.

Hill, J., Harrington, R. C., Fudge, H., Rutter, M., and Pickles, A. (1989). Adult personality functioning assessment (APFA): An investigation-based standardised interview. *British Journal of Psychiatry, 161,* 24–35.

Hirschfeld, L., and Gelman, S. (1994). *Mapping the Mind: Domain Specificity in Cognition and Culture.* New York: Cambridge University Press.

Hobson, R. P. (1993). *Autism and the Development of Mind.* London: Lawrence Erlbaum.

Hofer, M. A. (1984). Relationships as regulators: A psychobiologic perspective on bereavement. *Psychosomatic Medicine, 46* (3), 183–197.

Hofer, M. A. (1990). Early symbiotic processes: Hard evidence from a soft place. In: R. A. Glick and S. Bone (Eds.), *Pleasure Beyond the Pleasure Principle* (pp. 13–25). New Haven, CT: Yale University Press.

Hofer, M. A. (1995). Hidden regulators: Implications for a new understanding of attachment, separation and loss. In: S. Goldberg, R. Muir, and J. Kerr (Eds.), *Attachment Theory: Social, Developmental, and Clinical Perspectives* (pp. 203–230). Hillsdale, NJ: Analytic Press.

Hoffman, M. L. (2000). *Empathy and Moral Development: Implications for Caring and Justice.* Cambridge, U.K.: Cambridge University Press.

Hopkins, J. (1992). Psychoanalysis, interpretation, and science. In: J. Hopkins and A. Saville (Eds.), *Psychoanalysis, Mind and Art: Perspectives on Richard Wollheim* (pp. 3–34). Oxford: Blackwell.

Horowitz, M. J. (1995). Defensive control states and person schemas. In: T. Shapiro and R. N. Emde (Eds.), *Research in Psychoanalysis: Process, Development, Outcome* (pp. 67–89). Madison, CT: International Universities Press.

Howe, M. L., and Courage, M. L. (1993). On resolving the enigma of infantile amnesia. *Psychological Bulletin, 113,* 305–326.

Howe, M. L., and Courage, M. L. (1997). The emergence and early development of autobiographical memory. *Psychological Review, 104,* 499–523.

Hughes, C., and Russell, J. (1993). Autistic children's difficulty with mental disengagement from an object: Its implication for theories of autism. *Developmental Psychology, 29,* 498–510.

Isabella, R. A. (1993). Origins of attachment: Maternal interactive behavior across the first year. *Child Development, 64,* 605–621.

Isabella, R. A., and Belsky, J. (1991). Interactional synchrony and the origins of infant–mother attachment: A replication study. *Child Development, 62*, 373–384.

Izard, C. E. (1977). *Human Emotions*. New York: Plenum Press.

Izard, C. E. (1978). Emotions as motivations: An evolutionary–developmental perspective. In: J. H. E. Howe (Ed.), *Nebraska Symposium on Motivation, Vol. 26* (pp. 163–199). Lincoln, NE: University of Nebraska Press.

Izard, C. E. (1979). *The Maximally Discriminative Facial Movement Coding System (MAX)*. Newark, DE: University of Delaware, Office of Instructional Technology.

Izard, C. E. (1991). *The Psychology of Emotions*. New York: Plenum Press.

Izard, C. E., Dougherty, L. M., and Hembree, E. A. (1983). *A System for Identifying Affect Expressions by Holistic Judgements (AFFEX)*. Newark, DE: University of Delaware, Office of Instructional Technology.

Izard, C. E., and Malatesta, C. Z. (1987). Perspectives on emotional development. In: J. D. Osofsky (Ed.), *Handbook of Infant Development* (2nd ed., pp. 494–554). New York: John Wiley.

Jacob, F. (1998). *Of Flies, Mice and Men* (trans. G. Weiss). Cambridge, MA: Harvard University Press (original work published in 1997).

Jacobovitz, D., and Hazen, N. (1999). Developmental pathways from infant disorganization to childhood peer relationships. In: J. Solomon and C. George (Eds.), *Attachment Disorganization* (pp. 127–159). New York: Guilford Press.

Jacobovitz, D., Hazen, N., and Riggs, S. (1997). Disorganized mental processes in mothers, frightening/frightened caregiving and disoriented/disorganized behavior in infancy. Paper presented at the Biennial Meeting of the Society for Research in Child Development, Washington, DC.

Jacobson, E. (1953). On the psychoanalytic theory of affects. *Depression: Comparative Studies of Normal, Neurotic, and Psychotic Conditions*. New York: International Universities Press, 1971.

Jacobson, E. (1964). *The Self and the Object World*. New York: International Universities Press.

Jaffe, J., Beebe, B., Feldstein, S., Crown, C. L., and Jasnow, M. D. (2001). Rhythms of dialogue in infancy. *Monographs of the Society for Research in Child Development, 66* (2).

James, S. (1997). *Passion and Action: The Emotions in Seventeenth Century Philosophy*. Oxford: Clarendon Press.

James, W. (1884). What is an emotion? *Mind, 9*, 188–205.

James, W. (1890). *Principles of Psychology*. New York: Henry Holt.

James, W. (1892). *Psychology: The Briefer Course*. New York: Henry Holt.

Jeannerod, M. (1994). The representing brain: Neural correlates of motor intention and imagery. *Behavioral and Brain Sciences*, 187–246.

Jeannerod, M. (1997). *The Cognitive Neuroscience of Action*. Oxford: Blackwell.

Jeannerod, M. (1999). To act or not to act: Perspectives on the representation of actions. *Quarterly Journal of Experimental Psychology, 52A* (1), 1–29.

Jenkins, J., and Astington, J. W. (1996). Cognitive factors and family structure associated with theory of mind development in young children. *Developmental Psychology, 32*, 70–78.

Joffe, W. G., and Sandler, J. (1967). Some conceptual problems involved in the consideration of disorders of narcissism. *Journal of Child Psychotherapy, 2*, 56–66.

Johnson, J. G., Cohen, P., Brown, J., Smailes, E. M., and Bernstein, D. P. (1999). Childhood maltreatment increases risk for personality disorders during early adulthood. *Archives of General Psychiatry, 56*, 600–605.

Johnson, M. K., and Multhaup, K. S. (1992). Emotion and MEM. In: S. Christianson (Ed.), *The Handbook of Emotion and Memory: Research and Theory* (pp. 33–66). Hillsdale, NJ: Lawrence Erlbaum.

Johnson, S. C., Slaughter, V., and Carey, S. (1998). Whose gaze will infants follow? The elicitation of gaze following in 12-month-olds. *Developmental Science, 1*, 233–238.

Johnson-Laird, P. N. (1983). *Mental Models: Towards a Cognitive Science of Language, Inference and Consciousness*. Cambridge, U.K.: Cambridge University Press.

Johnson-Laird, P. N., and Byrne, R. M. (1991). *Deduction*. Hillsdale, NJ: Lawrence Erlbaum.

Johnson-Laird, P. N., and Byrne, R. M. (1993). Precis of deduction. *Behavioral and Brain Sciences, 16*, 323–380.

Jordan, M. I., and Rumelhart, D. E. (1991). Forward models: Supervised learning with a distal teacher. *Occasional Paper 40*. Cambridge, MA: Massachusetts Institute of Technology, Center for Cognitive Science.

Jorm, A. F., Prior, M., Sanson, A., Smart, D., Zhang, Y., and Easteal, S. (2000). Association of a functional polymorphism of the serotonin transporter gene with anxiety-related temperament and behavior problems in children: A longitudinal study from infancy to the mid-teens. *Molecular Psychiatry, 5* (5), 542–547.

Joseph, B. (1985). Transference: The total situation. *International Journal of Psycho-Analysis, 66*, 447–454.

Joseph, B. (1989). *Psychic Equilibrium and Psychic Change: Selected Papers of Betty Joseph.* London: Routledge.

Jurist, E. (1997). Review of John Steiner's *Psychic Retreats. Psychoanalytic Psychology, 14,* 299–309.

Jurist, E. (1998). The unexamined life is not worth living: Michael Stocker on emotions. *Metaphilosophy, 29,* 223–231.

Jurist, E. (2000). *Beyond Hegel and Nietzsche: Philosophy, Culture and Agency.* Cambridge: MIT Press.

Kagan, J. (1989). *Unstable Ideas: Temperament, Cognition and Self.* Cambridge, MA: Harvard University Press.

Kagan, J. (1992). The conceptual analysis of affects. In: T. Shapiro and R. N. Emde (Eds.), *Affects: Psychoanalytic Perspectives.* Madison, CT: International Universities Press.

Kandel, E. R. (1998). A new intellectual framework for psychiatry. *American Journal of Psychiatry, 155,* 457–469.

Kandel, E. R. (1999). Biology and the future of psychoanalysis: A new intellectual framework for psychiatry revisited. *American Journal of Psychiatry, 156,* 505–524.

Kaplan-Solms, K., and Solms, M. (2000). *Clinical Studies in Neuro-Psychoanalysis: An Introduction to Depth Neuropsychology.* London: Karnac.

Karmiloff-Smith, A. (1992). *Beyond Modularity: A Developmental Perspective on Cognitive Science.* Cambridge, MA: MIT Press.

Katsuragi, S., Kunugi, H., Sano, A., Tsutsumi, T., Isogawa, K., Nanko, S., and Akiyoshi, J. (1999). Association between serotonin transporter gene polymorphism and anxiety-related traits. *Biological Psychiatry, 45* (3), 368–370.

Kaye, K. L., and Bower, T. G. R. (1994). Learning and intermodal transfer of information in newborns. *Psychological Science, 5,* 286–288.

Kelemen, D. (1999). Function, goals and intention: Children's teleological reasoning about objects. *Trends in Cognitive Sciences, 12,* 461–468.

Kendler, K. S., Neale, M. C., Prescott, C. A., Kessler, R. C., Heath, A. C., Corey, L. A., and Eaves, L. J. (1996). Childhood parental loss and alcoholism in women: A causal analysis using a twin-family design. *Psychological Medicine, 26,* 79–95.

Kernberg, O. F. (1967). Borderline personality organization. *Journal of the American Psychoanalytic Association, 15,* 641-685.

Kernberg, O. F. (1976). *Object Relations Theory and Clinical Psychoanalysis.* New York: Jason Aronson.

Kernberg, O. F. (1982). Self, ego, affects and drives. *Journal of the American Psychoanalytic Association, 30,* 893–917.

Kernberg, O. F. (1983). Object relations theory and character analysis. *Journal of the American Psychoanalytic Association, 31*, 247–271.

Kernberg, O. F. (1987). Borderline personality disorder: A psychodynamic approach. *Journal of Personality Disorders, 1*, 344–346.

Kernberg, O. F. (1995). An ego psychology–object relations theory approach to the transference. *Psychoanalytic Quarterly, 51*, 197–221.

Kernberg, O. F., and Clarkin, J. F. (1993). Developing a disorder-specific manual: The treatment of borderline character disorder. In: N. E. Miller, J. P. Barber, and J. P. Docherty (Eds.), *Psychodynamic Treatment Research: A Handbook for Clinical Practice* (pp. 227–246). New York: Basic Books.

Kernberg, P. F. (1984). *Reflections in the Mirror: Mother–Child Interactions, Self-Awareness, and Self-Recognition.* New York: Basic Books.

Kihlstrom, J. F., and Hoyt, I. P. (1990). Repression, dissociation, and hypnosis. In: J. L. Singer (Ed.), *Repression and Dissociation* (pp. 181–208). Chicago, IL: University of Chicago Press.

Killen, M., and Nucci, L. P. (1995). Morality, autonomy and social conflict. In: M. Killen and D. Hart (Eds.), *Morality in Everyday Life* (pp. 52–86). Cambridge, U.K.: Cambridge University Press.

King, P., and Steiner, R. (1991). *The Freud–Klein Controversies: 1941–45.* London: Routledge.

Klauber, J. (1987). *Illusion and Spontaneity in Psycho-Analysis.* London: Free Association Books.

Klein, M. (1935). A contribution to the psychogenesis of manic-depressive states. In: *Love, Guilt and Reparation and Other Works: The Writings of Melanie Klein, Vol. 1* (pp. 262–289). London: Hogarth Press, 1975.

Klein, M. (1940). Mourning and its relation to manic-depressive states. In: *Love, Guilt and Reparation and Other Works: The Writings of Melanie Klein, Vol. 1* (pp. 344–369). London: Hogarth Press, 1975.

Klein, M. (1945). The Oedipus complex in the light of early anxieties. In: *Love, Guilt and Reparation and Other Works: The Writings of Melanie Klein, Vol. 1* (pp. 370–419). London: Hogarth Press, 1975.

Klein, M. (1946). Notes on some schizoid mechanisms. *International Journal of Psycho-Analysis, 27*, 99–110. In: M. Klein, P. Heimann, S. Isaacs, and J. Riviere (Eds.), *Developments in Psychoanalysis* (pp. 292–320). London: Hogarth Press.

Klinnert, M. D., Campos, J. J., Sorce, J. F., Emde, R. N., and Svejda, M. (1983). Emotions as behavior regulations: Social referencing in infancy. In: R. Plutchhik and H. Kellerman (Eds.), *Emotion: Theory, Research, and Experience.* New York: Academic Press.

Kohut, H. (1971). *The Analysis of the Self.* New York: International Universities Press.

Kohut, H. (1972). Thoughts on narcissism and narcissistic rage. *Psychoanalytic Study of the Child, 27,* 360–400.

Kohut, H. (1977). *The Restoration of the Self.* New York: International Universities Press.

Kohut, H. (1984). *How Does Analysis Cure?* Chicago, IL: University of Chicago Press.

Koós, O., and Gergely, G. (2001). The "flickering switch" hypothesis: A contingency-based approach to the etiology of disorganized attachment in infancy. *Contingency Perception and Attachment in Infancy,* ed. by J. Allen, P. Fonagy, and G. Gergely. *Bulletin of the Menninger Clinic, Special Issue,* 397–410.

Koós, O., Gergely, G., Gervai, J., and Tóth, I. (2000). The role of infant-generated stimulus contingencies in affect regulation and the development of attachment security. Paper presented at the Twelfth Biennial International Conference on Infant Studies (ICIS), Brighton, U.K.

Krause, R. (1997). *Allgemeine psychoanalytische Krankheitslehre. Grundlagen.* Stuttgart: Kohlhammer.

Krystal, H. (1988). *Integration & Healing: Affect, Trauma, Alexithymia.* Hillsdale, NJ: Analytic Press.

Kumakiri, C., Kodama, K., Shimizu, E., Yamanouchi, N., Okada, S., Noda, S., Okamoto, H., Sato, T., and Shirasawa, H. (1999). Study of the association between the serotonin transporter gene regulatory region polymorphism and personality traits in a Japanese population. *Neuroscience Letters, 263* (2–3), 205–207.

Kusche, C. A., and Greenberg, M. T. (2001). PATHS in your classroom: Promoting emotional literacy and alleviating emotional distress. In: J. Cohen (Ed.), *Caring Classrooms/Intelligent Schools: The Social Emotional Education of Young Children.* New York: Teachers College Press.

Laakso, A., Vilkman, H., Kajander, J., Bergman, J., Haaparanta, M., Solin, O., and Hietala, J. (2000). Prediction of detached personality in healthy subjects by low dopamine transporter binding. *American Journal of Psychiatry, 157,* 290–292.

LaHoste, G. J., Swanson, J. M., Wigal, S. B., Glabe, C., Wigal, T., and King, N. (1996). Dopamine D_4 receptor gene polymorphism is associated with attention deficit hyperactivity disorder. *Molecular Psychiatry, 1,* 121–124.

Laible, D. J., and Thompson, R. A. (1998). Attachment and emotional understanding in pre-school children. *Developmental Psychology, 34,* 1038–1045.

Lakatos, K., Tóth, I., Nemoda, Z., Ney, K., Sasvari-Szekely, M., and Gervai, J. (2000). Dopamine D4 receptor (DRD4) gene polymorphism is associated with attachment disorganization in infants. *Molecular Psychiatry, 5* (6), 633–637.

Lange, C. G. (1885). *Om Sindsbevaegelser.* In: Rand, B. (Ed.), *The Classical Psychologists.* Boston: Houghton Mifflin, 1912.

Laplanche, J., and Pontalis, J. B. (1973). *The Language of Psychoanalysis.* New York: Norton. Reprinted London: Karnac, 1988.

Laufer, M., and Laufer, E. (1984). *Adolescence and Developmental Breakdown.* New Haven, CT: Yale University Press.

Lazarus, R. (1984). On the primacy of cognition. *American Psychologist, 39,* 124–129.

Lazarus, R. (1991). *Emotion & Adaptation.* Oxford: Oxford University Press.

Lazarus, R. (1994). Meaning and emotional development. In: P. Ekman and R. Davidson (Eds.), *The Nature of Emotion.* Oxford: Oxford University Press.

Leach, P. (1997). *Your Baby and Child: New Version for a New Generation.* London: Penguin.

Lecours, S., and Bouchard, M.-A. (1997). Dimensions of mentalization: Outlining levels of psychic transformation. *International Journal of Psycho-Analysis, 78,* 855–875.

LeDoux, J. E. (1994a). Cognitive–emotional interactions in the brain. In: P. Ekman and R. Davidson (Eds.), *The Nature of Emotion.* Oxford: Oxford University Press.

LeDoux, J. E. (1994b). The degree of emotional control depends on the kind of personal system involved. In: P. Ekman and R. Davidson (Eds.), *The Nature of Emotion.* Oxford: Oxford University Press.

LeDoux, J. E. (1994c). Emotion, memory and the brain. *Scientific American, 270* (6), 50–57.

LeDoux, J. E. (1995). Emotion: Clues from the brain. *Annual Review of Psychology, 46,* 209–235.

LeDoux, J. E. (1996). *The Emotional Brain: The Mysterious Underpinnings of Emotional Life.* New York: Simon & Schuster.

Lee, D., and Aronson, E. (1974). Visual proprioceptive control of standing in human infants. *Perception and Psychophysics, 15,* 529–532.

Legerstee, M. (1991). The role of people and objects in early imitation. *Journal of Experimental Child Psychology, 51,* 423–433.

Legerstee, M., and Varghese, J. (2001). The role of maternal affect mirroring on social expectancies in 2–3-month-old infants. *Child Development, 72,* 1301–1313.

Lesch, K. P., Bengel, D., Heils, A., Sabol, S. Z., Greenberg, B. D., Petri, S., Benjamin, J., Muller, C. R., Hamer, D. H., and Murphy, D. L. (1996). Association of anxiety-related traits with a polymorphism in the serotonin transporter gene regulatory region. *Science, 274,* 1527–1531.

Leslie, A. (1984). Infant perception of a manual pick up event. *British Journal of Developmental Psychology, 2,* 19–32.

Leslie, A. (1987). Pretense and representation: The origins of "Theory of Mind." *Psychological Review, 94,* 412–426.

Leslie, A. (1994). ToMM, ToBy, and agency: Core architecture and domain specificity. In: L. Hirschfeld and S. Gelman (Eds.), *Mapping the Mind: Domain Specificity in Cognition and Culture* (pp. 119–148). New York: Cambridge University Press.

Leslie, A. (1995). A theory of agency. In: D. Sperber, D. Premack, and A. J. Premack (Eds.), *Causal Cognition: A Multidisciplinary Debate* (pp. 121–149). Oxford: Clarendon Press.

Leslie, A., and Happe, F. (1989). Autism and ostensive communication: The relevance of metarepresentation. *Development and Psychopathology, 1,* 205–212.

Leslie, A., and Keeble, S. (1987). Do six-month-olds perceive causality? *Cognition, 25,* 265–288.

Leslie, A., and Roth, D. (1993). What autism teaches us about metarepresentation. In: H. T. S. Baron-Cohen and D. J. Cohen (Eds.), *Understanding Other Minds: Perspectives from Autism* (pp. 83–111). New York: Oxford University Press.

Leslie, A., and Thaiss, L. (1992). Domain specificity in conceptual development: Neuropsychological evidence from autism. *Cognition, 43* (3), 225–251.

Levinson, A., and Fonagy, P. (2000). Attachment classification in prisoners and psychiatric patients. Unpublished manuscript.

Lewicka, M. (1988). On objective and subjective anchoring of cognitive acts: How behavioral valence modifies reasoning schemata. In: W. J. Baker (Ed.), *Recent Trends in Theoretical Psychology* (pp. 285–301). New York: Springer-Verlag.

Lewis, C., Freeman, N. H., Kyriakidou, C., Maridaki-Kassotaki, K., and Berridge, D. (1996). Social influences on false belief access: Specific sibling influences or general apprenticeship? *Child Development, 67,* 2930–2947.

Lewis, C., and Mitchell, P. (1994). *Children's Early Understanding of Mind: Origins and Development.* Hillsdale, NJ: Lawrence Erlbaum.

Lewis, M., Allessandri, S. M., and Sullivan, M. W. (1990). Violation of expectancy, loss of control and anger expressions in young infants. *Developmental Psychology, 26* (5), 745–751.

Lewis, M., and Brooks, J. (1978). Self-knowledge and emotional development. In: M. D. Lewis and L. A. Rosenblum (Eds.), *The Development of Affect* (pp. 205–226). New York: Plenum Press.

Lewis, M., and Brooks-Gunn, J. (1979). *Social Cognition and the Acquisition of Self.* New York: Plenum Press.

Lewis, M., and Granic, I. (2000). *Emotion, Development, and Self-Organization: Dynamic Systems Approaches to Emotional Development.* Cambridge, U.K.: Cambridge University Press.

Lewis, M., and Michaelson, L. (1983). *Children's Emotions and Moods: Developmental Theory and Measurement.* New York: Plenum Press.

Lichtenberg, J. D. (1987). Infant studies and clinical work with adults. *Psycho-Analytic Inquiry, 7,* 311–330.

Lichtenberg, J. D. (1995). Can empirical studies of development impact on psychoanalytic theory and technique? In: T. Shapiro and R. N. Emde (Eds.), *Research in Psychoanalysis: Process, Development, Outcome* (pp. 261–276). New York: International Universities Press.

Lieberman, A. F. (1977). Preschooler's competence with a peer: Relations of attachment and peer expenses. *Child Development, 55,* 123–126.

Lillard, A. S. (1993). Pretend play skills and the child's theory of mind. *Child Development, 64,* 348–371.

Linehan, M. M. (1993). *Cognitive–Behavioral Treatment of Borderline Personality Disorder.* New York: Guilford Press.

Liotti, G. (1999). Disorganization of attachment as a model for understanding dissociative psychopathology. In: J. Solomon and C. George (Eds.), *Attachment Disorganization.* New York: Guilford Press.

Liu, D., Diorio, J., Tannenbaum, B., Caldji, C., Francis, D., Freedman, A., Sharma, S., Pearson, D., Plotsky, P. M., and Meaney, M. J. (1997). Maternal care, hippocampal glucocorticoid receptors, and hypothalamic–pituitary–adrenal responses to stress. *Science, 277,* 1659–1662.

Londerville, S., and Main, M. (1981). Security of attachment, compliance, and maternal training methods in the second year of life. *Developmental Psychology, 17,* 238–299.

Luborsky, L., and Luborsky, E. (1995). The era of measures of transference: The CCRT and other measures. In: T. Shapiro and R. Emde (Eds.), *Research in Psychoanalysis* (pp. 329–351). Madison, CT: International Universities Press.

Luquet, P. (1981). Le changement dans la mentalization. *Revue Français de Psychanalyse, 45,* 1023–1028.

Luquet, P. (1987). Penser-parler: Un apport psychanalytique a la théorie du langage. In: R. Christie, M. M. Christie-Luterbacher, P. Luquet (Eds.), *La Parole Troublée* (pp. 161–300). Paris: Presses Universitaires de France.

Luquet, P. (1988). Langage, pensée et structure psychique. *Revue Français de Psychanalyse, 52,* 267–302.

Lyons-Ruth, K. (1999). The two person unconscious: Intersubjective dialogue, enactive relational representation and the emergence of new forms of relational organisation. *Psychoanalytic Inquiry, 19* (4), 576–617.

Lyons-Ruth, K., Bronfman, E., and Atwood, G. (1999). A relational diathesis model of hostile-helpless states of mind: Expressions in mother–infant interaction. In: J. Solomon and C. George (Eds.), *Attachment Disorganization* (pp. 33–70). New York: Guilford Press.

Lyons-Ruth, K., Bronfman, E., and Parsons, E. (1999). Atypical attachment in infancy and early childhood among children at developmental risk. IV. Maternal frightened, frightening, or atypical behavior and disorganized infant attachment patterns. *Typical Patterns of Infant Attachment: Theory, Research and Current Directions,* ed. by J. Vondra and D. Barnett. *Monographs of the Society for Research in Child Development 64,* 67–96.

Lyons-Ruth, K., and Jacobovitz, D. (1999). Attachment disorganization: Unresolved loss, relational violence and lapses in behavioral and attentional strategies. In: J. Cassidy and P. R. Shaver (Eds.), *Handbook of Attachment Theory and Research* (pp. 520–554). New York: Guilford Press.

Maccoby, E. E. (2000). Parenting and its effects on children: On reading and misreading behavior genetics. *Annual Review of Psychology, 51,* 1–27.

Maccoby, E., and Martin, J. A. (1983). Socialization in the context of the family: Parent–child interaction. In: E. M. Hetherington (Ed.), *Handbook of Child Psychology: Socialization, Personality and Social Development, Vol. 4.* New York: John Wiley.

MacLean, P. (1990). *The Triune Concept of the Brain in Evolution: Role in Paleocerebral Functions.* New York: Plenum Press.

MacLean, P. (1993). Cerebral evolution of emotion. In: M. Lewis and J. Haviland (Eds.), *Handbook of Emotions.* New York: Guilford Press.

Magai, C. (1999). Affect, imagery and attachment: Working models of interpersonal affect and the socialization of emotion. In: J. Cassidy and P. Shaver (Eds.), *Handbook of Attachment*. New York: Guilford Press.

Magyar, J., and Gergely, G. (1998). The obscure object of desire: "Nearly, but clearly not, like me." Perceiving self-generated contingencies in normal and autistic children. Poster, International Conference on Infant Studies, Atlanta, GA.

Mahler, M., and McDevitt, J. B. (1982). Thoughts on the emergence of the sense of self, with particular emphasis on the body self. *Journal of the American Psycho-Analytic Association, 30*, 827–848.

Mahler, M., Pine, F., and Bergman, A. (1975). *The Psychological Birth of the Human Infant: Symbiosis and Individuation*. New York: Basic Books.

Mahoney, M. J., and Freeman, A. T. (Eds.) (1985). *Cognition and Psychotherapy*. New York: Plenum Press.

Main, M. (1991). Metacognitive knowledge, metacognitive monitoring, and singular (coherent) vs. multiple (incoherent) model of attachment: Findings and directions for future research. In: C. M. Parkes, J. Stevenson-Hinde, and P. Marris (Eds.), *Attachment across the Life Cycle* (pp. 127–159). London: Tavistock/Routledge.

Main, M. (1997). Attachment narratives and attachment across the lifespan. Paper presented at the Fall Meeting of the American Psychoanalytic Association, New York.

Main, M., and Cassidy, J. (1988). Categories of response to reunion with the parent at age 6: Predictable from infant attachment classifications and stable over a 1-month period. *Developmental Psychology, 24*, 415–426.

Main, M., and Goldwyn, R. (1991). *Adult Attachment Classification System, Version 5*. Berkeley, CA: University of California, Berkeley.

Main, M., and Goldwyn, R. (1994). Adult attachment rating and classification system. Manual in draft version 6.0. Berkeley, CA: University of California, Berkeley, unpublished manuscript.

Main, M., and Hesse, E. (1990). Parents' unresolved traumatic experiences are related to infant disorganized attachment status: Is frightened and/or frightening parental behavior the linking mechanism? In: M. Greenberg, D. Cicchetti, and E. M. Cummings (Eds.), *Attachment in the Preschool Years: Theory, Research and Intervention* (pp. 161–182). Chicago, IL: University of Chicago Press.

Main, M., and Hesse, E. (1992). Disorganized/disoriented infant behavior in the Strange Situation, lapses in the monitoring of reasoning and discourse during the parent's Adult Attachment Interview, and dissociative states. In: M. Ammaniti and D. Stern (Eds.), *Attach-*

ment and Psychoanalysis (pp. 86–140). Rome: Gius, Laterza and Figli.

Main, M., Kaplan, N., and Cassidy, J. (1985). Security in infancy, childhood and adulthood: A move to the level of representation. *Growing Points of Attachment Theory and Research*, ed. by I. Bretherton and E. Waters. *Monographs of the Society for Research in Child Development, 50* (Serial 209, 1–2), 66–104.

Main, M., and Solomon, J. (1990). Procedures for identifying infants as disorganized/disoriented during the Ainsworth Strange Situation. In: M. Greenberg, D. Cicchetti, and E. M. Cummings (Eds.), *Attachment during the Preschool Years: Theory, Research and Intervention* (pp. 121–160). Chicago, IL: University of Chicago Press.

Main, T. (1957). The ailment. *British Journal of Medical Psychology, 30*, 129–145.

Malatesta, C. Z., Culver, C., Tesman, J. R., and Shepard, B. (1989). The development of emotion expression during the first two years of life. *Monographs of the Society for Research in Child Development, 54*, 1–104.

Malatesta, C. Z., and Izard, C. E. (1984). The ontogenesis of human social signals: From biological imperative to symbol utilization. In: N. A. Fox and R. J. Davison (Eds.), *The Psychobiology of Affective Development* (pp. 161–206). Hillsdale, NJ: Lawrence Erlbaum.

Maldonado-Duràn, M., Helmig, L., Moody, C., and Millhuff, C. (in press). Difficoltà iniziali d'alimentazione e la loro correlazione con le disordine di regulazione [Early feeding difficulties and their correlation with regulatory disorders]. *Psychiatria de l'infanza e del'adolescenza*.

Maldonado-Duràn, M., Helmig Bram, L., Moody, C., Fonagy, P., Fultz, J., Velissarios Karacostas, T. L., Millhuff, C., and Glinka, J. (in press). The Zero to Three diagnostic classification in an infant mental health clinic. Its usefulness and challenges. *Infant Mental Health Journal*.

Mandler, G. (1984). *Mind and Body: Psychology of Emotion and Stress*. New York: Norton.

Mandler, G. (1985). *Cognitive Psychology: An Essay in Cognitive Science*. Hillsdale, NJ: Lawrence Erlbaum.

Marans, S., Mayes, L., Cicchetti, D., Dahl, K., et al. (1991). The child-psychoanalytic play interview: A technique for studying thematic content. *Journal of the American Psychoanalytic Association, 39*, 1015–1036.

Marenco, S., and Weinberger, D. R. (2000). The neurodevelopmental hypothesis of schizophrenia: Following a trail of evidence from cradle to grave. *Developmental Psychopathology, 12* (3), 501–527.

Marty, P. (1968). A major process of somatization: The progressive disorganization. *International Journal of Psycho-Analysis, 49,* 246–249.

Marty, P. (1990). *La psychosomatique de l'adulte.* Paris: Presses Universitaires de France.

Marty, P. (1991). *Mentalization et Psychosomatique.* Paris: Laboratoire Delagrange.

Marvin, R. S., and Britner, P. A. (1999). Normative development: The ontogeny of attachment. In: J. Cassidy and P. R. Shaver (Eds.), *Handbook of Attachment: Theory, Research and Clinical Applications* (pp. 44–67). New York: Guilford Press.

Masten, A. S., and Braswell, L. (1991). Developmental psychopathology: An integrative framework for understanding behavior problems in children and adolescents. In: P. R. Martin (Ed.), *Handbook of Behavior Therapy and Psychological Science: An Integrative Approach.* New York: Pergamon Press.

Masten, A. S., and Garmezy, M. (1985). Risk, vulnerability and protective factors in developmental psychopathology. In: B. B. Lahey and A. E. Kazdin (Eds.), *Advances in Clinical Child Psychology* (pp. 1–52). New York: Plenum Press.

Matas, L., Arend, R. A., and Sroufe, L. A. (1978). Continuity of adaptation in the second year: The relationship between quality of attachment and later competent functioning. *Child Development, 49,* 547–556.

Mayes, L. C., and Cohen, D. J. (1992). The development of a capacity for imagination in early childhood. *Psychoanalytic Study of the Child, 47,* 23–48.

McDougall, J. (1978). *Plea for a Measure of Abnormality.* New York: International Universities Press.

McDougall, J. (1989). *Theaters of the Body: A Psychoanalytic Approach to Psychosomatic Illness.* New York: Norton.

McLoyd, V. C. (1990). The impact of economic hardship on black families and children: Psychological distress, parenting, and socioemotional development. *Child Development, 61,* 311–346.

McLoyd, V. C. (1998). Socioeconomic disadvantage and child development. *American Psychologist, 53,* 185–204.

Mead, G. H. (1934). *Mind, Self and Society.* Chicago, IL: University of Chicago Press.

Meichenbaum, D. (1997). The evolution of a cognitive-behavior therapist. In: J. K. Zeig (Ed.), *The Evolution of Psychotherapy: The Third Conference* (pp. 95–104). New York: Brunner/Mazel.

Meins, E., Fernyhough, C., Russel, J., and Clark-Carter, D. (1998). Security of attachment as a predictor of symbolic and mentalizing abilities: A longitudinal study. *Social Development, 7,* 1–24.

Mele, A. R. (1992). *Springs of Action: Understanding Intentional Behavior.* New York: Oxford University Press.

Meltzoff, A. N. (1990). Foundations for developing a concept of self: The role of imitation in relating self to other and the value of social mirroring, social modeling and self practice in infancy. In: D. Cicchetti and M. Beeghly (Eds.), *The Self in Transition: Infancy to Childhood.* Chicago, IL: University of Chicago Press.

Meltzoff, A. N. (1995). Understanding the intentions of others: Re-enactment of intended acts by 18-month-old children. *Developmental Psychology, 31,* 838–850.

Meltzoff, A. N., and Gopnik, A. (1993). The role of imitation in understanding persons and developing a theory of mind. In: S. Baron-Cohen, H. Tager-Flusberg, and D. Cohen (Eds.), *Understanding Other Minds: Perspectives from Autism* (pp. 335–366). New York: Oxford University Press.

Meltzoff, A. N., and Moore, M. K. (1977). Imitation of facial and manual gestures by human neonates. *Science, 198,* 75–78.

Meltzoff, A. N., and Moore, M. K. (1989). Imitation in newborn infants: Exploring the range of gestures imitated and the underlying mechanisms. *Developmental Psychology, 25,* 954–962.

Meltzoff, A. N., and Moore, M. K. (1997). Explaining facial imitation: Theoretical model. *Early Development and Parenting, 6,* 179–192.

Meltzoff, A. N., and Moore, M. K. (1998). Infant intersubjectivity: Broadening the dialogue to include imitation, identity and intention. In: S. Braten (Ed.), *Intersubjective Communication and Emotion in Early Ontogeny* (pp. 47–62). Cambridge, U.K.: Cambridge University Press.

Menzel, E., Savage-Rumbaugh, E. S., and Lawson, J. (1985). Chimpanzee (Pan troglodytes) spatial problem solving with the use of mirrors and televised equivalents of mirrors. *Journal of Comparative Psychology, 99,* 211–217.

Michels, R. (1984). Introduction to panel: Perspectives on the nature of psychic reality. *Journal of the American Psychoanalytic Association, 32,* 515–519.

Miles, D., and Carey, G. (1997). Genetic and environmental architecture of human aggression. *Journal of Personality and Social Psychology, 72,* 207–217.

Miller, N. E. (1969). Learning visceral and glandular responses. *Science, 163,* 434–445.

Miller, N. E. (1978). Biofeedback and visceral learning. *Annual Review of Psychology, 29,* 373–404.

Minuchin, S., Baker, L., Rosman, B. L., Liebman, R., Milman, L., and Todd, T. (1975). A conceptual model of psychosomatic illness in children: Family organization and family therapy. *Archives of General Psychiatry, 32,* 1031–1038.

Mischel, W. (1973). Toward a cognitive social learning reconceptualization of personality. *Psychological Review, 80,* 252–283.

Mitchell, P., and Lacohé, H. (1991). Children's early understanding of false belief. *Cognition, 39,* 107–127.

Mitchell, P., and Riggs, K. J. (Eds.) (2000). *Children's Reasoning and the Mind.* Hove, Sussex, U.K.: Psychology Press.

Mitchell, R. W. (1993). Mental models of mirror self-recognition: Two theories. *New Ideas in Psychology, 11,* 295–325.

Mitchell, S. A. (1997). *Influence and Autonomy in Psychoanalysis.* Hillsdale, NJ: Analytic Press.

Mitchell, S. A. (2000). *Relationality: From Attachment to Intersubjectivity.* Hillsdale, NJ: Analytic Press.

Modell, A. (1963). Primitive object relationships and the predisposition to schizophrenia. *International Journal of Psycho-Analysis, 44,* 282–292.

Moore, C., and Corkum, V. (1994). Social understanding at the end of the first year of life. *Developmental Review, 14,* 349–372.

Moran, G. (1984). Psychoanalytic treatment of diabetic children. *Psychoanalytic Study of the Child, 38,* 265–293.

Morris, H., Gunderson, J. G., and Zanarini, M. C. (1986). Transitional object use and borderline psychopathology. *American Journal of Psychiatry, 143,* 1534–1538.

Morton, J., and Frith, U. (1995). Causal modeling: A structural approach to developmental psychology. In: D. Cicchetti and D. J. Cohen (Eds.), *Developmental Psychopathology, Vol. 1. Theory and Methods* (pp. 357–390). New York: John Wiley.

Morton, J., and Johnson, M. H. (1991). CONSPEC and CONLEARN: A two-process theory of infant face recognition. *Psychological Review, 98,* 164–181.

Moses, L. J., and Flavell, J. H. (1990). Inferring false beliefs from actions and reactions. *Child Development, 61,* 929–945.

Moss, E., Parent, S., and Gosselin, C. (1995). Attachment and theory of mind: Cognitive and metacognitive correlates of attachment during the preschool period. Paper presented at the Biennial Meeting of the Society for Research in Child Development, Indianapolis, Indiana (March–April).

Muir, D., and Hains, S. (1999). Young infants' perception of adult intentionality: Adult contingency and eye direction. In: P. Rochat (Ed.), *Early Social Cognition* (pp. 155–187). Mahwah, NJ: Lawrence Erlbaum.

Mundy, P., and Hogan, A. (1994). Intersubjectivity, joint attention, and autistic developmental pathology. In: D. Cicchetti and S. L. Toth (Eds.), *Rochester Symposium on Developmental Psychopathology, Vol. 5. Disorders and Dysfunctions of the Self* (pp. 1–30). Rochester, NY: University of Rochester Press.

Murphy, C. M., and Messer, D. J. (1977). Mothers, infants and pointing: A study of a gesture. In: H. R. Schaffer (Ed.), *Studies in Mother–Infant Interaction.* London: Academic Press.

Murray, L. (1992). The impact of postnatal depression on infant development. *Journal of Child Psychology and Psychiatry and Allied Disciplines, 33,* 543–561.

Murray, L., and Trevarthen, C. (1985). Emotional regulation of interactions between two-month-olds and their mothers. In: T. M. Field and N. A. Fox (Eds.), *Social Perception in Infants.* Norwood, NJ: Ablex.

Nadel, J., Carchon, I., Kervella, C., Marcelli, D., and Reserbat-Plantey, D. (1999). Expectations for social contingency in 2-month-olds. *Developmental Science, 2,* 164–173.

Nadel, J., and Tremblay-Leveau, H. (1999). Early perception of social contingencies and interpersonal intentionality: Dyadic and triadic paradigms. In: P. Rochat (Ed.), *Early Social Cognition* (pp. 189–212). Mahwah, NJ: Lawrence Erlbaum.

Neiderhiser, J., Reiss, D., and Hetherington, E. M. (1996). Genetically informative designs for distinguishing developmental pathways during adolescence: Responsible and antisocial behavior. *Developmental Psychopathology, 8,* 779–791.

Neisser, U. (1988). Five kinds of self-knowledge. *Philosophical Psychology, 1,* 35–59.

Neisser, U. (1991). Two perceptually given aspects of the self and their development. *Developmental Review, 11,* 197–209.

Nelson, C. (1987). The recognition of facial expressions in the first two years of life: Mechanisms of development. *Child Development, 58,* 889–909.

Nelson, K. (1992). The emergence of autobiographical memory at age 4. *Human Development, 35,* 172–177.

Nelson, K. (1993). The psychological and social origins of autobiographical memory. *Psychological Science, 4,* 7–14.

Neu, J. (1992). Genetic explanation in *Totem and Taboo.* In: R. Wollheim

(Ed.), *Freud: A Collection of Critical Essays* (pp. 366–393). Garden City, NY: Anchor Books.

Nguyen, P. V., Abel, T., and Kandel, E. R. (1994). Requirement of a critical period of transcription for induction of a late phase of LTP. *Science, 265,* 1104–1107.

Nigg, J. T., and Goldsmith, H. H. (1998). Developmental psychopathology, personality, and temperament: Reflections on recent behavioral genetics research. *Human Biology, 70,* 387–412.

Noam, G. G. (1990). Beyond Freud and Piaget: Biographical world—interpersonal self. In: T. E. Wren (Ed.), *The Moral Domain* (pp. 360–399). Cambridge, MA: MIT Press.

Nussbaum, M. (1994). *The Therapy of Desire.* Princeton, NJ: Princeton University Press.

Oakley, J. (1992). *Morality and the Emotions.* London: Routledge.

Oatley, K., and Johnson-Laird, P. N. (1987). Towards a cognitive theory of emotions. *Cognition and Emotion, 1,* 29–50.

O'Connell, S. (1998). *Mindreading: An Investigation of How We Learn to Love and Lie.* London: Arrow Books.

O'Connor, T. G., Caspi, A., DeFries, J. C., and Plomin, R. (2000). Are associations between parental divorce and children's adjustment genetically mediated? An adoption study. *Developmental Psychology, 36,* 419–428.

O'Connor, T. G., Deater-Deckard, K., Fulker, D., Rutter, M., and Plomin, R. (1998). Genotype–environment correlations in late childhood and early adolescence: Antisocial behavioral problems and coercive parenting. *Developmental Psychology, 34,* 970–981.

Ogden, T. (1979). On projective identification. *International Journal of Psycho-Analysis, 60,* 357–373.

Ogden, T. (1985). On potential space. *International Journal of Psycho-Analysis, 66,* 129–141.

Olds, D., Henderson Jr., C. R., Cole, R., Eckenrode, J., Kitzman, H., Luckey, D., Pettitt, L., Sidora, K., Morris, P., and Powers, J. (1998). Long-term effects of nurse home visitation on children's criminal and antisocial behavior: 15-year follow-up of a randomized controlled trial. *Journal of the American Medical Association, 280,* 1238–1244.

Olson, D., and Campbell, R. (1993). Constructing representations. In: C. Pratt and A. F. Garton (Eds.), *Systems of Representation in Children: Development and Use* (pp. 11–26). New York: John Wiley.

Osher, Y., Hamer, D., and Benjamin, J. (2000). Association and linkage of anxiety-related traits with a functional polymorphism of the serotonin transporter gene regulatory region in Israeli sibling pairs. *Molecular Psychiatry, 5* (2), 216–219.

Oster, H. (1978). Facial expression and affect development. In: *The Development of Affect* (pp. 43–76). New York: Plenum Press.

Oster, H., Hegley, D., and Nagel, L. (1992). Adult judgements and fine-grained analysis of infant facial expressions: Testing the validity of a priori coding formulas. *Developmental Psychology, 28*, 1115–1131.

Oster, H., and Rosenstein, D. (in press). *Baby FACS: Analyzing Facial Movements in Infants.* Palo Alto, CA: Consulting Psychologists Press.

Owen, M. T., and Cox, M. J. (1997). Marital conflict and the development of infant–parent attachment relationships. *Journal of Family Psychology, 11*, 152–164.

Pacherie, E. (1997). Motor-images, self-consciousness, and autism. In: J. Russell (Ed.), *Autism as an Executive Disorder* (pp. 215–255). Oxford: Oxford University Press.

Paikoff, R. L., and Brooks-Gunn, J. (1991). Do parent–child relationships change during puberty? *Psychological Bulletin, 110*, 47–66.

Pancake, V. (1985). Continuity between mother–infant attachment and ongoing dyadic peer relationships in preschool. Paper presented at the biennial meeting of the Society for Research in Child Development, Toronto (April).

Panksepp, J. (1998). *Affective Neuroscience: The Foundations of Human and Animal Emotions.* Oxford: Oxford University Press.

Papousek, H., and Papousek, M. (1974). Mirror-image and self recognition in young human infants: A new method of experimental analysis. *Developmental Psychobiology, 7*, 149–157.

Papousek, H., and Papousek, M. (1987). Intuitive parenting: A dialectic counterpart to the infant's integrative competence. In: J. D. Osofsky (Ed.), *Handbook of Infant Development* (pp. 669–720). New York: John Wiley.

Papousek, H., and Papousek, M. (1989). Forms and functions of vocal matching in interactions between mothers and their precanonical infants. *First Language, 9*, 137–158.

Paris, J., Zweig-Frank, H., and Guzder, H. (1993). The role of psychological risk factors in recovery from borderline personality disorder. *Comprehensive Psychiatry, 34*, 410–413.

Park, K., and Waters, E. (1989). Security of attachment and preschool friendships. *Child Development, 60*, 1076–1081.

Parker, G., Barrett, E., and Hickie, I. B. (1992). From nurture to network: Examining links between perceptions of parenting received in childhood and social bonds in adulthood. *American Journal of Psychiatry, 149*, 877–885.

Parker, S. T., Mitchell, R. W., and Boccia, M. L. (Eds.) (1994). *Self-Awareness in Animals and Humans: Developmental Perspectives.* New York: Cambridge University Press.

Patrick, M., Hobson, R. P., Castle, D., Howard, R., and Maughan, B. (1994). Personality disorder and the mental representation of early social experience. *Developmental Psychopathology, 6*, 375–388.

Patterson, G. R. (1976). *Living with Children: New Methods for Parents and Teachers* (rev. ed.). Champaign, IL: Research Press.

Patterson, G. R. (1982). *Coercive Family Processes*. Eugene, OR: Castalia.

Perner, J. (1990). Experiential awareness and children's episodic memory. In: W. Schneider and F. E. Weinert (Eds.), *Interactions among Aptitudes, Strategies, and Knowledge in Cognitive Performance* (pp. 3–11). New York: Springer-Verlag.

Perner, J. (1991). *Understanding the Representational Mind*. Cambridge, MA: MIT Press.

Perner, J. (2000a). About + Belief + Counterfactual. In: P. Mitchell and K. J. Riggs (Eds.), *Children's Reasoning and the Mind* (pp. 367–401). Hove, Sussex, U.K.: Psychology Press.

Perner, J. (2000b). Memory and theory of mind. In: E. Tulving and F. I. M. Craik (Eds.), *The Oxford Handbook of Memory* (pp. 297–312). Oxford: Oxford University Press.

Perner, J., and Lang, B. (1999). Development of theory of mind and executive control. *Trends in Cognitive Sciences, 3* (9), 337–344.

Perner, J., Leekam, S. R., and Wimmer, H. (1987). Three-year-olds' difficulty in understanding false belief: Cognitive limitation, lack of knowledge, or pragmatic misunderstanding? *British Journal of Developmental Psychology, 5*, 125–137.

Perner, J., Ruffman, T., and Leekam, S. R. (1994). Theory of mind is contagious: You catch it from your sibs. *Child Development, 65*, 1228–1238.

Perry, B. (1997). Incubated in terror: Neurodevelopmental factors in the "cycle of violence." In: J. Osofsky (Ed.), *Children in a Violent Society* (pp. 124–149). New York: Guilford Press.

Perry, D. G., Perry, L. C., and Kennedy, E. (1992). Conflict and the development of antisocial behavior. In: C. U. Shantz and W. W. Hartup (Eds.), *Conflict in Child and Adolescent Development* (pp. 301–329). Cambridge, U.K.: Cambridge University Press.

Petit, G. S., Bates, J. E., and Dodge, K. A. (1997). Supportive parenting, ecological context, and children's adjustment: A seven year longitudinal study. *Child Development, 68*, 908–923.

Pettersen, L., Yonas, A., and Fisch, R. O. (1980). The development of blinking in response to impending collision in preterm, full-term and postterm infants. *Infant Behavior and Development, 3*, 155–165.

Piaget, J. (1936). *The Origins of Intelligence in Children.* New York: International Universities Press, 1952.

Pickens, J., and Field, T. (1993). Facial expressivity in infants of depressed mothers. *Developmental Psychology, 29,* 986–988.

Pillemer, D. B., and White, S. H. (1989). Childhood events recalled by children and adults. In: H. V. Reese (Ed.), *Advances in Child Development and Behavior, Vol. 21* (pp. 297–340). New York: Academic Press.

Pinker, S. (1997). *How the Mind Works.* New York: Norton.

Pipp-Siegel, S., Siegel, C. H., and Dean, J. (1999). Neurological aspects of the disorganized/disoriented attachment classification system: Differentiating quality of the attachment relationship from neurological impairment. *Atypical Attachment in Infancy and Early Childhood among Children at Developmental Risk,* ed. by J. Vondra and D. Barnett. *Monographs of the Society for Research in Child Development, 64,* 25–44.

Plomin, R. (1994). *Genetics and Experience: The Interplay between Nature and Nurture.* Thousand Oaks, CA: Sage.

Plomin, R., and Bergeman, C. S. (1991). The nature of nurture: Genetic influences on "environmental" measures. *Behavior and Brain Sciences, 14,* 373–386.

Plomin, R., Chipuer, H. M., and Neiderhiser, J. M. (1994). Behavioral genetic evidence for the importance of non-shared environment. In: E. M. Hetherington, D. Reiss, and R. Plomin (Eds.), *Separate Social Worlds of Siblings* (pp. 1–31). Hillsdale, NJ: Lawrence Erlbaum.

Plomin, R., and Daniels, D. (1987). Why are children in the same family so different from one another? *Behavioral and Brain Sciences, 10,* 1–16.

Plomin, R., DeFries, J. C., McLearn, G. E., and Rutter, R. (1997). *Behavioral Genetics* (3rd ed.). New York: W.H. Freeman.

Plomin, R., Fulker, D. W., Corley, R., and DeFries, J. C. (1997). Nature, nurture, and cognitive development from 1 to 16 years: A parent-offspring adoption study. *Psychological Science, 8,* 442–447.

Plotsky, P. M., and Meaney, M. J. (1993). Early, postnatal experience alters hypothalamic corticotropin-releasing factor (CRF) mRNA, median eminence CRF content and stress-induced release in adult rats. *Brain Research. Molecular Brain Research, 18,* 195–200.

Polan, H. J., and Hofer, M. (1999). Psychobiological origins of infant attachment and separation responses. In: J. Cassidy and P. R. Shaver (Eds.), *Handbook of Attachment: Theory, Research and Clinical Applications* (pp. 162–180). New York: Guilford Press.

Povinelli, D. J., and Eddy, T. J. (1995). The unduplicated self. In: P.

Rochat (Ed.), *The Self in Infancy: Theory and Research* (pp. 161–192). Amsterdam: Elsevier.

Povinelli, D. J., Landau, K. R., and Perilloux, H. K. (1996). Self-recognition in young children using delayed versus live feedback: Evidence for a developmental asynchrony. *Child Development, 67,* 1540–1554.

Povinelli, D. J., Landry, A. M., Theall, L. A., Clark, B. R., and Castille, C. M. (1999). Development of young children's understanding that the recent past is causally bound to the present. *Developmental Psychology, 35,* 1426–1439.

Povinelli, D. J., and Simon, B. B. (1998). Young children's understanding of briefly versus extremely delayed images of the self: Emergence of the autobiographical stance. *Developmental Psychology, 34,* 188–194.

Power, M., and Dalgleish, T. (1997). *Cognition and Emotion.* Hove, Sussex, U.K.: Psychology Press.

Premack, D. (1990). The infant's theory of self-propelled objects. *Cognition, 36,* 1–16.

Premack, D., and Premack, A. J. (1995). Intention as psychological cause. In: D. Sperber, D. Premack, and A. J. Premack (Eds.), *Causal Cognition: A Multidisciplinary Debate* (pp. 185–199). Oxford: Clarendon Press.

Prinz, W. (1997). Perception and action planning. *European Journal of Cognitive Psychology, 9,* 129–154.

Pulver, S. (1971). Can affects be unconscious. *International Journal of Psycho-Analysis, 52,* 347–354.

Quine, W. V. O. (1960). *Word and Object.* Cambridge, MA: MIT Press.

Quinton, D., Rutter, M., and Liddle, C. (1984). Institutional rearing, parenting difficulties, and marital support. *Psychological Medicine, 14,* 107–124.

Rapaport, D. (1953). On the psychoanalytic theory of affects. In: *The Collected Papers of David Rapaport.* New York: Basic Books, 1967.

Reddy, V. (1991). Playing with others' expectations: Teasing and mucking about in the first year. In: A. Whiten (Ed.), *Natural Theories of Mind: Evolution, Development and Simulation of Everyday Mindreading* (pp. 143–158). Oxford: Blackwell.

Reiss, D., Hetherington, E. M., Plomin, R., Howe, G. W., Simmens, S. J., Henderson, S. H., O'Connor, T. J., Bussell, D. A., Anderson, E. R., and Law, T. (1995). Genetic questions for environmental studies: Differential parenting and psychopathology in adolescence. *Archives of General Psychiatry, 52,* 925–936.

Reiss, D., Neiderhiser, J., Hetherington, E. M., and Plomin, R. (2000).

The Relationship Code: Deciphering Genetic and Social Patterns in Adolescent Development. Cambridge, MA: Harvard University Press.

Repacholi, B. M., and Gopnik, A. (1997). Early reasoning about desires: Evidence from 14- and 18-month-olds. *Developmental Psychology, 33*, 12–21.

Rey, J. H. (1979). Schizoid phenomena in the borderline. In: A. Capponi (Ed.), *Advances in the Psychotherapy of the Borderline Patient* (pp. 449–484). New York: Jason Aronson.

Reznick, J. S. (1999). Influences on maternal attribution of infant intentionality. In: P. D. Zelazo, J. Astington, and D. R. Olson (Eds.), *Developing Theories of Intention* (pp. 243–269). Mahwah, NJ: Lawrence Erlbaum.

Ricketts, M. H., Hamer, R. M., Sage, J. I., Manowitz, P., Feng, F., and Menza, M. A. (1998). Association of a serotonin transporter gene promoter polymorphism with harm avoidance behavior in an elderly population. *Psychiatric Genetics, 8* (2), 41–44.

Riviere, J. (1936). On the genesis of psychical conflict in early infancy. *International Journal of Psycho-Analysis, 55*, 397–404.

Robbins, W. T., and Everitt, B. J. (1999). Motivation and reward. In: M. J. Zigmond, F. E. Bloom, S. C. Landis, J. L. Roberts, and L. R. Squire (Eds.), *Fundamental Neuroscience* (pp. 1246–1260). San Diego, CA: Academic Press.

Rochat, P., and Morgan, R. (1995). Spatial determinants in the perception of self-produced leg movements in 3- to 5-month-old infants. *Developmental Psychology, 31*, 626–636.

Rochat, P., Neisser, U., and Marian, V. (1998). Are young infants sensitive to interpersonal contingency? *Infant Behavior and Development, 21* (2), 355–366.

Rochat, P., and Striano, T. (1999). Social–cognitive development in the first year. In: P. Rochat (Ed.), *Early Social Cognition* (pp. 3–34). Mahwah, NJ: Lawrence Erlbaum.

Rogers, R. D., Everitt, B. J., Baldacchino, A., Blackshaw, A. J., Swainson, R., Wynne, K., Baker, N. B., Hunter, J., Carthy, T., Booker, E., London, M., Deakin, J. F., Sahakian, B. J., and Robbins, T. W. (1999). Dissociable deficits in the decision-making cognition of chronic amphetamine abusers, opiate abusers, patients with focal damage to prefrontal cortex, and tryptophan-depleted normal volunteers: Evidence for monoaminergic mechanisms. *Neuropsychopharmacology, 20* (4), 322–339.

Rogers, S., and Pennington, B. (1991). A theoretical approach to the deficits in infantile autism. *Development and Psychopathology, 3*, 137–162.

Rogoff, B. (1990). *Apprenticeship in Thinking: Cognitive Development in Social Contexts.* New York: Oxford University Press.

Rorty, A., and Flanagan, O. (Eds.) (1990). *Identity, Character and Morality.* Cambridge, MA: MIT Press.

Rosenfeld, H. (1964). On the psychopathology of narcissism: A clinical approach. *International Journal of Psycho-Analysis, 45,* 332–337.

Rosenfeld, H. (1971). Contribution to the psychopathology of psychotic states: The importance of projective identification in the ego structure and object relations of the psychotic patient. In: E. B. Spillius (Ed.), *Melanie Klein Today* (pp. 117–137). London: Routledge, 1988.

Rosenfeld, H. (1987). *Impasse and Interpretation.* London: Tavistock Publications.

Rosenthal, N. E., Mazzanti, C. M., Barnett, R. L., Hardin, T. A., Turner, E. H., Lam, G. K., Ozaki, N., and Goldman, D. (1998). Role of serotonin transporter promoter repeat length polymorphism (5-HTTLPR) in seasonality and seasonal affective disorder. *Molecular Psychiatry, 3* (2), 175–177.

Rotter, J. B. (1966). Generalized expectancies for internal versus external control of reinforcement. *Psychological Monographs, 80* (1).

Rovee-Collier, C. K. (1987). Learning and memory in infancy. In: J. D. Osofsky (Ed.), *Handbook of Infant Development* (2nd ed.). New York: John Wiley.

Rowe, D. (1994). *The Limits of Family Influence: Genes, Experience and Behavior.* New York: Guilford Press.

Rowe, D., Stever, C., Giedinghagen, L. N., Gard, J. M., Cleveland, H. H., Terris, S. T., Mohr, J. H., Sherman, S., Abramovitz, A., and Waldman, I. D. (1998). Dopamine DRD4 receptor polymorphism and attention deficit hyperactivity disorder. *Molecular Psychiatry, 3,* 419–426.

Ruffman, T., Perner, J., Naito, M., Parkin, L., and Clements, W. (1998). Older (but not younger) siblings facilitate false belief understanding. *Developmental Psychology, 34* (1), 161–174.

Rumelhart, D. E., and McClelland, J. L. (1986). *Parallel Distributed Processing.* Cambridge, MA: MIT Press.

Russell, B. (1905). On denoting. *Mind, 14,* 479–493.

Russell, J. (1991). Culture and the categorization of emotions. *Psychological Bulletin, 110,* 426–450.

Russell, J. (1996). *Agency: Its Role in Mental Development.* Hove, Sussex, U.K.: Lawrence Erlbaum.

Russell, J. (1997). *Autism as an Executive Disorder.* Oxford: Oxford University Press.

Rutter, M. (1987). Psychosocial resilience and protective mechanisms. *American Journal of Orthopsychiatry, 57*, 316–331.

Rutter, M. (1993). Developmental psychopathology as a research perspective. In: D. Magnusson and P. Casaer (Eds.), *Longitudinal Research on Individual Development: Present Status and Future Perspectives* (pp. 127–152). New York: Cambridge University Press.

Rutter, M. (1999). Psychosocial adversity and child psychopathology. *British Journal of Psychiatry, 174*, 480–493.

Rutter, M., Dunn, J., Plomin, R., Simonoff, E., Pickles, A., Maughan, B., Ormel, J., Meyer, J., and Eaves, L. (1997). Integrating nature and nurture: Implications of person–environment correlations and interactions for developmental psychology. *Development and Psychopathology, 9*, 335–364.

Rutter, M., Silberg, J., O'Connor, T., and Simonoff, E. (1999a). Genetics and child psychiatry: I. Advances in quantitative and molecular genetics. *Journal of Child Psychology and Psychiatry and Allied Disciplines, 40*, 3–18.

Rutter, M., Silberg, J., O'Connor, T., and Simonoff, E. (1999b). Genetics and child psychiatry: II. empirical research findings. *Journal of Child Psychology and Psychiatry and Allied Disciplines, 40*, 19–55.

Ryle, A. (1997). *Cognitive Analytic Therapy and Borderline Personality Disorder: The Model and the Method.* Chichester, U.K.: John Wiley.

Sameroff, A. J. (1995). General systems theories and developmental psychopathology. In: J. Cicchetti and D. J. Cohen (Eds.), *Developmental Psychopathology: Vol. 1. Theory and Methods* (pp. 659–695). New York: John Wiley.

Sander, L. W. (1970). Regulation and organization of behavior in the early infant–caretaker system. In: R. Robinson (Ed.), *Brain and Early Behavior.* London: Academic Press.

Sandler, J. (1976). Countertransference and role-responsiveness. *International Review of Psycho-Analysis, 3*, 43–47.

Sandler, J. (1987). *Projection, Identification, Projective Identification.* London: Karnac.

Sandler, J. (1992). Reflections on developments in the theory of psychoanalytic technique. Paper presented at the Thirty-seventh Congress of the International Psychoanalytical Association: Psychic Change: Developments in the Theory of Psychoanalytic Technique, Buenos Aires, Argentina, 1991. *International Journal of Psycho-Analysis, 73* (2), 189–198.

Sandler, J., Dare, C., and Holder, A. (1992). *The Patient and the Analyst* (2nd ed.). London: Karnac.

Scarr, S. (1992). Developmental theories for the 1990s: Development and individual differences. *Child Development, 63*, 1–19.

Schachter, D. L. (1992). Understanding implicit memory: A cognitive neuroscience approach. *American Psychologist, 47*, 559–569.

Schachter, S., and Singer, J. (1962). Cognitive, social and physiological determinants of emotional state. *Psychological Review, 69*, 379–399.

Schmuckler, M. A. (1996). Visual-proprioceptive intermodal perception in infancy. *Infant Behavior and Development, 19*, 221–232.

Schneider-Rosen, K., and Cicchetti, D. (1984). The relationship between affect and cognition in maltreated infants: Quality of attachment and the development of visual self-recognition. *Child Development, 55*, 648–658.

Schneider-Rosen, K., and Cicchetti, D. (1991). Early self-knowledge and emotional development: Visual self-recognition and affective reactions to mirror self-image in maltreated and non-maltreated toddlers. *Developmental Psychology, 27*, 481–488.

Schneier, F. R., Liebowitz, M. R., Abi-Dargham, A., Zea-Ponce, Y., Lin, S.-H., and Laruelle, M. (2000). Low dopamine D_2 receptor binding potential in social phobia. *American Journal of Psychiatry, 157*, 457–459.

Schore, A. N. (1999). Commentary on Freud's affect theory in light of contemporary neuroscience. *Neuro-Psychoanalysis, 1*, 49–55.

Schuengel, C. (1997). *Attachment, Loss, and Maternal Behavior: A Study on Intergenerational Transmission.* Leiden, The Netherlands: University of Leiden Press.

Schuengel, C., Bakermans-Kranenburg, M., and van IJzendoorn, M. (1999). Frightening maternal behavior linking unresolved loss and disorganized infant attachment. *Journal of Consulting and Clinical Psychology, 67*, 54–63.

Searle, J. R. (1983). *Intentionality: An Essay in the Philosophy of the Mind.* Cambridge, U.K.: Cambridge University Press.

Segal, G. (1996). The modularity of theory of mind. In: P. Carruthers and P. K. Smith (Eds.), *Theories of Theories of Mind* (pp. 141–157). Cambridge, U.K.: Cambridge University Press.

Segal, H. (1957). Notes on symbol formation. *International Journal of Psycho-Analysis, 38*, 391–397.

Segal, H. (1964). *Introduction to the Work of Melanie Klein.* New York: Basic Books.

Sellars, W. (1963). *Science, Perception and Reality.* London: Routledge.

Serketich, W. J., and Dumas, J. E. (1996). The effectiveness of behavioral parent training to modify antisocial behavior in children: A meta-analysis. *Behavior Therapy, 27*, 171–186.

Shachnow, J., Clarkin, J., DiPalma, C. S., Thurston, F., Hull, J., and Shearin, E. (1997). Biparental psychopathology and borderline personality disorder. *Psychiatry, 60,* 171–181.

Sherman, N. (2000). Emotional agents. In: M. Levine (Ed.), *The Analytic Freud.* London: Routledge.

Shiffrin, R., and Schneider, W. (1977). Controlled and automatic human information processing: II. Perceptual learning, automatic attending, and a general theory. *Psychological Review, 84,* 127–190.

Shweder, R. (1994). "You're not sick, you're in love": Emotion as an interpretive system. In: P. Ekman and R. Davidson (Eds.), *The Nature of Emotion.* Oxford: Oxford University Press.

Slade, A. (1987). Quality of attachment and early symbolic play. *Developmental Psychology, 17,* 326–335.

Slade, A. (1999). Attachment theory and research: Implications for the theory and practice of individual psychotherapy with adults. In: J. Cassidy and P. Shaver (Eds.), *Handbook of Attachment.* New York: Guilford Press.

Slade, A., Belsky, J., Aber, L., and Phelps, J. L. (1999). Mothers' representations of their relationships with their toddlers: Links to adult attachment and observed mothering. *Developmental Psychology, 35* (3), 611–619.

Slade, A., Bernbach, E., Grienenberger, J., Wohlgemuth-Levy, D., and Locker, A. (1998). *Addendum to Reflective Functioning Scoring Manual (Fonagy, Steele, Steele, and Target): For Use with the Parent Development Interview (Aber, Slade, Berger, Bresgi, and Kaplan).* New York: City College.

Slomkowski, C., and Dunn, J. (1992). Arguments and relationships within the family: Differences in children's disputes with mother and sibling. *Developmental Psychology, 28,* 919–924.

Smalley, S. L. (1997). Genetic influences in childhood-onset psychiatric disorders: Autism and attention-deficit/hyperactivity disorder. *American Journal of Human Genetics, 60,* 1276–1282.

Smalley, S. L., Bailey, J. N., Palmer, C. G., Cantwell, D. P., McGough, J. J., Del'Homme, M. A., Asarnow, J. R., Woodward, J. A., Ramsey, C., and Nelson, S. F. (1998). Evidence that the dopamine D4 receptor is a susceptibility gene in attention deficit hyperactivity disorder. *Molecular Psychiatry, 3,* 427–430.

Smith, D. J. (1995). Youth crime and conduct disorders: Trends, patterns and causal explanations. In: M. Rutter and D. J. Smith (Eds.), *Psychosocial Disorders in Young People: Time Trends and Their Causes* (pp. 389–489). Chichester, U.K.: Academia Europea.

Smith, P. K. (1996). Language and the evolution of mind-reading. In: P.

Carruthers and P. K. Smith (Eds.), *Theories of Theories of Mind* (pp. 344–354). Cambridge, U.K.: Cambridge University Press.

Snow, C. E. (1972). Mothers' speech to children learning language. *Child Development, 43,* 549–566.

Solms, M. (1997a). *The Neuropsychology of Dreams: A Clinico-Anatomical Study.* Mahwah, NJ: Lawrence Erlbaum.

Solms, M. (1997b). What is consciousness? *Journal of the American Psychoanalytic Association, 45,* 681–703.

Solomon, J., and George, C. (1996). Defining the caregiving system: Toward a theory of caregiving. In: C. George and J. Solomon (Eds.), *Defining the Caregiving System (Infant Mental Health Journal, 17).* New York: John Wiley.

Solomon, J., and George, C. (1999). *Attachment Disorganization.* New York: Guilford Press.

Solomon, J., George, C., and Dejong, A. (1995). Children classified as controlling at age six: Evidence of disorganized representational strategies and aggression at home and at school. *Development and Psychopathology, 7,* 447–463.

Spangler, G., Fremmer-Bombrik, E., and Grossmann, K. E. (1996). Social and individual determinants of infant attachment security and disorganization. *Infant Mental Health Journal, 17,* 127–139.

Spangler, G., and Grossmann, K. E. (1993). Biobehavioral organization in securely and insecurely attached infants. *Child Development, 64,* 1439–1450.

Spelke, E. S., Phillips, A., and Woodward, A. L. (1995). Infants' knowledge of object motion and human action. In: D. Sperber, D. Premack, and A. J. Premack (Eds.), *Causal Cognition: A multidisciplinary Debate. Symposia of the Fyssen Foundation* (pp. 44–78). New York: Clarendon Press.

Spence, D. (1982). *Narrative Truth and Historical Truth. Meaning and Interpretation in Psychoanalysis.* New York/London: Norton.

Spence, D. (1984). *The Freudian Metaphor.* New York: Norton.

Sperber, D., and Wilson, D. (1995). *Relevance: Communication and Cognition.* Malden, MA: Blackwell.

Spillius, E. B. (1992). Clinical experiences of projective identification. In: R. Anderson (Ed.), *Clinical Lectures on Klein and Bion* (pp. 59–73). London: Routledge.

Spillius, E. B. (1994). Developments in Kleinian thought: Overview and personal view. *Psychoanalytic Inquiry, 14,* 324–364.

Spinoza, B. (1994). *The Ethics.* London: Penguin.

Spock, B., and Rothenberg, M. B. (1985). *Dr. Spock's Baby and Child Care* (5th ed.). London: W. H. Allen.

Squire, L. R. (1987). *Memory and Brain.* New York: Oxford University Press.

Sroufe, L. (1979). Socioemotional development. In: J. Osofsky (Ed.), *Handbook of Infant Development* (pp. 462–516). New York: John Wiley.

Sroufe, L. (1983). *Infant–Caregiver Attachment and Patterns of Adaptation in Preschool: The Roots of Maladaptation and Competence, Vol. 16.* Hillsdale, NJ: Lawrence Erlbaum.

Sroufe, L. (1986). Bowlby's contribution to psychoanalytic theory and developmental psychopathology. *Journal of Child Psychology and Psychiatry and Allied Disciplines, 27,* 841–849.

Sroufe, L. (1990). An organizational perspective on the self. In: D. Cicchetti and M. Beeghly (Eds.), *The Self in Transition: Infancy to Childhood* (pp. 281–307). Chicago, IL: University of Chicago Press.

Sroufe, L. (1996). *Emotional Development: The Organization of Emotional Life in the Early Years.* New York: Cambridge University Press.

Sroufe, L., and Rutter, M. (1984). The domain of developmental psychopathology. *Child Development, 83,* 173–189.

Sroufe, L., and Waters, E. (1977a). Attachment as an organizational construct. *Child Development, 48,* 1184–1199.

Sroufe, L., and Waters, E. (1977b). Heart rate as a convergent measure in clinical and developmental research. *Merrill-Palmer Quarterly, 23,* 3–28.

Steele, H. (1991). Adult personality characteristics and family relationships: The development and validation of an interview-based assessment. Ph.D. diss., University College London.

Steele, H., Steele, M., and Fonagy, P. (1996). Associations among attachment classifications of mothers, fathers, and their infants: Evidence for a relationship-specific perspective. *Child Development, 67,* 541–555.

Stein, A. (1994). An observational study of mothers with eating disorders and their infants. *Journal of Child Psychology and Psychiatry and Allied Disciplines, 35* (4), 733–748.

Stein, R. (1990). *Psychoanalytic Theories of Affect.* Westport, CT: Praeger.

Steiner, J. (1992). The equilibrium between the paranoid-schizoid and the depressive positions. In: R. Anderson (Ed.), *Clinical Lectures on Klein and Bion* (pp. 46–58). London: Routledge.

Steiner, J. (1993). *Psychic Retreats: Pathological Organisations in Psychotic, Neurotic and Borderline Patients.* London: Routledge.

Stern, D. (1977). *The First Relationship: Mother and Infant.* Cambridge, MA: Harvard University Press.

Stern, D. (1984). Affect attunement. In: J. D. Call, E. Galenson, and R. L. Tyson (Eds.), *Frontiers of Infant Psychiatry, Vol. 2* (pp. 3–14). New York: Basic Books.

Stern, D. (1985). *The Interpersonal World of the Infant: A View from Psychoanalysis and Developmental Psychology.* New York: Basic Books.

Stern, D. (1994). One way to build a clinically relevant baby. *Infant Mental Health Journal, 15,* 36–54.

Stern, D. (1995). Self/other differentiation in the domain of intimate socio-affective interaction: Some considerations. In: P. Rochat (Ed.), *The Self in Infancy: Theory and Research* (pp. 419–429). Amsterdam: Elsevier.

Stern, D. (1998). The process of therapeutic change involving implicit knowledge: Some implications of developmental observations for adult psychotherapy. *Infant Mental Health Journal, 19,* 300–308.

Stern, D., Hofer, L., Haft, W., and Dore, J. (1985). Affect attunement: The sharing of feeling states between mother and infant by means of inter-modal fluency. In: T. M. Fields and N. A. Fox (Eds.), *Social Perception in Infants.* Norwood, NJ: Ablex.

Stern, D., Sander, L., Nahum, J., Harrison, A., Lyons-Ruth, K., Morgan, A., Bruschweilerstern, N., and Tronick, E. (1998). Non-interpretive mechanisms in psychoanalytic therapy: The "something more" than interpretation. *International Journal of Psycho-Analysis, 79* (5), 903–921.

Stern, D., Spieker, S., Barnett, R., and Mackain, K. (1983). The prosody of maternal speech: Infant age and context related changes. *Journal of Child Language, 10,* 1–15.

Stocker, M., and Hegeman, E. (1996). *Valuing Emotions.* Cambridge, U.K.: Cambridge University Press.

Stuss, D. T. (1983). Emotional concomitants of psychosurgery. In: K. M. Heilman and P. Satz (Eds.), *Advances in Neuropsychology and Behavioral Neurology* (pp. 111–140). New York: Guilford Press.

Stuss, D. T. (1991). Self, awareness and the frontal lobes: A neuropsychological perspective. In: J. Strauss and G. R. Goethals (Eds.), *The Self: Interdisciplinary Approaches* (pp. 255–278). New York: Springer-Verlag.

Stuss, D. T., Gallup, G. G., and Alexander, M. P. (2001). The frontal lobes are necessary for "theory of mind." *Brain, 124* (2), 279–286.

Suomi, S. J. (1991). Up-tight and laid-back monkeys: Individual differences in the response to social challenges. In: S. Brauth, W. Hall, and R. Dooling (Eds.), *Plasticity of Development* (pp. 27–56). Cambridge, MA: MIT Press.

Suomi, S. J. (1997). Early determinants of behavior: Evidence from primate studies. *British Medical Bulletin, 53,* 170–184.

Suomi, S. J. (2000). A biobehavioral perspective on developmental psychopathology: Excessive aggression and serotonergic dysfunction in monkeys. In: A. J. Sameroff, M. Lewis, and S. Miller (Eds.), *Handbook of Developmental Psychopathology* (pp. 237–256). New York: Plenum Press.

Suomi, S. J., and Levine, S. (1998). Psychobiology of intergenerational effects of trauma. In: Y. Danieli (Ed.), *International Handbook of Multigenerational Legacies of Trauma* (pp. 623–637). New York: Plenum Press.

Swanson, J. M., Flodman, P., Kennedy, J., Spence, M. A., Moyzis, R., Schuck, S., Murias, M., Moriarty, J., Barr, C., Smith, M., and Posner, M. (2000). Dopamine genes and ADHD. *Neuroscience and Biobehavioral Reviews, 24* (1), 21–25.

Swanson, J. M., Sunohara, G. A., Kennedy, J. L., Regino, R., Fineberg, E., and Wigal, T. (1998). Association of the dopamine receptor D4 (DRD4) gene with a refined phenotype of attention deficit hyperactivity disorder (ADHD): A family-based approach. *Molecular Psychiatry, 3,* 38–41.

Target, M., and Fonagy, P. (1996). Playing with reality II: The development of psychic reality from a theoretical perspective. *International Journal of Psycho-Analysis, 77,* 459–479.

Taylor, C. (1985). *Philosophical Papers I: Human Agency and Language.* Cambridge, U.K.: Cambridge University Press.

Taylor, M., Gerow, L., and Carlson, S. M. (1993). The relation between individual differences in fantasy and theory of mind. Paper presented at the biennial meeting of the Society for Research in Child Development, New Orleans (March).

Thompson, A. E. (1985). The nature of emotion and its development. In: I. Fast (Ed.), *Event Theory: An Integration of Piaget and Freud.* Hillsdale, NJ: Lawrence Erlbaum.

Thompson, A. E. (1986). An object relational theory of affect maturity: Applications to the Thematic Apperception Test. In: M. Kissen (Ed.), *Assessing Object Relations Phenomena.* Madison, CT: International Universities Press.

Thompson, R. (1990). Emotion and self-regulation. In: R. Thompson (Ed.), *Socioemotional Development.* Lincoln, NE: Nebraska University Press.

Thompson, R. (1994). Emotion regulation: A theme in search of definition. *Monographs of the Society for Research in Child Development, 59,* 25–52.

Thompson, R. (1998). Empathy and its origins in early development. In: S. Braten (Ed.), *Intersubjective Communication and Emotion in Early Ontogeny* (pp. 144–157). Paris: Cambridge University Press.

Thompson, R. (1999). Early attachment and later development. In: J. Cassidy and P. R. Shaver (Eds.), *Handbook of Attachment: Theory, Research and Clinical Applications* (pp. 265–286). New York: Guilford Press.

Tienari, P., Wynne, L. C., Moring, J., Lahti, I., and Naarala, M. (1994). The Finnish adoptive family study of schizophrenia: Implications for family research. *British Journal of Psychiatry, 23* (Suppl. 164), 20–26.

Tobias, B. A., Kihlstrom, J. F., and Schachter, D. L. (1992). Emotion and implicit memory. In: S. Christianson (Ed.), *The Handbook of Emotion and Memory: Research and Theory* (pp. 67–92). Hillsdale, NJ: Lawrence Erlbaum.

Tolman, E. C., Ritchie, B. F., and Kalish, D. (1946). Studies in spatial learning: I. Orientation and the shortcut. *Journal of Experimental Psychology, 36,* 13–24.

Tomasello, M. (1993). On the interpersonal origins of the self. In: U. Neisser (Ed.), *The Perceived Self: Ecological and Interpersonal Sources of Self-Knowledge* (pp. 174–184). Cambridge, U.K.: Cambridge University Press.

Tomasello, M. (1995). Joint attention as social cognition. In: C. Moore and P. Dunham (Eds.), *Joint Attention: Its Origins and Role in Development* (pp. 103–130). New York: Lawrence Erlbaum.

Tomasello, M. (1999). *The Cultural Origins of Human Cognition.* Cambridge, MA: Harvard University Press.

Tomasello, M., and Call, J. (1997). *Primate Cognition.* Oxford: Oxford University Press.

Tomasello, M., Strosberg, R., and Akhtar, N. (1996). Eighteen-month-old children learn words in non-ostensive contexts. *Journal of Child Language, 23,* 157–176.

Tomkins, S. (1995a). *Exploring Affect: The Selective Writings of Silvan Tomkins.* Cambridge, U.K.: Cambridge University Press.

Tomkins, S. (1995b). *Shame and Its Sisters: A Silvan Tomkins Reader.* Durham, NC: Duke University Press.

Trevarthen, C. (1979). Communication and cooperation in early infancy: A description of primary intersubjectivity. In: M. M. Bullowa (Ed.), *Before Speech: The Beginning of Interpersonal Communication.* New York: Cambridge University Press.

Trevarthen, C. (1980). The foundations of intersubjectivity: Development of interpersonal and cooperative understanding in infants. In:

D. R. Olson (Ed.), *The Social Foundations of Language and Thought: Essays in Honor of Jerome Bruner*. New York: Norton.

Trevarthen, C. (1993). The self born in intersubjectivity: An infant communicating. In: U. Neisser (Ed.), *The Perceived Self* (pp. 121–173). New York: Cambridge University Press.

Trevarthen, C., and Hubley, P. (1978). Secondary intersubjectivity: Confidence, confiding and acts of meaning in the first year. In: A. Lock (Ed.), *Action, Gesture and Symbol: The Emergence of Language*. New York: Academic Press.

Trivers, R. (1971). The evolution of reciprocal altruism. *Quarterly Review of Biology, 46*, 35–57.

Tronick, E. (1989). Emotions and emotional communication in infants. *American Psychologist, 44*, 112–119.

Tronick, E. (1998). Dyadically expanded states of consciousness and the process of therapeutic change. *Infant Mental Health Journal, 19*, 290–299.

Tronick, E., Als, H., Adamson, L., Wise, S., and Brazelton, T. (1978). The infant's response to entrapment between contradictory messages in face-to-face interaction. *Journal of Child Psychiatry, 17*, 1–13.

Tronick, E., Als, H., and Brazelton, T. (1977). Mutuality in mother–infant interaction. *Journal of Communication, 27*, 74–79.

Tronick, E., and Cohn, J. F. (1989). Infant–mother face-to-face interaction: Age and gender differences in coordination and the occurrence of miscoordination. *Child Development, 60*, 85–92.

Tronick, E., Ricks, M., and Cohn, J. F. (1982). Maternal and infant affective exchange: Patterns of adaptation. In: T. Field and A. Fogel (Eds.), *Emotion and Early Interaction* (pp. 83–100). Hillsdale, NJ: Lawrence Erlbaum.

Turkheimer, E. (1998). Heritability and biological explanation. *Psychological Review, 105*, 1–10.

Uhl, G., Blum, K., Noble, E. P., and Smith, S. (1993). Substance abuse vulnerability and D2 receptor genes. *Trends in Neuroscience, 16*, 83–88.

Uzgiris, I. C., Benson, J. B., Kruper, J., and Vasek, M. E. (1989). Contextual influences on imitative interactions between mothers and infants. In: J. Lockman and N. L. Hazen (Eds.), *Action in Social Context: Perspectives on Early Development* (pp. 103–127). New York: Plenum Press.

Uzgiris, I. C., and Hunt, J. M. (1975). *Assessment in Infancy: Ordinal Scales of Psychological Development*. Chicago, IL: University of Chicago Press.

van der Kolk, B. (1994). The body keeps the score: Memory and the evolving psychobiology of post-traumatic stress. *Harvard Review of Psychiatry, 1,* 253–265.

van IJzendoorn, M. H. (1995). Adult attachment representations, parental responsiveness, and infant attachment: A meta-analysis on the predictive validity of the Adult Attachment Interview. *Psychological Bulletin, 117,* 387–403.

van IJzendoorn, M. H., Juffer, F., and Duyvesteyn, M. G. C. (1995). Breaking the intergenerational cycle of insecure attachment: A review of the effects of attachment-based interventions on maternal sensitivity and infant security. *Journal of Child Psychology and Psychiatry and Allied Disciplines, 36,* 225–248.

van IJzendoorn, M. H., Kranenburg, M. J., Zwart-Woudstra, H. A., Van Busschbach, A. M., and Lambermon, M. W. E. (1991). Parental attachment and children's socio-emotional development: Some findings on the validity of the Adult Attachment Interview in the Netherlands. *International Journal of Behavioral Development, 14,* 375–394.

Van Tol, H. H. M., Wu, C. M., Guan, H. C., Ohara, K., Bunzow, J. R., and Civelli, O. (1992). Multiple dopamine D_4 receptor variants in the human population. *Nature, 358,* 149–152.

Vygotsky, L. S. (1966). *Development of the Higher Mental Functions.* Cambridge, MA: MIT Press.

Vygotsky, L. S. (1967). Play and its role in the mental development of the child. *Soviet Psychology, 5,* 6–18.

Vygotsky, L. S. (1978). *Mind in Society: The Development of Higher Psychological Processes.* Cambridge, MA: Harvard University Press.

Waddington, C. H. (1966). *Principles of Development and Differentiation.* New York: Macmillan.

Ward, M. J., and Carlson, E. (1995). Associations among Adult Attachment representations, maternal sensitivity, and infant–mother attachment in a sample of adolescent mothers. *Child Development, 66,* 69–79.

Wartner, U. G., Grossmann, K., Fremmer-Bombrik, E., and Suess, G. (1994). Attachment patterns at age six in South Germany: Predictability from infancy and implications for pre-school behavior. *Child Development, 65,* 1014–1027.

Waters, E., Merrick, S., Albersheim, L., Treboux, D., and Crowell, J. (1995). From the strange situation to the Adult Attachment Interview: A 20-year longitudinal study of attachment security in infancy and early adulthood. Paper presented at the Society for Research in Child Development, Indianapolis (May).

Watson, J. S. (1972). Smiling, cooing, and "the game." *Merrill-Palmer Quarterly, 18,* 323–339.

Watson, J. S. (1979). Perception of contingency as a determinant of social responsiveness. In: E. B. Thoman (Ed.), *The Origins of Social Responsiveness* (pp. 33–64). New York: Lawrence Erlbaum.

Watson, J. S. (1984). Bases of causal inference in infancy: Time, space, and sensory relations. In: L. P. Lipsitt and C. Rovee-Collier (Eds.), *Advances in Infancy Research.* Norwood, NJ: Ablex.

Watson, J. S. (1985). Contingency perception in early social development. In: T. M. Field and N. A. Fox (Eds.), *Social Perception in Infants* (pp. 157–176). Norwood, NJ: Ablex.

Watson, J. S. (1994). Detection of self: The perfect algorithm. In: S. Parker, R. Mitchell, and M. Boccia (Eds.), *Self-Awareness in Animals and Humans: Developmental Perspectives* (pp. 131–149). New York: Cambridge University Press.

Watson, J. S. (1995). Self-orientation in early infancy: The general role of contingency and the specific case of reaching to the mouth. In: P. Rochat (Ed.), *The Self in Infancy: Theory and Research* (pp. 375–393). Amsterdam: Elsevier.

Wegner, D. M., and Wheatley, T. (1999). Apparent mental causation: Sources of the experience of will. *American Psychologist, 54* (7), 480–492.

Weinberg, K. M., and Tronick, E. Z. (1996). Infant affective reactions to the resumption of maternal interaction after the Still-Face. *Child Development, 67,* 905–914.

Weiskrantz, L. (1986). *Blindsight: A Case Study and Implications.* Oxford: Oxford University Press.

Wellman, H. (1990). *The Child's Theory of Mind.* Cambridge, MA: Bradford Books/MIT Press.

Wellman, H. (1993). Early understanding of mind: The normal case. In: S. Baron-Cohen, H. Tager-Flusberg, and D. J. Cohen (Eds.), *Understanding Other Minds: Perspectives from Autism* (pp. 40–58). New York: Oxford University Press.

Wellman, H., and Banerjee, M. (1991). Mind and emotion: Children's understanding of the emotional consequences of beliefs and desires. *British Journal of Developmental Psychology, 9,* 191–214.

Wellman, H., and Phillips, A. T. (2000). Developing intentional understandings. In: L. Moses, B. Male, and D. Baldwin (Eds.), *Intentionality: A Key to Human Understanding.* Cambridge, MA: MIT Press.

Werner, E. (1990). Protective factors and individual resilience. In: S. J. Meisels and M. Shonkoff (Eds.), *Handbook of Early Childhood Intervention* (pp. 97–116). New York: Cambridge University Press.

Werner, H., and Kaplan, B. (1963). *Symbol Formation.* New York: John Wiley.

West, M., and George, C. (in press). Abuse and violence in intimate adult relationships: New perspectives from attachment theory. In: D. G. Dutton (Ed.), *Treatment of Assaultiveness.* New York: Guilford Press.

Westen, D. (1997). Toward a clinically relevant and empirically sound theory of motivation. *International Journal of Psycho-Analysis, 78,* 521–548.

Whiten, A. (1991). *Natural Theories of Mind.* Oxford: Basil Blackwell.

Willatts, P. (1999). Development of means–end behavior in young infants: Pulling a support to retrieve a distant object. *Developmental Psychology, 35* (3), 651–667.

Wimmer, H., Hogrefe, G.-J., and Perner, J. (1988). Children's understanding of informational access as source of knowledge. *Child Development, 59,* 386–396.

Wimmer, H., Hogrefe, J.-G., and Sodian, B. (1988). A second stage in children's conception of mental life: Understanding informational access as origins of knowledge and belief. In: J. W. Astington, P. L. Harris, and D. R. Olson (Eds.), *Developing Theories of Mind.* New York: Cambridge University Press.

Wimmer, H., and Perner, J. (1983). Beliefs about beliefs: Representation and constraining function of wrong beliefs in young children's understanding of deception. *Cognition, 13,* 103–128.

Winnicott, D. W. (1960a). Ego distortion in terms of true and false self. In: *The Maturational Processes and the Facilitating Environment* (pp. 140–152). New York: International Universities Press, 1965.

Winnicott, D. W. (1960b). The theory of the parent–infant relationship. In: *The Maturational Processes and the Facilitating Environment* (pp. 37–55). New York: International Universities Press, 1965.

Winnicott, D. W. (1962). Ego integration in child development. In: *The Maturational Processes and the Facilitating Environment* (pp. 56–63). London: Hogarth Press, 1965.

Winnicott, D. W. (1963). Morals and education. In: *The Maturational Processes and the Facilitating Environment* (pp. 93–105). New York: International Universities Press, 1965.

Winnicott, D. W. (1965). *The Maturational Processes and the Facilitating Environment.* New York: International Universities Press.

Winnicott, D. W. (1967). Mirror-role of mother and family in child development. In: *Playing and Reality* (pp. 111–118). London: Tavistock, 1971.

Winnicott, D. W. (1971). *Playing and Reality.* London: Tavistock.

Wolff, P. H. (1996). The irrelevance of infant observations for psychoanalysis. *Journal of the American Psychoanalytic Association, 44,* 369–392.

Wollheim, R. (1995). *The Mind and Its Depths.* Cambridge, MA: Harvard University Press.

Wollheim, R. (1999). *On the Emotions.* New Haven, CT: Yale University Press.

Wood, D., Bruner, J. S., and Ross, G. (1976). The role of tutoring in problem solving. *Journal of Child Psychology and Psychiatry, 17,* 89–100.

Woodward, A. (1998). Infants selectively encode the goal object of an actor's reach. *Cognition, 69,* 1–34.

Woodward, A., and Sommerville, J. A. (2000). Twelve-month-old infants interpret action in context. *Psychological Science, 11*: 73–77.

Youngblade, L., and Dunn, J. (1995). Individual differences in young children's pretend play with mother and sibling: Links to relationships and understanding of other people's feelings and beliefs. *Child Development, 66,* 1472–1492.

Zahn-Waxler, C., and Radke-Yarrow, M. (1990). The origins of empathic concern. *Motivation and Emotion, 14,* 107–130.

Zajonc, R. B. (1984). On the primacy of affect. *American Psychologist, 39,* 117–123.

Index

Hembree, E. A., 216
"Henrietta" [clinical illustration], 19, 410–433
Herbst, J. H., 116
Herrera, C., 58
Hesse, E., 119, 175, 194, 382
Hetherington, E. M., 99, 104, 105, 110
Hewitt, J. K., 6
Hickie, I. B., 102
Hicks, L., 207
Higgitt, A., 12, 42, 43, 344
Higley, J. D., 116
Hill, J., 26, 27, 118
Hirschfeld, L., 146
historical-causal self-concept, 247
Hobson, R. P., 155, 193, 210, 300
Hochman, J. A., 344
Hofer, L., 133, 181
Hofer, M. A., 37, 90, 95, 133
Hoffman, M. L., 220, 238
Hogan, A., 34
Hogrefe, G.-J., 245
Holder, A., 432
Holder, J., 131
homeostasis, 37, 95
homunculus, 79
Hopkins, J., 26
Horowitz, L. M., 134
Horowitz, M. J., 40
hovering attention, therapist's, 315
Howard, R., 193
Howe, M. L., 241, 246
Hoyt, I. P., 40
Hrncir, E., 47
Hubley, P., 183, 225
Hughes, C., 245
Hughes, P., 119
Hull, J., 1
Hullian learning-theory research, 1
Hume, J., 70, 81
humor, 26, 432, 447, 449, 452, 453, 467
Hunt, J. M., 222
Hurry, A., xiii
hyperactive mentalizing, 383, 431

identification:
  primary, 380

projective: *see* projective identification
identifying affects, 437–440
imagination, 24, 294, 297, 298, 311, 439
  child's, importance of, 261–265
imitation, 150, 182, 183, 189, 215, 227
  -based attribution of emotional states, 149–152
  infantile, 182, 219
  intramodal, 183
  neonatal, 34, 183, 210, 211, 215
impulse control, 471
impulsivity, 251
  in BPD, 346, 360–362, 369
incest, 122
inclusive fitness, 122
independent teleology position, 232, 233
individuation, 264, 320, 321
  separation–, 320
infant-directed speech, 177
inference, 74, 127, 132, 159, 231, 242, 355, 368
  of mental state of other, 29
innate modularist approach, 243
"Insecure"/"Dismissing" individuals, 39
"Insecure"/"Preoccupied" individuals, 39
instability, emotional, in BPD, 346, 359, 362
instrumental action state, 34
intelligence, 91, 130
  quotient (IQ), 131
  social, 124
intentional action, 4
  "intention-in-action," 361–362
intentional agent, self as, 206, 237–242
intentional idioms, 147
intentionality:
  attribution of, 215, 236
  development of, 11, 286
  of mental states, 147
  sense of, 26, 54, 64, 145, 184, 197, 287
  of symbols, 294

philosophical perspectives, on affect regulation, 67–70
physical agent, self as, 207–209
physical self, 31, 129, 143, 205, 207, 208
physical stance, in prediction of behavior, 25
Piaget, J., 167, 207–209, 222, 226, 229, 322
Pickens, J., 157
Pickles, A., 118
Pillemer, D. B., 40, 41
Pine, F., 44
Pinker, S., 91
Pipp, S. L., 60
Pipp-Siegel, S., 119
Platz, D. L., 102
play, 130
    pretend: *see* pretend play
    reality-, traumatizing, clinical illustration: "Mat," 301–316
    symbolic: *see* symbolic play
playing with reality, 18, 144, 253–289
pleasure, 68, 72, 79, 85, 291
Plomin, R., 99, 104–107, 110, 114
Plotsky, P. M., 115
pointing, 46, 146, 159, 184, 225, 257
    declarative, 206
    protodeclarative, 220, 236
    protoimperative, 221, 235, 236
Polan, H. J., 90, 133
Polyphemos, 457–458
Pontalis, J. B., 255
postnatal depression, 421
potential space, 279, 284
Povinelli, D. J., 206, 241, 242, 245–247
Power, M., 74
prediction, 55, 124, 132, 224, 232, 349
    of action, 239
    of behavior, 25, 33, 160
Premack, A. J., 215
Premack, D., 215, 225
"preoccupied" attachment patterns, 39, 98, 135, 193, 249, 343, 344, 351, 354
    –"dismissive," 134

preoccupied caregiver, 43, 52
present self, 242, 247
pretend mode of communication, 178
pretend mode of functioning, 9, 57, 200, 253, 261–265, 439, 475, 478
    in BPD, 369, 375, 378, 380, 381
        clinical illustrations: "Emma," 388–410; "Henrietta," 410–433; "Sandra," 383–386
    and development, 296, 297
        clinical illustration: "Rebecca," 270–289
    Ogden on, 267
    and psychic equivalence mode, 2, 57, 144, 199, 257, 292–293, 320
        integration of, 263–265, 267, 293, 409
    vs. real, 25
pretend play, 47–48, 51, 54, 174, 178, 180, 257, 278, 369, 377, 407
    affect-regulative use of, 291–316
        clinical illustration: "Mat," 301–316;
pretense, 24, 47–53, 199–202, 232, 243, 296, 301–306, 312
    in BPD, 378, 379
    in play, clinical illustration: "Rebecca," 270–289
    see also pretend mode of functioning
Primary Access and Self-Awareness Assumption, 215
primary circular reactions, 167
primary identification, 380
primary object relationships, 4
primitive defenses, 251
principle of mental coherence, 239, 365
principle of rational action, 33, 224, 225, 228, 230, 239, 361
Prinz, W., 205
prior intentions, 206, 237, 238, 361–362
procedural memory, 40, 41
projection, 9, 198, 277, 295, 339, 473, 477
    of alien self, 328